Mystery & History In Georgia

(Volume I)

By R. Olin Jackson III
B.A., M.Ed.

Published by Whippoorwill Publications, LLC
Roswell, GA 30075

Copyright 2021 by R. Olin Jackson III
All Rights Reserved, including the right to reproduce this book in portions thereof or in any form whatsoever.

ISBN: 978-0-578-92142-6
Library of Congress Control Number: 2021912350

Cover design by Jess LaGreca, Mayfly Design

Publisher's Cataloging-In-Publication Data
(Prepared by The Donohue Group, Inc.)
Names: Jackson, Olin, author.
Title: Mystery & history in Georgia / by R. Olin Jackson III, B.A., M.Ed.
Other Titles: Mystery and history in Georgia
Description: Roswell, GA : Whippoorwill Publications, LLC, [2021-] | Includes bibliographical references and index.
Identifiers: ISBN 9780578921426 (v.1: paperback) | ISBN 9780578932064 (v.1: hardback) | ISBN 9780578932071 (v.1: ebook)
Subjects: LCSH: Curiosities and wonders—Georgia. | Georgia—History. | Georgia—Miscellanea.
Classification: LCC F286.6 .J33 2021 (print) | LCC F286.6 (ebook) | DDC 975.8—dc23

Also By R. Olin Jackson:
A North Georgia Journal of History, Volumes I – IV
Georgia's Doc Holliday
Old Mills in the Georgia Hills
Georgia Backroads Traveler
Tales of the Rails in Georgia
Moonshine, Murder, & Mayhem in Georgia
John Henry "Doc" Holliday: A Study in Survival

Co-Author with Dan Roper of:
Traced with Fire, Written in Blood
We Shall Die Together

Grateful appreciation is expressed herewith to Daniel M. Roper and Legacy Communications, Inc., Rome, GA, for reprint rights to selected articles within this publication.

Contents

Bartow County

Mysterious Mansion at Barnsley Gardens 1
The North Georgia Birthplace of Gangster "Pretty Boy" Floyd 10
The Bloody Battle at Allatoona Pass 17
Famed Author of "A Circuit Rider's Wife" 24
The Anderson Family Lived in a Railroad Boxcar during the Civil War 28
The Jackson Brothers Helped Build Early Cartersville 33
The Neel Family: Early Settlers of Bartow 40

Bibb County

The Mystery of the Woolfolk Murders 48

Carroll County

The Murder of Chief William McIntosh 60

Cobb County

Andrews' Raiders & the Real "Great Locomotive Chase" 70
The History & Preservation of Historic Concord Covered Bridge 82

Columbia County

The Birthplace of Hollywood Star Oliver Hardy 89

Dawson County

Champion Racers & Moonshine Makers of Dawson 94
The Gold Mining Russell Brothers – Founders of Denver 101
Traces of the Early Pioneers in the Etowah River Valley 110

Fayette County

The Mysterious Murder of Postman James Langston 117

Floyd County
Relic from De Soto's Conquistadors 122

Forsyth County
The Mystery of the Murder & Burial of Chief James Vann 129

Gilmer County
The Doublehead Gap Gunfight 137

Gordon County
The Astounding Story of Stand Watie 141
The Mystery of Sequoyah's Grave 155

Habersham County
Early Adventures on the Tallulah Falls Railroad 157
Remembering the Historic Tallulah Falls Railroad 165
The Mysterious Tallulah Falls Firestorm of 1921 172

Hall County
Chestnut Mountain, GA: The Early Days 179
Old West Bandit Bill Miner's Capture in North Georgia 184
The Hudgins Family of Jackson & Hall Counties 194
The Life & Times of Bandit John A. Murrell 205
The Rare Gold Coins of Templeton Reid 209
The Terrible & Devastating 1936 Gainesville Tornado 217

Heard County
Night of Terror at Merrill's Mill 226

Lumpkin County
The Gunfights and Mysterious Life of Pioneer Harrison Riley 231
Cunning Union Guerrillas of the North Georgia Mountains 246
Old West Bandit at the Historic London Home-Place 256
Remembering "Turner's Corner" and "Smoky" the Bear 262
The Amazing Life & Legend of Capt. Whit Anderson 267
The Captivating Life & Legend of "Boney" Tank 275
The Tragic Civil War Graves on Bearden's Bridge Hill 281

Monroe County
Filming *Fried Green Tomatoes* at Juliette, GA 293

Murray County

The Mysteries of Fort & Blood Mountains 297
The Mystery of Cherokee John Martin's House 303

North Georgia

Re-Tracing the Historic Alabama Road (Part 1) (Upper Route) 308
Re-Tracing the Historic Alabama Road (Part 2) (Lower Route) 319
Three Cherokee Families & Their Georgia Legacy 327

Pickens County

The Mysterious Night Riders of Pickens 334
The 1923 Pickens County Jail-Break 338
County Policeman Lee Cape Murdered Over Moonshine 341
The North Georgia Moonshine War 348
The Strange Murder Case of Kate Southern 356

Polk County

Railroad Destination to Devastation: The 1926 Rockmart Wreck 369
A Mysterious Cherokee Photo & the Naming of Collard Valley 379
Frontier Gunfighters from Yesteryear – The Asa Prior Family 387
High Times & High Crimes at Esom Hill 399
Old Piedmont Institute and a Famous Author 408
The Gravatt Family – From Holland to Polk County 416

Union County

Historic Walasi-Yi Center on the Appalachian Trail 421
The Life & Times of Ranger Arthur Woody 424
The Mysterious Petroglyphs of Track Rock Gap 432

White County

Col. James Hall Nichols Rebuilds A Devastated Life 436
"I Remember When Hollywood Came To North Georgia" 444
I'd Climb the Highest Mountain – Again 454
Mysterious Remnants of Early Spanish Explorers 465
The Old England Gold Mine – A Bottomless Pit 471

Whitfield County

The Murder of Joseph Standing 476
The Wreck of the W&A RR at Willowdale 481

Mysterious Mansion at Barnsley Gardens

The ruins of an immense antebellum Italianate mansion and its still-amazing gardens enthrall historians and visitors alike. Here, when Georgia was still essentially an unsettled wilderness, the ultra-talented Godfrey Barnsley lost the love of his life, and the U.S. Civil War brought terror and destruction as it spilled down into Georgia.

Like a small replica of the magnificent castle-like structure known as "Biltmore House" in North Carolina, the historic structure in north Georgia known today as "Barnsley Gardens" was originally built as a gift to his wife by wealthy Englishman Godfrey Barnsley. The saga surrounding the Barnsley family and the as yet awe-inspiring remnants of the Englishman's former mansion in the north Georgia mountains is as fascinating today as it is compelling and mysterious.

In 1824, when he was eighteen years of age, Godfrey Barnsley arrived in America from England. He was virtually penniless with little more than four shillings in his pocket, but as a result of his intelligence and honesty, he did at least have prospects. He was unusually adept and skilled in the financial realm, and within only ten short years, he literally had become one of the wealthiest men in Georgia, having made his fortune in the South as a cotton broker.

In building his brokerage firm, Barnsley established offices in Savannah, New York, New Orleans, and Liverpool, England. Since they were not completely filled with his primary product, his fleet of ships carried not only cotton, but other cargo as well – salt, wine, and carpeting – to all parts of the world.

And then there was his integrity. Above and beyond his super intellectual business acumen, Godfrey Barnsley – contrary to many in his profession – was also scrupulously honest, and this simple honesty paid him big dividends. He ultimately earned the favor of captains of industry throughout the United States and Europe, winning contracts other less-honest brokers would have been denied. In the Barnsley archives today there are still many letters from ministers of trade from throughout the world commending him for his high moral and professional standards.

A Wife of Letters

William Scarborough II, yet another prosperous shipping merchant, was instrumental in building the first steamship to cross the Atlantic. The U.S.S.

Mystery & History in Georgia

Barnsley Gardens (circa 1900) – Photographed prior to its deterioration from weathering and neglect, "Woodlands" manor house with its fine architectural lines is visible above much as it appeared during Godfrey Barnsley's day. Little more than the ruins of this structure exist today. *(Photo courtesy of Clint Coker)*

Savannah made her maiden voyage in May of 1819, but William would have an impact upon Godfrey Barnsley far beyond steamships. William's daughter – Julia Henrietta Scarborough – to the utter joy of the talented cotton broker, accepted Godfrey's proposal of marriage in 1828.

From that point forward, Godfrey Barnsley's goals in life included not only the creation of a successful business empire, but the happiness of his new bride whom he loved unconditionally. No need of hers was too great. No desire too manifest to bestow upon her.

With his fortune finally secure, Godfrey's most compelling immediate desire became the creation of a breath-taking mansion in the serene northwest Georgia mountains to present to Julia as a gift. He set about achieving this objective with a passion unmatched by his previous endeavors. Tragically, however, before this project could be completed, his beloved became ill with a terrible incurable disease – consumption (tuberculosis).

The knowledge of the suffering being experienced by his lovely wife was almost too much for Godfrey to bear, and so he immersed himself in his work. Nevertheless, despite the unbelievable health set-back, Barnsley continued work toward creation of the mansion in northwest Georgia for Julia. It was his hope that the cooler – and possibly drier – mountain air would be beneficial to his beloved's health, even though there was no "cure" at that time for the fatal disease she had contracted.

Toward this endeavor, in 1840, Barnsley acquired 3,560 acres of land in what is now Bartow (originally Cass)

County that had become available for purchase as a result of recent treaties with the Cherokees. It was here that his mansion was to be built – in an area wild and serene which had only been vacated by the native Indians two years earlier. He decided to name his new estate "Woodlands" and referred to it with the British word "manor" instead of the usual Southern term "plantation."

Despite the fact that his financial and marketing acumen had already earned him a fortune in products brokerage, Godfrey continued tirelessly in his pursuit of excellence in his profession. His work often kept him far from the "Woodlands" project, so he hired an Irishman named John Connoly as overseer of the manor's construction for the sixteen years it took to build it.

In the meantime, despite Julia's illness, the couple had borne "fruit" domestically. Six children eventually were born to them, bringing happiness where Julia's illness had brought only sadness. Godfrey brought his family to northwest Georgia where he had directed that a large log home be built as a temporary residence for his family while the larger and luxurious Woodlands home was being constructed.

Julia absolutely loved Woodlands, but her letters also reveal that she was quite lonely during Godfrey's long absences. Her health did improve somewhat during the hot dry summers, but the winters, conversely, were cold and damp, and had the opposite effect upon her health. The unerring deterioration of her health continued essentially unabated.

By the winter of 1844, Julia's health had declined even more drastically. This change in her condition occurred not long after the death of her son – Godfrey, Jr. – who had lived only eighteen months after birth. Despairing from this loss and with her own health in more rapid decline, Julia apparently realized that she now desperately needed the talents of a medical professional for herself if she wished to prolong her life.

She traveled southward first on the Western & Atlantic Railroad to Atlanta, and then changed trains to travel southeastward to Savannah, to be attended by her physician there. Despite the skilled medical attention, Julia nevertheless languished, and when her declining health reached the point of no return, she soon died in February of that year.

Godfrey, understandably, was overcome with grief. He subsequently lost all interest in continuing to build Woodlands after his beloved Julia's death. Devoting himself instead to his business, he traveled constantly between his seaport offices in New Orleans, Mobile, Savannah, and Liverpool. It was while he was in Mobile that he attended a séance after being approached by a friend who professed to be a spirit medium, telling him that it was possible for him to communicate with his dead wife.

Godfrey's gradual and desperate interest in spiritualism led to a renewed involvement at Woodlands, and his diaries and letters of that time indicate that he strangely believed he indeed could communicate with Julia in the gardens there. He renewed his construction efforts at Woodlands, and poured himself into this work.

Hand-crafted Beauty

Godfrey hired a local carpenter – Robert Freeman – to help with the work. He hand-crafted much of the elegant interior woodwork. Freeman often took unusual instructions from Barnsley which Godfrey indicated had come from his late dearly beloved. "I didn't know what to think when Mr. Godfrey told me 'Miss Julia' wanted something done such-and-such a way, and her being dead and all," Freeman later explained to his grandson, "but I just done what he told me."

Despite the traditional Greek Revival style which was so pervasive and popular in the South at this time, Godfrey instead wanted a structure in the style of a grand Italian villa for his mountain home. He spared no expense in constructing his 28-room manor house or in furnishing it, importing marble from Italy and great doors and paneling from his native England.

In that day and time, the luxurious domicile was as unique as it was attractive. At a time when they were virtually unknown in the United States, Woodlands boasted not only flush toilets, but both hot and cold running water as well – supplied by a 300-gallon water tank in the home's tower, and another beside the central chimney.

Barnsley also made use of the latest mechanical innovations in the home as well. He installed a "water ram" – which is a unique hydraulic pumping device – in a freshwater spring near the home, and designed it to pump fresh water to the holding tanks whenever the water level had dropped to a certain level. Even the overflow water was not wasted, it being piped to the large fountain in the formal boxwood gardens.

According to Emma Pritchett (1868-1960), a black servant at Woodlands, "People would come there from everywhere to see the place in them old days. It was so pretty that when folks would come over the main road on stage or buggies, they would stop and get out just to look at the place and get a drink from the spring. Oh, it was fine water too - the best in the country."

The first floor of the main structure at Woodlands contained a reception hall, dining room, library, and two drawing rooms. Bedrooms and water closets (bathrooms) were located on the second floor, as was Godfrey's office containing a massive roll top desk, a solid gold clock, and a collection of paintings and other art objects from all over the world. The third floor tower afforded Godfrey a full view of his domain in all directions.

The frame house in which the family had earlier lived, became a guest house known as "the left wing." The brick structure into which the Barnsleys had moved circa 1842 became "the right wing" of the main building. It contained a billiard room, quarters for the housekeeper, a wine cellar stocked with the finest imported wines and Godfrey's own peach and apricot brandies from the Woodlands orchard, and the kitchen, which was especially noteworthy because of its stove.

Constructed from plans drawn by the renowned Leonardo Da Vinci and imported from England, the stove had a rotisserie turned by heat rising up the chimney. A spigot attached to a lead pipe running through the fire area provided hot running water. The stove was capable of cooking meals substantial enough to feed 150 people. Many years later (in 1929), Henry Ford wanted to buy this remarkable stove for one of his museums, and offered a large sum of money for it, only to learn that it was considered a permanent portion of Woodlands, and was not for sale.

Breath-taking Gardens

Godfrey's formal gardens received his minute attentions as well. They were stocked with rare plants which were shipped to him from many parts of the world.

The main entrance to the house was

accessed through a geometrically-patterned English boxwood garden with a central fountain. Other areas of the grounds at Woodlands contained rock gardens with statuary, rose gardens, an Oriental garden with a fish pool encircled by Chinese fir trees, a British-style deer park, and a sunken bog garden planted with more than 5,000 aquatic plants. Woodlands was noted in particular for its rare roses, including several of Godfrey's own creation. One of these was a unique "green" rose.

"Aunt Fannie" Colston who was born at Woodlands in 1874 and lived until 1971, remembered it as a breath-taking sight. "You could see all the bright floral plants covering the big hill long before you got to the gates," she explained. "There was just about every kind of flower in the world growing in Woodlands. People would come from all around to have weddings and picnics there."

Godfrey also planted many rare trees on the grounds, including cedars from Lebanon, gingers from China, lindens from Germany, and sequoias from California. The Woodlands archives contain receipts for sixty almond trees and a letter from Godfrey's daughter commenting that *"the bananas and oranges are ripening quite well."* The tropical fruit trees are believed to have been kept in tubs in the sunny bay windows on the south side of the drawing room, and thus were protected from any freezing cold temperatures during the winter months.

Godfrey traveled far and wide collecting beautiful and rare items with which to ornament the manor house, including a life-size autographed portrait of Napoleon. Toilet articles once belonging to Queen Marie Antoinette became part of the decor of Woodlands Manor. Dinner guests sat at a 40-person mahogany dining room table that was once in the

Another view of the manor house at Barnsley Gardens prior to its destruction from a tornado and weathering. *(Photo courtesy of the GA Dept. of Archives & History, Atlanta)*

palace of Emperor Don Pedro of Brazil.

The original main staircase to the structure was ordered all the way from England and was actually shipped to New York. From there, it was transported by rail as far as Nashville, but it never made it to Woodlands, due to the outbreak of the U.S. Civil War.

Others of Godfrey's imported treasures were still in their shipping crates when the war came to Woodlands. Godfrey had business associates in both the North and the South, and attempted to remain neutral on the basis of his British citizenship which he maintained. He, however, remained convinced that it was only a matter of time before England entered the war on the side of the Confederacy, because of Britain's dependence upon Southern cotton.

Godfrey had nearly a hundred servants, and records indicate that he paid taxes to the state of Georgia for sixteen slaves. He, however, never referred to them as slaves, treating them instead as his Woodlands family, believing that "no man owns another, because all men belong to the supreme ruler of all things."

Onslaught of the War

When the western flank of General William Sherman's Union army finally arrived on the outskirts of the Woodlands property on May 18, 1864, Godfrey hoisted up the Union Jack, but that was not enough to convince the Federal forces of his neutrality, particularly after they discovered Confederate war bonds in Godfrey's safe and learned that his sons were fighting for the Confederacy.

A skirmish between the invading Federal forces and Confederates attempting to repel them was drawn by a sketch artist and published in *Harper's Weekly*, July 1, 1864. The commanding officer of the Confederates in this engagement – Col. Richard Earle – was a personal friend of the Barnsleys. He was killed as he left the Barnsley manor house after riding to warn Godfrey to "hide the women and children in the basement because the Yankees are coming." Col. Earle was buried beneath the redwood tree to the rear of the manor. His gravesite and tombstone may still be viewed there today.

Union troops eventually occupied Woodlands, but General J.B. McPherson was so impressed with the beauty of the place that he amazingly ordered that nothing be damaged. He described Woodlands as *"a little piece of heaven itself."* One has to believe today that Barnsley's neutrality must have had an impact, since there were many Southern mansions and plantations of exquisite beauty at that time which ultimately were burned to the ground by the destructive Union invaders. One of McPherson's soldiers published his ***Diary of an Illinois Soldier*** in 1882, in which he wrote that Woodlands was *"the most beautiful spot I've ever seen."*

Aside from the picket fences which became fuel for campfires, very little destruction ultimately took place at Woodlands while McPherson occupied the site, but when he moved on to Kingston, stragglers and looters moved in behind him and ransacked the Barnsley home, taking everything, right down to the silver latches on the windows. After invading the wine and brandy cellar, the intoxicated looters threw many now priceless Woodlands treasures (some of which were still in their shipping crates) into a huge bonfire.

The Barnsleys' Irish housekeeper – Mary Quinn – is reported to have described General McPherson as "a fine gentleman surrounded by rogues and thieves." When a Union soldier asked Godfrey for the time of day, only to snatch the gold watch out of Barnsley's hand and run, Mary reportedly exclaimed "I'm sick of the devils" and proceeded to chase the soldier and rake him with her fingernails. He escaped only after hitting her in the side with the butt of his musket.

Picking herself up, Mary then stormed into General McPherson's encampment, accusing him of failing to protect them as he had promised. McPherson, a true gentleman to the

Earle was buried beneath the redwood tree to the rear of the manor. His gravesite and tombstone may still be viewed there today.

Mysterious Mansion at Barnsley Gardens   Bartow County

end, lined up his soldiers, interrogating them until he had discovered the guilty party and recovered the watch. Godfrey Barnsley's great-great-grandson (also named Godfrey Barnsley) still owns the watch today, thanks in part to McPherson's moral fiber.

Former Barnsley historian Clent Coker was able to interview some of the Woodlands servants who were still alive in the 1950s, including "Aunt Molly" Curtis who gave him the following account of the invasion:

"Some of de soldier mens slipped aroun de place, stealin' ever' thang dey could, takin' de wine from de cellar and giving it to de rest of 'em... dey took near ever' speck of food we had. And some of dem kept on comin' through tryin' to take ever' thang.... Sho was hard times for a long time after dat ol' war." Godfrey, still considering himself a British subject, presented a carefully itemized list of damages in the amount of $155,000 to the British Consulate in Washington, D.C., but was never reimbursed.

Wreckage of the War

By the time the war had ended, Godfrey's shipping business was virtually nonexistent, due to the damage wrought by the Union blockades in the Southern ports. Two of Godfrey's ships had been sunk while trying to run the blockades, and he was nearly bankrupt. He spent most of his time at his only remaining office in New Orleans attempting to recoup some of his losses.

Two of Godfrey's sons, George and Lucian (who served in the Rome, Georgia Light Guard), returned safely but refused to take the Oath of Allegiance to the United States government. They eventually migrated to Brazil along with a group of other ex-Confederate colonists. Their descendants remain there today.

Heroic Ride – Col. Richard C. Earl (C.S.A.), commander of the Confederate forces engaging Union troops under the command of Gen. J.B. McPherson (U.S.) in the vicinity of the Barnsley estate during the U.S. Civil War, rode to the manor house to warn Barnsley of the impending danger to his family in the summer of 1864. As he attempted to leave the estate, Earl was fatally shot from his horse. He was buried on the grounds of the Barnsley estate and his grave may still be viewed there today.

Godfrey and Julia's oldest son, Harold, established a import-export business in Hong Kong and disappeared mysteriously in 1859.

Godfrey and Julia's daughter, Adelaide, died in 1858, two weeks after giving birth to her first child.

It then fell to the surviving daughter, Julia, and her husband, Captain James P. Baltzelle (who had served as a staff officer under General Robert E. Lee), to return to Woodlands after the war and attempt to restore it in Godfrey's absence. They traveled with their infant daughter,

Addie, who had been born in Savannah on December 14, 1864.

According to interviews with former Woodlands servants, it was Captain Baltzelle who taught the Woodlands servants how to can food in order to preserve it – a practice that had just been perfected during the Civil War. "The captain, he kept them all alive and taught them to survive after that 'ol war," said Elizabeth Morrow.

The restoration zeal at Woodlands however, was short-lived. Tragedy struck the family once again when Capt. Baltzelle was killed in 1868 as he helped rebuild a railroad bridge. A load of logs apparently shifted onto him, crushing him. Julia and Addie ultimately abandoned Woodlands, joining Godfrey in New Orleans.

Godfrey's attempts to re-establish himself as a cotton broker were unsuccessful. The South and any efforts which involved shipping – particularly the marketing and shipment of products such as cotton – were just too broken and destroyed to be regenerated anytime soon. When Godfrey died – virtually a pauper – in 1873, Julia brought his body back to his beloved Woodlands in a sealed copper casket for burial.

Julia's daughter, Addie, eventually married B.F.A. Saylor. The couple and Julia had returned to Woodlands once again, but the once-fine manor house was now in a sad state of disrepair. Saylor, a chemist and mineralogist by trade, believed he could develop a formula for aluminum from bauxite ore he had discovered on the property at Woodlands – a venture which ironically might possibly have resurrected the family fortune with any luck at all. It was not to be, however.

In a laboratory built for Saylor by Julia with funds from the family's rapidly-diminishing assets, the mineralogist did come up with the formula for making a new product he called "rayon," and was the first to apply for a patent for the fiber, but sadly, he never realized any income from his creation.

Almost exactly like the mythical "Tara" in famed author Margaret Mitchell's now legendary **Gone with the Wind**, much of the Woodlands estate ultimately was sold in later years to provide for taxes and general maintenance. When the roof of the manor was blown off by a tornado in 1906, there was no money to pay for the costly repairs, so the Saylors were forced to move into the right (kitchen) wing of the manor house. Following the tornado and exposure to the elements, the main structure continued to deteriorate over the years, along with what remained of the family fortune. When Julia's daughter, Addie Saylor, died in 1942, the trustees of the will held an auction to liquidate the estate and pay off the mortgage.

Renewed Life

Subsequent owners of Woodlands also lacked the necessary funds to restore the proud old structures, and the sad deterioration of the buildings and grounds continued until 1988. At that time, the property was purchased by Prince Hubertus Fuerst Fugger-Babenhausen of Germany. Under the guidance of

Julia brought his body back to his beloved Woodlands in a sealed copper casket for burial.

Carl H. Cofer, the U.S. business manager of Fugger-Babenhausen, an organization called Stonewall Limited Partnership ultimately did restore much of Woodlands' former magnificence, and stabilized the remainder as a historic site for posterity. Well over $2,000,000.00 was spent simply undoing damage which had been wrought by the forces of nature, time, war, and vandalism.

One of the first projects was the elimination of the kudzu that had engulfed the overseer's house, springhouse, and commissary, steadily advancing on the manor house itself which was already covered with wisteria vines. Large trees had grown up within the walls of the manor house, and portions of the walls had crumbled and fallen. The once immaculate and breath-taking gardens had also disappeared among the weeds and required rehabilitation.

Much of the ruins ultimately were stabilized. Master masons Bill Corey and Kenny Herron rebuilt crumbled walls so skillfully that they are indistinguishable from the original portions.

Landscapers under the direction of Gardens Manager Steve Wheaton restored the gardens with duplicates of the plants that Godfrey Barnsley had collected from around the world with his fleet of sailing ships. The prolific letters that Godfrey wrote almost 200 years ago for instruction of his gardeners at that time, saw second service as guides and blueprints for the restoration process.

An Atlanta sculptress was commissioned to create a fountain in the style of the Italian marble original which once graced the center of the parterre boxwood garden in front of the manor. And the neighboring rock gardens were covered with ferns and flowering bulbs.

Two parallel borders of old-fashioned roses and herbaceous plants (both annuals and perennials) were replanted behind the manor. Climbing roses and vines ornament the graceful lines of the ruins of the manor itself, which provides sanctuary for colorful peafowl.

A magnificent arbor, constructed in Atlanta, was installed on the south slope overlooking the Bog Gardens which once again teem with exotic flowers lotuses and Japanese carp. Breath-taking paths wind through azalea and rhododendron gardens.

The scene described by the English poet, William Wordsworth, in his famous poem, *I Wandered Lonely as a Cloud*, will be experienced by visitors to Woodlands in springs to come when they behold *"a host of golden daffodils fluttering and dancing in the breeze."* Thirty-thousand bulbs were planted – three times more than Wordsworth described seeing.

The main manor house reportedly will remain as a historic ruin, for it would be difficult to recreate Woodlands Manor as Godfrey Barnsley had created it. The right wing is in good condition, however, and has been converted into a museum to house Barnsley artifacts and also Native American artifacts discovered in the area. Professional archaeologists have conducted digs at Woodlands and uncovered implements, prehistoric arrow-points, and a ceremonial pipe that has been dated to be over a thousand years old.

One of the rooms in the museum has been devoted to the Civil War relics/memorabilia from the skirmishes and encampments at Woodlands during the conflict.

Many visitors in the years ahead undoubtedly will continue to witness and be amazed by this unique remnant of a day which has truly disappeared forever.

The North Georgia Birthplace of Gangster "Pretty Boy" Floyd

Though little-known today, one of America's most infamous criminals was born and lived his formative years in the town of Adairsville, Georgia.

Little-known to Georgians and many historians alike, one of the most notorious criminals in U.S. history was born in the sleepy north Georgia town of Adairsville. Though he died in a hail of gunfire in Ohio, and lived most of his life in Oklahoma, Charles Arthur "Pretty Boy" Floyd is Georgian by birth.

The house in which Floyd was born still stands (as of this writing) at 102 Railroad Street[1] in Adairsville. Many members of the Floyd, Murphey, Pinson, Echols, Gaines, and other families, many of which still reside in the area are related to the outlaw. These families came to Cass (now Bartow) County from South Carolina shortly after the removal of the Cherokees in 1838.[2]

Family Roots

Charles Floyd's great-great-great-grandfather, Roger Murphey, Jr., migrated to Cass from Laurens County, South Carolina. He and his father had both held property in Laurens, giving them a financial base from which to acquire land in the Georgia counties of Forsyth, DeKalb, and Cass.[3]

The two men apparently entertained the prospect of becoming part of the "planter elite" class then taking hold in the South. This becomes even more obvious when considering their real estate investments, and their known desire to acquire slaves and engage in large-scale agricultural endeavors.

Though their intentions were good, they never quite achieved the status they desired. They were able to purchase a number of slaves to help in their farming efforts, but they ultimately wound up laboring right along beside their workers just to be able to claim a profit at the end of each growing season. Such was the lot of many yeoman farmers in the pre-Civil War South.

In 1854 when Roger passed away, his estate was divided among his children. His home and property were purchased by his son, John, who used a portion of the slaves to continue farming.[4]

According to tradition, John Murphey's wife, Frances, has been described as a hearty individual. According to accounts of her life, she often saddled up her horse and rode the many miles back to South Carolina to visit relatives and friends. This was no easy trek, particularly for a woman in the mid-19th century, and the fact that she accomplished it alone makes it even more amazing.[5]

When John and Frances Murphey died, their farm was purchased by a daughter and son-in-law, Redding and Katherine Murphey Floyd. Redding was the son of Samuel and Patience Pinson Floyd. The Pinsons were of the Particular Baptist faith. A number of Pinson family members worked as millwrights in South Carolina and continued their tradition in Cass County, Georgia, constructing a number of water-powered mills in the area.[6]

Hard Times

Charles Arthur Floyd's great-grandfather, Redding Floyd, had two brothers – Newport and Jasper. Floyd family members, for various and sundry reasons, had begun moving away from Cass County prior to the U.S. Civil War. Newport and Jasper migrated to Arkansas circa late 1850s.

According to family lore, the pair had gotten as far as Arkansas when they stopped at a cabin to inquire about directions to Fort Smith. An elderly gentleman who lived in the cabin provided the requested information, then, apparently in the process of a conversation learned the site from which the two men had come, and then no doubt the fact they were Floyds from Cass County, Georgia. Somewhat stunned, the elderly gentleman then exclaimed that he was their father – Samuel Floyd.

It seems that in years prior, Samuel and Patience Pinson Floyd had split up. Samuel had moved away and the family had never heard from him again.

Apparently determined never to lose his "family" again, the old gentleman seems to have accompanied Newport and Jasper to their new home, because the 1860 Census of Arkansas indicates that he was living in Newport's household at that time.[7]

Charles Arthur "Pretty Boy" Floyd was photographed following an arrest in Colorado. (Photo courtesy of Western History Collection, University of Oklahoma Library)

Meanwhile, back in Georgia, the boys' other brother – Redding – had decided to remain behind, farming the old Murphey place. At the time of the Civil War, he owned three slaves and the farm, which apparently produced a reasonable living for his family.

In November of 1862, Redding enlisted in Company F of the 12th Georgia Cavalry in Kingston, Georgia. His brother-in-law, Matthias Murphey, wrote a letter to Redding on January 18, 1863, not knowing that Redding had already enlisted. His letter, in part, indicates that even at that early date, morale was a definite problem within the Confederate forces:

".... I understand that you have a couple of heirs (referring to Redding's recently born twins) at your house and I wish you great sicess (sic) in raising of them. . . Red, between me and you and the Gait post we have got the meanest Colonel in

Mystery & History in Georgia

The Echols family lived in the Towes Chapel area of Bartow County, near Cassville. Charles Arthur Floyd (front row, 1st from left) was photographed here with his Echols relatives circa 1909.

the confederate service. I never shall like Abda Johnson (later mayor of Cartersville, Georgia) any more as long as I live... . Red the Soldiers are all getting very tired of this war and if it is not stopt shortly they will stop it themselves by throwing down their muskets and going home. I am going to stay til July and if they don't let me come home on fair terms I am coming on fowl terms. This is the worst place we have been camped at yet bad water bad beef and bad weather."[8]

Starting Anew In The West

The advent of the U.S. Civil War had a devastating impact upon general farming in the South. Slaves became more and more difficult to manage; necessary products became more and more difficult to obtain as naval blockades eliminated the shipping avenues; and the Confederate dollars purchased less and less as the war progressed.

As a result, with the culmination of the war and the devastation it had wrought, many Southerners – the Floyds and Murpheys included – yearned for a new beginning and struck out for the West. From Anderson County, Texas in 1870, C.M. Murphey wrote to his brother-in-law, Redding Floyd, about the great promise of post-war Texas:

"Texas looks like a world of cotton. People kill all their meat out of the woods as fat as they are in georgia when we feed them 10 Bushels of corn apiece. use cast plows never sharpen them. cheaper than iron plows on Georgia. Water better than I expected to find."[9]

Redding Floyd received the same kind of mail extolling the virtues of Pike County, Arkansas from his brother, Jasper. This love affair with the West continued in the Floyd and Murphey families, but Redding, strangely, was never enticed to leave his native Bartow County farm, despite the devastation and poverty all around him.

One reason Redding never departed was his elderly mother for whom he cared. He reportedly did not want to uproot her and take her on the long, dangerous journey westward.[10]

Though Redding chose to remain behind, a second wave of emigration of Floyds and their allied kin occurred around the turn of the century, continuing until around 1915. This relocation was ignited by the opening of the Indian territory and the opportunity to acquire fertile agricultural lands at limited or no cost. An opportunity such as this was just too much of a temptation, particularly for those young enough and eager to start anew in a more productive location.

Formative Years Of "Pretty Boy"

One of the families that went West during this second exodus (around 1912) was that of Redding's grandson, Walter Floyd.[11] Within this family was included young Charles Arthur Floyd, called "Charlie" by the family. He had been born in Adairsville on February 3, 1904, living most of his formative years in the community.

Walter Floyd had married Mamie Echols in 1897 in Bartow County. Mamie's mother Emily Elizabeth Gaines Echols – wife of Elmer Echols – hailed from one of the South's most illustrious families – the Gaines – of Culpepper County, Virginia.[12]

Charles Arthur "Pretty Boy" Floyd is remembered primarily as a bank robber in the annals of U.S. criminal history. From time to time, however, he is also anointed with the mantle of a folk hero. He was referred to occasionally as "the Robin Hood of the Cookson Hills."

While robbing banks in that area, Floyd reportedly tore up first mortgages, hoping they had not been recorded. This act, if true, freed many of the destitute Depression-era families from loan

The house in which Charles Arthur Floyd was born and lived the early part of his life still stands as of this writing (2021) at 102 Railroad Street in Adairsville, GA.

obligations when hard cash was almost nonexistent.[13]

Today, the official FBI file on the career of "Pretty Boy" Floyd is in excess of 15,000 pages. Books, magazine articles, and movies have chronicled his life and times, often substituting fiction for fact to embellish circumstances.

One of the little-known ironies of the "Pretty Boy" Floyd story is the fact that his brother, E.W. Floyd, served many terms as sheriff of Sequoyah County, Oklahoma, and was highly respected in the law enforcement community.

A cousin, Duff Floyd, was a famed revenue officer of north Georgia. On one occasion when he was asked what he would have done had "Pretty Boy" crossed his path, Duff reportedly replied "I would have arrested him like any other criminal."[14]

Today, it is unknown for certain whether or not Charles "Pretty Boy" Floyd ever returned to Georgia to the land of his youth. According to folklore, however, he did once hide out in a house on Montgomery Street in Cartersville, Georgia.

Beginning A Life Of Crime

Floyd's first run-in with law enforcement personnel occurred in Akin,

Mystery & History in Georgia

The home of Redding Floyd, great-grandfather of Charles Arthur Floyd, still stands as of this writing (2021) in Folsom, GA. Redding and his wife, Katheryn, are buried nearby in Macland Cemetery. *(Photo courtesy of Father Phillip Paul Scott)*

Oklahoma, in 1922. According to accounts of the incident, he took $350 in pennies from the post office there. He was convicted and sentenced to probation.

For a short period of time, Charles apparently followed "the straight and narrow," moving to Sallisaw, Oklahoma, where he found work as a plumber and baker. Two years later, he married 16-year-old Wilma Ruby Hardgrave. Marriage and the grind of a daily job however apparently proved to be a lifestyle to which Charles could never adjust.

It wasn't long before he was back up to his old tricks. In 1925, he and an accomplice robbed a St. Louis, Missouri Kroger store of $11,984. Floyd was ultimately arrested at his home in Sallisaw. He was eventually convicted of the crime and sent to the Missouri State Penitentiary at Jefferson City for five years.

While Charles was in prison, Ruby gave birth to their only son, Jack Dempsey Floyd. Though she loved their son, Ruby apparently had given up on Charles, and divorced him shortly after Jack's birth. Later, the couple reconciled for a short period of time – without "benefit of clergy," – but then separated permanently.

After he was released from the state penitentiary, Charles resumed his criminal lifestyle. He and a friend, Bert Walker, stole a car and robbed a bank in Sylvania, Ohio.

By coincidence, while making a raid on a Kenmore Boulevard home, Officer Sherman Gandee of the Akron Police encountered Floyd and Walker. During an ensuing gun battle, Officer Harland F. Manes was shot dead by Walker.

A phone number discovered in the Kenmore Boulevard house led to another house on Lodi Street in Akron where Floyd and Walker were subsequently captured. Walker eventually earned an appointment with the electric chair for his deeds. Meanwhile, Floyd, on his way to the Ohio State Penitentiary, jumped out of a train window and successfully escaped.

The First Murders

Charles eventually found his way to Toledo, Ohio, where two brothers, William and Wallace Ash, befriended him. It was a friendship, however, that apparently was not reciprocated by Floyd. The Ash brothers were later discovered dead from gunshot wounds to the head. Their wives and Floyd had left town and later turned up in Kentucky.

Bowling Green, Kentucky, was the scene of Charles' next crime spree. He, William "Baby Face Billy" Miller, and the Ash women were at a Bowling Green hardware store when Officer Ralph Castner reportedly approached their car. Witnesses, who later identified Floyd, stated he opened fire on the policeman who was killed in the fray along with Miller. A ballistics analysis later matched the bullets in the policeman with those from the heads of the Ash brothers.

By this time, Floyd was now a suspect in three murders. In his career, he ultimately stood accused of killing twelve men, ten of whom were officers of the law.

From May through December of 1931, Floyd allegedly committed some fifteen bank robberies in Missouri, Kansas, and Oklahoma. When the governor of Oklahoma posted a $1,000.00 reward for Floyd's capture, the daring criminal promptly sent the good governor a letter.

"You either withdraw that $1,000 at once or suffer the consequences," Floyd penned. "No kidding, I have robbed no one but moneyed men. Floyd."

Despite the reward (which was not withdrawn), Floyd was not caught. From June through December of 1932, he continued his odyssey, staging robberies in some 40 additional banks.

On June 16, 1933, Floyd, Adam "Eddy" Richetti, and Vern Miller, allegedly made an unsuccessful attempt to free their friend, Frank Nash, who was being transferred to a federal prison. The effort, which was made at Union Station in Kansas City, resulted in a shootout between federal officers and Floyd and his accomplices. Agent Raymond J. Caffrey of the Federal Bureau of Investigation lived just long enough to identify his attackers as a group led by "Pretty Boy" Floyd.

Kansas City Massacre

Following the "Kansas City Massacre," as it came to be known, the Kansas City Police received a postcard from the ever-colorful Floyd.

"Dear Sirs:

"I, Charles Floyd, want it made known that I did not participate in the masacree (sic) of officers at Kansas City. Charles Floyd."

The postcard had been mailed in Oklahoma which prompted Gov. Murray to send the National Guard into Floyd's old lair in the Cookson Hills again. They did indeed flush the criminal out, but the ever-wily criminal escaped once again.

Floyd next turned up in Cresco, Ohio. The police in Cresco also cornered Charles, but he shot his way out to freedom once again. Accompanied by two women, he and Adam Richetti reunited and made their way to Wellsville, Ohio, where their car developed mechanical problems.

While the two women took the car to be repaired, Floyd and Richetti hid out in the nearby hills. A suspicious local resident spotted the two men and reported them to the Wellsville Police Department.

Chief John Fultz, along with his deputy, Grover Potts, went to investigate the reported strange men. A gun battle ensued. Richetti was captured, but Floyd escaped once again. He had lost his machine gun, but he still had his two .45 caliber pistols.

His Last Day

On Monday, October 22, 1934, Mrs. Ellen Conkle was scrubbing her floors when she noticed a man in her driveway. She did not know it at the time, but she was face-to-face with one of the most notorious criminals of all time.

Floyd said he needed a ride into

Floyd allegedly committed some fifteen bank robberies in Missouri, Kansas, and Oklahoma.

Youngstown, and Mrs. Conkle replied that her brother could oblige. Floyd was already seated in the car with Mrs. Conkle's brother when two other cars drove up the driveway.

Realizing that the cars contained police officers, Floyd jumped out and ran for cover behind the Conkles' corn crib. East Liverpool officer, Chester Smith, saw Charles and advanced on the corn crib. Floyd ran again, and Smith fired two shots at the elusive outlaw. One of the rounds hit Floyd in the back and knocked him off his feet.

The account of what next transpired depends upon what one wishes to believe. According to one respected account, FBI agent Melvin Purvis closed in on Floyd, who was seriously wounded in the shoulder, and disarmed him. He then reportedly ordered an agent named Hawless to go ahead and shoot Floyd again, which the agent did, firing point-blank into his chest.

The life and bloody career of Charles "Pretty Boy" Floyd thus ended on a lonely Ohio farm, a long way from the criminal's north Georgia roots. In an ironic twist of fate, most modern-day references to Floyd list his hometown as Akin, Oklahoma, and it was to that locale that his body was conveyed for burial.

Today, no historic marker identifies the house (which still stands) in which Floyd was born and in which he lived during his early years in Adairsville, Georgia. As of this writing, an effort is underway to identify the site at which Floyd died in Ohio.

Endnotes

1. Interview with Mrs. Bessie Darby, March, 1995. Also, telephone interview with city clerk, city of Adairsville, Georgia, March, 1995.

2. Early deed books in the office of the Clerk of the Superior Court of Bartow County indicate many titles recorded to these families in the 1830s and '40s. See also the 1840 U.S. Census Population Schedule for Cass County, Georgia.

3. See land title records, Laurens County, South Carolina and Forsyth, DeKalb and Cass counties, Georgia. The Murphey farming operation in DeKalb County seems to have been conducted by Roger's son, Charles, while the farm in Cass County was managed primarily by Roger and John. Little is known about the Forsyth County Land.

4. Letters of Administration, Administration Returns, and Inventories for 185556, Office of the Probate Judge, Bartow County, Georgia.

5. Fannie Mae Floyd Moss interview, 1983. Fannie Mae Floyd Moss owned the old Redding Floyd farm until her death. She was the custodian of the old farm, and also was an unofficial repository of a wealth of folklore and stories involving the family line of Charles Arthur Floyd.

6. Pinson genealogical data in the files of the author.

7. Pike County, Arkansas population schedule for the 1860 and 1870 Censuses of the United States.

8. Fannie Mae Floyd Moss papers. Photo copy in the collection of the author.

9. Fannie Mae Floyd Moss papers in the custody of Katheryn Floyd, Ed.D.

10. Fannie Mae Floyd Moss interview, 1983.

11. Dale Floyd interview (Walter Floyd's grandson), 1992. As of this writing, Mr. Floyd resides in Oklahoma and is the nephew of Charles Arthur Floyd.

12. Mary Kathryn Gaines Korstian, "History Of The Gaines Family," Rome, Georgia: Brazelton-Wallis, 1973.

13. Sandy Lesberg. "A Picture History Of Crime," New York: Haddington House, 1976, pp 109110. Most of the material concerning Charles Arthur Floyd's career after he left Georgia was drawn from an extensive feature in the Sunday Magazine of the "Akron Beacon Journal," Akron, Ohio, October 20, 1974.

14. Telephone interview with Katheryn Floyd, Ed. D., daughter of Duff Floyd. The author personally recalls hearing Mr. Floyd recount this statement once at a family reunion.

The Bloody Civil War Battle at N. Georgia's Allatoona Pass

It is often missed as a travel destination by those seeking historic U.S. Civil War battle sites, and Allatoona Pass near present-day Cartersville was the locus of one of the bloodiest of the war. This battlefield, on a section of the old grade of the Western & Atlantic Railroad, offers not only a scenic hiking trail today, but a unique glimpse of a battlefield where the Blue and Gray fought not once, but several times to control this strategic site.

Visitors to Allatoona Pass today are immediately struck by the immenseness of the bluffs on each side of the road-bed where the trains of the Western & Atlantic Railroad once sped back and forth through this unusual break in the mountains. And following a visit to the site, it is also very easy to understand why it was so important, and why the Confederate Army – though severely outnumbered by this point, starving, and bereft of munitions – was so willing to fight for it not once, but several times.

On a "hazy drowsy Indian summer day" of October 5, 1864, two huge armies met in fierce engagement over the battlements which once made up Allatoona Pass. Though the "steel ribbons" of rail are gone today, the 100-foot long 65-foot-deep dug-out gulch still bisects the Allatoona Mountain Range.

It is quiet today, but approximately 160 years ago (as of 2021), it was a strategic spot at which a railroad could descend from the uplands of northwest Georgia down into the flatter country southward toward Atlanta. It was a strategic site deemed worthy of pursuit – time and again – in battle, because it was the only such railroad from the north into Georgia at that time, and as such, it was the sole method of re-supplying the weary troops engaged in battle to the south.

This once-vital link through the pass is little more than a dirt trail today, and it is difficult to even imagine how manual labor was able to dig such a gap to allow trains to navigate the pass. The silence and peacefulness of this site today belie its bloody history.

Most all of the casualties in the battles here were eventually removed to burial sites in Marietta, but for years after the war, bodies were still being found. Some were buried along the railroad. Some were buried around the one or two homes near the pass that survived the battle. The Union armies often enjoyed what they apparently felt was the diminishment of homes in the South by

The Mooney family, owners today of the Clayton-Mooney home at Allatoona, were photographed in front of the historic residence in 1994. The graves of 21 unknown soldiers have been located by the U.S. Army Corps of Engineers and are protected in the backyard of their home. *(Photo by Olin Jackson)*

excavating the yards in front and to the rear to bury the war dead.

One such historic edifice – the Clayton House – has been owned by several generations of the Mooney family in more recent years. It is a two-story clapboard residence across Old Allatoona Road from the pass. John Clayton, one of the original Bartow County settlers, is believed to have been a wealthy miner.

Mr. Clayton built this home in the 1830s, at a time when most local dwellers could afford little more than rustic log cabins. The Cherokee Indians still resided in the region and it was as yet a wild and untamed wilderness. After surviving those hard times, Mr. Clayton died one month after the battle, reportedly at least partly as a result of the shock of the incident.

Battle Scars

From May through October of 1864, the Clayton House served as a headquarters for the Union Army in this vicinity, but during the battle, the house at one time or another, served both sides as a hospital, such was the fierceness of combat and shifting nature of this battlefield.

Today, bullet holes are still visible in the upstairs walls, as is a dark blotch on one floor that is believed to be blood which soaked into the porous pine as a result of the many surgeries which took place in the home. In earlier days, new owners of such a home would have repaired and covered-over such blemishes, but today, ironically, they actually add value to a home. The Mooneys however, preserve them solely in the memory of those who died.

A white marble marker in the front yard of the home commemorates the battle and the men who died here. With the help of a U.S. Army Corps of Engineers archaeologist, the Mooneys have located the graves of 21 unknown soldiers buried in their backyard.

In addition to the importance of the railroad through this pass in 1864, a dusty trail through the mountains which passed by the Mooney home also represented the rustic byway for foot and cart traffic from Kingston to Marietta and then on to Atlanta, so it was vital as well.

On his zigzag march southward in early June of that year, Gen. William T. Sherman sought a depot where supplies could be safely stockpiled for the remainder of the Atlanta campaign. He selected Allatoona Pass and ordered that forts be built on either side of the pass to protect these supplies.

Log stockades with abatis (obstacles formed of trees – their tips cut into a point – felled toward the enemy), thickly-laced with telegraph wire, and outer rows of trenches, protected the forts. Even with overwhelming troop numbers

The Bloody Battle at Allatoona Pass   Bartow County

Photographed shortly after the initial battle of Allatoona Pass, this view shows one of the forts – of which there were two, one on each side of the tracks – and the materials used around their perimeter for defense. The identity of the men pictured is unknown. *(Photo by George N. Bernard, Photographic Images of Sherman's Campaign)*

in their favor (which was a rarity for the Confederate army) in this engagement, still the men in gray struggled on this day to gain control of the strategic site.

In the fall of 1864, the village (named for nearby Allatoona Creek by the Cherokee Indians which once had resided in the area) located at the south end of the cut included eight merchant shops, eight homes, a railroad depot, and several large new warehouses for the storage of large quantities of rations of hardtack stockpiled by Sherman.

Interestingly, 9,000 head of cattle also grazed nearby beside the Etowah River near Emerson. Today, very little remains of the former community of Allatoona Pass, the railroad station long gone, and the dirt road having been long ago circumvented by a more direct and finer U.S. Highway 41 – and still later by the large new and more modern Interstate 75 which overtook the usefulness of Highway 41.

The Battle Begins

In 1864, after Atlanta had fallen, federal supply troops returned to Allatoona Pass to retrieve the stores of hardtack which would be needed to feed the hungry soldiers continuing on the remainder of Sherman's *"March To The Sea."* The railroad from Atlanta, southward, had been destroyed at several places – again, by both the Union and Confederate forces at differing times, depending upon who controlled the area at what time. The Confederate Army obviously wanted to eliminate – or at least detain – any Federal re-supply of their troops, since any army "travels on its stomach."

To eliminate the railroad supply line, Confederate Lt. Gen. John G. Hood sent Maj. Gen. S.G. French with approximately 2,500 men to capture Allatoona Pass and "to fill up the deep cut at Allatoona with logs, brush, dirt, and debris, etc." to forbid access by trains. Hood obviously hoped to deny Sherman the use of this portion of the Western & Atlantic Railroad.

In the midst of an autumn downpour, Gen. French and his men left Big Shanty (present-day Kennesaw, GA) and trudged up the railroad through Acworth and across Allatoona Creek.

Mystery & History in Georgia

In this crude artist's concept of that day, Confederate forces (foreground) assault Allatoona Pass (right-center, distance).

Photographed several weeks after the Battle of Allatoona Pass, the forts atop the railroad pass are visible in the distance, and the Clayton-Mooney House – the only structure from this photo still standing today – appears upper left. *(Photo by George N. Bernard, Photographic Images of Sherman's Campaign)*

It is important to understand that, despite all the myriad and multiple roads, highways, and even pig-trails which exist today in north Georgia, in 1864, there were virtually none whatsoever, so the army which controlled the one or two roads – and the railroad – controlled the war in Georgia.

At 7:00 a.m., French's artillery commenced firing upon the federal guns at Allatoona which returned the fire.

French then sent in a courier with the following message for Gen. John M. Corse (who had recently hurried down from Rome with 1,054 men to reinforce the already strong garrison at Allatoona Pass): *"I have placed the forces under my command in such positions that you are surrounded, and to avoid a needless effusion of blood, I call on you to surrender your forces at once."*

Corse reportedly replied: *"Your communication demanding surrender of my command I acknowledge receipt of, and respectfully reply that we are prepared for the 'needless effusion of blood' whenever it is agreeable with you."*

French later claimed he never received the reply, and the fighting resumed. With bloodcurdling screams, Confederates leaped from the forest surrounding the fort and charged forward. Corse later wrote that *"a solid mass of gray advanced from the woods and started up the hill, with artillery support from the rear."*

Men were killed steadily in hand-to-hand combat, using bayonets and swords to stab and slash, and rifles and even rocks to club and crush. The federals fired their repeating rifles so rapidly that they became too hot to hold.

In the end, French realized he would be unable to accomplish his mission – that of interrupting and damaging the rail line at Allatoona Pass. Midway through the afternoon, French reluctantly ordered his troops to retire – the intense abatis and other defensive measures around the Pass coupled with the Federals' repeating arms simply too much for the war-weary Confederates with single-shot muskets to overcome.

In seven hours of fighting, 1,505 men – nearly one-third of the 5,000 engaged – were killed or wounded. French reportedly lost 700 men, but the up-hill fighting Confederates were still able to bring a greater number of casualties to Corse. Nevertheless, records seem to indicate it was unsuccessful French who was the most regretful.

"History will record the Battle of Allatoona Pass as one of the most sanguinary of the war," he wrote in a communique. In his postwar book, *Two Wars*, French bitterly recalled Allatoona as a mistake. *"It was Hood's ignorance of the enemy's position that caused the battle; it should never have been made."*

Both Sides Now

As suggested above, Allatoona Pass had been strategically contested by both Union and Confederate forces at various times of the war. It was through this same Allatoona Pass that James J. Andrews, a contraband merchant and spy, and his coterie of raiders sped on April 12, 1862, having just hijacked the *General*, Engine #3 from Big Shanty Station in Kennesaw.

"With a full head of steam, the locomotive, tender and three boxcars raced from Big Shanty, beginning what is often said to have been the most daring American railroad adventure ever attempted," wrote Joe F. Head in the March, 1994 issue of the *Etowah Valley Historical Society*'s newsletter – a rather flowery description of Andrews' abortive effort.

Andrews' objective, ironically enough, was to burn bridges and destroy as much of the railroad as possible – but this time, it was being done so that *Confederate* troops wouldn't be able to use the line for supplies. The destruction would have more quickly enabled Union troops to advance upon Chattanooga, and would have prevented Confederate troops in Atlanta from moving northward to defend against the invading Yankees, but it essentially was a fruitless effort.

After speeding past Hugo – a wood and water stop in Bartow County – the train with Andrews and his raiders went past the Clayton House and hurtled onward into Allatoona Pass. Not too far behind, William A. Fuller, conductor of the *General*, and fellow Confederates, pursued hotly. When the engine ran low on fuel in Ringgold near the Tennessee state line, Andrews abandoned it, and he and most of his men were captured shortly thereafter, and many of them shot as spies – including Andrews himself.

Unknown Grave(s)

As would be expected with a battlefield of this nature, there ultimately were numerous burials on the spot as bodies – which began decaying quickly in the summer heat – could not be removed in time for burial in established cemeteries. As such, it was not uncommon for the dead to be buried near where they fell.

Today, approximately one-half mile south of the entrance to Allatoona Pass, the body of an unknown soldier was buried – shortly after the battle – in quiet repose beside the railroad bed. Over the years, more than one explanation has gained traction to explain sites such as this.

One story maintains the remains in this grave are those of a young man whose lifeless body was being shipped home by rail in a box labeled simply as "Allatoona, Georgia." The container – which by that point had been traveling on the rails for several days – was understandably very ripe. It reportedly showed no origin of the body, nor identification.

As the story goes – and to their credit if true – six young women took over a job normally reserved for the men, who by that point in the war were in short supply.

In what could only be interpreted as an attempt to ascertain identity, the women bravely pried off the lid of the box with a crowbar. Inside, they

Major-General S.G. French was the commander in charge of Confederate forces in the Battle of Allatoona Pass. Despite the fact that his forces suffered considerably fewer losses than the Union Army, the injuries were so sanguinary that he later declared the assault of the forts atop the Pass should not have been made.

reportedly found only a young man dressed in Confederate grey. With him lay a rolledup, broadbrimmed black hat, but nothing else.

The women reportedly reattached the top to the box – with several if not all of them no doubt retching in the process – then collected themselves and dug a grave, placing a crude marker upon it to mark it for posterity.

In the 1940s, when Allatoona Dam was being constructed, the gravesite would have been buried beneath the waters of the lake rising behind the dam. As a result, the body reportedly was exhumed and then reburied a short distance from the original site, reportedly so that the gravesite could be respectfully maintained by the railroad's maintenance crew.

Even that effort, however, proved to be in vain, since the railroad line itself was also relocated sometime later to accommodate the lake construction, leaving the lonely grave in an abandoned field – known only to God. In 1980, a group of surveyors reportedly erected a gravestone at the site.

Some people today disagree with the above story of the origin of the body in the grave – including Acworth resident Don Armstrong. He maintains that his grandfather – John Armstrong – who was a carpenter, came from North Carolina after the war and built the aged brick building – which once was a general store – just south of the Clayton House in Allatoona. Armstrong says he grew up listening to old soldiers talking around a pot-bellied stove in the old store, and from their comments, he believes that a more accurate explanation would be that workers – no doubt clearing the line of debris, etc. to reactivate the line – found the body of a soldier along the tracks and simply buried it where they found it – end of story.

Yet another explanation for the identity of the body in the gravesite has been offered by Robert White, former stationmaster of the Cartersville, Georgia Depot, and the late Colonel Thomas Spencer, a journalist and historian. According to these two men, there are two unknown graves at Allatoona Pass, not merely one, and the bodies were originally buried on opposite sides of the former track bed.

According to Etowah Valley Historical Society member Joe Head who researched the information from these two gentlemen, *"the lesser-known grave site lies within the pass on the east side of the original track bed and has no marker.*

It is assumed that this Confederate soldier was buried a few days after the battle (quite possibly the same burial as the one associated above with the women of Allatoona)."

The Abernathy family (relatives of Head) of Cartersville is credited by Head with this lesser-known burial. Unfortunately, the location of this grave is virtually unknown today, because it has not been maintained by the railroad and the vicinity of the grave was repeatedly disturbed by relic hunters prior to the establishment and protection of a park at the site.

Head says the second and more visible grave (near the northern entrance of the pass and a few feet west of the tracks) was dug for *another* soldier who died in the battle.

"*Local historians believe this is the grave site of Private Andrew Jackson Houston of the 135th Mississippi Regiment who fell during the Battle of Allatoona,*" he recorded. "*In 1950, the railroad relocated and marked this grave approximately one-half mile south of the pass and a few yards west of the existing tracks.*" This grave is maintained today by area residents, and is the best-known of a number of unknown solder graves in the area.

Finally, in his publication entitled *The Western & Atlantic Railroad / Marietta: The Gem City Of Georgia*, former Georgia Governor Joseph Emerson Brown, an ardent student of history – and in particular the history of the Western & Atlantic Railroad – wrote a description of this soldier's gravesite in 1887.

"*The most characteristic memorial of this bloody and famous struggle which now salutes the eye of the tourist, as the train darts through the deep, fern-lined (Allatoona) pass, is a lone grave at its northwestern end, immediately by the track, on the west side. This is the resting-place of a Confederate soldier, who was buried on the spot where he fell. For years past, the trackhands of the Western & Atlantic Railroad have held this grave under their special charge. . . A neat marble headstone has been placed there on which is the following inscription: An Unknown Hero. He Died For The Cause He Thought Was Right.*"

General William T. Sherman, commander of the Union Army moving through Georgia, needed the supplies of hardtack stored at Allatoona Pass to feed his men as they advanced upon Atlanta. Though he repeatedly suffered more losses and could not directly penetrate the Confederate defenders confronting him north of Atlanta, he enjoyed far-greater man-power and war munitions than did the Confederates, and was more than willing to sacrifice both in his lust to "make Georgia howl."

Bartow County Phenomenon:

Author of the Bestseller
A Circuit Rider's Wife

Corra Harris is memorialized as the author of the best-selling book, *A Circuit Rider's Wife*, which later earned even more acclaim after the film rights were purchased by Hollywood for a major motion picture entitled **I'd Climb the Highest Mountain**. Unbeknownst to many, other historic aspects of Harris's past still exist in Georgia's Polk and Bartow Counties.

As of this writing, Corra Harris has now been gone for almost 100 years, but her most famous work – *A Circuit Rider's Wife* – is still read by young and old alike, though not in the numbers enjoyed at the height of its popularity in the 1950s. The book was written as a memorial to her own experiences as the wife of a Methodist minister, and contains many snippets of her life with her husband in their early years.

It is not known by this writer all of the locales where Corra and her husband, Lundy, spent their earliest years, but one spot which is known, is Rockmart, in northwest Georgia's Polk County. The Harris family moved to Rockmart after Lundy received a teaching position there at Piedmont Institute.

It was here in Rockmart that Corra wrote a now controversial letter to the *New York Independent Magazine* in defense of the lynching of a Black male in Newnan, Georgia. Despite its contents and message, the editor of the magazine found the letter so well written that he published it in 1899. It, ironically, was the interest stirred by publication of this article which became the catalyst launching Harris' writing career.

Following publication of the 1899 letter, Corra began regularly writing articles, editorials, and book reviews for multiple different news outlets, so she was quite active journalistically-speaking while living in Rockmart. Because of the growth in her creative writing during her stint in Rockmart, it is quite possible that she at least began work on *A Circuit Rider's Wife* while living and working there, particularly during the long hours she had to "while-away" as a "dorm-mom," while her husband earned their living as a teacher of Greek and Latin across the street at Piedmont Institute. If such was the case, and if Mrs. Harris was in fact living at that time in the girls' dorm – known then as Ballenger Hall

Lundy Harris, husband of Corra Harris, was employed as a teacher at Piedmont Institute in Rockmart, Georgia in the early 1900s. The Institute, pictured here, was built in 1890, and once stood not far from the site at which old Rockmart High School (present-day Rockmart City Hall) stands today at the corner of Piedmont Avenue and College Street. (Photo courtesy of GA Dept. of Archives & History, Atlanta)

– then there may well be an unmarked and unpreserved historic structure in this small northwest Georgia town.

Old Ballenger Hall – now weathered and forlorn – still stands today on Piedmont Avenue directly across the street from the present-day Rockmart City Hall complex (old Rockmart High School). Its credentials include not only having been the residence of a nationally-famous author, but quite possibly also the site at which at least a portion of a nationally-renowned best-selling work was written which later spurred the filming of a major motion picture based upon Harris' book

After publication of her book, Corra Harris went on to become Georgia's first woman writer to gain national prominence.

entitled – ***I'd Climb The Highest Mountain*** – starring famous Hollywood actors Susan Hayward, Rory Calhoun, and William Lundigan.

It is unfortunate that the former Rockmart dormitory has not been preserved and its historic significance chronicled in a historic marker of some form or fashion at the site. Time and circumstances do not favor the aged structure.

After publication of her book, Corra Harris went on to become Georgia's first woman writer to gain national prominence. Today, sadly, few people even remember Harris, and that's doubly unfortunate,

Built circa 1887 as the residence of Rev. E.W. Ballenger, head of historic Piedmont Institute in its early years, the structure pictured here later became "Ballenger Hall," the female dormitory of the Institute. Corra Harris and husband Lundy Harris lived here, supervising the females, while Mr. Harris was a teacher. Mrs. Harris is believed to have begun writing her best-selling novel, **A Circuit Rider's Wife**, while living here. This book was later brought to the silver screen (1950) by 20th Century Fox Film Company in a movie entitled **I'd Climb The Highest Mountain**, filmed in northeast Georgia's White County. *(Photo by Olin Jackson)*

because she once held court with powerful politicians and influential businessmen. She earned her clout through her literary achievements, and she was able to do this, because Corra Harris wrote at a time when women weren't normally acknowledged as writers.

Above and beyond her other personality traits, Corra was simply an interesting woman. She chronicled the life and times of the 1920s and 1930s in rural sections of the state, particularly as involved women.

She began her writing career as a minister's wife, and as her life progressed, she became something of a phenomenon in the literary world. In some odd ways, she could probably be considered one of the early advocates of women's liberation, even though she deplored most aspects of the movement.

Harris's mildly-disguised autobiographical best-seller concerned an itinerant Methodist preacher and his wife, and was published in 1909. At the time, it created a sensation by tweaking the church for certain practices. Shortly after its publication, the book gained even more prominence when it was serialized by *The Saturday Evening Post*.

Despite her literary successes, Harris must be viewed at best as a tragic figure, married at the age of 15 to a roving minister who, amazingly, was also a drug addict and alcoholic. As a result, Mrs. Harris endured an early life fraught with financial insecurity and depression. Her husband – Lundy – rarely held onto a job for more than a year or two, and the couple sometimes never knew from whence might come their next meal.

Harris also outlived all her immediate family. Her husband tragically succumbed to his depression and committed suicide in 1910. Prior to his death, Corra and Lundy had become the parents of several children, only to watch as, strangely, every single one of them died either in infancy or early childhood. Corra also was forced to nurse and watch her beloved sister, Faith, waste away and die at an early age, and, to her further dismay, ultimately found herself alone and desperately lonely in the world.

Corra's husband committed suicide by overdosing on morphine at the home of a friend in tiny Pine Log, Georgia in Bartow County. Following his death, Corra purchased her home that she called *In The Valley* located in nearby Rydal, Georgia, close to where Lundy had died. The rustic and spartan dwelling – actually an aged former Cherokee Indian cabin a few miles from Rydal in Bartow County – became her home for the rest of her life.

Though she continued to write

prolifically, her novels following *A Circuit Rider* were not of high literary merit, and never reached the prominence of her best-seller. In much of her work she, ironically, repeatedly praised femininity and condemned in general the women liberals of her day, while at the same time approving of such things as women's right to vote.

In her day, Corra held court with a long list of "up and coming" politicians, as well as with dignitaries who had already achieved a position of prominence. She enjoyed a reputation for hospitality, wit, and sparkling conversation, not to mention that of a powerful journalistic talent, all of which kept her constantly in demand.

The devoted writer eventually produced some 20 books, and even served as the first female war correspondent covering the war in Europe during World War I. She endured many hardships during her life, and was deeply affected by the deaths in her immediate family.

Corra Harris obviously resented the Methodist Church's harsh requirements for ministers and their wives during her day. She thought that no other organization was so opposed to the recognition of women as was the governing body of the church. She even resented the writings of the apostle Paul in the *Bible*, because of what she believed were prejudices therein against women in religious work.

When the opportunity presented itself, Corra eagerly accepted two writing assignments from *The Saturday Evening Post*. One was to report on the differences between women in Europe and those in the United States. After researching the topic at length, she decided that it wasn't the women in these locales who were different, but the men.

The early 1930s found Corra back

Following Rev. Lundy Harris's death by suicide, Corra Harris purchased an original former Cherokee Indian cabin outside Rydal, Georgia, which she renovated and dubbed "In The Valley." For the remainder of her life, Mrs. Harris lived at this home. This structure, which still stands today, is owned as of this writing (2021) by Kennesaw State University in Marietta, Georgia, and is the site of her burial.

at home in the little crossroads of Rydal, near Cartersville, Georgia. Here, she bullied and pampered the country folk, and continued to hold open house for state politicians, newsmen, writers, and churchmen (or churchwomen) of that day.

Corra's final journalistic efforts involved a column in *The Atlanta Journal* called *"Candlelit,"* which was syndicated nationally. Her literary career began to come to an end when her health began failing her in the mid-1930s. She ultimately passed away in Atlanta, Georgia, after suffering a fatal heart attack in 1935.

Corra Harris is buried at her home *In The Valley* in Rydal, Georgia. Prior to her death she instructed that a chapel be built over her gravesite there.

For many years thereafter, Corra's home and gravesite suffered from neglect. A prominent insurance executive in Bartow – Mr. Jody Hill – purchased the property and paid to have the home partially restored before donating it to Kennesaw State University in 2008.

The O.D. Anderson Family:

"We Lived in a Railroad Boxcar During the U.S. Civil War"

O.D. Anderson and his family were fated to not only live during the dark days of the U.S. Civil War, but also to be caught in the vortex of the terrible onslaught of General William Tecumseh Sherman's infamous "March To The Sea" through Georgia in 1864. Like many Georgians of that day, they were made of strong stock, and managed to survive and persevere.

The name "Anderson" translates to "son of Andrew." Variant forms of the name include "Anders" and "MacAndrews." The family line originates from Ireland, and usually is of immigrant origin, having been introduced into Ulster Province by settlers and traders who arrived from Scotland and England, especially during the seventeenth century. The name is particularly common of Scots-Irish settlers of colonial America in the Pennsylvania and Virginia sections of the 18th Century.

According to records, the line of Andersons from which Oliver Davis Anderson descends – as far back as can be traced by this writer – did in fact originate in Scotland, but also possibly from an ancient Celtic tribe in pre-history. Beyond the above-quoted possible sources, the O.D. Anderson family ancestors undoubtedly originated – as did multitudes of early American settlers – from immigrants seeking a better life in the New World during this country's colonial days.

Isaac Anderson was born in 1668, and married **Martha Bell**, born in Ireland in 1703. From them descended **James** (b. 1720, Ireland); James' son, **Robert** (b. 1763, York, PA); Robert's son, **Isaac (the younger)** (b. 1795, Rockbridge Co., VA); and then Isaac's son, **Oliver Davis "O.D.,"** (b. 04/05/1824 in Maryville, Blount Co., TN).

Isaac Anderson (the younger) moved his family from Tennessee to what soon would become Cassville and Cass County in 1834, when O.D. was still a small boy. Growing up in what then was the American frontier, the Andersons lived among the native Indians (most probably Muscogee or Cherokees) who still owned the land and would continue to reside in this vicinity until 1838 when they were removed in the tragic "Trail of Tears."

O.D., possessing very blond hair, apparently was one of the first – if not the first – fair-haired child witnessed by the native Cherokees there. O.D. later would relate to his grandchildren how the Indians would pick him up and carry him about exuberantly upon their shoulders, continuously frightening his mother.

Upon reaching maturity, O.D. married *Amelia Gaines* in 1845, moving to Adairsville to operate a hotel there (1847). He also later entered the mercantile business. O.D. and his young family show up in the *1850 Federal Census* in Cass County, Georgia, where he is listed as *"merchant,"* with real estate valued at $1,000.00, which at that time was a fairly modest existence, the equivalent of slightly less than $34,000.00 in 2021 dollars.

Sometime around 1858, O.D. decided to move his family to Arkansas to follow his parents who were emigrating westward. Life in the harsh realities of the west, however, apparently did not agree with O.D., though he spent nearly a year with his family there before returning to Georgia.

O.D. next shows up in the *1860 Federal Census* of Adairsville, Cass County (later Bartow Co.), Georgia, where he is listed as *"Postmaster."* At the time of the U.S. Civil War, O.D. was depot agent of the newly-completed Western & Atlantic (W&A) Railroad, and postmaster at Adairsville.

O.D. later would relate to his grandchildren how the Indians would pick him up and carry him about exuberantly upon their shoulders, continuously frightening his mother.

As one might imagine, the W&A was vitally important to the war effort, and O.D.'s job shortly became a very busy post. He was refused service by the regular Confederate Army because he had a defective eye, but he did serve as a member of what was called "the Georgia State Troops," possibly a home-guard unit. His talents with the manipulation of the railroad rolling stock were shortly put to good use by the Confederacy.

As the war progressed, O.D. was kept busy buying supplies for the Army in addition to his position with the W&A Railroad. As the battle front moved inexorably southward toward Adairsville in the war's later years, in part naturally following the route of the vital supply line of the W&A, it soon became apparent to O.D. that his home was about to be caught within the teeth of the conflict, and he and his family would have to refugee southward down into Georgia.

While the *Battle of Resaca* was taking place – where, incidentally, the father (Capt. Joseph Lockhart Neel, C.S.A.) of O.D.'s future son-in-law (James Monroe Neel) was involved in desperate fighting – O.D. was preparing his family to flee southward. Due no doubt to his employment with the W&A, and the vital necessity of his professional manipulation of the rail line's Georgia rolling stock in the war effort, O.D. and his family, interestingly, were permitted to have a railroad boxcar assigned to them for their personal use. They loaded it with household goods and were soon being transported by rail southward.

Due no doubt to the severe limitations of space within the confines of the boxcar, O.D.'s young son, James, who is believed to have been approximately 13 years of age at the time, amazingly traveled *on foot* with the family's slaves through what then was the very densely-forested north Georgia countryside. Making this feat even more unbelievable for a youngster of James' age is the fact that north Georgia in the 1860s was a trackless wilderness with virtually no roads whatsoever other than occasional game trails and a few very crude and aimless wagon roads. It is unknown today just how he was able to navigate his way southward and reach the vicinity of Atlanta, let alone locate his family in the rail car at Stone Mountain to which they had traveled, but locate them he did.

When O.D. and family had reached Atlanta, their boxcar had been sent out eastward on the Georgia Railroad, no doubt at the direction of O.D., whose talents by this point were being actively used by the Confederacy. O.D.'s responsibilities with the railroad soon required him to be separated from his family, and they continued onward alone into east Georgia.

According to family records, the Andersons traveled as far as Stone Mountain where they spent approximately two months on a railroad siding in that small town living within the strict confines of the boxcar. It is unknown by this writer if these circumstances involved freezing winter weather within the boxcar, or the unbearable boxcar heat generated by a harsh Georgia summer. Either way, however, their stark existence under these circumstances is almost unthinkable – but those were anything but "normal" times, and thousands of war-weary refugees had no roof over their heads whatsoever.

Nevertheless, apparently tiring of the harsh environment of their boxcar home, the Andersons eventually set out northeastward on foot to Monroe, Georgia, where they somehow obtained a home – either by renting or squatting – where they remained until the raids by Federal troops became so frequent and deadly, that they decided to move on once again – no doubt fleeing with retreating Confederate troops – into South Carolina, still amazingly traveling on foot.

After reaching South Carolina and

> *Making this feat even more unbelievable for a youngster of James' age is the fact that north Georgia in the 1860s was a trackless wilderness with virtually no roads whatsoever other than occasional game trails and a few very crude and aimless wagon roads.*

finding the accommodations and options for survival even worse, Amelia and her children decided to return to Monroe where they remained until the end of the war. The children reportedly even went to a rustic school in Monroe and made many friends there.

Meanwhile, O.D., according to family records and lore, was in South Georgia (quite likely Barnesville), where he continued to manage the Georgia state railroad rolling stock for the Confederacy – a task at which he apparently had become quite adept, moving it continuously around the state to keep as much of it as possible out of the hands of Federal troops. He continued in this capacity until the end of the war.

With the war concluded, both Amelia and her family in Monroe, and O.D. in south Georgia, traveled back across the war-torn, lawless, and devastated Georgia countryside to return to their home in Adairsville to see if anything remained to salvage. It is unknown today how they communicated with each other while separated, or what they discovered when they arrived back at their home in Adairsville. No family lore or ancient letter has been discovered which recorded those circumstances for posterity. Suffice it to say that historic records of the war which do exist describe a devastated Georgia, particularly along the route of the Western & Atlantic Railroad which would include Adairsville and present-day Bartow County.

Just as did many others, the Anderson family somehow struggled along and scratched out a meager existence in what was left of a culture literally *"gone with the wind."* O.D. initially attempted to survive by farming, but when that failed, he turned back to something about which he knew a bit more – the mercantile business – interestingly the same pursuit in the same town as the father of his future son-in-law, James Monroe Neel.

O.D. was able to survive within that profession, no doubt due to his many and close relationships with the people of his community. Bessie Bevins, one of O.D.'s grandchildren, described him during those days as follows: *"He had many noble characteristics. He was much more intelligent than the average man of his time, and his tiny frame bore a heart of gold. Kind and considerate of everyone, he was a very polite man and a devout Christian."*

Raised as a Presbyterian, O.D. joined the Baptist Church with his wife and was staunch in his belief. He was clerk of Oothcaloga Baptist Church outside Adairsville for many years. A friend once told him he made himself poor feeding preachers. He was a great believer in Sunday school and a faithful attendant for many years.

Anna Anderson, the future wife of James Monroe Neel later of Cartersville, was the third of O.D.'s six children. James Monroe Neel also grew up in Adairsville, probably in the same church as the Andersons. A daguerreotype described by the Neel sisters once showed a very pretty Anna with brown hair and eyes. She talked of wrapping bandages around the poor and desperate Confederate soldiers during the war.

Ella, O.D.'s eldest child, married Zachariah McReynolds in 1869, and began the flight of some of the family to Texas with her husband. Some of their descendants can still be found in Texas today.

Julia Margaret Anderson who was six years younger than sister Anna, was a pretty 19-year-old at the time of Anna's marriage to James Monroe Neel. She would later marry James herself following the untimely death of her sister.

In February of 1875, sister Laura Anderson married a Confederate veteran and cousin, Augustus Marcellus Foute. They eventually moved to Cartersville, an up and coming town on the W&A, ultimately building a fine home next to the James Monroe Neel home at 119 South Avenue. Old Cass County in which Adairsville had existed prior to the war had been totally devastated, with its county seat of government – Cassville – reduced to a charred ruin, never to be rebuilt. Cartersville, also on the newly-rebuilt Western & Atlantic Railroad, was the new "up and coming" community selected as the new county seat of government, offering new hope to both the Anderson and Neel families.

Brother Jimmy Anderson who had married the previous year carried a reputation as the family mischief-maker, and was continuously keeping things lively. He lived in Kingston with his wife Hepatia Bowden Anderson.

O.D. Anderson shows up in the **1880 Federal Census** of Cartersville, Bartow County, Georgia, with Julia Margaret and Frank still living at home with him and wife Amelia. O.D. is listed in this head-count as *"furniture merchant."*

Several years after the death of his wife Amelia in 1881, O.D. married her sister, Susan Gaines. Ever the vigorous seeker of new horizons, O.D. sought in Susan the same lust for life which he had enjoyed in Amelia.

No one can ever claim O.D. was not adventurous. With all of his experiences behind him to date, he chose – at almost 60 years of age – to strike out yet again in one last professional adventure. He and Susan apparently sold their Adairsville property and purchased, of all things, an orange grove in Apopka, Florida, and moved there to raise and market oranges. Both O.D. and Susan show up in the **1885 Federal Census** of Orange County, Florida where he is identified as *"orange grower."*

O.D. labored greatly and his orange groves flourished, but Lady Luck just did not favor the hard-working transplanted Georgia. Nothing could save him from the unexpected "great freeze of 1892." O.D. lost his entire livelihood for the second time in a little over 25 years, a situation which would have crushed and devastated a lesser man.

O.D. and Susan ultimately were forced to move back to Cartersville to live with his daughter and her husband – the Foutes – next door to his daughter and son-in-law James Monroe Neel. Those were family-centered times, when family stood strongly beside those who were struggling, and took in those who were homeless. Such was the case with O.D. and what remained of his family when the Foutes took them in.

The year 1909 must have been an even more difficult year for the Anderson family. O.D., who had reached the ripe old age of 85, tragically tumbled off the high front porch of James Monroe Neel's home (which still stands on South Avenue in Cartersville), possibly as the result of a stroke. He lingered for three days before passing.

Though the method of his death was tragic, O.D. nevertheless had enjoyed a full and rich – if overly difficult – life with a large and extended family, living out his final years next door to the substantial Neel homestead and many nieces, nephews, and grandchildren in Bartow County. He was remembered fondly by all who knew him and his name has been passed down to descendants.

The Jackson Brothers: Early Builders in Bartow

They were prominent in the construction industry in Bartow County as early as the 1850s – almost 175 years ago. The Jackson brothers left a standing legacy which is visible in many of the wonderful antebellum and post-bellum homes which still grace the landscape of the county even today.

A solitary entry on a page from an ancient receipts book (which, as of this writing, still hangs on the wall of the **Bartow History Center** in downtown Cartersville) lists the donors to the construction of the first courthouse in Cartersville. *"Milton C. Jackson"* is listed among those donors, and, as is explained below, undoubtedly was at least one of the original builders of that historic structure. In fact, he and his brother were instrumental in the construction of a number of the early commercial and residential structures of Bartow.

According to records, Milton was a skilled designer, and the "architect" side of a contracting partnership with his equally-skilled builder-brother, Zimri. Their trademark was large two-story homes with soaring gables and fancy trim-work ("gingerbread") on the porches and around the eaves of the homes. These homes were also often built with distinctive pointed Gothic Revival windows.

Zimri W. Jackson (1824-1894), was born in North Carolina, and migrated southward circa 1835-1840 to Pickens County, Georgia, with his father, Thomas Frederick Jackson (1782-1850) and the rest of their family. Both Thomas Frederick and his wife, Elizabeth Ann Patterson, are buried in old Hinton Cemetery in Pickens. As recently as the late 1980s, their sizeable historic family home – complete with the classic "soaring 'Jackson' gables" – still stood in Hinton before being tragically consumed by a fire reportedly set by vandals.

Accompanied by his brothers, Zimri migrated from Hinton to Cassville (old Cass County), Bartow County, GA, in the early 1850s, no doubt shortly after the death of their father in Hinton. By 1849, Cassville, the seat of Cass County, had grown into the largest town in northwest Georgia, with four hotels, two colleges, four churches, a two-story brick courthouse, and many commercial and private business endeavors. Business was booming there and it was a powerful magnet for young men searching for their destinies. It was a place in particular which offered many new construction opportunities for builders such as the Jacksons.

Mystery & History in Georgia

Located at 124 Etowah Drive, the structure known today as the Trammel House was built by the Jackson brothers, and carries the distinctive triple-gabled Gothic Revival lines which was a hallmark of their style. *(Photo by Olin Jackson)*

At 2 Cedar Lane, the beautiful and immense home of George Jackson – one of builder Zimri Jackson's sons – still stands today. It is not known for certain that this home was built by the Jackson Brothers, but it carries all the same distinctive Jackson architectural characteristics of soaring gables and pointed cathedral Gothic Revival windows. *(Photo by Olin Jackson)*

Zimri would have been 26 years of age at that time, and already skilled in the building profession, no doubt having learned his trade at his father's knee, judging from the impressive Hinton home which still survives today in photographs. In all early censuses in which Zimri appears, his profession is listed as either "master carpenter," or "builder," or "master builder."

On page 21 of the *Bartow County Heritage Book, Volume I*, Zimri W. Jackson is listed as *"among the important persons entering the Civil War from Bartow County."* He had enlisted circa 1862 in Company I, 40th Regiment, Georgia Volunteer Infantry, but when his prowess as a builder was discovered, he, according to tradition, was sent instead to Savannah, Georgia, where he reportedly built ships for the Confederate Navy.

Back in Cassville, between May 19 and November 5 of 1864, the entire town – including most of the residential homes – was all but erased forever, after being torched by federal troops. Only the churches and a smattering of homes used for hospitals and the quartering of troops survived. Following this utter devastation, the town was never rebuilt, the charred chimneys standing in mute testimony to the unconscionable destruction wreaked in Sherman's infamous *"March to the Sea."*

For many years, the scores of scorched chimneys in the former downtown area were a stark reminder of the dead town. Though Cass County had been absorbed into and renamed Bartow County in 1861, and though the town of Cassville had been relieved of its designation as the county seat of government, it nevertheless had continued to persevere until being burned to the ground by Sherman. Nearby Cartersville on the commerce-producing *Western & Atlantic Railroad* was named the new county seat.

Zimri's home, also built in 1861 on the Cassville Road, was one of the few in the Cassville area which miraculously survived the war and the heavy fighting

The Jackson Brothers: Early Builders in Bartow   Bartow County

At 23 Attaway Drive, the Jackson partners built the Attaway family – Jeffie Gilreath home which sits impressively on a knoll. (Photo by Olin Jackson)

On Mission Road, the brothers built Zimri's son – William Anthony – this classic plantation-style home with its distinctive "planter's porch," from which instructions were given each morning to field hands. This home is still in the Jackson family today. (Photo by Olin Jackson)

which had occurred in and around old Cass County. The talented builder returned to this home – which still stands today – and resided there for the remainder of his life after the war.

Several federal censuses of the late 1860s list the births of several of Zimri's children in "Cassville." The *Federal Census of 1870*, however, lists his residence as "Cartersville." Since Zimri had built his Cassville Road home (513 Cassville Road) approximately mid-way between Cassville and Cartersville, and since he lived there until his death in 1894, his "new" address listed in the 1870 Census undoubtedly resulted simply from the fact that Cassville proper had essentially disappeared, and the nearby growing Bartow township of "Cartersville," had become the new county seat of government and Zimri's new census address of record.

Among the earliest of the exceptional homes built by Zimri and Milton was this Cassville Road home. It has been owned for many years by the Joe L. Myers family. The late Mrs. Joe Myers is the granddaughter of Thomas Patterson Jackson, a younger brother of Zimri and Milton. Today, this impressive home is owned and occupied by Joel Myers and his wife Camille.

The huge 10 by 8-inch hand-hewn sills of this home are constructed with mortise and tenon joints, and pegged with wooden pegs. The corner posts are all heart pine and all the doors were hand-planed and constructed with pegs. All the floors – even the front porch floor – are basically still composed of the original wide boards laid down over 150 years ago.

To the rear of the aged Jackson-Myers home, evidence existed for many years of a ditch which was dug by the Jacksons to hide their valuables from the advancing Union troops. Mrs. Jackson reportedly also hid her nearly-grown son, along with the family livestock, in the woods to the rear of the home.

Another historic structure credited to the Jacksons is the original Bartow County Courthouse on the old Cartersville town square. In their youth in the 1950s, a number of the Jackson descendants of the area were told by grandparents and other long-time residents of Bartow on numerous occasions that their ancestors had been the builders of that structure (which today houses the *Bartow History Center*). There is substantive evidence to support this claim.

Mystery & History in Georgia

Located at 513 Cassville Road, Zimri built this home for himself in 1861, living here until he died suddenly one morning at the breakfast table. It is one of the few homes in the Cassville, Georgia, vicinity which were not burned by contingents of Union Gen. William T. Sherman during the U.S. Civil War. This structure is also still in the Jackson family, owned as of this writing by Joel and Camille Myers. *(Photo by Olin Jackson)*

On North Erwin Street, the Jackson brothers built partner Milton's spacious home which was owned in later years by the Rowland family and is occupied as of this writing (2021) by Strands Salon. *(Photo by Olin Jackson)*

An article on Zimri and Milton entitled *"Builders of Cartersville – the Jackson Brothers"* was published on November 11, 1975, in the **Cartersville Daily Tribune News**. This article documents their construction legacy in the county. The writer, Mr. Clyde Jolley, was well-known with that publication for many years, and a very active member of the **Etowah Valley Historical Society** (EVHS). Mr. Jolley describes in great detail the numerous homes in Cartersville – many of which are still standing – which were built by the Jacksons, and in his article he credits them with construction of the courthouse as well.

"By 1869, they (the Jackson brothers) had completed Bartow County's new courthouse which was to remain the county seat of government until 1902," Jolley wrote. His reference for this statement is unknown today, but his historical society credentials and his detailed article imply he researched the topic in depth.

Jolley also knew where the Jackson brothers' shop once had stood (corner of Carter and Railroad Streets) in Cartersville, a detail which had been thought by most to have been lost through time. A follow-up article in the May, 1994 issue of the EVHS's periodical again identifies the Jackson brothers as builders of the Bartow County Courthouse *"which remained the county seat of government until 1902."*

Even more compelling is an article published in *The Courant American* of Cartersville on May 26, 1892, page 4, which announced Zimri's death to the county. Among the many laudable accomplishments reviewed in this article, it states very clearly, *"Mr. Jackson was a successful farmer during his latter days, but earlier a prominent contractor, and was connected with the construction of Bartow's courthouse besides a number of Cartersville's business structures."*

As noted by the ancient receipts book page hanging today on the Bartow History Center wall in downtown Cartersville, Milton Jackson's name on this document clearly indicates he was a major donor to the courthouse construction at the height of his contracting partnership with his brother. Since

Elizabeth Ann Hill Jackson, wife of Zimri Jackson. *(Photo in author's collection)*

Zimri Wilson Jackson *(Photo in author's collection)*

he and Zimri literally "made their living" by building such structures in Bartow, it is highly unlikely they would have been contributing to the coffers of a competitor in the building trade in their own community.

To the contrary, Milton and Zimri almost certainly were in fact making a contribution toward a construction project with which they undoubtedly expected to be involved. In the *Bartow County Heritage, Volume I*, printed in 1995 and compiled by the *Bartow County Genealogical Society*, page 25 states as follows: *"The construction of the two-story brick courthouse began in 1867. There were contract disagreements between Wallis-McElreath* (the presumed initial builders) *and the county's building committee which caused a legal battle that stalled work that was stretched into 1869. Work started up again in 1870. The work was probably completed in 1873."*

At that point, since construction is listed as beginning in 1867, and ceased in 1868 – with the courthouse uncompleted – and since solid evidence on the History Center wall today lists Milton C. Jackson as a major donor to the construction, logic would dictate that the Jackson brothers almost certainly took over the project sometime in late 1869 or early 1870, following the legal settlement, and completed construction of the courthouse. After a substantial legal battle such as this which occasionally occurs in small town politics, it is highly unlikely the town fathers would have retained the Wallis-McElreath builders to continue work on the project, particularly if they had a "master builder" such as Zimri and his talented architect brother waiting in the wings who were even willing to donate to the construction cost.

Regarding the home-building talents of the Jackson brothers, evidenced today by the numerous historic structures still extant, one needs only to drive around the city and the outlying county to begin recognizing the signature marks of the Jacksons with the soaring gables, Gothic

According to the best indications and records, the building firm of Wallis-McElreath began construction of the original Bartow County Courthouse in 1867. Following contractual disagreements between them and the county's building committee, a legal battle ensued and construction ceased in 1868. In 1870, when the Jackson brothers are believed to have assumed the mantle of builders of the courthouse, work was recommenced and the structure was completed circa 1873. It was photographed here in 2020. *(Photo by Olin Jackson)*

Revival windows, and unique "ginger bread" trimmings upon these homes.

In *Historic Bartow County, Circa 1828 – 1866*, published in 1981 by the *Etowah Valley Historical Society*, it states, *"One style of architecture popular in the county just before and immediately after the Civil War was the gabled, early Victorian or Gothic Revival house, two stories high and embellished with fancy scrollwork on the balustrades and around the eaves; usually the gables of these houses were topped with carved finials. Pre-Civil War homes in the area (thought to be the products of contractors Zimri and Milton Jackson) that are in the Gothic Revival mode include the Jackson-Myers house, the Billy Jackson house, the Munford house and the Dr. Wilson Hardy house."*

According to records, the unique construction skills of the Jackson brothers were employed in a variety of ways in the county, but were most instrumental in the construction of very eye-pleasing residences. Among the many homes they built, those still standing as of this writing (2021) include:

On Mission Road, they built the former residence of William A. "Billy" Jackson, Zimri's son, which still remains in the Jackson family today. This fine plantation-style structure has the classic "Planter's Porch" from which instructions were given each morning to the field hands. Though this home is slightly in disrepair as of this writing, it once was a show-piece of the county.

At 124 Etowah Drive, the Jackson brothers built a signature home for the Trammel family.

On North Erwin Street, they built Milton's spacious home which was owned in later years by the Rowland family and is occupied today by Strands Salon.

At 23 Attaway Drive, the partners built yet another eye-pleasing creation for the Attaway family which was later owned by the Jeffie Gilreath family and, as of this writing, by Mr. Jim Hunter.

On West Avenue, they built a fine home for the Lumpkin family. When a fire partially destroyed the upper level of this residence, the Jacksons' trademark soaring gables were replaced by a conventional roofline. This home, having lost its architectural beauty lines, was later torn down to make room for new construction.

At 2 Cedar Lane and West Avenue, George Jackson, another of Zimri's sons, lived in an impressive domicile which still stands. It is not known positively today whether or not this home was built by the Jackson brothers, but it has all the ear-marks of their work, right down to the soaring gables and pointed cathedral gothic windows, both of which were clearly their trademarks appearing on their other homes.

On Cherokee Avenue, they built a home for the Gaz White family which was later owned by City Manager Walter Mahone. This home later incurred a major fire in 1987, and was relocated to an unknown location.

Out in Peeples Valley, the Jackson brothers built, in 1859, a home for Lewis Martin Munford later owned by Oscar Peeples. It was subsequently sold and moved to a site in Cobb County, Georgia, circa 1983.

An imposing nine-room home located east of Cassville on White Road was built in the 1850s for Dr. Weston C. Hardy. It was one of only three Cassville homes spared by federal troops during the war, and a compelling case can be made for its construction by Zimri and Milton. This home, which was used as a hospital by both the Confederacy and federal troops during engagements, was built only a very short distance from Zimri's Cassville Road home. It also has unusual front porch pillars which are identical to the ones which appear in the photograph of the Hinton, Georgia, home of Frederick Jackson, father to Zimri and Milton. The Hardy home also has the identical single soaring front gable so often incorporated into the Jackson creations.

Milton was the younger of the two brothers in the Jackson partnership, but he passed away relatively early in life at the age of 45 on February 14, 1872. Knowing that death was eminent, Milton designed an elaborate tomb which was constructed according to his specifications to house his last remains on the summit of historic Oak Hill Cemetery in Cartersville.

Zimri lived considerably longer, dying of what appears to have been a heart attack or stroke on May 20, 1892, at the age of 70, while seated at the breakfast table of his Cassville Road home.

Though of poor quality, this photo of the boyhood home of Zimri and Milton Jackson – built circa early 1840s by their father, Frederick, in present-day Hinton, GA – no doubt served as a learning experience in home-building for both young men and was valuable in their later endeavors. (Photo courtesy of Joe L. Myers)

He reportedly reached the table on the morning of his death, sat down and stated that he felt ill, and then simply collapsed into his morning meal. Interestingly, he is buried in Cassville Cemetery, not Oak Hill in Cartersville.

There no doubt were other homes built by the Jacksons in the vicinity of Bartow which were either destroyed during the Civil War or later by fire, neglect and other causes. Nevertheless, travelers and residents alike often still encounter impressive two-story historic homes in the Bartow County vicinity with either one, two or three "soaring gables," fancy trimwork, and oftentimes "pointed" Gothic windows. These homes invariably may be credited to the long-ago efforts of the Jackson brothers who were instrumental in the development of the county in the last half of the 19th Century.

(Zimri W. Jackson is the great-great-grandfather of the children of the late Ralph Olin Jackson, Jr. and the late Marilyn Jordan Jackson of Rockmart, Georgia, as well as of many other Jackson descendants in the Polk, Bartow and Hall County, Georgia areas.)

The Neel Family: Early Settlers of Bartow

The Neel family was among the first settlers in Bartow County, Georgia, and instrumental in the re-establishment of order and civility in that area following the devastation wrought by the U.S. Civil War. Family members volunteered for service and were wounded in action in the U.S. Civil War; were often elected to public office, serving in posts such as representatives to the Georgia State Legislature and U.S. Presidentially-appointed positions; and received Georgia state gubernatorial appointment to judgeship.

Joseph Lockhart Neel (09/22/1826 – 03/09/1909) came first to Adairsville (ne Gordon County) in the early 1840s and was prominent in the foundation of that community. He appears in the *1850 Federal Census of Gordon County*. There, on November 2, 1848, he married Mary Ann Swain and began business as a merchant. This early involvement in northwest Georgia occurred barely ten years after the Cherokee Indians had been removed from this and other regions of Georgia on the infamous "Trail of Tears."

According to the *History of Bartow County* (1933) by Lucy Josephine Cunyus Mulcahy, *"Adairsville was incorporated in February, 1854, with D.A. Crawford, Joseph Lockhart Neel, H.G. Lawrence, A.C. Trimble, and John W. Parrot appointed as town commissioners."* On page 85 it also states that in 1857-1858, Joseph Lockhart Neel was elected to and served in the Georgia State Legislature, and also as a member of the Masonic Lodge in both Adairsville and Cartersville.

In 1862, shortly after the onset of the war, "Captain" Neel organized, at Adairsville, a company of volunteers for service in the Confederate Army as a part of Company H ("Veach Guards," Bartow County, GA), 40th Regiment, Georgia Volunteer Infantry, Army of Tennessee, C.S.A., commanded by Col. Abda Johnson.

According to historic records at the Georgia Department of Archives & History in Atlanta, Captain Neel's unit was assembled with other northwest Georgia contingents at Camp McDonald near Big Shanty (present-day Kennesaw), Georgia, and initially brigaded with the 41st, 42nd, 43rd, and 52nd Georgia Infantry Regiments.

Engagements

The 40th was first sent to Tennessee, then Mississippi, where it was placed in

Barton's Brigade, Department of Mississippi and East Louisiana. The 40th participated in the conflicts at Chickasaw Bayou and Champion's Hill, and were part of the garrison which was forced to surrender during the siege of Vicksburg on July 4, 1863. Captain Neel, as were many others, was wounded in this conflict. It is worth noting, that while the Union forces were able to surround and starve the Confederates into surrender, they were less able to actually defeat them in battle during the early years of the war. However, as disease, malnutrition, starvation and other deprivations began taking a toll upon the Confederates during the later years of the war, their losses began to accumulate progressively.

After undergoing a prisoner exchange, the 40th Georgia was reorganized and attached to General Stovall's Brigade, which again included the 41st, 42nd, 43rd, and 52nd Georgia Infantry Regiments and, the 1st Georgia State Line Troops.

The 40th (including Capt. Neel) ultimately served on numerous battlefields from Chattanooga to Nashville and in many of the major engagements in the Georgia Campaign, including the brutal clashes at Shiloh, Chattanooga, Resaca, Chickamauga, Missionary Ridge, the Hundred Days Battles, New Hope Church, Kennesaw Mountain, Peachtree Creek, and the Battle of Atlanta.

According to Sam Watkins, author of the now well-known book, *Company Aytch*, and a line soldier of Company H of the First Tennessee Infantry Regiment, Army of Tennessee from the opening of the war until its close, some 5,100 troops who originally composed the First Tennessee had been reduced to roughly 125 officers and men at the conclusion of the conflict in 1865, such was the bloody and destructive nature of the engagements in which this army served.

The other infantry units of the Army of Tennessee fared little better. During this time, Captain Neel was one of many individuals in this group who found themselves fighting through their own towns and communities and, indeed, their own shattered homes and former properties, as they sought – though severely outnumbered – to turn back the tide of invasion by Union General William T. Sherman whose army was relentlessly ransacking, thieving, pillaging and burning its way down through Georgia in the spring and summer of 1864. It is still a point of pride among many Southerners, that despite the fact that Sherman's troops – according to the general's own figures – numbered in excess of 100,000 troops during his march through Georgia, and the Confederate forces confronting him numbered less than 60,000 troops at best, the Federal forces still were unable to consistently defeat the men in gray in head to head combat, and were forced to perform constant flanking movements in order to reach and ultimately surround Atlanta to lay siege to the city.

After his withdrawal from Atlanta with the 40th, Captain Neel later also saw action in the horrendous desperate engagements at Franklin and Nashville, Tennessee, and finally, at Bentonville, North Carolina, where he witnessed the conclusion of the war, surrendering on April 26, 1865. By this point, only a handful of the original enlistees in the 40th Georgia remained to return to northwest Georgia where they found their families scattered, their homes and farms totally destroyed, and their way of life erased from the landscape forever. Many once-prosperous towns and communities of northwest Georgia,

Capt. Joseph Lockhart Neel, dressed in his Confederate uniform, reveals how a portion of his hand had been shot-away during engagements of the U.S. Civil War. Capt. Neel organized a company of volunteers in 1862 at Adairsville, Georgia, and served until the surrender of the South in 1865.

dismal December day when the line of battle was formed... As we marched on down through an open field toward the rampart of blood and death, the Federal batteries began to open and mow down our men... a scene so sickening and horrible that it is impossible for me to describe it... A sheet of fire was poured into our very faces, and for a moment, we halted as if in despair as the terrible avalanche of shot and shell laid low those brave and gallant heroes... Never on this earth did men fight against such terrible odds... The earth was red with blood. It ran in streams, making rivulets as it flowed... Dead soldiers filled the entrenchments. The firing was kept up until midnight when it gradually died away."

Wounded In Action

Such was the dramatic and terrible specificity of Watkins' recollections and observations, that they have been quoted numerous times, not only in every segment of *The Civil War*, the acclaimed 1990 television series by noted Civil War authority Ken Burns, but also frequently in the multi-volume *Time-Life* series *The Civil War*. Captain Neel fought in all of these engagements.

including Van Wert in Polk, Cassville in old Cass County, Etowah, Stilesboro, and Allatoona in Bartow – among numerous others – never recovered from the devastation, some of them disappearing completely from the landscape.

Watkins described the terrible Battle of Franklin (in which Captain Neel participated) near the end of the war as *"the blackest page in the history of the war of the Lost Cause. It was the bloodiest battle of modern times in any war. It was the finishing stroke upon the independence of the Confederacy. I was there. I saw it. My flesh trembles and creeps and crawls when I think of it today... It beggars description. It was four o'clock on that dark and*

Where many of the Southern troops joined for only a one or two-year enlistment and then returned home, Neel and others like Watkins endured what undeniably were unbelievable hardships in their day-to-day quest for survival for the entire duration of the war. From the day he volunteered his services, Captain Neel never hesitated nor wavered in his military commitment, serving long after many others had quit.

It would, in fact, have been quite easy for Captain Neel to simply retire from the field and return home as did many of his compatriots. He suffered from a number of wounds and literally passed right by what was left of his home in Adairsville during the Army of Tennessee's retreat in the face of the overwhelming numeric superiority of Sherman's Army in July of 1864. Neel, however, remained resolutely devoted to his unit. Quitting was not an option.

According to the official Muster Roll of Company H, 40th Regiment, Georgia Volunteer Infantry, Army of Tennessee, CSA, Captain Joseph Lockhart Neel – as was also the case with countless of these noble souls – was wounded at Vicksburg, Mississippi, on July 4, 1863; in Atlanta, Georgia (during the Battle of Atlanta) on July 22, 1864; and in Bentonville, North Carolina on March 19, 1865. He was listed in the Greensboro, North Carolina hospital on April 26, 1865, and paroled at Charlotte, North Carolina, on May 6, 1865.

According to reminiscences of his experiences which were written down prior to his death by his daughter, Leonora Neel, Captain Neel was directed by Col. Abda Johnson of the 40th Regiment to *"take charge"* one day. *"After several color bearers had been shot down before another could be appointed, Capt. Neel could not bear to see the (Confederate) flag trail in the dust any longer,"* Ms. Neel recorded. *"Of course the enemy frequently aimed at the color-bearer* (since he served as the rallying point for the troops and attracted significant attention) *and he* (Capt. Neel) *was therefore wounded in the hand on this occasion. Many times he was in hard-fought battles, and

From the day he volunteered his services, Captain Neel never hesitated nor wavered in his military commitment, serving long after many others had quit.

was wounded no less than three times."* On one occasion (date unknown) Captain Neel was photographed in uniform with his arm held aloft, showing the missing portion of his hand which had been shot away.

One incident – somewhat humorous today if such is possible of so terrible an event – recorded by Ms. Neel of Captain Neel's reminiscences involved a fellow soldier. *"When falling back during Sherman's campaign through Georgia, one of Capt. Neel's soldiers became so exhausted – or stubborn about giving up his homeland – that he stopped and stated that he would not go another step further, and subsequently dropped down into a fence corner. It was at about that time, as fate would have it, that a shell struck the fence (near) where this soldier was resting, causing him to immediately reassume the march – double-quick – running ahead of Capt. Neel who asked him in passing why he was running so fast. The startled soldier reportedly paused only briefly to reply, 'Because I can not fly!'"*

After the war, according to records, since Adairsville had not been completely destroyed, Captain Neel rejoined his wife, Mary, in that community to engage in farming and the mercantile business once again with his brother-in-law, W. Jesse Swain, helping to rebuild that shattered community. He was active in educational, civic, and political affairs locally, and was elected once again to represent his region in the Georgia General Assembly for the 1876-1877 term.

James Monroe Neel, an early attorney, city judge, and son of Joseph Lockhart Neel in Cartersville.

In 1882, Mr. Neel removed to live in Cartersville, near his son who had become prominent in the development of that community. Though he had remained active in his community endeavors even after returning from the terrible experiences of the war, Captain Neel, reportedly, was never the same man, his spirit reportedly broken. He died 27 years later in 1909 at the age of 83, in his home on "Neel Street" in Cartersville.

It quite possibly was Captain Neel, as a farmer upon the Neel lands in Cartersville – or possibly even one of the field-hands tilling his land – who discovered a large Native American hand-axe/tomahawk today in the possession of one of Mr. Neel's descendants. This hand-axe was kept in the Neel family at their home – coincidentally not far from present-day Etowah Indian Mounds in Cartersville – for many years. Mr. Neel's granddaughter, Isabelle Neel Jackson, often told family members prior to her death that her mother and father, interestingly (and ironically), had used the stone "to tenderize steaks."

James Monroe Neel

Captain Neel's eldest surviving son, James Monroe Neel (01/22/1850 – 11/30/1930) was a young boy during the days of the Civil War in Georgia. He attended the common schools of Bartow and then the University of Kentucky. He taught school for two years while studying law with his great-uncle, David W. Neel of Gordon County, and was admitted to the Georgia Bar on February 1, 1874.

Records indicate that in 1875, James had opened a law office in Adairsville, but soon relocated to Cartersville where he became associated with the firm of Gen. W.T. Wofford. Approximately two years later, he became a partner with Judge Robert B. Trippe.

In 1881, James became principal owner of the law firm of Neel, Conner and Neel (W.J.) of Cartersville, but this partnership was dissolved when his brother, W.J., received a government appointment from President Grover Cleveland. During a later period, James was the principal of Neel & Peeples (O.T.) of Cartersville.

Also in 1875, James married Anna Anderson of Adairsville. Their children were Ella, born in 1876, Joseph Francis, born in 1878, and Oliver Anderson, born in 1881. To James' utter despair, Anna died from what was described as "child-bed fever" 26 days after Oliver's birth. From that point forward, Oliver was devotedly raised by James' spinster sister, "Aunt Nora" (Leonora).

On January 4, 1883, James married once again, this time to Julia Margaret Anderson, the sister of his beloved late wife, Anna. According to genealogical notes by Jule Brooke which she transcribed from conversations sometime in

The extended Neel family photographed in front of the family residence at 119 South Avenue in Cartersville. From left to right (rear, standing) as can best be identified are: Blanch Hall Neel (Joe Neel's wife); Juliet Anderson "Dootz" Neel-McClatchey; Oliver Anderson "Uncle Poly" Neel; Mary Ella Neel; James Monroe "Syl" Neel, Jr.; Robert William "Bob" Neel; Julia Anderson Neel (James Monroe Neel's wife); and Joseph Francis Neel. (Seated in chairs, left to right): Joseph Norris Neel (eldest son of James Monroe holding baby Gladys); Gladys Neel; Roland Hall Neel; Susan Gaines Anderson (O.D. Anderson's wife); Oliver Davis (O.D.) Anderson; James Monroe Neel, and Joseph Lockhart Neel (far right). (Seated on the ground): Fredrick Donald Neel; Blanche Neel; and Isabelle Neel Jackson (beside pillow).

the mid-1900s with James' three daughters – Ella ("Aunt Neely"), Juliet ("Aunt Dootz"), and Isabelle ("Izzie") – James and Julia Margaret were married *"in the Hedden's home on Bartow Street"* in Cartersville. More children were born into the family from Julia Margaret. Bob was born in 1890, Isabelle in 1894, and Fred in 1898.

Life on South Avenue

As his law practice prospered and family grew, James knew that a larger home would be necessary, so he contracted with a builder for the construction of a substantial residence on South Avenue (present-day 119 South Avenue) in Cartersville. This fine structure was within easy walking distance of James' law offices downtown, and still stands today. It has been said that James' wife, Julia Margaret, could always tell in later years when James was homeward bound as she could hear his walking cane tapping on the sidewalk as he walked up South Avenue.

On one side of the large Neel home stood another home where the Foute family lived. Julia Margaret's other sister, Laura Anderson, had married Augustus Marcellus Foute who was a cousin. Augustus had lost an arm in the war, but he never allowed this handicap to slow him in the least. He and Laura produced four children: Augustus, Jr.; Anna; Julia; and Mary.

On the other side of the Neel home (toward rear?) stood the final abode of Captain Neel where he, his wife, Mary; his daughter, Leonora ("Aunt Nora"); and Oliver Neel lived. As indicated earlier, Oliver was the third child of James Monroe and his first wife, Anna, and was raised by Aunt Nora.

Two magnolia trees which ultimately grew to a substantial height were planted in the front yard of the 119 South Avenue home. This yard also contained pink oleander, parina, double violets, tulips, white ferns or asparagus, and a 3 to 4-foot lemon tree that reportedly produced delicious fruit "as large as oranges."

To the rear of the home was a large field for the family cow. The Neel sisters vividly remembered one occasion when they were sent hunting for the cow – which had "escaped" on a rainy day – and their irritation with Grandpa Neel at sending them off to fetch the wayward beast.

The smokehouse where corn shucks were burned to smoke sides of bacon, hams, and sausage, was located to the rear of the home. The hogs were kept in a pen nearby. The barn to the rear of the home was the domain of "Plugola," an aged, dark-coated horse once used to

This fine structure was within easy walking distance of James' law offices downtown, and still stands today. It has been said that James' wife, Julia Margaret, could always tell in later years when James was homeward bound as she could hear his walking cane tapping on the sidewalk as he walked up South Avenue.

pull the wagon which provided transportation in earlier days.

In the 1920s, mischievous grandchildren – who were constantly exploring the grounds – chanced upon a keg of whiskey which had been secreted away in the barn. It was a discovery which became a part of the family lore in those days of "abstinence," particularly in a community which sported the likes of nationally-famous and fiery evangelist Sam Jones who lived just a few blocks away in his elegant mansion.

The big Neel home was the center of much activity over the years with the advent of all the children and grandchildren and cousins. The home had shutters on the windows, but no screens except in the dining room. A large sofa in the living room was remembered as being "hard," and due to its lack of use, the hounds were allowed to sleep on it. Upstairs there were double-beds in every room for the many children who lived, laughed, loved, and played throughout this happy domain until they reached the age to go out into the world on their own.

The children were all devout Baptists, just as were their parents, and were regulars in the nearby Baptist Church. Judge Neel was a member and a deacon there for many years, but the elder Captain Neel strangely did not attend church. He often explained that he had decided to abstain from church services ever since the day he had fallen into a deep ditch alongside one of the dark streets while walking home after attending a prayer meeting one night. He always claimed he was shocked to still be alive, and insisted it was a "sign" that he should avoid church from that point forward.

Community Service

In 1892, James, just like his father before him, ran for and was elected to the Georgia State Legislature. During the 1893 session, he wrote and introduced the *Neel Pleading Act* which was passed into law (Acts of 1893, page 56) in Georgia. It regulated the pleading procedure in civil actions in Georgia courts, and is still in use in the courts today (as of this writing, 2021).

By 1907, James Monroe Neel was recognized as one of the foremost legal minds in the state. He was appointed by Governor McDaniel in 1885 as the first judge of the City Court of Cartersville. A retiring and modest man in public, James, according to records, was masterful in the courtroom and highly respected as a legal force who was always supremely-prepared when trying a case.

James' counsel eventually was widely sought throughout the state, and indeed, in some corners nationally. His clients were many and varied, and included the Seaboard Airline Railway, the North Carolina and St. Louis Railway ("N.C. & St. L."), the Louisville and Nashville Railroad ("L. & N."), the First National Bank of Cartersville, the American Textile Company, and many others.

The year 1909 must have been a difficult one for James. Oliver Davis ("O.

D.") Anderson (Julia Margaret's and Anna's father who was 85 years of age) fell off the porch of the Neel home on January 25th, and died three days later. Captain Neel – who had weathered many a storm, not the least of which was his service through almost four years of deadly combat in the Civil War – died in March of that year at the age of 83, in his home next to James' home.

As is the case ultimately with all men, James Monroe Neel eventually reached the age at which he was forced to retire, and his tapping cane was no longer heard on South Avenue. His legal practice was carried on by two of his sons – James Monroe Neel Jr. ("Syl") and Fred – and by a grandson, James Monroe Neel III. Descendants of the family still practice law under the Neel banner in Cartersville even today.

The 1883-1884 Cartersville City Directory states as follows: *"J.M. Neel – attorney at law. Judge Neel is one of the most talented lawyers of north Georgia. He is a native of Bartow, was raised in Adairsville, and studied Blackstone in Calhoun, being admitted to practice in 1874. He has since built up a large clientage among the leading people of this and adjoining counties. He has a neat and comfortable office to the north of the hotel on the public square. In his two years' service as City Judge he has shown fine judgement and profound knowledge of law. He is a member of the State Bar Association and is one of the energetic citizens of Cartersville."*

(Joseph Lockhart Neel is the great-great-grandfather of the children of the late Ralph Olin Jackson, Jr. and the late Marilyn Jordan Jackson formerly of Rockmart, Georgia, as well as many other branches of the family, including the McClatchey, Brooke, and Aldred families to name just a few.)

The Mystery of the Woolfolk Murders

It was one of the most horrible crimes in Georgia history, and it almost certainly occurred as a result of mental derangement. In a modern trial for such a crime, Tom Woolfolk possibly would have been ruled as criminally insane. Instead, he received a "Guilty" verdict in a few minutes, then was hung for eighteen minutes until dead. Today, questions about this trial and the actual perpetrator of this crime remain unanswered.

As of the date of this writing (2021), it has now been over 130 years since the horror which occurred on August 6, 1887, in Bibb County, Georgia, yet distant members of the family who carry the name of the defendant still cannot escape association with this tragedy – for obvious reasons.

Though the crime occurred in Bibb approximately 12 miles west of Macon, its roots lie on Pulaski Street – just off Prince Avenue – in Athens, Georgia, not far from the sprawling campus of present-day University of Georgia. Though few are aware of it today, this impressive Athens neighborhood became the spawning ground for one of the most notorious and heinous murders in Georgia's long and storied history.

It was in this Pulaski Street home that a youngster – raised in a privileged realm – found security and hope. It was here that he became accustomed to a life which eventually was harshly taken from him as a child, casting him into another world which was alien and foreign, and which resigned him to a life over which he had no control and in which he could not bear to live. But I digress -

Tom Woolfolk's (pronounced "Wool-fork") father – Richard Franklin Woolfolk[1] – was graduated from the University of Georgia in 1854, and soon thereafter was married to a Miss Susan Moore, daughter of Mr. Thomas Moore in Athens. Susan and Richard moved to Bibb County, Georgia, where the Woolfolk family owned a plantation, and it was here that they settled to live their lives.

Richard's father – Thomas Woolfolk – hailed from a prominent North Carolina family. He (Thomas) had migrated to the Macon area to seek his fortune when much of that area was still a virgin wilderness inhabited by the native Creek Indians.

Why Thomas chose Bibb County in south Georgia for his home is a mystery today. Perhaps he recognized the possibilities for growth in the area coupled with the extremely inexpensive

48

nature of the real estate there at that time. Whatever the circumstances, he purchased a one hundred-acre tract of land which he ultimately developed into a substantial enterprise, allowing him the latitude to play a major role in the early growth of Macon.

Following his marriage to Susan, Richard returned to his father's plantation to take up the reins of the family businesses. All went well for the early years, but there were dark clouds on the horizon.

Early Life

From the union of Susan and Richard came three children – two little girls and a darkly quiet little boy. The two females were named Floride and Lillie. The little boy – Thomas G. Woolfolk – was born on June 18, 1860, just prior to the U.S. Civil War.

Susan, sadly, died soon after her son's entry into this world. The circumstances in rural Bibb County in the 1860s were primitive, so Susan's death is understandable. Childbirth often resulted in the death of the mother in the days prior to hospital births.

There was not even a nearby cemetery in which to bury Susan, so she reportedly was interred in the yard of the Woolfolk home, where a holly bush was planted to mark the site for posterity.

Shortly thereafter, Richard answered the call to service in the Confederate Army. With no direct parental

Though few are aware of it today, this impressive Athens neighborhood became the spawning ground for one of the most notorious and heinous murders in Georgia's long and storied history.

supervision remaining on the plantation north of Macon, young Tom was sent to Athens to be raised by his mother's sister, Fannie Moore Crane, who was married to John Ross Crane, a builder of some renown in that city prior to the war.[2]

Tom spent the first seven years of his life in the Pulaski Street neighborhood in a substantial house that John Crane had built in 1842. This structure still stands today, and has been occupied for many years by the University of Georgia chapter of Sigma Alpha Epsilon (SAE) fraternity.[3]

As the fighting no doubt raged in the far off confines of Virginia and Maryland as the U.S. Civil War progressed, Aunt Fannie fed, bathed, and clothed young Tom in an all-encompassing security in Athens, Georgia. She quite likely pushed him in an infant carriage down Prince Avenue on some days, past the magnificent Taylor-Grady mansion (which still stands as of this writing) and other well-known Athens edifices during the early 1860s.

Though they escaped most of the destructive nature of the war – since Athens was not a priority target of the Gen. William Tecumseh Sherman and the Federal Army – there nevertheless were sacrifices to be made until the South recovered. A limited amount of these, however, touched the Cranes and young Tom.

A few years later, during Georgia's "Reconstruction" days, Tom no doubt continued playing happily, without any hint of the dark evil possibly lurking within him. The Cranes had chickens and other farm produce upon which to survive, and as a center of higher education, Athens was not a poverty-stricken area like much of the rest of the state.

At war's end, Richard Woolfolk returned to Georgia and remarried. At that point in his life, there were many more females living in Georgia than males as a result of the decimation caused by the war, and returning soldiers often could take their pick among the most eligible females. Richard's new bride was Mattie E. Howard, a graduate of the Forsyth Female Collegiate Institute in nearby Monroe County.

Richard and Mattie began a new family which, by 1887, included six more children – two boys and four little girls.[4]

At age seven, young Tom was suddenly returned to his father back at the Woolfolk family plantation twelve miles north of Macon, where his life began anew with his father and step-mother. It no doubt was a harsh adjustment, since by that point, there were a total of nine children in the Woolfolk household, and instead of being the sole focus of Aunt Fannie's attentions, young Tom was relegated to a home filled with large strangers, and in which he received scant attention from his new step-mother. One can only imagine today the fears and misgivings he must have harbored all those years of early youth.

The "cracks" in the façade of what he now called "home" were obvious too. Almost immediately, there were problems. He reportedly never warmed to his step-mother Mattie, and no doubt missed his Aunt Fannie terribly since she had served as his center of stability and safety since his earliest days. He, in fact, openly rebelled against Mattie to the degree that she and his father often gave up in exasperation, and returned him periodically to Aunt Fannie in Athens to live. But then, just as soon as he had re-adapted to that secure environment, they returned to take him back to the farm in the wilderness.

First Failures

Despite the on-going problems with young Tom, the Woolfolk family adapted to the circumstances as best they could with nine children to clothe and feed. Richard's successes on the plantation and in his other business and civic endeavors however continued to mount. Young Tom received less and less loving attention.

Upon reaching maturity, Tom sought a profession of his own, attempting numerous business endeavors, almost all with the financial support of his father. He, nevertheless, ultimately was a miserable failure in each one, including stints at running a separate plantation, managing a store, driving a streetcar in Macon, and owning a grocery store.

Nothing seemed to work for Tom Woolfolk; everywhere he turned failure loomed. Was it a continuous intentional rebellion on his part? Was it, in his mind, a way to punish

Nothing seemed to work for Tom Woolfolk; everywhere he turned failure loomed.

his father for the loss of his mother and/or Aunt Fannie and the ostracizing inattention he had received? We'll never know.

Despite his shortcomings, money and property nevertheless became an obsession with Tom as he matured – no doubt in a constant quest for the security he had never received at home. He told his "friends" (who more often than not were merely acquaintances or "hangers-on") that he hoped to get his father's estate. However, as more children were born to his father and Mattie, it became increasingly obvious this dream quite likely would never be fulfilled.

As a result of this frustrating obsession, Tom became more and more embittered toward not only his step-mother, but his father as well, as he matured and time passed. His step-mother became a target for his unpleasantness, and the object of blame for his deprivation of an inheritance.

When he was 27, Tom married Georgia Bird, the daughter of a well-to-do farmer. In what could only be described as a rather strange ceremony, Tom and Georgia boarded a train at the Holton, Georgia, depot in Jones County where Georgia's family lived. The train was a south-bound passenger headed to Macon, and Tom and Georgia were married in the aisle as the train proceeded fullspeed ahead.

Following the wedding, Tom promised his new bride that he would take her "to a fine mansion in Macon." In reality, however, he had nowhere to take her except to the home of his older sister. Unsurprisingly, his new bride was not impressed, and his marriage, just as all his business endeavors, was very short-lived, lasting all of three weeks.

Strange behavior, however, had become the norm for Tom. Prior to his wedding, he had already attracted considerable attention to himself for highly questionable activity. He had begun openly carrying a sidearm – even when visiting Aunt Fannie in Athens – which was yet another indication of his growing insecurity and mental illness.

Following his failed attempt at marriage, Tom told one acquaintance that everybody was "against him," and that he had no friends – yet another indication of growing illness. He also said that he was a fool for marrying Georgia, because she was "no good," and that he might have had "to frail her out" (beat her) – yet another indicator of destabilization.

The Murders

After his professional and marital failures, Tom returned to the Woolfolk plantation since he had no other home or form of support. Since he was far too old to just take back as a family member to be raised with his brothers and sisters, his father "put him on wages," at $9.00 per month (the equivalent of $251.00 per month or roughly $60 per week in 2021 dollars). His labors in this capacity undoubtedly were a rude awakening – far from the privileged life he had anticipated and craved.

It is unknown for certain today, but at some point shortly after beginning work for his father on the farm, Tom's anger, jealousy and resentment finally boiled over. The life to which he had been relegated was just more than he could bear mentally, and he finally lashed out in insanity early one fateful morning, sending his life careening into a dark void from which he would never recover.

On Saturday, August 6, 1887, between 2 and 4 a.m., Tom reportedly knocked on the door of a local cabin where he awoke Green Locket, a black man who worked for the family. He told Green that something awful had happened. "Someone got into the house and killed my family," he reportedly blurted.

Upon their arrival at the Woolfolk plantation, Tom tried to persuade Locket to enter the house to investigate. Locket, however, apparently decided discretion was the better part of valor in this situation. His mama hadn't raised a fool. He instead elected to go get neighbors for help.

When the neighbors of Hazzard District of Bibb County arrived, Tom repeated his story of someone entering the house and murdering the Woolfolk family. He said he had escaped by jumping through a window.

In what may have been a tragic twist of fate, later testimony indicates one of the neighbors who had gathered on the scene that night had remarked that he heard a noise in the house. Tom, reportedly, immediately reentered the house to investigate. According to eyewitnesses, he remained inside the house for twenty to thirty minutes, and when he returned, he told the men outside that he could find no one alive. Tragically, this action quite possibly cost the life of one barely-surviving family member inside the house who might have been saved if those present had been aware of the true circumstances afoot.

The following is an account of the murder scene as published in the October 30, 1890 issue of the **Macon Telegraph** newspaper.[5] It undoubtedly was a reprint of the original news report of 1887. This account is provided in an abbreviated format, since the full account is considered far too graphic for this article.

"Finally it was decided to make an investigation, and not until then was the whole horror of the butchery discovered.

"In the back room on the left of the hall the bodies of Capt. Woolfolk and his wife were found lying on the bed with their skulls crushed by fearful blows. Across the foot of the same bed was the body of the baby (eighteen months), also with its head crushed.

"Across the foot of the same bed and half on the floor was Miss Pearl (age 17). She had dreadful cuts on the back of the neck as well as on the hand, which showed that she had defended her life with desperate courage, and the position of the body showed that her murderer had killed her either in another room or in the hall and then dragged the body across the floor and thrown it where it was found.

"Just inside the door of the same room, the body of Charles H. Woolfolk, a small boy (age 5) was found. It was evident that he had entered the room and a single blow had crushed in his skull and his body had been left lying where it fell.

"A little further in the room was the body of Richard Woolfolk, Jr., a young man of 20, and it was evident that he, too, had made a struggle for life and had not been killed easily. His forehead and part of his face were disfigured with numerous small gashes, which gave rise to the theory that he had seized the axe in the hands of the murderer and had held to it until the sharp edge had pushed into his face so often that he became blinded with his own blood and could struggle no longer with his opponent. The coup de grace was delivered in the top of the head, crushing the skull....

"Across the hall was the body of Mrs. Temperance West,[6] an aged lady who was on a visit, and those of Rosebud, aged 7 years, and Annie, aged 10, were found (as well). Mrs. West had been struck while asleep and one hand still rested under the head which was horribly crushed. On the floor, little Rosebud was stretched, and near the window, half covered with a sheet, was Annie. It was evident that

Annie had been the last victim, and that she had dragged the sheet from the bed in a wild effort to hide herself, and that while crawling to the open window to make her escape, she had been overtaken by the murderer and slaughtered like the rest of her family by blows from an axe."

Convincing Evidence

From the outset, most individuals immediately suspected Tom as the guilty party. According to the *Telegraph*, the neighbors, even before law enforcement authorities arrived, had gone to Tom and *"with hard-set faces and determined voices, told him that he was under arrest for murder, and if he attempted to escape he would be killed like a dog."*

As could be imagined, a heinous murder such as this brought out the "looky-looks" in droves. Word of the murder spread like wildfire, and hundreds of curious people reportedly arrived at the scene the following morning. Every clue in the investigation continued to point at Tom.

Bloody footprints were found in all of the rooms of the house. Surprisingly, Tom didn't even try to claim that they might have belonged to someone else. He no doubt was clearly aware of this condemning evidence from the outset, and possibly had initially hoped to lure Green Locket into entering the premises in order to frame him for the crime.

In the room that Tom shared with his brothers, it was found that the floor had been scrubbed with soap and water within a few hours of the murders. Tom attempted to explain this away to investigators by saying he had washed his feet because they were bloody and that he had then, for inexplicable reasons, *"wiped up the floor."* It, nevertheless, was abundantly clear to all who investigated the crime that had anyone other than Tom been the perpetrator of the crime, that individual could not have avoided leaving bloody footprints in the house, yet Tom's tracks were the only tracks found.

The gathering crowd also noticed that Tom had on a dirty shirt and trousers which were much too large for him. Later, the clothes were proven to be the property of his murdered brother. Tom, again obviously guilty, neither could nor would explain what had become of his own clothes.

Remarkably, despite the heinous nature of the crime, Tom had displayed – from the outset – an unusually calm attitude. As news of the terrible crime spread and more and more people began arriving, Tom, reportedly, sat beneath a tree outside, totally emotionless. No tears were shed and *"not a muscle quivered in agitation"* in his body. It was almost as if he had slain a monster, and his world was secure once again.

In another strange turn, Tom asked that a china cup be filled with water from the well and brought to him. When the water arrived, however, Tom reportedly looked at the cup for a second, touched it to his lips, and then strangely dumped the water on the ground.

Local tradition maintains that it was this clue which caused Sheriff Cooper to discover the critical evidence which was used against Tom. According to one version of this story, Cooper went to the well and drew a bucket of water, offering Tom a drink. When Tom became visibly repulsed at the offer, it aroused Cooper's suspicions. He reportedly sent a man down into the well where Tom's bloodstained clothes were discovered.

Newspaper accounts, however, offered a slightly different version of the story. In these reports, a Sheriff Westcot is credited with the discovery:

"A bundle of clothes, soaked in blood,

was brought up, and they were identified beyond the peradventure of a doubt as having belonged to Tom. There was a shirt, an undershirt, a pair of trousers, and a pair of drawers. They were all dyed a deep red, except the drawers and even they were terribly stained. They had been rolled up in such a way that the water had not been able to soak it (the blood) out and on the leg of the drawers, just above the knee, on the inside, was the imprint of a hand, with the fingers pointing up, just as they would have been if a struggling person had grasped the murderer by the leg."

The bloody footprints inside the house, the bloody hand-print on the leg of his clothing, Tom's repulsion at the water from the well, and his otherwise unusually calm demeanor following such a shattering event, collectively became the damning primary evidence used at his later trial. Even worse, Tom hardly tried to deny any of it at all. Following the discovery of the clothes, Sheriff Westcot immediately arrested Tom and removed him to the Macon jail, because the incensed crowd was threatening to lynch him on the spot.

Upon arrival at the jail, Tom was stripped of all his clothing and searched. According to reports, on the inside of his bare leg, in exactly the same spot corresponding with the hand mark on his underclothing, was a similar imprint dyed into his flesh. Tom argued that he had rested his hand when it was wet with his own blood on his leg. It soon became obvious, however, that in order for him to have successfully placed his hand on his leg in such a manner, he would have been *"obliged to assume an acrobatic posture, as the fingers pointed up instead of down."*

Coroner Hodnet conducted an inquest that same day. Tom was stripped yet again to reveal the bloody handprint to the coroner's jury. They, as a result, became convinced there was enough evidence to try Tom for capital murder. He was moved shortly thereafter from Macon to Atlanta to prevent mob violence.

Questionable Journalism

The **Atlanta Constitution** newspaper reporter(s) immediately began covering the Woolfolk murders and the story eventually was carried in papers as far away as the **Cincinnati Enquirer** and even on the front page of the **New York Times**. The **Times** called it *"the bloodiest, blackest chapter in Georgia criminal history."* Other papers called it a crime *"without parallel in the criminal history of the South if not the world,"* and *"the bloodiest tragedy in the annals of crime."* It was the press which first labeled the accused murderer as *"Bloody Tom."*

It, however, was a Macon photographer who captured the true grisliness of the crime. Traveling to the Woolfolk home the morning following the crime, before even any part of the scene had been disturbed, he photographed the mangled corpses and bloodstained walls and furniture. The photos sadly were sold on the streets as collectables, and mailed out to various newspapers.

Thankfully, none of the photos taken in 1887 are known to still be in existence today. A copy of the October 29, 1890 issue of the **Macon Evening News** however, offered a glimpse of the carnage of the terrible crime scene, with sketches likely drawn from the photos taken by the photographer. The illustrations show not only a bloody murder scene, but also a vivid reminder that Annie, the child of ten, had tried desperately to escape. The sketch shows how she made it to the window, but no farther, as the terrible blows from the ax rendered her unconscious, her hands still clutching the open window sill.

The *Evening News* also detailed the layout of the home. It was described as a one-story four-room structure with a porch of six columns. It had a central hallway with three bedrooms and a parlor.

The boys slept in the front bedroom on the left, across the hallway from the parlor which was on the right. Captain and Mrs. Woolfolk occupied the back bedroom on the left. The baby's cradle was in their room too. The girls and the guest, Mrs. West, slept in the third bedroom in the right rear portion of the house. Six of the victims were found in one room and three in another.

According to reports, a Macon undertaker was the individual responsible for going to the scene of the tragedy and preparing the bodies for burial. The task took longer than expected, and it reportedly was Sunday morning around 6:00 a.m. when the funeral procession left the plantation and headed to Rose Hill Cemetery.

The nine murdered Woolfolk family members were laid to rest in two rows of Rose Hill Cemetery in Macon under an ancient tree on a hill just above Macon's Civil War veterans. The Ocmulgee River flows peacefully in the background.

The Woolfolk graves are topped by rectangular brick and are unmarked. The only identity is the name *Woolfolk* engraved upon the steps that lead down to the graves.

According to reports, the five adults were buried in black coffins and lie in one row. The only indication of who rests beneath each of the brick coverings is the slight difference in the length of the last two brick overlays. The slightly shorter overlays obviously indicate where Richard Jr. and Pearl were placed.

These rectangles also suggest the order of the first row (from left to right): Richard F. Woolfolk, Mattie H., Temperance West, Richard Jr., and Pearl. The four small children undoubtedly lay in the second row, probably also in order of age: Annie, Rosebud, Charles, and the baby, Mattie.

Tom (understandably) and his two older sisters were not buried with the family.

The Trials

Interestingly, Aunt Fannie Crane and Tom's two older sisters, Floride Woolfolk Edwards Shackelford and Lillie Woolfolk Cowan, stood by him – despite the overwhelming evidence – to the very end.

The sisters reportedly greeted Tom with a kiss upon their arrival in court each day. When someone in the audience shouted "Hang him! Hang him!" during the closing arguments of the first trial, Tom's sisters threw their arms around him as if to protect him from the mob in the courtroom.

Despite their show of support, Tom was quickly (understandably) found guilty by a Bibb County jury which rendered a verdict in only twelve minutes. John C. Rutherford, Tom's lawyer, immediately asked for a new trial.

And Aunt Fannie, as devoted as the sisters, was there to pin a bouquet of violets on Tom in 1889 when he was granted the new trial. The three stood by Tom without hesitation during the proceedings of the first trial in Bibb County, the second in Houston County, and during hearings in the Georgia Supreme Court for a third trial. The three always arrived with flowers, fruit and a kiss, and all three testified to Tom's affection for the whole family.

As for Tom, he strangely continued to exhibit the total disinterest he had demonstrated the night the bodies were discovered – again, as if a huge burden had actually been lifted from his back. During the second trial, he resorted to outright disrespect by spending most of his time reading Joel Tyler Headley's ***Napoleon And His Marshals***.

Tom had hired John C. Rutherford of Athens as his lawyer. The Rutherfords were prominent Athenians as were the Cranes. John C.'s father had been a professor at the University of Georgia. John's sister, Mildred, was principal of The Lucy Cobb Institute, a historic education facility which still stands today on Milledge Avenue in Athens.

During his defense of Tom in the Bibb County trial in December of 1887, Rutherford was understandably unable to blame the slaughter on anyone else, and though the evidence in law terms was "circumstantial," it was also considered very strong. There simply was no one else at which to direct the vehemence of those wishing to convict Tom, and he did make a very convincing target.

Many clearly understood Green Locket, in refusing to enter the premises that night, had foiled Tom's original plan for an alibi. Most believed it was Tom's intention to get Locket inside the house that night, then either kill him, and accuse him of committing the heinous butchery, or to simply get Locket's footprints imprinted on the bloody floor with his (Tom's) own, in order to accuse him in that manner.

And then there was the question of what Tom had been doing when, after noises were heard inside the home, he inexplicably reentered and remained inside for some 20 or 30 minutes. In the account of the murders in the ***Macon Evening News***, it was speculated that Pearl had actually revived early that morning after the neighbors arrived. She quite likely made the noise that unfortunately drew Tom (instead of friendly forces) so quickly back inside the house.

Many believed that Pearl received the initial blows from the axe in the hallway, but since her body was found lying across the foot of the bed on which her father and mother lay, she possibly had revived from the early blows and had made it to the bed, and was struggling there when Tom returned inside the home to finish her.

Tom reportedly showed no nervousness or anxiety whatsoever during the first trial. His calmness was recorded over and over in news accounts.

The Georgia Supreme Court ordered a new trial in February of 1889. Tom was to be re-tried for the murder of his father, but the presiding judge warned him that even if he were found *"Not Guilty,"* there were still eight other indictments on which he could be tried.

The new trial took place in Perry, Georgia, in May of 1889. Once again, in less than an hour, the Houston County jury quickly brought back the verdict of *"Guilty."*

Some ladies in Macon strangely sent Tom flowers, fruits, and "delicacies" after the second *"Guilty"* verdict. His ex-wife, however, openly rejected him. She had successfully sued him for divorce, and had taken back her maiden name – Bird. She had no intention of being associated with the name "Woolfolk" ever again, and wanted everyone to know it.

Undeterred in the first two losses, Rutherford filed for a third trial. It was denied. Rutherford then appealed to the Georgia Supreme Court. Some said Rutherford was a determined lawyer and would take the case all the way to the United States Supreme Court if he lost the appeal. Unfortunately, he apparently did not enter a plea of "Insanity" for Tom, which might have actually been the appropriate defense.

The Mystery of the Woolfolk Murders   Bibb County

The Georgia Supreme Court heard arguments in June of 1890. In July of 1890, the Court upheld the second conviction of Tom Woolfolk and refused to order another trial. Rutherford became ill soon thereafter, and was unable to handle Tom's case any further. Many believed at the time that had Rutherford not become ill, Tom Woolfolk might not have been hanged for the murders. However, such was not the case, and Tom was finally sentenced, and his date of execution was set for October 29, 1890.

Execution

In a valley where Big Indian Creek joins Fanny Gresham Branch beneath the Dr. A.C. Hendrick Memorial Bridge, a gallows was built for the disposition of the death sentence of Tom Woolfolk. On the day of the execution, a reporter from the **Macon Telegraph** wrote that a *"noticeable feature of the day is the immense number of ladies and children in attendance."* Local folklore maintains some of the onlookers even munched on 'possum sandwiches as they awaited the fateful event.

The *Telegraph* report continued by explaining that *"the Perry Rifles, who had recently won a prize at a state drill in Atlanta, were marched to the jail under the command of Capt. W.C. Davis, and formed a line"* in front to maintain order.

"Soon, Sheriff Cooper and Deputy Sheriff Riley escorted Tom Woolfolk to a carriage waiting in front. Under the escort of the Rifles, the carriage moved to the scene of execution, moving past the red brick courthouse. The crowd, estimated at from 7,000 to 10,000, followed."

The *Telegraph* reporter also described the appearance of the execution site. *"Meanwhile, as the hour of noon came near, the multitude began to gather about the gallows, which had been erected in a little valley half a mile from the courthouse and on the Central road. A small stream flowed through the depression which was surrounded by hills almost shutting it in on all sides and forming a natural coliseum. On the one side was the railroad crossing the brook on a low trestle. On the other was the town cemetery. It was on a hill top, looking down upon the scene with its white monuments confronting the victim as he stood upon the scaffold. Three negro churches crowned the hill tops around. The white gallows stood in the middle of the little valley.*

"A circular space of 150 feet had been roped off at the scaffold for those who had tickets, around 200 people. The military marched inside the enclosure and with fixed bayonets assisted the deputies in keeping the mass of people from pressing upon the reserved space. Tom Woolfolk declared his innocence from the scaffold and prayed with his head upraised toward heaven. A few seconds before the drop fell, Tom said 'God bless you all.'"

According to reports, the fall through the scaffold trap-door unfortunately did not break Tom Woolfolk's neck, even though the noose positioning and the rate of fall are designed to accomplish that task. The noose however, had slipped from its proper position under Tom's right ear.

The wrenching rope partially tore the black death shroud from Tom's head, revealing his stretched neck. Seven minutes later, Woolfolk's pulse reportedly was amazingly still beating. Every ten or twenty seconds, his breast would heave and his shoulders would draw up. Eleven minutes later, however, his body had given up the ghost and his pulse had ceased. He was pronounced dead at 1:58 p.m.

The body was cut down, placed in a coffin, and sent by hearse to Hawkinsville.

Final Resting Place

Tom Woolfolk was buried in Orange Hill Cemetery in Hawkinsville, and his older sister, Floride Shackelford, was later buried beside him. The tombstone – undoubtedly provided by his Aunt Fannie, or his elder sisters, or even all three – appears to have been vandalized at some point in time, and then repaired. The name engraved upon it, "Thomas G. Woolfolk," is barely discernable as of this writing.

Prior to his death, Tom had been concerned about his place of burial. It was he (not another family member) who requested that he not be buried in Macon with his murdered family. He had also requested that no one view the body except his brother-in-law, Mr. Cowan, husband of Lillie Cowan. His grave was dug in Orange Hill Cemetery, the body placed therein, and walled with brick and cemented.

Tom never admitted to the murders. However, even Aunt Fannie and one sister stated that he had exhibited strange behavior just prior to the murders.

In an interview in the *Athens Weekly Banner Watchman* shortly after the crime, Floride and Aunt Crane said they had discussed Tom and had agreed that he must be losing his mind. Floride said she had told her father of their conclusion but that Captain Woolfolk had not agreed.

Curiously, evidence revealed years after Tom's execution, placed a modicum of doubt upon his guilt. Unexpected confessions to murders for which others have paid the penalty, while not unusual, almost always are fabrications, but in Tom Woolfolk's case, at least two of them gave pause to the confidence of those who convicted him so readily.

Articles in the August 6, 1987 issue of the *Telegraph* and in the August 7, 1987 issue of the Anderson (SC) *IndependentMail* revealed that ten years after Tom's execution, a criminal named Simon Cooper had been lynched in South Carolina and a note found in his diary stated ominously: *"Tom Woolfolk was mighty slick, but I fixed him. I would have killed him with the rest of the damn family, but he was not at home."*

And in 1893, a letter appeared in the *Pittsburgh Dispatch* which stated that the writer of the letter had met a tramp who killed not only the Borden family of Massachusetts in that highly publicized crime, but a farm family near Macon, Georgia. The tramp confessed that he and some friends were in Macon a few years earlier where they had trouble with a farmer. He said they went into his house and killed all but one son that had escaped. They said they took some of his clothes and threw them, with blood on them, into the well.

A reprint of the article appeared in the *Macon Telegraph* on August 28, 1893. It identified the similarities of the two crimes. Both Tom and Lizzie were at odds with their parents over money. Both had step-mothers. Both exhibited extraordinary self-control during the subsequent investigations and trials. Both murders included an axe, and both occurred in early August. The Bordens were murdered on a Thursday, August 4.

There is also one other similarity: the massive sensationalistic publicity which occurred as a result of both crimes which quite possibly contributed to the outcome of both trials. However, in the case of Lizzie Borden, positive newspaper coverage quite possibly contributed not to a *"Guilty"* verdict, but instead to a *"Not Guilty"* verdict.

Tom Woolfolk, by comparison, received considerable negative publicity well in advance of his two trials, and quickly received *"Guilty"* verdicts in both instances. He was in fact virtually convicted in newspapers all over the state.

Sometime after the hanging, the Woolfolk plantation land in Bibb County was divided between the two sisters and then sold. The old house where the violent murders took place stood vacant for many years.

In 1909, the home, interestingly, became, for a short while, the headquarters of the Macon Auto Club. Then it stood vacant again for more years.

In 1964, Merton E. Coulter, history professor at the University of Georgia, visited the site when writing an article for the *Georgia Historical Quarterly*. In his article, he described how *"nothing was left except two large piles of brick and stones marking the chimney places, a depression, appearing to have been the cellar, a well nearly filled up near a cedar tree, some shrubbery, and a large holly tree, undoubtedly marking the spot where Susan M. Woolfolk, Tom's mother, had been buried all those years ago."*

Today, individuals visiting the notorious site – unless they are archaeologists or skilled historic researchers who are familiar with such investigations – will find absolutely nothing at all. The terrible crime scene, which no one wished to purchase or live upon since that terrible day, has disappeared appropriately from the landscape.

Endnotes:

1. Richard F. Woolfolk was one of four sons born (1832) to Thomas Woolfolk.

2. John Ross Crane was responsible for the construction of the University Chapel (1832) and New College (1832) on the old campus of the University of Georgia, the First Presbyterian Church, and a number of very prominent homes, including the Ferdinand Phinizy house (1857) in Athens.

3. Several previous articles have stated that Tom Woolfolk grew up on Prince Avenue. The home supposedly was located at 716 Prince, and was described as having been demolished. However, following research on the work of John Ross Crane in Athens, it was discovered that his home was still in existence. Crane built a home for himself in 1842 on Pulaski (an extension of Prince). In 1924, the house was sold out of private ownership to the Athens Lodge and then again in 1929 to Sigma Alpha Epsilon (SAE) fraternity. As of this writing, it continues to serve as the fraternity house. Crane died in 1866, leaving the home to Fannie Moore Crane. In Longstreet's *Annals Of Athens*, there is a reference to a Mrs. Ross Crane. She was living on Prince in the home of a Col. Billups. This house, destroyed by fire, was not the fine home built by John Ross Crane (as previous articles have erroneously indicated). Research indicates Fannie Crane sold her large home on Pulaski Street following her husband's death in 1866, moving into the Billups home shortly thereafter. Former writers undoubtedly were confused by the recorded fact that Mrs. Ross Crane's last known residence (which was quite near the 1842 home built by her husband), was destroyed by fire, deducing they were one and the same. It is therefore quite likely that Tom Woolfolk was raised for seven years in the fine structure which today houses SAE fraternity in Athens. It was shortly after John Ross Crane's death in 1866, that young Tom was sent back to Macon. Therefore, when he visited Athens from that point forward, he may indeed have stayed with Aunt Fannie Crane at her home (the old Billups house) on Prince Avenue, but it and the 1842 house on Pulaski Street were not one and the same.

4. In 1887, the day of the murders, Richard F., Jr. was age 20; and Charles age 5. The girls included Pearl, age 17, a student at Wesleyan Female College; Anne, age 10; Rosebud, age 7; and Mattie, eighteen months.

5. The account was republished in the Wednesday, October 29 1890 issue of the *Macon Telegraph* following the hanging.

6. Temperance West was Mattie Howard's aunt.

(Grateful appreciation is acknowledged herewith to Kathryn Gray-White who provided most of the information contained in this article.)

The Shocking Murder of Chief William McIntosh

It marked the beginning of the end for the once-great nation of the Creek Indians in what today is the southeastern United States. On a spring night in 1825, Creek warriors set ablaze the home of one of their most prominent leaders – William McIntosh – on the Chattahoochee River near present-day Carrollton, Georgia, and then summarily executed the famed Indian in a defiant act of retribution.

Not even the faintest clue foretold the terrible events about to unfold on the morning of Saturday, April 25, 1825, as the fatal day dawned at the home of Creek Indian Chief William McIntosh in what today is known as Carroll County, Georgia. Though he had no inkling of the situation – since his Creek brethren had been keenly diligent in stalking his home – he was only moments away from terrible death and total destruction.

At that time, the Creek Indians of Alabama and Georgia knew only that McIntosh had committed a fatal deed – the sale of the tribe's native lands in Georgia – and now he must pay a price. Depending upon which side one takes in the issue, the Creeks were about to either murder or legally execute one of their major chiefs in retribution for his signing of the *Treaty of Indian Spring* which dealt their lands to the white man, dispossessing the Creeks in Georgia forever. Two other Creek leaders who had also participated in the treaty would receive the same punishment shortly.

The Indians' rage could be understandable. As a result of the treaty, the last remaining Creek Indian lands in Georgia were ceded to the U.S. Government for inclusion as a portion of the state.

Negotiations for ratification of that treaty had been on-going for a number of years, because Georgia had been pressing for more land to enable the expansion of her frontiers westward, but the Creek Nation as a whole did not wish to part with their land. The Creeks, in fact, viewed with alarm their diminishing homeland, and were reluctant to part with another large consignment to land-hungry pioneers and settlers.

Caught in the vortex of these negotiations were Georgia Governor George Troup and his cousin – mixed-blood Creek Indian Chief William McIntosh. The two were related through Governor Troup's mother who was a sister of

McIntosh's father, making the two leaders first cousins. Both men were astute politicians in their own domains, and both essentially conspired to cede the Creeks' last vestige of lands in today's Georgia to the encroaching whites, in return for a substantial payment to McIntosh.

In the 1820s, despite the constant immigration of colonists into the region, most of Georgia was still a dense frontier; and the native Indians, by and large, still lived by their own code of ethics and morals. Warnings had been sounded through the years by other chiefs in the Creek Nation, extolling to all who would listen, the punishment which would be meted out to any member of the Nation involved with any further diminishment of the Nation's land. But McIntosh, with his cousin in the position as head of the rapidly growing white government in Georgia, chose to ignore these threats, thus sealing his fate. He assumed – to his detriment – that his position as a Creek "headman" exempted him from the punishment of such a death.

On February 12, 1825, McIntosh, along with a contingent of lower chiefs, signed the now infamous *Treaty of Indian Spring*, so-called because the signing was conducted at the site of another of McIntosh's homes which still stands as of this writing in present-day Butts County, Georgia. This fine structure, though unprotected and unpreserved in later years, somehow managed to survive intact to the 21st Century, and is today preserved and maintained at Indian Spring by the Butts County Historic Society.

In payment for signing the treaty, the U.S. Government agreed to pay the Creek Nation (McIntosh) the sum of $200,000.00 *"as soon as practicable after ratification of this treaty."* It is totally understandable that a large portion of

A painting of Chief William McIntosh in full regalia – including a checkered shirt possibly in homage to his Scottish heritage – was done in the spring of 1825 prior to his murder. As a major chief of the Creek Indians of the Southeast, he was a man of dignity and intellect, but was assassinated by his Creek brethren after signing away his tribe's lands in the Treaty of Indian Spring. (Reproduction from the McKenney-Hall Portrait of American Indians)

the Creek Nation living in what today is Georgia and Alabama would be outraged. Their homeland was sold from beneath them and they were to be forced to relocate to a strange land, and they did not even receive any of the $200,000.00 paid to McIntosh. The Creek chief also received other considerations as well, including his large reservation and home on the Chattahoochee River in present-day western Georgia.

For years, a pervading myth has maintained that McIntosh was paid the $200,000.00 in person and in gold. One tale even relates how many wagons were necessary to transport the gold back to McIntosh's Chattahoochee

River plantation. No evidence, however, has ever surfaced to substantiate these stories, and no mention of gold was made in the language of the treaty. Despite this fact, rumors persist to this day, and searches continue for "McIntosh's gold" all along the road from Indian Spring in Butts County to the site of McIntosh's Chattahoochee River home.

Immediately after the treaty was signed, the Creek chiefs who had opposed the signing met in secret at several sites in the Creek towns of east-central Alabama, where they began discussion of retaliation against those individuals who had signed away the tribal lands. It was decided that William McIntosh would die, as would his son-in-law, Samuel Hawkins. Hawkins lived on the Tallapoosa River near the Creek towns which once existed in today's central Alabama.

Within the secret meetings, detailed and careful instructions were provided to a group of the tribe's warriors on how they were to meet and advance upon McIntosh at his plantation on the Chattahoochee. The exact number of Creeks involved in this group of executioners is unknown today; best estimates range from 170 to 400, according to several different sources which recorded events at that time. The number of warriors assigned to the task is an indication of the respect they yet held for McIntosh.

The group, principally from Ocfuskee and Tookabatchee – both large Indian towns in east-central Alabama

In payment for signing the treaty, the U.S. Government agreed to pay the Creek Nation (McIntosh) the sum of $200,000.00

– met and advanced on foot in single file toward Georgia. They traveled so silently that they were completely undetected on their journey, reaching the neighborhood of McIntosh's Chattahoochee plantation near the evening of the second day. The warriors reportedly stationed themselves on both sides of an intersection about one mile northwest of McIntosh's home, and awaited the wee hours of early morning to carry out the assassination.

It was on the evening of the warriors' arrival, that an ironic incident befell the group. According to later accounts, McIntosh and his son-in-law, Samuel Hawkins – both of whom were slated for execution by the Creeks – met at the very intersection where the Indians were concealed, totally unaware of the vengeful warriors surrounding them, so well concealed was the group. McIntosh and Hawkins remained upon their mounts as they conversed at length. The assassination warriors were so quiet that, even though they could almost have reached out and touched the two unsuspecting men, they remained completely undiscovered.

Interestingly, the warriors could easily have killed the two men on the spot, but they had been specifically instructed that for maximum effect, McIntosh was to be executed *"in his own yard, in the presence of his family, and to let his blood run upon the soil of that reservation which the Georgians had secured to him in the treaty which he had made with them."*

After concluding his meeting with McIntosh, Hawkins reportedly turned and headed home, with McIntosh riding a short distance beside him. Turning back toward his own home shortly thereafter, McIntosh again passed right through the hidden Indians, and again they had an opportunity to kill him, but did not. As Hawkins continued westward to return to his farm on the Tallapoosa River (near present-day Talladega, Alabama), a chosen few of the warriors separated from the main group and silently followed him, intent upon an equally bloody demise for him. *(Interestingly, it would be at this very site at Horseshoe Bend on the Tallapoosa that the Creeks would shortly be annihilated into total submission by Andrew Jackson and his band of volunteers.)*

The main body of the Creek warriors reportedly remained in the woods until about 3:00 a.m. of the fateful morning, at which time, they gathered "fat lighter" (the flammable resinous heartwood of aged pine trees) to use to burn McIntosh's house. They quietly surrounded the house, and at daybreak, set the structure ablaze to force McIntosh and his family outside.

For a number of years, McIntosh (as did several other prominent Indian chiefs during this period in Georgia history) had operated an inn as well as a ferry near his home on the Chattahoochee River. The inn provided accommodations for travelers using the "Alabama

The assassination warriors were so quiet that, even though they could almost have reached out and touched the two unsuspecting men, they remained completely undiscovered.

Road" which passed beside the site.

Inside this inn on the night of the fatal attack, five persons were sleeping, including Chilly McIntosh, son of the doomed William. As he was also one of the signers of the ill-fated treaty, and undoubtedly knew his life was in grave danger, Chilly quite likely quickly sized up the situation upon hearing the commotion in the yard outside. He no doubt decided that discretion was the better part of valor, and leapt from a rear window of the inn and then plunged into what could only have been the very cold April waters of the Chattahoochee to swim to the opposite shore and safety.

The Creek warriors, meanwhile, had had the presence of mind to bring a white man (named Hudman or Hutton; records differ on the spelling of the name) with them, in order to certify that no harm had come to any whites in the inn. There were whites sleeping there, including one white peddler. Accounts of the day maintain that the peddler "became a most wretched man" after the commotion began, until Hutton reassured him that no harm would come his way. The Indians, true to their word, left the peddler unharmed, but destroyed his wares, along with everything else in sight.

Yet another of the signers of the Indian Spring Treaty, a minor Creek chief named Toma Tustinugee who was also sleeping in the inn, was not so lucky. The

Shouting "McIntosh we have come for you!" the Creek Indian warriors no doubt horrified this one-time respected chief as they exacted their revenge upon him for signing the Treaty of Indian Spring relinquishing the Creek lands in what today is Georgia. McIntosh's lonely grave has existed undisturbed a few feet from the site of his assassination for over 200 years as of this writing (2021) in what today is a Carroll County, Georgia park approximately four miles south of Whitesburg. A reproduction of the home which the Creek warriors burned here has been constructed on the original site of his home.

warriors, totally unexpecting this additional prize, removed Toma to the yard, where, in the light of the burning building, they executed him summarily by firing some fifty bullets into his body.

McIntosh, in the meantime, was having problems of his own. The flames from his home threw a bright light over the yard, giving his astonished family a clear view of the terrifying painted warriors surrounding the house. To the warriors' credit, they allowed McIntosh's two wives and his children to remove themselves from the burning house; no harm befell them. They, however, did not allow the women or children to remove any articles with them from the burning structure. Consequently, the women were wearing only their night clothes, and the children were naked.

After the women and children were removed, McIntosh reportedly barricaded the front door and stood near it until it was forced open. He then retreated to the second floor, guns in his hands, returning the fire from the warriors.

His attackers stood in his yard shouting "McIntosh! We have come! We have come! We told you, if you sold the land to the Georgians, we would come!" The Creek assassins continued to discharge their weapons into the burning house. McIntosh's wives, in the meantime, were imploring the assailants to spare their husband, or at least to remove him from the burning house before shooting him.

They screamed to the Creeks that McIntosh was an Indian like themselves, and, as a brave man, did not deserve to die a horrible death in the flames.

In short order, the burning house forced McIntosh to return to the first floor, where he was met by a hail of bullets. He fell to the floor and was seized by the legs and dragged to the yard outside by the warriors. While lying in the yard, and while blood coursed from numerous wounds, he reportedly raised himself on one arm and surveyed his murderers with a look of defiance. At that moment, an Ocfuskee Indian plunged a long knife to the hilt into McIntosh's breast. It is recorded that he took one long breath before collapsing and dying.

The Indians, however, were far from finished. Their appetites had only been whetted and their wrath was far from depleted. They proceeded to plunder the out-houses and to kill every domesticated animal in sight. Anything they could not carry with them, they destroyed with vehemence. Hogs were shot and left lying in the yard beside the dead men. All the peddler's goods were removed from the inn and destroyed.

One of McIntosh's wives went to the warriors and requested that they give her a white suit in which to bury her husband. This request was quickly refused. McIntosh was subsequently scalped and left lying in the yard where he had died. Later, after the warriors had departed, McIntosh's body was buried in the yard a short distance away.

After looting and destroying the plantation, the Indians returned to their Alabama homes, carrying McIntosh's scalp with them. It later was exhibited in the public square at Ocfuskee. The scalp was a warning to others who might be tempted to take similar measures with the remaining Creek lands.

Samuel Hawkins suffered a similar fate. After following Hawkins home to Alabama, the Creek warriors assigned to him quietly surrounded his farmhouse where they remained until daybreak. Following instructions, Hawkins was not killed out-right, but was taken prisoner until the fate of McIntosh became known. About 3:00 p.m., after word had been received of McIntosh's death, Hawkins also was killed and scalped. The latter trophy was displayed with that of McIntosh's in Ocfuskee Town.

The resulting repercussions of these killings were felt all the way to the halls of Congress. Called "murder" by the whites, and "a legal execution" by the Indians, the incident was actually an act of desperation by a nation of people quickly being displaced from their homeland by an on-rushing tide of white settlers. It would only be a short ten years before the state and federal governments would remove the Indians completely from their remaining lands in Alabama, shipping them west to present-day Oklahoma.

Today, one can visit the site of the McIntosh killing in a Carroll County park located about four miles southwest of Whitesburg. It is a beautiful, quiet and secluded spot overlooking the scenic Chattahoochee River that holds no hint of the horrors perpetrated there in April of 1825.

The remains of a later house built on or near the site of McIntosh's burned home actually stood until the late 20th century. The later structure, however, eventually was almost completely destroyed by greedy "treasure hunters" and vandals, many of whom were ridiculously searching for McIntosh's mythical gold. As of this writing, a replica of McIntosh's burned home has been reconstructed at the site, and is preserved there today.

If one visits the intersection of the park road with GA Highway 5, just north of the old home-place, he or she will be in the exact spot where McIntosh and Hawkins conversed on that fateful night so long ago.

For those who desire to retrace the original McIntosh Road westward from Indian Spring, the following directions are provided:

Leaving Indian Spring in a southwestwardly direction, the old road passed just north of present-day Mt. Vernon Church and by Elgin and Liberty Churches, before going through an area once known as "Sandy Plains."

The road next passed through the old ghost town of Waltham, before reaching Spalding County on today's GA Highway 16. It continued by Union and Ringgold Churches to the intersection of GA Highways 16 and 156. At that crossing there was once a well-known stagecoach stop known as "Double Cabins" (the Militia District today retains the name: "Cabin District").

Double Cabins was due north of present-day Griffin and the McIntosh Road in running through the former town, missed Griffin completely. Along that stretch, the old road was once known as the "Old Madison Alabama Stage Road," and also as "Upper Cabin Road."

Passing on through the upper fringes of Experiment, the McIntosh Road took the left fork at McIntosh School, before going through Rio and Vaughn and crossing the Flint River into Fayette County. It ran on westward through Brooks and Senoia, passing just north of Turin to go through Sharpsburg and Raymond, close on GA Highway 16, before reaching Newnan on McIntosh Street, a name obviously retained from the original McIntosh Road.

From Newnan, the old thoroughfare turned northwest to cross the Chattahoochee River near the mouth of Pearsons Creek. At that stream, the McIntosh Road crossed over McIntosh's Ferry into present-day Carroll County where it reached the settlement of William McIntosh.

As of this writing, there is an area on McIntosh's old reservation just west of the Chattahoochee River where an abandoned remnant of the old original roadway is still discernible. Turning up the hill from the river, the road passes the site at which McIntosh's home and inn once existed - the site of his murder.

Continuing northward for a short distance, the old road reached an intersection just west of today's Rotherwood. It was at that intersection that William McIntosh and Sam Hawkins conversed while the silent Indians surrounded them.

From this point, the McIntosh Road turned directly westward to run on GA Highway 5 all the way into Alabama,

As of this writing, there is an area on McIntosh's old reservation just west of the Chattahoochee River where an abandoned remnant of the old original roadway is still discernible.

passing through Lowell, Roopville, and Tyrus along the way. It was along the latter stretch that Sam Hawkins made the final trip to his home in Alabama before dying at the hands of his Creek brethren.

Today, there is a great interest in the McIntosh saga. In Peachtree City, just north of the actual route of the road, there is a McIntosh Opry as well as a McIntosh High School. In fact, all along the way from Indian Spring in present-day Butts County westward, remnants of the name are retained, and many persons living today along the old route are familiar with details concerning the McIntosh legend.

Though he has departed this earth, and though the worldly possessions of Chief William McIntosh have been scattered and lost, the historic milestones of this once-prominent member of the Creek Indian Nation live on . . . as does McIntosh's legend.

Today, archived at the University of Georgia Libraries are two letters, one written by two of the three wives of Chief William McIntosh, and another written by the daughter of the third wife. The letters were written immediately following McIntosh's murder.

The letters were sent to white leaders of that day in 1825. They represented the McIntosh family's desperate pleas for help. These plaintive documents vividly describe the horror and anguish suffered by Peggy and Susannah McIntosh (two of the wives), and of Jane Hawkins (a daughter of the third wife). The letters also provide a clear indication of the oftentimes harsh and unforgiving circumstances encountered by 19th Century American Indian leaders (and, subsequently, their families) who dared to negotiate with and bargain away tribal lands to the U.S. government. These letters are maintained in the Telamon

An abandoned portion of the original McIntosh Road in the former McIntosh Reserve of present-day Carroll County, Georgia, is still clearly visible through the forest. The ancient former Indian trail, identified by Marion Hemperley, former deputy surveyor-general of Georgia prior to his death, is just north of and parallel to the Chattahoochee River in the Reserve. *(Photo courtesy of Marion Hemperley)*

Cuyler Collection at UGA Libraries, and are provided in their entirety below.

May 3, 1825. Line Creek, Fayette Co.

To Col. Duncan G. Campbell and Major James Meriwether U.S. Commss

Gentlemen,

When you see this letter stained with the blood of my husband the last drop of which is now spilt for the friendship he has shown for your people, I know you will remember your pledge to us in behalf of your nation, that in the worst of events you would assist and protect us. And when I tell you that at day light on Saturday morning last, hundreds of the Hostiles surrounded our house, and instantly murdered Genl McIntosh & Tom Tustunnuge, by shooting near one hundred balls into them (Chilly and Moody Kennard making their escape thro' a Window) they then Commenced burning and plundering in the most unprincipled way, so that here I am driven from the ashes of my smoking dwelling, left with nothing but my poor little naked hungry children, who need some immediate aid from our white friends, and we lean upon you white, you lean upon your government.

About the same time of the morning that they committed the horrid act on the General, another party caught Col Saml Hawkins, and kept him tied until about 3 o'clock when the chiefs returned from our house and gave orders for his execution in the same way, and refused to leave his impliments to cover his body up with, so that it was left exposed to the Fowls of the Air and the beasts of the Forest, and Jinny and her child are here, in the same condition as we are - this party consisted principally of Oakfuskies, Talledegers & Muckfaws, tho' there were others with them - The Chiefs that appeared to head the party were Intockunge of Muckfaw, Thloc-co-cos-co mico of Arpachoochee, Munnawho, but I know not where he was from, who said they were ordered to do it by the Little prince and Hopoeth Yoholo, and that they were supported and encouraged in it by the Agent and the chiefs that were left after the Big Warriors Death in a council at Broken Arrow where they decreed that they would murder all the Chiefs who had any hand in selling the Land, and burn & destroy and take away all they had, and then send on to the President that he should not have the Land - I have not heard of the murder of any others but expect all are dead that could be catchd.

But by reason of a great freshet in the Chattahochee they could not get Col Miller nor Hogey McIntosh nor the Darisaws, and they and Chilly are gone to the Governor. Our country is in a most ruined State so far as I have heard (tho' by reason of the high waters word has not circulated fast) all have fled from their homes in our parts and taken refuge among their white friends, and I learn there are now at Genl Wares (near this place) from 150 to 200 of them who are afraid to go to their homes to get a grain of what little corn they have to eat, much more to try to make any more, and if You and Your people do not assist us, God help us - we must die either by the Sword or the famin.

This moment Genl. Ware has come in and will in a few minutes start with a few men and a few friendly Indians to try to get a little something for us to eat. I hope so soon as you read this, You will lay it before the Governor and the President that they may know our miserable condition, & afford us relief as soon as possible, I followed them to their camp about one and one-half miles to try to beg of them something to cover the dead with, but it was denied me. I tryed also to get a Horse to take my little children and some provisions to last us to the White Settlements which was given up to me and then taken Back - and had it not have been for some White men who assisted in burying the Dead and getting us to the White Settlements, we should have been worse off then we were if possible - before I close I must remark that the whole of the party so far as I knew them were hostile during the War.

Peggy & Susannah McIntosh
Fayett County, 3rd May, 1825

Colo Campbell and Major Meriwether,

My dear friends, I send you this paper, which will not tell you a lie, but if it had ten tongues it could not tell you all the truth. On the Morning of the 30th of April at break of day, my Fathers house was surrounded by a party of Hostile Indians, to the number of several hundred, who instantly fired his dwelling, and Murdered him, and Thomas Tustunnugee by shooting more than one hundred balls into them, and took away the whole of Fathers money and property which they coud carry off, and destroyed the rest leaving the family no clothes (some not one rag) nor provision. - Brother Chilly was at Fathers and made his escape through a Window under cover of a Travelling white man who obtained leave for them to come out that way, It being not yet light, he was not discovered.

While those hostiles were Murdering my beloved Father, they were tying my Husband (Colo Saml. Hawkins) with Cords, to wait the arrival of Itockchunga, Thloccocoscomicco and Munnawwa, who were the commanders at Fathers, to give orders for the Colos execution also, which took place about 3 oclock the same day. And these barbarous men, not content with spilling the blood of both my Husband and Father to attone for their constant friendship to both your Nation and our own; refused my hands the painful previledge of covering his body up in the very ground which he lately defended, against those Hostile Murderers, and drove me from my home, stript of my two best friends in one day, Stript of all my property my provision, and my clothing, with a more painful reflection than all these, that the body of my poor murdered husband should remain unburied, to be devoured by the birds, and the beasts. (Was ever poor woman worse off than I?).

I have this moment arrived among our white friends, who altho they are very kind, have but little to bestow on me, and my poor helpless infant, who must suffer befor any aid can reach us from you, but I can live a great while on very little, besides the confidence I have on you, and your government. For I know by your promise, you will aid and defend us, as soon as you hear from our situation.

These Murderers are the very same Hostiles who treated the whites 10 years ago as they have now treated my husband and Father, who say they are determined to kill all who had any hand in selling the land, and when they have completed the work, of Murdering, Burning, plundering and destruction, they will send the President word that they have saved their Land, and taken it back and that he and the white people never shall have it again. Which is the order of the heads of the Nation, by the advice of the Agent.

We expect that many of our best friends are already Killed, but have not heard, by reason of the waters being too high for word to go quick, which is the only reason Colo Miller and others on his side of the River were not Killed. We are in a dreadful Condition, & I dont think there will be one ear of corn made in this part of the Nation, for the whole of the friendly party have fled to Dekalb and Fayett Counties two much alarmed to return to their houses to get a little grain of what corn they left, for themselves and their families to subsist on, much more to stay at home to make more, and we fear every day that what little provision left will be destroyed.

I am afraid you will think I make it worse, but how can that be, for it is worse of its self than any pen can write, my condition admits of no equal, & mocks me when I try to speak of it. After I was stript of my last Frock but one, humanty and duty called on me to pull it off and spread it over the body of my dead Husband, (which was allowed no other covering) which I did, as a Farewell witness of my Affection, I was 25 miles from any friend (but sister Catharine, who was with me) and had to stay all night in the woods, surrounded by a thousand hostile Indians, who were constantly insulting and affrighting us. And now I am here with only one old coat to my back, and not a Morsel of Bread to save us from perishing, or a rag of Blanket to cover my poor little boy from the sun at noon or the due at night, & I am a poor distracted orphan and Widow.

Jane Hawkins

"They're Stealin' The Train !"

Confederate Camp McDonald and Great Locomotive Chase

Conceived as a method to sabotage the vital Western & Atlantic Railroad between Atlanta and Chattanooga to interrupt the supply of men and munitions to Confederate forces, a group of Union raiders achieved the impossible simply by being a daring and brave group of men. Their objective was to hijack a locomotive parked right under the noses of thousands of Confederate troops in a military training camp.

If one visits the city streets of Kennesaw, Georgia, today, modern development and a reasonably historic town square bisected by a still-busy railroad are the basic components that will be encountered. On April 12, 1862, a sea of tents and other temporary structures at Confederate Camp McDonald housing thousands of troops existed at this site on the west side of the tracks, and on the other side, a few commercial buildings, a modest train depot, and the Lacy Hotel composed the hamlet of "Big Shanty" where a momentous event was about to take place.

During a twenty-minute breakfast stop at the Lacy Hotel on the morning route of the Western & Atlantic train out of Atlanta, a small coterie of daring Union Army spies moved silently onto the idling train and took control of the locomotive General. The locomotive already had steam in the boiler and after engaging the drive mechanism and opening up the throttle, the train began lumbering up the track toward Chattanooga – all without firing a shot. A hijacking was taking place!

The parade grounds and tent city which once composed the Confederate army training site known as Camp McDonald are long gone today. Commercial buildings and the city streets of the town of Kennesaw, Georgia, have replaced the tents, pickets, horses, military equipment and temporary structures which formerly occupied this historic ground, but Camp McDonald is anything but forgotten. It is the spot where 20 Federal saboteurs stole a huge

Confederate Camp McDonald And Great Locomotive Chase   Cobb County

Confederate locomotive and three boxcars from right under the noses of thousands of Confederate troops.

The line once known as the Western & Atlantic Railroad still exists today at this site in downtown Kennesaw, but today, it is used almost exclusively by modern freight trains. Nearby, inside a museum on the east side of the railroad tracks is the fabled "General," the locomotive stolen by the Yankee saboteurs who came to be known as "Andrews' Raiders."

Although most historians today agree that the seizure of the train was accomplished with extraordinary daring, they are divided on the actual role played by Governor Joseph Emerson Brown in the creation of a vulnerable defense posture at Camp McDonald. As the commander-in-chief of the Georgia military, Brown was responsible for the local defense of Georgia. Evidence suggests that his actions and orders as commander caused Camp McDonald and the Western & Atlantic Railroad to be exceedingly vulnerable to Federal espionage agents – and Federal strategists apparently had noticed.

A Weak Defense

With the war beginning to take a more serious toll upon the manpower and military munitions of the South by 1862, the Confederate War Department notified all the Confederate governors that more troops were needed. Georgia was asked to supply twelve regiments which would be armed and supplied by the Confederacy, and each soldier would receive a $50 bounty for enlisting.

As a result of this action, Governor Brown ordered that Camp McDonald be re-opened in March of 1862. He had first opened the camp in June of 1861 to organize and train the 4th Brigade of

In 1862 Georgia Governor Joseph E. Brown ordered 10,000 pikes be manufactured for use in arming his troops when no firearms were available.

Georgia Volunteers, but had closed it in July of that same year after the regiments of the brigade had been sent to the front in Virginia.[1]

As William Smedlund described in his book on Georgia's camps, there were no fortifications or walls of any kind around Camp McDonald since it was located in the "rear area" of the war effort, and was therefore considered inviolable from attack by Northern invaders. The large rolling fields made ideal camping areas and drill fields, and fresh-water springs in the vicinity provided ample water for the troops. Sentries were posted about the camp – but for guard training purposes only – since there was no concern about an enemy attack at this site.[2]

There is evidence that Governor Brown was more a student of the warfare of "antiquity" than that of a military strategist of the 1860s. He, in fact, is noted in history as having been the

This present-day photo was taken looking south from the former site of Camp McDonald on the west side of the railroad tracks at Big Shanty (present-day Kennesaw). In the foreground are three stone markers. The one on the left remembers William A. Fuller, conductor of the stolen train who gained fame for his tenacious pursuit of the raiders. The stone marker on the right marks the spot at which the locomotive "General" was idling as it was seized by Federal raiders on April 12, 1862. Across the railroad tracks on the east side (in the background) is the present-day depot which did not exist in 1862. Just south of this depot, the Lacy Hotel (which was burned in 1864) once stood. It was at the Lacy that the train crew was having breakfast when their train was stolen. *(Photo courtesy of Joe Griffith)*

This modern photograph looking southward, was taken from the approximate spot where James J. Andrews, leader of a band of 20 Federal raiders, climbed aboard the locomotive "General" and seized the train on April 12, 1862. A sentry at Camp McDonald, armed with a "Joe Brown Pike," stood near the locomotive at this spot. *(Photo courtesy of Joe Griffith)*

brain-child of at least one arms manufacturing enterprise which was truly bizarre.

With virtually no basis in logic whatsoever, Brown had publicly stated that any enemy upon Georgia soil must be driven away *"by the use of cold steel at close quarters."*[3] To emphasize and underline this bizarre statement – made in the day and time of gun powder arms – he introduced his dream weapon which he dubbed "the Georgia Pike." With considerable ridiculous aplomb, he assured fellow Georgians that by using this pike, any Northern invader would be driven *"from our genial territory back to his frozen home."*[4]

Instead of funding and spearheading the production of modern weapons for Georgia troops, Brown instead appealed to the mechanics of Georgia to put aside all unnecessary work and make "ten thousand pikes." As an earnest advocate of the pike, he argued that *"if the defenders at Fort Donelson had been armed with pikes, the outcome of that battle would have been quite different."*

Brown backed up his claims with the assertion that *"the long-range gun might fail to fire or miss its mark, thus wasting ammunition, but the short-range pike and terrible knife. . . . wielded by a stalwart patriot's arm, never fails to fire, and never wastes a single load."*[5] He somehow failed to take into consideration all those Confederate troops who were falling before the rifled repeating arms of the Union Army while Southern troops were fighting with single-shot weapons – and usually with nothing more than antique muskets – and his "Georgia Pikes." (And still, somehow, the South won battles.)

Brown's initiative not only was amazingly naïve, it truly was bizarre. For each pike accepted by the Confederate Arsenal, Brown instructed the government to pay $5. For each side knife with tipped scabbard, belt, and clasp, the government paid $4.60. In all, 7,099 pikes and 4,908 side knives amazingly were actually manufactured and received into the arsenal at Milledgeville.[6] *(In an ironic turn of circumstances, the Joe Brown Pikes today fetch amazing prices on the auction and collectibles market.)*

Rodney Brown, in his *American Polearms* reported that new recruits at camps of instruction such as Camp McDonald in Georgia were issued pikes which were used for training drills and as primary infantry weapons in sham battles. The ancient devices were also used by sentries on guard duty in rear areas, as was the case at Camp McDonald in 1862. Nevertheless, to even consider them as a training weapon was absurd if they were never to actually be used on the battlefield, and to this writer's knowledge, few – if any – were ever actually used.

The pikes and knives were also issued to some coastal defense units as their primary weapon in lieu of a musket. On 12 February, 1862, the *Southern Banner* newspaper of Athens, Georgia, reported that *"a perfect novelty,"* a company of volunteers from the hills of Habersham County, Georgia, and armed with pikes, passed through town on their way to defend the coast.[7]

According to accounts of that day, few soldiers were thrilled to be issued the archaic pikes. One might logically surmise that none of troops receiving the pikes preferred them – understandably – over long-guns and pistols. According to Rodney Brown, some recruits simply laughed at the idea of using a sharp pointed stick against an enemy who was armed with a large caliber long-gun which in many cases were being updated with repeating arms. With great

James J. Andrews as he appeared at the time of the daring raid at Big Shanty, Georgia.

hilarity, the Confederate trainees chased each other around the camp brandishing their medieval-looking weapons.

I.G. Bradwell wrote, in the *Confederate Veteran*, that when he enlisted, his regiment was promised they would be issued new Enfield rifles. However, when, instead, wagon loads of pikes arrived for issue, there was a near riot among the soldiers until the pikes were laid aside and the men were issued not the coveted Enfield rifles, but old smooth-bore muskets. In the end, the soldiers treated the whole idea of using pikes in battle against an enemy with firearms as a cruel joke.[8] With logic and strategies such as this, it is amazing the South ever won any of the engagements in which it was involved.

Biographer Joseph E. Parks pointed out that Gov. Brown was particularly eager to issue his pikes and accompanying side knives to his troops because he was being ridiculed by members of the Georgia General Assembly for his wastefulness of scarce defense dollars on outdated and impractical weapons. As a result of this embarrassing predicament, pikes

Mystery & History in Georgia

Captain William A. Fuller, conductor of the stolen train, was photographed in March of 1904, some 42 years after the raid. *(Photo courtesy of GA Dept. of Archives & History, Atlanta)*

ultimately were issued only to recruits at rear area installations such as Camp McDonald, and even guard duty was performed by sentries armed with what were, by that time, being mockingly referred to as "Joe Brown Pikes."[9]

Camp McDonald

The troop strength at Camp McDonald, according to reports, was indeed impressive, despite the paucity of actual weapons. What was not impressive was the fact that they literally had no legitimate arms whatsoever unless they brought their own. They were bivouacked for a great distance southward along the west side of the Western & Atlantic Railroad. One special row of tents on the high ground to the northwest end of the camp housed the camp commander and the commander-in-chief of the Georgia Army, Governor Brown.

Brown, who lived a short distance away near what today is Canton, Georgia, reportedly spent a great deal of time at Camp McDonald. He thought camp life might improve his health. The dispatches he issued from there were signed "commander-in-chief." He, however, was not held – understandably – in great esteem by the troops inhabiting the camp with him.

Nearby were the tents of the cadets from Georgia Military Institute in Marietta. Having been professionally-trained in the techniques of military drill on a daily basis at the Institute, they were put into service as drillmasters and instructors for the recruits. In early April of 1862, there were at least five regiments and a separate battalion of infantry consisting of the 39th, 40th, 41st, 42nd, 43rd, and 52nd Georgia Volunteer Infantry Regiments and the 9th Battalion Georgia Volunteer Infantry undergoing training at the camp. As a result, the camp was more crowded in 1862 than when it first opened in the summer of 1861.[10]

Planning The Raid

Meanwhile, Gen. Don Carlos Buell commanded the Union Army in middle Tennessee in the spring of 1862. A spy named James J. Andrews was normally in the employ of Gen. Buell, and had traveled in disguise down into Georgia on several occasions to scout targets, as well as the potential for sabotage. Andrews had provided valuable information to the Union Army in the first year of the war, and was about to attempt an even more daring escapade into Confederate Georgia.

In March of 1862, Buell had sent Andrews and a party of eight men on a secret mission to burn the bridges west of Chattanooga, but the raid had failed due to a lack of expected cooperation

This war-time illustration from Harper's "Pictorial History of the Great Rebellion," shows Chattanooga, Tennessee, from the north bank of the Tennessee River.

from local townspeople. After that defeat, Andrews had visited the Atlanta area posing as a blockade runner. He inspected all of the Confederate rail lines in that vicinity and northward to Chattanooga. He then returned to Buell with a plan for a second attempt to destroy the bridges.[11]

On the eve of his march from Shelbyville, Tennessee, to Huntsville, Alabama, Buell sent Andrews to Union Brigadier General Ormsby Mitchell who commanded a division of Buell's troops. Andrews and Mitchell discussed the details of the proposed raid.

Mitchell ultimately approved the plan and authorized Andrews to lead a party of twenty-four men into enemy territory to capture a train, then proceed back northward on a railroad sabotage mission, burning bridges along the northern portion of the Georgia State Railroad and on the East Tennessee Railroad where it approached the Georgia border.

The destructive mission was intended to block any reinforcement from the south and thereby isolate Chattanooga. When the blocking mission was completed, Mitchell could then move into a virtually undefended Chattanooga with ease, and without further concern for a rapid enemy response by rail from Georgia. It was a bold – and perhaps foolhardy – plan.[12] And as things turned out, it not only was foolhardy, but cost Andrews his life, as well as the lives of many of his men.

For the proposed raid, 23 soldiers from three Ohio regiments were selected for their courage and combat experience. In addition to Andrews, there was one other civilian – William Campbell of Salineville, Ohio. He happened to be visiting a friend in the camp at the time Andrews was seeking men.

All of the 24 men selected were told the mission would be secret, very dangerous, and conducted behind enemy lines. According to William Pittenger, who was one of the soldiers, *"not a man chosen declined the perilous honor."* The men were also told they would not be in uniform and would wear ordinary civilian

Chattanooga, Tennessee, was photographed here in 1863 during the war. Lookout Mountain is faintly visible in the distance. The objective of the raid being conducted by James J. Andrews was to cut off supply lines and the support of Chattanooga from the south. *(Photo courtesy of National Archives)*

dress. In other words, they would be spies, and could be shot if captured. Each man would be provided with clothing, Confederate money, and a small caliber revolver to be carried in a holster on the rear of his belt hidden from view under his coat.

Dressed as a businessman for this trip, Andrews was adept at his disguises. He wore a top hat and frock coat, and carried saddle bags on his left arm to set him apart as a man of authority. He was tall and bearded, which added to the effectiveness of his Southern upper-crust disguise.[13]

As the men traveled southward, they passed Big Shanty – where the train was to be seized the following morning – about eight miles north of Marietta. Upon reaching Big Shanty, the men discovered to their shock and dismay that a huge sprawling Confederate camp – humming with thousands of troops – surrounded the very train they were to steal. No one had confided to them this little additional detail.

Looking out of his train window at the busy military camp, Pittenger recalled his thoughts at the time. He wrote:

"To succeed in our enterprise, it would be necessary first to capture the engine in a guarded camp with soldiers standing around as spectators, and then to run it from one to two-hundred miles through the enemy's country, and to deceive or overpower all trains that should be met – a large contract for twenty men."[14]

Pittenger also didn't mention the fact that a steam locomotive takes a certain amount of time to build up enough speed to avoid being overtaken by someone on foot. Its sluggish start would leave him and his fellow spies at the mercy of what he presumed would be the thousands of Confederate muskets opening up fire upon them as they slowly chugged away from the Lacy Hotel. Though he didn't know it at the time, he fortunately had only to outrun the foot traffic.

By Friday night of April 11, 1862, Pittenger confirmed that Andrews and twenty-one of his raiders were staying at two different hotels in Marietta, Georgia. Most took rooms at what is known today as the Kennesaw House (which still stands as of this writing) alongside the Marietta railroad depot. The remainder took quarters at the nearby Marietta House on the town square.

The man-power of the saboteurs was unexpectedly cut from 25 to 22 (counting Andrews) – in yet another unexpected turn of events – when one man did not show up at all and two others had come under suspicion near Chattanooga on the way down and had been forced to join the Confederate Army near Jasper, Tennessee, just as they had said they wanted to do when questioned by authorities.[15]

Determined Leader

The morning of Saturday, April 12 was cold, wet and miserable as the men were aroused shortly before daybreak at about 4:00 a.m. Always the perfectionist, Andrews left nothing to chance, going from room to room to review the details of each man's role in the raid. They spoke in whispers in order to avoid being overheard through the thin walls of the hotel rooms. According to Pittenger, Andrews quietly instructed each man thusly:

"When the train stops at Big Shanty for breakfast, keep your places till I tell you to go. Get seats near each other in the same car, and say nothing about the matter on the way up. If anything unexpected occurs, look to me for the word. You, you, and you [designating the men] will go with me on the engine; the rest of you will go on the left of the train forward of where it is uncoupled, and climb on the cars in the best places you can, when the order is given. If anybody interferes, shoot him, but don't fire until it is necessary."[16]

In his writings, Pittenger also explained that one of the men – Sergeant Major Ross – was against continuing the raid and protested that *"the circumstances have changed since we set out and . . . that many more troops were at Big Shanty*

The Kennesaw House, at which James J. Andrews and a portion of his men over-nighted prior to beginning their famous episode in history, still stands in downtown Marietta beside the same (albeit modern) railroad tracks.

than formerly; that we had noticed the crowded state of the road as we came down, and that Mitchell's movements would make it worse." Therefore, Ross respectfully asked Andrews to either postpone or abort the raid.

Andrews, in response, quietly admitted to Ross that everything he said was true, but countered by pointing out the opportunities inherent in the situation:

"The military excitement and commotion, and the number of trains on the road will make our train the less likely to be suspected," Andrews said. *"And as to the troops at Big Shanty, if we do our work promptly, they will have no chance to interfere. Capturing the train in the camp will be easier than anywhere else, because no one would believe it possible, and there will therefore be no guard."*[17]

Pittenger reported that all did not go as planned in the attempted sabotage – in fact, very little actually went according to the method in which it had been originally conceived. Prior to boarding the train in Marietta – despite Andrews' explanation to Ross – several other raiders joined in the respectful protest against continuing with the raid.

Mystery & History in Georgia

The historic locomotive "General" was photographed here (date and place unknown) with its tender still bearing the inscription "W&A R.R."

Andrews reportedly listened to their complaints and then closed the meeting by saying: *"Boys, I tried this once before and failed; Now, I will succeed or leave my bones in Dixie."* (He possibly suspected it, but did not know just how prophetic his words would turn out to be.) Then, according to Pittenger, Andrews grasped the hands of each of the raiders and they left the room to go next door to the depot to catch the morning train to Big Shanty as a misty rain descended upon them.[18]

In order to maintain the subterfuge of their effort, the raiders had purchased tickets at the depot before 5:00 a.m., and each ticket was for a different stop farther up the line in order to avoid attracting suspicion by all going from Marietta to Big Shanty. At boarding time, two of the raiders who were staying at the Marietta House failed to appear, having overslept, thus reducing the number of raiders to 20 as the train pulled out at 5:15 a.m.

William A. Fuller was the conductor of the train on this route. Always efficient and thorough, he entered the passenger car and began taking tickets. He was keeping an eye out for deserters because he had been warned about their possible presence on the line, but he strangely was not suspicious of the raiders even though they had all boarded the train at Marietta.[19] He did, however, recognize the "businessman" Andrews, who had previously ridden his train, but he did not know him by name.[20]

Sleight of Hand

The first stop after leaving Marietta was Big Shanty. After approximately a 45-minute trip at 6:00 a.m., the train approached Big Shanty and Camp McDonald. The white tents of the enemy soldiers could be seen with the sentries walking their posts. Pittenger described it thusly:

"Big Shanty had been selected for the seizure because it was a breakfast station, and because it had no telegraph office. When Andrews had been here on the previous expedition, few troops were seen, but the number was now greatly increased. It is difficult to tell just how many were actually here, for they were constantly coming and going; but there seems to have been three or four regiments, numbering not far from a thousand men each. They were

In 1962, almost 100 years after the "Great Locomotive Chase," the General went on tour, retracing the route of the famed incident from Marietta to Ringgold, Georgia, still using some of the old wooden trestles such as the one in this photo. *(Photo courtesy of Adairsville History Museum)*

encamped almost entirely on the west side of the road, but their camp guard included the railroad depot."[21]

This stop at the Lacy Hotel was a regular pause for the train crew. They made it every morning. The train had hardly rolled to a stop before the entire crew – including the engineer, fireman, and conductor, and most of the passengers – got off and went quickly into the hotel for breakfast. They all apparently relished the meal at the Lacy, and no guard was even left on the train!

Demonstrating the utmost patience in the face of mortal danger, the raiders kept their seats, awaiting a signal from Andrews. As the last passengers going to breakfast cleared the front door of the coach, Andrews and Knight fell in behind them, but instead of going off on the right side of the train, they got off on the left side next to the camp. As a result, they were hidden from the view of anyone in the hotel as they went about their espionage.

The men first had to confirm that their hijacking of the train was even possible at that point. They reportedly walked confidently forward together to see if the tracks ahead were clear. When they had confirmed that no train obstructed their departure, they walked back to the rear of the third empty boxcar where Andrews told Knight to uncouple the remaining cars and wait for him there. Then, Andrews walked back to the passenger car where the remaining raiders were waiting and, in a calm voice, said: *"Come on boys; it's time to go."*[22]

Stealth was as much a necessity as was a daring temperament. Pittenger explained that the raiders left the coach car quietly so that the remaining passengers – who had not gone up to the Lacy for breakfast – would not be alarmed. Andrews immediately went forward and Knight, seeing him coming, also hurried forward and climbed aboard the engine.

At this point, Knight cut the bell rope that was tied to the Big Shanty loading dock; put his hand on the throttle, and stood ready, his eyes fixed on Andrews awaiting a signal to depart.[23] Andrews stood on the lower step of the engine, leaning back to see his men running forward and scrambling aboard the empty boxcars. An extra engineer and a firemen among the raiders ran forward to the engine to their posts beside Knight in the cab.[24]

Meanwhile, as Pittenger pointed out in his recounting of the incident: *"All this time a sentry was standing not a dozen feet from the engine quietly watching, as if this was the most ordinary proceeding, and a number of other soldiers were idling but a short distance away."*[25]

The late Wilbur G. Kurtz, Sr., a long-time Atlanta artist and respected historian and the son-in-law of conductor William Fuller, interviewed many of those involved in the raid. In the postscript to the MacLennan Roberts book, *The Great Locomotive Chase*, he wrote that recruits at Camp McDonald were armed with the "Joe Brown Pikes" because of a shortage of firearms. Kurtz interviewed Henry Whitley of Company F, 56th Georgia Regiment, who was the sentry who stood and watched the raiders steal the train that day. Whitley told him that he also was armed with nothing more than a pike.[26]

Pittenger added that when everything was ready and the last raider was pulled into a boxcar, Andrews climbed aboard the engine and nodded to Knight, who opened the engine throttle. The great locomotive spun its wheels before gaining traction, then slowly began gaining momentum toward the curve in the rail line, leaving Camp McDonald in its wake and taking the 20 men to a date with destiny.

All of this happened so quickly that none of the camp's soldiers raised their useless weapons, sounded an alarm, or even showed any sign that they suspected anything was wrong as the engine – with only three boxcars attached – pulled away. The theft of a train at Camp McDonald in the midst of thousands of enemy soldiers had been done by twenty raiders "without firing a shot or even an angry gesture."[27]

Flight To Eternity

The remainder of this daring incident from the U.S. Civil War is a matter of history today. Though he was imminently successful in his theft of the locomotive called *General*, James J. Andrews and his men ultimately failed in their mission. After a dramatic flight northward up the railroad, the raiders eventually abandoned the train two miles north of Ringgold, Georgia, having completed only moderate damage to the railroad and failing to destroy any bridges.

The saboteurs were all eventually captured as they fled on foot into the north Georgia countryside. Several were later executed in Atlanta, and several amazingly even managed to successfully escape, fleeing back to the North where they later were awarded the Medal of Honor.

Meanwhile, back at Camp McDonald, an enraged cadre was trying to put the best face on a very embarrassing incident. The railroad raid at the camp was an extraordinary feat of daring, but as Andrews had predicted at Marietta on the morning of the event, their success in capturing the train was enabled by the lack of a local defense preparedness by both the railroad and camp authorities. This lack of preparedness ultimately fell upon the shoulders of the lone governor of the state, Joseph Emerson Brown.

Endnotes

1. Allen D. Candler, ed., The Confederate Records of the State of Georgia, 5 vols. (Atlanta, GA: Charles P. Byrd, State Printer, 1909), vol. 2, p. 187-195 (hereafter referred to as CR, 2:187-195); Joseph H. Parks, **Joseph E. Brown of Georgia** *(Baton Rouge, LA: Louisiana State University Press,*

1977), 182-83; William S. Smedlund, **Camp Fires of Georgia's Troops, 1861-1865** (Lithonia, GA: Kennesaw Mountain Press, 1994), 201-205; **War of the Rebellion: Official Records of the Union and Confederate Armies**, 70 vols, in 128 pts. (Washington, DC: Government Printing Office, 1880-1901), ser. 4, vol.1:902 (hereafter referred to as OR).

2. CR, 2:89-91; Smedlund, 201-205; Sarah Blackwell Gober Temple, **The First Hundred Years: A Short History of Cobb County in Georgia** (Atlanta, GA: Walter W. Brown Publishing Company, 1935; reprint, Athens, GA: Agee Publishers, Inc., 1989), 238-241.

3. CR, 2:194-198; OR ser. 4, vol. 1:917.

4. Rodney Hilton Brown, **American Pole Arms 1526-1865** (New Milford, CN: N. Letterman & Company, 1967), 118-135; CR 2:199; Parks, 184. The "Georgia Pike" was a pole arm that had a long double-edged blade secured to its six foot wooden shaft by a ferrule made out of brass or iron and two long wrought iron side straps. The butt end usually had a cap or long cast iron shoe to prevent splintering. The Georgia pattern pikes were normally produced at the Confederate armories. The principal pike manufactured in Georgia and known as the "Joe Brown Pike" was of the "clover-leaf" design which means it had the usual ten inch double-edged blade and two additional side "bridle-cutter" blades which gave it the clover-leaf or cross appearance. The side blades were used as bridle cutters to engage cavalrymen and cut the reins of their horses, thus rendering them out of control and making the rider vulnerable to a thrust from the pike's main blade.

5. CR, 2:199-200; Louise Biles Hill, **Joseph E. Brown and the Confederacy** (Chapel Hill, NC: University of North Carolina Press, 1939), 249.

6. CR 2:349-353.

7. "A Perfect Novelty," **Athens Southern Banner**, 12 February 1862; Rodney Brown, 134; Kenneth Coleman, **Confederate Athens** (Athens, GA: University of Georgia Press, 1968), 43.

8. I.G. Bradwell, "Soldier Life in the Confederate Army," Confederate Veteran 24, no. 1 (1916): 21; Rodney Brown, 134.

9. Henry H. Kurtz, Jr., "Hijack of a Locomotive: The Andrews Raid Revisited," **Atlanta History: A Journal of Georgia and the South** 34, no. 3 (1990): 2; MacClennan Roberts, **The Great Locomotive Chase** (New York: Dell Publishing Company, 1956), postscript by Wilbur G. Kurtz, Sr., 155; Parks, 242.

10. Parks, 151-154; Smedlund, 11-12.

11. William Pittenger, "**Locomotive Chase in Georgia**," **The Century Magazine**. 36, No. 1 (1888): 141-142; Wilbur G. Kurtz, Sr., "The Andrews Raid," Atlanta Historical Bulletin 13, no. 4 (1968): 12.

12. William Pittenger, **Daring and Suffering: A History of the Great Railroad Adventure Into Georgia In 1862** (New York: The War Publishing Company, 1887), 97; Derry, 95-96; John A Wilson, **Adventures of Alf. Wilson: A Thrilling Episode of the Dark Days of the Rebellion** (Marietta, GA: Continental Book Company, 1972), 17.

13. Pittenger, **Locomotive Chase in Georgia**, 142; Wilbur G. Kurtz, Sr., "The Andrews Railroad Raid," Civil War Times Illustrated 5, no. 1 (1966): 8-13; Wilson, 15-18.

14. Pittenger, **Locomotive Chase In Georgia**, 143; Wilson, 18-25.

15. Pittenger, **Daring and Suffering**, 98-99; Daniel O. Cox, Telephone interview with the author, 20 February, 2002; Wilson, 26.

16. Pittenger, **Daring and Suffering**, 99-100; Charles Kendell O'Neill, **Wild Train: The Story Of Andrews Raiders** (New York: Random House, 1956), 129.

17. Pittenger, **Daring and Suffering**, 100-101.

18. Ibid, 101.

19. Fuller, 10, 21; Kurtz, Sr., "The Andrews Raid," 17; O'Neill, 131-32.

20. Pittenger, **Daring and Suffering**, 102.

21. Pittenger, **Daring and Suffering**, 102-103; O'Neill, 132-133; Wilson, 28.

22. Pittenger, **Daring and Suffering**, 102-103; Fuller, 30; O'Neill, 135-36; Wilson, 29.

23. Pittenger, **Daring and Suffering**, 103; Wilson, 29.

24. Pittenger, **Daring and Suffering**, 104-105.

25. Ibid, 105.

26. Pittenger, **Daring and Suffering**, 105; Lillian Henderson, ed., **The Rosters of Confederate Soldiers of Georgia**, vol. 5 (Spartanburg, SC: The Reprint Company, 1982), 883; Kurtz, Jr., 6; O'Neill, 137; Roberts, 155; Wilson, 28-29.

27. Pittenger, **Daring and Suffering**, 105; O'Neill, 137; Wilson, 29.

Aged Structure From Yesteryear:

The History & Preservation of Concord Covered Bridge

It has stood the test of time now for over 150 years, but the increased modern traffic over the historic structure does not bode well for its future.

Many people think Concord Covered Bridge over Nickajack Creek is an antebellum structure (built before the Civil War). Not true. It was actually built in 1872, but even at that age, it is almost 150 years old, as of 2021. Since the historic bridge amazingly has been in continuous use all this time, and is still used (as of this writing) for motorized traffic is amazing in itself. That the bridge is still in existence at all is even more amazing.

Americans began covering bridges in the late 1700s in an effort to get more life out of the important structures. It was easier to replace a roof on a bridge than the heavy support beams beneath them which crossed the creeks and rivers.

Concord Covered Bridge – along with an adjacent additional two historic structures, Ruff's Mill and the former mill operator's home – have all been placed on the National Register of Historic Places, and as such, receive decent protection, but time is not on the bridge's side.

According to records, the ownership of Concord Covered Bridge was transferred to Cobb County in 1888. Since that time, literally millions of dollars have been poured into its preservation, but the fact that the 150-year-old structure remains as a portion of an important artery of travel between Marietta and Smyrna makes its destiny highly questionable.

Modern Protection

How can a structure so valuable to the state's history be allowed to be continuously used for heavy vehicular traffic? It is one of only two such historic covered bridges remaining in metro-Atlanta. All the rest have disappeared – victims of "progress." Each time something like this occurs, at least a measure of the priceless history of our state once again is victimized.

Due to the fact that age and incessant use had caused the bridge to begin leaning, new work was required in 2017. A special local option sales tax (SPLOST) was enacted and over

The History & Preservation of Concord Covered Bridge   Cobb County

Though listed on the National Register of Historic Places, Concord Covered Bridge is the only such historic structure in the Atlanta metro-area amazingly used by present-day motorized traffic. It was the scene of the Battle of Ruff's Mill on July 4, 1864, during the U.S. Civil War.

The historic Martin Luker Ruff home near Nickajack Creek was built in the 1840s. With his brother – Robert Daniel Ruff – he established several mills in this vicinity.

$800,000.00 in additional monies were spent to correct the problem.

"We will do whatever it takes to keep that bridge intact," said Bill Shelton, head of Cobb's road maintenance at the time.

As of this writing, heavy-duty protective steel guard bars on either side of the entrance to the bridge keep oversized and abusive vehicular traffic from damaging the bridge these days. The big metal barriers are designed to break partially while forbidding the entrance of oversized vehicles, trucks, and trailers.

And whenever someone does attempt to drive an oversized vehicle or trailer into the bridge and breaks the barrier, it's expensive. At last check, the fine was $600.00.

Over the years, a number of supports have been added to the bridge in a continued effort to preserve it. Heavy concrete piers were added beneath the bridge in 1966 to supposedly make it sturdy enough to support heavy traffic, but as the years go by, the materials being hauled over the ancient structure grow heavier and heavier.

Will the county ever get the message and construct a new bridge alongside the historic structure in order to retire it from service and genuinely preserve it for posterity? At the time of this writing, Cobb County was awaiting word from the U.S. Army Corps of Engineers on whether or not the Corps approved of the county's revised plan for a four and three-quarter mile segment of highway which will cross the historic district. But even that plan is seriously flawed according to historians and may fall by the wayside.

Future Preservation Plans

A permit from the Corps for new preservation measures was first sought in 1989, but a public uproar over the original route prompted Cobb commissioners to alter the route – a plan which was still unacceptable to many. The new route still included a stretch of asphalt which would run between Hicks Road and South Cobb Drive, coming within 500 feet of the historic Martin L. Ruff house and family cemetery and isolating the property from the remainder of the 158-acre historic district.

This newly proposed plan, however, with its revised highway route and official park designation, is a significant improvement over the previous design which would have included the

Mystery & History in Georgia

Ruff's Gristmill, powered by an over-shot waterwheel, dates to the 1850s. It is listed on the National Register of Historic Places.

development and paving of a four-lane highway only 700 feet north of historic Concord Covered Bridge. The new plan places the highway some 1,350 feet north of the bridge.

Unfortunately, the passage of time can have a dramatic impact upon one's perception regarding "progress." Back in the days when Georgia was still being settled – prior to the removal of the Cherokee Indians – the development of the Concord Bridge area was a top priority of most every citizen in the area.

In 1838, the town of Smyrna was begun with a Methodist campground. Sometime around 1845, the first railroad – the Western & Atlantic (chartered in 1836) – was built through Smyrna, and the town's growth began taking off.

Pioneer Developers

Martin L. Ruff, who obtained land in the *1832 Land Lottery of Georgia*, moved his family into the area of Concord Covered Bridge near present-day Smyrna sometime in the 1840s. According to the *Georgia Land Lottery* files, *"On 28 June, 1843, a Goss, M.L. Ruff, & a Mobeley assigned a lawyer to act as their agent with regard to land in Cobb County."*

The *1851 Tax Digest* reported that Ruff was the owner of *"two slaves and 695 acres of land"* in Cobb County. In 1856, Ruff purchased land lots which included a gristmill, the miller's house and the covered bridge, from a farmer. The mill came to be known as "Ruff's Mill."

In 1850, Robert Daniell moved to Cobb County and purchased land in the same area along Nickajack Creek. He entered into a partnership with Ruff and the men built and operated the Concord Woolen Mills and a sawmill – in addition to the gristmill – along the creek. Available water-power in areas adjacent to pioneer gristmills often encouraged the construction of a sawmill as well at the sites.

This partnership in what then was a sparsely-settled area marked the beginning of the development of an early mill community. A general store was opened near the gristmill, and was described as *"a small wooden building, erected 20 or 30 yards opposite the mill entrance."* It was stocked with groceries – canned goods and other basic necessities of life. This building was demolished in the early 1900s.

The thriving community also contained several residences, churches, and a school. A map from the Georgia Department of Archives and History in Atlanta shows that a settlement known as "Mill Grove" existed in this vicinity as early as 1847.

State Senator John Gann who represented Cobb in the Georgia State Legislature in 1842, was a pioneer settler in the county. He received land in the lottery and built the Gann House in 1853. This structure, which still stands today, is located about one-quarter mile west of Concord Bridge, and is a basic component of the present-day historic district.

Mill Grove Post Office, established on September 28, 1837, once existed near the Gann House. Mail came to the post office by pony.

Gann was also a founding member of Concord Baptist Church in 1833. Still in existence today, it is the oldest church in Cobb County.

U.S. Civil War Impact

The woolen mill on Nickajack Creek – an important cog in the production of uniforms and other materials for the Confederacy – was often mentioned in the official records of the Union and Confederate armies at the time of General Sherman's advancement into Georgia. Gordon Ruckart (who, with his wife, bought the Reed House and gristmill in 1976), maintained that this mill produced some of the South's finest

The Henry Clay Ruff house on the southeast side of Concord Covered Bridge is believed to date to the beginning of Ruff Mill. It was the residence of the first miller – Henry Ruff – and has been extensively renovated over the years.

woolen fabrics in its day – actually winning awards for its *"cassimeres and jeans."*

For this and other reasons, it was no accident that a significant Civil War engagement – the "Battle of Ruff's Mill" – took place in this vicinity in July of 1864. It was just one of several skirmishes that Sunday and Monday of 1864, as Sherman's armies moved from Kennesaw Mountain toward Gen. Joe Johnston's new Confederate line along Nickajack Creek.

Today, the ruins of this historic old woolen mill are barely 550 feet from the proposed new highway. Many preservationists and area residents alike are appalled at the possibilities for damage to the mill site during the highway construction. Cobb officials steadfastly maintain the site(s) will be preserved.

An article published in the *Atlanta Journal* on July 6, 1958, recorded remembrances of Gann's grandson who said that *"John Gann and his wife were forced to billet 15 Yankee officers – captains through colonels."* Mrs. Gann and the few remaining slaves had to cook and wash and iron for the outfit, and Mr. Gann, according to his grandson, was

The Ruff family cemetery is located in the vicinity of the Martin Luker Ruff house.

forced to shine boots, chop wood, and perform other menial chores.

Despite the invasion of their property, the Ganns were spared the devastation of having their home burned. The woolen mill, however, was not so fortunate. It was destroyed by the federals because of the Confederate uniforms being made there.

Concord Bridge (according to some sources) and the sawmill were destroyed as well. The gristmill, since it was a refining point of food for residents, was spared.

Post-War Rebuilding

After the war, in the autumn of 1868, the woolen mill was quickly rebuilt, resuming operations in 1869 with 32 looms, 600 spindles, and 52 operators. The rebuilt sawmill produced most of the lumber used in reconstructing the state-owned Western & Atlantic Railroad in the Cobb area too.

The *Marietta Journal*, on March 5, 1869, reported: *"One of the greatest Southern enterprises that Southern ingenuity and capital has brought into existence is the Concord Manufacturing Company. The machinery from New York is being received and skillful and efficient machinists are engaged in putting it up ready for operation. This factory is calculated with the preparations made to turn out as fine woolen fabrics as are manufactured (in the) north and the benefits that will spring from this factory to the county and state are incalculable."*

In 1880, Martin Ruff's widow managed the gristmill after Martin passed away. Demonstrating her prowess and determination, Mrs. Ruff hired one male who operated the mill 12 hours a day in the summer and 20 hours a day in the winter, and who earned a daily wage of $1.50 for an annual salary of $234.00. He produced annually some 3,000 bushels of wheat, in addition to corn meal and feed.

A post office named *"Nickajack"* also existed at the Concord site in the late 1800s. The name *"Concord"* had been rejected by the postal department since that name was already being used by another community in the state.

By 1882, two rail lines had been constructed through this area. Southern Railroad had a line to the south, and Seaboard Airline had a line north of the woolen mill and gristmill.

By 1888, the loose-knit community had succumbed to tradition and was being called "Concord," despite postal service objections according to the *Marietta Journal* of August 30 of that year.

The Concord Mills were destroyed by fire yet again in 1889. This time, the owners rebuilt the factory downstream and east of the Concord Covered Bridge. The community, hard-hit by the fire, rebounded with the reconstruction.

A newspaper article from 1895 describes the community as *"the smallest place in the state where there is free mail delivery,"* and a community with *"telegraph, telephone, electric lights, free schools, water works, and literary and social clubs."*

Later Families

One of Ruff's eleven children – John Wesley Ruff – purchased the gristmill, miller's house (Henry Clay Ruff house) and family home-place from his father's estate in 1889. The Ruff family cemetery, typical of its day, is near the house.

In 1897, Ruff sold the *"Ruff and Daniell Mill"* to Parker M. Rice, who, in turn, sold it to two Martin brothers. The gristmill was run by Asbury Martin as *Martin Feed and Grain*, ca. 1914-1930. When Martin sold out, he took the mill works with him to a new location.

In the early 1900s, the Seaboard Airline railroad built a depot to the north of the mill complex. The new stop was known as "Rice Station."

John Rice, a son of one of the owners of the woolen mill at that time, built a residence which ultimately became known as *"The Rock House."* After purchasing the mill, he nevertheless soon sold it to Annie E. Johnson of Rome, Georgia.

Despite efforts to the contrary, the woolen mill eventually fell victim to rising competition from the north and to changing technologies in the industry. It went into receivership in 1916.

According to Harold Glore (now deceased) – a Mableton historian with direct connections to the community through his grandmother (a sister of Gann) – the area comprising what once was the vibrant Concord community had surprisingly become a literal ghost-town by 1910, such was the still undeveloped and uninhabited nature of the area.

In 1930, Dr. Clinton Reed, an Atlanta physician, bought 313 acres which included *"a rock house, store house, and several operatives' houses."* Dr. Reed also became the owner of the gristmill and Henry Clay Ruff house (old miller's house). He first planned to visit the property for weekend retreats only, but eventually moved permanently to the miller's house and employed William C. Pauley, a noted landscape architect, to create a formal garden and terraces at the site. Dr. Reed continued living there until his death.

The woolen mill was never reopened following its bankruptcy. The gristmill, with its machinery and waterwheel removed, never functioned again either.

The dams along Nickajack Creek which provided the waterpower to operate the mills eventually fell victim to time and the elements. One of the dams broke during a flood in the 1960s, and large stones were washed downstream where they were reclaimed for use as a portion of the wall which encloses the old miller's (Henry Clay Ruff) house property.

The Current Situation

The gristmill, miller's house, John Rice's rock house, and the Martin L. Ruff house are all privately owned as of this writing. Concord Covered Bridge, the Henry Clay Miller house, the Gann house and the Ruff gristmill, are all listed on the ***National Register of Historic Places***.

The Ruff home remained in the family until an English couple bought it in 1943. Mr. and Mrs. J. Harold Ivester purchased that home in 1976.

"We restored the home, rather than remodeled it," emphasized Mrs. Ivester, who lived as of this writing in the North Fulton County community of Crabapple.

Mystery & History in Georgia

Known today as the Rice house, this structure is made uniquely of creek and field stones, and was built by John W. Rice in 1907. Rice was an owner of the woolen mill at Concord Covered Bridge which he purchased from his father – Zachariah Armistead Rice.

The house, very historic in its own right, sheltered wounded soldiers during the Battle of Ruff's Mill. "Oh, the ghost stories we heard while living there!" Mrs. Ivester once stated.

Concord Covered Bridge is one of the few covered bridges – if not the only one – in Georgia still in use today. It also enjoys the distinction of being the only covered bridge still in use on a public highway in the metropolitan Atlanta area.

Ironically, despite its age and historic nature, Concord Covered Bridge is also the most heavily used covered bridge in the state. It is only 16 feet wide and 13 feet high, with clearance for only one vehicle at a time.

Most historians today maintain the current bridge was constructed (having possibly been burned during the Civil War) in 1872. Mr. Harold Glore once noted that an abutment beneath the wooden structure bears the date of 1848, undoubtedly marking the date the structure was originally built as a flat-decked bridge, later to be covered when a dam was built upstream beside it.

There is considerable debate as to whether the bridge was actually burned during the Battle of Ruff's Mill. Some sources maintain that Ruff and Daniell built the present bridge after the previous one was destroyed during the battle. Harold Glore, however, said that his grandmother remembered that the bridge did not burn at all.

"I've grappled with this question on several occasions," Dr. Thomas Scott, a history professor at nearby Kennesaw College stated. "I think Harold Glore's grandmother's memory of the intact bridge is a good reason to believe it was never destroyed. Possibly, the original bridge, not covered, underwent a later renovation and expansion that has since been reported as a *complete rebuilding*."

Scott emphasizes the bridge's historic significance. "Concord Covered Bridge is an important part of Smyrna's history," he explains. "There's as much history around that site as in any other part of the county."

In the nomination form submitted to the ***National Register of Historic Places***, Mr. and Mrs. Gordon Ruckart wrote: *"The stonemasonry supports are original and may date from an antebellum bridge at the same location. The concrete supports were added in 1965 to strengthen the bridge so that it could accommodate modern automobile traffic."*

Concord Covered Bridge was included in the ***World Guide To Covered Bridges*** published by the National Society For The Preservation Of Covered Bridges in 1972. The beauty and uniqueness of the bridge, as well as that of the homes and old mill in the historic district surrounding it, are unmatched anywhere else in the state, say many historians. Only time will tell to what degree this site is preserved for the future.

Another Fine Mess !

The Birthplace of Oliver Hardy

If one listens closely to the old films of the famous Hollywood comedy team of Laurel and Hardy – which occasionally are re-broadcast on one of the cable channels – one can hear the faintest sweet Southern accent in funnyman Hardy's voice. That accent isn't happenstance. Hardy was born and spent his formative years in Georgia, and carried that identity the rest of his life.

The rotund Oliver Norvell Hardy is actually claimed by three Georgia cities today: Harlem in Columbia County, Madison in Morgan County, and Milledgeville in Baldwin County. Several other Georgia communities have lesser ties to Hardy, but simply can't let go. Hardy and his partner – Stan Laurel, who migrated to Hollywood from England – ultimately comprised one of the most famous motion picture comedy teams of all time.

Oliver Hardy was born January 18, 1892, in Harlem, Georgia, the only son of Oliver and Emily Norvell Tant Hardy. When he was born, Oliver was given his mother's maiden name – "Norvell" – as his first name. His father, Oliver, died ten months after Hardy's birth, so he never even knew of his son's eventual fame. Norvell, perhaps to honor his father, took his name – Oliver – as his own, all the way down the road to eternal celebrity, becoming known thereafter as "Oliver Norvell Hardy."

Twice widowed, the elder Oliver Hardy, who appears to have been a foreman on the Georgia Railroad through Harlem, and previously tax collector of Columbia County, married Emily Norvell Tant in 1890. In May of 1890, "Emmie" Oliver, as she was known, purchased a small house behind what formerly was the city hall in Harlem. By 1891, however, the couple had moved to nearby Madison where Oliver, Sr. managed the Turnell-Butler Hotel at the corner of East Jefferson and Hancock Streets.

Records indicate Emmie returned to Harlem in January of 1891, perhaps to her mother's home, to give birth to Norvell, returning a short time later back to Madison.

It is not known by this writer if the elder Hardy carried the excess weight so characteristic of his son, but either poor health, or perhaps the stress of his occupation, eventually took its toll upon Oliver, Sr. He passed away unexpectedly at the age of 50 on November 22, 1892, and

Following employment in a movie theatre and growing admiration of the flickering images moving across the big screen, Oliver Norvell Hardy became fascinated with motion pictures. When a friend returned from a vacation and informed him about a new actors' colony in Florida, the rotund young man set out to seek his fortune, later to become famous as the heftier half of the comedy duo, **Laurel & Hardy**, starring in a multitude of Hollywood films.

was returned to Harlem for burial in the city cemetery beside his second wife.

Oliver's death understandably came as a shock to Emmie. She was now widowed yet again, this time not only with her four children by her first marriage, but also with her infant by Oliver.

The bad news was compounded when she was informed by the owners of the Turnell-Butler Hotel that she would not be retained as the proprietor of the hotel her husband had managed. Perhaps the news that he was about to be dismissed was the news which had sent her husband "over the edge." We'll never know.

Whatever the circumstances, Emily Norvell Tant Hardy was no quitter. She also, interestingly, had a knack for business.

One of the first things Emmie did after learning of her discharge from the Turnell-Butler Hotel was to petition the local county probate court for a year's support from her late husband's estate, and she was awarded $628.00. This amount of money as the norm for "a year's support" may seem like a paltry sum today, but in 1892, it was a fair-sized sum of money.

Emmie didn't spend the stipend frivolously either. She promptly invested it in "cigars, bedding, crockery, lamps, silverware, coal, and a showcase." It was obvious that her position was "If the mountain won't come to Mohammed, Mohammed will go to the mountain." Emmie had decided to set up her own hotel – *The Hardy House* – in Madison in a rented building near the railroad depot on West Jefferson Street.

Emmie Hardy operated her new hotel from early 1893 until the autumn of 1897. According to records, she left the business briefly, then returned in January of 1899.

Despite her tenacious attitude, fortune did not smile upon Emmie's endeavors. Whatever rates were offered in The Hardy House were undercut by the Turnell-Butler Hotel, and the quality of the Turnell-Butler undoubtedly exceeded that of The Hardy House as well. Emmie steadily lost business until she could no longer meet the cost of her overhead, and was forced to close the hotel on May 1, 1899.

Records indicate Emmie rented a house on Main Street in Madison for approximately a year, and then departed shortly thereafter with her family, leaving Madison behind forever. Little remains today of the Norvell Hardy era in Madison.

The Turnell-Butler Hotel met its demise sometime around 1930, when it reportedly burned to the ground *"in a spectacular blaze."* It was never rebuilt.

Interestingly, after the Turnell-Butler went out of existence, the former Hardy House carried on under new ownership, eventually becoming *"The White House"* around 1913. It soldiered on for many more decades before being closed and torn down in the 1970s.

Unfortunately, it didn't take a tragic fire to bring it to an end. Both the Turnell-Butler Hotel and the White House had suffered the fate being foisted upon most of the formerly beautiful turn-of-the-century hotels in the railroad towns across the South. Once railroad passenger service ceased in the early 1960s, the traveling public and businessmen who had provided the life-blood of the hotels disappeared. At that point, the end was inevitable.

One of the few remaining relics in Madison which does still have ties to Norvell Hardy – the massive Victorian brick school he attended, known at that time as the Madison Grammar School – today houses the Madison-Morgan Cultural Center on Main Street. Norvell's former first grade room, which the future comedian undoubtedly occupied during the 1898-1899 school year, is a reception room as of this writing. Norvell reportedly was overweight even at that early date.

For several years after 1900, relatively little is known about the Hardy family. Those days, undoubtedly, were very difficult and trying times.

In May of 1900, Emmie Hardy moved to Athens to lease the Victoria Hotel – still attempting to pursue the profession with which she was most familiar – but ultimately left Athens for unknown reasons after only a short period of time. An unverified report maintains she briefly managed the Button Gwinnett Hotel in Lawrenceville, Georgia.

The family later appears to have lived in the Atlanta area where young Norvell reportedly pursued training in the performing arts (singing) profession, since he had a keen appreciation for music. He was blessed with an excellent tenor voice which occasionally was given brief feature in his later acting roles.

It was also during this period that Emmie is believed to have married yet again, this time to a Mr. Jackson, about which virtually nothing is known. The marriage however did result in the birth of two more daughters.

Emmie relocated to Milledgeville sometime after 1901, perhaps as late as 1908 or 1909. This move appears to have coincided with growing adolescent problems involving young Norvell. The young man no doubt missed the father he had never known, and his older half-brother, Sam Tant, 12, had been tragically drowned in the Oconee River.

Food appeared to provide solace for Norvell. And it quickly became obvious. By age 15, he already weighed 250 pounds.

For brief periods of time, Norvell found outlets for his energy not only in the performing arts but in baseball as well. Interestingly, he eventually acquired the nickname of "Babe." He, reportedly, was the hit of school plays, and was greatly admired as well as an umpire for local baseball teams.

Norvell also briefly attended Georgia Military Academy at Milledgeville, Young Harris College in the mountains of north Georgia, and the Atlanta Conservatory of Music. He just could never seem to "find his place." This would soon change.

It was during this period, that Emmie operated the dining rooms of two hotels in Milledgeville – the Wayne Street Hotel, and, later, the Baldwin Hotel, the largest and finest hostelry in the city. Both have since been torn down – additional victims of the scourges of time as explained above.

Stan Laurel and Oliver Hardy with their wives, circa 1930s.

One of the jobs the by then very large and tall teenaged Norvell disliked was carrying the sandwich boards around Milledgeville advertising the dinner fare at the Baldwin's dining room. But someone had to do it, and his family's income was dependent upon the numbers of customers served by the dining room.

It was while attending the Georgia Military Academy at Milledgeville that young Norvell fell into the habit of carrying the books of Althea Miller (later Mrs. Althea Horn). Mrs. Horn's daughter, Amelia Tennille of Milledgeville, later recalled that her mother once described how young Norvell was quite a performer even in those days. "She said he was always singing and dancing all the way to school each day, and as a result, she often ended up carrying not only her books, but his too!"

As he was quickly reaching adolescence, it wasn't long before young Oliver Norvell Hardy began looking for more lucrative opportunities for his musical talents. He briefly left town with a traveling minstrel show that had stayed at one of the hotels. He also briefly studied opera at the conservatory in Atlanta.

During this period, Oliver Norvell also increasingly "played hooky" from school to sing at a local movie house where he was able to indulge his passion for the performance of popular tunes. It was at that movie house that he was accidentally introduced to another career which was to change his life forever – acting in "the movies."

In 1910, a movie house was opened in the ground floor of the Opera House building in downtown Milledgeville. This aged building still stands as of this writing, and when it opened its doors for the first time, 18-year-old Oliver Hardy applied there for work. He reportedly became a virtual jack-of-all-trades, collecting tickets with a jaunty air, sweeping the floor, singing during the showing of the illustrated glass plate slides featured as the reels were being changed, and much more.

Oliver also was the projectionist, which in those days undoubtedly meant he turned a crank to move the silent movie film through the projector and past the flickering lens. He even acted as manager when his boss was away.

As he filled any time available working in this theater, the flickering pictures on the big screen began to hold more and more of an allure for the heavyset – but very agile – young man. This was something *he* could do, he no doubt thought dreamily, as he watched the images move across the screen.

It was shortly thereafter, around 1912, that a friend returned from a vacation and told Hardy there was a growing actors' colony in Jacksonville, Florida. That was just too much of a temptation for Oliver to resist. In early 1913, he packed his bag and left, never again to return to Milledgeville.

The nearest Hardy ever came to returning to the last town of his Georgia residence was the trip he made to Macon, Georgia, on November 17, 1913, when he married his first wife, Madelyn Saloshin. Emmie, his mother, was furious, but at that point, she once again was having financial problems, so she had little time – or even wherewithal – to be cross with her son.

Oliver, interestingly, acted in numerous silent movies shot in Florida, New York, and, finally, Hollywood, where he joined the Hal Roach Studios in 1924. Stan Laurel, a British-born Vaudeville comedian, broke into the movies in 1917, joining Roach in 1920.

In their early years, Laurel and Hardy appeared together in comedies, but not as a team – until they shared top billing in *Putting Pants On Philip* in 1927. The pair turned out to be so hilarious, that their future became academic.

The comedy team of *Laurel and Hardy* made a successful transition to talking pictures ("talkies") two years later. A list of even their feature movies is too lengthy to provide here. Their antics in *Pardon Us, Babes In Toyland, Fra Diavolo, A Chump At Oxford, Saps At Sea, The Flying Deuces*, and many others, kept audiences in stitches, and assured the duo's future. These movies continue to delight audiences even today.

Laurel and Hardy appeared in their final film together in *Atoll K*, shot in 1951. Today, memories of the bumbling pair are kept alive through re-runs, videos, and the *Laurel and Hardy* appreciation society – *The Sons Of The Desert* – named after another of their films. Each local chapter is called a tent, and is named after one of the movies in which *Laurel and Hardy* appeared.

Stan Laurel and Oliver Hardy, circa 1920s.

Oliver's mother, Emmie, eventually left Milledgeville herself for Atlanta about 1916. In later years, she refused to settle near her famous son in southern California, despite two trips to the West coast, preferring instead to remain in the South. This can only be considered ironic, since her son never returned to the South.

Mary Page Walker of Madison, Georgia, had a fleeting acquaintance with Emmie (who by then had reverted back to her famous son's name – Mrs. Oliver Hardy, Sr.), when both of them lived at the *Georgian Terrace Hotel* at Peachtree and Ponce de Leon Streets in Atlanta during the mid-1940s. "Mrs. Hardy was a very large, short woman who probably weighed 250 pounds," Ms. Walker explained. "She was very plain-spoken, but very proud of her son, who, according to gossip, contributed very generously to her welfare."

Mrs. Oliver Hardy, Sr., died on November 16, 1948, and was interred the next day in the mausoleum at Atlanta's Westview Cemetery. Her death certificate listed her age as "About 88."

Oliver Norvell Hardy, her famous son, was married three times, but had no children. He died on August 7, 1957, at the age of 66. His ashes were interred in the Garden of Valhalla Memorial Park in North Hollywood, California.

Champion Racers and "Moonshine" Makers of Old Dawson County, GA

For many years now, Dawson County has been known as a "moonshine" mecca, producing in turn some of the fastest race car drivers alive. Bill Elliott has reigned as the most celebrated racing champion from Georgia (and indeed, the nation) in recent years, but he's not the only famous competitor to emerge from Georgia – not by a long shot.

One needs only to mention stock-car racing today, and Dawson County, Georgia, immediately is included in the mix of the conversation. And almost on an equal level of fame (or infamy) is the county's storied past in the history of "moonshining," which had a huge impact upon the development of a number of the county's racing champions.

You see, it was because the illicit liquor producers had to outrun the local police and "revnoor" agents that they ultimately became so fast and adept at driving in the first place. They learned how to rebuild their automobile engines with immense horsepower and to reconfigure the vehicle suspensions to carry extra weight yet still be fast and agile enough to maintain an advantage over their law enforcement pursuers. It is a legacy which lives on today.

It was also a life replete with danger and death at every turn. In a lonely graveyard overlooking downtown Dawsonville today, the stark tombstone of Lloyd Seay stands in mute testimony to this life. He is just one of these racing legends for which the county has gained fame and fortune. Others, both living and deceased, still dominate the folklore of the state – and even the entire nation in one instance.

Of course, not every early racing champion in the South evolved from outrunning state or federal revenue agents, "but a good many of them did," explained Dawsonville businessman and racing historian Gordon Pirkle, Sr. Bill Elliott and his progeny are merely the "latest and greatest."

Pirkle owns the Dawsonville Poolroom, the management of which has been turned over to his son, Gordon Pirkle, Jr. As of this writing, Pirkle, Sr. fills his days at the *Georgia Racing Hall of Fame* in Dawsonville – a museum filled with NASCAR racing memorabilia

Many of the racecars guided to victory lane by "Awesome Bill" Elliott are displayed in the Elliott Museum near Dawsonville, GA. (Photo by Judy Bates)

The now-famous Dawsonville Poolroom enjoys a long association with racing history and memorabilia, thanks to long-time owner Gordon Pirkle.

generated over the years by the county's favorite sons.

The Dawsonville Poolroom itself isn't "short" on racing remnants and souvenirs from days gone by. The moment one walks inside it, he or she instantly realizes that it isn't just another pool hall in yet another slow-paced Georgia town. To the contrary, Mr. Pirkle's place is quite literally a museum and a shrine in its own right.

Located at 9 *Bill Elliott Street*, just a short block from the central traffic circle around the historic county courthouse, the Poolroom displays a plethora of memorabilia of Elliott's glory days – along with that of the county's other legends as well. Elliot's racing collectibles nevertheless dominate by far, because his credentials are almost too numerous to mention.

"Awesome Bill" won the *1988 Winston Cup* Championship, ultimately racking up 44 wins in that series, including two *Daytona 500* victories in 1985 and 1987, three *Southern 500* victories in 1985, 1988, and 1994, one *Winston 500* victory in 1985, one *Brickyard 400* victory in 2002, and a record four consecutive wins at Michigan International Speedway in the 1980s.

Bill is the owner of many other records as well. He holds the track record for fastest qualifying speed at *Talladega* at 212.809 miles per hour (342.483 km/h) and *Daytona International Speedway* at 210.364 miles per hour (338.548 km/h), both of which were set in 1987 (the mark at *Talladega* is the fastest qualifying speed for any NASCAR race ever). With the current usage of restrictor plates at Daytona and Talladega beginning since 1988, it is highly unlikely that these two qualifying speed records will ever be topped again.

In 1985, Elliott also made racing history by winning the first ever *"Winston Million,"* a million dollar bonus to any driver that could win three out of the four crown jewel races of NASCAR: The *Daytona 500* at Daytona, the *Winston 500* at Talladega, the *World 600* at Charlotte, and the *Southern 500* at Darlington. In a year dominated by Elliott, he went on to win 11 races (with 4 "season sweeps": *Atlanta, Pocono, Michigan,* and *Darlington*) and 11 poles, with three of those 11 wins being in the *Daytona 500*, the *Winston 500*, and the *Southern 500*, earning Bill the vaunted *"Winston Million Dollar Bonus"* and the nickname *"Million Dollar Bill."*

Elliott also won *NASCAR's Most Popular Driver Award* a record 16 times

(1984-1988, 1991–2000, 2002). He withdrew his name from the ballot for that award after winning it in 2002. In 2005, the Georgia State Legislature declared October 8 as *Bill Elliott Day* in the state of Georgia. He was inducted into the *Motorsports Hall of Fame of America* on August 15, 2007 and into the 2015 class of the *NASCAR Hall of Fame*. Elliott has also been honored by the state legislature with a stretch of roadway (the entirety of Georgia State Route 183) in his native Dawson County renamed *Elliott Family Parkway*.

Though not being honored with as lengthy a list of awards as Elliott, others in the county were nonetheless champions of their day as well. Just east of the Poolroom, *Gober Sosebee Street* crosses *Main*. To the west, the names of long-ago trailblazers *Raymond Parks, Roy Hall* and *Lloyd Seay* adorn additional signs.

Interestingly, in an earlier day at the Dawsonville Poolroom, the game of billiards was really all it offered. It was a local hang-out for individuals with "idle time" on their hands. Racing legends and moonshine weren't really the focus.

But that was then. Today, "this place ain't about pool," Pirkle, Sr. has intoned about his establishment since Elliott's emergence in the racing world. "It's about racing."

And indeed, every wall in the building is covered with information about the sport. Newspaper clippings and pictures stretch from ceiling to floor, attesting to the fame of not only local and national hero, Elliott, but to many of the other Dawson County notables from yesteryear as well, including Gober Sosebee, Lloyd Seay, and Roy Hall, to mention a few.

"Lloyd and Roy were both known to run liquor," said Pirkle with a smile.

"I don't know if Gober ran any or not, but man, he burned those backroads and racetracks plumb up."

A visit to the Dawsonville Poolroom is not complete without viewing at least one of the many films of old races Pirkle has collected over the years. He has hundreds of them scattered around the Poolroom, and it is amazing that such collectibles do not enjoy tighter security.

The races of choice of yesteryear, according to Pirkle, most often were those that were run half on low-tide beach sand and half on the paved surface of Atlantic Avenue in Daytona Beach, Florida, during the early years of the famed *Daytona 500*.

And while you're watching the film of one of these races, Pirkle recommends you try the house specialty – a bacon cheeseburger "with the works." It seems the Poolroom has earned quite a reputation not only as a site of racing memorabilia, but for tasty food as well.

The guest register at the front door of the Poolroom includes testimonial after testimonial from satisfied customers too. The addresses there represent racing fans from all across the U.S., and even the world. Somehow, they have sought him out in little downtown Dawsonville for decades, and today, they continue to come to this racing mecca from whence are coming the younger and latest generation of racers – including Bill's son – Chase Elliott – all of whom are now carving out their own niches in NASCAR history.

The comments of visitors to the Poolroom reflect their enthusiasm for both the racing history and the Poolroom's dining fare: *"The best ol' fashion burger in the state, if not the world." "Go Big Bill." "Super fries and burgers, just like when I was a kid." "Bill is back!"*

Racers & "Moonshine" Makers of Old Dawson   Dawson County

Dawsonville native Gober Sosebee poses beside his 1939 Ford coupe. He raced it to victory in the 1950 and '51 Daytona 500s. "I came in first in '49 too," he laments, "but they disqualified me."

Page after page of the comments alternate between praise for the homemade burgers and fries and encouragement for Dawson County's favorite son, and now, for Elliott's son, Chase, who won the *2014 NASCAR Nationwide Series* championship, becoming the first rookie to win a national series championship in NASCAR and the youngest champion in that series. Most recently, in 2020, Chase won the *Cup Series Championship*. Suffice it to say, the racing memorabilia and the food are where the interest lies at the Dawsonville Poolroom today. No mention is ever made anymore of the game of pool.

"We serve hundreds of burgers every day," Pirkle explains with a flourish. "We do it the old-fashioned way. We pat out the fresh beef patties several times a day and fry them on the grill. The fries are hand-cut from big ol' Idaho baking potatoes."

One never knows just who will be stopping by the Poolroom for a visit either – whether a racer from yesteryear, or a "revenoor" from yesteryear. Charley Weems, a former ATF (*Alcohol Tobacco & Firearms*) agent for the U.S. Treasury Department in the 1950s and '60s, was active during the same time that many of the racing legends were in their heydays in Dawson County. When he has visited the Poolroom, the stories of his adventures have filled hours of time, just as they fill the pages of his two books: *A Breed Apart* and *Agents That Fly*.

"I was alone one night," Weems explained as he described one incident from his colorful career, "and I came up behind a vehicle I recognized. You know the man that was in it," he says to Pirkle with a smile, whispering the name to him. "He was from around here.

"I ran him down and he jumped out of the passenger side and tumbled down a kudzu-covered bank in the dark. I didn't want him to get away, so I just jumped out into the night and landed smack on top of him. I knew the minute I landed that I had hold of a big, strong man, and that I was in trouble.

"Well, I weighed about 165 pounds in those days," Weems continued. "I knew I either needed a real good plan, or I was about to get one heck of a beating. I hollered out, 'It's okay Coppe! I've got him,' to suggest to the fellow I'd just landed on that I wasn't alone," Weems added with a smile. "Every violator in the state at that time knew Carl Coppe. You might say he was a very 'dedicated' officer, and most of the liquor law violators not only respected him, they feared him.

"When we got back up the bank, my prisoner asked 'Where's your partner?' I just told him that he was over at the car and behind the lights.

"It wasn't until I got him cuffed and secured in the car that he finally figured out that I was alone," Weems smiled.

Talk in the Dawsonville Poolroom just naturally seems to drift back and forth between great car races, race-car drivers and illegal whiskey "day-trippers" who transported the coveted spirits down to Atlanta and elsewhere. As often as not, the race driver and day-tripper were the same person.

"There's plenty of folks around here try to separate the racing from the whiskey-makin' and transportin'," Pirkle grinned. "To me, that's just so much wishful thinkin.'"

The production of illegal or untaxed liquor of course evolved in north Georgia generations before the days of stockcar racing. Immigrants from the Ulster region of what today is Northern Ireland brought their liquor distilling skills to America, spreading the craft throughout the Appalachians as they settled in the region.

Pirkle credits two incidents in the history of our nation for the evolution of "moonshining" as a big-time illegal money-making enterprise.

"It was the *Depression* and *Prohibition* that done it," he explains without hesitation. "The poultry industry and tourism were (still far away) in the future; the forests were long gone, having been cut for lumber production (eliminating the timber industry); the ground wouldn't grow good crops; and there just wasn't many other ways to make a livin'." And from the production and distribution of illicit liquor sprang the race-car drivers.

There is obvious pride in Pirkle's voice when he speaks of Bill Elliott, racing champion and multi-winner of that premier stock-car race, the *Daytona 500*.

Interestingly, the Poolroom is just a block away from Georgia's Highway 9. Both Bill and Chase have steadfastly been car #9 during their NASCAR racing careers. There's a reason for that too. In the early days of moonshine production in Georgia, Highway 9 was famous as a lifeline for whiskey trippers transporting their outlawed goods to market. It was one of the original "Thunder Road" routes. The blacktop snakes from the foot of the Southern Appalachians all the way to Atlanta.

"Visitors will ask me if Bill is the first Dawson County driver to win at Daytona, or they'll ask if he was the only winner from around here," Pirkle says, "and I'll tell them 'Neither.' He's the latest, but about the sixth to win it.'

"There was Gober Sosebee. He won it three times. Of course we're talking about the '40s and '50s, when it was the *Daytona Beach Race*, and it was run at low tide, half on the beach and half on Atlantic Avenue. It was some race in them days.

"Then there was Lloyd Seay and Roy Hall, Bernard G. Long, and a lady (believe it or not) by the name of Carleen Rouse. All in all, Dawson County drivers have won at Daytona more than ten times."

It was at this point that Pirkle enjoyed explaining a peculiarity of big city sports reporting involving Dawson County racers. "It's interesting," he smiled . . . "Whenever one of our drivers won a race anywhere, the Atlanta papers used to always declare 'Atlanta driver wins at so and so.' But just let that same driver get caught running white likker the next week, and those same papers would all say 'Dawson County violator arrested.'"

Perhaps one of the most charismatic of the early Dawson County racers was a handsome and lead-footed devil-may-care driver known as Lloyd Seay.

"Lloyd could drive," Pirkle agreed. "The law couldn't catch him at all. There's no tellin' how far he could have gone as a race driver if he had 'alived."

Unfortunately, Lloyd Seay didn't live beyond his 21st birthday, and the manner of his death both shocked and disgusted the world of racing in the 1940s.

The circumstances surrounding the tragedy were so insignificant, they verged upon the pathetic. The whole incident involved a simple disagreement about "sugar." Seay reportedly had purchased a large amount of the sweetener for the family's whiskey-making enterprise. He apparently had used a cousin's line of credit – without obtaining the obligatory prior permission from that cousin – to buy the sugar. Unfortunately, that just wasn't done in the illicit liquor world of the Appalachian Mountains.

In the "moonshine bidness," one's ability to produce a product depended upon one's ability to obtain sugar, which was – and continues to be – important in the distilling process. When Lloyd Seay maxed-out his cousin's sugar quota, that shut down his cousin's moonshining operations – and that was a serious infraction of the social mores of the area. As a result, Woodrow Anderson, Lloyd's cousin, was hot.

The previous day, Seay had won the then-prestigious *Lakewood 100* race in Atlanta on the old Lakewood Speedway. It was Labor Day, 1941, and Seay had won in his newly-numbered open-top '39 Ford roadster. He had always run with #7 painted on the side of his racer, but on the day of the *Lakewood 100*, for unknown reasons, Seay painted #13 on his doors – an unlucky omen of the events which would transpire in less than 24 hours.

According to reports of the tragedy, after the race, Seay had gone to the tiny hamlet of Burtsboro, between Dawsonville and Dahlonega, to spend the night at the house of his brother Garnett Seay. Early the next morning, Woodrow Anderson appeared at the home, insisting that Seay "go with him to settle-up."

Anderson said they would go to the house of another family member – an aunt to all three of them – who was respected by all and who would settle the dispute. Lloyd Seay, his brother Garnett, and Anderson, left together, but they never reached Aunt Monnie's house.

After stopping briefly at his own house, Anderson drove to the house of his father, Grover Anderson, reportedly "to put water in the car radiator." At this point, Woodrow invited Garnett Seay to get out of the car "if you don't want to get mixed up in somethin'."

According to court records, Garnett's account of the incident sent Woodrow Anderson to prison for life.

Lloyd Seay, a well-known racer from Dawsonville in the late 1930s and early '40s, was murdered outside the small town during a dispute over moonshine supplies. The day prior to his death, he had won the Lakewood 100 at the old Lakewood Speedway in Atlanta.

He (Garnett) testified that when he refused to get out of the vehicle, Anderson jumped on Lloyd and began striking him with his fists.

"Then he pulled a gun out of the bib of his overalls and shot me in the neck," Garnett explained in his court testimony. "He shot Lloyd right through the heart and told me he would finish me off if I ever said anything about it."

When word got out that local celebrity Lloyd Seay had been killed, the people in Dawson County were in stunned, particularly since Seay had just won the *Lakewood 100*. It was a big deal.

Lloyd Seay's funeral drew friends, relatives, and fans in numbers never previously witnessed in the little town of Dawsonville. Seay's tombstone in Dawsonville City Cemetery was purchased by Raymond Parks who owned the cars that Seay raced. Parks also was one of Seay's biggest fans, and the flamboyance of the tombstone clearly reflects this admiration.

Carved into the stone is the requisite image of a racecar of the 1940s. It has a large #7 (not #13) on the door. At the wheel of the vehicle sits Lloyd Grayson Seay, his photograph frozen forever in a block of crystal, smiling his best winning smile back to his fans for eternity.

Gober Sosebee, also a Daytona Beach Race winner, is often a topic of conversation in the Poolroom. Sosebee, tragically, was killed in an agricultural accident at his home in 1996, and had been a popular fixture in Dawsonville lore for generations. Sosebee won two *Grand National Series* races, one in 1952 and one in 1954. He also was a three-time winner of the *Daytona Beach* race in 1949, 1950, and 1951, and had 33 "Top Ten" finishes in NASCAR races.

A drive to Sosebee's home only a short distance from the Poolroom rekindled a lot of memories for both Weems and Pirkle as they pointed out first a former "still" location and then the home of a former moonshiner.

"That's old Snuffy's place," says Pirkle.

"I remember him," Weems replied. "We just passed over the place back there where his son, Clifton, had a head-on collision with Doug Denney and James Stratigos (former ATF agents). Three people died from that, counting the boy riding with Clifton. James was nearly killed too, but he managed to survive."

"I wonder why Gober never made it into the *Racing Hall Of Fame*?" asks Weems. "There's plenty of men in there who can't hold a candle to him and who never won *Daytona* - not even once."

"It sure don't seem right," agrees Pirkle. "I'm sure that for many years, it was because of hard feelings on (Bill) France's part, and now, so many years have gone by."

Gold Mining Russell Brothers, Founders of Denver, Colorado

The Russell Brothers sought gold in the hills and streams across the United States. They were adventurers of the first order, surviving Indian battles, the U.S. Civil War, disease, injuries and numerous deprivations to become wealthy men, but their adventures all began in Lumpkin County, Georgia.

They learned the business of gold mining at their father's knee, for the precious yellow metal existed all around them in their native north Georgia. Today, however, few people are aware of the fact that this adventuresome family by the name of Russell not only are credited with the initiation of the Pike's Peak gold rush, but also with the founding of Denver, Colorado.

It is no coincidence that the community which was created at the site of the Georgia gold rush and the city of Denver once shared the same name - "Auraria." It is a name, when translated, that loosely means "golden place," and it was intentionally bestowed upon the Colorado locale by the Georgia miners in memory of their old home.

It was in February of 1858, that a rough-shod group of miners was organized by the Russell brothers (William Greenberry "Green," Levi, and Joseph Oliver) from Leather's Ford near present-day Dahlonega, Georgia. Despite the fact that gold mining was still active in the north Georgia mountains, all the "easy gold" had been reached by the mid-1800s, and the Georgia miners had long since begun looking elsewhere for opportunities.

The Russells had learned the trade of gold mining from their father, James Russell. James had supplemented his gold mining income with income from various surveying jobs. Both professions were difficult work in the 1830s. In 1835, a fatal illness suddenly claimed James' life, and Green became the patriarchal head of the household, a position he would hold for the rest of his life.

"Go West Young Man"

The Russell brothers were lured west by Indian and fur-trader accounts of sightings of gold in the peaks and valleys of the present-day Rocky Mountains. They had intermarried with and befriended the Cherokees in north Georgia, and it is believed today they learned of the possible location of the precious yellow metal in the Rockies from their Cherokee brethren who themselves traveled and traded widely with other Native Americans and trappers across the West.

Joseph Oliver Russell eventually separated from his two wanderlust-struck brothers and traveled to Texas with his wife to live out his life in the cattle business.

On the appointed day, the Russells – led by brother Green – reportedly set out up old Gold Diggers Road (the present-day course of Georgia Highway 9 from Auraria to just north of Dahlonega where its course has been abandoned across the mountains) for the journey. Green was highly admired and respected by his brothers, of which there were actually four (another brother, John, who is described in some references as being older than Green and in some others as younger, did not accompany the group to Colorado to prospect). It was the lure of gold, newly discovered in California in 1848, which had aroused the interest of the brothers, and which ultimately sent them packing for Colorado after they heard rumors of the presence of the precious yellow metal there.

Though it might seem today like a daunting task to set out on foot to cross the wild western portion of the North American continent, such a trip was not a novel undertaking for the Russells. Green and John had been among the first 35,000 gold seekers to travel overland to California in 1849 for the gold rush there. By the end of the year, they had amassed a sizeable fortune and had returned to Georgia by way of the Isthmus of Panama and New Orleans.

From this venture, Green was able to pay (according to written accounts) $10,000 cash for the 540-acre Savannah Plantation on the Etowah River, one of the most beautiful parcels of land in present-day Dawson County, approximately 20 miles from his family's old Leathers' Ford home. Savannah Plantation would be the seat of the family activities for the next 20 years. John was able to purchase a mercantile business and a place of his own as well.

The lure of the search for gold ran deepest in Green. Before the end of 1850, he had returned to California a second time - a remarkable achievement in that day and time when Indians and deprivations abounded in this portion of what today is the western United States. This time, he took along with him his two younger brothers - Levi and Oliver.

The men remained in the California gold fields roughly two years before returning home to Georgia, and again, were lucky in their efforts. Levi had acquired enough to pay for his tuition and costs for medical school at the Pennsylvania College of Medicine and Surgery from which he was graduated in 1856.

Interestingly, little more than 15 years after Levi's graduation from medical school in Pennsylvania, another Georgian who would earn lasting fame out West – Dr. John Henry "Doc" Holliday – was also graduated (1872) from this same institution. He too would be lured out West, but not for the same reasons as the Russell brothers.

Holliday was diagnosed with tuberculosis shortly after his graduation, and was advised to reside in a dryer climate in the West for health reasons. In order to support himself, he lived in numerous mining towns in Kansas, Arizona and Colorado, plying the gambling trade at which he was an adept player. He ultimately died in the mining town of Glenwood Springs, Colorado in 1887.

Colorado Prospecting

Following a return from his California gold mining ministrations, and with a seemingly secure future, Green and his brothers eased into a life of leisure in Georgia. At Savannah Plantation, Green became a typical small Southern planter. He is listed as a member of the Blue Mountain Masonic Lodge (an affiliation which served him well more than once during his adventures out West).

Green's brothers enjoyed similar success in other professions. John was a merchant, and Levi practiced medicine *(Editor's Note: Until the 1980s, Levi's old doctor's office still stood near the site of Green's Savannah Plantation. The office, unfortunately, was not protected, and eventually succumbed to termites and the ravages of Georgia's weather, ultimately collapsing unfortunately into a pile of rubble.)*

Except for the money panic of 1857 immediately prior to the U.S. Civil War, the Russells' interest in gold prospecting might well have been ended with the California trips. Green and Oliver however, were both reportedly overextended in various investments. They planned a trip to what was known as "Kansas Territory" to invest in cheap land and to investigate the source of rumors they were

Dr. Levi Jasper Russell attended the same School of Dentistry in Pennsylvania as did another later and even more famous Georgian by the name of John Henry "Doc" Holliday of Griffin, Georgia.

encountering from trappers and Cherokee Indian friends about sightings of gold in this region.

There apparently was never any thought of leaving Georgia permanently at this point, for the brothers' families remained at home with the various farming and business enterprises there. Quick riches from gold mining, and new investment opportunities, seemed to be the only motive for the trip.

This initial trip ultimately focused upon what later became the vicinity of present-day Denver, Colorado (then part of the Kansas Territory). It, however, apparently resulted in little more than an exploration of the area and minor investments in land in the region. *(Despite their nearness to the bloody border*

Mystery & History in Georgia

William Greenberry "Green" Russell was the undisputed leader of his gold-mining brothers.

wars raging along the Smokey Hill River near present-day Manhattan, it does not appear that the Russell brothers were involved in any of the violent activities there.) The Russells soon returned home to their livelihoods in Georgia.

This trip nevertheless had introduced the brothers to a half-breed Baptist preacher named John Beck, who was to rekindle their interest in their quest for gold in the West. Beck had been a member of a party led by Lewis Ralston seven years earlier to California. In the Rocky Mountains area, Beck remembered discovering promising signs of gold and was able to interest Green in returning to the site to search it more closely.

It wasn't long thereafter that the group was loaded with supplies and headed for Ralston's Creek in Colorado. Led by Green, the group of 104, nineteen of which were from Georgia, 27 picked up in Missouri, and others from various other states including approximately 50 Cherokees from the Cherokee Nation, set out on the trek. The wives of both Green and John Russell were of Cherokee descent and the Russell family accordingly enjoyed close ties to the Cherokees.

Leaving Georgia with Green, Oliver, and Levi, were six other men: Lewis Ralston, William Anderson, Joseph McAfee, Solomon Roe, Samuel Bates, and John Hampton. Just as they had ten years earlier in the trip to California, the group moved up old Gold Diggers Road toward Tennessee.

A Courageous Leader

A trip across America in the mid-1800s was not a simple affair, as one might well imagine. The trip to Kansas Territory (present-day Colorado) proved to be an arduous undertaking, rife with sickness and hostile Indians. After arriving in the Rockies, the group's luck didn't change much either, at least not initially. They panned and prospected for weeks with little success.

Despite their close ties with the Cherokee Indians, the Russells' group was not welcomed in Kansas Territory in 1858. The region was the home of the Cheyenne and Arapahoe Indians and was not considered "open for settlement." The white men were considered invaders, and as a result, skirmishes with the Indians of the area were not unusual, a situation which often required Levi to put his medical training to good use, once even on himself, when he, amazingly, had to cut an arrow from his own hip.

By late June of 1858, the disappointment was beginning to take its toll. Luke Tierney, the self-proclaimed journalist of the group wrote: *"On the twenty-sixth, most of the men spent the day prospecting.*

On their return to camp, the spirits were very much depressed. . . . The prospect was so far short of their expectations and feverish hopes that many began to show signs of mortification. They no doubt expected to find lumps of gold like hailstones, all over the surface."

According to Tierney, it wasn't long before most of the group decided to head back home... all of them that is, except Green Russell.

"Gentlemen," he reportedly said, "You can all go, but I will stay if but two men will stay with me. I will remain to satisfy myself that no gold can be found."

This statement remained indelibly imprinted for the remainder of their lifetimes in the memories of the twelve men who decided to stay on with Green, for their decision to remain loyal to him proved to be a fortuitous one. Green Russell apparently possessed an uncanny sense of knowing "where to pan" for gold. He also had received a good education in the profession of gold mining from his father.

To his good fortune - and that of the twelve men who remained behind with him in the wilds of the Kansas Territory in 1858 - Green Russell ultimately did discover gold. The rest is history. In the process, he initiated the Pike's Peak gold rush, ushering in the beginnings of the history of the state of Colorado.

Green Russell very likely, was the only man in U.S. history connected with all three gold rushes of the last century. His first strike in Colorado was at Little Dry Creek, located in the present-day Denver suburb of Englewood. His discovery of the rich mining section known as "Russell's Gulch" nearby in Colorado is credited with starting the settlement of Central City, Colorado, once described as *"the richest square mile on earth."*

The gold rush was on, but so was

One of the primitive early roads across Georgia called "the Alabama Road," is visible over Gober Hill near "Big Savannah" plantation in present-day Dawson County. It was photographed here in 1990. Many early pioneers – including the Russell brothers – traveling to the West followed this trail to reach their destinations. In 1991, Highway 53 West was re-graded by the Georgia Department of Transportation, eliminating a substantial portion of the historic road in this vicinity.

another event of epic proportions in America at that time - the U.S. Civil War. With the outbreak of the war, the Russells decided to return to Georgia. Their investments and mines in Colorado had made them wealthy men for their day and time.

Bringing The Fortune Back To North Georgia

In September of 1859, a Denver newspaper reported that Green Russell and three of his men were in Denver City, dispatching 103 pounds of gold back home to Georgia. A packet of 103 pounds of gold was quite a fortune in the 1850s, and certainly nothing to be sniffed at today as well. A year later, 22 men from the Russell Gulch area headed back to "the states" with three wagons hauling what then amounted to $110,000 in gold bullion.

Despite a rising tide of anti-Southern sentiment in Colorado in 1859, Green and Levi returned to the region

Known today as "McClure Cemetery," this early burial ground exists a short distance from the rear of the historic Silas Palmour/Green Russell home-site in Dawson County. Many of the Russell family members are interred here, including the matriarch of the Russell clan – Elizabeth M. Russell (1793-1855) (foreground); Green Russell's wife, Susan (1827-1893); two of Green's sons, Thomas (1856-1859) and Benjamin H. (1858-1859); Levi's son, Charlie (1858-1858); and John Oliver's daughter, Francis (1855-1859). *(Photo by Olin Jackson)*

once again the following year, to divest themselves of their mining interests there, which were many and varied. Oliver had remained in Colorado over the winter, and reportedly had endured *"dynamitings"* to mining properties and other property damages. The Russell brothers' strong Masonic ties with many of the Union partisans apparently staved off serious problems until the brothers could sell off their holdings (reportedly at a rate far below market value) and return home to Georgia.

Deciding to leave the Colorado Rockies was one matter. However, actually being able to leave proved to be an entirely different situation. Almost all customary routes to the South were, by this time, held by Union forces, a situation which promised trouble for the Southerners. The best route, the Russells felt, lay through New Mexico and Texas on the Fort Smith Road known then as *"the back door to the Confederacy."*

In the end, this route proved to be flawed too. In the Texas panhandle, some 200 miles from present-day Las Vegas, the group was detained and imprisoned by a troop of Union cavalry under the command of a Lieutenant Shoup. On February 14, 1863, having found no legitimate reason to hold the Russells further, Lt. Shoup ordered that the men be released and their property restored.

Once again, the Masonic ties of the Russells apparently had been advantageous. They had been instrumental in the development of good relations with the Union commander and his men, and ultimately resulted in the release of the Russells and the restoration of their property - which amazingly included their gold!

The harsh trip to Georgia still remained ahead for the Russells, but it proved to be much less troublesome than it could have been. The Russell luck was still holding.

The brothers subsequently took a stagecoach to St. Joseph. They were granted passes as far as Louisville, Kentucky, by a Union soldier. From the Ohio River however, they had to hide by day and travel by night, and often within earshot of both Confederate and Union soldiers. The trip, which should have taken but a couple of weeks, reportedly was stretched to several additional weeks in length.

Amazingly, the Russells, somehow reached Savannah Plantation with their gold intact. Reports indicate that Green, an ardent Democrat, spent much of his Colorado gold outfitting a Confederate cavalry company. On August 11, 1863,

Gold Mining Russell Brothers — Dawson County

This artist's concept depicts the life of miners at Gregory Gulch and Central City, Colorado. The Russell brothers are credited with the discovery of gold in the Colorado mountains and with the initiation of the Pike's Peak gold rush of the 1850s. *(Illustration courtesy of Denver Public Library Western Collection)*

Captain William Green Russell's company, Georgia Cavalry, was mustered at Dawsonville, Georgia. Oliver Russell was named a lieutenant, and even Green's 16-year-old son John joined as a trooper.

The company reportedly never numbered more than 50, nor is it likely they saw service outside of Georgia. Accounts indicate Captain Russell's company spent most of its time rounding up deserters and recruiting new men, duties which did not earn him or his brothers great popularity in the region at this time.

Civil War Desolation

When the South surrendered in 1865, things became even worse. The uncertain and quickly-unraveling of circumstances in Georgia at this time undoubtedly were the impetus for the brothers' decision to leave Georgia again shortly after 1865. Also, Georgia at that time was terribly impoverished, and the Russells undoubtedly realized that the restoration of order and prosperity would be long in coming.

Green was eager to return to Colorado, this time permanently with his family. Levi had become disinterested in gold mining and Colorado altogether. He wanted to go to Texas. Oliver's wife, Jane, had relatives in Texas, and wished to go there too. John's wife, Frances, being part Cherokee, had friends and relatives in the Cherokee Indian Territory in Oklahoma which she longed to see. She also was entitled to land there as a result of her heritage, so this became

Mystery & History in Georgia

When her husband, Green Russell, passed away in 1877, Susan Russell reportedly could not bear the sadness of the event, and ultimately returned to a locale at which she had enjoyed many happy memories of her youth – "Big Savannah" plantation in present-day Dawson County – to live out the remainder of her life in the home pictured here. Though unknown for certain, it is believed she had retained more than enough of her husband's wealth from his mining strikes to live comfortably, and this home, which still stands today, seems to indicate such security. *(Photo by Olin Jackson)*

their destination. (Green's wife, also of Cherokee lineage, decided to accompany Green back to Colorado.)

Though saddened to be separating from his brothers with whom he had experienced so much over the years, Green nonetheless was irresistibly attracted back to Colorado and the Huerfano Valley where he owned a ranch. Many of his old Georgia friends and prospectors had recently returned to the valley for similar reasons, so he knew he would hardly be lonely there.

The Colorado country reportedly was beautiful that fall, especially on Apache Creek where Green lived. For the first two years, Green and his son John, now 25, turned most of their attention to building a cattle and horse ranch in the valley. Mrs. Russell and the six younger children soon came to share the men's enthusiasm for the region.

The End Of The Line

It wasn't long however, before it became apparent that the Russell luck was running out. Green's son, John, was killed in a tragic mining accident in 1874 (Green and his son apparently could never fully abandon the urge to mine gold.). Grasshopper plagues and droughts depleted cash reserves needed for ranching. A change was inevitable.

Green eventually decided to move nearer to his brother John in the Cherokee Indian Territory (in Briartown) in present-day Oklahoma. Green's wife and six children, as a result of their

Cherokee blood, had land title rights in the territory.

In the winter of 1877, with John's help, Green selected 600 acres on the Canadian River three miles southeast of Briartown, and settled down for a new life there. The bad luck continued however. The following June, malaria, perhaps complicated with typhoid, struck every member of the family.

By this point, Green apparently had had his fill of the Oklahoma climate. He reportedly longed for the cool crispness of the north Georgia mountains. Unfortunately, he never made it back to his beloved north Georgia mountains.

On August 14, William Greenberry Russell suffered a massive stroke or some type of similar affliction, possibly a heart attack, while chopping wood in his yard. Ten days later, he died. He was buried in Briartown Cemetery.

As one of the most colorful figures in the gold rush history of the United States, and a pioneer of the early explorations of the American West, the contributions of Green Russell have been largely overlooked. He has been called the "Sutter of Colorado," and was sought out for counsel by the likes of Kit Carson (when he was sent into the Kansas Territory by the United States government to form a pact with the Arapaho and Ute tribes); Horace Greeley (when he came to Colorado in 1859 researching his book *An Overland Tour To San Francisco* which is crowded with material furnished by Russell); and many others.

Demise Of The Brothers

According to records, Dr. Levi Russell became a practicing physician in Texas and died and was buried in Menardsville in 1908. Joseph Oliver Russell, apparently believing there was more money in the cattle business than in gold mining, moved to Texas also, and became a rancher, dying there in 1906.

After Green's death, John decided to stay in the Cherokee Nation in Oklahoma where he owned a fine ranch. He and his wife lived a long and fruitful life together, and are buried there.

Interestingly, Green's wife, Susan, moved her family back to Georgia to live again at Big Savannah Plantation in Dawson County, where it had all begun for the Russells so many years earlier. The old family home still stands there today, and remains as part of the legacy earned through all the hardships suffered by Green Russell and his brothers.

In the family cemetery near the original Dawson County home-site rest the remains of many of the descendants of the Russell family, pioneers in the truest sense, and history-making adventurers recorded in the annals of at least five states.

In an ironic twist of fate, the Colorado State Historic Society corresponded with the county historian near Auraria, Georgia in 1931, requesting information on the Russell brothers. (A historic marker in Confluence Park in downtown Denver, Colorado commemorates that site as the spot where the Russells discovered gold and began the gold rush culminating in the founding of Denver.). The fortunes of Auraria, Georgia, had sunk so low by 1931 that the former gold rush town had all but disappeared. There was no longer any information available there on the Russells at all.

Adding insult to injury, *Webster's Geographic Dictionary*, published in 1949 either did not know of the Georgia community, or just decided to ignore it. The listing for Auraria that year read: *"First settlement in Colorado; established in 1858."*

Traces of the Early Pioneers in the Etowah River Valley

Remnants of the earliest pioneers to present-day Dawson County are still visible in a number of secluded sites if one knows where to look, but they are fast disappearing.

The peaceful valley not more than 40 minutes north of Atlanta, carved over eons of time by what today is known as the Etowah River, in Dawson County, Georgia, is still reasonably quiet. In pioneer days, it was known as "Big Savannah Plantation." Historic farms and plantation homes still dot the countryside in this valley at various sites. And if one digs beneath the surface, real nuggets of gold can be found – as well as some nuggets of the county's history.

Wagon trains of pioneers who had given up on the north Georgia gold fields in the 1840s left for the new strikes in California, and later, in the 1850s, for the new discoveries in Colorado. Remnants of the old pioneer roads traveled by these early residents of present-day Dawson still exist in the Etowah River Valley if one knows where to look.

Many of the historic homes and farms of these early residents also still exist in Dawson, but it is a perilous existence. "Development" is inexorably gobbling up the county's real estate, imperiling the historic gems hidden there.

Despite the value of these homes and property today, it is ironic that some of the early owners of these now-historic sites simply walked away from them in the first half of the 19th Century, such was the lure of gold out West.

Bishop Family Home

One of the historic structures which still exists on Etowah River Road is the old Bishop family home, located back in a hollow beyond the first mountain ridge above the Etowah River. Wiley T. Bishop purchased the property sometime in the 1880s, and the farmhouse on it was built circa 1870.

As of this writing, the property, though abandoned, was untouched by pilferers and thieves. One reason for this is the isolation of the property. There is only one way into the site and it is a treacherous mountain trail which dead-ends at the property.

It was almost like stepping back through time. The old farm implements were still there - wooden buckboard wagon and all. Among its treasures, the house still had the ancient primitive wooden clothing armoires in which clothing was stored.

Though isolated in those days prior

Traces of the Early Pioneers in the Etowah River Valley — Dawson County

Built circa 1880, the Silas B. Palmour home still stands in the Etowah River Valley in Dawson County. It is located off old Highway 9-E (Alabama Road), and is one of several homes built by this once-prominent planter. *(Photo by Olin Jackson)*

Photographed in the late 1980s, this structure is believed to have been the original Silas B. Palmour homestead, built circa 1845 near the pioneer community of Landrum, on the old Alabama Road, just off old Highway 9-E in present-day Dawson County. *(Photo by Olin Jackson)*

to the advent of the "horseless carriage," the Bishop farm residents were very self-sufficient. They had to be in order to survive. According to Arch Bishop (yes, that's really his name) a descendant in the family, they raised hogs and a few beef cattle, and had bee hives for honey, fruit trees for fresh fruits, and enough farmland to grow a variety of row crops.

The Bishop family even had "indoor plumbing" "before indoor plumbing was cool" in the 1920s in the north Georgia mountains. In an innovative use of the resources at hand, the Bishops redirected – via small pipe – a stream of water from the creek out back of the farmhouse, creating a continuous flow of fresh water into the kitchen where it drained through a kitchen sink and then down a drain pipe and out the side of the home back into the stream a short distance away.

A mud-daubed chimney in the old home undoubtedly provided a cozy warmth on cold winter days, despite the uninsulated nature of the home. The chimney in the back kitchen however, wasn't constructed of stone. Never one to waste anything, the Bishops had collected the old piping once used in the big water canals of the hydraulic mining ditches constructed during gold mining days near the farm. In the early 1900s, hydraulic mining – using water which generated great force as it surged down canals from high in the mountains and then into the pipelines – replaced the more traditional methods of gold mining. The water pressure contained in the water lines was used to "spray" down the soil from the mountainsides. The soil was then collected by various devices and separated from the gold.

When hydraulic gold mining ceased in Lumpkin and Dawson counties, a lot of the old heavy metal pipeline was just abandoned. The ever-resourceful Bishops simply repurposed it as a chimney in their kitchen.

The Palmour Family

Another historic structure on Etowah River Road is the large two-story former Palmour family home. The Palmours were yet another of the pioneer families in Dawson County and, according to Forsyth County Historian Don L. Shadburn in his seminal *"Cherokee Planters in Georgia, 1832-1838,"*

Palmour Gristmill - Built circa 1906, this structure once existed beside the original bridge across the Etowah River (approximately 100 yards north of present-day State Road 53 Bridge) at Dougherty, Georgia, a former Cherokee Indian community. Pictured in the photo to are: Elizabeth Hardy (l) and Dessie Black, daughter of Dick Black.

a number of them were Indian countrymen with Cherokee Indian families.

Built by John D. Palmour (b. ca. 1807) prior to the Civil War, the impressive home (for that day and time) is a visual reminder of the wealth which once permeated this valley. Though they disappeared long ago from weathering and the elements, there once were slave quarters to the rear of this structure.

Mr. Palmour reportedly would give his slaves Christmas holidays for as long as the log used in his hearth to build the fire Christmas day would last. According to local folklore, the slaves would get an old blackgum tree, soak it in the creek for several weeks, and then build the fire with it on Christmas day. The log, reportedly, would last for several days as it simmered and steamed. It is unknown today if old Mr. Palmour ever knew what was going on, but folks said he always kept his word about the holidays.

According to historian Shadburn's findings, Silas Palmour was among the first pioneers in the Etowah River Valley in what today is Dawson County. *"Long before the gold rush years, several white men had taken Cherokee mixed-bloods for their spouses, built homes in the fertile valleys and cleared farmland in the county. Silas Palmour (1797-1878), a white man at "Big Savannah" was a citizen of the Cherokee Nation by right of his marriage to Sarah Dougherty, a mix-blood daughter of James Dougherty, Jr. and Mary Dean. His* (Silas's) *extensive improvements on the river were assessed at $2,786.00"* Shadburn wrote.

"These (improvements) included 16 acres of upland, 81 acres of river bottom-land, a hewed log house, a gristmill and sawmill, and one other house (unfinished when he lost the land).

"Notable among this class of Indian countrymen" Shadburn added, *"and recognized as leading planters of the period were Lewis Ralston,* **Silas Palmour,** *Daniel Davis, John Satterfield, and James Landrum. "Lumpkin County (present-day Dawson) with its extensive water power, gold mines, and about one-half of the land tillable, had 54 Indian families, 6 intermarried white men, and 43 slaves in 1835. Cherokees and the families of Indian countrymen were concentrated largely at the town sites on the Etowah River. Altogether, they claimed 91 farms, 234 houses, and 1,300 acres of land. . . . Whites and mixed bloods who owned slaves in the county (included)* **Silas Palmour,** *1; Charles Landrum, 1; James Crittenden, 1; Sam Downing, 2; and Nelly Downing, 7."*

According to the Palmour family memoirs passed down through the family, though some members of the family may have gone West during the Cherokee removal in the 1830s, some of the family also obviously remained behind:

"After allotments were let, they secured homes for four brothers and one sister: Silas Palmour, Aaron Palmour, John Palmour (not the John D. Palmour mentioned above), Solomon Palmour, and a sister, probably Mary.

"The land consisted of ten miles on both sides of the Etowah River; their homes adjoining.

"Aaron Palmour acted as local banker, discounted notes, loaned money, and was a stock raiser and farmer. The others were all farmers.

"Aaron built a small fort on the 'Big Savannah' as the property was called. Port holes were arranged so as to give protection from enemy on any side of the building. This building was destroyed several years ago by fire."

It is not difficult today to imagine quite a plantation along Etowah River Road in Dawson County, if the Palmour property extended "ten miles on both sides of the Etowah River." Small wonder that he needed slaves to farm the property.

Today, the old John D. Palmour home harkens back to a day when the rich farmland in the river valley was broadly cultivated by antebellum planters. The house appears (as of this writing) to still be in good condition, despite having been used in recent years as a rental property. Records appear to indicate that John D. Palmour was a son of the original Etowah River Valley Palmours – Aaron, John, Solomon, Silas, and Mary.

According to records, Silas Palmour married an Indian octoroon, Nancy. Nancy and their children, according to Georgia law, were admitted to Georgia citizenship. Aaron Palmour, who never married, lived with his sister Mary for her lifetime. John Palmour married a Miss Nancy Boone, "a relative of

Old Dougherty Post Office – Built circa 1938, approximately 100 years after the Cherokee Indians had been relocated out West, the small structure in the center of this photo was the town's post office. This photo was taken at the Gober home on Highway 53 in Dawson. The young lady is Ophelia Stowers.

a Daniel Boone" (but apparently not *the* Daniel Boone of Squire Boone). Solomon Palmour married a Miss Nix.

Records also appear to indicate that John D. Palmour was the nephew of the John Palmour who married Nancy Boone, and possibly was the son of Solomon Palmour.

These hardy pioneers not only farmed for a living, but also sought out the gold buried in the hills and streams of the area. When the gold gave out, many of these homesteaders simply "pulled up stakes" and moved on in the spirit that had originally brought them to this region. Their legacy can be found as far away as California. The Palmours, however, despite no doubt being devastated by the Cherokee removal, the later trials of survival during the U.S. Civil War and freedom of the slaves, and other unfortunate circumstances, somehow hung onto much of their property in the Etowah River Valley.

The seclusion of the homes and relative isolation of the Etowah River valley in Dawson County have combined

John D. Palmour home – Built circa 1850s and photographed here in 1989, this historic home at the intersection of New Bethel Church and Etowah River Roads was one of the few antebellum plantation homes constructed in Dawson County. This home was over 170 years old as of this writing (2021). Foundation stones from the former slave shanties still existed to the rear of this home when the photo was taken. *(Photo by Olin Jackson)*

to preserve many of these historic structures for well over one hundred years now, but it is a fragile preservation at best. It is destined to be tested as more and more of the adjoining countryside is populated through northward expansion made possible by nearby Georgia-400 thoroughfare.

The Russell Family

Another of the historic homes in this valley is the aged William Greenberry Russell estate. This structure, yet another treasure, was also originally built by the Palmour family – more specifically, Silas Palmour. It came into the possession of the Russell family of gold rush renown sometime in the 1850s.

It is hard to imagine today why anyone would want to leave such a beautiful setting and such an impressive home for the wilds of the West in the 1840s and 50s, but Greenberry ("Green") and his brothers were adventurers of the first order, anchored to no place in particular. They left the Etowah River Valley in Dawson County not once, but several times as they made treks out west to Colorado (then part of Kansas Territory) and California.

It was at the Green Russell home that the wagon-train westward to Colorado was organized to search for gold there. Green Russell, according to folklore, paid Silas Palmour upwards of $10,000.00 for the home and adjoining property from gold he had accumulated in the early 1850s on a prospecting trip to California during the 1849 gold rush.

When the Russell brothers left for the West for the last time in the 1860s, the Palmour family reportedly regained possession of the Green Russell property. It later was passed on to the McClure family who were heirs of the Palmour family.

According to records, Silas Palmour married twice, the first time to the Indian named Nancy (as explained above), and the second time to a Widow McClure (possibly the widow of a Robert B. McClure). Silas had no children from either marriage, but the Widow McClure had a son from her former marriage. His name was Robert McClure.

Since Silas had no children, his home (the former Green Russell home) was passed on to his step-son Robert. It is for this reason that the home and the old cemetery a short distance behind it are known today as the "McClure" house and "McClure" Cemetery (when not referred to as the Silas Palmour or Green Russell house).

The Russells, with only a few exceptions, left Georgia permanently shortly after the Civil War, living in Colorado, Oklahoma, Texas, and other places out West. They were among the many Georgians whose homes, properties,

Traces of the Early Pioneers in the Etowah River Valley   Dawson County

Silas Palmour/Green Russell home – This home was originally constructed and owned by Silas Palmour, one of the original settlers in the Etowah River Valley in present-day Dawson County. This domicile later was owned by adventurer and gold-miner Green Russell, later credited with the discovery of gold in Colorado and as one of the founders of Denver, Colorado. *(Photo by Olin Jackson)*

methods of income, and general stability, had been decimated by the U.S. Civil War, and particularly by the destructive actions of General William Tecumseh Sherman in his *"March To The Sea"* in 1865.

Interestingly, when Green Russell died in 1877, his wife Susan (1827-1893), though part Cherokee Indian, decided to bring her children back home to Georgia to live, and in fact returned to Savannah Plantation to live. Her grave and the graves of many other members of both the Russell and Palmour families are in the "Russell/Palmour/McClure" cemetery behind Green's old home.

The mystery surrounding Susan Russell is exacerbated by the fact that when she returned to Georgia in 1877, she did not return to her former "Green Russell house." She instead chose to live in a larger home a short distance down the road. Perhaps she was unable to regain possession of her former home from the Palmour family, or perhaps her memories of her late husband conjured up by the old home were simply too poignant to bear. The actual details undoubtedly will never be known.

Preservation

The home to which Susan Russell returned to live at Big Savannah Plantation has been owned in more recent years by another "Susan" – more specifically, Bill and Susan Adamson, formerly of Alpharetta. This home is known by long-time Etowah River Valley (Big Savannah) residents simply as "the home to which Susan Russell returned." The Adamsons reportedly rescued this home, since prior to their purchase and

Mystery & History in Georgia

Aaron Palmour/Levi Russell home – Originally built at the intersection of Seed Tick and Etowah River roads in Dawson, this pioneer log cabin was moved to this location on Ridge Road in Dawson by a later owner. Built circa 1830 by Aaron Palmour, it was designed as a portion of the original fort-type compound constructed by the Palmour family after first arriving in Dawson (Lumpkin County at that time) in the early 1800s. It originally stood in the flood plain near the river, and probably was moved up to the intersection of Seed Tick and Etowah River by Dr. Levi Russell in the 1880s.

renovation, the structure was amazingly slated for demolition, despite its historic nature.

The Palmour and Russell family histories are unique not only to Georgia history, but indeed to U.S. history as well. Green Russell very likely was one of only a few men in American history connected with all three major gold rushes of the 19th century – the Georgia gold rush of 1829, the California gold rush of 1849, and the Colorado gold rush of 1859.

Indeed, the Russell brothers enjoyed many adventures out West in the days in which it was still "Indian country," and are credited with many historic accomplishments. This includes their founding of the city of Denver, Colorado, proclaimed today by a historic marker in downtown Denver, (but, ironically, not in Dawson County, Georgia); their initiation of the Pike's Peak gold rush; and their discovery of "Russell Gulch" (Central City), once described as the "richest square mile on earth."

Despite all these accomplishments; despite the pioneer history of the Palmour family in Dawson County, and even the history of the Stowers family which coincides with the Palmours and Russells in these homes, no historic marker identifies these homes, nor explains the historic significance of these pioneer Dawson County families and their residences here in the Etowah River valley.

A sad example of the inevitable results of such neglect may be found in what remains of the historic home of Green's brother – Dr. Levi Russell – one of the oldest if not the oldest domicile in the county. It was built (ca. 1830) by Aaron Palmer (b. ca. 1771) as part of the original fort-type compound constructed by the family when they first arrived in Dawson (formerly Lumpkin) County.

The home was later moved in the mid-1800s by Dr. Levi Russell to a site near the intersection of Etowah River Road and Seed Tick Road where it remained intact until the mid-1980s. At that time, however, the old homestead was purchased and taken apart piece by piece, and moved to another site for use as a "summer home" by a wealthy family. Just that quickly, this historic structure was erased from the area, and a valuable part of the heritage of Dawson County was lost forever.

The memory of Dawson County's pioneers will live on in a history book here and in a legend or tale there. But the tangible evidence of the former existence of the county's most noteworthy inhabitants is slowly, but inexorably, slipping away.

The Mysterious Murder of Postman James Langston

On a crisp morning in 1922, a U.S. postman was methodically murdered on a backroad just south of Atlanta. The perpetrators – all revenge-minded moonshiners – were pleased with their capture of the postman, until they realized they had the wrong man. Then they killed him anyway. The reason for this crime has never been fully explained.

"*Neither rain, snow, heat, nor gloom or dark of night shall stay these couriers from their appointed rounds.*" That well-known U.S. Postal Service motto was intended to include many unattractive circumstances, but not the horrible act which interrupted mail delivery on October 28, 1922 in Fayette County, Georgia.

James C. Langston had been a U.S. Postman for a number of years. According to the late Marvin Rivers, he was a tall, popular man who resided in downtown Fairburn. He also was known for his big feet – so big in fact – that the foot pedals on his Ford automobile had to be specially rebuilt for him by a local blacksmith.

On a Saturday morning in late October, Langston knew nothing of the fate awaiting him as he left the Fairburn Post Office on his rural mail route. He stepped into his Ford, adjusted the clutch with his special peddle, and drove off on his route. It was a trip from which he would never return.

Deadly Chain Of Events

A series of events had been set into motion in late September of 1922 which, sadly, destined Langston for doom. Fayette County Sheriff Tom Kerlin and U.S. Revenue Agents Milam and T. B. Harris had raided an illegal liquor ("moonshine") distillery ("still") just off Kite Bridge Road in upper Fayette. They were accompanied on their mission that night by at least one other person – Abner (Ab) Davis – a peddler who lived in the nearby Kenwood community about two miles east of the still site.

The moonshine distillery itself (remnants of which still existed in the 1990s) had a 50-gallon capacity, and was located on the property of John Waller just off Kenwood Road on Kite Road. John and his brother – Charlie – were well-known bootleggers in the illicit trade and enjoyed a steady business in the countryside south of Atlanta. They were also shrewd criminals.

When buyers approached them for moonshine, they (the Wallers)

117

instructed the clients to walk back into the garden and look under a certain cabbage plant. A bottle of "shine" would be awaiting pickup there.

An informant eventually alerted law-enforcement officials to the presence of the Waller brothers' operations – an action which culminated in the night raid by Sheriff Kerlin. Ab Davis was with the officers and assisted in the destruction of the still.

As the party was leaving the still site, they were observed from cover by another moonshiner – Ora Whittle – who was quick to note Ab Davis' presence in the group. Davis was well-known in the area because he often peddled his wares along the road.

Word of Davis' involvement in the incident spread quickly in the close-knit community. On the following Sunday morning, a group of the moonshiners consisting of Ora Whittle, John and Charlie Waller, and Rainey Cauthen, met at the home of John Waller. They discussed plans to punish Davis for his actions.

According to later court testimony, John Waller wanted to "whip Davis," but Charlie Waller and Ora Whittle said it "would be better to kill him." The argument reportedly continued until the men eventually reached an agreement whereby they would pay Cauthen approximately $125.00 to "whip Davis." Though that may seem like a paltry sum, $125.00 was the equivalent of just over $1,600.00 in 2021 dollars, so it would have been a nice payday for Cauthen.

The more the men pondered this punishment, however, the more they felt it to be inadequate. Another meeting eventually was scheduled at John Waller's house the following Wednesday and at this session, the plans were changed from whipping Davis to killing him. The deed was set to be accomplished the next Saturday morning, since Davis was known to travel down Kite Road each Saturday.

The men originally planned to use a firearm of some sort to murder Davis. However, after further consideration, it was decided that a gun would make too much noise, and an axe and a maul were selected instead, since they were silent in their deadliness.

By this time, a total of eight moonshiners were included in the group conspiring to kill Davis. According to later news accounts and courtroom testimony, the murderous group was ultimately enlarged to include Arthur Alexander, Melvin Brown, Oscar Dutton, and Melvin Windham.

The Murder Site

Kite Bridge Road, Kite Lake Road, or South Kite Road as the route was variously known in recent years, turns northward from Kenwood Road and immediately begins a gentle downhill descent to a small tributary of Morning Creek before continuing up the next hill. A bridge at the bottom of the hill was to be the site of the killing, and an ambush was carefully planned for that spot. Today, this site is well-developed with numerous homes, but in 1922, it

By this time, a total of eight moonshiners were included in the group conspiring to kill Davis.

was a very secluded spot with no residences near the bridge or creek.

John Waller's home, located approximately 150 yards up the hill, was the nearest residence to the creek. Today, in retrospect, the selection of an ambush and murder site so near to the headquarters of the perpetrators was an infantile decision. It was one of many aspects of this gruesome crime which defied logic, and which remain unexplained today.

A few longtime Fayette residents still remember the very good spring which once existed at the bottom of the hill. Travelers often stopped at the spot for a cool drink in the early 1900s. Fayette native Woodrow Harris said the postman always stopped at that spring for a drink and usually ate his lunch there. This, however, somewhat contradicts the murderers' testimony.

According to courtroom testimony in the later murder trial, just before 11:00 a.m. on the appointed day of October 28, 1922, Postman Jim Langston crested the hill in his Ford automobile, his bag of mail in the seat beside him. He drove on down the slope and was surprised when Rainey Cauthen stepped out of the bushes along the roadside and flagged him to a stop.

Langston immediately informed Cauthen that he was unable to provide him with transportation, saying, "I'm a government man and can't give you a ride."

It was at this point that Langston's heart must have jumped into his throat, because Melvin Brown jumped out into the road and covered the by now dumbfounded Langston with his shotgun.

"What are you fellows going to do with me?" Langston reportedly implored.

"We're going to teach you how to report stills," Cauthen reportedly responded, as Ora Whittle, an axe in his hands, and Oscar Dutton, hefting a large wooden maul, jumped menacingly from their hiding spots nearby.

Despite the fact that Langston obviously was not the intended victim (Ab Davis), the men, for some unknown reason, nonetheless proceeded with their grisly plans. Were they simply so eager for revenge that they were willing to exact retribution from Langston (a federal official) too? Or were they simply too eager, mistakenly stopping Langston, and then fearing he would later implicate them if they released him and then subsequently committed the ill deed on Davis? The true circumstances likely will never be known.

The Murder

"You're not going to kill me for nothing?" the by-now terror-stricken Langston reportedly croaked, realizing the men had a bloodthirsty gleam in their eyes. These words, reportedly, were the last ever uttered by Jim Langston.

By this point, Rainey Cauthen must have begun having second thoughts, because he reportedly instructed the group to "Let the man go. We were going to whip him, not kill him."

"Alright," Whittle replied deceivingly. He and Dutton reached in and literally yanked Langston through the driver-side window and out of the vehicle, obviously indicating they had no intention of halting their murderous actions.

Again Cauthen repeated "We weren't going to hurt anyone, but whip Ab Davis." It was at this point that Windham also said to Dutton and Whittle "Turn him loose."

Langston, apparently thinking he might escape unharmed after all, went

Mystery & History in Georgia

around to the front of his car to re-crank it. It was the last move he ever made. According to courtroom testimony – and for reasons still unexplained today – Whittle suddenly struck Langston viciously in the back of the head with his axe.

Langston immediately collapsed, falling to his knees. Dutton, his own thirst for violence peaking, then struck Langston again with his heavy maul, crushing the entire top of Langston's head. The mailman fell onto his face, flat on ground, instantly dead.

It must have been about this time (if at all) that reality began to dawn upon the murderers. If they had not previously noticed the mail bag, and if for some unknown reason they still believed that Langston was Davis, the existence of the mail must have tipped them off to their mistake.

Accounts differ somewhat as to the actions of the men immediately following the murder. Newspapers of that day state that all the men literally ran in different directions and later met at Kite's Lake, trying all the while to disguise their trails with a turpentine and camphor mixture which they spread liberally behind them to confuse the bloodhounds they knew would follow shortly.

It would almost seem comical today, had not the crime been so heinous. Before departing the murder scene, Whittle hid the axe in nearby woods. No mention of the disposition of the wooden maul was ever made in courtroom testimony.

All the murderers (again defying logic) met at approximately 12:00 or 12:30 p.m. at John Waller's house (near the top of the hill and amazingly just a short distance from the murder site).

At this point, according to later testimony, John Waller stated "Well, we got the wrong man," to which Whittle replied "Yes, but it's too late to pray after the devil's done got you."

The Murder Investigation

Meanwhile, Rosa Porch, sometimes known as "Lizzie," was a black lady who lived on the corner of Kenwood and Kite Roads, just above John Whittle. It was she who informed Fayette County Sheriff Tom Kerlin of the murder. Kerlin immediately contacted U.S Department of Revenue Officer T. B. Harris before speeding to the crime scene.

When Kerlin arrived, he noted Langston's car on the bridge in the center of the road with Langston stretched out in front of the automobile, his skull crushed and the U.S. Mail bag and its contents strewn in the road along the side of the car.

By 3:00 p.m., Revenue Agent Harris had arrived from his office in Newnan, Georgia. He began assisting in the investigation. U.S. Postal Inspector J.W. Cole also aided in the investigation. He was replaced sometime later by Inspector Frank Ellis, who in turn was assisted from time to time by Inspectors J.R. Smith and W.W. Hodge.

Strangely, no records remain today of the investigation conducted by the federal government, and none of the men involved in the murder were ever charged with any federal crimes, although a number of charges could have been brought against the men for interference with the U.S. mails. The U.S. Postal Service officials apparently were content to allow local officials to investigate, arrest and prosecute the perpetrators solely for the crime of murder, which is a state, not a federal offence.

The authorities instantly suspected the Waller brothers. After all, they

The Mysterious Murder of Postman James Langston Fayette County

were known bootleggers and John lived almost within sight of the murder scene.

John and Charles Waller, as well as George B. Samuels, were all arrested the following week on suspicion of murder. Samuels was "a Spaniard who had been in the World War" and who lived with Lula Waller, daughter of John. All these men denied any knowledge of the crime and were released.

Over the span of the next two years, Ora Whittle and John Waller were both arrested, but were only charged with possession of intoxicants. They were both subsequently found "Not guilty" and released.

Despite the difficulties involved in solving this case, the local authorities did not give up. Finally, three years later in May of 1925, Oscar Dutton and Ora Whittle were arrested as suspects in the case. Dutton was sent to the Coweta County Jail in Newnan and Whittle was held in Atlanta, both probably for safekeeping. Both men had flatly denied any connection with the murder and openly proclaimed their innocence. While in jail, however, Dutton eventually confessed and implicated some of the others, including John Waller who was promptly arrested.

The Trial & Sentences

A special June session of Superior Court was called in 1925 to try Whittle and Dutton for the murder of James Langston, and also to try John Waller as an *"accessory before the fact"* of the murder. The *Fayette County News* reported that despite a June heat wave, large crowds attended the trial and the Fayette County Courthouse was completely filled. Overflow spectators surrounded the building, hoping to hear some of the trial through the open windows.

All three men ultimately were found *"Guilty"* on July 3, 1925, but surprisingly were given life sentences with recommendations for mercy. Existing records are not clear as to how the other perpetrators were implicated in this case, but by December, all eight men involved had been tried and found *"Guilty."*

Melvin Brown, Rainey Cauthen, Arthur Alexander, Melvin Windham, Oscar Dutton and Ora Whittle were also given life sentences with recommendations for mercy for the murder. John and Charlie Waller drew the same sentence for being accessories to the others.

All eight men were sent to different prison camps to serve out their sentences. Some longtime Fayette County residents today can still remember Dutton and Whittle serving on the local "chain gang," once located just east of Fayetteville.

Despite the bloodthirsty nature of the crime, most of the men served relatively short sentences. Charlie Waller was paroled in July of 1932, and his brother, John, in November of 1935. Melvin Windham received a parole in September of 1933, and Oscar Dutton was granted parole in January of 1935. No record has been located for the release date of Ora Whittle, Melvin Brown, Arthur Alexander or Rainey Cauthen.

Meanwhile, Ab Davis, the object of all the hatred and vicious bloodletting on an October morning in 1922, continued peacefully in the produce business and in later years ran a store in Kenwood. He lived out his life without incident.

(Author's Note: Information on the murder of Jim Langston is a matter of public record in the Fayette and Spalding County courthouses, the Georgia Department of Archives and History, and the archives of the local newspapers.)

Mysterious Spanish Sword Discovery:

Relic of De Soto's Conquistadors Unearthed in Floyd County, GA

Archaeologists and historians alike have, for over a century, pondered the question of Spanish explorer Hernando De Soto's actual route through the southeastern United States. An ancient Spanish sword discovered on a Floyd County farm by several young men may have solved the mystery.

One favorite Saturday morning pastime of young fellows in the South in years past has been to go to a recently-plowed pasture owned by a father, or grandfather, or another relative or friend, and search the ground for prehistoric Indian artifacts. Such was the case with three men in 1982, but they didn't find prehistoric Indian artifacts. Instead, they hit the jackpot.

The location was a field near Rome, in northwest Georgia's Floyd County. That, by the way, is not the locale one would expect to find a genuine ancient Spanish artifact, but find it they did.

At the time, these young men didn't really know what they had found. They just knew it looked ancient, and they intended to hang onto it for the time being. They didn't realize it at the time, but they were about to set into motion a series of events which may have solved not one, but two previously mystifying events of important historic significance.

On the day of the discovery, the men knew they had a high likelihood of finding at least some minor historic relics. The field they were searching alongside the muddy Coosa River is a documented aboriginal Indian village site within a large loop of the river known as "Foster Bend." Prehistoric aboriginals of what today is the southern United States often built their villages at such a bend in the river if the water depth was in excess of 8 or 10 feet, since the site then was already easily defensible on three sides.

Foster Bend has been a favorite of relic hunters for several generations, often yielding arrow tips, spearheads, banner stones, stone celts, bits of pottery, and the like. These young men were just enjoying a leisurely Saturday afternoon.

On the day that the men walked across the field, signs of a professional archaeological dig which had been

Relic of De Soto's Conquistadors — Floyd County

The three discoverers of the Spanish sword uncovered in 1982 at the archaeological "King Site" near Rome, Georgia, are pictured with their treasure. Left to Right: Gary Hamilton (attorney); Larry Itson of Cave Spring; Steve Redden of Centre, AL; Jeffrey Raymond of Rome; and Gene Richardson (attorney). *(Photo courtesy of William S. Autry)*

conducted at the site some eight years earlier were still evident. At the time the archaeologists had inspected the site, they determined that the prehistoric village – named the King Site – had been occupied for about fifty years in the sixteenth century.[1] The scientists had also discovered inexplicable slash marks and rodent gnawings on the bones of some of the aboriginals in gravesites there.

Aside from the marks on the bones, another mystery concerning north Georgia has also perplexed historians and researchers for many years – that being the actual route taken by Hernando De Soto during the Spaniard's now-famous exploration of the southeastern United States in 1540. Though considerable research has been conducted over the years, and even Spanish artifacts discovered at other sites in the present-day southeastern United States, De Soto's actual route has remained an intriguing mystery.

This is what makes the discovery by the young men at the King Site in Floyd County so significant. As one of the men scanned the ground ahead of him, he noticed what he thought was a rusty strap of steel which had been unearthed earlier by a plow. It resembled any number of modern-day metal bands used for an assortment of purposes involving in the binding/bundling of various modern agricultural products.

On an impulse, the young man reportedly kicked idly at the rusted piece of metal. As he no doubt noticed the rusty relic's sword-like design, he wrenched it from the dirt. He then realized to his immense curiosity, that the piece did in fact resemble a sword.

He decided to take it home and clean it up for better inspection. All of the men agreed that this sword-like piece of rusted metal appeared to be something other than just a piece of modern day agricultural junk.[2]

After returning home and cleaning up what they now were strongly suspecting as a historic relic of some type, the men discovered it was indeed a sword of some age – perhaps a relic from the U.S. Civil War. They had no idea that it might actually be an ancient Spanish explorer relic of great historic significance.

After news of the men's discovery reached the scientific community, it first became necessary for researchers to confirm whether or not the supposed relic was merely a boyish hoax. One archaeologist – Keith Little – proceeded step by step through the possibilities, interviewing eyewitnesses and examining the site of the discovery. He concluded the discoverers not only were telling the truth – they "lacked the knowledge or expertise to perpetuate a hoax of this magnitude with such detail."[3]

The question now became, how could the archaeologists who supposedly had carefully excavated the King Site eight years earlier have missed this sword? Answer: They had only excavated two-thirds of the five-acre historic area during their research.[4]

Years later, a graduate from Rome's Shorter College who had worked on the dig as a senior stated with obvious chagrin, "When I found out exactly where the sword was found, I realized that was the King Site which we had spent months excavating. And I used to eat my lunch practically on top of where it (the sword) must have been buried."[5]

During the archaeological dig, the researchers had discovered the King Site contained ample artifacts, as well as remnants of a sixteenth century aboriginal Indian village. It was in the late nineteenth century that modern-day floods first exposed the site. A volume of history written about the Rome, Georgia, area in 1922 states that a wide variety of Indian artifacts were discovered at this spot.[6]

In 1928, an archaeological examination reportedly uncovered a "burned structure" at the site, and in the 1970s, extensive excavations were carried out by a number of college archaeological teams.[7] As the evidence accumulated, a picture began emerging of a prehistoric Indian village once located in the vicinity of the King Site on the Coosa River. The village apparently was a portion of a chiefdom or province which is believed to have extended northeast to about Knoxville, Tennessee, and southwest to about Childersburg, Alabama.[8]

More importantly, the village reportedly has also yielded artifacts such as metal knives and chisels (found in burial sites) which indicate almost certain contact between Spanish explorers and the aboriginal Americans, a discovery which excited the archaeologists of the 1970s.[9] The researchers, however, remained perplexed by the strange slash marks and rodent gnawings discovered on the aborigines' bones in the gravesites.

Following extensive research and examination, the archaeologists determined that the sword discovered by the men was in fact an authentic Spanish artifact of over 400 years in age. The grip or hilt ends in a large pommel which acted as a counterweight for the mass of the blade. *(A shiny modern replica of the sword weighs almost three pounds.)*[10] The weapon measures almost 48 inches in length and has a straight, 40-inch long, double-edged blade.

During its long exposure in the

University of Georgia archaeological students excavate the King Site near Rome, Georgia, in the early 1980s. A number of perplexing discoveries were made at the time which later lent credibility to the ultimate identification of the sword.

acidic red clay soils of north Georgia, the sword blade not only had been severely corroded, it had been damaged in two spots – undoubtedly the result of plowshares over the years. Preservative coatings applied by the archaeologists revealed deep pitting of the steel in a uniform black patina. In other words, it definitely looked its age.

The relic was given a "complete physical." X-rays which understandably were superfluous, were not excluded, but they, just as understandably, revealed nothing useful.[11] Following an electrolytic cleaning, inscriptions, excitingly, became visible on the sides of the blade. One side was so corroded that the inscription there was unreadable, but the other side revealed lettering clearly enough to provide a clue – that being the lettering style.

In situations of this nature, archaeologists must be resourceful in ferreting out the clues in a scientific capacity. Keith Little therefore assumed the role of a Sherlock Holmes in search of a Spanish connection to the sword. He forwarded descriptions, measurements and photographs of the relic to Dr. Helmut Nickel, curator of arms and armor at the Metropolitan Museum of Art in New York.[12]

The indistinct inscription on one side of the sword seemed to spell "*Christ*," and the capital letters appeared to be somewhat square in design.[13] According to Dr. Nickel, however, Spanish inscriptions would have had what's known as "uncial" or more rounded lettering. Nickel therefore advised that the blade must have been made "by a swordsmith in northern Italy, or possibly even southern Germany (instead of in Spain)."

This determination, however, still did not exclude a "Spanish" explorer connection, since many Spanish soldiers and adventurers often acquired and used weapons of German, Italian, or French design. It therefore would not have been unusual at all for De Soto himself to have carried a sword of German or Italian origin.

The corroded remnant of a hilt on the King Site sword lacks any unusual characteristics such as were found on the blade.[14] Today, the elaborate rings which protected the hand and allowed the swordsman to parry opposing thrusts are only twisted vestiges of their former beauty and utilitarianism. In their day, however, they represented an important aspect of state-of-the-art weaponry, "of a fairly international type found almost everywhere in sixteenth century western Europe," Dr. Nickel added. Features such as the "short grip, large pommel, and particularly the flaring top part of the un-swept knuckle-bow (knuckle-guard)," date the sword to the mid-sixteenth century.

These characteristics then begged the question, "Could the sword be connected to the De Soto expedition of 1540?" Aside from De Soto's venture, chronicles of Spanish explorations of the Southeast have included the Luna

Artist Ken Townsend's conception of the village which once existed at the King Site on the Coosa River in present-day Rome, Georgia. The rendering was made based upon information revealed by several professional archaeological digs at the site. It conforms to the classical example of a fortified prehistoric Indian village of what today is the southeastern United States. *(Illustration courtesy of Ken Townsend)*

expedition in 1560 and the Juan Pardo expedition in 1567.[15] Later European explorers visited the area, but they were too late to qualify as suspects.

So which expedition then lost the sword? The clues so far place a mid-sixteenth century sword in an aboriginal Indian village of that same period. That much falls into place neatly enough. After considerable investigation of the known information of the other possible Spanish explorers of the Southeast – Pardo, Luna, et alle – and the routes which they took, it becomes clear that they should be eliminated as possibilities for the former owner of the sword. That leaves only the De Soto expedition.

The archaeological investigators next re-focused their attention upon the skeletal remains recovered from the site. It was a revealing and grisly clue which ultimately tipped them off.

It finally dawned upon the researchers that the slash marks on the bones were much more than simply wounds inflicted by aboriginals upon aboriginals. If the Indians had been killed by other Indians, there would have been more fatal puncture wounds to the torso, and crushed skulls from the war clubs they used upon their enemies. There would have been few – if any – slashed arms and legs. To the contrary, however, there were in fact many unhealed slashing cuts on the bones of the extremities and on the skulls of the Indians – evidence of violent deaths attributable only to metal weapons such as those of Europeans.

When initially examined in the laboratory at Georgia State University, the cuts on the bones had been duly noted, but they didn't seem significant enough to warrant being intensely studied.[16] However, following the discovery of the Floyd County sword, the slash marks on the bones in the aboriginal graves suddenly became an exceedingly important issue.

The marks were then re-examined and tallied, and a pattern began emerging – something the researchers had not previously considered. They realized the wounds not only were indeed battle wounds, but were in fact injuries which had been inflicted with European-style weapons, and not by the aborigines themselves.

To confirm this hypothesis, the King Site injuries were then compared to European battle wounds recorded from the skeletal remains of 1,500 fallen dead at the Danish Battle of Wisby in 1361.[17] Seventy-eight percent of the wounds from each site *(the King site and the Wisby site)* proved to be cut marks. The remainder were punctures – both strongly indicative of sword and knife-inflicted wounds.

It was also clear that the weapons used in both conflicts were weapons which obviously had a long blade as was plainly evidenced by slash marks which continued across two bones at the same angle.[18] Spanish soldiers, trained to cut down opponents wearing body armor by slashing their arms, legs, and heads, almost certainly did the killing at the King Site.

Nevertheless, even though the time-frame now became approximately correct for the De Soto expedition to have committed the ill deed, there still was no hard evidence of that possibility. That is, not until one of the accounts of the expedition – an account maintained by De Soto's men themselves – was reviewed in detail.

According to that report, there was a pitched battle – perhaps one of the first conflicts between Europeans and aboriginal North Americans – between De Soto's men and Indians on Monday, October, 18, 1540.[19] It is this battle which quite possibly provides the vital connection between De Soto and the sword in present-day Rome, Georgia.

The account of the incident indicates the Spaniards had rounded up Indians – both men and women – from the village at the King Site. The Indians were to serve as slaves and were force-marched west with the explorers.[20]

At some point in the march, at a place called "Mabila" in present-day Alabama, the Spanish walked into a trap, and a great battle ensued. Records of the "Battle Of Mabila" today are considered indisputable.

When the fighting ended, the De Soto party – according to the account – spent a month recuperating before leaving Mabila. Approximately 2,500 Indians or more were reported killed in the battle. Considering the wounded that died later, some authorities have set the casualties even higher. The Spanish casualties were listed at 18 killed and 150 wounded.[21]

With this information in hand, a relationship between the King Site dead (cut marks on the bones, the sword, etc.) and the battle of Mabila became all the more credible, particularly when the cause for the previously unexplained rodent gnawings (teeth marks) on the bones suddenly became obvious. The Indians – always reverent of their dead – were forced to wait the month for the Spaniards to leave, before they could recover their dead from the battle site at Mabila. In the interim, field mice, opossums, and untold numbers of other wildlife gnawed at the moldering remains of the dead between the time they died and the point at which they were buried back at their homes (at the King Site) as was customary.

At this point also, any hypothesis concerning burrowing animals (digging into gravesites at the King Site) were ruled out as the source of any gnaw marks, since, of all the remains at the King Site, only the battle victims' remains exhibited gnaw marks.[22]

With this and additional evidence, the cause for the curiously gnawed and nicked ancient bones can now be explained. Further, a relatively-firm case can also now be made that Hernando De Soto's expedition passed quite near today's Rome, Georgia, identifying for posterity at least a portion of the mystery of the infamous explorer's route.

As revelations (and supposition) such

The Indians were to serve as slaves and were force-marched west with the explorers.

Historians and archaeological researchers have long pondered the route taken by Hernando De Soto in his exploration of the Southeast. Several other discoveries of possible Spanish relics have been uncovered over the years, including in northeast Georgia's White County. *(Readers please see "Mysterious Remnants of Early Spanish Explorers in White" in the White County section of this book.)*

As this come to light, the history of our nation (and of the state of Georgia) must constantly be updated. Dr. Charles Hudson, an anthropologist at the University of Georgia in Athens, working with numerous colleagues, has created what he calls "*The De Soto Trail Study*," an updated reconstruction of the assumed route of the De Soto expedition of 1539-43.[23]

And what became of the now-famous sword referred to quite often as "the De Soto Sword?" After centuries of lying forgotten in the red Georgia clay, the weapon suddenly became embroiled in a heated battle once again – except this time it was a court battle which was concluded in 1990. The "boys" (as to whom they are still referred by locals) who discovered the sword are fast approaching "middle age" as of this writing in 2021. The judge in the case awarded them possession of the relic after ownership was disputed by the owner of the property on which it was found. It is unknown today what further has occurred with the relic.

Endnotes:

1. Hally, David J., "*Archaeology and Settlement Plan of the King Site*" in Blakely, Robert L. (ed.), *The King Site: Continuity and Contact in Sixteenth Century Georgia*, Athens, Georgia: University of Georgia Press, 1988.

2. Fortenberry, Bill, 1990. "*Sword's Discoverers Hold History In Their Hands*," **Rome** (Georgia) *News Tribune*, March 25.

3. Little, Keith J., 1985. "*A Sixteenth Century European Sword From A ProtoHistoric Aboriginal Site In Northwest Georgia*," *Early Georgia*, Vol. 13, Nos. 12, p. 3.

4. Ibid, p. 3.

5. Harris, Bob, 1991. Personal communication. April 17.

6. Battey, George M., Jr., 1922. *A History Of Rome And Floyd County*, Webb and Vary. Atlanta.

7. Little, op. cit., p. 3.

8. Hudson, Charles, Chester DePratter and Marvin Smith in Blakely, op. cit., p. 122.

9. Hally, op. cit., p. 6.

10. Harris, op. cit.

11. Little, op. cit., p. 6.

12. Ibid.

13. AP. 1989. "*Floyd County Judge Says Historic Sword Belongs To Finders*," **Atlanta Journal & Constitution**, July 3.

14. Little, op. cit., p. 8.

15. Hudson, Charles, Chester DePratter, and Marvin Smith in Blakely, op. cit., p. 119.

16. Blakely, Robert L., 1989. "*A Coosa Massacre*," *Archaeology*, May/June, p. 30.

17. Mathews, David S., in Blakely, op. cit., p. 109111.

18. Blakely, op. cit.

19. Hudson, Charles, 1990. "*A Synopsis Of The Hernando de Soto Expedition, 15391543*," National Park Service. *De Soto National Historic Trail Study, Final Report*. March, p. 8889.

20. Hudson, Charles, Chester DePratter, and Marvin Smith in Blakely, op. cit., p. 130.

21. Mathews, David S., in Blakely, op. cit., p. 113.

22. Ibid, p. 105108.

23. Hudson, *Trail Study*, op. cit., p. 77.

The Mysterious Murder and Burial Of Cherokee Chief James Vann

On a frigid winter night in 1809, at an inn located on the Federal Road at what today would be the county line between Forsyth and Cherokee counties, an important chief of the Cherokee Nation was brutally murdered in cold blood. Though he was buried and his grave clearly marked in Blackburn Cemetery, the specific location of his grave has been strangely lost through time. Today, no one knows for certain where the last mortal remains of Chief James Vann now lie, nor even where he was murdered.

Most historians today who are familiar with the Cherokee Indians in north Georgia are aware of the story and legacy of James Vann. Descriptions of his stately mansion at Spring Place (near present-day Chatsworth, Georgia), stories of his wealth and wide-spread business affairs, and finally, his murder at Buffington's Tavern near the present-day Forsyth/Cherokee County line in Georgia, have been handed down from generation to generation. But how many people really know the actual site of Vann's final resting place? I'll tell you how many. . . . . Not a single person.

Much of the controversial issue of the location of Vann's grave stems from a tendency of the general public – and even of some respected historians – to perpetuate myths and false stories created in the absence of factual information.

Vann's grave no doubt exists in the general vicinity of the site suspected by researchers. It, however, has been totally confused with other graves and other landmarks.

Vann was a prominent and wealthy leader of the Cherokees in the Southeast in the early 1800s, and the owner of impressive plantations, complete with slaves, and extensive business enterprises. The development of the Federal Road between Athens, Georgia, and Nashville, Tennessee, formally permitted by the Cherokees in the Treaty of Tellico in 1805, created tremendous commercial opportunities for Vann, and he quickly took advantage of them, achieving enormous wealth for that day.

In addition to his previously-mentioned plantations, he also operated a stagecoach stop, trading post and tavern on the Federal Road near Eton, Georgia,

The magnificent plantation home of Cherokee Native James Vann II was constructed in 1804 at his home in Spring Place in what today is Murray County in north Georgia. Vann was exceedingly wealthy for his day and time, owning over 1,000 acres at this property alone. *(Photo courtesy of the GA Dept of Natural Resources, Historic Sites Division, Atlanta)*

as well as a ferry and inn where the Federal Road crossed the Chattahoochee River in present-day Forsyth County, and a second plantation near that same location. At the site where the Federal Road crossed the Conasauga River just west of Spring Place he owned yet another ferry, as well as a mill on Vann's Mill Creek, a tributary of the Conasauga. *(Note: The Federal Road crossed the Conasauga on Lot #149, District 9, Section 3, according to the 1832 surveys of old Cherokee County by David Duke, D.S., June, 1832).*

Though described as having occurred at several different sites throughout most of the more than two centuries since it transpired, Vann's murder undoubtedly took place at an early inn by the name of Buffington's Tavern (the site of which unsurprisingly is also a controversy; the physical portion of Buffington's no doubt disappeared long ago).

Many individuals for many years identified an old log structure which once existed across the road from the former site of the Sherrill home on the Old Federal Road in Forsyth County as the remains of Buffington's Tavern, but nothing could be further from the truth, according to the late Forsyth County Historian Don L. Shadburn who did considerable research on the topic, and who has written extensively on the Cherokees of Georgia in his seminal *"Cherokee Planters, 1832-1838"* (1989).

"That's true," Shadburn confirmed in an interview prior to his death. "Vann was killed at Buffington's Tavern, and Buffington's Tavern was on the old Federal Road not far from the Sherrill Place, but it (Buffington's) isn't the old structure across the road from Sherrill's. That structure is part of what used to be Lewis Blackburn's Public House built around 1820. It (Blackburn's Public House) is very historic in its own right, but it is not Buffington's Tavern."

The structure which once existed across from the old Sherrill home to which Shadburn refers has recently been moved from that site to the Cumming, Georgia, fairgrounds where it has been put on public exposition. According to reports, the relocation committee – Forsyth County Historic Society – has (as of this writing in 2021) declared this structure to have been the actual site of Vann's murder. Unfortunately, there is no solid evidence to support this claim.

Constructed of heavy log timbers 20" x 6" x 32', Blackburn's Public House is immensely sturdy, accounting for its endurance over the years. It is awe-inspiring to stand in the doorway of this building and understand the history that has both entered and passed from its doorstep over the past 200+ years.

"Part of the confusion between Buffington's Tavern and Blackburn's Public House centers around the fact that Lewis Blackburn married Tom Buffington's widow after Tom died," Shadburn added. "Lewis and the former Mrs. Buffington lived at Buffington's Tavern for a short while before moving to Blackburn's Public House at the site of the present-day Sherrill home-place. (In contrast), Buffington's Tavern actually existed on up the old Federal Road from the Sherrill Place, and was on the right, just across the Cherokee County line."

This specification by Shadburn that Buffington's Tavern existed "on the right" side of the road is a critical detail. It is known for a fact that the public house formerly existing on the Sherrill property and removed to the Cumming Fairgrounds was originally built on the "left" side of the road as one proceeds toward Canton, not on the right. The information in Ebenezer Newton's (who was an eye-witness) Diary seems to confirm this, and the Sherrill family have stated they moved the historic public house on their property from the left side of the road (as one travels toward Canton) to the right, in order that they might build their home on that site many years ago. The former Sherrill property public house (now on exposition in Cumming) almost certainly has to be Lewis Blackburn's Public House, and therefore NOT the site of Vann's murder.

Shadburn said another myth involving Vann and his death included Vann's sister – Nancy Falling/Fawling – who supposedly lived across the road from Buffington's Tavern. "That's just another case in which the facts have been embellished and twisted," he explained. "Nancy lived south of Spring Place at Vann's home near present-day Chatsworth."

For years, local folklore has maintained that Nancy's supposed residence across the road from Buffington's Tavern in some way connected her with Vann's death. Vann was, in fact, responsible for the death of Nancy's husband – John Fawling – but no definite connection between her and Vann's death has ever been

Very similar to Buffington's Tavern, Blackburn's Public House was one of the first such structures on the Georgia frontier in the early 1800s when this area was still controlled by the native Indians. In the public house pictured here – the identity of which has not been confirmed but which once existed at the old Sherrill homeplace in Forsyth County – the late Clifford Ruddell stands beside the stairs leading to the upper level where rooms for overnighting exist. (Photo by Olin Jackson)

established. Most historians today do agree however, that it quite probably was Falling's family which was in fact responsible for Vann's death, as was the Cherokee custom at the time.

Despite his enterprising and peaceful nature when sober, James Vann has been characterized by historians as a very violent, arrogant, and abusive person when under the influence of alcoholic beverages which he reportedly consumed in ever-increasing quantities during his later years in life. It was during one of these fits of anger, that he reportedly was responsible for the death of Fawling.

It is ironic that history has chosen to characterize Vann as violent and abusive.

An argument could be made for the fact that he was a victim of circumstances beyond his control in a quest to best portray his section of the Cherokee Nation as law-abiding and socially acceptable in the face of an advancing tide of white settlers who were by this time openly seeking reasons to displace the natives.

It is well documented that Vann ordered the use of such devices as painful whippings, etc., for the punishment of criminals, a practice which no doubt enhanced his reputation as a man of cruelty. The fact that is not so well documented, is that in doing so, Vann was actually carrying out Cherokee law as decided by the entire Cherokee Nation.

Indeed, in the *Laws of the Cherokees*, published in the *Cherokee Advocate* at Tahlequah, Oklahoma in 1852, a glimpse into Indian life on the frontier is provided. One of the laws (in an order from the chiefs and warriors in National Council at "Broom's Town" on September 11, 1808, the year prior to Vann's murder) provided for the formation of *"regulating companies"* of one captain, one lieutenant and four privates each, for the purpose of arresting horse thieves and protecting property.

The penalty in the Cherokee Nation for stealing a horse was 100 lashes on the bare back of the thief, be it male or female, and fewer lashes for things of less value, and if a thief resisted the regulators with gun, axe, spear or knife, he or she could be killed on the spot. This law was signed by Black Fox, principal chief; Charles Hicks, secretary to the Council; Path Killer; and Toochalar, all of whom formed the inner circle of Cherokee leadership at the time.

Even more interesting, this same National Council barely a year and a half later on April 10, 1810 (a year after Vann's death) passed the following law: *"Be it known that this day the various clans and tribes which compose the Cherokee Nation have agreed that should it happen that a brother, forgetting his natural affection, should use his hand in anger and kill his brother, he shall be accounted guilty of murder and suffer accordingly; and if a man has a horse stolen, and overtakes the thief, and should his anger be so great as to cause him to kill him, let his blood remain on his own conscience, but no satisfaction shall be demanded for his life from his relatives or the clan he may belong to."*

One of the more enlightened and enduring achievements of Vann was his association and support of Moravian missionaries whom he allowed to establish a mission near his home at Spring Place. It is from the diaries kept by the Moravians that one of the most reliable accounts of Vann's murder is described. On February 21, 1809, the following entry was made:

"We received the startling news of the murder of Mr. Vann. Here and there, he and his had punished Indians for stealing. When one of them refused to surrender, Vann ordered him to be shot.

"For a few days thereafter, Vann stopped at the tavern of a half-breed, Tom Buffington, about 56 miles from here. While there, he drank heavily and became involved in altercations with some of his friends for whom he had

It is from the diaries kept by the Moravians that one of the most reliable accounts of Vann's murder is described.

taken a violent dislike. He feuded with them, was most abusive, and made violent threats.

"Toward midnight, Vann stepped out of the tavern and stood before the open door, when suddenly, a shot was fired from without which pierced his heart. He fell lifeless to the floor without his perpetrator being seen.

"After hearing the shot, Joseph, his son, and a Negro rapidly gathered up the belongings of father and son, including Vann's 'pocketbook' with a considerable amount of cash and bank notes. Wrapped in a blanket, Joseph with the Negro fled to his father's plantation on the Chattahoochee River, 13 miles from Buffington's Tavern.

"At the crack of dawn, Mrs. Vann and other members of the family fled to Buffington's but before they arrived, Vann's body had been buried in the woods not far from the road."

It was this and similar descriptions which have led historians and residents to believe that Vann's grave was located in present-day Blackburn Cemetery, situated not far from the old tavern site.

"That's right," Shadburn continued. "There's no doubt that Blackburn Cemetery or its general vicinity is the burial site. In October of 1818, an individual by the name of Ebenezer Newton was traveling on the Federal Road from Athens, Georgia to Tennessee. In a journal describing his trip, he details how his travels led him to Vann's Tavern on the Chattahoochee River. The following morning, he describes how he continued on up the road toward Tennessee, crossing the Hightower (Etowah) River, and suddenly encountering a grave on the right 'on an eminence, paled in' (to keep out livestock), and painted, with a headboard and inscription which read: "Here Lies The Body Of James Vann Who Departed This Life February, 1809, Aged

In the early 1980s, Rev. Charles O. Walker, a noted historian and illustrator recreated this historically accurate depiction of Vann's grave on the Federal Road, based upon a description recorded in Ebenezer Newton's diary of 1818. It is worth noting that the public house in this depiction is accurately placed on the "left" or "south" side of the road as one travels toward Canton, as was the original case with the historic public house removed from the old Sherrill home-place in 2004. Conversely, the site at which Vann was murdered – Buffington's Tavern – was on the "right" or "north" side of the road, a critical detail for researchers in the determination of the actual site of his murder. (Illustration courtesy of Rev. Charles O. Walker)

40.'" Newton's description of the location of Vann's grave almost perfectly fits the description of present-day Blackburn Cemetery," Shadburn added.

But, the story doesn't end there. In the 1960s, when a team of what has been described as "amateur archaeologists" and a descendant of Vann – J. Raymond Vann of Mt. Vernon, New York – exhumed what they and many others assumed to be the remains of Vann, they received a surprise. According to an associated article in the *Atlanta Journal*, of August 29, 1962:

"Dalton archaeologist Wayne Yeager has confirmed that he removed the skeleton of Chief Vann from his grave near Ball Ground, Georgia, and brought the remains to a local funeral home which he declined to name.

"The local archaeologist said it took

Mystery & History in Georgia

The late Clifford Ruddell was one of the workers who exhumed the remains claimed to have been those of James Vann II from Blackburn Cemetery in 1962. He points to the site at which the exhumation was made. *(Photo by Olin Jackson)*

seven hours to exhume the remains from the old Blackburn family cemetery on the Etowah River between Ball Ground and Cumming. Mr. Yeager said the skeleton is in good condition considering that it has been 153 years since Chief Vann's death.

"Mr. Yeager said he is positive that he has the right skeleton because of several factors:

"No. 1 is that local residents pin-pointed the grave from local common knowledge, although it was not marked.

"No. 2, the upper right arm bone had been fractured as if by a bullet. Mr. Yeager said Chief Vann fought a political duel from horseback with his brother-in-law, John Fawling, shortly before his death, and accounts of the duel say that Fawling was killed and Chief Vann was hit in the right arm by a bullet.

"No. 3, Mr. Yeager has compared the shirt buttons found in the grave and the buttons of a shirt of the same era, and found them to be the same. The shirt used for comparison belonged to Tarleton Lewis, an ancestor of Mr. B.J. Bundy, (a Dalton historian).

"*Mr. Yeager said the grave was located on property owned by Mr. and Mrs. Ernest Sherrill, and that Mr. Sherrill's 94-year-old aunt, known only as 'Becky,' stated that she could remember when the grave was marked with a wooden slab.*

"In fact, after the Georgia Historical Commission established the location of the grave, Mr. Sherrill piled brush over it and refused to tell curious historians where it was located in fear that they might dig into the grave.

"However, Mr. Sherrill did show the grave to Raymond Vann and Mr. Vann secured an order from Forsyth County Ordinary A.B. Tollison to exhume his ancestor. Mr. Tollison acted as an official witness during the excavation.

"Found in the grave were seven glass buttons, approximately 50 nails from the coffin, and a belt buckle. Mr. Yeager said the bottom of the grave was in the exact shape of the old-time wooden coffins.

"*Mr. Yeager (also) said two gold rings were discovered on the hands of the skeleton,* and these rings are now being cleaned by Jack Zbar, another Dalton archaeologist and chemist. The rings appear to be inscribed, but the cleaning process has not been finished."

On the surface, the exhumation described in the *Atlanta Journal* article sounded very conclusive, and seemed to convincingly identify Vann's grave, but was it accurate? Actually, it appears not.

In the early 1990s, Clifford Ruddell had lived in the vicinity of Blackburn Cemetery most of his life, and he well remembered the day the remains were removed from the grave site. He was one of the diggers hired to perform the labor.

"We dug for a good long while, and then all of a sudden, we were into the bones," he explained. "They told us to get out of the hole, and they jumped in with all these little tools and brushes.

"Eventually, when they had collected all they wanted from the grave; they put it in bags and then left," he continued. "I don't remember exactly how long it was, but later on, they came back, and I think they put the bones or something back into the grave, and then they covered it all back over. That always struck me as kinda strange."

Strange indeed. For far from ending a controversy, the exhumation of this grave actually began spawning additional ones.

In the **Dalton Daily News** of August 29, 1962, a bold headline proclaimed *"Vann Excavation Stirs Controversy."* The article went on to describe how state and local officials were casting considerable doubt on the findings of Yeager and Zbar as well as their credentials. The article stated:

"...Dalton amateur archaeologist Wayne Yeager has stirred a controversy among historians and archaeologists throughout the state. Doubt has been expressed on the part of at least one archaeologist, Clemens deBaillou, as to whether the remains of Chief Vann have actually been found.

"However, on the other hand, the Rev. Mr. Yeager, a Baptist minister, said today that an inscription uncovered on one of the gold rings found on the hands of the skeleton (leaves no) doubt in his mind that he found Chief Vann.

"The Rev. Mr. Yeager said one of the plain, gold rings was inscribed with a 'V', and he doubts very much that anyone else

buried in the Blackburn Cemetery in Forsyth County near Ball ground would have had a name starting with the letter 'V.'"

Ironically, the proclaimed discovery of the ring with the "V" inscribed in it greatly complicated (rather than simplified) the issue of identification of the remains. In the April 25, 1971 issue of the **Chattanooga News-Free Press**, *Dalton Historian Mrs. B.J. Bandy said that her investigation of the census records of the early 1800s time-period indicated no one in that area had a name starting with a "V" except the Vanns. Therefore, the likelihood of anyone but James Vann being in possession of, not one, but <u>two gold rings</u>, particularly a ring inscribed with a "V," would have been extremely remote.*

Imagine the surprise and disappointment then of all involved, when the analysis of the remains – which were supposed to have been James Vann's bones – indicated that the bones were Negroid.

"...the man appointed by the Georgia Historical Commission had been against the whole thing from the start," Mrs. Bandy continued. *"He was determined that it wasn't Vann. He insisted it was a slave, although I never heard of a slave with a gold ring. He turned in a documentary report against it, so there was nothing we could do.*

"I was just sick," Bandy added, *"but when you have done all you can, you can't do anything else. I took the bones back and re-buried them where we got them (in Blackburn Cemetery)."*

Where then rest the remains of Cherokee Chief James Vann? Do they lie moldering still in some unmarked grave in or around Blackburn Cemetery? Or were those really James Vann's bones unearthed on a hot summer in August of 1962?

Could James Vann have been part Negro, thus accounting for the bone

James Vann II was traveling to his public house (pictured) on the Chattahoochee River near the present-day Forsyth – Hall county line, when he was assassinated while pausing at Buffington's Tavern in present-day Cherokee County. Built around 1800, Vann's Tavern survived the ravages of time, but was about to be inundated by the rising waters of newly-constructed Lake Lanier in the 1950s, when it was rescued, dismantled and removed to the state historic site, New Echota, near Calhoun, Georgia, where it was reconstructed for permanent display. New Echota was the last capital of the Cherokee Nation in the southeast prior to relocation to the West.

analysis? Or could there have been a misinterpretation as Negroid instead of Mongoloid?

"At the very least, I am convinced those were definitely not the bones of Vann exhumed in 1962," explained historian Don Shadburn. "There were just too many conclusive facts to the contrary. Even the nails used in the coffin were of a type not in existence in 1809. I've seen that report, (by the Georgia Historic Commission done in 1962) and their conclusions were very thorough."

Archaeologists Yeager and Zbar and Historian Bandy later returned to Forsyth County seeking another court order from County Ordinary A.B. Tollison for the exhumation of yet another grave believed to be Vann's, but by that time, Mr. Tollison had had enough. He denied their request.

The exact location of Vann's grave now may never be known, other than the fact that it is somewhere in or near Blackburn Cemetery in Forsyth County. Despite all of the above, just as some individuals have irresponsibly claimed to have "identified" a historic structure (which may actually be Blackburn's Public House) as Buffington's Tavern, these same individuals have also placed a grave-marker in Blackburn Cemetery "identifying the grave of James Vann II."

The positive identification of the actual sites of Buffington's Tavern and Blackburn's Public House is, in all likelihood, virtually impossible, so it would be much better to just leave well enough alone. And as for the positive identification of Vann's actual remains and grave site, the only way that will occur now is if bodies are continuously exhumed in the vicinity of the supposed gravesite until remains which can be proven to be Vann's can be found, and that's never going to happen.

One important sidebar to this whole affair is the fact that at the time the 1962 exhumation was done, it is painfully unfortunate that a DNA comparison could not simply have been done of Mr. Raymond Vann and his ancestor, James Vann II, to ascertain identity in that manner, but at that time, such an option obviously did not exist.

It's probably just as well, that Vann simply be remembered for his remarkable achievements, such as the home at Spring Place, and the nurturing of the Moravian Mission there which provided the diaries revealing the style and substance of pioneer life in north Georgia in the early 1800s. At this point, as far as the grave site and the delineation between Buffington's Tavern and Blackburn's Public House are concerned to "responsible" historians, these items undoubtedly will simply have to remain almost totally as speculation.

The Doublehead Gap Gunfight

The "frontier" in America is often deemed synonymous with what today is known as "the old West." In reality, the frontier actually started on the eastern seaboard of what today is the United States, and moved westward as the lands became settled and areas "civilized." Accordingly, there not only were "shoot-outs" and gunfights in the old West, but in the eastern United States as well. One such event occurred in 1884 in Gilmer County, Georgia.

From the onset of the U.S. Civil War up through the period known as "Reconstruction" in the South, ill feelings – and yes, downright hate – persisted as a result of the devastation the war had wrought upon that region and the elimination of ways of life held dear. A principal participant within the vortex of this climate of hate in north Georgia was an individual by the name of Walter Webster "Web" Findley of Pickens (and later Fannin) County.

Findley was born on May 20, 1841, the son of James R. and Catherine Findley. The Findley family members were ardent secessionists, with many political connections within the area's Democrat Party.

Though many of the weapons owned by Southerners had been confiscated by Union authorities at war's end, many weapons also still existed, due to the lawless and hostile climate in the South at war's end.

The Findley family members made no bones about their often-hostile attitude regarding "Unionists" (Southern residents who remained loyal to the Union following secession) during the Civil War. Web Findley's brother was Col. James Jefferson Findley, a Dahlonega, Georgia resident well-known for his still-strong pro-Confederate attitude after the war. Web, himself, had served as a second lieutenant in the Gilmer County militia during the war, and had also gained a reputation as a pugnacious adversary of his pro-Union neighbors in the mountainous portions of north Georgia.

A sometime lawman, Web won fame and fortune by tracking down and bringing to justice Jackson County murderer Sanford Pirkle in 1875, Fannin County killer Ayers Jones in 1876, and Pickens County murderess Kate Southern in 1877. Findley's home was frequently used as a headquarters by revenue agents, including Web, during raids on illegal liquor ("moonshine") distilleries in north Georgia. His career as a lawman might have been even more extensive had he learned to read and write.

Interestingly enough, however, Findley – as did many mountaineers during this period – sometimes worked the other side of "the straight and narrow" too when it suited his sense of "right" and "wrong." During the war and for a number of years thereafter, north Georgia was a lawless and often uncivilized environment, as is often the case during and after major conflicts. Kinship and friendship, rather than the U.S. legal system, often determined the actions and allegiances of area residents. This apparently was a motivating factor for Findley's actions which ultimately resulted in the shoot-out at Doublehead Gap.

The production and sale of home-produced corn liquor were considered a "Godgiven" right by mountaineers, and the income derived from such "moonshine" was important to the very limited incomes of these hardy early pioneers. Any tampering with these rights – especially by the U.S. government authorities – was very serious business.

John A. Stuart, who had the misfortune of being a north Georgia Unionist during the war, was the Deputy Collector of Internal Revenue following the war. His quick but effective law enforcement methods earned him a reputation as an effective lawman who was respected despite his political stance. In a massive raid during one period of time, he led posses which destroyed fourteen illegal liquor distilleries in Fannin, Towns, and Union counties. Actions such as this, however, could get a man killed, no matter what his position of authority might be.

During the war and for a number of years thereafter, north Georgia was a lawless and often uncivilized environment, as is often the case during and after major conflicts.

The "moonshiners," led in this instance by none other than Walter Webster Findley, retaliated against Stuart by attacking his farm in the early morning hours of April 6, 1880, burning the storehouse and slightly wounding Stuart's son when the attackers fired upon the sheriff's home.

Twenty men – who, interestingly, included both former Unionists and former Confederate soldiers – were later indicted for the attack. Those arrested were: Benjamin M. Tilly, John D. Fricks, S.J. Simmons, Cub Newberry, J.W. Vandergriff, Bud Hill, J.F. Bingham, William Crisp, James Findley, Samuel White, Jasper Long, Charles Smith, Walter W. Findley, Jackson Bearden, R.V. Hughes, Bud Roberts, William Teague, Milton Dill, Wilson Bryant, and George Sparks.

The two Findleys, Bearden and Sparks were the first of the group to be tried. All but Sparks were found "Guilty" in federal court in Atlanta on October 14, 1882.

Amazingly, following the reading of the verdict, the Findleys (who, incidentally, were father and son) and Bearden brandished pistols and ran. Bearden was quickly subdued, but James escaped (later to be recaptured in Gilmer County in 1886). Walter W. Findley had an injured hip, and, not being able to run, surrendered.

Web Findley was sentenced on February 10, 1883. He received two years in the terrible Erie County Penitentiary in Buffalo, New York.

After he had served six months in the Erie County Pen, Findley made application to the President of the United States (a Democrat) for a pardon. To strengthen his plea, a petition campaign calling for his release came from Lumpkin, Fannin, Gilmer, Hall, Pickens, White, and Forsyth counties, as well as, surprisingly, from the prison authorities themselves. Both of Georgia's U.S. senators and a congressman wrote letters of endorsement as well, and several members of the Georgia State Legislature signed a pro-Findley petition.

At the same time, however, another petition signed by church members, ministers, and the Fannin County sheriff, requested the President NOT grant Findley a pardon, a plea seconded by the United States Attorney General. The anti-pardon campaign interestingly was led by Robert P. Woody (1838-1901), a native north Georgian, Unionist, and a Union Army officer during the Civil War.[1]

Woody was injured during the war, and was receiving a federal pension as a disabled veteran. He had assisted the prosecution in its conviction of Findley. Although Woody and Findley held opposing political views, they, ironically, had once been friends.

To the surprise of the anti-pardon contingent, the President granted Findley the pardon over the loud objections of his attorney general. The trial judge and the U.S. Pardon Attorney had recommended the pardon, pointing out that Findley's sentence had nearly expired anyway, counting the time that he had spent in jail in Atlanta. The U.S. Attorney for North Georgia consented because of reports of Findley's poor health, and also no doubt in view of his past law enforcement record.[2]

Following Findley's release, he and Woody, though residing in the same locale, refused to greet or even acknowledge each other in passing. As time passed, their hatred of each other grew more pronounced.

Finally, on Sunday, September 28, 1884, the animosity between the two men "came to a head," when they chanced to meet at Mt. Pleasant Church, Doublehead Gap, near the Gilmer-Fannin County Line. Woody had traveled to the site with his wife for a church meeting.

At the time the two men accidentally met at the church, night had fallen, but a full moon provided reasonably-good visibility. Woody was bringing up his ox-drawn wagon when he was greeted by several friends who later stated they knew trouble was brewing when they smelled liquor on Woody's breath.

According to Woody's version of the events which transpired that night, he was helping his wife out of the wagon when Findley loudly remarked: "By God, roll her out Woody." Mrs. Woody was over-weight, but Findley later claimed that his remarks were not directed toward her, but to Jesse Bailey and a saddle blanket.

Woody, in fairness, was very nearly deaf, and could have mistaken Findley's comments. Whatever the circumstances, Woody, in response to Findley's remarks, angrily replied, "By God, I'll roll you down," and then cursed Findley as

Woody was injured during the war, and was receiving a federal pension as a disabled veteran.

a thief, house-burner, and a jailbird. Findley responded in kind, calling Woody a "lie swearer."

The two men – who both were carrying arms as was customary in that day – drew pistols and began firing at each other at the murderous range of only fifteen to thirty feet. Several shots were exchanged as the two men drew even nearer, and both attackers, in their anger, ignored the several individuals between them who were attempting to stop the fight.

Woody was wounded in the hand on the first exchange, but he managed to get off a second shot. Findley's second shot passed harmlessly through Woody's vest and Woody's third shot nicked Findley's shirt. Woody's pistol then began misfiring, and Findley wounded him again – this time seriously – in the stomach.

Both men fell to the ground. Findley apparently fell simply because someone had hit him in the head with a rock in order to stop the fight. A bystander – William Kimsey – lay with them, mortally wounded before he was able to evade the gunfire.

That neither Findley nor Woody was killed in the exchange is not nearly as amazing as the fact that more bystanders were not hit. The pistols of that day often were crude and inaccurate instruments, but they also could understandably be quite deadly nonetheless.

When order was finally restored, Woody was arrested. He subsequently was found guilty of assaulting Findley and served one year in the Georgia State Penitentiary. He and Findley were both

The feud between the two men, surprisingly, ended without further bloodshed.

tried for the murder of Kimsey and were acquitted.[3] Findley later successfully gathered information which caused Woody's Disability Pension to be revoked as fraudulent. Woody, however, gained a measure of revenge by being appointed U.S. postmaster at the community of Dial.

The feud between the two men, surprisingly, ended without further bloodshed. According to a Woody relative – Willis Rackley – Woody eventually tired of Findley's public insults (mainly in the form of public snubs). On one such occasion shortly after the gunfight at Doublehead Gap, he demanded that Findley either have the courtesy to speak to him in public and treat him civilly, or the two of them would end the matter once and for all. From that day forward, the feud ceased to exist.[4]

Walter W. Findley died in Fannin County on June 9, 1910.

Endnotes

1. *A transcript of a proWoody official report of the events leading to the gunfight is available in Lawrence L. Stanley's* **A Little History Of Gilmer County**, *(1975), and in the Robert Barker Collection, Knoxville Public Library.*

2. *Findley's pardon papers are on record in the National Archives, Washington, D.C., in Record Group 204.*

3. *A transcript of the Woody trial (The State versus Robert Woody) is available in the Gilmer County Court Case Papers, Record Group 1611211, Box 24, Georgia Department of Archives and History.*

4. *Information on Robert P. Woody came from Willis Rackley and an article by William C. Farmer in* **Facets Of Fannin: A History Of Fannin County, Georgia**, *(1989).*

Courage in the Face of Certain Death:

The Astounding Story of Stand Watie

This brave Native American knew he almost certainly would suffer a harsh death at the hands of his Cherokee brethren – just as did his brother, cousin and uncle – for signing the Treaty of New Echota in 1835. Stand Watie, however, also knew it was the best choice for the survival of his race and he was willing to make that sacrifice. Amazingly, he not only survived the Cherokee death squads, but later rose to the rank of brigadier general in the Confederate Army. Though his sacrifices were legion, he has been virtually forgotten by the modern-day residents of his former homeland.

He was born on December 12, 1806[1], in the village of Oothcaloga south of New Echota in the Cherokee Nation. He was originally named Ta-ker-taw-ker which, when translated into English meant "to stand firm," and the rest of the Cherokee Nation would soon learn just how firm a stance he could actually take when necessary. It would not be long before Stand Watie would earn both fame and fortune[2] as a result of his strength of character, so he was well-named.

He later was formally named according to tribal custom as "De-gado-ga," which meant "he stands on two feet." Somewhat later still, his preferred name evolved to a combination of a shortened form of the English translation of his Cherokee name – "to stand firm" – and a contraction of his father's name – "Oo-Wa-tie" – which led to the name – "Stand Watie" – by which he was more famously known.[3]

He spent his boyhood years along the creek that flowed gently through the pleasant valley[4] of what today is Gordon County, Georgia, and was later baptized into the Moravian Church and given the Christian name "Isaac."

In his youth, Stand Watie lived in a comfortable home built in the 1790s by his father, David Watie *(the double Oo, as in "Oo-Wa-tie" was, at some point, dropped from his name)*. In addition to the income from his plantation, David operated a ferry on the Hightower (Etowah) River from 1825 to 1831.

141

Mystery & History in Georgia

On June 29, 1995, the U.S. Post Office issued a set of 20 commemorative stamps showing 16 individuals and 4 battles of the U.S. Civil War. Brigadier General Stand Watie (1806-1870) was one of the individuals selected to appear on the stamps. He is pictured here, on horseback, following a raid on a Union river boat.

Futile Assimilation

By this point in time, the Cherokees had adopted many of the ways of the white settlers in the area in a desperate attempt to assimilate into White culture, but no matter how much the Cherokees tried, the White settlers always wanted more, and that meant being pushed farther and farther to the West out of their native homeland. It also didn't help that gold had been discovered in Georgia at about this same time, and the mad dash to grab land and seek fortunes from the precious yellow metal had seized the White race, and became the death knell of the Cherokees' existence in the East.

Interestingly, the assumption of the customs of the White man by the Native Americans included by default the custom of owning black slaves to work the Indian plantations of the wealthy

Stand Watie (1806-1871), was the brother of Buck Watie (Elias Boudinot), and the nephew of Major Ridge, prominent Cherokees, all three. He was a plantation owner in what today is Gordon County and also a member of the Treaty Party. By a stroke of luck, he was absent from his home the day Major Ridge, John Ridge and Buck Watie were brutally assassinated. He later became the highest ranking Indian officer in the U.S. Civil War, rising to the rank of brigadier general in the Confederate Army. *(Image courtesy of Western History Collection, University of Oklahoma Library)*

upper-crust Cherokees. Young Stand Watie nevertheless was raised by his father to work alongside the slaves in the fields. After his chores for the day had been completed, he often went hunting in the forest to bring in fresh meat for the family.[5]

Even more interesting, these Native Cherokees were so intent upon assimilation that they readily even took up arms to defend the issues of the White man, including the submission of the "Red Stick" Creek Indians in what today is southern Alabama, who were violently opposing the White settlers, as opposed to the peaceful assimilation practiced by the Cherokees.

When Stand Watie was only six or seven years of age, his father, David, was appointed as a captain in a regiment of 600 Cherokee volunteers – mostly mixed-bloods – commanded by his brother, Major Ridge. Under the overall command of Andrew Jackson, the regiment was a portion of a larger force sent to fight the Red Stick faction of the Creek Nation in present-day Alabama.

In March of 1814 at the Battle of Horseshoe Bend on the Tallapoosa River, the Andrew Jackson forces crushed the Red Stick uprising, quite nearly killing all of the Red Stick Creeks in the process. It was during that campaign that Major Ridge acquired his first name when he was commissioned as a major in the United States Army by Andrew Jackson.[6]

It can only be considered bitterly ironic today, that it would soon be "President" Andrew Jackson who was the driving force in denying the Cherokees the retention of their ownership of their Georgia homeland, even though the U.S. Supreme Court had ruled in favor of the tribe. Despite all of this, Stand Watie, his father, Major Ridge, and the rest of the "Treaty Faction" were firm in their stance of a peaceful and orderly settlement with the Whites.

White Education

Stand Watie, who spoke only his native tongue until he was twelve years of age, learned to speak, read, and write English at the Moravian Mission Schools, attending classes at both the school at Spring Place and another at Brainerd, Tennessee. It is amazing today to understand the lengths the Cherokees were

Buck Watie, also known as Elias Boudinot (1802-1839), was editor of the *Cherokee Phoenix* newspaper. His support for the Removal Treaty caused him to be replaced as editor of the paper, and later, to be assassinated by a Cherokee Death Squad at his new home in Park Hill, Arkansas. *(Image courtesy of Western History Collection, University of Oklahoma Library)*

willing to go to attempt assimilation, and still they were denied.

When not pursuing his studies at the Moravian Mission Schools, young Watie was especially interested in sports. He was small in stature, but reportedly was an outstanding athlete as well as an excellent rider. He was considered one of the best players in the games of ball in the "challenge" competitions in the Cherokee Nation.[7]

Stand Watie had a brother who was four years older than he named Kilakeena, meaning "stag" or "male deer." He was commonly known as "Buck" Watie. In time, the two boys were joined by other siblings for a total of eight children – four boys and four girls.

Buck Watie and his cousin, John Ridge (the son of Major Ridge), were

Mystery & History in Georgia

The stern visage of Major Ridge reveals the seriousness of the 1830s in the Cherokee Nation. He was speaker of the lower house in the Cherokee Council. He also was chief of the Cherokee police, a close advisor to Chief John Ross, and a strong supporter of the treaty being urged by the United States government which would cede the Cherokee lands to the Whites. His support for this treaty eventually cost him his life. *(Photo courtesy of GA Dept. of Archives & History, Atlanta)*

sent to complete their education at the American Board of Commissioners for Foreign Mission Schools at Cornwall, Connecticut. While there, in addition to a higher education, Buck gained a new name, and both Buck and John gained New England girls as their wives.

According to a common practice at the time, Cherokees who had been assisted in life by a benefactor took that benefactor's name as their own in tribute to the individual. Buck Watie accordingly adopted the name of his white benefactor – Elias Boudinot – who was a Philadelphia philanthropist. In 1827, Buck (now called Elias Boudinot) married Harriet Gold and brought her home to live at New Echota.[8]

Eastern Cherokees

In 1819, the sprawling Cherokee settlement of "New Town" was established on the south bank of the Oostanaula River just below the confluence of the Coosawattee and Connasauga rivers. In 1820, at New Town, a law was passed by the tribal council dividing the Cherokee country of Georgia, Alabama and Tennessee into eight territorial and judicial districts. Although Stand Watie and Major Ridge lived 30 miles apart, they both lived within the Coosawattee District.[9]

In 1825, New Town was designated as the new Cherokee National Capital and renamed "New Echota" (Echota being the Cherokee term for "town"). New Echota was (and the historic remnants still are) located east of present-day Calhoun, Georgia, in Gordon County, off GA Highway 225 at the present-day locus of New Echota State Historic Site.[10]

About eight miles south of New Echota, the Indian town of Oothcaloga once stood in the Oothcaloga Valley. Christianity was strongly held in the community as witnessed by a large number of converts made during the revivals held there in 1819-20. Soon thereafter, a prominent group of Cherokee leaders requested that a Moravian Mission be established in their neighborhood to conduct regular church services.

Many of the Cherokees – and not only those of higher education – were strong advocates of Christianity, and held firm to their beliefs. They also had realized the positive benefits of learning all facets of White culture in order to blend with that race, and, in doing so, retain possession of their properties in the East.

Major Ridge, his wife, Susanna, and

their son, John, were among the first to invite the Moravians to come to the valley. In addition, David Watie and his wife, Susannah, and their sons, Elias Boudinot and Stand Watie, encouraged the establishment of both a church and a school. Thus, from 1822 to 1833, the Oothcaloga Mission Station was operated by the Moravian Church in the valley.[11]

According to the **Cherokee Constitution** adopted on July 26, 1827, the Cherokee Supreme Court was authorized to appoint a clerk to a term of four years. Stand Watie was appointed as clerk in 1828, and at age 22, began a long career in legal work that eventually gained him a license to practice law in the Cherokee Nation[12] – which was no small achievement.

The Watie Family

During the time of his residence in the East, Stand Watie married three of the four wives with whom he was associated during his lifetime. These wives all had Christian names and there were no children from any of these marriages.

His first wife was Elizabeth "Betsy" Fields, who sadly died in childbirth, as did the child in late March of 1836.

His second marriage – in September of 1836 – was to the former wife of a deceased Cherokee neighbor Eli Hicks. Her name was Isabella Hicks, and she had a son by the previous marriage.

Watie's third marriage was to Eleanor Looney. No details of this marriage are known today.

It was a tragedy almost beyond comparison, since they had struggled so tirelessly to simply be accepted into White culture.

Stand Watie married his fourth wife – Sarah (Sallie) Carolina Bell – after he was a resident in the western Indian Territory in 1843. With Sarah, Stand Watie had five children – three sons and two daughters.[13]

When they reached maturity, the three cousins – Stand Watie, Elias Boudinot and John Ridge, along with the older Major Ridge, came to be not only a tight family group, but, in 1832, the leadership core of a pro-treaty party favoring the removal of the tribe to the West. They had ultimately realized that assimilation into White culture of the East was a futile effort. There simply were too many European settlers arriving in successive waves. The tide seemed endless.

Therefore, resettlement in the West after obtaining fair reimbursement in the sale of their properties in the East seemed the only logical option for the pro-treaty party, particularly in view of the fact that they also understood that if they did not take this step, their lands and properties in the East would simply be taken from them by the Whites. It was a tragedy almost beyond comparison, since they had struggled so tirelessly to simply be accepted into White culture.

In order to achieve these objectives, the pro-treaty group (Stand Watie, Elias Boudinot, John Ridge, Major Ridge, etc.) were seeking to gain control in the Cherokee Nation over the anti-treaty faction, which opposed the tribe's removal. The anti-treaty faction was led by the principal chief of the Cherokees, John Ross.[14]

Mystery & History in Georgia

John Ross (1790-1866), principal chief of the Cherokee Nation from 1828 until his death, appeared to have much more white blood than he did Cherokee blood, and in fact, he did. He was an eighth-blood Cherokee. He also was unflinchingly opposed to the treaty which would cede the Cherokee lands to the Whites, and led the punishment of those who signed the Treaty of New Echota. *(Photo courtesy of Western History Collection, University of Oklahoma Library)*

After Andrew Jackson, the U.S. Congress, and the state of Georgia recognized the pro-treaty faction as the legitimate delegation of the Cherokee Nation, they (the pro-treaty faction) took the lead in negotiating the Treaty of New Echota in 1835, surrendering the Cherokees' ancestral homes in the Southeast for new lands in the West.[15]

On December 29, 1835, at Elias Boudinot's house at New Echota, the Watie-Ridge-Boudinot-led faction signed the Treaty of New Echota. They gave up all claims to their land in the East in return for new land west of the Mississippi River and just compensation for any improvements made on their land in the East.

Other Cherokees, however – led by John Ross – were not present for the signing of this treaty, and bitterly opposed it and the removal of the tribe.

In order to exact revenge for what they considered to be an unpardonable sin, the anti-treaty group vowed to exact retribution from the Watie-Boudinot-Ridge pro-treaty faction. Nevertheless, the United States Senate quickly ratified the treaty after it was executed by the pro-treaty faction and three years later, the United States army enforced the Cherokee removal in what came to be known as the "Trail of Tears."[16]

Western Cherokees

In the spring of 1837 – prior to the forced removal of those Cherokees who refused to leave the Southeast – the Stand Watie, Elias Boudinot and Ridge families began their voluntary migratory journey to the Indian Territory in the West. Upon arrival, they joined forces with the "Old Settlers" – those earlier Cherokees who had also voluntarily relocated to the Indian Territory in 1817 long before the signing of the Removal Treaty.

Contrary to their expectations, the Watie-Boudinot-Ridge families and their allies among the Old Settlers were unable to gain leadership over the Cherokee Nation in the West. Their old treaty opponent – John Ross, who had arrived in the West in mid-March of 1839 in the wake of the forced removal – still retained the allegiance of the majority of the Cherokees.[17]

On June 21, 1839, at Double Springs in the Indian Territory, a secret meeting of the Cherokees who had opposed the removal treaty was held to judge those who had violated the "blood law," and, without authorization, sold the Cherokee lands in the East. A verdict of death was passed against all the signers and endorsers of the Treaty of New Echota.

On the next day on June 22, the sentences were carried out by execution squads and three of the most prominent signers – Major Ridge, who was Stand Watie's uncle; John Ridge, who was Stand Watie's cousin; and Elias Boudinot, who was Stand Watie's brother – were all brutally murdered. Stand Watie, however, who was also marked for execution, was warned about the death squads, and managed to escape the assassins.[18]

For his protection, Stand Watie organized a band of warriors at Old Fort Wayne as a personal bodyguard. The next few years were a time of murderous internal feuding between the two treaty factions. Relations between the factions bordered on civil war, with many acts of vengeance and retaliation carried out by both sides.

Eventually, a restless calm emerged in the Indian Territory, and Stand Watie, who had attained prominent social and political stature in the territory, joined the Tribal Council where he served from 1845 to 1861. During that time, he participated in the leadership of the Cherokee Nation until the beginning of the War Between the States.[19]

The U.S. Civil War

In the spring of 1861, the Union abandoned all of its military posts in the Indian Territory. The Confederates quickly took advantage of this situation and occupied these forts.

As a prosperous planter and slave owner, Stand Watie was sympathetic to the Southern cause, but his dedication undoubtedly had little to do with his loyalty to the Southern states. In all likelihood, he envisioned his involvement

This historic structure exists on the Bray Farm near Calhoun, Georgia, in Gordon County. Local lore maintains that the core of this home is an early log cabin built by David Watie – father of both Stand Watie and Elias Boudinot - in the 1790s. Many historians believe both Stand Watie and Boudinot were born in this cabin. *(Photo courtesy of Joe Griffith)*

in the White's war as an opportunity to get rid of his old treaty party enemies – the John Ross regime, which was pro-Union.

When Confederate emissaries approached Stand Watie for his support, he readily agreed to organize a cavalry unit. With the outbreak of the war, he, due to his leadership capabilities, was made a colonel in the Confederate army and he raised a regiment of mostly mixed-blood, pro-slavery soldiers known as the Cherokee Mounted Volunteers.[20]

As a military unit, the Cherokee Mounted Volunteers fought as a band of very irregular cavalry. They wore odd colored shirts and pants, moccasins, and hats with feathers sticking out of them. Despite their support of the Southern cause, they were not supplied by any normal Confederate unit. As such, they had no reliable source of arms or munitions, so they depended upon captured Union supplies and equipment for their logistical support. Interestingly, the Union weapons were the most modern of that day and time, so in a few rare instances,

Major Ridge, the uncle of Stand Watie, departed for the West in 1837. The structure in this photograph has an Indian log cabin at its core which was Ridge's actual home in which he resided in Indian Territory in what later grew to become Rome, Georgia. Ridge also operated a ferry and several other business endeavors at this site in the 1820s and '30s. Today, this structure is called Chieftains Museum, and is a National Historic Landmark dedicated to the preservation of the heritage of the Cherokees.
(Photo courtesy of Joe Griffith)

the Cherokees were better supplied than the line Confederate units.

In cold weather, the Cherokee Mounted Volunteers were known to wear captured pieces of Yankee blue uniforms and overcoats. Watie and his men – armed mostly with shotguns, knives and tomahawks – preferred to fight on horseback, conducting slashing raids on unsuspecting enemies in the tradition of the guerrilla tactics of Francis Marion, the "Swamp Fox," in South Carolina during the American Revolution. Watie and his men operated with the same dash and daring as they ambushed wagon supply trains, steamboats, and military escorts during the war, gaining renown and generating fear in their opponents.[21]

It is a matter of record, however, that Watie and his men did participate in one traditional infantry battle. On March 7-8, 1862, his unit was part of Confederate Major General Earl Van Dorn's 16,000-man army in the vicinity of Fayetteville, Arkansas. Van Dorn was trying to encircle the right flank of Major General Samuel R. Curtis' Union Army of 12,000 men.

Curtis was defending "good ground" about 30 miles to the northeast of Fayetteville at a place called Pea Ridge. He apparently was well-prepared for an attack and managed to fight off the Confederates in two days of fierce battle, forcing Van Dorn's forces to retreat in complete disarray.[22]

Ironically, in that defeat, Stand Watie's reputation as a fierce fighter and capable combat leader was displayed "front and center," earning him a revered place in the combat lore of American forces. In a driving snow storm, Colonel Stand Watie's men, who were for the first time being employed on foot as regular infantry, were aligned with other units on the left flank of the attacking force. During the attack, Watie's men charged a Union artillery battery of three guns protected by dismounted Union cavalry.

As they ran across the open field screaming a blood-curdling Rebel yell and brandishing the cold steel of their weapons, Watie's men caused the startled Yankees to break from their positions and flee in terror. In the process, three cannons were captured – an accomplishment which was considered a great victory at that time. As a result of this courage in the face of terrible fire, Watie and his men were cheered by the other Confederate units.[23]

Interestingly, despite the great victory in the capture of the cannons, Watie had no horses or harnesses to move the cannons to the rear. He therefore directed his men – still under heavy hostile fire from other Union artillery units – to drag the captured pieces into the woods where they were secured. Unfortunately, Watie's advanced position became untenable as other Confederate forces in the line began retreating, and he was forced to withdraw with them.

Thus, Watie and his men had successfully fought in their one and only battle deployed as traditional infantrymen, despite the Confederate loss. Unfortunately, by the end of the day, the battle had become a crushing defeat for the Confederates.[24]

Following the defeat at Pea Ridge, John Ross – who initially had supported the Confederacy – became a turncoat and suddenly switched sides. He realigned his Cherokee supporters with the Union army and cause, deciding that instead of bravely fighting on in loyalty to his original cause, he decided instead to simply "join the winning side."

A short time later, a Union force – with the cooperation of Ross and his people – invaded the Indian Territory. This invasion divided the already shattered Cherokee Nation into its former two treaty factions once again.

As a result, pro-Union Cherokees battled pro-Confederate Cherokees, with the Ross faction once again bitterly fighting the Watie faction. Following four years of violence based almost entirely upon tribal animosity rather than U.S. Civil War conflicts, the Cherokee homeland in the West was generally laid to waste. Many of the Cherokees began leaving their resettlement homes to resettle once again south of the Red River in Texas. It is for this reason that a Cherokee population ultimately evolved in this vicinity.

It took more than four long years for the Union armies to defeat the starving weaponless Confederacy but it eventually occurred. This culmination of the war returned John Ross to his position of control over the Cherokee Nation. Factional violence within the Nation essentially ended at the conclusion of the U.S. Civil War, but bitterness and hatred endured well into the next century.[25]

Prior to war's end on May 6, 1864, Stand Watie had been promoted to the rank of brigadier general, becoming the highest ranking Indian to fight in the Civil War. In 1995, the United States Post Office issued a set of commemorative stamps featuring distinguished individuals and battles of the United States Civil War. In the foreground on one of those stamps, the image of a Cherokee Indian who also was a brigadier general in the Confederate Army, is prominently displayed riding on horseback. It is not difficult to discern the identity of the Indian.

In the distant background on this same commemorative postage stamp, smoke can be seen rising from the burning hulk of the Federal steam-driven ferryboat – the J.R. Williams – on the Arkansas River. Watie and his men ambushed this vessel during the U.S. Civil War on June 15, 1864.

While the J.R. Williams was steaming upriver on its way to Fort Gibson in the western Indian Territory, the vessel was fired upon and disabled by Watie's artillery. The Indians made their assault "Indian-style" from behind bushes on a bluff overlooking the river – almost invisible to the boat crew. Blasted out of control, the boat ran aground on a sandbar on the north side of the river.

The outnumbered Federal soldiers aboard the boat were taken completely by surprise. Those who survived the ambush fled on foot southward back toward Fort Smith from whence they had come. The boat's crew deserted to the Confederates.

Watie's men swarmed over the captured vessel, looting the boat of its cargo of commissary stores, quartermaster supplies and subtler goods intended for

Mystery & History in Georgia

Following the removal of the Cherokees in 1838, the town of New Echota fell into ruin and the land reverted to agricultural usage. In the foreground in this photo, the last remains – a few foundation stones and the outline of the original hand-dug well – of the Buck Watie aka Elias Boudinot home are visible. Buck was the older brother of Stand Watie and served as the first editor of the *Cherokee Phoenix* newspaper. Buck constructed a large two-story home on this site in 1827. He was among those assassinated at the Cherokee reservation in Park Hill, Oklahoma, for his support of the Treaty of New Echota. *(Photo courtesy of Joe Griffith)*

Fort Gibson. After they had gathered up what booty they could carry, most of the Indians fled the scene to rejoin their destitute families who were living along the Red River in Texas where they had taken refuge from the invading Union Army.

Watie loaded up as much of the supplies as he and his remaining Cherokee soldiers could carry away with them, then set fire to the boat. He then departed for his camp on the Limestone Prairie in the Cherokee Nation, because he knew a strong Federal reaction force would be arriving at the site of the burned ferryboat in short order.[27]

The Stand Watie stamp commemorates this amazing leader's many years of perseverance and devotion to both the Cherokee Indian and Confederate American lost causes. Despite being cast as a fighter for two major losing causes, his loyalty never wavered. As a three-quarter-blood Cherokee aristocrat, prosperous slaveholding planter, and leader of his mixed-blood allies, he somehow survived the many years of bloody tribal feuding in both the East and the West.

As a Confederate Army Brigadier General, Watie also survived this conflict despite regular service in combat situations. He was the highest-ranking Native American to fight in the Civil War – on either side.[26] On June 23, 1865, over two months after General Lee's surrender, Stand Watie became the last Confederate general to surrender his forces.

Following the war, Watie tried unsuccessfully to rebuild his fortune, but the constant combat – both in the Civil War and against the anti-treaty faction – had taken a heavy toll upon his normally strong constitution. With his body weakened and ill, he died on September 9, 1871, at his home on Honey Creek in Delaware County, Oklahoma, near the northwest corner of Arkansas.[27]

Vestiges of Stand Watie In Georgia Today

Back at Stand Watie's old homesite in what today is northwest Georgia, there is no commemorative marker of any type at the birth-site of this amazing Cherokee. The only recognition of any type whatsoever is found in the form of The Sons of Confederate Veterans, General Stand Watie Camp #915 in Calhoun, Georgia, which honors his name. If one knows where to look, however, there are still vestiges of Watie's former existence in the area.[28]

The first site of interest undoubtedly would be the spot where Stand Watie was born in 1806. The actual location of this site, however, may be in question. The *Calhoun Times and Gordon County News* reported on March 11, 1998, that *"The site [the Bray farm] includes a historic home-place historians estimate was built around 1796 by*

Oo-Watie [David Watie], *'The Ancient One,' brother of Major Ridge*. [David Watie's sons] Elias Boudinot and Stand Watie, a leading family of the Cherokee Nation, were both born on the site."[29]

Others claim the old home place at Bray Farm (also known as "Daffodil Farm"), was built by a Methodist minister, Bannister Bray in 1837. For example, Jewell B. Reeve in her book **Climb The Hills Of Gordon** writes, *"There, near a grove of oak and cedar trees surrounding three springs, he built a house of logs covered with white clapboard and faced with a row of six majestic white columns."*[30]

Regardless of the circumstances, a historic farmhouse is located on Land Lot 119, District 15, Section 3, about five miles south of downtown Calhoun, Georgia, in Gordon County. The farm on which this structure exists was purchased by Dr. J. Brent Box in the year 2000.

According to Dr. Box, he has investigated the claim that Stand Watie was born in the house on his property, but to date, no evidence has been found to confirm or deny this claim. Dr. Box, however, says he has researched the construction of the house, and has been informed that the current structure actually has an earlier log structure at its core, similar in style to that of the Cherokee dwellings of the early 19th century.[31]

Another historic house of interest is the large two-story home of Stand Watie's uncle – Major Ridge. This structure is well-preserved in Rome, Georgia, beside the Oostanaula River, approximately 30 miles south of New Echota.

"The Ridge," as he was called, reportedly migrated to the Oothcaloga Valley in what today is north Georgia as a young man. He was one of the first Cherokees to adopt the farming and herding methods of the white man. He acquired black slaves and established an efficient plantation.

As a National Historic Landmark, his former home presently houses the *Chieftains Museum*, an interesting repository of memorabilia and artifacts relating to the Cherokee Indian culture of the 18th and 19th centuries. At the core of this house – which has been renovated numerous times – is the original four-room "dog-trot style" log structure which was built by Ridge after 1794. In the museum is a small wall exhibit with a photograph and information about the life of Ridge's famous nephew, Stand Watie.[32]

The site of the home of Stand Watie's older brother – Elias Boudinot – is located at the northwest corner of the New Echota town square on the New Echota State Historic Site near Calhoun, Georgia. Boudinot served as the first editor of the **Cherokee Phoenix** newspaper, and a short distance from the printing shop where he published the paper, he built a two-story frame house in 1827.

It was at Boudinot's house that, on December 29, 1835, the **Treaty of New Echota** was signed by twenty Cherokees, including Major Ridge and Elias Boudinot. Stand Watie and John Ridge later signed the treaty in Washington City (D.C.) on March 1, 1836. Sadly, today, only corner stones and an abandoned well remain to mark this historic site.

The New Echota State Historic Site has a visitors center and a museum, and is open daily for a self-guided tour of the historic buildings and archaeological sites.[33]

According to James F. Smith in his book **The Cherokee Land Lottery**, Stand Watie's personal property as an adult was located in the 14th District, 3rd Section in present-day Gordon County, Georgia. Specifically, the property was located in and adjacent to the town of

Pictured here is a reproduction of the print house constructed on the grounds of New Echota in Gordon County by the Georgia Historic Commission. Elias Boudinot, aka Buck Watie, was the brother of Stand Watie. He also was the editor of the *Cherokee Phoenix* and published the unique Cherokee language newspaper in this structure. Stand Watie assisted his brother with the paper from time to time, and was acting editor in 1832 during his brother's absence. *(Photo courtesy of Joe Griffith)*

On November 15, 1836, his improvements were appraised at $2,392.00 by the land lottery surveyors.

New Echota near the confluence of the Coosawattee and Connasauga rivers. Survey notes indicate that most of Watie's improvements (e.g. buildings, outbuildings and orchards) were located astride the convergence of Land Lots 92, 93, 124 and 125. In addition, some improvements were scattered along a line between Land Lots 93 and 94.[34]

To date, the actual site upon which Stand Watie's home (during his adult years in the Southeast) once stood has not been located or identified. He may possibly have lived near his brother, Elias Boudinot, at New Echota. Land Lottery records indicate Stand Watie owned 95 additional acres of improved land in the Oothcaloga Valley as a part of Land Lot 156 in the 15th District and 3rd Section of present-day Gordon County, Georgia. This property might also possibly have been the site of his home in his adult years in the Southeast.

Land Lot 156 is located approximately six miles south of downtown Calhoun, Georgia. Oothcaloga Creek runs north through this tract of land which is just west of the present-day intersection of Highway 41 and Taylor Bridge Road about a mile north of the lower Gordon County line. On November 15, 1836, his improvements were appraised at $2,392.00 by the land lottery surveyors.[35]

Interestingly, Isabella Watie, Stand Watie's third wife, did not migrate with him to the West, and claimed separate improvements on Oothcaloga Creek. These improvements included 80 acres of improved land, buildings, and orchards for which she was paid $3,095. This property quite possibly was owned by Isabella's first husband - Eli Hicks – and willed to her following his death.[36]

As previously mentioned, the site at which Oothcaloga Mission Station once stood may be viewed today approximately three miles to the northeast of the Stand Watie property. The mission was located on Land Lot 209. The Ridge and Watie families attended church there from 1822 to 1833.

To visit the Oothcaloga Mission Station site, start at the intersection of present-day Highway 41 and Taylor Bridge Road. Proceed north on Highway 41 approximately 1.8 miles to Union Grove Road. Turn right and proceed eastward one mile to Belwood Road and turn left. Proceed north for approximately two-tenths of a mile to a site overgrown with trees and brush on the left side of the road.

The structures at historic Oothcaloga Mission Station no longer exist. Sadly, the two-story frame main building fell into ruin in recent years and has virtually disappeared.

At this same location, but on the opposite side of the road, is a dirt road. Approximately 100 yards up that road to the east is old Morrow Cemetery. John Gambold, the first Moravian missionary at Oothcaloga Mission Station in 1822, was buried in this cemetery in 1827. Gambold not only was a missionary, but also the only known Revolutionary War veteran buried in Gordon County.[37]

Vestiges Of Stand Watie In The West

In the former Indian Territory in the West, historic monuments, markers and national historical sites honor Stand Watie in present-day Oklahoma, Arkansas, Missouri and Texas.

The courageous Cherokee's grave may be visited in old Ridge Cemetery (later known as Polson Cemetery) in present-day Delaware County, Oklahoma. Outside the cemetery, a historical marker provides details of his life for travelers.

There are additional markers and monuments at Honey Creek, Old Fort Wayne, Park Hill, Cabin Creek and Doaksville. Three miles east of present-day Gore, Oklahoma, at the original capital of the Cherokee Nation in the West, there is an exhibit honoring the Watie, Boudinot and Ridge families at Tahlonteskee Museum. At Sequoyah's home in Sequoyah County, Oklahoma, there is an exhibit honoring Stand Watie and his cousin John Ridge.

At the Pea Ridge Civil War Battleground in Arkansas, there is an exhibit commemorating Stand Watie's participation in that famous battle.

Endnotes

1. Don L. Shadburn, *Cherokee Planters In Georgia, 1832-1838* (Roswell, GA: W.H. Wolfe Associates, 1990) 25.

2. Frank Cunningham, *General Stand Watie's Confederate Indians* (Norman, OK: University of Oklahoma Press, 1998), 2-4.

3. Frank Cunningham, *General Stand Watie's Confederate Indians* (Norman, OK: University of Oklahoma Press, 1998), 2-4.

4. Franks, *Stand Watie*, 2-3.

5. Franks, *Stand Watie*, 2-3.

6. Don L. Shadburn, *Cherokee Planters In Georgia, 1832-1838* (Roswell, GA: W.H. Wolfe Associates, 1990) 25.

7. Roger Aycock, "Stand Watie Strong Leader In Times Of War And Peace," *Rome* (Georgia) *News-Tribune*, 10 October 1971, 8-B.

8. Franks, *Stand Watie*, 4.

9. George Magruder Battey, Jr., *A History Of Rome and Floyd County* (Atlanta, GA: Cherokee Publishing Company, 1979) 27,51.

10. Ibid, 27.

11. William G. McLoughlin, *Cherokees and Missionaries, 1788-1839* (New Haven, CN: Yale University Press, 1984), 146.

12. Battey, *A History Of Rome*, 26-28; Franks, *Stand Watie*, 10-12; James F. Smith, *The Cherokee Land Lottery*, "Field Notes" (Atlanta, GA: Records of the Georgia Surveyor-General Department, nd), 256-263.

13. Battey, *A History Of Rome*, 211-212; Cunningham, *Confederate Indians*, 16; Franks, *Stand Watie*, 8, 37, 9-41; Gary E. Moulton, ed., *The Papers*

Mystery & History in Georgia

Georgia Governor George R. Gilmer fought for the removal of the Cherokees but he lost his political support (and his office) for promoting state ownership of gold mines as a means of reducing property taxes for wealthy Georgia planters.

Of Chief John Ross, Volume II, 1840-1866 (Norman, OK: University of Oklahoma Press, 1984), 738.

14. Franks, *Stand Watie*, 2-3.

15. Ibid, 13, 14-36.

16. Franks, *Stand Watie*, 26-27; Shadburn, *Cherokee Planters*, 17-19.

17. Franks, *Stand Watie*, 8.

18. Battey, *A History Of Rome*, 89-90.

19. Franks, *Stand Watie*, 96-97.

20. Ibid, 114-118.

21. Cunningham, *Confederate Indians*, 1-3.

22. Franks, *Stand Watie*, 124-125.

23. Ibid.

24. Ibid.

25. Ibid, 126-212 passim.

26. George Magruder Battey, Jr., *A History of Rome and Floyd County* (Atlanta, GA: Cherokee Publishing Co., 1979) 47.

27. Kenny A. Franks, *Stand Watie and the Agony of the Cherokee Nation* (Memphis, TN: Memphis State University Press, 1979), 160-164.

28. The Sons of Confederate Veterans, General Stand Watie Camp #915 of Calhoun, GA.

29. "Bray Farm To Hold Annual Open House," *The Calhoun Times and Gordon County News*, 11 March 1998.

30. Gordon County Bicentennial Committee, *A Historical Tour of Gordon County Celebrating 1976, American's Bicentennial Year* (Calhoun, GA: Published by GCBC, 1976), 1-3; Jewell B. Reeve, *Climb The Hills Of Gordon* (Easley, SC: Southern Historical Press, 1979, c 1962), 218-225.

31. Telephone conversation between Joe Griffith, the author, and Dr. J. Brent Box, the current owner of the Bray farm, 26 January 2002.

32. Battey, *A History Of Rome*, 37, 50; Sesquicentennial Committee of the City of Rome, *Rome and Floyd County: An Illustrated History* (Charlotte, NC: The Delmar Company, 1986), 14-15; McLoughlin, *Cherokees and Missionaries*, 1788-1839, 85.

33. New Echota State Historic Site, *New Echota Self-Guiding Trail Guide*, Calhoun, Georgia.

34. Franks, *Stand Watie*, 10-12; Shadburn, *Cherokee Planters*, 34; Gary E. Moulton, ed., *The Papers Of Chief John Ross, Volume II, 1840-1866* (Norman, OK: University of Oklahoma Press, 1984), 738.

35. Franks, *Stand Watie*, 39; Shadburn, *Cherokee Planters*, 34, 38.

36. Franks, *Stand Watie*, 39-41; Shadburn, *Cherokee Planters*, 13, 34.

37. Kenneth W. Boyd, *The Historical Markers of North Georgia* (Atlanta, GA: Cherokee Publishing Company, 1993), 84-87, 89-90; John M. Brown, ed., *Yesterdays 1830-1977* (Calhoun, GA: Gordon County Historical Society, Inc., 1977), 8.

(Grateful appreciation is expressed herewith to Joe Griffith who provided detailed factual information necessary to complete this article.)

The Mystery of Sequoyah's Grave

Though prominent in Cherokee Indian affairs in the area known today as north Georgia, Sequoyah - architect of the amazing Cherokee alphabet - spent his last days in south Texas, but his burial site is unknown today.

The six-foot one-inch statue of Sequoyah proudly commands an imposing position in the anthropology hall of Corpus Christi Museum in southern Texas. But what is the statue of a Cherokee Indian doing in a Texas museum? The mystery of his final days may solve the puzzle.

Sculptor Dennis Silvertooth, whose father was three-quarters Indian (Cherokee and Shawnee), fashioned the work and explains that Sequoyah himself provides the connection with south Texas. History notes that this section of North America was the land of the Karankawa Indian peoples. Sequoyah and other Cherokees, however, visited the area.

Contemporaries said Sequoyah usually wore a homespun jacket with a red fringe, and on his head he wore a shawl, much like a turban. He also wore buckskin leggings and unadorned moccasins. Around his neck was a silver medallion presented by the Cherokee Nation in 1825 as a tribute to him for his marvelous invention of the Cherokee alphabet.

"He is of middle stature, of rather slender form. . ." reported the **Arkansas Gazette** in an early 19th century account. "His features are remarkably regular, and his face is well-formed and handsome. His eyes are animated and piercing, showing indications of a brilliancy of intellect far superior to the ordinary portion of his fellow men."

Sculptor Silvertooth's work fits written descriptions of Sequoyah - the cane, bad leg, turban, medallion, piercing gaze and noble demeanor. The figure, which holds a tablet of the alphabet, is larger than life. It also has a vague resemblance to a Karankawa Indian, but then, that's probably as it should be.

Sequoyah quite possibly would have liked Silvertooth's image, even though it's located a long, long way away from his native homeland in the mountains of present-day north Georgia.

Sequoyah was a half-blood Cherokee, born in Tennessee in 1776. His parents were Nathaniel Gist, a prominent Tennessean, and a Cherokee woman. He was raised with the Cherokees, and never learned to read English.

Sequoyah also was crippled from youth; one leg was shriveled, possibly from polio. Despite the disability, Sequoyah served nobly on the American forces in the Creek War of 1813, fighting at Horseshoe Bend with General Andrew Jackson.

Mystery & History in Georgia

Super Intellect – Born circa 1776 in the Cherokee town of Taskigi in present-day Tennessee, Sequoyah was a mixed-blood Cherokee. His creation of the Cherokee alphabet and written language can only be viewed today as an incredible achievement, and an amazing advancement for his race. *(Illustration courtesy of the Georgia Dept of Archives & History, Atlanta)*

Sequoyah eventually noted that whites communicated through the written word, and he realized that it was a powerful asset. He decided he would provide the same knowledge for the Cherokee Nation.

Developing an alphabet is extremely difficult work. Alphabets of other races were oft-times painstakingly developed over a thousand years or more, and involved many people. Sequoyah, amazingly, developed an alphabet which Cherokee-speaking peoples could master and read in a week. He, quite possibly, is the only man in history to single-handedly develop an alphabet, and especially in the short span of time which it took.

History maintains that Sequoyah's work unified the Cherokee Nation as had no other event. As a result, the Cherokees established a capitol in 1825 at New Echota, near present-day Calhoun, Georgia, and a social structure almost the equivalent of the white settlers then flooding the region.

The *Cherokee Phoenix* was the first newspaper printed in the language of the Cherokees, and the Indians used the white man's newspaper medium to battle the laws and courts in an effort to save their territorial lands. Despite heroic effort, their attempts sadly fell short.

It was also at New Echota that the "Trail of Tears" began, a process which eventually resulted in the removal of the Cherokee Nation from the Southeast. Sequoyah himself had earlier resettled in Arkansas Territory, so when his people were evicted from Georgia, he helped them to settle in the new land. He served as a spokesman in Washington for the Western tribes, and was a personal friend of Sam Houston.

Houston was a strong advocate for the Indians, particularly the Cherokee with whom he lived, on and off. He supported resettlement into Texas the displaced Indians from the East.

When Mirabeau B. Lamar became president of the Republic of Texas in 1839, he unfortunately decided to reverse Houston's Indian settlement policy. He drove the Cherokees (many of whom had settled in Texas) across the Red River, an event which resulted in numerous Cherokee Indian deaths.

A few years later in 1843, Sequoyah traveled through south Texas to visit the displaced Cherokees who had been forced into Mexico, and who were then camping near the U.S.-Mexico border in Mexico. He reportedly died there in a town recorded by the Cherokees as "Sanfernando." Unfortunately, the exact location of his gravesite in this region has been lost to history.

Early Adventures Working On The Tallulah Falls Railroad

He was a fireman on a locomotive for many years, then an engineer on the scenic Tallulah Falls Railroad which once ran between Cornelia, Georgia, and Franklin, North Carolina. The little mountain short-line is long gone today, but Hoyt Tench remembers many adventures on the fabled line.

Railroading gets into your blood. If you don't believe it, just ask Rev. Hoyt Tench of Cornelia, Georgia, who spent thirty-eight years keeping the engines fired and the trains rolling.

Tench and his bride, Catherine Dalton, were married May 27, 1939. He admits to being only eighteen years of age at the time. "And you're not supposed to ask how old my bride was," he says, his eyes a-twinkle.

Her father, Beecher Dalton, was employed by the Stewart and Jones Company and Doubletrack, and worked in railroad construction. Mr. Dalton's work on the Tallulah Falls (TF) Railway made it possible for a young Hoyt Tench to be one of the first to know when an employment opening existed.

In 1942, an engineer transferred from the Tallulah Falls Railroad to the Southern Railroad. A fireman was promoted to engineer and an opening was suddenly available for a new fireman. Hoyt Tench "hired on," beginning a railroading career which lasted until 1980, a total of thirtyeight years.

Of course all of those thirty-eight years weren't spent on the Tallulah Falls line, since it went out of business in 1961, but for nineteen of those 38 railroad years, Tench said he had many adventures on the old TF.

Early Disaster

The first day on the Tallulah Falls Railroad almost became the last for young Tench. It began with the new fireman shoveling coal into a cart which he then rolled to the train and dumped into the engine tender (coal car). This effort was repeated four or five times until enough coal was loaded to make the trip from Cornelia, Georgia, to Franklin, North Carolina and back.

Once the coal loading was completed, the engineer next began teaching young Tench all the things he needed to observe and do during the trip. The duties included watching the tracks ahead to make sure no obstructions were on

The Rev. Hoyt O. Tench spent thirty-eight years as an employee on the railroads of north Georgia, a large portion of which was spent on the Tallulah Falls Railroad. He is pictured here with wife, Catherine Dalton.

them, as well as looking backward to insure that none of the boxcars had jumped the track or developed "hot boxes" in the wheel bearings.

Shortly thereafter on his first trip, Tench found himself making numerous interesting stops along the way at spots like Clarkesville, Demorest, Lakemont, Tiger, Clayton, Mountain City, Dillard, and on and on until they reached Franklin, North Carolina. There, the engine was turned around, the box cars were disengaged and parked for removal by another later train, and new cars were hooked to the engine for the return trip home to Cornelia.

As the train moved southward, it soon passed back through the little hamlet of Mountain City in northern Rabun County, Georgia. The train picked up speed, entered a curve, and then suddenly began to shake and rattle like an earthquake.

A backward glance by the new fireman revealed a sight which would strike terror in the hearts of even the most inveterate of railroad men. Dust was flying, cars were bouncing, and a derailment seemed imminent.

Tench immediately alerted the engineer who gradually slowed the train to a halt. Miraculously, only one boxcar had jumped the track, and it had remained hooked to the other boxcars. The task now was one of getting the heavy derailed boxcar back onto the tracks.

Crew members, accustomed to the chore, began removing huge jacks – specially designed for this purpose – from the train. It took hours of "jacking and chocking," "jacking and chocking," until the errant boxcar could again be "righted" onto the tracks, and the train allowed to proceed.

By the time the train reached Cornelia, Hoyt Tench had just about decided that railroading was a job he'd be happy to let someone else do. The work was too hard. The hours were too long. There was too much to learn, and it was very dangerous. After a good supper at home and a much-needed night of rest, however, he decided to give it another try.

The second day was much less eventful. The instructions and duties didn't seem quite so formidable this time out either. Thus began a railroad career spanning a time period from the second World War to the 1980s.

Hospitality On The Rails

Neighborliness has long been a characteristic of north Georgians. This sense of camaraderie and compassion was demonstrated many times by the people who lived along the rails, as well as by the railroad men themselves.

When a wreck or derailment occurred, citizens living nearby rushed to the scene to render whatever aid could be given. In cases of injury, neighbors along the tracks were the first to summon help and render first aid.

Sometimes the roles were reversed too. Train workers on one occasion noted that certain families living near the

Working On The Tallulah Falls Railroad — Habersham County

The Panther Creek trestle on the Tallulah Falls Railroad was considered one of the most hair-raising, but the Wiley trestle (pictured above in 1939) with its five decks, was by far the most dangerous.

tracks were clad in threadbare clothing and some children didn't have shoes, even on the coldest days of winter as they waved to the train crew.

Inquiring about the children, crew members learned that they were not in school because of inadequate clothing. The good-hearted trainmen discreetly learned the number of children, the ages, sex and approximate sizes of each, then purchased clothing and had it distributed to the children. Santa Claus was an exciting event that year – for both parents and children at this spot.

Dealing With Danger

During the years the Tallulah Falls Railroad was in service, numerous frightening events occurred. Hoyt Tench, though much more fortunate than most, witnessed his share of accidents and natural disasters.

One disaster in which he thankfully

The weakened wooden bridge over the creek, unable to support the weight of the train, collapsed, spilling the engine and its crew to the ground.

was not involved, occurred on February 7, 1927, when one of the Tallulah Falls trains was passing over the high trestle over Hazel Creek. The weakened wooden bridge over the creek, unable to support the weight of the train, collapsed,

Mystery & History in Georgia

Accidents were an accepted hazard of the trade in railroading. This derailment on August 23, 1920, of the TF south of Tiger was responsible for the death of the engineer, and the fireman was badly injured. The train was carrying children to a summer camp, and the accident was instrumental in the eventual permanent cancellation of passenger service on the TF. *(Photo courtesy of GA Dept. of Archives & History, Atlanta)*

A Tallulah Falls freight train was photographed near Demorest, Georgia in 1951. *(Photo courtesy of Goldman Kimbrell)*

spilling the engine and its crew to the ground. Three people were killed.

The accident undoubtedly would have been even more disastrous had not a piece of timber fallen across the whistle arm, releasing steam from the engine. It otherwise, undoubtedly would have exploded, according to Tench.

The engine – though severely damaged – was retrieved by a wrecker, rebuilt and placed back into service. Hoyt Tench was fireman for this rebuilt engine (#73) for a period of time.

On a return trip from Franklin on another occasion, Tench and his crew experienced a scare similar to the trestle-spill of Engine 73. As they approached the high trestle just north of Dillard, everything appeared to be in very good order, but in the middle of the trestle, a loud pop sounded as the train was passing over it. The engine gave a lurch, but the entire train passed over safely.

A repair crew dispatched to the trestle site discovered that a main supporting timber had indeed snapped. If the train had been heavily loaded as it crossed, the entire trestle would no doubt have collapsed, spilling the train and causing a loss of life as had occurred with #73.

Another experience vivid in Hoyt Tench's memory – and he had many of them – happened during a severe thunderstorm one summer afternoon. The train was returning from Franklin. Lightning flashed constantly.

Suddenly, a huge bolt of lightning struck some distance ahead of the train, then something akin to a "ball of fire" began traveling up the rails straight toward the engine. The tremendous charge reportedly passed over the driver wheels on the engine and continued along the entire train – as if it followed the rails until it reached a wheel – then flashed up, over and down the wheels, and on over the rails, continuing until it had run the entire length of the train, then continuing on beyond it farther down the rails.

Miraculously, neither engineer nor fireman was injured. At the next stop, Tench and the engineer talked to other crew members. They, too, had witnessed the phenomenon and equally amazingly were not harmed by the lightning. Amazingly, no damage was suffered by the train either.

Working On The Tallulah Falls Railroad   Habersham County

A Tallulah Falls Railroad diesel-electric mail car or "Dinky" is being loaded in downtown Cornelia in the early 1950s. *(Photo courtesy of Thomas Frier)*

The dinky was photographed in 1953 on Queen's trestle just south of Mountain City in Rabun County. *(Photo by R.D. Sharpless, from the collection of Frank Ardrey, Jr.)*

Pranks On The Rails

"Boys will be boys," as the saying goes. Some who lived along the railroad tracks delighted in a past-time that was as dangerous and troublesome for the train crew as it was exciting and fun for the little trouble-makers who initiated it.

The deed was usually performed on a portion of the rails that were slightly inclined up a slope. Such places were easy to find along the mountainous terrain of the Tallulah Falls Railroad. Slight inclines were common through the mountains of north Georgia and North Carolina which was the route of the TF.

Once the spot was located, the mischief-makers applied grease to the rails for a short distance. Of course, the quantity of grease necessary to achieve the wheels slippage wasn't that easy to come by from the 1930s through the 1950s, so the prank often was tell-tale for the perpetrators.

If the next train traveling the tracks was heavily loaded or proceeding slowly, the engine would immediately lose traction when the wheels hit the grease, and stall. In order to extract the train from the slick rails, the engineer had two choices. He could either reverse the engine, back it up a considerable distance on the tracks and then try to gain enough momentum to pass over the grease, or he could stop the train so that the crewmen could wipe the grease off the rails and place dirt on them for traction.

Runaway Engine

Cold weather always presented special problems on the Tallulah Falls Railroad. Crew members had to check equipment to insure that it was in tiptop shape. They examined signal lights, signal flags, switch controls and the mechanism of the engines as well.

When bitter cold weather arrived, it was necessary for a crew member to remain on duty at night to keep all the engines fired so the water in them would not freeze (antifreeze being still somewhat in the future in those days). One man was always assigned to watch over the engines parked in the yard at night.

On one particularly cold night, Hoyt Tench had railroad yard-watch duty. About halfway between midnight and dawn, he returned from checking each engine and was warming himself by a coal-fired heater.

Suddenly, Tench said he heard a strange sound and opened his door to listen. All, however, seemed quiet. He closed the door and returned to his heater. Again the sound came. He opened the door again and walked a few steps

Mystery & History in Georgia

Photographed March 25, 1961, the final year the Tallulah Falls Railroad was in operation, engineer Goldman Kimbrell smiles down from the cab of one of the line's diesel-electric engines. *(Photo courtesy of Goldman Kimbrell)*

into the train yard. The sound came a third time, and this time, Tench recognized it immediately. One of the engines, amazingly, was moving out of the yard!

"Somebody's trying to steal an engine," he thought, trying to decide what to do. But then, as he peered closer at the engine, he realized there was no one at the controls.

Tench then exercised the only option available to him. He made a quick dash to catch up with the locomotive, climbing into the cab as the engine gained momentum. He applied the brakes immediately, and the engine slowed to a stop.

Once it was halted, Tench released the brakes as was customary, and was amazed to see the engine lunge forward again, even though he had not touched the throttle. Quickly checking the device, he discovered that the throttle had been moved from the park position. He repositioned it back into park and waited. After a few moments, the engine again moved forward, and Tench realized that a valve in the throttle mechanism was leaking, thus allowing the engine to move.

As he made temporary repairs to the controls to make certain the engine was stable, he broke out into a cold sweat. He realized what havoc might have occurred had that engine moved onto the main line and met another train, or had it struck a vehicle or person at a crossing or derailed while advancing too swiftly into a curve.

Other Dangers

"Blow-up" can be a somewhat confusing railroad term. As a fireman, Tench's job was to keep the firebox hot enough to produce steam to run the train. On steep grades like those from Lakemont to Tiger, the train sometimes had to be stopped so the fireman could "double." To stop and get up double steam is known as "blowing up" (building up the steam for steep inclines).

A fireman's reputation hung on how few times he had to stop the train to blow up steam. Fireman Tench remembers one such instance in which he almost overdid his responsibilities.

"One day, Jim Brown and I got Engine 75 too hot," he recalled. "The engine walls never did cave in, but back in the yards at Cornelia, Noah Ward, the boiler man, had to fix all the stay bolts because they were so weak from the excessive steam (pressure) from that Tiger (Georgia) pull.

"You see, there were spaces, just like a wall (on the inside periphery of the big boiler on the engine)," he explained. "The firebox was on the inside, and there was a wall between it and the

Working On The Tallulah Falls Railroad   Habersham County

Train #501 with its diesel-electric engine travels north across Tallulah Lake circa 1950s. In the foreground is the old Highway 441 bridge which still exists today in Tallulah Gorge State Park. Though the rails were removed long ago, the large concrete piers pictured on the Tallulah Lake railroad bridge also still exist today in Tallulah Lake. *(Photo courtesy of Buck Snyder)*

water which generated the steam when heated, and then a wall between the water and the outside," he said. "Water and steam were around that stay bolt, too, that went from one sheet (of metal on the outside) to the other (on the inside of the firebox). We almost burned the stay bolts in the crown sheet, and water was leaking all in the firebox on my fire. That's when we almost blew up the engine literally. We managed somehow to get it back into Cornelia without having an explosion."

Traveling over the many trestles between Cornelia, Georgia, and Franklin, North Carolina, was a perilous experience too. "They always said the Panther Creek trestle was the highest, but I think the Wiley trestle was the most dangerous and boogerish-looking, because it had five decks," Tench explained.

It was on the Wiley Trestle that the cab on the TF once jumped the tracks. It went on running right across the crossties according to Mr. Tench. "We just braked it light and let it come to a stop," he noted with a smile. "It never did get off the trestle.

"Mr. John Snyder was the conductor that day; Brawner Walker was the

We almost burned the stay bolts in the crown sheet, and water was leaking all in the firebox on my fire.

brakeman and Alec Dillard was the flagman. We used the 're-railers' to get the cab back on the tracks. As you might imagine, there was very little room to work on that trestle – it was so narrow. And one mistake could have sent men and train plummeting down into the gorge. It was scary and dangerous as all getout."

Another danger to the railroading men, especially to the fireman, was what was known as "getting a monkey." In the peak-heat summer months, the heat in the engine and near the firebox could reach horrendous proportions, causing a condition known today as heat exhaustion or heatstroke. Symptoms included delirium, hallucinations and other serious disabilities. "But back then, we just knew it made people go crazy. That's why we called it 'getting a monkey,' I guess," Tench remembered. "You might see snakes, monkeys or all manner of other things."

Changing Times

Hoyt Tench eventually worked himself up to the position of engineer. Technology was changing about that time, and steam power was giving way to diesel.

On March 25, 1961, the Tallulah Falls Railroad ceased operation – a victim of its own good service. Highways had been built back into the mountains allowing trucking firms to move products and merchandise more inexpensively and more precisely. The timber had all been harvested and transported to mills by the TF until the supply was exhausted.

Finally, in the 1950s, passenger service was discontinued on the line, and the fabled railroad eventually was unable to generate enough income to support itself.

Hoyt Tench moved on, working as an engineer for the Southern Railroad. He also became an ordained minister in 1948, managing two careers until his retirement from the railroad.

Not much remains of the old line today. The old depots that do still remain intact may be seen at Cornelia, Tallulah Falls, and Demorest.

The Demorest TF depot was used as a film site for one of the scenes in the major motion picture *I'd Climb The Highest Mountain*, shot in 1950 around Cleveland, Georgia, and starring Susan Hayward, Rory Calhoun, and William Lundigan. The TF's steam engine # 75 was brought out of retirement so that it might steam across the steel trestle over Lake Tallulah for film scenes used in the movie's opening credits.

The diesel mail/ express unit was purchased and placed by old US 441 north of Clayton by a local entrepreneur originally intending to open a diner.

A former TF caboose along with other memorabilia is on display at Cornelia; another former caboose is on display on a short piece of grade in Tallulah Falls. The diesel mail/express unit was purchased and placed by old US 441 north of Clayton by a local entrepreneur originally intending to open a diner.

Now that it is gone, the captivating Tallulah Falls Railroad has captured the public attention, and virtually any memorabilia associated with the former line is now a collectible.

Sadly, so scenic was the Tallulah Falls Railroad that no lesser a person than showman/television and movie impresario Walt Disney himself attempted to purchase the line after it had ceased operations. Disney reportedly had big plans to develop a rough equivalent to Orlando's *Walt Disney World* in the scenic north Georgia mountains, but the individuals controlling the TF bankruptcy proceedings turned down his offer. Just think of what might have occurred if that had come to pass.

Remembering Historic Tallulah Falls Railroad

It was one of the most scenic railroads in the entire eastern United States, and was in operation for over half a century, but poor decisions and even poorer funding eventually spelled doom for the fabled rail line.

For over half a century (54 years to be precise), an exceedingly scenic mountain railroad short-line called the Tallulah Falls Railroad (TF) operated continuously through some of the most rugged and beautiful mountain vistas in the entire eastern United States, connecting Cornelia, Georgia, with Franklin, North Carolina. Though many people are not aware of it today, the north Georgia region – and indeed the entire state – lost an exceptional opportunity, as well as a unique way of life, when the final train on this little rail line whistled its way into oblivion on March 25, 1961.

Actually organized in 1881 (the same year as the Earps and Clantons shot it out at the O.K. Corral in Tombstone, Arizona), the Tallulah Falls Railroad was originally known as "the Rabun Gap Route," indicating the original designers fully intended all along to extend the rail line at least to the Georgia state line at North Carolina.

By 1882, track had been laid from Cornelia, Georgia, to the scenic tourist town of Tallulah Falls. Since this original portion of the route was created much earlier than the ultimately-completed route between Cornelia and Franklin, North Carolina, it therefore was also obviously in business much longer (a total of approximately 80 years) than was the completed Cornelia to Franklin route.

For many years, once the train reached Tallulah Falls on the 1882-completed portion of the route, it turned around (reversed direction) on a railroad "wye" which once existed not far from the depot, and then headed back to Cornelia. During these years, the line provided passenger service for tourists and residents, as well as freight service for the timber industry and, eventually, the supplies necessary for the lake impoundments built on the Tallulah River.

Builders of the rail line advanced its construction across the Tallulah River via a wooden trestle in 1903, and the railroad arrived in Clayton in 1904. In subsequent years, track was laid to Rabun Gap and then on to Otto and Franklin, North Carolina.

Though most of this former line has disappeared completely from the landscape today, significant portions of the old rail bed can still be seen if one knows

Mystery & History in Georgia

For many years after the bankruptcy of the Tallulah Falls Railroad (TF), Caboose #5 was still lovingly maintained behind the old Southern Railway Depot in Cornelia by a railway equipment dealer.

Pictured here is a section of the former TF track which still stretches approximately two miles between Cornelia and Demorest, Georgia. It has occasionally been used in recent years as a storage area for various incidentals by other railroads.

where to look. Today, some history and railroad buffs like to retrace the route of this historic line, imagining what life in northeast Georgia would be like if it were still in existence.

Many old-timers in northeastern Georgia who remember the TF speak almost reverently of this famed shortline whose familiar and dependable trains made daily runs through Demorest, Clarkesville, Hollywood, Turnerville, Tallulah Falls, Lakemont, Wiley, Tiger, Clayton, Passover, Mountain City, Rabun Gap, Dillard, Otto, and on to Franklin, North Carolina. Veterans of the line included individuals like Roy Shope of Rabun Gap, former trestle foreman, and Carl Rogers of Dillard, former station agent at Clayton. Just as did many others, they mourned the loss of this once dynamic railroad, and the familiar dependable service it brought to the mountain towns.

Though now completely erased from the landscape, most of the former locations of the 42 wooden trestles which once dotted the 58 miles of track on the TF could still be easily be pointed out by the likes of Shope and Rogers. According to them, it was the expense of the maintenance of these trestles, coupled with other factors, which were major causes for the demise of the line.

Long stretches of the old roadbed – in various states of erosion or abandonment (or erased completely by new development) – can still be seen across three counties, clearly visible in some spots, and virtually lost in the undergrowth in others. The Tallulah Falls roadbed, sadly, was never embraced by such preservation-minded groups as the *Rails To Trails* Conservancy which has preserved hundreds of other railroad beds of lesser beauty and magnificence nationwide in hiking and biking trails.

Had it been preserved, the former route of the old TF undoubtedly would have provided one of the most remarkably scenic *Rails To Trails* opportunities in the eastern U.S. One short portion near the rail line's namesake town of Tallulah Falls thankfully has been preserved by Georgia State Parks, but it is the lone surviving segment.

Remnants more tangible than the faded roadbeds could also be found until just recently at numerous points along the old route. Just behind the neat

The only steel and concrete trestle on the TF stretched over Tallulah Lake, the concrete pylons of which may still be seen in the lake today. It was the constant expensive maintenance requirements of the many wooden trestles on the line which eventually contributed heavily to its demise.

The former Tallulah Falls Railroad Depot in Demorest is one of only two which still remain intact from the former line. It served as the location for the filming of the opening scene in the major motion picture *I'd Climb The Highest Mountain* in 1950, starring Hollywood stars Susan Hayward, Rory Calhoun, and William Lundigan. It may still be viewed in that movie footage today.

former Southern Railway station at Cornelia, Georgia, the bright red TF Caboose #5 was lovingly maintained for many years by a railway equipment dealer with TF roots. Its location today is unknown.

Another portion of now-unused weed-choked TF track – though unprotected – still stretches (as of this writing) for about two miles out of Cornelia toward Demorest. It is unknown who owns this historic stretch today. Much of the remainder of the roadbed of the line between these two communities, however, has been buried beneath new state highways.

The old TF station in Demorest – one of only two remaining – silently awaits an entrepreneurial investor to bring it back to life. It, interestingly, has been amply preserved for posterity by serving as the movie location for the opening scene of the major motion picture *I'd Climb the Highest Mountain*, filmed in 1950 around nearby Cleveland and Helen, Georgia, by famed Hollywood director Henry King. It starred Susan Hayward, William Lundigan, Gene Lockhart, Barbara Bates,

Alexander Knox, and young rising star Rory Calhoun (all now deceased).

In the opening segment of this scene at the Demorest Depot, the Tallulah Falls Railroad locomotive (subbing for the movie locomotive) pulls slowly into the station. As of this writing, this historic depot – its Hollywood legacy seemingly forgotten – has essentially been abandoned.

The scenic town of Tallulah Falls, formerly one of the most splendid resorts in the eastern U.S., has the only *other* remaining depot. Today, this substantial tile-roofed former station still stands proudly at its original site alongside U.S. Highway 441 in this former resort town, and is one of the most visible – as well as best-preserved – landmarks of the railroad.

Back in its heydays, the northward-constructed TF tracks, clinging at one point to the very rim of the rugged Tallulah Falls Gorge – north Georgia's answer to the Grand Canyon – was an awe-inspiring ride before the train pulled into the TF station at Tallulah

Mystery & History in Georgia

The depot in Tallulah Falls was photographed here shortly after a tornado had torn some of the tiles from its roof. It was quickly repaired and is still a popular shop and tourist attraction today.

Falls. Visitors to the now historic "Scenic Overlook Loop" off Highway 441 just prior to entering Tallulah Falls can still look down in amazement at the beauty and majesty of the gorge rim section of the old railroad.

Although many of the tiles were ripped off the roof of the Tallulah Falls Depot by a disastrous tornado in March of 1994, the remainder of the sturdy structure stood firm. The current owners of the aged depot – which today is used as a unique gift shop – thankfully quickly restored it.

This former bastion on the line still boasts its station sign, and even the original chalkboard announcing the arrival and departure times of the trains. Period photographs and local paintings of the site in days gone by have captured and preserved the former activity of the locomotives which once dominated this station.

North of the Tallulah Falls Depot, the railroad at one time literally leaped over the little village via a huge wooden trestle, before crossing over Tallulah Lake on rails supported by huge concrete piers and then plunging into the woods on the opposite side. The five towering concrete piers and abutments remain today in what once represented the only steel and concrete bridge on the line – 585 feet long and 100 feet high – built when Georgia Power impounded the Tallulah River and formed Tallulah Falls Lake.

A historic marker with old photos of the TF has been permanently emplaced on the roadbed at the point at which the railroad once transitioned from the steel and concrete bridge back onto terra firma (at the north end of the high bridge piers across Tallulah Falls Lake). From there, the roadbed – still visible through the forest – twists around several hills as it climbs up-grade through Lakemont and Tiger on its way to Clayton.

Some years ago, the old Lakemont Depot was purchased and removed to a site on Lake Rabun where it was put to new use as a summer home. It is unfortunate that it could not have been preserved at its original location in Lakemont, just as have a number of the original Lakemont commercial buildings which have survived, and which today serve as unique shops and businesses in that quaint historic mountain fiefdom.

A similar fate befell the old Clayton, Georgia TF depot, which was demolished for commercial development sometime after the line ceased operations in 1961. Prior to its removal, the Clayton Depot was used as a film site for yet another major motion picture on the TF line – *The Great Locomotive Chase* (1957) – starring Fess Parker, Jeffrey Hunter, Slim Pickens and others. It was filmed in Clayton and on more northern sections of the Tallulah Falls line near Otto, North Carolina, by *Walt Disney Productions*, with the famed creator of Disneyland and major motion pictures himself actually visiting the site in 1956.

One of the "Disney boxcars,"

imported for the movie and then left behind after filming was completed, could still be found south of Clayton for many years. Other remnants of the railroad can also still be seen if one knows where to look today.

Disney, who had a definite appreciation for historic and scenic rail lines, reportedly toyed with the idea of purchasing and preserving the entire scenic Tallulah Falls Railroad line – and he obviously had the financial backing to do it – but the plan fell through for a number of ironic reasons. Had that idea reached fruition, tranquil Rabun County might today resemble the likes of Anaheim, California, or Orlando, Florida, instead of the current sleepy confines of Clayton, Georgia. Some people would have been happy with that. Others would not.

At north Clayton, the body of the gasoline-powered motor car which had performed yeoman service as the railroad's passenger train when the steam locomotives were not running, had been recycled into a unique private home for many years by one enterprising resident, but its status as of this writing is unknown.

Unbeknownst by many of the rail line's enthusiasts, a "phantom" railroad – begun in the 1850s and once planned to be routed through the outskirts of Clayton – played a vital role during the original construction of the TF. At this juncture, builders of the TF encountered – and happily made use of – a short stretch of the roadbed of the legendary, and abandoned, *Black Diamond Railroad*, also once known as the *Blue Ridge Railroad*.

The Black Diamond/Blue Ridge was financed by John C. Calhoun, the fiery Civil War-era senator and former vice president of the United States from

The very scenic Lakemont depot on the Tallulah Falls Railroad was photographed here in the 1930s after either a dusting of snow or sleet. Some years after the TF had ceased operations, this depot was removed to one of the lots on nearby Lake Rabun for use as a summer home. A few of the historic commercial buildings in Lakemont survived into the 21st Century, and have been renovated into popular summer shops today. *(Photo courtesy of GA Dept. of Archives & History, Atlanta)*

South Carolina. Calhoun wanted the rail line to connect Charleston, South Carolina, with Cincinnati, Ohio, in order to redouble the commercial growth of his state. Though most of the infrastructure of the rail line was completed, bankruptcy (just as with the TF) and the U.S. Civil War succeeded in killing the Black Diamond in the tri-state area before any rails were laid. Today, several partially-completed railway tunnels and portions of the old railroad bed can still be found near Clayton.

Though the TF itself had no tunnels, it had numerous expensive wooden trestles. Roy Shope worked for the TF for 21 years, much of it as the bridge foreman and as a brakeman. "We could have filled in many of those (42 trestles) for less cost than it took to maintain them," he lamented. "I don't know why the railroad never did that.

"We had seven men who worked on the trestles between Cornelia and Franklin," he continued. "Toward the end, they cut them all off (released them)

Mystery & History in Georgia

A Tallulah Falls freight train was photographed near Demorest, Georgia in 1951. *(Photo courtesy of Goldman Kimbrell)*

before they stopped running (ceased operations), and that left only me."

Roy says he'll never forget the time several boxcars loaded with heavy pulpwood derailed atop the trestle just south of Mountain City. "Two or three cars went off, but they didn't hurt the bridge," he explained. "We didn't have a wrecker like the big railroads, so we had to use manpower and Norton jacks to raise them a few inches at a time."

At Rabun Gap, a remarkably well-preserved piece of roadbed embankment – at one time kept in topnotch condition by its owner as a memorial to the TF – is still clearly visible (as of this writing), marking where this section of the railroad crossed a field on its way to Mountain City.

From Mountain City to Franklin, the TF roadbed parallels the east side of Route 23. However, in many places, it swings far out away from the highway. At other spots, new development has shaved the roadbed down to the point that it is barely recognizable.

The Georgia Power Company played a large role in the life of the TF. Five separate branch lines off the TF were built by the big utility company to reach the new hydroelectric power plants being constructed to take advantage of the waters dammed behind several different impoundments along the course of the Tallulah River. Georgia Power was also responsible for the construction of the railroad's only non-wood trestle spanning the Tallulah Falls Lake.

As previously mentioned, the maintenance of the many trestles along the route was a constant (and some say unnecessary) financial drain on the TF. On most larger railroads, trestles were laid across the low spots during the initial construction of the lines, then those spots were gradually filled in as time passed to create a permanent raised roadbed. That practice apparently was too much of a luxury for the TF.

The routinely-destructive mishaps and wrecks – often occurring as a result of collapsing trestles – eventually took a toll. And then there was the fact that the TF literally hauled in the supplies to build the new highways and hauled out the natural resources – such as timber and mining products – until they were exhausted, to eventually put itself out of business.

Passenger service (or the lack thereof) on the TF played a lesser role in the line's eventual bankruptcy, but had an impact nonetheless. Even though the service was important to area residents and tourists, the income generated by passengers was minimal – yet it still helped to pay the bills. In 1946, however, passenger service was abruptly discontinued forever on the line following a crossing accident with a truck that broke several coach windows, spraying the startled passengers with broken glass. For the next fifteen years, the TF operated without any passenger service income whatsoever.

This somewhat dramatic photograph shows a Tallulah Falls train at Wiley Junction in 1939. Today, this immense picturesque trestle - just like most of the rest of the Tallulah Falls Railroad - has disappeared completely from the landscape. *(Photo courtesy of GA Dept. of Archives & History, Atlanta)*

The TF flirted with several brief insolvencies before it slipped permanently into its final bankruptcy in 1923 – well in advance of the *Great Depression*. It continued in financial limbo for the remainder of its life – another 38 years – until the line's credit was exhausted.

In 1961, the TF suffered its final indignity when a scrap dealer brought in heavy equipment to rip out the rails from the ties one by one, and then truck them out to be melted down for other products. When the rails disappeared, there was no question that the line was finished forever.

The day after the final run of the old TF was a sad day indeed for area residents all up and down the former route of the line. No whistle sounded any longer as no trains approached a station or road crossing. No staccato chant of the steam escaping the locomotive's jets met the ears anymore. The train which, since 1907, had daily chugged up and down the beautiful hills and around the majestic curves and precipices of the mountains of northeast Georgia from Cornelia to Franklin, North Carolina, and then back again, was no more.

Sometimes, on bitterly cold nights, the wind can be heard blowing through the Tallulah Falls Gorge. If one listens real close, interspersed with the whistling wind, the dull staccato chant of a steam locomotive can almost still be heard once again - almost.

By all accounts, the old Tallulah Falls Railroad is dead and gone, but according to some grassroots research, there are a lot of folks who, if given the latitude, would bring it back in an instant!

The Tallulah Falls Firestorm of 1921

In the late 1800s and early 1900s, Tallulah Falls in northeast Georgia carried a cachet as a top tourist destination in the Southeast, but when the waters of the Tallulah River were impounded to generate electricity for Atlanta in 1912, the huge waterfall was silenced, seriously damaging the site as a tourism attraction. When a monstrous fire swept through the town on a cold winter night in 1921, the site's attraction as a tourism destination was basically completely destroyed.

Prior to the burgeoning electrical needs of Atlanta, Georgia, at the turn of the 19th century which required the Georgia Power Company to generate more electricity, the small community of Tallulah Falls in northeast Georgia had evolved into one of the top tourist attractions in the Southeast. It was not long, however, before the dream came to a screeching halt, when the waters of the river were impounded, silencing the dramatic waterfall, and a huge fire swept through the community, burning most of it to the ground.

Prior to the above disasters, the impressive whitewater created by the crashing Tallulah River was awe-inspiring in its day, and tourists were drawn to the site in droves. Magnificent hotels and mountain inns were built all along the precipice of the huge gorge through which the falls thundered, and all manner of entertainment was created for the many tourists which flocked to the site.

But the city of Atlanta needed more electricity, and part of the answer lay in water-generated electrical power such as that which could be provided by lake impoundments and generation plants on the Tallulah River. And then one cold night in December of 1921, despite the fact that the town and its hospitality industry had already been dealt a severe blow when the falls were choked off by electrical development, a huge fire decimated the remaining commercial infrastructure of Tallulah Falls completely, sweeping through the town and burning with abandon most of the hotels along the precipice of the gorge – even incinerating the huge wooden trestle over the town which carried the scenic and vital Tallulah Falls Railroad.

The devastation wrought by the terrible fire in 1921 sounded the death knell of this fabled and scenic mountain community. It was a devastating blow to the acclaimed resort – one from which Tallulah Falls has never recovered.

In The Beginning

No description of the devastating fire of 1921 would be complete without an accounting of the four decades of immense development which had preceded the fire. Tallulah Falls had blossomed as a tourist mecca from 1882 – the year the Tallulah Falls Railroad first chugged into town – until 1912, when the falls were silenced by electrical generation, and then withered and died in 1921, the year of the fire.

Though other factors were already negatively impacting the town's tourism economy by 1921 (such as the dams built on the Tallulah River by Georgia Power Company), the community of Tallulah Falls had continued to persevere – albeit at a dramatically-reduced level – because of the still-grand hotels which had continued to beckon invitingly from the top of the gorge.

Tucked away in the northeast corner of the state, the popularity of Tallulah Falls had grown progressively, thanks to word-of-mouth publicity and writers such as David Hillhouse whose account of the falls was widely published in the United States. Assisting this growth was a new trail which had been cut through the forested mountainsides of northern Habersham County, facilitating access to the site by a new mode of travel – the automobile.

Despite the lure of the site in its earliest days, many travelers found they needed a guide just to find their way to the falls, such was the nature of the trackless and untamed mountain wilderness, but still they came – in droves. According to researcher and educator Dr. John Saye in his *The Life And Times Of Tallulah. . . . the Falls, the Gorge, the Town* (available in shops in Tallulah Falls), "*By 1840, visits to the falls by groups of men, women, and even children had become

Photographed shortly after the huge fire which had destroyed the town of Tallulah Falls, the Tallulah Falls Railroad crews had quickly rebuilt the huge trestle over the town – such was the importance of the daily income to the line. *(Photo courtesy of GA Dept. of Archives & History, Atlanta)*

quite common.*" By conservative estimates, nearly 2,000 visitors reportedly had journeyed to the falls in the remote corner of northeast Georgia by 1877.

Perhaps Tallulah Falls' resort era actually began in 1870 with the construction of the Shirley Hotel on the brow of the gorge. Just a year later, the hotel began expanding to handle the increasing numbers of visitors. With two more hotels built during the 1870s, the resort's popularity as a travel destination seemed to be assured for the foreseeable future. But there were clouds on the horizon which no one expected.

The Tallulah Falls Railroad

The next decade witnessed the arrival of a convenience which brought "boom-times" to the town of Tallulah Falls – the railroad. By the 1880s, travelers no longer were required to brave the rough trip to the falls via a mountain trail. The Tallulah Falls Railroad had been completed to the rim of the gorge, making the destination even more appealing.

Actually organized in 1881 (the same year as the Earps and Clantons shot it out at the O.K. Corral in Tombstone,

The Cliff House, contrary to many modern-day accounts, was one of the few large mountain inns at Tallulah Falls which amazingly were not destroyed by the fire. It, nevertheless, did fall victim to a fire several years later, and also was not rebuilt. It appears to be hosting a large group of youngsters in this photo. *(Photo courtesy of GA Dept. of Archives & History, Atlanta)*

Engine #77 of the Tallulah Falls Railroad was purchased by the line in 1923, indicating this photograph was taken after the fire of 1921, and confirming the existence of the Cliff House following the 1921 conflagration. Pictured in the left edge of the photo is the Cliff House and in the right edge, the Tallulah Falls Depot. *(Photo courtesy of GA Dept. of Archives & History, Atlanta)*

Arizona), the Tallulah Falls Railroad was originally known as "the Rabun Gap Route," indicating the original designers fully intended in its early stages to extend the rail line at least to the Georgia state line at North Carolina, and undoubtedly further.

By 1882, track had been laid from Cornelia, Georgia, to Tallulah Falls. Accordingly, this original portion of the route was created much earlier (circa 1882) than the ultimately-completed route between Cornelia and Franklin, North Carolina, and therefore was also obviously in business much longer (a total of approximately 80 years) than was the completed Cornelia to Franklin route. It, coupled with the huge hotels at the falls, became the life-blood of the tourism industry at Tallulah Falls.

For many years, once the train reached Tallulah Falls on the 1882-completed portion of the route, it turned around (reversed direction) on a railroad "wye" which once existed not far from the depot, and then headed back to Cornelia. During these years, the line provided passenger service for tourists and residents, as well as freight service for the timber industry and, eventually, the supplies necessary for the lake impoundments built on the Tallulah River.

Builders of the rail line advanced its construction across the Tallulah River via a wooden trestle in 1903, and the railroad arrived in Clayton in 1904. In subsequent years, track was laid to Rabun Gap and then on to Franklin, North Carolina.

Many early travelers to Tallulah Falls came by train (L&N Railroad) from Atlanta and Athens to Cornelia, Georgia, where they changed trains, boarding the Tallulah Falls train. An hour and fifteen minutes later, they stepped off at the community of Tallulah Falls.

A variety of hotels at the falls offered accommodations for travelers. Author John Saye describes it this way:

"At its peak, there were seventeen hotels and boarding houses in and around town. Guests could stay in a large, grand hotel, or in a small, intimate establishment. They could stay in the heart of the bustling little town, or in the peaceful forest surrounding Tallulah Falls."

From 1882 to 1904, the railroad ended at Tallulah Falls, and the area's

The Tallulah Falls Firestorm Of 1921

The Tallulah Falls City Hall exists today where a three-story automobile service garage once existed. The great fire of 1921 began in this garage.

The J.D. Harvey store, one of numerous businesses destroyed in the fire once existed on this site.

tourist industry thrived. However, some seventeen years later in 1921, the community literally went up in smoke.

A Windstorm & A Fire

"I have never seen nor heard the wind blow so hard as it did that night," said Bertha Burrell, a Tallulah Falls resident. "That windstorm carried burning bark and shingles as far away as Tugalo." Bertha had arrived home from Athens Normal School for the holidays and hadn't even unpacked.

Drucy Turpen remembered the fire all too well too. "We lived on a hill on the other side of town. I was sleeping in the front room.

"Granny Harvey lived just below us. She came up to the house hollering that the town was burning," Drucy said sadly, tears filling her eyes at the memory. "We stood on the porch and watched it. It was just awful. It even burned the railroad trestle and my daddy's store."

Valiant town residents and businessmen put in yeoman effort to save their community. Some rang dinner bells to awaken the sleeping citizens. Others fired shots from rifles and pistols. Anything to alert and wake everyone so they at least wouldn't burn up in their homes and in the hotels.

It soon became clear, however, that there was no stopping this fire. The town of Tallulah Falls was caught "flat-footed," with virtually no fire department to speak of, so everyone soon realized that all they could do was stand back and watch their way of life go up in smoke, with flames reaching to the heavens. Never before had there been a windstorm like this in Tallulah Falls – or anyplace else as far as most of the residents were concerned.

"Most everybody lost everything," recalled a still-distraught Gussie Harvey. Her father lost a store and a car in the fire. The Maplewood Inn and the Robinson Annex and some dozen other hotels went up in flames – reduced to ashes in a matter of hours.

Culprit of the Fire

The actual cause of the inferno is still a matter of conjecture even today, but some residents apparently highly suspect one individual. Several differing accounts, however, exist.

One story maintains that a man whose car had become stuck in the mud had stopped at a local garage for help. The garage was on the street level of a

Mystery & History in Georgia

The Glenbrook Hotel – Photographed here prior to 1928, the Glenbrook was located a short distance from the old downtown area, and also survived the 1921 firestorm. It still existed – though in abandoned ruins – in recent times.

This aerial view, photographed in the 1950s, shows the immense trestle which once extended over the town of Tallulah Falls for the Tallulah Falls Railroad. This substantial wooden structure was destroyed by the 1921 fire, but was quickly rebuilt.

three-story building. The owner, who lived upstairs, reportedly had no intention of getting out in the freezing cold weather, and simply told the chilled stranger to come back later.

It was shortly after those remarks that the town went up in flames. Apparently angry at the lack of help, the stranger with the mired car is suspected by many residents of having torched the town.

"He even broke into the garage to steal what tools he needed to repair his car," says Drucy Turpen. "He then set fire to the garage to cover up the break-in."

Ironically, according to local sources, it is believed that the guilty party was himself consumed by flames several years later, when he mistakenly used gasoline instead of what he thought was kerosene to start a fire.

Regardless of the cause of the conflagration, the results were indescribably horrifying. A barn with livestock was also consumed. "I remember the screaming, mooing, and braying of those poor animals," recalled Bertha Burrell. "It was terrible." Most of the animals perished. Some were more fortunate, breaking out of the barn and racing maniacally up Main Street.

"There was no fire department in those days, and certainly no water mains," Bertha added. "People had spring water for their own use, but little else. There was nothing to do but watch the town burn. We saved our house by putting bags of cottonseed meal on the roof."

Gussie Harvey recalled the destruction of the railroad. "About half of the trestle was burned, stopping passenger service to Clayton, Georgia, and Franklin, North Carolina," she explained, still wide-eyed at the memory. "There was a freight train that came down from Franklin, so benches were put in some of the freight cars for passengers.

"I remember," continued Gussie, "my father went to town in his bare feet. He came back the next day badly blistered. He had poured CocaCola syrup all over our store to try to save it, but the fire was just too hot for the syrup."

Gussie's sister also remembered the livestock running panicked up and down the street. "Many of them just dropped dead from exhaustion, and some of the animals were on fire," she said.

After The Fire

When the smoke had cleared and the flames died down, the horror of what they faced became painfully obvious to area residents and businessmen. Little, if anything, remained, and virtually none of the hotels, inns, and businesses were rebuilt after the fire. There simply was no reason.

Although the fire was the final death blow to the town, other factors contributed to its ultimate demise. The extension of the railroad to Clayton and Franklin, North Carolina, inevitably lured visitors deeper into the mountains, causing many of them to bypass Tallulah Falls.

"Many people had been coming here from South Georgia for health reasons," explains Jim Turpen, a local Methodist minister. "Once they realized they could go even further into the mountains on the railroad, that's exactly what they did."

The construction of the massive dam just above the falls and at other sites farther upriver also completely changed the town's character. The once-mighty falls were virtually extinguished, eliminating much of the original charm and beauty of the site. The focus of leisure pursuits then shifted from the falls to fishing and lifestyles around the various lakes created behind the dams. Though that satisfied some people, the real lure of Tallulah Falls was gone.

Cost was another reason for the town's demise. In those days, few people had insurance coverage on their homes and property, and those that did were invariably caught short, since the cost of rebuilding the hotels was prohibitive – certainly more than their insurance coverage.

Guests were photographed on the porch of the Cliff House circa 1906. It was one of the few hotels to survive the fire, but succumbed to yet another conflagration several years later, supposedly ignited by sparks from a passing Tallulah Falls Railroad locomotive. *(Photo courtesy of GA Dept. of Archives & History, Atlanta)*

By the mid- to late-1930s, all of the grand hotels had completely disappeared from the brow of Tallulah Gorge. If the 1921 fire didn't get them, another fire or destructive element eventually did.

By the 1950s, passenger service had been discontinued on the Tallulah Falls Railroad, further depleting tourism to the area. And in 1961, the railroad itself ceased to exist – a victim of its own success. The transportation system which had made all of the original growth at the falls possible, had outlived its usefulness.

Ironically, the TF had made possible the construction of the dams which choked off the beautiful falls; it had transported the felled trees from the area until the logging industry expired; and it had brought in the building materials necessary for the construction of U.S. Highway 441. With the advent of the highway, trucking firms could then transport products and materials more economically and precisely than the railroad. Each year, the revenues from the Tallulah Falls Railroad became less and less until bankruptcy was inevitable.

This view of Tallulah Falls reveals a community almost devoid of human activity, suggesting the photograph may have been taken some months or years following the fire. It shows the view first seen by travelers as they reached the town from the south. *(Photo courtesy of GA Dept. of Archives & History, Atlanta)*

The Future

Today, despite its decline, Tallulah Falls still vies for a slice of the tourism pie dollars in Georgia. Travelers still want to view the beautiful gorge and the remnants of the scenic little town.

A new state park in Tallulah Falls (actually in and around Tallulah Gorge) has helped immensely. It was established in the 1990s to preserve as much of the gorge and its environs as possible for posterity. Area residents are hopeful the new park will facilitate new growth in the little town.

The community of fewer than two hundred residents (as of this writing) still welcomes tens of thousands of visitors who pause – if only briefly – to admire the gorge, and perhaps reminisce a bit about the glory days of the town of yesteryear. Also, the Georgia Power Company periodically opens the flumes on Tallulah Dam to allow the beautiful waterfalls to once again come to life.

The old Tallulah Falls Railroad depot, which somehow survived the firestorm of 1921, also escaped serious damage during a devastating tornado in the 1990s. It serves today as a crafts store, displaying the wares of local mountain crafts-persons.

Tallulah Falls School still attracts students from throughout Georgia and other states for its excellent programs, and continues to grow and expand. The area also boasts a rehabilitation center and an adult education center.

Nevertheless, unless the falls are permanently freed once again to crash and roar unrestrained into the huge gorge, recreating the wonderland which caused Indians to anoint the site as a sacred place and tourists to flock to northeast Georgia by the trainload, it is highly unlikely that this scenic spot will ever again recapture the vibrancy it enjoyed prior to the terrible fire in the winter of 1921.

Chestnut Mountain: The Early Days

Though it still shows up on maps even today, the actual original commercial district of this tiny former pioneer community disappeared long ago. Nevertheless, it is still well-known, and until 1986, included one of the oldest gristmills in the state.

An 1895 map of Hall County identifies a community there called "Chestnut Hill." Old-timers maintain that at one time, visitors to this spot could fill pockets and bags with the delicious fruit from the trees, lending an identity which has remained with this spot for the past 125 years, despite the fact the chestnut trees disappeared long ago (victims of a blight) just as the tiny town's once-vibrant little commercial district.

An old Gazette records that Chestnut Mountain was a post-village of Hall County and in 1900 reported a population of 84 – quite a difference from the better than 25,000 in the community today, and the more than 200,000 living in surrounding Hall County today. *"It is located about four and one-half miles northeast of Flowery Branch and about 14 miles from Gainesville,"* the pioneer article explained.

Chestnut Mountain, to be certain, was one of the early communities in northeast Georgia, having been settled originally as a portion of Jackson County, established in 1796. Many early marriage and deed records for this community are still found today in the Jackson County Courthouse in Jefferson.

Chestnut Mountain was among a large portion of north Georgia counties originally parceled out in the 1820 Land Lottery. It became a farming district early-on, and narrow roads through the community eventually linked Gainesville with Hoschton, Braselton and Jugtown (presentday Winder).

The first roads or lanes followed trails established ages earlier by native aboriginals. These early trails were usually little more than two or three feet wide, since the Indians traveled in single-file, one after the other. This was often by necessity, since prior to European inhabitation and the harvesting (and sometimes outright decimation) of the original timber, the virgin forests contained thick growths of immense trees and almost impenetrable undergrowth.

The early trails used by the aborigines invariably had been originally created by migrating buffalo, antelope, deer and other wildlife who followed the routes of least resistance around hills,

Mystery & History in Georgia

The tiny historic graveyard in which James Bevely Hudgins and Jane Bell Hudgins were buried is easy to miss without proper directions. *(Photo by Olin Jackson)*

mountains and across bodies of water, and these trails ultimately were adopted by the natives.

The *Federal Road*, the first vehicular route in northeast Georgia, was opened in 1805 through what today is Hall County, an area which at that time was still included in the Cherokee Nation. When this occurred, the creation of Hall County was still thirteen years in the future.

The *Federal Road* soon became the main thoroughfare for pioneer travelers from Jackson County to west Georgia and the western territories, and was vitally important to early settlers. Many of these original travelers followed this route to Vann's Ferry on the Chattahoochee River before crossing and proceeding westward on the *"Alabama Road"* or northwestward on the *Federal Road*.

Old deed records show the *Federal Road* once passed the property of Irvin Strickland, Jr., and descendants say it also crossed the property of Jesse Lott, Sr. Irvin (also spelled Ervin/Erwin) Strickland, Jr. of Chestnut Mountain was the son of Irvin, Sr. and the grandson of John Strickland.

Irvin, Sr. was married in 1807 in Jackson County, Georgia to Patsy Crow, and was enumerated in the *1820 Census of Hall County*. Loyd Strickland, the founder and owner of Crystal Farms in Chestnut Mountain, is a descendant of this family.

Jesse Lott, Sr. was born in 1771 in South Carolina, and died in Hall County in 1854. He was married to Nancy Martin who was born in Ireland. When Lott settled in Hall County in the Chestnut Mountain area, he bought 1,200 acres of land and an old log house which stood on the property.

In later years, Lott's house, which was two-storied, had a cellar which was

180

used as a tavern or inn. Farmers who were driving livestock to market often over-nighted at the spot, as did travelers along the road. Livestock shelters and fences were built to maintain the animals during the night.

A family story still related by Lott descendants maintains that Jesse, Jr. operated a store in the neighborhood. As the story goes, two men came in inquiring about buying meat one day. Jesse, who kept his money in a small wooden box under the stairway, was overpowered by the bandits who threw red pepper in his eyes and then robbed him.

After this experience, Jesse, according to family lore, buried his money for safekeeping. Some descendants today believe his hoard, which included gold coins, may still be buried near the old home site.

By the late 1820s, stagecoach lines operated over most of the main routes, including the route to Chestnut Mountain. Post riders, however, had begun traveling the *Federal Road* in 1819. Mail was delivered to the Carmel Mission (later called old Carmel Church and today known as Chestnut Mountain Baptist Church) and later to Chestnut Mountain on a weekly basis.

Ambrose Kennedy was named postmaster in 1865 and the old family cemetery is located along Highway 23. Kennedy was born in South Carolina and was married to Martha "Patsy" Gideon in Jackson County, Georgia. At one time he owned more than 5,000 acres in Hall and Jackson counties,

operating a tanning yard and government distillery. He also served a term as sheriff of Hall County in 1850 and represented the county at the state capital in Milledgeville from 1863 to 1865.

Ambrose and Patsy were the parents of fourteen children. Sarah Jane, a daughter, was married to a gentleman named Thomas Jefferson Benton. Sarah Jane apparently did not know her husband had served with the Union Army during the U.S. Civil War until Thomas began receiving a pension. Sarah never quite forgave her husband for that. It is said that today, a fence still divides their graves in the Kennedy Cemetery. (Sarah also believed that marriage was a permanent bond.)

Ruth Smith Waters, a noted historian, has written that Chestnut Mountain once boasted a post office, an academy, and later, a three-story high school which also housed a masonic hall. The school burned in 1940 and the principal – George Dunagan – drove three miles to summon the Gainesville Fire Department – an effort which was in vain, as the structure was nevertheless completely destroyed. Two nearby churches – Baptist and Presbyterian – were then used to house students who continued to pursue studies at the site.

Three country stores were managed by W.A. McEver, J.T. "Thomps" Reed, and J.J. "Seif" Braselton. The names "McEver" and "Braselton," obviously familiar, would later become very prominent as identities of other nearby civic endeavors in later years.

By the late 1820s, stagecoach lines operated over most of the main routes, including the route to Chestnut Mountain.

Prior to being burned by arsonists in 1986, historic Tanner's Mill was one of the oldest remaining intact gristmills in the state, and the oldest by far in Hall County. *(Photo courtesy of GA Dept. of Archives & History, Atlanta)*

A portion of Chestnut Mountain was included in Journey Cooper's farm and he planted cotton on the hill or "mountain" top. It is not known just how many mills (grist, etc.) existed from time to time in this area, but at least some of the operations were founded by Thomas Cooper and later operated by Journey. Thomas was married to Martha Meeks and son Journey married Mellie Bell.

Tanner's Mill, one of the oldest gristmills in Georgia and the oldest in Hall County, was located on the Walnut Fork of the Oconee River in the vicinity of Chestnut Mountain. It tragically was burned by vandals in 1986, erasing an important landmark forever in the blink of an eye.

Matthew Tanner, Jr. was one of the first Tanners to migrate to this section of the South, buying 250 acres in Jackson County from pioneer Elisha Winn. The property was located on both banks of the South Mulberry Fork of the Oconee River in Jackson.

A son of Matthew – David Tanner – purchased the acreage where Tanner's Mill was built. David and his wife had eleven children, four of whom fought for the Confederacy in the Civil War.

Many old family and early church cemeteries are located in the Chestnut Mountain vicinity. One is the old Liberty Church Cemetery which was first established in Jackson County (later Hall County). It is believed that Francis Bell, a veteran of the American Revolution is interred here. He was the son of Thomas Bell and the family was originally from Virginia. Today, the grave of Francis Bell is unmarked, but many of his descendants in this same cemetery have headstones inscribed with family information.

Francis Bell married his first wife – Esther Montgomery – in 1770. Their daughter, Jane, born August 27, 1781, was married to James Beverly (1777-1850) (also spelled Bevely) Hudgins in January of 1801 (also recorded as June 6, 1801).

James Beverly Hudgins's *(Readers please see "The Hudgins Family of Jackson and Hall Counties" in the Hall County section of this book.)* father-in-law, Francis Bell, gave him property in Hall County, GA, in the days when the area was still an unsettled wilderness with most of the land still in the possession of the native Indians. James Beverly reportedly built a five-room log house on this land near a place called "Macedonia Settlement." He is listed in the *1820 Hall County Census* as *"Beverly Hudgeons"* (page 71), and again in the *1850 Hall Census* (page 790).

From the union of James Beverly

and Jane Bell came Beverly, Jr.; Virginia B.; Gregory; Dessie; Mary Ann; Zacharia (a.k.a. "Zaccharia," "Zachus," and "Zacheus"); Holder; Esther; Francis Bell; and Iverson Delaprierre.

James Beverly and wife Jane Bell's graves may still be viewed in Hall County near Chestnut Mountain if one knows where to look. The small graveyard may have been no more than a family cemetery, and can be easily missed. To reach it: Travel to GA 53 South from Gainesville past Lanier Raceway/Road Atlanta to Macedonia Church on the left. Turn left just beyond this church onto J.J. Lott Road. Follow this road until it dead-ends into another road and then turn left once again. The cemetery will be on the right just a short distance away. Be aware that in the past, thick undergrowth has often concealed this tiny cemetery from the road.

Descendants of the Bell, Montgomery and Hudgins families still live throughout the Chestnut Mountain area today, as well as in many other parts of the state.

A descendant of Beverly and Jane Bell Hudgins – Iverson Daniel Hudgins – but for the interruption of World War I in 1914, would have been known as an international botanist. He was considered one of the foremost authorities on botany in America, and was visited at the time by botanists in the employment of King George of England and Kaiser Wilhelm of Germany.

The settlement of Beverly's estate

James Beverly and wife Jane Bell's graves may still be viewed in Hall County near Chestnut Mountain if one knows where to look.

is listed in the Hall County Ordinary's office. Sons Zacheus & Holder Hudgins were administrators. James Beverly Hudgins's old farm was passed to his wife, Jane, upon his death, and to their son, Francis Bell Hudgins, upon Jane's death, and to Francis's son, Jim, upon Francis's death.

In more recent years, Beverly's former property was owned by a Mr. J.J. Lott, and has been the site of frequent Hudgins family reunions over the years. Old Liberty Methodist Church at Chestnut Mountain disappeared long ago, as did the little community of Chestnut Mountain itself, though it (the community name of Chestnut Mountain) still may be found on maps even today.

As of this writing, pioneer James Beverly Hudgins's lonely grave – which was well-marked at last check – still amazingly exists with a handful of other graves today at Chestnut Mountain, Hall Co., Georgia.

[Zacharia/Zacheus Hudgins was the great-grandfather of the late Essie Hudgins Jordan – mother of the late Marilyn Jordan Jackson (both of Rockmart, Georgia) and the late Patricia Jordan Nixon (formerly of DeKalb County, Georgia). Marilyn's children: Patricia Jackson Hughes, Ralph Olin Jackson III, and David Anderson Jackson, have homes in the Rockmart (Polk County), Georgia, area as of this writing. Patricia Nixon's children: Hal, Eve, Dave and Melinda, reside in the Gwinnett, DeKalb, and Cobb County areas.)

Old West Bandit Bill Miner's Capture in North Georgia

He haunted the stagecoach and train routes throughout the old West, robbing and pillaging at will, but always with a polite manner. Though captured and imprisoned numerous times, he always escaped to continue his high crimes... that is, until age and infirmity, and a trip to Georgia combined to bring his days to a close.

George Anderson of Jackson County, Kentucky, was born in 1843. Instead of the normal law-abiding life of most citizens, George apparently decided early-on that he was better suited for a life of crime. In fairness, as the son of a sometime school teacher mother and a fly-by-night father who abandoned his family before George was even ten years of age, the youngster was "running against the wind" before he ever reached manhood.

Without proper supervision, young George quickly earned a reputation as a dare-devil and irresponsible youth – traits by which he would live for the rest of his "devil-may-care" life. Throughout his life, in order to maintain a measure of anonymity, he used a variety of names, including George Morgan, California Billy, George Edwards, George Bud, and Louis Colquhoun, among many others, but he was known most notoriously as "Bill Miner."

Shortly before the U.S. Civil War, Miner (Anderson) left home for the gold fields of California where he landed a job as a pony express rider. He, however, either quickly tired of this job, or else it tired of him. Whatever the circumstances, he soon began robbing stagecoaches, igniting the life of crime from which he never wavered.

The nation watched in interest, as young Billy the Kid, Jesse James, Black Bart, Cole Younger, the Daltons, Butch Cassidy and the Sundance Kid, and the other notorious outlaws of the old West rose to prominence and then faded into

Whatever the circumstances, he soon began robbing stagecoaches, igniting the life of crime from which he never wavered.

the mists of time. Miner was cut from the same cloth and was considered by many to have been even more notorious than his counterparts. To be certain, he was one of the last surviving members of this fraternity, and was still robbing trains well into the 20th century.

Early on the cold morning of February 18, 1911, Miner held up Southern Railway's *Train No. 36* near the White Sulphur Station north of Gainesville, Georgia. How he progressed all the way from California to Georgia in his life of crime is unknown today, but he also has a criminal record as far north as Canada, so he was wide-ranging to say the least. He had no way of knowing it at the time, but his days of crime were fast coming to a close, as this final episode of his life of theft began unfolding in Georgia.

According to reports, at approximately 3:15 A.M. on the appointed morning, engineer David J. Fant of Atlanta might have cursed had he not been known as a railroad evangelist. Southern Railway No. 36 was already late when he took it out of Atlanta at 12:15 that morning. On this, of all mornings, Fant had H.E. Hudgens, general superintendent of the railroad on board in a private car at the rear, and now someone was flagging down the train, further delaying the train's schedule.

As Fant peered through the darkness and rain of that cold early morning, he saw that someone up ahead was waving a red lantern. The engineer knew he had to stop. He assumed a lineman or a farmer had discovered a broken rail and was trying to save the train from wrecking.

As the train coasted to a halt, Fant slid down from the engine cab and called out, inquiring if the track was being repaired. Out of the darkness, two other men suddenly appeared, brandishing

This photo is believed to have been taken of George Anderson, alias Bill Miner, following a robbery attempt in Canada. Just as described by countless lawmen and victims alike, Miner "appeared" to be anything but an outlaw, with more of a friendly grandfatherly visage than that of a dangerous outlaw who robbed stagecoaches and trains from California to Georgia, and was reportedly responsible for more than one murder. *(Photo courtesy of Canadian Marshals Service)*

revolvers. To Fant's dismay, they announced the obvious. Southern Railway No. 36 was being robbed!

The three bandits, all wearing masks and calling each other "captain," "number four" and "number five," ordered Fant's black fireman Rufus Johnson to "disappear," a command to which the normally affable trainman, the whites of his terrified eyes clearly visible in the dim light, quickly complied.

While the bandit with the lantern watched Fant, the other two robbers walked down to the express car with the intention of releasing the train from that point rearward, so that the robbery could be completed farther up the track,

The late Ray Shaw, former U.S. Postman in Gainesville, Georgia, was photographed in 1987 at the site at which Southern Railway's Train #36 was flagged down and robbed by Miner and his accomplices near White Sulphur, Georgia, on a cold February morning in 1911. *(Photo by Olin Jackson)*

without having to contend with a lot of panicky, confused passengers.

Shortly thereafter, flagman C.H. Shirley and conductor Walter T. Mooney, both of Atlanta, began walking up to the engine to find out what was happening. Seeing the man with the lantern, Mooney called out but received no response from the suspicious-looking man. The conductor later recalled that he "assumed he was dealing with a blockhead," and he grabbed the man's arm and gave him a shove, demanding to know why the train had been stopped.

The no-nonsense bandit replied by sticking a revolver in Mooney's face, and announcing the holdup. Thinking this was all just a bad joke, the conductor exclaimed "cut out this foolishness. I've got to look after my train." Only then when the masked man responded with a string of obscenities and was on the verge of pistol-whipping him, did Mooney realize the full implication of the situation, and that he had come very close to being shot.

Once out of the bandit's view, the conductor told Shirley to try to slip past the rear of the train and get help. The flagman did just that, running to White Sulphur Station, a small railway depot about a mile away.

Meanwhile, Walter B. Miller, in the express car, had learned of the robbery and was desperately attempting to quickly lock all of the doors to thwart the bandits' efforts, but despite his best efforts, the men entered through a door he had overlooked, and demanded the keys to the two safes. Luckily, the keys were not kept on the train, so the bandits would have to use more powerful measures if they were to succeed in this theft.

Disappointed but undeterred, Miner (George Anderson) had come prepared for this possibility. He brought Fant and a shovel from the engine. With dirt from the outside, the bandits packed dynamite under the safes, lit the fuses, and fled the car. The resulting explosion tore holes through the roof and sides of the car, shattered the windows, and even put out the train's lights. When the smoke had cleared, however, to the bandits' immense disappointment, only the smaller of the two safes was open.

With time running out, "the captain" filled a bag with what little "loot" was available, and then he and his two accomplices semi-panicked and ran into the woods. They, however, made good on their escape, *"disappearing as if the earth had swallowed them up,"* according to a subsequent newspaper report.

Fant started up his damaged train and since the rolling stock was still operational, he engineered the train to the nearby community of Lula where he shortly telegraphed a report of the robbery. Meanwhile, ten minutes prior to Fant's report, Shirley had reached the White Sulphur Station, where he hurriedly reported the news of the robbery to local law enforcement authorities.

As could be expected under the

Old West Bandit Bill Miner's Capture in North Georgia — Hall County

circumstances, initial reports of the robbery became twisted and distorted as the news was passed from person to person. Two mythical additional bandits were included in early reports as having been passengers on the train. The gang's escape was described in various accounts as involving an automobile, a buggy, and even as involving a ride hitched on the underside of the very train they had robbed.

No complete account of the items/money stolen was ever made, but at the very least, approximately $800.00 in U.S. currency, $770.00 in Mexican pesos, an unknown amount in several other foreign currencies, a number of legal papers of no value to the robbers, a pair of pearl ear screws, and a watch were taken. Had the bandits known what they had left behind in the larger safe which they had failed to blow, they undoubtedly would have been truly disappointed. Still intact within the confines of that container, $65,000 in gold and cash had been left untouched, an amount equivalent to $1,755,000.00 in 2021 dollars. It would have ranked among the most valuable robberies in U.S. history. Nevertheless, even the $800.00 in U.S. currency (equivalent to $21,600.00 in 2021 U.S. dollars) in Miner's loot was a nice payday for the bandits.

Miner recruited his two accomplices for the Gainesville robbery – Charlie Hunter and James Handford – in Pennsylvania and Virginia respectively, in 1910. Hunter, a thirty-year-old Irishman from Michigan agreed, after some persuasion, to accompany the old bandit to a locale in the South, "to try holding up a Southern train." The pair worked for two months in a Virginia sawmill where they completed their group by recruiting thirty-three-year-old Handford from Nebraska.

White Sulphur Road at the intersection with the old Southern railroad in Hall County was photographed in 1987. Some 110 years earlier in 1911, the train depot at White Sulphur stood at the approximate location of the warning signal pictured here. It was to this point that flagman C.H. Shirley ran to report the robbery of Train #36. *(Photo by Olin Jackson)*

The trio moved on to Georgia to prepare for what was almost unthinkable at that time – a Wild West-style train holdup in the East. The week before they finally struck Southern Railway No. 36, Hunter pawned Miner's watch in Atlanta, using the money to buy whiskey and a lantern later used in the robbery. A track wrench later found at their camp indicated that they had considered derailing and wrecking the train.

The first reports of the incident were met with incredulity by a disbelieving Gainesville populace. According to newspaper accounts of that day, most of the townspeople dismissed the news of the robbery, thinking it was a joke. Most were dumbfounded when they learned the truth.

"*The truth dawned at last,*" the newspaper said, "*and they were confronted with the fact that here in a free, civilized, God-fearing, and law-abiding community, a train robbery was committed that would abash the most God-forsaken Wild West country to be found. That such*

Taking On Supplies – The home of Merritt M. London which formerly existed at the intersection of Long Branch Road and Highway 60 in Lumpkin County, is pictured in this primitive print. While fleeing lawmen in February of 1911 following the robbery of Southern Railway's Train #36, Bill Miner and his accomplices reportedly paused at the country grocery in front of this home to purchase supplies. Pictured in this photo are: Merritt M. London (with white beard and hat in center). His wife, Mary Neisler London stands beside the tree. Sons Frank (in the wagon) and Bob (2nd from left) also appear. The identity of the individual in overalls is unknown. *(Photo courtesy of Annie Lou Dobbs of Toccoa, GA, daughter of Frank and Annie Kemp London)*

a daring hold-up could take place right at our doors was inconceivable."

The Atlanta newspapers had a field day with the event. The *Atlanta Journal* filled the first two pages of the February 18 issue with the news. The train crew, all of whom were Atlanta residents, were interviewed and their photographs published.

When the report of the robbery reached the Hall County Police Office in the early morning hours of February 18, Sheriff W.A. Crow was home sick with the mumps. He arose from his sick bed to organize a posse by telephone.

Assembling his deputies, Crow gave them a pep talk: "I want you to go out into the country and mountains now, and don't come back here until you bag these train robbers," he instructed. "Bring them back alive if you can.... But if not, just bring them along anyway."

These initial efforts in locating the bandits proved futile. Deputy Sheriff Little, with the help of county officials and railroad detectives, began a search of Gainesville, to see if the robbers might have been in town all along.

The posse sent to the robbery site was delayed, waiting for the bloodhounds to be brought from Gwinnett County. By the time the dogs arrived, the rain and pepper and snuff reportedly scattered by Miner and his two accomplices had effectively obscured the trail.

To Sheriff Crow's posse were added the Pinkertons, a deputy U.S. marshal, and detectives of the Southern Railway and Express. All local law enforcement officials also went into the field, using the promise of a $1,500 reward (almost more than the bandits actually took) offered by the State of Georgia and the Southern Railway, to enlist men and boys for their posse. Despite all these efforts, the ultimate capture of the train robbers was accomplished, as the editor of the 1911 *Dahlonega Nugget* explained, "*by mountaineers skilled in tracking.*"

Only a few days after the robbery, the search efforts were losing steam. Officials conducting the man-hunt were sitting around the main room of the old Dixie Hunt Hotel – their headquarters in Gainesville – so despondent, that they hardly noticed when the telephone began ringing. When one of the lawmen finally picked up the receiver, the caller turned out to be ex-Lumpkin County Sheriff Jim Davis calling from Dahlonega to announce that he believed he had found the train robbers in an abandoned house nearby. How the bandits had made it through the rough north

Georgia mountains toward Dahlonega in such a short time is unknown today, but they had to have been making really good travel time through some really rough country where roads were almost nonexistent.

Davis had learned of the men earlier, and both he and Lumpkin County Sheriff John Sergeant began having doubts about them. They claimed to be prospectors and had overnighted at Sergeant's hotel in Dahlonega. However, between them, the three strangers had no prospecting tools other than one broken and split shovel.

When Lumpkin County resident Pete Carmichael reported the three men near his farm, Sergeant became even more suspicious. He set out for the Carmichael place where he picked up two sets of tracks. The bandits apparently had split up at this point, and Sergeant decided to follow the single set of tracks.

Sergeant assembled a posse which included the aforementioned Jim Davis and Davis' two sons – Rufus and Joe. The trail at length led the group to the Elbert Kendall farm some 17 miles northwest of Dahlonega in the present-day Nimberwill community. The Kendalls reported that they did have a male boarder who was sleeping on a cot upstairs in a loft.

Davis and his sons reportedly mounted the stairs where they found a person who appeared to be asleep. As Davis pulled the blanket away, the stranger aimed a .45 revolver at him. Davis' salvation was found in his two sons who had a shotgun and a .22 rifle directed at the old man who in fact turned out to be George Anderson, alias Bill Miner.

Rufus Davis was still alive in 1987, and lived in Cartersville, Georgia. Though in his nineties at the time, Rufus still remembered details of this day. He

The historic Merritt M. London home-place at the intersection of Long Branch Road and GA Highway 60 was photographed here in 1993 just a few years prior to its unfortunate demolition.

also still possessed the set of handcuffs used to restrain Miner after his capture.

Jim Davis eventually collected the reward offered for the capture of the train robbers *(Miner's accomplices in the robbery had been arrested earlier in the day prior to Miner's arrest.)* Sheriff Sergeant unsuccessfully sued Davis for part of the reward, claiming the last capture was really his work.

Despite all the clamor of the event, the detectives, sheriffs, and other officials in the manhunt still had no idea who they had actually captured even after Miner was clapped in chains. The old bandit identified himself by his real name – George Anderson – and all the official Georgia police and criminal records relating to him identified him by that name. It was probably the first time in many years that he had used his actual name for identification purposes. Interestingly, when the name by which he was commonly known – "Bill Miner" – was learned by the authorities, it was assumed that that was his actual name, and that the moniker "George Anderson" was an alias.

While waiting in the Lumpkin County jail, Anderson (alias Bill Miner) talked of the great potential of

The manhunt for the bandits who robbed Southern Railway's Train #36 was headquartered at the Dixie Hunt Hotel in Gainesville. This structure, built in 1882 on the corner of Main and Spring streets, was photographed here in 1900. A portion of this building still exists today in downtown Gainesville. *(Photo courtesy of GA Dept. of Archives & History, Atlanta)*

Dahlonega's inactive gold mines in such a way that the *Dahlonega Nugget* published his remarks as if he were a prominent geologist, stroking local civic pride. It is ironic to note that Miner began his life of crime at the site of the second great gold rush in California and ended it at the site of the first U.S. gold rush in Dahlonega, Georgia. And even as he was captured, he was preaching the merits of the gold mining industry.

After his capture in Dahlonega, Miner was transported to Gainesville for trial. His arrival by automobile in Gainesville was greeted by crowds of hundreds of people, gathered as if to see a street parade, and caused Miner to remark "They must think I am a bear."

A special session of the Hall County Superior Court was held on March 3, 1911, to try the train robbers. Charlie Hunter confessed his role in the robbery, and became the state's chief witness against Miner. Hunter received a sentence of fifteen years, but escaped within a year, and surprisingly, no effort was ever made to recapture him. James Handford also pleaded guilty, received the same sentence, and was granted a parole in 1918.

Miner however, differed from his henchmen in that he demanded, for unknown reasons, a jury trial. Despite the fact that witness after witness testified against him, Miner sat impassively. Some observers believed that Miner believed his almost flawlessly polite manners might carry the day in the trial and somehow set him free, but it was not to be, as the Hall County jury steadfastly returned with a verdict of "*Guilty*."

Miner's only show of emotion in the verdict came when Howard Thompson, special attorney for the express company, spoke of the dynamite used in the express car potentially "*blowing into eternity sleeping women and children on the train.*" A reporter witnessed Miner answer that charge "*with a most vengeful, glaring, and hateful glance.*"

When Judge Sims sentenced Miner to twenty years in prison, the old gentleman bandit reportedly thanked him, stood up and turned to a group of college girls and ladies and proceeded to provide a moral for the story they had witnessed unfolding before them: "*When one breaks the law, one must expect to pay the penalty. I am old, but during all my life, I have found the golden rule the best guide to man in this world,*" he said. He then smiled and sat down.

Though one of the most cold-blooded and notorious thugs in the colorful history of train robberies in the U.S., Miner is routinely described as "*looking less like a criminal than almost any man one might imagine.*" Yet, this kindly-looking old man reportedly methodically gunned down virtually all of a group of posse-men pursuing him from the scene of a stagecoach robbery in 1881 in California. He was also identified as associated with numerous other capital crimes throughout his life.

Books have been written and even modern feature-length movies have been made about Bill Miner, some of them actually portraying him as somehow justified for some or all of his crimes. Though this final event in Georgia ended forever Miner's stagecoach/train robbing days, it did not bring to a close his ability to continue to cause mayhem and galvanize public attention.

Above and beyond his notoriety as a train robber, Miner was also literally a legend as an escape artist. Prior to his crimes in Georgia, he had escaped from numerous prisons in Canada and elsewhere and often boasted that no prison could hold him indefinitely. He had been so successful that he had been dubbed "*The Grey Fox*" by the news media.

William Pinkerton, head of the well-known detective agency of the same name, was a spectator at the Gainesville trial, and warned the press that he doubted that any Georgia prison could hold the old man. His comments proved prophetic. Miner escaped not once, but twice from prison in Milledgeville, Georgia, after his incarceration there. Had it not been for his aging condition and lack of resistance to exposure and the elements after his escapes, he might not have been recaptured. If anything, the man was just short of amazing.

Following the trial in Gainesville, the convicted trio was sent to Georgia's huge prison camp in Newton County. Life in the camp did not suit Miner, however. A personal appeal to Robert E. Davison, then chairman of the State Prison Board, finally earned him a transfer to the state prison farm for the infirm in Milledgeville.

While at the farm, Miner recruited the services of convicted murderers John B. Watts and Tom H. Moore for an escape. Late one night, Watts somehow managed to remove the peep-hole apparatus out of the door of his cell, and squeeze through the opening. He took the keys and a pistol from a sleeping guard, and released Miner and Moore. The trio made a clean getaway.

Following his escape, Miner was even brazen enough to mail a letter to Robert Davison, thanking him for giving him his opportunity for escape. *"My dear sir,"* he wrote, *"I want to thank you for your kindness in putting me at Milledgeville. My dear sir, don't trust a prisoner, don't matter how sick he is or makes out he is. Yours truly, B. Miner"*

The chairman's embarrassment was also the embarrassment of the state of Georgia and the newspapers and citizens as well who had urged that the *"sick old man be allowed to die in peace"* at the lightly-guarded prison farm. The ***Atlanta Journal*** proclaimed that *"wherever Bill Miner is, he is probably grinning and the joke is on Georgia."*

It wasn't long however, before Miner was recaptured. He and Moore had headed for Augusta, Georgia. At a tiny community nearby called Keysville, a J.W. Whittle overheard a brakeman talking to two "bums" in a boxcar. When it was realized that the two matched a description of two escaped convicts, Whittle summoned help.

The boxcar was shortly thereafter surrounded by a posse, and Miner recaptured yet again. Moore, however, chose not to return – at least not alive. He reportedly fired a single shot in the vicinity of the posse, and then in turn was killed by a single shot to the face. Inside the boxcar, members of the posse found dynamite and fuses which Miner explained *"were good for catching fish."* Old Bill had

Mystery & History in Georgia

Photographed in front of the old Lumpkin County Jail (which still stands today in Dahlonega), are: (L to R) Sheriff James M. "Jim" Davis, Gordon Davis, Joe Davis, William S. "Bill" Davis, Charles C. Davis, and Rufus Tilman "R.T." Davis. Bill Miner was captured by newly-elected Sheriff John Sergeant, Former Sheriff Jim Davis, and Davis's two sons – Rufus and Joe. Following this capture, Miner was incarcerated in this jail. *(Photo courtesy of C.C. Davis, Jr.)*

been a breath away from yet another train robbery.

Returned to his prison cell in Milledgeville, Miner boasted that he would escape again at the first opportunity. His guards, understandably, took no chances against any future embarrassment. One can only imagine their total humiliation, when on the morning of June 27, 1912, they found the *Grey Fox* gone yet again, his ankle and arm bracelets locked to his bunk, the window bars sawed out, and the bedding made into a rope which he had used to climb to the ground. It was literally the stuff of legends.

Accompanied by convicts W.J. Windencamp and W.M. Wiggins, Miner was once again making good his escape. The trio took a boat into the Oconee River this time, with the plan of reaching a port where they could ship out as deck hands. However, the boat reportedly capsized, drowning Windencamp. It is not known today for certain if that was the actual circumstance.

For three days afterwards, Miner and Wiggins were lost in an almost endless boggy swamp near Oconee, Georgia, living on blackberries and unable to find safe drinking water. When they finally came out near Toombsboro, they offered no resistance to a posse which found them at a home begging for breakfast. Miner's escape this time had lasted only five days, and his age and failing constitution were fast catching up with him.

The reception the old outlaw

Old West Bandit Bill Miner's Capture in North Georgia — Hall County

The old Lumpkin County Jail in Dahlonega, Georgia, in which Miner was incarcerated was photographed in 1993. *(Photo by Olin Jackson)*

The grave of notorious outlaw Bill Miner in the convicts burial section of Memory Hill Cemetery in Milledgeville, Georgia. It was the one prison from which he finally could not escape.

received upon his return to Milledgeville this time even exceeded Bill's wildest imaginings. Driven in an open, heavily-guarded automobile and shackled securely, Bill was met in the downtown area by an extremely large crowd of admiring townspeople who reportedly literally applauded him and passed him money and cigars.

Always gracious, Miner stood up in the car and waved his hat to his fans. The *Union Recorder* claimed that *"for a short time, it looked like a hero had come to the city instead of a man who had wrecked and robbed trains."* This, however, was the last adventure for the grizzled old *Grey Fox* who had robbed trains from coast to coast.

Today, the exact circumstances of Miner's last days are unknown, but it is believed the hunger, exposure to the weather, and contaminated water he consumed during his escape, apparently took their toll on him, causing him to lapse into illness.

The *Atlanta Journal*, learning that Miner was near death in September of 1913, interviewed him one last time. Before they could get the story printed, however, the *Angel of Death* visited the cell of the *Grey Fox*, and spirited him away, granting him permanent freedom at last.

Though accounts of his actual burial site vary today, the final resting place of Bill Miner is in the old city cemetery known as *Memory Hill* in Milledgeville. Miner's grave is marked with a simple headstone, and is found on the southeast side of *Memory Hill* where the cemetery slopes toward Fishing Creek, a place where many convicts were buried when the penitentiary was located at Milledgeville. His headstone bears his pseudonym *Bill Miner*, since no one at the time was certain of his true name.

Treasure-hunters still ply the railroads and other sites suspected of holding the loot Miner supposedly left behind somewhere in Hall or Lumpkin counties in north Georgia. Interestingly, almost all of the money and valuables stolen by Miner and his henchmen in the robbery in Gainesville were recovered. Miner had personally provided Sheriff Crow (of Hall County) with directions to two caches of loot. Several other caches turned up later, satisfying most recovery efforts.

The site of the famed train robbery now bears mute testimony to the events of February 18, 1911. Today, the crossing at White Sulphur is known as *"Bill Miner Crossing."*

The Hudgins Family of Jackson/Hall Counties

They were among the pioneers on this early venue to the Old Alabama Roads westward across Georgia from the eastern seaboard. After reaching the vicinity of Cherokee territory in what later became Jackson County, the Hudgins family put down roots still existing today.

According to Dorothy Hudgins Shaw who spent many hours painstakingly researching the Hudgins family genealogy, there were Hudgins living in Virginia as early as 1642. Many of them were shipmasters. Grants of land owned by these Hudgins were recorded with deeds as early as 1634, and this original land was still owned by descendants of these hardy early settlers as recently as 1770.

It was only natural when the Hudgins family arrived in Virginia for them to associate themselves with a church. Some ultimately became active members of the Petsworth Parish Episcopal Church, while others became members of Kingston, Ware, or Abingdon Parishes.

In 1651 Gloucester County was formed out of York County. By an act of court order, the Grand Assembly of March 6, 1655, *"all counties not yet laid out into parishes shall be divided into parishes the next county court."* (Hening, **Statutes at Large, Volume 1**, *page 400*). The Church of England was the only church allowed in the new colony of Virginia, and it and its branches became the governing body in these early communities.

Petsworth Parish was west of Ware which was north of Abingdon Parish. Kingston Parish covered all the section east of North River. The first mention of Kingston Parish is found in the *Vestry Book*, dated November 15, 1679. At this time, the worship house was called North River Chapel. The land between North River and Blackwater Creek is still called Chapel Neck. This is the same area where records show that *"John Hodden"* owned 1,100 acres in 1643. Later, this land was still in the ownership of a John *"Hudgins."*

Few records of the Petsworth Parish exist today, but by some chance, the Kingston Parish Register survived the destruction of wars, time, and the elements, and is still preserved as of this writing in readable form (with the exception of a few missing and torn pages). In this document, the earlier instances of the Hudgins name are recorded as

The Hudgins Family Of Jackson/Hall Counties Hall County

"*Hudgen.*" Later, the name is recorded as "*Hudgin,*" then later as "*Hudgins,*" which is the spelling used today.

The Kingston Parish Register (KPR) includes births and baptisms for each year 1755 through 1777. The year 1778 is missing. Pages 167-170 (1779-1783) were recorded. After 1783 (and the Revolutionary War), very few Hudgins (Hudgen) births were recorded by the Kingston Parish. It is believed that, following the war, most of the Hudgins became associated with other churches, because they could then worship openly in any church of their choosing.

The Baptist faith, aided by the persistent ministrations of Robert Hudgins, had been brought to Gloucester County, Virginia, in 1775 by Iverson Lewis, pastor of Excel Church in King and Queen County. Robert had heard Elder Lewis preach, and had invited him to his home to preach to his family and friends. They had not been allowed to build a Baptist church prior to the conclusion of the Revolutionary War, because the Church of England was the only church allowed to exist in the colonies up to that point.

By 1790, the Baptists, led then by Robert Hudgins, had a sizeable congregation. After he was baptized, Hudgins was named their pastor. They then built a small church. They called it Petsworth Baptist Church. (This church was not in any way connected with Petsworth Parish.) Robert Hudgins led this church as pastor until his death in 1791. This church, built near Wolfe's Corner (present-day Meeting House Corner) is no longer standing.

In 1791, Kingston Parish was cut off to form Mathews County (*Colonial Churches of Tidewater Virginia* by George Carrington Mason). Some of the Hudgins descendants still live in Mathews County today. One small village in this county has a Baptist Church – Mathews Baptist – which was founded in 1777, shortly after the American Revolution. At that time, many Hudgins were active in this church, and their descendants continue to be active today. This little town is still known today as "Hudgins," Virginia (located at the intersection of VA 198 & VA 223).

Mathews Baptist was originally known as Kingston Church, and remained so until 1791, when the name was changed to Mathews Baptist. In 1905, the church was remodeled, leaving the balcony across the back.

Records of the church were not kept in the early years, but in 1790, it was recorded that Hugh Hudgins (probably a deacon) was ordered to cite two women – Mary Longest and Sister Westcombe – to appear before the church and account for their conduct in the practice of free communion. Also in 1833, it was recorded that Deacon Thomas Hudgins attended an Association meeting in Williamsburg.

In later years, Mathews Baptist was remodeled again and enlarged by adding a wing on both sides, as well as a new pastorium. Many Hudgins families still worship at this lovely church today in Hudgins, Virginia.

The early branch of the Hudgins family in Virginia from which the Hudgins in Hall County, Georgia, are derived today are descended as follows: John Hudgen, who married in Kingston Parish, Virginia, Mary Carney on 25 December, 1774; James Beverly (a.k.a. Beverly) Hudgen (b. 14 September, 1777) who married in North Carolina to Jane Bell; Zacharia (a.k.a. "Zacheus," "Zachus," and "Zaccharia") Hudgins (b. 1804 in Hall County, GA) who married Margaret (Peggy) Major (a.k.a. "Majors"); Richard Bennett Hudgins (b. 1831, Hall

195

County, GA, D. January 4, 1865, during service in the Confederate Army, in Raleigh, North Carolina) who married Arabella Pettyjohn; and James Zacheus Hudgins who, in Hall County, Georgia, married first, Elizabeth Harris in 1882, and second, Sarah ("Sallie") Elizabeth Tanner in 1895.

James Beverly (Bevely) Hudgen (Hudgins) received land from his father-in-law, Francis Bell, in Hall County, Georgia, in the days when that area was still a pioneer country with most land still in possession of the native Cherokee Indians. James reportedly built a five-room log house there near a tiny settlement called "Macedonia." He is listed in the 1820 Hall County Census as *"Beverly Hudgeons."*

The settlement of James Beverly Hudgins' estate is listed in the Hall County Ordinary's office. James' sons, Zacharia (a.k.a. "Zacheus," etc.) and Holder, were administrators. In his will, James' farm was passed on to his wife, Jane Bell.

Upon Jane's death, the farm was passed to James' and Jane's son, Francis Bell Hudgins. Upon Francis' death, the farm was passed on to Francis' son, Jim. The property eventually came into the possession of a Mr. J.J. Lott, and was the site of frequent Hudgins family reunions over the ensuing years. It is not known who owns this property today.

The graves of James Bevely Hudgen (a.k.a. "Beverly Hudgins") and Jane Bell Hudgen (a.k.a. "Hudgins") can still be viewed today in Hall County near Chestnut Mountain. This small graveyard may have been no more than a family grave plot, since there are few, if any, other graves in the vicinity of these two Hudgen (Hudgins) graves. *(Note: To reach James Bevely Hudgins' grave today, travel to GA 53 South from Gainesville,* past Lanier Raceway/Road Atlanta, to Macedonia Church (on left). Turn left just beyond this church onto J.J. Lott Road. Follow this road until it dead-ends into another road and then turn left again. The cemetery will be on the right just a short distance away. Be aware that the cemetery often is concealed from visibility by thick vegetation.)

Zacharia (a.k.a. "Zacheus," "Zachus," and "Zaccharia") married Margaret "Peggy" Majors on 16 March, 1825, in Hall County, GA. They had ten children. Records on Zacharia are sketchy. He died 9 November, 1879, in Hall County, GA.

Richard Bennett Hudgins was 29 years of age when, on August 27, 1861, he departed to serve in the Confederate Army during the U.S. Civil War. He left behind his wife, Arabella Pettyjohn, two daughters – Mary and Margaret – and a young son, James Zacheus Hudgins.

Family tradition maintains that Arabella, who had very straight black hair and other prominent Native American features, was possibly part Cherokee Indian, but no actual Native American blood connection has been established for her.

James Zacheus never remembered his father, who, while still in service in the Confederate Army, died in a Raleigh, North Carolina field hospital, after falling ill with pneumonia during the terrible winter of 1864. He passed away on January 3, 1865, and was buried January 4, 1865, in Raleigh's Oakwood Cemetery (Grave #356).

After the war, Confederate money of course was worthless and anything worth owning had mostly been pilfered and destroyed by marauding troops and other outlaws. Just as were most Southerners at that time, the Hudgins family was destitute. However, just as daylight follows darkness, "spring" soon followed the awful winter, and the family cow dropped a calf and the sow had a litter of pigs. The garden was planted from seeds hoarded from the previous year and there, thankfully, was enough to eat – at least for the time being.

Arabella had lost not only her husband, but also two brothers to the war. It was not easy to carry on, but carry on she did. One way or another, just like the mythical "Scarlett" in *Gone With The Wind*, she was determined for her family to survive.

In 1872, Mary married, and in 1876, so also did Margaret. By 1880, Arabella was 46 years of age, and James Zacheus was the only child left at home. At that time, he was 20 years of age, and would soon be leaving the nest himself.

In 1882, James married Elizabeth Harris. From this union came five children. The first child was named Richard, in honor of his grandfather. A second son was named after his mother's father – Silas. The following two children – a boy and a girl – died in childhood. A fifth child, Lucy May, was the only female to survive.

The mother of these children – Elizabeth – died before Lucy was two years of age. The cause of her death is unknown today. Arabella, the grandmother, though feeling her years, took James' family in and did the best she could to take care of them for several years.

By the time the children were ages five, eight and ten, James knew they needed a full-time mother. After all, Arabella was 66 years old by that point and needed to slow down.

James had his eyes on a pretty young girl who lived nearby at Chestnut Mountain. She wasn't only pretty, she could sew expertly and cook the best biscuits James had ever tasted. Despite her beauty, she was a tom-boy of sorts, and even had her own beautiful black horse (a gift from her grandfather), but she loved children too, and this was of obvious importance to James. Her name was Sarah "Sallie" Elizabeth Tanner.

James, for his day and time, was moderately successful, and therefore of obvious interest to eligible ladies. He owned a small mercantile business and was respected by his peers. He also had a good reputation as a family man and provider for his family, and was active as well in his church. These qualities no doubt earned him high marks in the eyes of David Tanner, Sarah's father.

James ultimately popped the question to the vivacious 16-year-old beauty, and, after her father, Mr. Tanner, had agreed to the union, Sallie responded with a resounding "Yes!" After her acceptance of his proposal, James went shopping and bought the prettiest dress he could find for his new bride. The photograph of the two taken on their wedding day was made without Arabella, but did include James' three small children.

The marriage took place on March 31, 1895. Interestingly, there was no honeymoon after this marriage. There was no new home, nor even new furniture. James was a straight-forward practical man, and, being extremely

Arabella had lost not only her husband, but also two brothers to the war.

frugal-minded, took his wife home to live in his mother's abode with his three children until he could provide them with a home of their own. And from the day she was married until the day he passed away, Sallie always referred to him as "Mr. Hudgins," and never as "James."

Both Sallie and James were devout Christians, and believed that the Bible meant that a wife submits herself to her husband, and if God meant for her to bear children, then she would have children. Sallie did not disappoint her husband either, and they were fruitful and multiplied.

While living in the house with Arabella, Sallie longed to have her own home. She wanted a kitchen that was hers and hers alone, so that she could bake good things without an "eye" looking over her shoulder. And if by chance her kitchen preparations didn't turn out right, she wouldn't then have to be concerned about any critical remarks either from the mother-in-law.

Interestingly, once while Arabella was napping, Sallie baked a cake and, for reasons unknown today, the cake didn't rise as it was supposed to. Sallie was so upset that she slipped out of the house and fed the cake to the hog. Arabella never knew of this little mishap, and Sallie never revealed it to anyone until many years later.

Sallie and James' first child was born one year and four months after the wedding. It was a beautiful baby girl. James thought she was the prettiest little girl he had ever seen, and he and Sallie named her "Daisy."

Two more children were born in quick succession while the family lived in Arabella's home: A son, Carl, and a daughter, **Essie**, were their names. Arabella's home was a log structure which once stood not far from the former community of Sugar Hill which once existed on the old Gainesville/Athens Highway *(formerly U.S. 129, but today called "Old Gainesville Highway," and officially re-identified as "GA 332" between Talmo and Pendergrass).*

By this time, James could see that it was time to build a larger house to accommodate his growing family. He had purchased 181 acres of land in lower Hall County (still in the vicinity of Sugar Hill) from the estate of **George Washington Tanner** – Sallie's grandfather. On this property, an original log home, tenant houses, a gristmill, and a nicer home into which James temporarily moved his family, already existed. This temporary home had a large front porch with a separate room built at one end of the porch. This room was a tradition during the late 19th and early 20th centuries in the South. It was designed exclusively for traveling salesmen and itinerant preachers ("circuit riders").

This temporary home also had a large hall ("dog-trot") in the center of the house which led from the front porch to the rear porch. There in the rear, a large kitchen existed at the end of the porch. The kitchen had a huge fireplace and hearth with an oven built into one side. This fireplace was capable of burning very large logs, and this kitchen was where the cooking – as well as the eating – took place.

The remainder of this home was composed of two rooms. One large room was used for family gatherings, and it included a large fireplace for warmth in the winter. It also had two beds for sleeping. The other room was also for sleeping.

By 1900, James had completed the construction of a large house up on the main road *(originally identified as U.S. 129, but today called "Old Gainesville*

Highway," and officially re-identified as "GA 332" between Talmo and Pendergrass), still in the vicinity of Sugar Hill and his mother's home. At the same time that he was building this new home, he was also building a new store nearer to the main Gainesville to Athens road. This mercantile business carried most of the things needed by country residents of that day.

Inside the Hudgins store were oil for lamps, flour and meal for those who failed to visit the local miller, sugar, crackers, candy, bananas, cheese, nails, tacks, leather for new soles for worn-out shoes – and if the customer didn't have money, he or she could trade eggs, hens or fryers for what they needed. If they didn't have anything to trade, James, who was generous to a fault, would allow these individuals to charge their purchases until harvest time.

And if the harvest failed, James would even allow his customers to carry their debt over until the next harvest. Family records clearly demonstrated that some individuals never paid off their debts to James, but he would hardly ever mention these debts, preferring instead to be charitable. This very Christian-like trait endeared James to his neighbors, but it would later come back to haunt his family following James's death.

Hudgins Store in short order became the hub of life in the community of Sugar Hill. In the early 1900s, the U.S. mail was delivered there by a carrier riding on horseback. James' daughter, Daisy, would always run to the store when the mailman was arriving.

The mailman carried two steer horns and a gun along with his pouch of mail. After all, that was only 45 or 50 years after the War Between the States, and rural Georgia was still unpredictable and unsettled for the most part. One of the mailman's horns held gunpowder for his gun, and the other was used both to summon help (should he encounter an emergency situation) and to announce his imminent arrival in a community as he neared the outskirts of a town.

On one memorable occasion, the mounted mailman sounded his approach to the Hudgins' Sugar Hill home, and Daisy ran out to meet him. He handed her his powder horn and told her he would not need it anymore. It was his last mail run. "Rural Free Delivery" was scheduled to begin the following day, and the aged man was retiring. In 1990, Daisy Hudgins Giles gave that powder horn to her nephew, Richard Shaw (namesake of Richard Bennett Hudgins), to preserve and pass along to future generations.

The Sugar Hill home is where James' children by Elizabeth Harris – Richard Braselton, Silas and Lucy – grew up and left the fold. Lucy surprised the family by getting married July 25, 1908, to Az McNeal at the Hopewell Church Celebration on Candler Road in Hall County. Richard Braselton entered service in the U.S. Army and died from pneumonia on an Army base in California on January 12, 1919. He is buried at Concord Baptist Church Cemetery in Clermont, Hall County, GA. Interestingly, his grandfather (and namesake) – Richard Bennett Hudgins – also died of pneumonia, also while serving in the army – the Confederate States of America army – as described earlier in this article. Silas Arthur Hudgins was married to Mamie Major.

The new Sugar Hill home was also where most of the rest of James's and Sallie's children were born. A fourth child, David, was born soon after moving into the home. Then came Clyde, then Mary Lou. Soon, another baby was on the way.

She was named Cora. Then came Ralph, Albert and Raleigh.

Before Sallie gave birth to Raleigh at Sugar Hill, she decided she would not have any more children. She felt ten children was a good number to "stop" on. However, shortly thereafter, Sallie became gravely ill with what ultimately was diagnosed as appendicitis. After being rushed to Downey Hospital in Gainesville, she was told that surgery was urgently required – immediately.

Following the removal of a ruptured appendix – an extremely serious condition – a tube was placed in Sallie's side for the drainage of fluid. In that day and age, most individuals would have died from such an illness. Sallie, however, later explained that she had prayed to the *Almighty*. It turned out to be a very poignant prayer. She revealed she had told God that if he would spare her life, she would never again complain about having children, and that she would have and love all the children he chose to allow her to conceive. The *Almighty* answered her prayer, and Sallie made good on her promise as well.

On June 19, 1904, Arabella Pettyjohn Hudgins, James's mother, finally passed away. She had endured an arduous life, and was not always pleasant to James' children during her later years, but by the same token, her life had never been easy. She was buried in Harmony Hall Baptist Church Cemetery in Hall County. *(Note: To reach Harmony Hall Baptist Church, take U.S. 129 east and turn left onto Blackstock Road in Hall County, then bear left onto Mangum Mill Road. Harmony Hall Baptist Church is on the left.)* Interestingly, Elizabeth Clementine Harris Hudgins (James' first wife) and two of her children are also buried near to Arabella.

As the children matured, James Z. and Sallie had come to the realization that they needed to make yet another move – one of the most important moves of their lives. James was a strong advocate of a good education, and wanted his children to have the best education reasonably available to them.

By this point, Daisy and Carl were already enrolled at Chattahoochee High School in Clermont, Georgia, and the other children would shortly need higher education as well. James decided that instead of sending his entire brood away to the Clermont boarding school, he would simply move to that community so that the children could live at home and he could be more involved in their educations.

In order to accomplish this, James first rented a house near Clermont at Wauka Mountain. In the spring of 1913, he began moving his family and all their possessions to this new north Hall homestead. Some of the family rode in a wagon and some in a buggy. Others took turns walking and leading the milk cow.

Help was needed to move the furniture. It was a 25-mile trip from Sugar Hill to Clermont. Sallie had a small baby in her arms and luckily was not yet pregnant again. The trip started at first light and ended at sundown. The children of modern America have no idea of the many times difficult trials endured by the children of pioneer America.

The Hudgins family had no sooner settled in their new home at Wauka Mountain before James got busy planning for the construction of a new home in downtown Clermont. It was to be the best and prettiest home he could build, and, as things turned out, he was successful. This lovely home – as of this writing in the year 2020 – still stands in Clermont on King Street.

This fifth house into which James moved his family was built with a large hall down the middle. It had a parlor (for receiving guests), six bedrooms, a large kitchen, and a dining room with a large table in order to accommodate the entire family for meals.

At the same time that he began building this new home, James set about also building a new store. It was located on Main Street just down the street from the hotel in Clermont, less than two blocks from the family home – and very near to the railroad tracks – for easy access to supplies and wares.

This new store carried all the same supplies that the store in Sugar Hill had carried, and some additional wares as well. The Gainesville and Northwestern Railroad had recently been completed to Robertstown in northeast Georgia where the huge supplies of virgin timber were being harvested. The tracks of this railroad passed directly through Clermont to the rear of James' new store. James also owned a warehouse near the railroad where additional supplies were stored.

Most of James' merchandise came by rail, but much of it also was supplied by mountaineers traveling through Clermont on their way to Gainesville where they annually sold the products they had grown and raised. James acquired many of their unique products seasonally each year to sell to the public. These included apples, sorghum, honey, chestnuts, turkeys, hogs, chickens, and many other unique mountain products. Most of these hardy mountain travelers simply camped out overnight in their mule- or ox-drawn wagons, but a privileged few were able to spend the night in the big hotel in Clermont.

After the big house on King Street was completed, the family was able to move in before the arrival of the eleventh child – Sarah – who was born 1914. Two more daughters were born in this home in Clermont – Dorothy and Marjorie – bringing the family total to 13 children.

Two additional children were born, but did not survive birth. They were buried in the Concord Baptist Church Cemetery in Clermont where both James and Sallie would one day be laid to rest. Sallie, who was 43 by this time, was a strong lady, but time and nature were not on her side. From that point forward, she was never again able to conceive a child.

Remarkably, all 13 children were graduated from Chattahoochee High School which had become a respected Baptist-affiliated school in Clermont. Some of the children attended college as well, and some were graduated from college. In the early 1900s, this not only was a tremendously admirable achievement, it was a remarkable one as well. Of James' and Sallie's children, seven taught school at one time or another, and three retired as school teachers.

James and Sallie continued to prosper in the growing community of Clermont. New buildings had been added to the town to supplement the large hotel on the square. The Gainesville and Northwestern Railroad brought additional commerce to the community. Life was peaceful and harmonious for the Hudgins family.

Sallie was a good mother and a good doctor to her children. They all eventually fell victim to – and survived – chicken pox, measles, mumps, and a variety of other childhood sicknesses. Interestingly, not one of the children ever had pneumonia or extremely serious illnesses.

In September of 2000, Dorothy, the next to last child born to James and Sallie, remembered that on one occasion, a Dr. Homer Lancaster in Clermont had two little girls, one of whom – Martha – had fallen ill with an extremely high fever. The doctor had applied all his medical knowledge and expertise in an attempt to break the little girl's fever but she showed no improvement whatsoever.

"Dr. Lancaster, who was related to Mother, looked on her as a second mother to his children," Dorothy explained. "He came to her with tears in his eyes and asked her if she knew anything else to do to cure his precious daughter, because he had done all he could."

It is not known today what instructions Sallie gave the good doctor, but it is known that the following morning, Dr. Lancaster was at Sallie's door with a big smile on his face. The little girl's fever had finally broken during the night, and she was steadily improving.

Life in Clermont was idyllic not only for Mr. and Mrs. Hudgins, but for the children as well. A few years prior to her death in 1999 at the age of 98, daughter Essie remembered that "Father had a soda fountain in the store and made carbonated drinks for customers. My favorite was called 'peach phosphate,'" she recalled in delicious remembrance.

"I loved to play tennis on the hard clay courts behind the Miller's (Clermont) hotel," Essie added. "Jean Rogers and I used to play together in our middy blouses and box-pleated knee skirts. She later married my older brother, Carl, and the wedding was held in the hotel."

Dorothy, Essie's younger sister, was friends with Jean's younger sister, Frances. Prior to her death, she also described many happy memories of Clermont at the tennis courts behind the hotel, a duck pond, and a see-saw behind the hotel where the girls played as children. She also described many nights in the hotel with her childhood friend, and remembered crying her heart out when the Rogers family moved to Gainesville in the early 1920s.

Dorothy also remembered that when she walked from the Hudgins home on King Street, she had to cross the railroad tracks to get to her father's store. She was deathly afraid of the trains when she was five or six years old, but later, she says she enjoyed buying a ticket and riding the train to Gainesville to visit her friend Frances.

Trains weren't the only frightful experience for the Hudgins family in Clermont. They had only been living in their new home on King Street for approximately a year when a "cyclone" (actually a tornado) roared through the community causing damage. The front porch was blown off the hotel, but luckily the now-historic structure suffered little other damage that day. Other structures in town, however, were not so lucky.

In an interview in 1998, Essie Hudgins Jordan remembered the day all too clearly. Experiences with tornadoes are difficult to forget.

"Father had gone to the store, and Mother had gone to visit my grandmother, **Rebecca Hawkins Tanner**, who was ill," Essie explained. "My brothers and sisters and I were eating breakfast when we heard a strange noise. We ran to the window and saw things flying up high into the air. Our first thought was that we needed to get to our parents, but my older brother insisted that it was safer to stay right where we were."

As things turned out, Essie's brother's instructions were sound counsel, for neither the Hudgins children, nor their home suffered any ill effects from the tornado.

Life soon returned to normal in Clermont. James' business continued to thrive. He always wore a white long-sleeved shirt and a little black bow-tie at his business. He also carried a very businesslike appearance according to family members, but also had a knack for the sales of merchandise.

"All the stories you read which describe pioneer life and the little general store where saddles, sunbonnets, barrels of apples, cheeses, dry goods, animal traps, and such were sold – that was very similar to Father's store," Essie continued. "On cold winter days, men gathered around an old pot-bellied stove in the store to play checkers. Father loved to play checkers," she smiled conspiratorially.

Eventually, as the years passed and the children grew and began seeking their own lives in the world, the idealistic life in Clermont began fading away for the Hudgins family. James' health began failing him, and he ultimately died from cancer of the liver in 1933. He was buried in Concord Baptist Church Cemetery with his two children who died in child-birth.

Following her husband's death, Sallie discovered there were outstanding uncollected debts owed by customers on accounts at James' store. She also discovered that sometime prior to his death, he had taken on a minor partner in his business – or at least that was the story she was given – and this "partner" claimed the outstanding uncollected accounts exceeded the value of the remaining assets of the store. It is unclear today why this "partner" was not just as responsible for these outstanding unpaid accounts as was James.

Sallie had strong doubts about the authenticity of the supposed partner's claim(s) to James' business, but with no firm knowledge of his business affairs, and no business acumen herself, Sallie was "out of her element" in fighting the lawsuit brought by the erstwhile "partner," and she ultimately lost the family business and source of income to the suspicious interloper who foreclosed on the unpaid notes. It was a cruel fate.

Interestingly, however, it was also at approximately this same time that the Gainesville-Northwestern Railroad – the life-blood of tiny Clermont – entered into Receivership and the rails were taken up forever, eliminating the supply line to Clermont and the old Hudgins store. The loss of the rail line rendered the town and commercial district virtually worthless. It seemed almost like Providence had intervened to deal with the "questionable partner."

Sallie continued to live at the Clermont home for two more years until the last child – Marjorie – was graduated from Chattahoochee High School. Then, in 1935, she moved to live at 32 East Washington Street in Gainesville.

Around 1937, Sallie moved to Atlanta to live with daughter Daisy and husband Charles Giles. They had a large old home on Juniper Street with five bedrooms which they operated as a "rooming house." They rented rooms out to travelers and area residents. Sallie lived with them for a number of years.

By 1945, World War II was nearing an end, and Daisy and Charles decided to close down their rooming house. Sallie then moved in with daughter Marjorie and her husband "T," living with them for several years.

In the last 30 years of her life, Sallie lived with one daughter then another before eventually discovering a nursing home by coincidence in Austell, no doubt during one of her trips to see daughter, Essie, in the northwest Georgia town of Rockmart a few miles beyond Austell. At the time, Sallie was living with daughter Mary Lou in Powder

James Bevely and Jane Bell Hudgins, the progenitors of much of the Hudgins descendancy from Hall and Jackson counties today, are buried in this tiny family graveyard in south Hall.

Springs, and after some thought, she reportedly stated, "When this is finished, I want to move in here," pointing to the Austell nursing home.

The nursing facility was newly-constructed at that time, and affiliated with a local hospital. Sallie, always a prudent and wise individual, apparently knew she was getting up in years and didn't want to become a burden to any of her children, even though she had raised every single one of them from childhood to adulthood. In short order, Sallie had made good on her statement, and moved into the nursing facility, living there for the last years of her life until she passed away on December 22, 1969.

On a cold winter day on this earth, her mortal body was buried alongside that of James, her two still-born babies and other relatives at Concord Baptist Church Cemetery in Clermont where their life had been so happy and content over half a century earlier. She no doubt smiled broadly as she entered *Glory* to rejoin husband James, and join hands with the Lord.

(Sarah Elizabeth Tanner Hudgins, descended from those pioneer Tanners who built such landmarks as Tanner's Mill at Chestnut Mountain, and James Zacheus Hudgins, descended from pioneers James Beverly Hudgins and wife Jane Bell, were all ancestors of the late Marilyn Jordan Jackson of Rockmart, and the late Patricia Jordan Nixon of Doraville, Georgia. Their children, grandchildren, and great-grandchildren – the Jacksons of Rockmart and Roswell; the Bradleys of Atlanta and Stone Mountain; and the Hughes of Rockmart, Marietta and Milton, Georgia, as well as the descendants of all the remainder of Sarah's and James' children, continue to grow the family today.)

Covered Bridges Outlaw Known as "Reverend Devil":

The Life & Times Of Bandit John A. Murrell

Some of north Georgia's treasured covered bridges were once the realm of a nasty band of outlaws.

Bandits, banditos, train robbers, and highwaymen. When we think of them, we usually think of the old West, but in point of fact, the state of Georgia has had its share of outlaws too, particularly during the days of the pioneers and early settlers. One such nasty group went by the name of "the Murrell Gang."

The Murrells were a loosely formed group of outlaws, led by one John A. Murrell, who roamed the north Georgia area in the early 1800s. Because of the nature of their "enterprises," the group plundered a wide territory, even reportedly ranging as far west as Texas, Arkansas, and the Choctaw Nation, but they hailed from north Georgia, and it was their base of operations.

Ironically, they might not have pillaged northeast Georgia at all, had it not been for a unique aspect of architecture there – the many covered bridges – which facilitated their evil ways. North Georgia – and northeast Georgia in particular – was once dotted with these structures. From the dark rafters of these always dimly-lit protective coverings of the many wooden bridges, a surprise attack could easily be launched upon unsuspecting travelers, businessmen, gold miners, stagecoaches, et cetera, creating an environment in which even seasoned travelers and former victims never knew when to suspect the next attack.

The notorious Bolding house which once existed near the Chestatee River in Hall County, Georgia, was a "headquarters" of sorts for the Murrells shortly after the discovery of gold in the area. And just beyond the Bolding home, Bolding Bridge likewise became a frequent site at which gang members reportedly pillaged travelers.

Even though law enforcement officials undoubtedly knew they were there, they couldn't catch them, since the Boldings used a sophisticated system of "early warning" to alert their brethren bandits in Bolding Bridge if they saw law enforcement officials approaching on the narrow road. And they didn't always use Bolding Bridge for their robberies either, moving all around northeast

205

Mystery & History in Georgia

Bolding Covered Bridge – This original covered bridge spanning the Chestatee River once linked Hall and Forsyth counties. Over the years it had gained a reputation as a dangerous spot for travelers and was the site of numerous robberies conducted by bandits such as James Murrell in the 1800s who would hide in the rafters of the bridge then drop down upon unsuspecting individuals. Mr. W.R. Bolding who owned it later sold this bridge to Hall County, and following the construction of Lake Lanier in 1956, Bolding Bridge was submerged beneath the lake waters. *(Photo courtesy of Chestatee Regional Library, Gainesville, GA)*

Georgia and even the Southeast in their criminal quest.

In the early days in north Georgia, there were few roads. People rode on horseback, or walked over rough trails which had been traversed by animals and Indians since time immemorial. These trails eventually began to widen, as carts and mule-drawn wagon traffic with increasingly more pioneers moved westward.

There were no bridges in these early years, and the task of crossing a stream with a loaded cart or wagon was often not only difficult but dangerous. Good river and creek fords usually were only available at shoals and low spots in the streams, usually during the dry season. Stream crossings were particularly dangerous during heavy rains.

Thus, the era of bridge construction was born, to insure year-round travel. And shortly thereafter, the wooden structures were covered with roofs and sides. Some said this was to keep the horses, mules and oxen from becoming frightened when seeing the water below. In truth, however, the wooden covers were designed to preserve the heavy timbers under-pinning the bridges, which were expensive and difficult to build and replace. And protect the bridges they did, but they at the same time exposed travelers to a new danger – the outlaw.

The Murrells came to north Georgia in the 1820s or '30s. The group, at best, was a strange family.

John A. Murrell, the leader of the group, was the son of a preacher. The Reverend William Murrell doubtless had some influence in the pulpit, but at home, "the old lady" ruled the roost.

John A. Murrell was born about 1800, and the exact site of his birth is not known today. When quite young, the family lived about 25 miles south of Nashville, Tennessee, near the village of Bethesda, a serene small community surrounded and half-hidden by the Cumberland Mountains. If Murrell was charmed by this picturesque setting, he never spoke of it.

From his earliest days, John Murrell was more interested in "speculations." He watched the traffic go by over the Natchez Trace and talked with travelers who roomed at a tavern operated by his mother. According to family tradition, young John never had aspirations to become a "man of God" like his boring and disrespected father. Instead, he listened to breath-taking stories of robberies and looting and adventures on the trail, dreaming of the day when he too could become a highwayman, seeking adventure, fame and ill-gotten fortune.

Down through the years, young John repeatedly maintained that it was his mother who began his life of crime. "My mother was one of the true grit; she learned me and all her children to steal as soon as we could walk," he reportedly once stated. "Whatever we stole, she hid for us, and dared my father to touch it. She made us hate the proud ones and go after those who had more than we did." Spoken like a true criminal in training.

It was at age 16, John stated years later, that he committed his first petty crime, swindling a storekeeper. Neighbors and acquaintances however, became suspicious and began watching him too closely. John decided his rural neighborhood was just too closely monitored for his ill deeds. He ultimately abandoned his Tennessee home to pursue his "speculations" on a grander scale in new places.

With a few accomplices, Murrell eventually traveled over much of the Southern states, stealing horses and robbing unsuspecting travelers wherever he went. He later returned to his home in Tennessee for a period of bragging, free-spending, and general carousing, but soon had spent all his ill-gotten gains.

To recoup his fortune, John set out to steal several horses nearby, but this time, he was caught in the act. After a speedy trial, the court's sentence stated: *"John A. Murrell shall receive on his bare back at the public whipping post in Davidson County thirty lashes, set in the pillory two hours on Monday, two hours on Thursday, and two hours on Wednesday, next, that he be branded on the left thumb with the letters H.T. (horse thief) in the presence of the court; that he be imprisoned twelve months from this day and be rendered infamous."*

From that horrible day forward, John Murrell was an embittered and unrepentant man with a passion for violence and revenge. In his prison cell however, he kept a stack of old books – the Bible and law books – but they were all a "smoke screen." He poured over these books day after day, learning each and every opportunity in which he might use the knowledge from the books to take advantage of an unsuspecting soul.

John Murrell later said that his study of criminal law and fundamental theology made him prepared for anything. His brother William Jr. met him when he stepped out the prison door as a free man, and another life of criminal activity began immediately. The two men rode off on two fine, freshly-stolen horses.

Making further

It was at age 16, John stated years later, that he committed his first petty crime, swindling a storekeeper.

Mystery & History in Georgia

Bolding Homestead – Located in Hall County on the old Dawsonville Highway at the Chestatee River, this landmark was also demolished in 1956, during the construction of Lake Lanier. It reportedly was frequented by John A. Murrell circa 1830s, who often posed as a traveling preacher. According to folklore, an opening at the edge of the ceiling above the porch (circled in white) was used to send signals to outlaws at a hideout on a hill a short distance away. *(Photo courtesy of Chestatee Regional Library, Gainesville)*

use of his studies, John turned to religion as a guise for his evil deeds. He often related to his cronies that as a child, he had been amused at the blind confidence a minister of the gospel could inspire, even a sorry minister like his father. John subsequently adopted the device of preaching, as a side-line profession, undoubtedly dipping into untold sums of money contributed to the church along the way.

His preoccupation with crime no doubt eventually forced his migration to Georgia. Men of unsavory reputations from all walks of life joined his band.

In that day, long coats and high-top hats were symbols of superiority, honor and intelligence. The arrival of an itinerant preacher was an event that brought settlers from miles around. Revival and camp meetings became regular devices for John. His gang members, needless to say, were very busy.

"Reverend" Murrell had found that these revival meetings furnished an excellent atmosphere for his work. During the campaigns, Murrell was quietly directing his lieutenants in horse-stealing, as well as various and sundry other criminal activities.

Despite the realm to which Murrell's operations had spread however, his intended goal in fact was much larger. The hatred and bitterness in him was welling more to the surface with each passing day. His vendetta was against the whole of established society in the South, and he was intent upon the destruction of as much of it as possible.

His plot, later uncovered and thwarted, was fabricated around the idea of a slave uprising (slaves in the South at that time usually outnumbered whites 40 to 1). The Blacks were being organized for just such an event on a certain day. According to Murrell's plans, all white people would be killed with the exception of some of the beautiful White women. Murrell promised the slaves (which he had been stealing now for many months and hiding away) their freedom, their own homes and money from the plantations they would plunder.

John Murrell's boldness, ruthlessness and lavish distribution of spoils attracted scores of followers and his band was reputed eventually to have numbered around 1,000 members. His operations, which extended over a number of states, included the robbery of mails, banks, stores, the piracy of river boats, and slave-kidnapping. Legend also attributes hundreds of murders to Murrell and his unholy crew.

Early Georgia Coin-Maker:

The Rare Gold Coins of Templeton Reid

Today, this former mint-operator's coins are among the rarest and most valuable in the world, yet the only sign of his former existence in Gainesville, Georgia, is a historic marker on the town square. In fairness, Reid did not leave many signs of his passing. He owned no home. He owned no business. He operated his mint in the town for only a brief few months. And when Templeton Reid – the purveyor of possibly the most valuable coins in the world – died, he was virtually penniless.

The gold coins minted by Templeton Reid in Gainesville, Georgia, in 1830, are today some of the rarest and most coveted coins in the world. The worth of some of his rarest coins is incalculable. In his day, he provided a highly-welcomed service to miners, but greedy dishonest competitors worked tirelessly to discredit his work and put him out of business – and they quickly succeeded. Ironically, it is due to the modern-day rareness of his coins that their value has sky-rocketed.

In 1977, an 1830 ten-dollar Reid gold coin sold for $41,000.00, and in 1979 a five-dollar Reid coin brought an astounding $200,000.00 in sale. The "1849 California Gold" coins minted by Reid after he left Gainesville are so rare that most coin books do not even attempt to place a value on them.

Records have indicated that at a minimum, Reid ran his Gainesville mint during part of July, all of August and September, and part of October, 1830. Dexter C. Seymour, who studied Reid's work extensively, stated in his *1830 Coinage of Templeton Reid* published by the American Numismatic Society in 1977, that he produced a total of approximately 1,600 coins, including approximately 1,000 quarter-eagles, 300 half-eagles, and 250 eagles.

The early history of Gainesville would not be complete without inclusion of the story of this early entrepreneur and his unique coinage practices. Reid was not a native of Gainesville. He merely took his business where the money was. He was actually only in Gainesville at the most for approximately one year, and possibly for as little as a few brief months, but in that short period of time – almost two centuries ago – his activities earned him renown with modern coin collectors throughout the world. An article which appeared in the July 24, 1830 edition of the Milledgeville, Georgia, *Southern Recorder* described Reid's new mint, and his coinage enterprise which he was bringing to Gainesville:

"We have examined, during the past week, with great pleasure, an apparatus constructed by our very ingenious fellow citizen, Mr. Temple Reid, for the purpose of putting gold into a shape more convenient than that in which it is originally found. He makes with great facility and great neatness, pieces worth ten, five and two and a half dollars. No alloy is mixed with it, and it is so stamped that it cannot be easily imitated. He sets out soon for the mines, and intends putting his apparatus into operation, as soon as he reaches them.

"About $1,500-worth of Georgia gold has been stamped by our ingenious townsman, Mr. Templeton Reid, with handsome dies, showing the actual value of each piece of metal, in parcels of $2.50, $5, and $10. The pieces of ten dollars have on one side this inscription: GEORGIA GOLD, 1830, and on the other, TEN DOLLARS, TEMPLETON REID. ASSAYER.

"The die of the five dollar is not inferior in execution to the stamp on the coins issued from the National Mint. Mr. Reid informs us that the gold dust stamped by him will be taken at the Mint and at most of the banks for the value it purports on its face to bear. This will give a pretty general currency, and make it answer the purpose of money.

"Mr. R. intends making an establishment in the gold region for the purpose of assaying and marking the gold as it may be found which will be a great convenience and saving to the miners, who have heretofore been obliged to part with the precious metal in its crude state at a loss from five to fifteen per cent. Reid's seven percent profit seems reasonable."

One can only imagine today the enthusiasm with which Templeton Reid's coin minting enterprise was met by the businessmen and crude exchangers of gold in the wilderness areas of what later became White, Lumpkin, Dawson and Hall counties. As long as Reid was in business exchanging his coins for gold dust being panned and mined in northeast Georgia, the slick purveyors in the backwoods would no longer be able to underestimate the value of the dust exchanged by them for food, funds, equipment and services. To say the least, Reid was not popular among those individuals, and they quickly sought to discredit him.

Early Life

The Reids were natives of Scotland. Templeton and his brothers had acquired many skills which enabled them to provide fine services and products. Templeton was an extremely-talented fine craftsman of a variety of goods which not only included the minting of fine gold coins, but the manufacturing of a number of finely-crafted items, including firearms, jewelry, and watches. He also was a fine silversmith. One also must not forget his mechanical skills as well, for someone had to design and build the detailed mint he used to create his coins.

Templeton's father, Alexander, and his brothers arrived in Georgia by way of northern Ireland and Lancaster County, Pennsylvania about 1745. A few years later they moved south, to the Rowan County district of North Carolina.

Alexander and four of his brothers, fought in the Revolution and after the war all qualified for bounty lands in

Georgia. They exercised their rights and the five families moved to the Greene County area between 1786 and 1792.

Alexander farmed, operated a ferry over the Oconee River, and with John Garner, owned a gristmill on the river near the crossing of the Eatonton-Greensboro road. Just as were his sons after him, Alexander was multi-talented.

The history of Greene County states that Templeton was born in 1789, when his father was 63 years old. This birth date may or may not be accurate, since it was reported at the time of his death that he born in 1786.

Alexander died in 1807 and his will does not mention Templeton by name, although it does provide for five unnamed minor children. This would lead one to believe that the 1789 date as Templeton's birthdate is correct, since that would make him a minor at the time of his father's death.

Nothing is known of Templeton's education, but it is evident that he received something better than the average individual for that day and time. It is also clear that he served a thorough apprenticeship in the metal-working trade, very possibly with other members of the Reid clan, since he demonstrated considerable talents in that profession. All his life he took pride in and demonstrated his fine craftsman skills.

Regrettably, Templeton did not demonstrate the same ability as a businessman. He also was something of a drifter, but was nevertheless a skilled silversmith as well. Some jewelry of his making is still in the possession of his descendants. Cutten's exhaustive study of this trade, *The Silversmiths of Georgia*, corroborates this and, in addition, reviews the careers of two other Reids – Elisha and Josephus – both also silversmiths. The three Reids are obviously related but the exact relationship is unclear today.

The earliest record of young Templeton Reid in the business world is a card (advertisement) in the *Milledgeville Argus*, of Aug. 10, 1813, wherein he advertises from Putnam County that he repairs watches and clocks and manufactures jewelry of all kinds. That same year he moved his shop to Milledgeville, where he *"had every material and convenience for working with dispatch."*

In 1814 and 1815, Templeton was a member of the firm T. and E. Reid. The E. in the firm was the Elisha mentioned earlier. The next year, Templeton was again working alone.

In 1817, Templeton undertook another line of business, becoming an officer in the short-lived Oconee River Navigation Company, an enterprise intended to operate freight boats on the Oconee River between Milledgeville and the mouth of Fishing Creek. The Fishing Creek terminus was the river port of Scull Shoals, a ghost town today.

For the next seven years, Reid pursued the watch repair and jewelry business in various Milledgeville locations. His cards appeared at irregular intervals in the *Georgia Journal*, the *Argus* and the *Recorder*.

In 1824, he announced that he was prepared to make rifles and rifle barrels of a superior order, priced from one to five hundred dollars. It is not known today how successful he was in this business, but it must have been a very limited market, judging from the fact that in 1824, $100 was the equivalent of $2,730.00 in 2021 dollars, and $500 was the equivalent of $13,653.00 in 2021 dollars – a hefty sum for any individual to have, wealthy or not.

It was in the summer of 1830, that Templeton Reid graced Gainesville with his presence. This in all likelihood was an exploratory trip to review the conditions then existing in the north Georgia gold fields and the viability of setting up a coinage business. Among his other talents, Templeton was an opportunist.

Georgia Gold Fields

As is commonly known today, gold was discovered in north Georgia in 1828. In spite of the lack of modern communications, word of the discovery spread rapidly. Benjamin Parks is quoted as saying, *"Within a few days it would seem the world must have heard of it, for men came from every state. They came afoot, on horseback and in wagons, acting more like crazy men than anything else."*

By 1830, the human wave was cresting. Thousands were combing the hills and wading the creeks in a search for the precious yellow metal. For the most part these men operated as individuals or in small cooperative groups. There were a few large mines, but in these heady early days most operations were simple pick and shovel affairs. The day of the big syndicates, the huge stamp mills and the elaborate water projects was yet to come.

Many of the miners found gold, if not in quantity, at least enough to provide food and to keep hopes high. Thanks to movies and television today, most of us are accustomed to visualizing a leather pouch or "poke" as the container of common usage by the miners for their "dust." No doubt there were such conveyances, but the average miner found the precious stuff in no such volume. In the Georgia fields the favorite container, amazingly, was a simple slender goose quill, carefully stoppered at each end. That was just how insignificant were the average "takes" by early gold miners.

Above and beyond the containers used to maintain the gold dust, the lucky miners still had a major problem.... How might they best "convert" their gold? Hard money was very scarce in 1830, particularly in the wilds of north Georgia. Banks, quick-stops, drug stores and the like obviously simply did not exist.

As has often been experienced in modern times with certain coin issues, speculation in gold and silver bullion can cause coins to disappear from circulation, and such was the case with many of these early coins too. The situation became so serious that President Thomas Jefferson had stopped all minting of the gold eagle and the silver dollar by 1806.

The absence of the dollar coins meant that the half-dollar was left to carry the burden of exchange and these promptly disappeared into bank vaults to be held as reserves or for use in large transactions. One historian has amazingly estimated that in 1830, there was only one good coin of Federal minting for each person in the country.

It also must be explained herewith that the "paper money" in America's pioneer days was issued **not** by the federal government, but by individual banks throughout the states, and these notes ranged from discountable to dubious to absolutely worthless in value. Early paper money literally was a "crap-shoot."

For these reasons, in 1830, most gold was bartered for supplies since it could not be easily converted into coins. Some was sold in the field to buyers and speculators and some more fortunate miners were able to send the yellow stuff to family or friends in distant places where a better exchange rate existed or a fair-rated mint of coinage was located.

The miners' dust varied considerably in both fineness and purity, and therefore in value for a given weight. As a consequence, businessmen and other

The Rare Gold Coins of Templeton Reid   Hall County

Templeton Reid's Georgia coins were produced from native metal and were of excellent fineness. Unfortunately, following an assay by a competitor, it was discovered the face value of each coin was slightly more than the actual gold content. A subsequent negative publicity campaign of letters published in area newspapers effectively ended Reid's career as a coiner.

Gold in its native state is always alloyed with other metals such as silver, tin, and copper. Templeton Reid believed his gold coins to be made of nearly pure gold, which ultimately has been proven incorrect. Nevertheless, his coins did contain purer gold than even those produced by the United States Mint.

sources of exchange of the gold dust automatically discounted the presumed value of the dust in order to avoid taking a loss. This almost always was to the disadvantage of the miners and others who owned the dust. It meant constant low gold prices for the hard-working miner, which became the source of constant agitation for a better system of marketing and barter of the metal.

And this didn't begin to take into consideration the miners' losses as a result of the hugely-inflated prices for all goods and services in general in the backwoods, so even though a miner might own a nice quantity of gold which would have been quite lucrative to convert in a big city where there was an established mint or goods which weren't tremendously-inflated in price, such was not the case in the wilds of north Georgia in 1830.

Reid's Mint

This demand from the miners for a fair exchange was to result, in a few years, in the establishment of the Dahlonega, Georgia, and the Charlotte, North Carolina, United States Branch Mints. And this, no doubt, was the opportunity Reid saw in 1830 in Georgia, prior to the availability of any mint in the area. He undoubtedly realized there was money to be made if he moved to a site near the mines, bought gold, and paid for the raw metal with coins of his own making.

Though the gold in his coins was of a higher purity even than that of the gold coins from the U.S. Mint, the actual quantity of the gold in his coins was slightly less than indicated by the face value of the coins. This was the method in which Reid maintained a profit margin, and it was perfectly legal and legitimate.

Gainesville was a natural choice as a location for Reid's new enterprise. According to the *U.S. Telegraph* of May 4, 1831, *"Gainesville, a small village on the borders of the gold region, also experienced a phenomenal growth. At the Elrod and Potosi mines were 3,000 workers and, in addition, Gainesville was a supply center for the Cherokee region. In 1830, the*

213

Mystery & History in Georgia

merchants took in $120,000.00 worth of gold and 8 or 10 streets were laid out." The claim of "3,000 workers" at the two mines undoubtedly was either an error or an intentional exaggeration. A number nearer 300 may have been more correct.

The first public notice of Reid's intentions in the minting realm is found in the *Milledgeville Recorder* of July 24, 1830, which read: *"About $1,500 of gold has been stamped by our ingenious fellow townsman, Mr. Templeton Reid, with handsome dies showing the value of each piece of metal, in parcels of $2 ½, $5 and $10. The $10 gold piece has the inscription "Georgia Gold, 1830" on one side, and on the other, 'Ten Dollars, Templeton Reid, Assayer.'"*

Reid is believed to possibly have been in operation in Gainesville even before this item appeared. Whatever the date, the first private operating mint in this country for the production of gold coins in dollar denominations was in Gainesville, Georgia. Before the days of the big gold rushes were over, nearly thirty firms would eventually mint such coins.

The Reid Mint is believed to have stood on West Washington Street, in a building that was later to become a blacksmith shop. Mr. W.A. Roper, writing as *"Cousin Arthur"* in *The Times* of Gainesville on August 4, 1959, stated that the shop was on Washington, between the Castleberry and the Looper properties. It is believed that the Castleberry home stood on the northeast corner of the block between Maple and Grove Streets, and that the Looper wagon yard was on the northwest corner.

The building in which Reid set up his coinage must have been rented or leased, as there is no record of a deed transfer. He also no doubt was only able to operate his private coin mint for a short time due to a growing chorus of negative publicity from jealous competitors

Negative Publicity

One such complainer – almost certainly one of the unscrupulous gold exchange operators and very possibly a competitive gold buyer – wrote to the *Georgia Courier* on the 16th of August, 1830, a letter obviously intended to cause Reid trouble. It read as follows:

Mr. Editor:

Although no assayer, I have taken the trouble of having a piece of Mr. Templeton Reid's coining, purporting to be worth $10 assayed at the mint. It was found to be but 22.5 carats fine; consequently (purported to be) worth a trifle more than Georgia gold dust. The actual value is $9.38c, giving Mr. Reid a profit of about 7 percent. The value of Mr. Reid's coin may be estimated as follows: $10 pieces - $9.38; $5 pieces - $4.69; $2.50 pieces - $2 and 34 cents.

(The letter was signed *"No Assayer."*)

The *Courier* letter of course was reprinted by other papers, and received national attention when a digest of it appeared in *Niles Register* – a publication considered to be the *Time* and *Newsweek* of its day – on October 9, 1830. The *Register* article was headed *"Strict Construction of the U.S. Constitution,"* and begins *"About two hundred and thirty thousand dollars-worth of Georgia gold is said to have been received in Augusta within the last nine months. Report says, Mr. Templeton Reid is coining and stamping at his mint in Gainesville not less than $700 of this gold per day. Allowing his profits to be 7 per cent, he is making about $16,000 per annum. This is better business than gold digging."*

The remainder of the article

discussed the legality of a private mint, quoting the *U.S. Constitution*, but in the end, the writer was forced to admit that there was nothing in the statutes which actually forbade private citizens from owning a mint and performing coinage, although it was unlawful for a state or territory to issue such coins.

Templeton Reid almost certainly was outraged at his detractors, and wasted no time in coming to his own defense. After all, jealous gold converters were doing their best to ruin his reputation and put him out of business.

Even before the *Register* article appeared, Reid directed the following notice to the *Georgia Journal* with a request that it be reprinted in other papers. From the *Athens Athenian*, September 21, 1830: *"Messrs Editors: I have just seen an article in the Courier, of the 16th inst., which I wish you to republish with my remarks on the same. It is over the signature of 'No Assayer.'* No Assayer begins by acknowledging he is no assayer, which was unnecessary; for I would expect everybody to know that – even before his expose on the subject of coin. But if he had ended by saying he was no calculator, nor knows anything about the standard worth of gold by the carat, he would deserve some credit for this candor."

Reid then went into a rather lengthy explanation of the problems of the gold buyer, the losses encountered in refining and the very slim margin of profit left to the operator. He concludes with this paragraph *"But as the currency and demand for my coin, and its credit in some of the Banks, seem to warrant the course, I shall continue to stamp and issue the Georgia gold in pieces of $10, $5 and $2 ½."*

However, due to the relatively short time Reid was able to remain in the business after the above negative publicity, one can only assume that his detractors achieved their objective in tainting his name and thereby forcing him to cease operations in the minting of gold coins.

Today, one can only guess at the number of coins actually minted by Reid in Gainesville. If, as many think, he was in business for at least a year, the total could amount to as many as 50,000 pieces, though other estimates give the total as small as 1,600. Nevertheless, today, these coins are extremely rare and consequently very valuable.

There is a full set of Reid coins in the Smithsonian Institution, and it is thought that a private collector holds one other set. Knowledgeable collectors estimate that there are no more than six pieces of each issue remaining in existence in the entire world.

.942% Gold

One explanation for the disappearance of the coins is the wide distribution they received. The merchants put them into channels of trade that even reached overseas, and miners sent them home.

The principle reason, however for the present-day rarity of Reid coins is the *exceptional honesty* of Templeton Reid. His coins were tested by the Philadelphia Mint in 1842 and were found to actually contain more gold rather than less gold than the face value would indicate. This completely discredits not Reid, but the above "No Assayer" and other detractors of his coins. With .942% fineness, Reid's coins are of a higher standard of purity than is found in any other gold coin of that day, not excepting those minted later by the government. He therefore, was making virtually no profit in his minting operations, which was yet another reason he was forced to cease operations.

In other words, Templeton Reid's coins were actually worth more as bullion than as coins. There is even a story

Mystery & History in Georgia

Pictured is a rare print of the United States Branch Mint which once existed upon the site occupied today by Price Memorial Hall at North Georgia State University in Dahlonega. Prior to construction of the federal mint in Dahlonega, Templeton Reid attempted to fulfill the need by Lumpkin County miners for coinage with his unique coining operation in nearby Gainesville, Georgia.

to the effect that they were so good that they were counterfeited. As a result of all of the above, most of Reid's coinage work ultimately went into the "melting pot," but ironically, the world is a better place for the few that have survived. There simply was no reason to allow Templeton Reid coins to remain in coin form prior to the days of collectibles.

Templeton Reid left Gainesville about as suddenly as he arrived. He is thought to have gone from there to Rutherford County, North Carolina, for part of 1831. In early 1832 he was back in Milledgeville and thence to Putnam County – but this time, his profession was that of a fine gun-maker and as a gunsmith.

In 1840, Reid moved to Columbus, Georgia, where he advertised in the *Enquirer* as *"the best gun-maker in the United States."* He supposedly was in California in 1849, but according to the *1850 Muscogee County Census*, he was back in Columbus. He died in that city on August 2, 1851.

A small number of coins bearing Templeton Reid's name were struck in California, but the exact mint site is unknown today. These coins were struck in $10 and $25 denominations. They were evidently only proof or "trial strikes." Only one of each denomination reached the East for the Philadelphia Mint, and the $25 specimen was stolen from the Mint in 1858.

To refute some misinformation in some books and magazines – which even to this day maintain that Reid's mint was in Lumpkin County and/or Dahlonega, – let us remember that neither the county nor town mentioned was in existence in 1830. Templeton Reid minted his coins in Gainesville.

And finally, to those who have persisted in falsely claiming that Templeton Reid's coins were made of lesser-pure gold and that he therefore was "run out" of the county for this deception, the aforementioned Philadelphia Mint tests in 1842 clearly indicated the actual purity involved.

(Grateful appreciation is expressed herewith to L.W. Richardson who provided the factual information necessary for this article.)

The Terrible and Devastating 1936 Gainesville Tornado

The day began ominously, with frightful black clouds, ringed with a fiery perimeter, gathering on the horizon. The air was deathly still just prior to the sound of a roaring howl the equivalent of which was later described as that of a huge freight train. And just that quickly, the city of Gainesville, Georgia, was left in ruins.

There are very few people still alive today who remember the terrible minutes during, and the worse hours following the terrible tornado which struck Gainesville and Hall County, Georgia, at approximately 8:28 a.m. on the morning of April 6, 1936. Those who do remember it would be very happy to have it removed from their memory banks forever. That event is still officially listed – as of 2021 – as the 5th worst tornado in U.S. history.

Weather specialists and other researchers today are still uncertain if the horrible creature was one, two, or three separate tornadoes at one time, but they do know it lasted only a couple of minutes. In that short period of time, a vibrant city was reduced to a landscape which more closely resembled a devastated urban battlefield.

According to the best assessments and witness reports of that day, at least one tornado paralleling the old Atlanta Highway (present-day Brown's Bridge Road) moved across Gainesville from the southwest. Another destroyed corridor appeared to have been the result of another tornado from the west which came up the valley between the Dawsonville Highway (Highway 53) and West Avenue. These two fields of destruction then appeared to combine on the western edge of Gainesville to form one immense funnel which then roared up to the town square, leveling it. This large funnel then apparently split apart again just south of the present-day Northeast Georgia Medical Center and continued its destructive path toward New Holland. A third separate tornado is believed to have spun off near Brenau College campus, rendering destruction there but causing no casualties.

In total, the twister (or twisters) roared along causing massive destruction for a total of approximately two minutes across approximately eight miles. It was finished before anyone could believe it, but its destructive path was massive and seemed to have caused so much damage that it appeared the city could never recover.

217

Mystery & History in Georgia

Survivors of the tornado on West Spring Street search for property and relatives following the devastating storm. *(Photo courtesy of Atlanta Journal)*

Destruction at 8:30 a.m.

At approximately 8:37a.m. (the time stamp in the wrecked Western Union office stopped at that moment) the two tornadoes came together west of Grove Street with a fury unmatched by anything prior to or since. Other "stopped watches" and clocks indicated times ranging from 8:28 a.m. to 8:31 a.m.

Nearly everything in an area four blocks wide in the heart of Gainesville exploded in ruins from the decompressive force and massive high velocity shrapnel flung by the gigantic weather anomaly. Buildings were crumpled like paper boxes. Stones, bricks and mortar man had used to shelter businesses and families for decades were ripped apart and hurled about like flotsam.

After a scant two minutes, the Gainesville town square lay in utter ruin. The structures which had miraculously escaped the storm, as well as those only partially destroyed, were shortly thereafter incinerated and consumed by the multiple fires which then were ignited.

Finally, having spent its fury, the combined tornadoes separated yet again and advanced on different paths out of town and onward – presumably into South Carolina.

The mythical *"Hammer of Thor"* could not have rendered a more thorough job of destruction or have left the people more dazed and bewildered. The whole town was stunned.

203 Dead

The actual number of dead from the disaster probably will never be known, but a total of at least 200 people may have lost their lives as a result of the huge twister(s). The United States Weather Bureau (National Climatic Center) has recorded the death toll at 203. So does the *World Almanac*, but it obviously used the weather bureau statistics.

The Red Cross, in its final report of the terrible disaster – which is on file at its national headquarters in Washington, D.C. – maintains that 132 persons were killed.

The *Gainesville Eagle*, in its April 16, 1936 edition, ten days after the disaster, carried a report credited to the local Red Cross, giving the death toll as 149.

The *Atlanta Journal* of April 7 – the day after the tornado – however, reports 158 killed, yet in its next day's edition the headline read: *Gainesville Prepares to Bury its 185 dead.*

The *Atlanta Georgian* of April 7 – also the day after the tornado – carried an article indicating 129 had been killed.

The last name-by-name list of victims found by *The Daily Times* researcher in the old *Eagle* counts **152 dead**.

The book, *A City Laid Waste* by W. M. Brice carries a table of statistics with 156 identified dead and six unidentified, bringing the total dead to 162.

The Times published the *Gainesville Eagle's* death list and asked for corrections, additions, etc. Only seven names were ultimately added, bringing the total to 159 identified dead.

There were four unidentified dead

The Terrible and Devastating 1936 Gainesville Tornado — Hall County

for whom memorial services were held. That brings the death list to 163. The old death list includes two charred unidentified bodies, putting the total at 165.

The 1936 Gainesville disaster is also rated as the tornado with the highest loss of life in a single building, with the fatalities suffered in the Cooper Pants Factory building.

"Missing Completely"

Since it is known for a fact that the bodies of some individuals listed as "Missing" were never found, the total tally for deaths is confused and incomplete at best. Irrespective of this fact, at the very least, the total number of dead is somewhere between 165 and the United States Weather Bureau's figure of 203.

It is unknown today how many – if any – of the "Missing" actually survived and never bothered to report themselves as alive and well. The Red Cross, as recorded in the April 16 issue of the *Eagle*, reported 17 missing and the *Gainesville News* of Aug. 14, 1947, reported eight still missing as of that date.

Almost certainly there were losses about which the circumstances will never be known, since even after many bodies were mutilated by the horrible shrapnel blown about by the tornado and torn by the unimaginable 150 to 200 mile-per-hour winds in the twister(s), they were then subjected to incineration by the many fires which were ignited as a result of ruptured gas lines and scattered wood stove coals, etc. By the time these bodies were reached by rescue operations, in many instances, very little remained but ashes – and sometimes, nothing remained at all.

Rescuers combed through the rubble for weeks after the disaster in the search for bodies – or even body parts. Sometimes grisly remains were

Following the horror of the huge tornado, victims next were forced to contend with numerous raging infernos as fires were ignited by overturned coal-stoves, ruptured gas mains and tinder-dry wooden structures. Pictured here are the blazing ruins of the C.V. Nalley Company and Pruitt-Barrett Hardware Company. *(Photo courtesy of Ramsey's Studio, Gainesville)*

discovered, and many times, as described above, nothing was discovered at all.

There is also a big question mark today as to whether or not bodies were lifted up in the storm and then carried far away to remote parts of the state or adjoining states, to be deposited in isolated locations, never to be discovered, their remains consumed by the elements and wildlife.

950 Reported as "Injured"

The number of "Injured" also is questionable. The United States Weather Bureau officially placed the number of injured at 934. Other sources list as many as 1,600 injured.

The national office of the Red Cross closed the Gainesville disaster file listing 546 as "Injured." In contrast the Red Cross, state and local figures in the old *Eagle* of April 16 say 733 were injured.

Here again, confusion reigned for weeks and even months after the disaster, and the confusing statistics leave much of the tragic losses still in question. The scope of the tornado(s) was so

Mystery & History in Georgia

Wreckage litters the town square, including many automobiles which were tossed about like matchsticks. *(Photo courtesy of the Atlanta Journal)*

great and the destruction so widespread, the exact number of dead will never be known, and the number of "Injured" will remain a question mark as well.

A 50th anniversary edition of the *Gainesville News* in 1947 stated the number "Injured" by the huge tornado was 950.

Regardless of the circumstances, it quite possibly would be reasonable to assume today that the actual number of injured was somewhere between 733 and 950 individuals.

Estimates of the property loss are not so mixed. The United States Weather Bureau table reported property damage at $13 million, based presumably on values of that time. In 2021 dollars, that loss would be the equivalent of $2.3 billion.

The *Gainesville News* of 1947 placed the loss at $16 million. Regardless of the reports, it is a known fact the town square was in ruins and much of what was left standing after the horrendous onslaught was destroyed by fires from ruptured gas mains.

Three Tornadoes

The tornado of 1936 almost certainly was a double-tornado, and quite possibly a "triplet." The official weather bureau map published in May of 1936 following the disaster graphically shows the disturbance as a triplet.

The funnel(s) approached the city from the west and southwest with a fury heretofore unmatched by any previous storm in Georgia history. A jittery populace which had already endured at least one previous – though not nearly as destructive – serious tornado, watched in mounting uneasiness as ominous black clouds, ringed by a fiery-appearing perimeter, appeared on the horizon and quickly approached the city on the fateful morning.

The first tornado recorded on the map reportedly came in from the west, struck Brenau College at 8:27 a.m., and moved on toward New Holland. The college was not badly damaged and there miraculously were no recorded casualties there.

Meanwhile, two other much larger funnels were striking the town square, rending and tearing and collapsing buildings, automobiles, and anything else in their paths. Objects as heavy as the huge one-ton cast-iron bell from the downtown courthouse were lifted like feathers and tossed blocks away. Some materials were carried far over into South Carolina.

Recovering From Shock

After a few horrible minutes, when they began to understand the disaster which had befallen them, residents of the town began coming to their senses. Many individuals acted quickly to rescue the trapped, assist the injured – and remove the dead. There were few in the town whose lives – one way or another – were not touched by the three-pronged hellish winds.

The Red Cross in its final report

The Terrible and Devastating 1936 Gainesville Tornado   Hall County

says 2,094 families were affected and 1,763 of these received Red Cross assistance. Red Cross close-out figures show 139 homes were destroyed and 198 damaged. The national office figures report 195 dwellings were either rebuilt or repaired by the Red Cross. Of this number 47 were completely rebuilt, along with 11 other structures. Six other buildings were repaired, the report shows.

"The building went to pieces!"

That is the way one of the survivors described the Cooper Manufacturing Company pants factory when the tornado collapsed the building that morning. The loss of life in the Cooper pants factory in Gainesville is still rated as the highest tornado-caused loss of life in a single building ever experienced in the United States.

The ill-fated individuals in this building met death in the twisted wreckage and a subsequent fiery furnace. The old *Gainesville Eagle* of April 18 says 100 bodies were recovered from the building.

Estimates differ as to how many workers were actually on the job at Cooper when the tornado struck. Some say 125, others say from 75 to 100 people were there.

Many of the workers were in the sewing room on the second floor and when it appeared as if the black cloud would envelope the plant they frantically rushed for the stairway, becoming trapped as the building was ripped asunder.

After the tornado struck, fires sprang up immediately as *"coal heaters burst and hot coals sprayed over cloth, dry wood and other inflammable materials"* and the building quickly became an inferno. Some people escaped, but many did not, perishing in the fire.

Workmen later dug in the ashes

South Main Street in Gainesville more resembles a war zone than a civilized city. *(Photo courtesy of the Atlanta Constitution)*

for days before bodies, horribly charred, were recovered.

Death & Destruction

All agree that the destruction of the Cooper pants factory was one of the more horrible aspects of the disaster. There were some miracle-like escapes, but for most of the workers it was simply "Doomsday."

"The dew stood on the screens of windows and doors that morning; mother told me not to report for work, but I went anyway," said one young girl rescued from the wreckage of the Pants factory. "I arrived at the plant at 8 a.m. and black clouds already completely hid the sun and the morning resembled night.

"One employee of the plant who faced a row of windows noticed a rolling cloud of dust and rain approaching. She yelled for someone to look, but by then, timbers were already flying through the air and the building was collapsing around us.

"Then the coal heaters burst and the hot coals sprayed over everything, turning it into an inferno," the survivor continued.

Another employee at the ill-fated factory blamed the tragic fires on the coal heaters which burst. She related her experiences during the very brief

221

A view from the Federal Building toward the old Hall County Courthouse, an area of utter destruction. Notice the many mutilated and buried automobiles inside the structure (foreground). *(Photo courtesy of the Gainesville Photographic Studio)*

– but seemingly infinitely-long – period in which many of her companions perished.

"I was working on the top floor of the plant after reporting to work as usual that morning," she explained. "The power went off very early, and the dark skies offered little light to the gloomy interior of the plant. Many of the workers gathered coats and made for the narrow stairway which led to a doorway on the first floor. Many were screaming before the tornado even struck, but the stairway (was a death-trap).

"I didn't reach the doorway. Timbers fell on me and a heavy safe lodged above me. This safe protected me from much of the fire which was raging through the rubble, but my clothes were scorched by the intense heat."

From News Reports:

THE GAINESVILLE EAGLE
Corteges Move Almost Hourly to City of Dead;
Services Will Extend Into Next Week for the Storm Victims

"Gainesville citizens set about the mournful task of burying their dead this weekend with funerals scheduled for nearly every hour of the day, while in the business section and throughout the storm-torn districts, workers continued to toil, clearing the debris and searching for those still reported as missing.

"The following paragraphs are of funerals already held and time and place of other funerals to be held this week-end and the first of next week, of those already recovered from the mass of twisted and broken wood, steel and brick which once were homes or business houses.

"MRS. H.L. GAINES AND MISS KATHERLEEN GERTRUDE GAINES, ages 58 and 32, respectively, wife and daughter of H.L. Gaines, were held Wednesday afternoon, at 4:30 o'clock, at the First Methodist Church, with Rev. R.L. Russell officiating, assisted by Dr. R.Q. Leavell, Mrs. and Miss Gaines are survived by their husband and father, H.L. Gaines, of this city, and one son and brother, Herman L. Gaines of Atlanta.

"MRS. FAY WATTSON, age 22,

who was killed in the Cooper Pants Factory, was held Wednesday afternoon, at 3:30 o'clock, at the residence, 70 West Broad Street. She is survived by her father and mother, Mr. and Mrs. Henry Robinson, of Anderson, S.C.

"MRS. BIRDIE MAE KEMP, at 19, was held at the residence, 88 N. Bradford Street, Wednesday afternoon at 3:30 o'clock.

"CLYDE B. CARTER, age 36, was held at the home of Mr. O. A. Carter on North Green Street, Tuesday afternoon, at 4 o'clock with Rev. R. Q. Leavell officiating."

Rescue workers search frantically for bodies in the debris. *(Photo courtesy of the Atlanta Georgian-American)*

Body of Man Covered by Flowers

"Covered by a bed of beautiful hothouse flowers, the body of the first victim found in the residential section since the clean-up crews left the business section was discovered Friday. The body was that of John Franklin, 65. His death brought the storm total to 184.

"He was blown out of his home by the tornado, carried across an alley and smashed through the glass shelter of the 'Jackson Green House.' His body was found in a bed of tulips in full bloom.

"Employees of the greenhouse had escaped death in the storm because a hail storm just before the tornado struck sent them huddling to the shelter of a heavy fence."

THE GAINESVILLE NEWS
Freaks of 1936 Storm

"Huge steel drum, used for transporting oil, found standing upright beside desk in Gainesville News office. It was never discovered from whence it came.

"One-ton bronze courthouse bell blown across three streets, landing 350 feet away against a residence.

"Sliver of wooden framing, two inches wide, three feet long driven through door-facing at meat market.

"Of the building, equipment and seats in a large church, only one piece found was ever recognized - part of the piano.

"Fire bell weighing over 600 pounds lifted across street, crashed through roof onto floor of business building 150 feet away.

"Piece of timber four inches square dropped and jammed into stove pipe leading from business house.

"Billheads from Gainesville store dropped at Toccoa, over 40 miles away, 17 minutes after storm struck.

"Three small Negroes skeeted under steps of a house when storm approached. House and its foundations completely destroyed, steps left, little Negroes unharmed.

"Business stationery from Gainesville was picked up at Tucapaw Mills, S.C., 130 miles away."

Victims of the Tornado

Compiled by W.M. Brice
in *A City Laid Waste*

White
1. Mr. Fred L. Grigg
2. Mrs. Fred L. Grigg
3. Cecil Chester Grigg

Mystery & History in Georgia

Gladys Tanner poses beside the huge bell from the Hall County Courthouse which was tossed some 350 yards by the tornado. *(Photo courtesy of the Atlanta Journal)*

4. Dinwiddy Grigg
5. Nora Ann Grigg
6. Malum Grigg
7. Pansy Estelle Kanady
8. John Egbert Owens
9. Guy Barrett
10. Clyde Carter
11. John Stewart Rogers
12. Dr. Robert Dinwiddie Grigg
13. Mrs. George Spain
14. Mrs. Hattie Strickland
15. Mrs. Laura Anna Gailey
16. Emmett Julian Lilly
17. Dorothy Ree Fleming
18. Rufus McMahan
19. Osler Doyle Bowman
20. E.H. Perry
21. Mrs. W.M. Bailes, Jr.
22. Mrs. W.M. Bailes, Sr.
23. Miss Kathleen Gaines
24. Frank William Benson
25. Mrs. H. Leon Gaines
26. Jesse C. Eades
27. Herbert Franklin Cochran
28. Spencer Morgan Means
29. John Henry Richardson, Jr.
30. Rev. Jesse M. Sheffield
31. Mrs. Stanton Cox
32. Clark Hubert Henry
33. Mrs. Mollie Kimbrell
34. John Kimbrell
35. Norris Theodore Sheridan
36. Gladys Opal Barker
37. Candler Martin
38. Mark Anthony Bolding
39. Mrs. Garland Anderson
40. Haywood Pethel
41. Frances E. Anderson
42. Edward Anderson
43. Mrs. Ernest G. Watson
44. Irene Kiser
45. Ernest Sewell Hancock, Jr.
46. Roy Martin
47. Mrs. Claude Foutes
48. David Gower Jarrett
49. Pauline Sullins
50. Frank Coyle
51. Mrs. Richard R. McMahan
52. John Latty
53. Miss Winnie Bryant
54. Charles Schubert
55. Mrs. Hoyt Dale
56. Mrs. Ralph Evans
57. Rosa Lee Tumlin
58. Mrs. Birdie Mae Kemp
59. Mrs. Glenn G. Stowe
60. Mrs. Joe Bryant
61. Sidney Glover
62. Talmadge DeWitt Stevens
63. James Barnes Palmour
64. Mrs. Mary Hudgins Evans
65. Lorene Wilson
66. Dean DeLong
67. Mary Addie Thomas
68. Miss Tommie Porter
69. Mattie Ethel Adams
70. Joe B. Adams, Jr.
71. Robert Adams
72. Olomon W. Apperson
73. Emma Austin
74. Mrs. Mamie Brooks
75. Claude Brown
76. John Burnett
77. Ola Barrett Burnett
78. Richard Ellis Bowles
79. Lorene Bailes
80. Mrs. Flora Burtz
81. Flora Helen Burtz
82. Dewey C. Cagle
83. John Cain, Jr.
84. Mrs. Annie Mae Cain
85. Paul E. Cox
86. Mrs. Hattie Mae DeLong
87. Gertrude DeLong
88. Dwane Dowdy
89. Miss Jessie Dunnigan
90. Clarence Osgood Ellis
91. Mrs. Clarence Ellis
92. John Franklin
93. Mrs. Omie Kanady Gilstrap
94. Miss Idell Gillespie
95. Mrs. Bell Hart
96. Birdie Hart
97. Virlin Hart
98. Mrs. J. Harrington
99. Mrs. Jamie Henderson
100. John Jacob Huessey
101. Mrs. J.J. Huessey
102. Dolores Huessey
103. Mrs. Gertrude J. Jackson
104. Mrs. John Jones
105. Mary Jones
106. Harvie Kerves

The Terrible and Devastating 1936 Gainesville Tornado　　　　Hall County

Heavy railroad boxcars in the Gainesville Midland Railway yards were also easily tossed about. The now-historic Gainesville-Midland Depot – which still stands today – is visible (left-rear). *(Photo courtesy of the Atlanta Georgian-American)*

107. Harvey Pinkerton Kervey
108. Samuel McCrary
109. John E. Murphy
110. W.H. Norris
111. Mrs. Becky Patterson
112. Mrs. Jessie L. Phillips
113. Authur Ernest Porter
114. Miss Olie Prater
115. Mrs. Lilly Onie Robinson
116. Wm. Robert Shields
117. Mrs. Lilly Richardson
118. Mrs. Shiloh Smith
119. Ruby Sullins
120. Grace Tate
121. Hubert Tumlin
122. Lilly Bell Tumlin
123. Infant Tumlin
124. Boy Unidentified
125. Unidentified Body
126. Unidentified Body
127. Unidentified Body
128. Girl Unidentified
129. Ben West, Jr.
130. Lois Whitehead
131. Missing-Tommy Brown
132. Missing-Tommy Cagle
133. Missing-Glaze
134. Missing-Tommie Smith
135. Missing-Mrs. M.H. Grindle
136. Missing-M.H. Grindle

Black

137. One Unidentified
138. Dee Byrd
139. Clifford Banks
140. Flora Bradley
141. George Cheek
142. Nicie Collier
143. Otis Couch

The destruction and loss of life was so severe that U.S. President Franklin D. Roosevelt traveled to the site and spoke from the rear platform of the Presidential Train to express his sympathy and support. The Gainesville disaster is still rated as the fifth-worst such tornado in U.S. history. *(Photo courtesy of the Atlanta Journal)*

144. Mary Nelle Davis
145. Carrie Louise Davis
146. Mary Dorsey
147. Lizzie Jones
148. Louise (Kitty) Moss
149. Montine Reynolds
150. Lizzie Reynolds
151. Louellen Sadler
152. Charles Welborn Singleton
153. Lloyd Singleton
154. LeRoy Strickland
155. Hattie Sadler
156. Joe Thompson
157. Ellen Waters
158. Edgar Lee Williams
159. Mollie Butts Williams
160. Carrie Lou Williams
161. Name not listed
162. Name not listed (White)

Night of Terror at Merrill's Mill

Approximately 140 years ago – as of this writing in 2021 – a terrible flood struck the tiny mill village of Franklin, Georgia.

In the next to last decade of the 19th Century, the Merrill and Roop families of rural Franklin, Georgia, operated a gristmill powered by the cold, usually-quiet waters of Hillabatchee Creek. Under normal circumstances, the individuals of this little fiefdom led the tranquil lives that would be expected of a rural agrarian family. All of that, however, changed abruptly on the night of April 23, 1883.

It was a fearsome night for the families inhabiting the small mill village. The weather that night was a precursor of the wrath about to descend from the heavens. At the time, however, the citizenry around Merrill's Mill were oblivious to their impending doom.

The few records which were kept for that date state that the sky over west Georgia was fearsome, dark and threatening, composed of deep hues of red, orange and blue during the day, and a seething black when the sun dipped below the horizon in the evening. It was almost as if nature were trying to warn area residents that it was time to flee – before the doom arrived.

As the evening approached, rain began to fall – lightly at first, then with more violence as the storm cell moved into the area. Mixed with hail, the deluge beat a cacophony reminiscent of bullets upon the tin roofs of homes. The terrible force of the storm was frightening almost immediately. Thunder reportedly played like the bass notes of a Sunday organ.

The dirt roads of the county quickly became rivers of thick sucking goo, creating everwidening rushing streams of dirty, red water, quickly becoming evident that one could not "leave" even if one wanted to at that point. Everywhere one looked, the water collected faster and faster, and the ground, which had already soaked up its limit that week, began to refuse further absorption.

The residents of Heard County didn't know it at the time, but vicious tornadoes from this storm had been spawned farther to the northwest, and were tearing up the countryside all across the Southeast. This destruction was headed straight toward Franklin.

With the torrential downpour becoming worse by the minute, Hillabatchee Creek also began to fail to shed the onslaught, dramatically swelling in size. Lightning flashed evilly across the darkened sky, and as was their custom, the families in the vicinity of Merrill's

Mill began huddling together to wait out the ever-increasing storm.

Sometime around midnight, according to later newspaper accounts of the tragedy, there was a lull in the storm. At this point, many of the families undoubtedly relaxed somewhat, thinking the worst had passed, and went to bed. It was a decision which would shortly cost many of them their lives.

According to news reports, the Roop and Merrill families were central characters in the disaster in the Merrill's Mill area.

The Families

Benjamin Jocephus "Ceph" Roop, 31, had moved to this mill village after marrying Georgia Merrill whose father, Robert, owned the gristmill and substantial property in the vicinity. Ceph's father – Martin Roop – was known as the founder of Roopville, Georgia. Census records from that time, amusingly, list Ceph's occupation as "huckster." The night of April 23rd, however, was anything but a laughing matter.

Ceph's house, unfortunately, was located on the low side of the creek – and even more chilling, it was just below the dam. It was a factor which would shortly prove devastating to his family. Of his household, he would be the only survivor of the on-coming disaster.

According to one newspaper report, Georgia Merrill Roop, (Ceph's wife) was not feeling well the night of the disaster.

Bula Roop, 5, was the oldest child of Ceph and Georgia.

H.D.R. (Homer), 3, was the middle child of Ceph and Georgia. Today, his worn tombstone lies broken – his initials on one portion and his surname on the other.

Ella Roop, 1, was the youngest child of Ceph and Georgia.

Thomas Roop was Ceph's brother, and had the misfortune to be overnighting at Ceph's home the evening of the disaster. His home was in Roopville where he was the town's first postmaster. He also helped his brother at the mill and store.

A black female provided house-tending and nursing services in the Roop home. Though unnamed in any newspaper accounts of the incident, she is remembered by some residents as the daughter of Harmon Ridley, 48, a black farmer with a large family who lived nearby.

Robert Merrill, 52, was Georgia's father. Robert and his wife, Sara, both survived the flood, but were fated to watch it and its horrible consequences as the events unfolded that night. Their home, which was on high ground, was across the creek from the Roop home.

Henry Albert (Bit) Merrill was Georgia's brother, and Lula Miller Merrill was his wife. Lula went into labor and gave birth to their first child, Carrie Lee Merrill (Cook), sometime during the storm. Family members maintain that when water began rising up into their home, Lula and Henry sought refuge with relatives (probably her parents who lived farther away from the creek).

Henry's house was also destroyed. No one in this household died that night, but all were fortunate they departed the premises in advance. Only one piece of furniture – a three-drawer chest with oval frame – was salvaged. Carrie Merrill Cook later gave this chest and frame to her youngest daughter, Vilwon Cook Gore.

The Storm

News reports place the time of the most destructive portion of the storm between midnight and 2:00 a.m.

Reporters described heavy rain, hail and intense thunder at this time.

According to an eyewitness account in the April 27, 1883 issue of the *Carroll County Times*, the lightning was so constant that for 80 minutes, it was almost as if it were daylight. *"It was the grandest display of electricity I ever saw,"* he stated. *"Several responsible persons inform me that hailstones fell from the size of hen eggs to as large as a man's fist...."*

A writer in the Thursday morning (April 26, 1883) edition of *The Atlanta Constitution*, written with a Hogansville dateline, very obviously was either an eye-witness or interviewed a witness. He wrote: *"Sunday night's storm was fearful around this place, but what we suffered was insignificant compared to the damage in Heard County. Every creek overflowed there and the bottomlands are almost ruined for the present year...*

"An awful story comes from a settlement six miles beyond Franklin," the article continued. *"Mr. B.J. Roop is one of the best-known citizens of Heard County. About midnight, the tempest lulled a little and the family was able to sleep. The rain seems to have continued up the creek (however), for the water kept on rising until it had swept beyond the highest mark it ever before had reached. The Roop family slept on, oblivious of the awful doom that was creeping on.*

"Between 1:00 and 2:00 a.m., the water had risen under the house high enough to lift it from its sills. It swayed to and fro in the awful tide. The motion aroused Mrs. Roop, who was trying to wake her husband when the torrent rushed in the doors and the house began to float down the stream.

"... The scene of terror must have been appalling. The children were screaming and the poor woman was almost frantic with grief. Roop, though almost a giant in form, stood helpless in the awful storm....

"... The house, turning and reeling, reached the current of the creek and dashed swiftly down the foaming water. After going a hundred yards or so, it struck a tree with such violence that the shock shivered it to a mass of floating ruins."

A Victim Survives

According to this newspaper account, Ceph Roop caught a floating mattress and was carried downstream. His wife, children and the house-maid girl struggled in vain for their lives. As Ceph Roop held desperately to the mattress, his family disappeared under the black tide as strobed lightning flashed on the nightmarish scene.

According to the *Atlanta Constitution* correspondent from Hogansville, Ceph Roop eventually climbed into a small tree as the mattress lodged against it momentarily.

"He climbed high enough to escape the current and was saved," the article stated. *"Though an expert swimmer, he could never have gotten out of the rushing current from which the tree saved him. Holding on to a limb all night long, he suffered untold agony for he realized that his loved ones must all have been lost."*

At daybreak, Ceph reportedly determined his whereabouts. He was three-quarters of a mile from home and 150 feet from "shore," according to the news account.

In the Friday morning (April 27, 1883) edition of *The Atlanta Constitution*, correspondent R.J. Gaines of Carrollton wrote:

*"... The last words Mr. B.J. Roop recollects of speaking to his brother, Thomas, was while they were standing in the yard, in front of the house. He told his brother to

take care of himself and he would try and save his family.

"He then hurried to the window and the water was, by this time, waist deep, and did all he could to extricate his wife and children from the impending danger. But with that unselfish love that only a mother can feel, (Mrs. Roop) refused to go unless her precious little ones could be taken at the same time, preferring to perish with them rather than leave them alone to the merciless fury of the raging waters.

"A few minutes more persuasion with his poor sick wife, who was not able to help herself, and all was lost. The dam above the house gave way and its tremendous volume of water came with all the force and terror of a mighty avalanche, sweeping everything before it.....

No vestige of dwelling, store or outbuildings was left to mark the spot where once dwelt this happy family."

The home of Henry Albert Merrill was also destroyed, according to the article in the *Constitution*. "He and his wife would have been lost had they not gone to spend the night with some of her relatives," the article explained.

A Search For Victims

Neighbors and relatives began the search for the missing individuals the next morning. The bodies of two of the children were the first to be found – about a mile away. One source said Ceph Roop found the bodies.

Volunteers searched all Monday and Tuesday for Mrs. Roop, Thomas Roop, the third child and Harmon Ridley's daughter. News accounts (*Carroll County Times*, April 27, 1883) indicate that later, the body of Thomas Roop was found about a mile below the mill site. Mrs. Roop and the house maid were also found. Some reports maintain the bodies were in trees and under debris left by the torrent.

The third child, according to the May 11, 1883 issue of the *Carroll County Times*, was the last unrecovered body, and was finally found Wednesday, May 2, "the buzzards indicating its locality. When found, the body was covered by the debris sufficiently to keep the buzzards from it. It was decently buried by the side of its mother."

No doubt overcome with grief and loneliness, Jocephus Roop left Heard County that fall (1883) with several men (William Garrison, Frank McWhorter, and J.H. Parham) for Bell County, Texas, according to a news item in the November 1, 1883 issue of *The LaGrange Reporter*. Ceph reportedly remarried and reared another family there.

One must remember this was barely 18 years after the devastating destruction wrought by Union troops and the U.S. Civil War in Georgia. Those still living in Georgia were barely surviving, and survival resources were still at a premium in 1883. Many people were leaving Georgia for a new start in Texas, and this is the reason so many families have relatives in Texas today.

As explained earlier in this article, Carrie Lee Merrill (Cook) was born sometime just before or during the storm. Because many records were destroyed when the Heard County Courthouse burned in the late 1880s, Carrie later had to prove her birthdate to qualify for a pension.

To accomplish this, Carrie asked a neighbor, the late Byrd Wood of Ephesus, if he remembered her birthdate.

"He said he sure did," related Carrie's daughter, Verna Cook Smith in a later interview. "He told her it was the night of the freshet. She took him to Franklin and he told the people in the

Very little remains of Merrill's Mill today. Merrill-Roop Cemetery is overgrown and quickly being reclaimed by nature.

courthouse and she went to drawin' (her pension)."

Eighty years after the terrible storm, Carrie finally expired from natural causes on February 2, 1963. The petite Godfearing mother and grandmother – with the help of her husband, Lucious Riley Cook – amazingly had raised 12 children.

Merrill-Roop Cemetery

The following individuals are buried in the Merrill-Roop Cemetery, near the original mill village site adjacent to Hillabatchee Creek:
- Sarah J. Merrill (May 4, 1827 Dec. 1, 1886)
- Georgia A. Merrill Roop (Oct. 15, 1856 April 23, 1883)
- Little Ella (Jan. 2, 1882 April 23, 1883)
- Bula Roop (Nov. 1, 1878 April 23, 1883)
- Homer D. Roop (broken headstone with initials H.D.R.) (April 15, 1880 April 23, 1883)

Interestingly, the gristmill on the Hillabatchee Creek was rebuilt after the flood, but the spirit of the community had been broken. No one trusted the site for security any longer. The Merrills, devastated by the tragedy, moved to another mill town in nearby Alabama.

Today, as of this writing, very little – aside from the tiny abandoned cemetery – remains to mark the mill village which once existed on this site. With the rush of the Hillabatchee just a short distance away, Mother Earth wraps her great arms around the remains of those buried quietly here in this final repository among the tall trees and briary weeds in the low hill country of Heard County.

The Gunfights & Mysterious Life Of Pioneer Harrison Riley

In the tumultuous days of the 19th Century, one of the early pioneers to the gold fields of Lumpkin County, Georgia, became renowned as a wealthy plantation owner and businessman, and even more so as an aggressive fighter who wasn't averse to a shoot-out on the town square if necessary.

Harrison W. Riley was a name which invoked a measure of admiration and respect, but also fear and trepidation in the hearts and minds of some of his contemporaries. He possibly was born dirt poor, but when he died, he quite likely was one of the richest men in all of north Georgia. Upon his final breath in 1874 at the age of 70, those with whom he had done battle in his lifetime undoubtedly felt not remorse, but relief, and possibly even a measure of vengeance.

Riley was the kind of person who evoked strong emotions from almost anyone who knew him, whether it be respect from the electorate, love from the women he squired, or hatred from his political adversaries and challengers in general. No one was neutral about Harrison Riley.

At least a portion of any ill feelings was based upon simple jealousy. Riley was never one to "rest upon his laurels."

He was a man of constant action. As such, he was successful in his pursuit of public office as well as in the accumulation of wealth during his lifetime. These qualities singled him out for acclaim, but also made him a target for animosity as well.

Several details and characteristics of Harrison W. Riley's life – even if taken singly – would make him considerably noteworthy in the history of north Georgia:

1/ If one considers both hard cash and real estate, Riley undoubtedly was the wealthiest man at least in the northeast Georgia region for a number of years.

2/ The full extent of all of his former real estate holdings possibly will never be known, due to the fact that a number of them were placed in the names of individuals he loved and cherished. It is known for certain, however, that he once owned several substantial plantations – including slaves – in Georgia, and at least one in Alabama.

3/ Throughout his early life, Riley had coveted a military position of high authority. Though he was never actually commissioned as an officer in either the U.S. military or the Confederate Army, he assumed the rank of – and was addressed as – "General" from the 1860s until his death. At one point in the 1860s, he assured Georgia authorities that he could raise a 1,000-man army for the Confederacy from the northeast region of the state.

4/ Riley was known far and wide as a "scrapper" who would fight with fists, dirks, or firearms and both challenge others and defend himself in the legal arena at the drop of a hat. He neither gave any "quarter" to his opponents, nor asked for any for himself. The court records of Lumpkin County are replete with accounts of his numerous battles – both legal and physical. He was fearless, and did not hesitate to engage even in pitched gunfights, several of which were waged on the Dahlonega, Georgia, town square with his enemies.

5/ When he died, Riley reportedly left a hidden treasure that, as of this writing, has never been found, or at least never *publicly acknowledged* if it was discovered. It could conceivably be worth millions of dollars today and is still being sought by treasure hunters. The property around his former home in White County resembles a lunar landscape today as a result of years of excavations made by treasure hunters in search of that gold.

6/ Riley served in the Georgia General Assembly as a representative from the Lumpkin County area for a number of terms. In fact, for a period of 30 years, it was a rare event when he did not hold public office. He so competitively sought service in the political arena that one of his outraged opponents once attempted to assassinate him as he stooped to light his pipe from the coals of a hearth.

7/ And finally, the aspect of his life which created the most notoriety of all, involved the numerous females with whom he consorted throughout his life. He reportedly was the father of numerous children, by several different women, and not once was he ever legally married.

Early Life

The first thirty years of the life of Harrison W. Riley are a mystery which quite possibly will never be solved. It is known, however, that he was born in North Carolina circa 1804.

One early newspaper article states that Harrison Riley was *"a penniless orphan boy"* when he came to Dahlonega. This statement, however, cannot be completely accurate. Riley certainly was not penniless and he was not an orphan, although it is possible that his father pre-deceased him at an early age. His mother, Mrs. Susan Riley, was still living and she along with another son, Jesse L. Riley, moved to Dahlonega at the same time as did Harrison.

It is also possible that there was a third Riley brother in the group. They were joined a few years later (about 1837) by a sister and a brother-in-law, Mary P. and John M. Harris, and their children.

A portion of the inscription on Susan Riley's grave marker reads *"She was born in Person Co., N.C. about the year 1787"* (1787 - Aug. 3, 1856). A search of the public records in Person Co., N.C. reveals that a William Riley posted a marriage bond there on January 24, 1802 (actual records of marriages were not recorded until years later).

William Riley owned property and lived in the Deep Creek section of

Person County, and the Riley name may still be found there today. Harrison Riley's family apparently followed the migratory trend of settlers moving from east to west in early pioneer days, traveling from North Carolina to Monroe Co., Tennessee prior to the family's move down into north Georgia.

Riley's sister, Mary, whose husband John M. Harris had died July 2, 1848 on his way home from the Mexican War, stated in a widow's pension application that she and her late husband were married about November 20, 1833 in Monroe Co., Tennessee. Mary was only 18 years of age at the time of her marriage and it is highly unlikely that she would have moved from North Carolina to Tennessee without her family, so the entire Riley family – including Harrison – most probably lived in Tennessee in the early 1830s prior to moving to the gold fields of north Georgia.

Lumpkin County at the time of Harrison Riley's arrival was a frontier land. Andrew Cain's *History of Lumpkin County (1832-1932)* describes it as follows:

"*The rush to the mines brought into the country thousands of men of great diversity and character, many of whom were of that reckless class who disregard the laws of God and man. . . .Gamblers and swindlers of all kinds thronged hither to cheat the miners out of their easily gotten gold. Drinking, gambling and fighting were rife and the laws were little known and less cared for.*"

Harrison Riley was one of the first settlers in Lumpkin, arriving shortly after the county was created on December 3, 1832, following the first land lottery from the Indian property confiscated by the state of Georgia. The state was insistent upon acquiring the land in order to enlarge its scope and gain access to the gold fields in the northern portion of the state. Riley no doubt had traveled to Lumpkin to seek his fortune either directly or indirectly via the gold fields.

According to period newspaper accounts, Riley arrived "*before a stick of timber was cut where the city of Dahlonega is situated today.*" At that time, the area which ultimately grew into the city of Dahlonega was a deep and dark wilderness, exceedingly difficult to penetrate, particularly since there simply were no roads.

It was the perfect situation for an opportunist vagabond such as Riley. He apparently decided that instead of back-breaking labor for himself, he would let others do the dirty work of finding the gold, and he would provide a place for the miners to come to spend their newly-discovered riches. It was infinitely easier to find gold with a deck of cards or by the sale of price-inflated merchandise, than it was with a pick and shovel. Riley, if anything, was always clever and resourceful.

Interestingly, it wasn't long before he erected the first store in Dahlonega on the east side of the town square, and soon began to accumulate his vast fortune. The origin of the funds required for this early mercantile development is a matter of high suspicion today.

It has been speculated that the beginnings of Riley's substantial wealth could have originated from a 1838 triple-murder in South Carolina. In a sale transaction involving slaves, three travelers were returning home from Dahlonega one day with their funds from the sale when they reportedly stopped to camp for the night at the Georgia border. Suddenly, out of the darkness two horsemen appeared (according to later court testimony) and set upon the three campers, killing them horribly by hacking them to death with a hatchet and then stealing their funds which supposedly were in gold dust, since very little coinage – and certainly no paper money – existed there in that day and time.

Lawmen eventually tracked – to Dahlonega – a suspect to the crime who, interestingly, turned out to be one of Riley's slaves named Isaac. They charged him with the crime after they discovered him in possession of some of the gold from the travelers.

In a bid to save himself from the gallows, Isaac testified in his trial in South Carolina that no lesser a man than Harrison Riley had promised to grant him (the slave) his freedom, and to even share a portion of the stolen gold with him (which must have been fairly substantial) if he would commit the crime.

Whether a portion of the bargain Riley supposedly struck with his slave involved the murder of the victims, or merely the theft of their money, is unknown today. Regardless, Isaac ultimately was convicted of the crime, but his testimony against his owner was not believed to be credible – at least not by those jurors – and Riley was never charged with any crime.

It was only a very short time later, that Riley the businessman began construction of his gold rush-era expansive hotel on the south side of the Dahlonega public square and also the accumulation of acreage all around north Georgia, as well as in Alabama. The sudden origin of the funds for these investments is unknown today.

As for Riley's prolific fatherhood, many of his children were born among 14 slaves he owned. Some estimated he had as many as 100 children, both black and white, but it was more likely 25 to 30. Most of his life, he didn't live with any of his women, maintaining separate residences for them and taking good care of them and their children. In his Last Will & Testament bequeathing property to various people, he didn't refer to any of the children as "his children," but rather as the children of whatever mother.

The *1834 State Census of Lumpkin County* shows #374 Harrison W. Riley, head of a household of 6. The *1838 Census*, however, indicates that Riley's fortunes had improved considerably in the previous four years. He was listed as the head of a household of 18, 14 of whom were slaves.

Interestingly, there also was a *"Wm. H. Riley"* listed in the *1834 Census* as the head of household #379, a family of 3. The exact relationship between Harrison W. Riley and William H. Riley is unclear today, although there are indications that they were related – if not the same person.

On June 1, 1835, William H. Riley purchased one-half of town lot #113 located at the present intersection of South Chestatee and West Main Streets and erected a tavern. Jesse L. Riley bought the same property on June 6, 1837 and Harrison W. Riley acquired it on March 4, 1841.

Riley (Harrison) had previously acquired a one-half interest in city lots #96 and #97 which were located on the corner of South Chestatee Street and the town square, lot #110 *(in front of the present-day Smith House)* and lots #111 and #115 *(present-day Chestatee Village)*. He and John M. McAfee bought them at a sheriff's sale on April 7, 1840 for $1,739.00, a substantial sum at that time equal to $52,952.00 in 2021 dollars.

Riley's brother Jesse bought out McAfee's share on April 15, 1841 for $1,000.00 *(He later sold his interest in this property to Harrison)*. With full control of this town property, Riley then

Gunfights & Mysterious Life of Harrison Riley — Lumpkin County

began construction of a substantial hotel on the courthouse square (city lots #96 and #97) which must have looked like a palace in the wilderness at that time in the 1840s. When completed, the Riley or "Eagle Hotel" was almost half a block long and had two elliptically arched doorways, six dormers with arched windows, and paneled rooms with hand-crafted mantels and heart-pine wainscoting.

His entrepreneurial skills growing by the day, the shrewd businessman no doubt realized that he could easily make back the cost of construction of the hotel in just a few short years with all the easy money floating around with the many miners and travelers who would frequent the Riley businesses as a result of their conveniently accessible location on the town square in the county seat of government.

According to Andrew Cain's *History of Lumpkin County, 1832-1932*, there was once an upstairs bridge across the street to Riley's tavern and gambling establishment (which once existed on the site of the present-day Chestatee Village) that he operated on the southwest side of the town square. The Eagle Hotel was such a fine structure that it was blue-printed through the federal government's *Historic Buildings Survey* for the Library of Congress.

Rough Road To Success

The land records of Lumpkin County offer an overview of Riley's rapid accumulation of property, but another section of the courthouse records – the *Writs and Bonds* – tell another side of the story.

Almost from the day he arrived in the gold fields, Riley was involved in legal scraps or physical altercations with a long line of competitors, swindlers, and

Harrison Riley looked the part of a man one did not want to "cross." Though a fearful foe to his detractors, challengers, and political opponents, he, nevertheless, reportedly was kind and strongly supportive of the women and children in his very extended family.

just careless businessmen. As a result, he was required to regularly appear in court – either in response to a suit he had filed, or in answer to a suit filed against him by someone else – for the rest of his life.

Interestingly, most of the suits filed against Riley were for *Assault and Battery*. One man suing Riley for $5,000.00 on March 10, 1838, described the beating Riley gave him as follows:

"Harrison W. with force and arms, to wit with swords, knives, dirks, sticks, rocks, fists, hands, feet and teeth furiously and violently assaulted and beat your petitioner and. . . violently caught hold of your petitioner and threw him upon the ground and then and there struck your petitioner a great many violent blows on the head and diverse parts of the body with the rocks, fists, sticks and weapons aforesaid

and shook and pulled about your petitioner and. . . . pulled a great quantity of hair from your petitioner's head by means of which said premise and ill treatment your petitioner was then and there greatly hurt, bruised and wounded and became and was sick, sore, lame and disordered so much that the life of your petitioner was then and there greatly despaired of. . . ."

The man said that he had spent $50 on medical treatment and was unable to work for a month. The court ruled in favor of the plaintiff but awarded him only $100.00 and court costs, which came to $14.31¼, a fine Riley easily paid.

Another suit filed against him on March 8, 1853, stated that Riley had ". . . with force and arms assaulted your petitioner. . . . with his fists and a large stick with great violence struck your petitioner upon the head and upon divers parts of the body by means whereof your petitioner was then and there greatly hurt, beat and bruised and then and there became sick, sore and lame. . . ."

The petitioner asked for the sum of $500.00 in damages. The most interesting part of this suit was the fact that the petitioner was a woman! Even more interesting, the court ruled in favor of Riley.

Riley was even sued May 29, 1856 by a slave owner named Daniel Weaver for alleged damages to *"a certain Negro man slave named Cesar (sic) of great value to wit of the value of one thousand dollars."* Weaver sued for $1,000.00 and swore that Riley ". . .confined said negro man in the common jail of said county for a long space of time to wit twenty-four hours. . . . petitioner was forced and obliged to and did necessary expend divers large sums of money. . . . .the sum of two hundred dollars in and amount recovering possession of said Negro man. . . ."

Once again the court ruled in favor of Riley. The voluminous court records indicate Riley won more suits than he lost. And in fairness to the man, it appears that many of the suits were brought against him simply because of his reputation and the fact that he was extremely wealthy, making him a good target.

Powerful Political Figure

Though it is clear from public records that Riley had many enemies, he also had a devoted group of friends and followers as well. He ran for and was elected to a number of different public offices. In fact, for a period of thirty years (1843-1873) he was seldom out of public office.

His first elected position in Lumpkin County was that of state representative. He was first elected in 1843 and served until 1845. He was again elected and served 1849-1851 and 1853-1855.

In 1858 Riley ran for and was elected to the Office of state senator. It appears that he was re-elected in 1860 since the next senator was Weir Boyd who took office in 1861 when Lumpkin, White and Dawson were combined to form the Thirty-Second Senatorial District.

It was about this time that Riley's political policies almost cost him his life. There are several versions of the attempted assassination of Harrison Riley after a particularly bitter campaign. Andrew Cain's **History of Lumpkin County** describes the incident as follows:

"During his long and stormy career, Riley received only one bullet; and that was planted in his shoulder by a political enemy. In that day and time everybody who smoked used a cob pipe or a clay pipe - the kind that was molded by Mrs. Rachel Medford and sold all over this section at a cent a piece. Now Riley was fully able to smoke the finest tobacco in a meerschaum, and to light his pipe with a match, even though matches

were then rare and expensive. But he did not care to do things that way. He smoked one of Mrs. Medford's one-cent pipes, and dipped it into the embers to light it.

"One day, just as he stooped to light his pipe preparatory to celebrating one of his political victories, an enemy who is said to have sworn that Riley would never again go to the Legislature, shot him; but the wound was not serious."

A story written in 1960 by Andrew Sparks in the *Atlanta Journal & Constitution* Sunday Magazine quotes Joe Thomas Sr., an old-timer who was born soon after Riley's death and lived near the old Riley plantation in White County.

"From all accounts he was a pretty rough citizen. But he never killed anybody that I know of and he never got shot but once. That was after he was elected to the Georgia Senate. Him and Dan Davis run, and Riley beat. Davis said Riley never would serve and he came to the house when Riley was stooped over at the fireplace lighting his pipe and shot him in the arm from the back. Riley got up and got him a gun and shot a hole in Davis's hat as he ran away."

Daniel Davis (2/8/1785 – 6/9/1868) was a very wealthy planter who lived in the Davis District of Lumpkin County. He was a leading citizen and had moved to the area when it was still a part of the Cherokee Nation.

A letter donated to the Dahlonega Courthouse Gold Museum by a descendant of Daniel Davis indicates another possibility altogether – that one of Davis' sons may have tried to kill Riley. The letter postmarked Grand River, Cherokee Nation and dated 17th December 1860, was addressed to L.D. (Lorenzo Dow) Davis (son of Daniel), Calhoun, Ga., and was written by a cousin, J.M. Lynch, at the request of Joseph C. Davis.

"Dear cousin,
I write you these lines to let you know that your brother Joe has arrived here safe and will remain with us until he hears from you - I have not yet seen Joe though he is at Les Thompson's about six miles from my house - he sent Les to my house on yesterday to get me to write this letter and send it to the post office, he wishes you to write to him everything in regard to his difficulty with Riley - whether Riley is dead or likely to recover and whether he has sent any one in pursuit of him or not....."

Riley did recover of course and Joseph Davis returned to Lumpkin County of his own free will. Davis, just another in the long line of political enemies of Riley, died of natural causes Aug. 27, 1889 and is buried in the Davis Cemetery in Lumpkin County.

Riley & the Civil War

At the time that Riley was serving in the Georgia General Assembly, the capital of Georgia – and therefore the General Assembly – was located at Milledgeville, Georgia. This was quite a trip for anyone to be making on a regular basis on horseback or by horse and buggy. It is unknown today exactly how Riley made the trip.

It is known, however, that he attended the Secession Convention in Milledgeville in January, 1861. Although his exact role is unclear, the unpublished *Diary Of Amory Dexter* notes: *"Jan. 20, 1861, Riley returned from Milledgeville and says Georgia out of the Union."*

Riley then sought a military commission from the Confederacy. The following letters, written by Harrison Riley shortly after the beginning of the Civil War, are on file at the Georgia Archives:

*Head Quarters
August 25th, 1861*

Second Brigade Seventh Division
To the Executive Department

Dear Sir,
Your order of the 27th inst received calling on the Major General, Brigadier Generals, Colonels and other officers for speedy organization of the militia of this state.

I not knowing whether the Major General of this brigade is living or not, I have assumed responsibility of responding to the call hoping that I have not done wrong in obedience to said order. I enclose to you a complete list of my staff. I also enclose my order for a thorough organization of the militia of my brigade.

I also state to you that I will with pleasure attend to and distribute any order that may come from your department. I am your most obedient servant.
H.W. Riley

Dahlonega
November the 12th 1861
General A. Hansell

Dear Sir,
After all due regard allow me to offer you some apology for troubling you at this time but circumstances are of such a pressing and urgent nature at this time that I am compelled to call on you as a special friend believing that you will do all you can to promote my interest.

I have just made the tour through my brigade. I have visited six counties and reviewed the troops in all those six counties. I find, on examining my Brigade Inspections Report of the strength of my brigade, that it is composed of three thousand one hundred and fifteen (3115) hale, hearty, stout warriors as ever breathed a pure mountain atmosphere all of them professed a perfect willingness to turn out in the defense of their native state for twelve months unless sooner discharged.

I took the companies, one at a time, in every county in the brigade and put the question in this way "that if the officers and men should be called on by the governor or his authority to go to the coast for twelve months unless sooner discharged - if there was any that had any excuse why he should not go for such a one to step two paces to the front." [Strange] to say not one came to the front, all stood firm which with the exception of some forty sick men which were excused.

Now my dear friend, I want you to use your influence with his Excellency the governor to secure a permit for me to raise a regiment or a battalion to go to the coast to rendezvous at Dahlonega to be called the Dahlonega Regiment or Battalion. I ask this favor of you knowing that you are well appraised that if I go at all it must be on a horse as it is impossible for me to walk owing to my bodily afflictions.

There is in White, Habersham and Hall about some one thousand good men who possess a perfect willingness to go if I can get any positive assurance that I will be received and that the governor will allow me I will take hold of it and you know I am not slow when I take hold. I will be at all the expense and trouble of raising the regiment or battalion whichever his excellency will allow.

Please attend to this for me on the spot and let me hear from you at your earliest opportunity dear sir. I have the honor to remain your most obedient humble servant.
To General Andrew I Hansell
Harrison W. Riley

Despite his obviously earnest and diligent efforts, Riley failed to get the commission he desired. Weir Boyd, a local lawyer, was elected colonel of the unit that became the 52nd Georgia Regiment. Nevertheless, Harrison Riley from that day forward was always addressed as "General," both in person and in print. His grave marker even has this title preceding his name.

The origin of Riley's rank is unknown today. In all likelihood, it represents little more than a local or honorary title due to his command of the local militia unit. Interestingly, there is no record in either the state or national archives of any military service – either in the U.S. or Confederate forces – served by Riley.

Final Battle

The Georgia House of Representatives in which Riley served several terms, honored him in 1873, near the end of his illustrious career, with the following resolution:

"Resolved that a seat upon the floor of this House be tendered to the 'unlearned' but stout old Champion of the People's Rights, and Representative, Man of the Mountains, General Harrison W. Riley of the County of Lumpkin."

This was the last year that Riley held public office and the year before he began his final battle in life. . . . one of the few battles that he did not win. The ravages of illness and time had finally caught up with him, and on November 1, 1874, in spite of the attention of four of the most prominent doctors in the area, he realized that his death was imminent.

On this day, three days before his death on November 4, he executed his *Last Will & Testament*. This remarkable document, (now on file in the office of the probate judge of Lumpkin County), is the most lasting evidence of the paradoxical nature of Riley's life.

It was also during this time that the legend of Riley's "hidden treasure" began. According to the legend, as well as various written accounts, Riley called two of his most trusted friends to his bedside and confided to them the location of $2,000.00 in gold that he had hidden.

Today, the ultimate disposition of this gold cache is unknown. Perhaps the treasure was quietly recovered years ago, or perhaps it has been lost forever. Regardless of the circumstances, the legend continues to this day. The following article, dated December 30, 1898, appeared in the *Mountain Signal* newspaper 24 years after Harrison Riley's death:

$2,000 Gold Buried

Judge Brittain is one of the few old landmarks that is left. He was a special friend to Harrison W. Riley who has long since passed away. Judge Brittain is one of two men to whom General Riley told where he hid about two thousand dollars in gold. The other old gentleman is still alive and lives out in the country. They are the only two persons that were told the whereabouts of the hidden treasure and will likely die without disclosing the secret. The Judge says that the money is not his and he is not going to tell it so as to create a lawsuit.

The name of the second person to which the above article refers, has been lost to history. If Riley's gold is still buried, how much would it be worth today?

In 1874, gold dust was selling for $20.76 per ounce. As of this writing (2021), the price is $1,737.00 per ounce, so if the buried gold was all dust, it would be worth approximately $167,341.00.

But what if the gold was in coins? In 1874, Dahlonega gold coins were quite common. Depending of course upon the year and denomination, $2,000 in Dahlonega gold coins could be worth millions today. If part of the gold included the extremely-rare "Templeton Reid" gold coins (minted in Gainesville), the current value could easily exceed tens of millions of dollars in value.

At the time of his death, Riley owned thousands of acres of land. However, most of the treasure hunting for his gold has occurred around his plantation in White County where Riley spent his final days. The ruins of this former home-site still existed in the 1990s, but the site was inaccessible except on foot, and difficult to reach.

During the last years of Riley's life and for several years thereafter, the house and plantation were the home of Elizabeth (Eliza) Wood and her son and daughter, reportedly two of Harrison Riley's many children.

Eliza Wood also raised a nephew, Sidney Dowdy. Sidney (1868-1944) was the son of Eliza's sister, Margaret, and her husband, Alfred J. Dowdy. Sidney was undoubtedly one of the last people who actually remembered Harrison Riley, the man, and not just the legend.

A grandson of Sidney Dowdy, Hoyt T. Booth of Bowman, Georgia, recalled many tales that his grandfather had told of Riley. According to Booth, Dowdy once described an incident during the Civil War revealed to him by his aunt Eliza.

According to the story, during the dark days of the U.S. Civil War, the plantation was raided by outlaws. Whether they were deserters from the Union or Confederate armies, or simply thieves taking advantage of an area in which law enforcement was nonexistent in the 1860s, is unknown today. What is certain, is that they were looking for Harrison Riley's gold.

Even in the 1860s, Riley's gold was legendary, and highly coveted. The raiders reportedly tore the home apart in search of the coins – even to the point of ripping open the bedding. The only place they did not search was a pile of dirty clothes strewn beneath the home's staircase.

When the raiders rode away empty-handed, they had no idea that they had overlooked much of Riley's treasure in the form of $20,000 in gold which according to the tale, had been hidden practically in plain view – beneath the pile of dirty clothes!

Harrison Riley's obsession with gold was so well known that at the time of secession in January, 1861, it almost caused an incident of statewide proportions. When Georgia seceded from the Union, there was a U.S. Branch Mint in operation in Dahlonega. It continued to operate for about a month, and the problem of protecting the stocks of bullion and coin on hand at the Mint swiftly became a source of major concern.

The assayer of the Mint at that time – Capt. Isaac L. Todd – explained it as follows:

"There were some rough characters in the mountains in those early days, and when the state seceded, one of them by the name of Harrison W. Riley threatened to organize a crowd and make a raid on the mint, as he declared that the money belonged to nobody in particular, and that he was as much entitled to it as anybody.

"We hears of the threatened raid and armed ourselves, closing the vaults and putting the keys in a place of safety. Riley evidently thought better of the matter, for he never put in an appearance."

Capt. Todd's version, while accurate, does not tell the entire story. Gov. Joseph Emerson Brown had grown up in Union County, just north of Dahlonega, and later lived near Canton, Georgia. He was well acquainted with Harrison Riley and knew precisely how to deal with him.

When the report of Riley's threat to seize the Mint was telegraphed to Gov. Brown, several leading men of the state pressured the governor to send in state troops at once and secure the Mint by force, to avoid allowing Riley or anyone else an opportunity to make an attempt of this nature.

The governor knew Riley well from his boyhood. He was satisfied that a very large element in his motivation for making this threat was a desire to attract notoriety, and that he was too shrewd to undertake a rebellion against the state in northeast Georgia – unless advantage was given him.

The governor was also well aware however, that with so large a proportion of Union sentiment as there was in that section of the state, if any difficulty was raised with Riley about the Mint, the popular sympathy quite probably would have been with the man from Dahlonega, thus putting the state in a ticklish position indeed.

Gov. Brown explained this to the men who approached him on the subject, and told them he knew Riley well. He added that he could manage the situation if they would just leave it to his discretion.

A few days afterward, the governor wrote to several prominent citizens of Dahlonega, telling them that he had heard such a report in reference to Gen. Riley, but had known him too long and had too high an appreciation of his good sense and patriotism to believe he would attempt such a thing, and that as old personal friends, he and Riley must have no collision.

The governor did not think it best to write to Riley personally or directly, but wrote instead to friends who he knew would communicate the facts to Riley. This course of action apparently had a soothing effect upon Riley, and toned him down.

The governor also notified the superintendent of the Mint that the state now held and possessed it. The superintendent formally recognized the authority of Georgia over the Mint, and consented to act under the executive who gave him written orders.

Governor Brown was criticized by the newspapers for not making a demonstration upon the Mint, but considering Riley's influence and following, Brown's actions seem almost a stroke of enlightened genius. Harrison Riley remained a strong political supporter of Gov. Brown for the remainder of his life.

Interestingly, the remaining gold bullion at the Mint – if such ever had been left behind by U.S. authorities as the war loomed – ultimately disappeared anyway, but that's a story for another day.

The Final Chapter

A great-granddaughter of Harrison Riley has reported that she grew up hearing that Riley fathered approximately 100 children. On the surface, this number seems somewhat exaggerated. Nevertheless, one thing is almost certain: Harrison Riley fathered several children by several different women – both black and white.

In the absence of birth and death records during Riley's lifetime, it is doubtful that it will ever be known, with any degree of certainty, just how many children Harrison actually fathered. In fact, it is doubtful that he knew exactly himself!

In 1838, Riley owned 14 slaves. It would not be realistic to assume he was the father of all the children born to the female slaves, but it is highly likely that he was the father of at least several.

Research is further complicated by the fact that some of his children used the last name Riley while others used their mothers' maiden names. It also appears that, except for the last few years

Riley's Eagle Hotel, from which he once waged a gun battle with a foe, served as his headquarters for many years, and was built by him at least as early as the 1840s. It was the site of many political campaigns and celebrations during his lifetime. During one gun-battle from the porch of this hotel, Riley's opponent fatally wounded his (Riley's) pet dog, and the building was pock-marked with bullet holes for years thereafter. Riley, however, was uninjured and drove off his attacker with returned gun-fire. *(Photo courtesy of GA Dept. of Archives & History, Atlanta)*

of his life, Riley never actually lived for any period of time with any of his female consorts. He maintained a separate residence for each of them and never presented them socially.

In the days when a "shotgun wedding" involved a real shotgun, one might wonder just how Riley managed to survive while living such an unorthodox lifestyle. How did he manage to avoid being gunned down by an irate father?

The answer seems two-fold. First of all, Riley took exceptionally good care of his consorts – and their children: They lived in substantial households; the children received the best educations; and the lifestyle of the mothers and children was considerably better than that of the average family in what then was a rugged mining country of north Georgia.

Secondly, Harrison Riley had proven beyond a shadow of a doubt that any challengers – or even assassins – were taking their lives in their hands by attacking him in any manner whatsoever. If he couldn't shoot them dead in an open gunfight, he'd file suit against them to see how much damage he might cause in that manner. He also was wealthy enough to simply hire someone to eliminate anyone attacking him. The residents of Dahlonega were all aware of these things.

Additionally, there was always the matter of Riley's fabled fortune. Any woman and/or children to whom Riley could establish lineage quite possibly would be denied any financial support if Riley perished in an attack. They knew it and he knew it, and this provided yet another measure of protection.

Descendants

A paragraph of Harrison Riley's *Last Will & Testament* reads as follows: "I hereby bequeath to Eliza Jefferson. . . . my farm known as Sprigg's Place in Dawson County. . . . at her death to Julia Rutherford and Susan Mathis and a little girl, the daughter of Lorena Witherow, deceased, now living with Susan Mathis, given name not recollected, also to Alice Pilgrim, and I further give to the said Susan Mathis, the farm she is now living on for and during her natural life. . . . at her death to her children."

Eliza Jefferson, born about 1819, was a former slave that Harrison Riley had purchased November 5, 1839, from R. A. Holt for the sum of $1,250.00. She was about 20 years of age and had four children: Henry, about 5 years old; Rial, a boy of about 3; June, a girl about 18 months old; and a female child about 6 months old.

Over the next 20 plus years, Eliza had seven more children, possibly more:

1. Goliath Riley, born 1841/43, was left $500.00 in Harrison Riley's will. He moved to Alabama.
2. Julia, born 1844/45, married (as Julia Riley) Franklin Rutherford on September 23, 1860. The marriage was performed by John C. Brittain, judge of the Inferior Court and one of the two men to whom Riley supposedly revealed the location of his buried gold. Franklin Rutherford was a white man who joined Co. C, 52nd Georgia Regiment, C.S.A. on March 4, 1862, and served until July 10, when he furnished a substitute. Julia is the same Julia Rutherford mentioned above in Harrison Riley's will.
3. Sarah Ann (known as Susan), born about 1847, married (as Susan Riley) Jasper Matthews on October 20, 1863. Susan is the same Susan Mathis mentioned above in Riley's will. The diversion in the last name is probably a spelling error or a transcription error at some point.
4. Jesse T., born August, 1850.
5. Charles, born about 1853.
6. Mary, born about 1855.
7. Son, born about 1858, was still not named at the time of the *1860 Census*. There were possibly other children born after the *1860 Federal Census*. Who were *"Lorena Witherow, deceased,"* and her *"little girl...given name not recollected?"*

On October 13, 1862, Harrison W. Riley sold to. . . . *"Alice Witherow, a female daughter of Alfred H. Witherow. . . . in consideration of the sum of four hundred seventy five dollars. . . . in the 1st Section, 13th District. . . . Land lot #44 (40 acres) a portion of Land lot 343 (35 acres), and Land lot 374 (40 acres). . . . if the said Alice Witherow dies before she becomes of proper age, the title to the above premises to remain to the said Alfred A. Witherow."*

A check of the census records in 1870 found the same family living in the Auraria section of Lumpkin County #3-3:
Alfred Witherow, age 60;
Nancy Witherow, age 30;
Alice Witherow, age 10;
John Witherow, age 5;
Kirby Witherow, age 3.
This undoubtedly means that when Harrison Riley sold 115 acres to Alice Witherow, Alice was only 2 years old!

Although Eliza Jefferson was purchased as a slave, her heritage must have included only a very small portion of Negro blood. Her children were light enough (even in pre-Civil War days) to be accepted as white children. Even before the war and emancipation of the slaves, Elizabeth Jefferson was living with her family in a house in town and working as a seamstress.

In another section of his *Will*, Riley bequeathed to: *"Eliza Wood (a white woman who lived at Riley's plantation in White County).... lot of land.... known as the Nix Place.... and bequeath to the said Eliza Wood.... lot of land.... known as the Gen. Field's place.... in her natural life and at her death to be equally divided between her children now in life, names as follows: David Sherman, about ten years of age, and Josephine, about nine years of age. I make the above bequeath as some compensation to the said Elizabeth Wood for waiting on me in my afflictions."*

Riley also bequeathed to Elizabeth Wood all his household and kitchen stock (except his old mare and mule) plus all present crops and provisions on same to be used for her support and the support and education of her children heretofore mentioned.

David Sherman Riley was born December, 1864, in White County, Georgia, and married Molly Margaret Hunt, May 11, 1884. They were the parents of six children, the first five were born in White County, Georgia and the sixth was born after they moved to Dallas, Texas:

1. Clarence Riley, born 1886.
2. Hattie Riley, born 1890.
3. Marley Riley, born 1892.
4. Lonnie Riley, born 1894, married Joe Monroe Epps, May 11, 1913, died 1938.
5. Roy Riley, born 1897.
6. Grace Riley, born 1907; still living as of the summer of 1986.

Josephine Callie Riley, (known as Callie) was born in White County in 1868. She married Frank Cleveland Hunt, brother of Molly Margaret Hunt. They were the parents of eight or more children. Callie died in 1915. Frank, born in 1861, died in 1939. Both are buried in Alta Vista Cemetery in Gainesville, Georgia (Hall County).

The last child mentioned in Harrison Riley's will was William Taylor Dowdy.

Taylor Dowdy's mother was Julia Ann Dowdy (1837-December 28, 1922) daughter of John M. Dowdy (1808-1892) and Anna Johnson Dowdy.

On March 4, 1862, when William T. Dowdy was just three years of age, Riley sold to Julia Ann Dowdy, for the sum of $50.00, 40 acres of land *".... being the same lot whereon the Rev. John Dowdy, father of Julia Dowdy now lives...."*

In his will, Riley stated:

"I hereby give and bequeath to Taylor Dowdy, all other lands to me belonging in Georgia, not heretofore mentioned, to be sold by his grandfather John Dowdy and the proceeds turned over to Taylor Dowdy."

Later in this will, Riley added a stipulation to the sale of 900 acres of land that he owned in Alabama:

"I hereby further direct that two hundred and fifty dollars be paid to Taylor Dowdy from the proceeds of said lands."

William T. (known as Taylor) was raised in the household of his grandfather, John M. Dowdy. John was a Baptist preacher and a school teacher. Taylor Dowdy grew up to become one of the best known and most beloved Baptist preachers in the Lumpkin County area.

Another missing piece of the Harrison Riley puzzle involves H.W. Riley, Jr., who enlisted in Company E, Phillips Legion, "Blue Ridge Rifles" C.S.A., on July 9, 1861. He gave his residence as Dahlonega, Georgia, and his age as 14.

H.W., Jr. apparently was wounded at Hanover Junction, Virginia, on May 27, 1864, and was received at General Hospital No. 9, Richmond, Virginia, on May 30. Records indicate that he

By the 1940s, Harrison Riley's beloved mountain hotel on the Dahlonega Public Square had been relegated to use as a men's dormitory (called Moore Hall) for North Georgia College. Tragically, on January 9, 1943, Riley's signature creation mysteriously burned to the ground.

had been shot in the left hip. He was given a 60 days medical furlough on July 11, 1864. On the final muster roll dated January 30, 1865, he is listed as being absent without leave (AWOL). No further records have ever been found of H.W. Riley, Jr. either before or after the Civil War.

Gen. Harrison W. Riley died on a cold Wednesday morning, November 4, 1874 at his plantation in White County and was buried two days later beside his mother in the Riley family plot in Mt. Hope Cemetery in Dahlonega. All the places of business in Dahlonega were closed respectfully for his funeral and the citizens of the town and the surrounding area turned out in mass to pay their final respects to this man who, during the forty-plus years since his arrival in the wilderness that was to become Dahlonega, had become the most famous (or infamous) character that north Georgia's gold rush produced.

There, no doubt, were others who came simply out of curiosity; maybe they sensed that they were witnessing the end of an era – the final passing from rough and tumble frontier to civilization. Still another group – possibly the larger – came just to see for their own satisfaction that Harrison Riley was really finally dead.

Today, the Dahlonega Courthouse Gold Museum receives numerous inquiries almost weekly, and certainly monthly, from family researchers all over the United States trying to prove a link to the infamous Riley. This man whose gravestone reads, *"Let his faults be buried with his bones,"* also inspired the lines: *"Harrison Riley... At the very mention of his name, Heaven blushes, Hell trembles, and the whole world shudders."*

(Grateful appreciation is acknowledged herewith to Jimmy Anderson of Dahlonega who provided much of the very detailed information in this article.)

Cunning Union Guerrillas In North Georgia's Mountains

Despite the fact that support for the Confederacy was dominant throughout the South, particularly in Georgia, there nevertheless were pockets of resistance in the mountainous areas where hardy independent-minded souls were not influenced by plantation loyalties. To counter this opposition, Confederate "Home Guard" units were created to quell "traitorous" activity, but that brought even more problems.

Support for the Confederate States of America in opposition to the North was almost unanimous in the South, particularly in the extreme southern states of Texas, Louisiana, Virginia, Mississippi, Alabama, Georgia, and South Carolina, but there nevertheless were pockets of resistance – primarily in the more independent-minded upland areas of Tennessee, north Georgia, and North Carolina. These hardy, isolated, mountaineers simply opposed the requirements which support for the Southern cause imposed upon them – particularly since the flashpoints of unfair taxation, states' rights, and slavery basically were not issues which concerned the mountaineers. And life in the mountains was difficult enough as it was.

When Confederate impressment officials began drafting males in the area for service in the war, and Home Guard units began robbing the mountaineers of their meager supplies, foodstuffs, and possessions, and a period of severe climatic drought began plaguing the region, the smoldering resentment of these families grew into a bonfire.

Problems such as these existed everywhere in the South, but they were particularly harsh for the residents in the mountains. At first, the vastness of the Blue Ridge and Great Smokies substantially increased the ability of many mountaineers to avoid some elements of these repressive activities, but eventually, the constant abuses took their toll, and nowhere was this more evident than in north Georgia.

The most common resistance to the Confederacy in north Georgia – and elsewhere in the South – was draft evasion and desertion from the Confederate forces. President Jefferson Davis authorized the first Conscription Act of the war on April 16, 1862. This legislation required all white males aged eighteen to thirty-five to serve three years of Confederate service if called. The act also obligated soldiers already in the military to then be obligated to serve an additional twenty-four months which certainly could not have made them happy.

Many of the troops served out of sheer loyalty – and it was a loyalty unseen since the Revolutionary War. Disease, malnutrition, untreated wounds, freezing rain, blazing heat, the constant vermin attacking their bodies, coupled with constant terror on the battlefield were all faced by these men on an almost daily basis. Nevertheless, most of the Southern enlistees and even draftees were so dedicated, that they remained to endure the harshness day after day, week after week.

This same loyalty and devotion, however, was not engendered in many of the mountaineers. Even the mountaineers who willingly volunteered many times did not fulfill their obligations. In mountainous terrain and among sympathetic mountain families, "hiding out" practically became a way of life, accomplished considerably more easily than in other parts of the Confederacy.

As a result, the state of Georgia was occasionally forced to make massive round-ups of these deserters to keep matters from getting out of hand. Oftentimes this was accomplished via the "Home Guards," who were sworn to protect the homes, possessions, and families of those off fighting in the war. Unfortunately, these "protective" home guards all too often were little more than vigilante outlaws, taking the law into their own hands, and plundering the defenseless homes and citizens left with no men to defend them.

When the Home Guards DID find deserters from the Army, there was no mercy whatsoever, nor even a legal trial in many instances. The offending former soldiers were simply hung on the spot from the nearest tree or shot, and the families harboring them became fair game for all manner of abuse as well.

The bloody Confederate victory at Chickamauga in northwest Georgia in 1863 was the final straw for many war-weary rebels. Of the north Georgians at Chickamauga, many simply quietly returned home without orders, despite the threat of execution by the Home Guards. These men also soon learned that a loosely organized "underground railroad" was already in existence to guide them to the Union lines in Tennessee, should they ultimately desire to flee from the South.

Once out of Confederate-held territory, deserters and draft evaders could – and often did – become traitors to the Southern cause, joining the Union Army or Navy, or even traveling north of the Ohio River to be otherwise employed by the U.S. government. For many, it was an easy decision to make. They simply left their families behind and changed allegiance. But woe be unto those who ever returned to their homes in the South to be captured by the Home Guard units.

As the incidents of desertion increased, so also did the ranks and viciousness of the Home Guard units, who became ever more vigilant. The torture and murder of deserters became commonplace, particularly as

The bloody Confederate victory at Chickamauga in northwest Georgia in 1863 was the final straw for many war-weary rebels.

247

the circumstances of the war became more desperate for the South. The folklore of north Georgia is replete with accounts of corpses found after the Home Guards had departed, and of men having their Achilles' tendons cut on the heels of their feet and being forced to agonizingly walk or crawl for miles before finally being hanged.

Many north Georgians loyal to the Southern cause claimed that the Home Guards were nothing more than officially sanctioned murderers and horse-thieves. In many instances, depraved criminals in the Home Guard ranks even preyed upon pro-Confederate families, forcing them to suffer, regardless of their loyalties to the South.

Conditions eventually became so violent and lawless that some loyal and devoted troops in the Confederate Army were forced to desert their units simply from the necessity of returning home to protect their families from the Confederate Home Guard units! By the mid- to late-1860s, virtually the entire southern region was a lawless cut-throat arena with all manner of depredations, unlawful executions and general persecution being meted out by guerrillas and vigilante units on both sides – both Northern and Southern.

When General Sherman's Union Army invaded north Georgia in 1864, they found that the same Southern traitors who had been helping men to evade the Confederate draft and desert from the army, were willing to act as spies and guides for the Union, including assisting Sherman's foragers in seizing property from the pro-Confederate homes, plantations, and businesses.

The Confederate Home Guards' response to this disloyalty was the stepped up practice of still-more raids and even more executions. Sherman, in turn, answered by sending Union troops into strongholds such as Pickens County and elsewhere to rescue the pro-Union families opposing the Confederacy, and to suppress the Home Guards. Union forces burned Canton, Georgia, in retaliation for atrocities committed there against north Georgia families.

North Georgia areas with large numbers of pro-Union families were often identified by the populace and shunned. Old "Union Hill" in Georgia's north Fulton County and "Union County" in the north Georgia mountains are two examples of regions where "disloyal" Southerners were known to live.

Federal officials believed that resistance to the Confederacy and the Home Guards could be channeled into practical support for the Union. On November 18, 1863, twenty-four-year-old Major Dewitt C. Howard of the 103rd Ohio Infantry was ordered to organize armed Georgia units who were loyal to the Union Army.

Howard himself was a Georgian, and, judging from the number of refugees he witnessed daily streaming into Federal camps in Chattanooga, he was convinced that he

The Confederate Home Guards' response to this disloyalty was the stepped up practice of still-more raids and even more executions.

248

could raise an entire brigade. After several months of detached duty however, he determined that he may have over-estimated the degree of Southern disloyalty, since he failed to enlist more than just a handful of men. In most cases they were willing to run away, but they weren't willing to return to fight against their family and neighbors. Desperate as the circumstances in the South had become, "disloyalty" was not a common trait in the South.

The attempt to recruit a Georgia unit for the Federal forces was revived in 1864 by James G. Brown, civilian chief of scouts for Union General George H. Thomas. Brown had organized a spy ring in north Georgia as circumstances in the South continued to degenerate, and often would conduct his own personal reconnaissance missions, sometimes even disguised as a member of a Confederate Home Guard unit, such was the degree of disorganization at that time!

On August 9, 1864, Brown was ordered by General James B. Steedman to enlist as many men as possible for use in the protection of General Sherman's supply lines in north Georgia. In response, Brown arranged for six companies of north Georgians to gather near their homes in Pickens, Dawson and Union counties on or about July 1. They included men brought to Cleveland, Tennessee, on July 10 by Dr. John A. Ashworth of Dawson County and a "Union Home Guard" company organized in Pickens County by Federal troops.

At the request of Ashworth, his brother-in-law Iley T. Stuart raised a company, and in Morganton, William A. Twiggs rallied enlistees with a stirring speech calling for the removal of the Confederates out of north Georgia.

By the end of August, 1864, James G. Brown had approximately 300 enlistees, but far from the 800 to 1,000 men he needed for a regiment.

As a result, one of the companies raised by Stuart went to Tennessee and became Company C of the 5th Tennessee Mounted Infantry Regiment, U.S. Army, on September 23, 1864. Others who had answered Brown's call served in an independent company in Fannin County under Twiggs that on February 1, 1865, became Company H of the 5th Tennessee.

Brown organized his remaining four companies as the 1st Georgia State Troops Volunteers, with himself as colonel, Ashworth as lieutenant colonel, and Henry L. Carroll of Union County as acting major. The men were all promised a bounty of $300.00, army pay, and clothing, in exchange for enlisting for three years to serve exclusively as guards for the railroads in Georgia, as the Union Army gained control of the lines. They were provided food, ammunition, and probably weapons, but apparently were compelled to take horses and mules from pro-Confederate families.

Despite the circumstances, Brown's men interestingly were never actually accepted into the U.S. Army as a regular unit. It seems the unsavory attitude, lack of professionalism, and deceitful tactics of Brown and his men labeled them as "just a little bit too far outside the law" for the taste of the regular Army commanders. The official reason, however, maintained that Brown and his men did not qualify as a regular unit because they did not meet one of the pre-conditions of the unit's original organization – that being that they would serve ONLY in Georgia.

Nor were the men of Brown's units brave and dependable. Col. L. Johnston, commanding the largely black garrison at Dalton, later blamed his forced surrender to General Hood's Confederate

Army on October 13, 1864, upon the cowardice of the men of Brown's 1st Georgia State Troops. Johnston claimed that the troops of the 1st Georgia not only failed to do their duty as scouts, but that they literally cut and fled to the mountains at the approach of Hood's gallant troops, just as they had done upon the approach of Wheeler's Confederate Cavalry on October 2.

On November 5, while on a raid to obtain horses and mules, Lt. Col. Ashworth, Capt. McCrary, and nineteen other members of Brown's command were caught off-guard and captured by Col. James J. Findley (of Dahlonega) and his 1st Georgia State Cavalry Home Guards in Bucktown in Gilmer County. Three others of Brown's command were wounded and four were killed in a minor engagement.

Of interest is the fact that captured with these men were papers that gave the names of all their local traitorous supporters, including such prominent men as Dawson County Sheriff George R. Robinson, Justices Cleveland Andrews and John Fouts, Lindsey Vaughters, and Hiram Brooks. As Findley took his command through Dawsonville, these civilians were abruptly arrested – no doubt much to their shock and terror – to be tried for treason.

A dozen of the men captured turned out to also be deserters from Confederate units. They were unceremoniously executed at Gainesville, Georgia, on November 7, 1864. Their bodies were later transferred by Union Army burial details to the National Cemetery at Marietta, Georgia, in July, 1867, where they were re-interred and identified as "heroes." Today, their graves may still be viewed in Section E, Numbers 6012-6023

Col. John Azor Kellogg, a Union escapee from a Confederate prison in South Carolina, had more positive experiences with Brown's men. A group of the 1st Georgia found Kellogg and his companions in Pickens County and, under Capt. McCrary, escorted them safely to the Union lines. Kellogg would remember these men as *"generous, hospitable, brave and Union men to the core."* He described them as effective guerrillas, providing armed protection for local farmers against the Confederate Home Guards.

However, if Kellogg's report to his superiors was as accurate as his memoirs, he must have also added that Brown's men were aiding and abetting not only Confederate deserters, but Union deserters as well, conducting raids to plunder pro-Confederate plantations in other counties, and refusing to accept offers of a truce by Capt. Benjamin F. Jordan's Cherokee County Home Guards. Hit and run ambushes between Brown's men and the Confederate Home Guards were apparently happening almost daily.

Col. Kellogg was sympathetic to Brown's men, but it is doubtful that his feelings were shared by the Union line officers and rank-and-file line troops. Brown's men were not trained, equipped, or led as regular soldiers, and as such, practiced almost solely as lawless vigilantes. They could not be scouts or guides at Dalton while their own families were left unprotected, nor could they allow themselves to be captured at Dalton (or anywhere else), since so many of them were also Confederate deserters.

The men of Brown's 1st Georgia however, regardless of the circumstances, could not be prevented from seeking revenge upon the Home Guards, now that they too were armed and organized. They were fighting a merciless guerrilla war against men who had abused them and their families and friends for several years now, and it had almost become a way of life for many of them.

After the Secretary of War and General Sherman finally decided not to allow the 1st Georgia to be admitted into the United States Army, Brown's men were ordered dismissed on November 2, 1864, and they formally disbanded on December 15, 1864. They received no pay, bounties, or compensation for their months of service and fighting. Today, one has to wonder if Sherman and the Secretary of War had simply preferred to disband the men, hoping to "sweep under the rug" a nasty little problem.

A few of Brown's men nevertheless refused to cease operations, and joined a new 1st Georgia. Dewitt C. Howard created his own 1st Georgia Infantry Battalion (at least on paper) at Marietta on October 31, 1864. Some of the men from Dawson County enlisted in Company A, and some from Pickens County joined Company B. The two companies were filled out with men recruited from Confederate POWs in Atlanta, after the city fell to Sherman. They guarded Sherman's rail and rear echelon supply lines in the northern part of the state until disbanded on July 19, 1865.

The problems of Brown's men did not end with the close of the war. Civil War related revenge killings continued long after the signatures had dried at Appomattox. For forty years, the families of Brown's 1st Georgia unsuccessfully petitioned Congress for financial compensation to which they felt they were entitled as a result of their affiliation with the Union cause. These efforts, however, were largely unsuccessful due to the known illicit nature of Brown's troops, and the fact that so few of the leaders of these families had survived to help with the petition.

James G. Brown remained a scout for General Thomas to the end of the war, and died in late 1866. Dr. John A. Ashworth died in Raleigh, NC *("by reason of starvation and ill treatment whilst a prisoner of war in the hands of rebel authorities")*, shortly after General Sherman's army freed him from the Confederates. Capt. George W. McCrary was killed by Confederate guerrillas on November 10, 1864. Ironically, he was not serving in Georgia at that time, contrary to the terms of his enlistment, but was in Tennessee.

Transcribed on the pages which follow are the rosters of Col. James G. Brown's 1st Georgia State Troop Volunteers, reproduced from memory by men from Brown's command. These records were obtained from the National Archives, Washington D.C., R 882, V.5., Box 842, Record Group 94. Microfilm of these records has been donated to the Georgia Department of Archives and History.

The original rosters and papers of this unit were destroyed in Hood's attack on Dalton in October, 1864. The names of Dewitt C. Howard's 1st Georgia Infantry are published in Robert S. Davis, Jr.'s *A Researcher's Library of Georgia*, (1987). Their compiled service records are available from the National Archives and on microfilm reel 279-34 at the Georgia Archives. Members of the 5th Tennessee and other Tennessee units are listed in Pt. II of *Tennesseans in the Civil War*, (Nashville, 1964)

The problems of Brown's men did not end with the close of the war.

Mystery & History in Georgia

(Information in brackets was added by the authors).

COMPANY A (Union County) (Roll prepared from memory January 10, 1870)

George W. McCrary, captain, killed in battle by guerrillas, November, 1864; Henry L. Carroll, 1st lieutenant, (Later in company B of Howard's 1st Georgia U.S. Infantry); Leander McCrarey; 2nd lieutenant; dead since service.

1/ Milton Nix, 1st sergeant, killed at Gainesville; prisoner of war; (Also called A.M. Nix; had been in Co. C, 52nd Georgia Confederate Infantry, buried at National Cemetery in Marietta, GA); 2/ Harper McCrarey, 2nd sergeant; 3/ Jesse Allen, 3rd sergeant; (later in Co. C, 5th Tennessee U. S. Mounted Infantry?); 4/ Henry Ducket, 4th sergeant; 5/ Willis McCrarey, 1st corporal; Killed by rebels in battle, November 1864; 6/ Robert Bennett, Jr., 2nd corporal; 7/ William Elkin, 3rd corporal; 8/ Jacob Denson, 4th corporal (later in Co. H, 5th Tennessee U.S. Mounted infantry).

Privates:

9/ Allen, David; 10/ Anderson, John W.; 11/ Ash, Henry; 12/ Blackwell, Daniel, killed at Gainesville, GA while a prisoner of war, November 1864. (Had been in Company C, 65th Georgia Confederate Infantry; buried in the National Cemetery, Marietta, GA.); 13/ Braidy, Lewis; (had been in Company D, 52nd Georgia Confederate Infantry; later in Co. H, 5th Tennessee U. S. Mounted Infantry); 14/ Braidy, Braxton; (Later in Company H, 5th Tennessee U. S. Mounted Infantry); 15/ Blackwell, Sidney; 16/ Bramblet, Jesse; 17/ Barrett, Thomas; 18/ Brown, Joseph N.; 19/ Brown, William (Later in Company B, Howard's 1st Georgia U.S. Infantry); 20/ Bramblet, Reuben E.; 21/ Colbert, James; 22/ Cockran, James (Later in Company H, 5th Tennessee U. S. Mounted Infantry); 23/ Dotson, William (Later in Company H, 5th Tennessee U.S. Mounted Infantry); 24/ Davis, Benjamin; 25/ Dowdy, James R. (Had been in Company D, 52nd Georgia Confederate Infantry; later in Company H, 5th Tennessee U. S. Mounted Infantry); 26/ Daniel, Albert; 27/ Edmonson, Thomas; killed by rebels while prisoner of war at Gainesville, GA, November, 1864. (Had been in Company D, 52nd Georgia Confederate Infantry?); 28/ Edmonson, William; (Had been in Company D, 52nd Georgia Confederate Infantry; had been in Company E, 30th Georgia Confederate Cavalry?); 29/ Eavens, George; 30/ Fowler, Johnson; 31/ Ford, John; (Later in Company F, 5th Tennessee U. S. Mounted Infantry); 32/ Free, Ebenezer; 33/ Gladen, William; (Had been in Company D, 1st Georgia State Line Regiment; later in Company H., Tennessee U. S. Mounted Infantry); 34/ Gilrith, John; 35/ Garrett, Martin L.; 36/ Griffith, John; 37/ Garrett, Joseph; 38/ Griffith, William; 39/ Garrett, Robert; 40/ Hix, James; 41/ Hopper, Charley; 42/ Ingram, John; 43/ Kerby, William; killed in battle, October, 1864; 44/ Lacky, Wm.; 45/ Long, James M; (Had been in Company B, 52nd Georgia Confederate Infantry); 46/ Long, Joseph; 47/ Long, John; 48/ Long, James, Sr.; 49/ Long, Connord; 50/ Long, Henry; 51/ Long, Jasper; (Had been in Company B, 43rd Georgia Confederate Infantry); 52/ Long, William; (Later in Company H, 5th Tennessee U. S. Mounted Infantry); 53/ Long, Nathaniel B.; 54/ Long, James, Jr.; 55/ Lovengood, William; killed in battle, October, 1864; 56/ Moore, Joseph; 57/ McCloud, William M.; 58/ Newberry, Jackson; 59/ Payne, John; (Later in Company B of Howard's 1st Georgia U. S. Infantry?); 60/ Payne, George W.; 61/ Rogers, Joseph; 62/ Ray, Joseph (Later in Company H, 5th Tennessee U. S. Mounted Infantry); 63/ Ray, Archable; (Had been in Company D, 52nd Georgia Confederate Infantry; later in Company H, 5th Tennessee U. S. Mounted Infantry); 64/ Ray, John D. (Later in Company H, 5th Tennessee U. S. Mounted Infantry); 65/ Ray, Martin; (Later in Company H, 5th Tennessee U. S. Mounted Infantry); 66/ Stanley, William, Sr.; 67/ Stanley, William, Jr.; 68/ Stanley, Braxton; 69/ Stanley, Reculious; 70/ Stanley, Samuel; 71/ Stanley, Elisha; 72/ Tuner (Turner?), William: (Later in Company F, 5th Tennessee U. S. Mounted Infantry); 73/ Thompson, James; (Later in Company H, 5th Tennessee U. S. Mounted Infantry); 74/ Woody, Robert; (Later in Company H, 5th Tennessee U. S. Mounted Infantry); Roll certified by Henry L. Carroll, January 10, 1870.

COMPANY B (Dawson County) (Roll prepared from memory January 10, 1870.)

Alvin W. Prince, captain; wounded in battle; Henry B. Chatlin, 1st lieutenant; James M. Reece, 2nd lieutenant

Martin P. Berry, 1st sergeant; killed by guerrillas; (Had been in Company 1, 52nd Georgia Confederate Infantry; later in Company H, 5th Tennessee U. S. Mounted Infantry); Thomas N. Mathews,

Cunning Union Guerrillas In North Georgia's Mountains   Lumpkin County

2nd Sergeant; Thomas Chatlin, 3rd sergeant; William A. Aarnhart, 4th sergeant; Nelson Bearden, 5th sergeant; John T. Spriggs, 1st corporal; James L. Griggs, 2nd corporal; (Had been in Company D 52nd Georgia Confederate Infantry); Jeptha Cochran, 3rd corporal; (Had been in Company D, 52nd Georgia Confederate Infantry; later in Company H, 5th Tennessee U. S. Mounted Infantry); John Reed, 4th corporal; Killed at Gainesville, GA, November, 1864; (John A. Reid; had been in Company D, 1st Georgia Confederate Sharpshooters; buried in National Cemetery, Marietta, GA,); Joseph Rider, 5th corporal; W. P. Turner, 6th corporal; (Later in Company F, 5th Tennessee U. S. Mounted Infantry).

Privates:

1/ Ayers, Elijah; 2/ Clayton, Elias; 3/ Burlison, William (Later in company A of Howard's 1st Georgia U. S. Infantry); 4/ Beardon, R. M.; 5/ Cochran, Francis M.; 6/ Cantrell, Andrew J. (Later in Company E, 7th Tennessee U. S. Cavalry; 7/ Dempsey, E. F.; 8/ Denny, Elisher; 9/ Dotson, William (Later in Company H, 5th Tennessee U. S. Mounted Infantry); 10/ Evans, John (Later in Company H, 5th Tennessee U. S. Mounted Infantry); 11/ Ewards, Thomas; 12/ Frix, Pleasant (later in company H, 5th Tennessee U.S. Mounted Infantry); 13/ Craine, Yerba; 14/ Garman, James (Had been in Company I, 52nd Georgia Confederate Infantry, later in Company I, 12th Tennessee U. S. Cavalry); 15/ Gladden, William (Had been in Company D, 1st Georgia State Line Regiment; later in Company H, 5th Tennessee U. S. Mounted Infantry); 16/ Lingefelt, John; 17/ Lively, John (Later in Company A of Howard's 1st Georgia U.S. Infantry? Jobry Lively?); 18/ Mincy, James; (Reported to have been in Company E, 30th Georgia Cavalry; captured at Bucktown, Gilmer County); 19/ McDugle (McCugle?), John C.; 20/ Morgan, Cunningham; died in service; 21/ Prince, Martin; (Later in Company K, 12th Tennessee U. S. Cavalry); 22/ Reed, Robert G.; killed in service; 23/ Ray, Joseph;(Later in Company H, 5th Tennessee U. S. Mounted Infantry); 24/ Ray, Archibald; (Had been in Company D, 52nd Georgia Confederate Infantry; later in Company H, 5th Tennessee U. S. Mounted Infantry); 25/ Reece, A. J.; 26/ Reece, (?) Jackson T.; 27/ Rider, Henry; 28/ Swaney, James C.; 29/ Scoogins, Mathew; 30/ Turner, O. P.; 31/ Williams, Wm. W.; (Later in Company A, 13th Tennessee U. S. Cavalry); 32/ Prince, Archibald A.; 33/ Reece, William; 34/ Newberry, Hegga. *Roll certified by Alvin W. Prince, January 10, 1870*

COMPANY C (Dawson County) (Rolls prepared from memory January 4, 1870.)

Elias Darnel, captain; (Had been in Company I, 38th Georgia Confederate Infantry); Calvin J. Lawless, 1st lieutenant John Kelly, 2nd lieutenant; Virgil D. Monroe, 1st sergeant; (Had been in Company I, 52nd Georgia Confederate Infantry; later in Company H, 5th Tennessee U. S. Mounted Infantry. In 1889, he wrote to the National Cemetery in Marietta enclosing the names of the men of Brown's 1st Georgia unit buried there as "one of their old comrades."); William A. Chumbly, 2nd sergeant; (Later in Company A of Howard's 1st Georgia U. S. Infantry); John Tatum, 3rd sergeant; paroled under Gen. Wofford; Thomas Darnell, 4th sergeant; Joseph M. Chamber, 1st corporal; paroled under Gen. Wofford; Josiah W. Haithcock, 2nd corporal; Pollard Kelly, 3rd corporal; Jordon Anderson, 4th corporal

Privates:

1/ Anderson, William, Jr.; died since the surrender; 2/ Anderson, William, Sr.; died since the surrender; 3/ Bennett, Jackson; 4/ Bennett, Robert; 5/ Bennett, William; 6/ Beck, John; paroled under Gen. Wofford; 7/ Brooks, Aaron T.; killed at Gainesville, GA in service, November, 1864. (Aaron Thacker "Zack" Brooks; had been in Company G, 8th Georgia Confederate Battalion, buried in the National Cemetery, Marietta, GA); 8/ Baird, James L.; 9/ Blackburn, Jesse W. (Later in Company H, 5th Tennessee U. S. Mounted Infantry); 10/ Braden, Elias W.; 11/ Carlisle, John; 12/ Chambers, Phillip; paroled under Gen. Wofford; 13/ Carnes (?), Marshall; paroled under Gen. Wofford; 14/ Carnes, Tandy W.; paroled under Gen. Wofford; 15/ Chambers, Barak; paroled under Gen. Wofford; 16/ Carney, Absolem; 17/ Chumbley, Thompson; 18/ Denson, Joseph; (Later in Company H, 5th Tennessee U. S. Mounted Infantry); 19/ Denson, George W.; (Later in Company H, 5th Tennessee U. S. Mounted Infantry); 20/ Denson, Jethro; 21/ Elkins, William; 22/ Elkins, Jordon; died in service; 23/ Evans, Nehe M; 24/ Evans, John (Later in Company H, 5th Tennessee U. S. Mounted Infantry); 25/ Fouts, John; 26/ Hyde, Asa A.; paroled under Gen. Wofford; 27/ Henry, Alexander; paroled under Gen. Wofford; 28/ Hix, John; 29/ Kelley, Pollard; 30/ Kelley, William; 31/ Ledbetter, Joseph;

Mystery & History in Georgia

paroled under Gen. Wofford; 32/ Monroe, Daniel P.; 33/ Monroe, Samuel L.; paroled under Gen. Wofford; 34/ Millsips, Solomon; (Later in Company H, 5th Tennessee U. S. Mounted Infantry); 35/ Monroe, Vanburen H.; paroled under Gen. Wofford; 36/ Martin, Morgan; 37/ McCrary, Julius; 38/ Millsaps, Stephen S.; (Later in Company H, 5th Tennessee U. S. Mounted Infantry); 39/ Nelson, Henry; 40/ Pinyan, Jeptha; paroled under Gen. Wofford; 41/ Pinyan, Abraham D.; 42/ Payne, Ambrose; 43/ Payne, Thomas; killed at Gainesville, GA, by rebels November, 1864, while in service. (Thomas W. Payne; had been in Company K, 52nd Georgia Confederate Infantry and Company G, 30th Georgia Confederate Cavalry; buried at the National Cemetery, Marietta, GA.); 44/ Robinson, Andrew J.; killed at Gainesville, GA by rebels November, 1864, while in service. (Had been in Company C, 7th Tennessee U. S. Cavalry?); 45/ Robinson, George R.; (Had been in Company I, 38th Georgia Confederate Infantry); 46/ Smith, Collins; 47/ Simmermon, Jacob; 48/ Simmermon, James; (Later in Company A of Howard's 1st Georgia U. S. Infantry); 49/ Stone, Jordon; killed at Gainesville, GA, by rebels while a prisoner of war. (Had been in Company D, 52nd Georgia Confederate Infantry; buried at the National Cemetery, Marietta, GA.); 50/ Stone, Jeptha; 51/ Sutton, Amos; 52/ Tesseneer, James; 53/ Tatom, Horatio; 54/ Turner, Tandy W.; 55/ Vaughters, Linza; died since service; 56/ Whitmore, Henry; 57/ Whitmore, William; (Had been in Company I, 22nd Georgia Confederate Infantry.); 58/ Whitmore, Charles; killed at Gainesville, GA, November, 1864, while in service. (Buried in the National Cemetery, Marietta, GA.); 59/ Willey, John; paroled under Gen. Wofford. (Later in Company H, 5th Tennessee U. S. Mounted Infantry.); 60/ Whitmore, Henry T.; hanged by General (?) ACock (?) In November, 1864; Certified by Elias Darnell, January 4, 1870.

COMPANY D (Pickens County) Roll prepared from memory January 14, 1870

George H. Turner, captain. (Had been in Company E, 23rd Georgia Confederate Infantry.); Robert B. McCutchen, 1st lieutenant. (Later in company B of Howard's 1st Georgia U.S. Infantry.); Hezekiah M. Paris, 2nd lieutenant; Thomas Taylor, 1st sergeant; killed in battle; William G. Brown, 2nd sergeant. (William T. Brown later in Company B of Howard's 1st Georgia U. S. Infantry?); Joseph Morris, 3rd sergeant; Samuel Brown, 1st corporal. (Later in company H, 5th Tennessee U.S. Infantry.)

Privates:

1/ Anderson, Woodville B.; 2/ Allred, Elias R.; paroled by Gen. Wofford; 3/ Berry, William A.; captured and killed. (William J. Berry; buried in the National Cemetery, Marietta, GA; had been in Company E, 23rd Georgia Confederate Infantry.); 4/ Berry, Milas D.; 5/ Bearden, Ancil; 6/ Bearden, William M.; 7/ Bennette, Hiram; 8/ Brooks, Isham A.; 9/ Brown, Robert S.; 10/ Brooks, Alexander (Later in Company K, 5th Tennessee U. S. Mounted Infantry.); 11/ Brock, John J.; 12/ Bruce, Madison; 13/ Bozeman, Henry B.; 14/ Bozeman, William A.; 15/ Brown, Thomas C.; 16/ Cowart, Thomas A.; 17/ Cowart, FrancesM. (Later in company K, 5th Tennessee U. S. Mounted Infantry.); 18/ Carney, L. B.; paroled by Gen. Wofford; 19/ Coffey, Martin V.; 20/ Carney, Edmond; paroled by Gen. Wofford; 21/ Carney, S.; paroled by Gen. Wofford; 22/ Cunningham, Robert (Later in Company K, 5th Tennessee U. S. Mounted Infantry.); 23/ Cook, Lemuel; 24/ Chapman, John (Later in Company K, 5th Tennessee U.S. Mounted Infantry.); 25/ Chambers, James; 26/ Chambers, william B. (Later in Company B, 6th Tennessee U. S. Infantry.); 27/ Dearing, Reubin; 28/ Darnel, Joshua; since died. (Later in Company K, 5th Tennessee U. S. Mounted Infantry.); 29/ Darnel, Sion A. Sen. (Later in Company K, 5th Tennessee U.S. Mounted Infantry.); 30/ Darnel, William J. (Later in Company K, 5th Tennessee U. S. Infantry.); 31/ Evans, G. M.; 32/ Evans, Mirey; 33/ Goode, M. H.; 34/ Goode, Abram; 35/ Griffeth, Robert; captured and killed; 36/ George, James; 37/ Green, Garland S. D.; 38/ Goode, Silome (Later in Company K, 5th U. S. mounted Infantry.); 39/ Hood, Tate; 40/ Honea, George M.; 41/ Heath, Griffin; died. (Later in Company K, 5th Tennessee U. S. Mounted Infantry.); 42/ Hendrix, John (Later in Company K, 5th Tennessee U. S. Mounted Infantry.); 43/ Hyde, A. A.; 44/ Howell, Russell; 45/ Howard, Samuel; 46/ Hood, Samuel; 47/ Howard, John L.; 48/ Jordan, John G. (Later in Company A of Howard's 1st Georgia U. S. Infantry.); 49/ Lovin, Reubin; killed by the enemy; 50/ Loveless, C. C.; 51/ Loveless, Abner L.; 52/ Manly, Lewis F.; 53/ Moss, John (Had been in Company I, 52nd Georgia Confederate Infantry.); 54/ Martin, William P. (Later in Company B, 5th Tennessee U. S. Mounted Infantry.); 55/ McHan, W. M. (Later in Company

K, 5th Tennessee U. S. Mounted Infantry.); 56/ Manley, Julius C.; 57/ Mann, Emsly O.; 58/ Mosley, Albert (Later in Company B of Howard's 1st Georgia U. S. Infantry.); 59/ Mullins, James P. (Later in Company b of Howard's 1st Georgia U. S. Infantry.); 60/ Mullins, Martin B. (Later in Company B of Howard's 1st Georgia U. S. Infantry.); 61/ Mullins, Green D. (Later in Company B of Howard's 1st Georgia U. S. Infantry.); 62/ McHan, Wilkie; 63/ McHan, Alfred; 64/ Mullins, George R. (Later in Company B of Howard's 1st Georgia U. S. Infantry.); 65/ McCravey, William; 66/ McHan, Henry; 67/ McCravey, D. S.; 68/ Nelson (?), William J. (Written over Joseph Morris?); captured and killed; 69/ Newman, James; 70/ Patterson, E.D. (Later in Company K, 5th Tennessee U. S. Mounted Infantry.); 71/ Pinyan, James H.; 72/ Pinyan, Jacob; 73/ Padget, Isaac (Later in Company B of Howard's 1st Georgia U. S. Infantry.); 74/ Payne, John W. (Later in Company B of Howard's 1st Georgia U. S. Infantry.); 75/ Patterson, Hix (Later in Company K, 5th Tennessee U. S. Mounted Infantry.); 76/ Patterson, Edward (Later in Company K, 5th Tennessee U. S. Mounted Infantry.); 77/ Patterson, Asa (Later in Company K, 5th Tennessee U. S. Mounted Infantry.); 78/ Pool, William(Later in Company K, Tennessee U. S. Mounted Infantry.); 79/ Presley, J. Marion; 80/ Padget, Alfred L.; 81/ Padget, William J. (Had been in Company I, 52nd Georgia Confederate Infantry, later in Company B of Howard's 1st Georgia U. S. Infantry.); 82/ Padget, John; 83/ Roe, Ancil C.; captured and killed; 84/ Russell, John; 85/ Ray, Thomas; 86/ Sizemore, A.; 87/ Stone, James J.; 88/ Shirly, Nathan (Later in Company B of Howard's 1st Georgia U.S. Infantry.); 89/ Swoffered, William M.; 90/ Turner, James (Had been in company I, 52nd Georgia Confederate Infantry.); 91/ Turner, Martin; 92/ Taylor, William (Later in Company K, 5th Tennessee U. S. Mounted Infantry.); 93/ Taylor, Cicero; 94/ Taylor, Lewis; 95/ Turner, David; has since died; 96/ Tally, John; 97/ Turner, Fielden; 98/ Turner, H. Green B.; 99/ Turner, Memory; 100/ Townsend, David; 101/ Wigington, James S.; 102/ West, Columbus J.; paroled under Gen. Wofford; 103/ Warren, Jeremiah; 104/ Watkins, Elias; 105/ Yancy, Obadiah; Certified by George H. Turner, January 14, 1870

OTHERS:

The compilers of these rosters admitted that omissions and errors had occurred. A newspaper account of the fighting at Bucktown, for example, mentions that James M. Weaver, a deserter from Company G of the 39th Georgia Confederate Infantry, was among the members of Brown's 1st Georgia taken prisoner. Weaver's name does not appear on the above rosters or the lists of the men buried at the Marietta National Cemetery. Similarly, a Lewis Lively of Company B appears on Virgil D. Monroe's list of the members of the 1st Georgia executed at Gainesville and on early burial records at the National Cemetery, but not in the rosters.

The persons listed below are found at the end of the microfilm of the compiled service records of Howard's 1st Georgia U. S. Infantry under the title of *"Cards Bearing Names That Do Not Appear on Rolls of the 1st Battalion Georgia Infantry."* A copy of this microfilm is reel 279-34 at the Georgia Department of Archives and History. Some of these men were members of James G. Brown's 1st Georgia State Troops Volunteers and others were probably men recruited by Dewitt C. Howard in late 1863 and 1864.

1/ Young, Wilson Abercrombie; 2/ Jesse C. Cox; deserted May 4, 1865; 3/ John Fitzgerald; deserted May 5, 1865; 4/ Sargent M. Holcomb; deserted May 24, 1865; 5/ John Jordon; deserted April 25, 1865; 6/ Henry H. Masis; deserted April, 1865; 7/ Richard Robison; deserted May 16, 1865; 8/ Andrew B. Stewart; deserted June 18, 1865; 9/ Leander J. Thompson; private; Company B, 1st Georgia Cavalry; 10/ Francis Wisdom; 11/ Col. J. H. Ashworth; prisoner-of-war; 12/ Capt. Wm. F. Curry (or Carry); Company A; wounded in the thigh, January 16, 1864; 13/ James Davis, died of typhoid, March 5, 1864; 14/ James B. Fowler; Company A 1st Georgia Cavalry; died December 12, 1864, of diarrhea; buried at Sharptop, Cherokee County, GA; 15/ William A Prewitt; died March 13, 1864; age 18; 16/ Meager Russell; Company B (A?); 1st Georgia Cavalry; died March 18, 1865; 17/ C. C. Spurlin; 1st Georgia Cavalry; died 1863; 18/ E. P. (J. B.?) Thompson; 19/ Tablah Vineyard; died August 21, 1864, of diarrhea; 20/ William Walden; died January 23, 1864, of measles.

(Grateful appreciation is herewith expressed to Robert S. Davis, Jr., for the research in acquisition and provision of the facts and details necessary for the production of this article. Appreciation is also extended herewith to Michael Musick and Tod Butler of the National Archives in Washington, D. C., for their research as well.)

Old West Outlaw At The Old London Homeplace

It was a landmark in the county for approximately 125 years before sadly succumbing to "progress" and being demolished for new construction at the Georgia 400 – Georgia Highway 60 intersection in Lumpkin. A famous old West outlaw – memorialized in best-selling books and at least one major motion picture – also once stopped by the house.

The intangible entity known as "progress" can be both a good thing, and a bad thing. When it comes to historic preservation, "progress" many times falls on the "bad" side of the spectrum. Such was the case with construction of the intersection of Georgia 400 Highway and Highway 60 south of Dahlonega, because it required the removal/demolition of one of the most historic homes in the county known as "the old London home-place."

It is unknown today exactly when the Old London home-place was built, but it quite possibly was constructed during the earlier gold mining days in Dahlonega. From the early 1920s until sometime around the mid-1990s, travelers driving on Highway 60 from Gainesville to Dahlonega caught a glimpse of the rear of a large imposing farmhouse on the right at the intersection of Long Branch Road. To most, it also seemed oddly situated, but that was easily explained. You see, it was built so long ago,

The home of Merritt M. London stood near the intersection of Long Branch Road and GA Highway 60 in Lumpkin County until construction of Georgia Highway 400 required its demolition in the mid-1990s. Outlaw George Anderson, alias "Bill Miner" and his accomplices paused at London's Store in front of this home just long enough to stock up on a few supplies, before continuing their flight from justice after having robbed Southern Railway's Train #36 at White Sulphur in Hall County.

that it faced a road which no longer existed in more modern times.

Merritt M. London, the builder and original owner, came to Dahlonega

Old West Outlaw At The Old London Homeplace — Lumpkin County

The "MM London & Sons Cash Store" was operated by Merritt London in his later years. It was at this store that outlaw Bill Miner reportedly briefly stopped to purchase a few supplies.

Photographed circa 1890, members of the Long Branch community participate in a "corn-shucking" at the Jim London farm. The young lady (second from right in front) is Myrtle London (born 1891). *(Photo courtesy of the GA Dept. of Archives & History, Atlanta)*

from Burke County, North Carolina. As the son of James Wadkins London and Elizabeth Conley London, Merritt prospered in his new north Georgia home, farming the rich bottom lands along the Chestatee River during the latter half of the 19th century.

London was twenty-eight years of age when he married 17-year-old Mary Neisler in Lumpkin County in 1859. Mary's father – Daniel Neisler – was one of the earliest settlers in the area.

Today, much of Georgia Highway 60 follows an old wagon trail once known as "Neisler's Road." Mary's sister – Frances "Fannie" Neisler – married William H. Early and lived in a house which still stands on Long Branch Road a short distance from the former site of the Merritt London home.

Most of the present-day information about Merritt and Mary N. London came from two of their descendants who, until recent times, lived in Gainesville, Georgia. Merritt and Mary had nine children – four boys and five girls. The late Mary Annie Hope, the daughter of Merritt and Mary's youngest daughter – Flossie – was 89 years of age in 1994 when she was interviewed.

"I could hardly wait for school to let out so I could go visit Grandpa and Grandma London's farm outside Dahlonega," Miss Hope reminisced. "Since we lived in Gainesville, I rode with Uncle Bob in his covered wagon pulled by a pair of mules.

"Grandpa raised cows, hogs, chickens, ducks, and geese," Miss Hope continued. "I remember helping to pluck the geese to make pillows. It has to be done at a certain time, or the feathers won't pull out easily and it hurts the skin. It takes twenty pounds of feathers to make a feather mattress, and Grandma gave each of her girls a feather bed when they married.

"The hens always made their nests in the grass at the edge of the woods, and I loved to go hunting for their eggs," she added. "Grandma was always anxious to get a hen to set so she could get some early fryers. It was such a pretty sight to see a gang of little chicks running around in the yard.

"Grandpa farmed the bottomlands all the way to the river. He grew a lot of corn for his stock, but he didn't believe much in cotton – just enough to pay his taxes.

Mystery & History in Georgia

The Jim London family were photographed here circa 1897. (Seated L-R): Fannie Martin London and Jim London. (Standing L-R): Dave, Julia Martin, Myrtle, Floyd ("Doc"), (female beside him is unidentified), Clarence (with banjo), Eve, Emma, and Tom. *(Photo courtesy of GA Dept. of Archives & History)*

Merritt M. London Home-place – Photographed circa 1897, the London home had changed little prior to its ultimate demolition circa 1990s. Pictured are: Merritt (center, with white beard & hat); his wife Mary Neisler (beside tree); his sons, Frank (in wagon) and Bob (second from left). *(Photo courtesy of GA Dept. of Archives & History, Atlanta)*

"I don't know how old the house was, but I do know that Grandpa had the timbers cut and the bricks burned for it," she explained. "Water was piped into the house from a spring, and there were two wooden troughs on the porch where the water flowed through. I used to love to wade in the branch in the summertime.

"Some men who worked on the dredge boats that mined the Chestatee River for gold used to board with Grandma and Grandpa, and they always paid off in gold dust. Grandma used it to have gold rings made for Mama and her sister, Mollie.

"Mollie married George Moore, the son of Col. Robert Hughes Moore, who came to Dahlonega in 1839 to mine for gold. George and Mollie moved to Gainesville where he started the G.W. Moore Coal Company.

"I don't remember Grandpa London very well, since he died in 1908 when I was only five years old. The last time I visited the farm was in 1913, because Grandma moved to Gainesville after that.

"Mama (Flossie) married Charlie Hope, a mule trader like his father, 'Doc' Hope, who used to run a livery stable in Dahlonega in the 1880s. Before they moved to Gainesville, Grandpa and Grandma Hope lived in one of the oldest houses in town."

{Author's Note: Even though it passed through many other hands after A.A. Hope sold it in 1891, the historic structure, built circa 1845, continued to be known as the "Hope House" through the years. It was built and for many years stood in front of the present-day Smith House Restaurant in Dahlonega, prior to being moved from that site (in 1985) to a spot known as "Mountain Music Park" on Highway 60 South where it may still exist today.}

Merritt and Mary's daughter – Alice – married James "Jimmy" Elrod, and their daughter, Mae, was the mother of Mrs. Clara Belle Eades, who lived for many years on Thompson Bridge Road outside Gainesville. She, too, remembered visiting the Merritt London farm when she was a small girl.

Mrs. Eades also recalls the tragic story of Merritt and Mary's son, Ben,

Old West Outlaw At The Old London Homeplace — Lumpkin County

Historic W.H. Early home – Built at roughly the same time and almost a twin-construction of the London homestead, the historic Early home still exists as of this writing (2021) on Long Branch Road. Merritt M. London married Mary Neisler of nearby Neisler's Ford. Mary's sister – Frances "Fannie" Neisler – married William H. Early who built and lived in the W.H. Early home.

Merritt M. London, the family patriarch, is pictured above as he appeared in his later years.
(Photo courtesy of Annie Lou Dobbs)

who reportedly went out to tend the sheep one winter night. When his little dog returned without him, Grandma London burst out crying and said, "If some of you don't go see about Ben, I will!"

Following a search of the property, members of the family found Ben leaning over a fence rail – dead of unknown causes. After that day, Grandma London never again enjoyed snowfall. She also lost another son – Willie – who had a twin sister named Mattie.

When Grandpa Merritt got too old to work in the fields, his surviving sons – Bob (who never married) and Frank (who married Annie Kemp) – reportedly built him a country store not far from the London homeplace.

Today, a family legend and local folklore maintain that the infamous outlaw – Bill Miner – entered the store with one or more of his accomplices one day in 1911, to purchase supplies. Whoever was tending the store at the time – likely one of Grandpa Merritt's sons – remembered that the stranger was in an awfully

Today, a family legend and local folklore maintain that the infamous outlaw – Bill Miner – entered the store with one or more of his accomplices one day in 1911, to purchase supplies.

big hurry, and thought it unusual, until the posse tracking him arrived shortly thereafter.

Miner was wanted in California and numerous other spots for murder and train and stagecoach holdups, and had just robbed Southern Railway's Train Number 36 just north of Gainesville. *(Readers please see "Old West Bandit Bill*

London's Cash Store, once operated by "Uncle" Merritt, was photographed at the old London homestead in 1993, just prior to its demolition for construction of Georgia 400 Highway.

Miner's Capture in North Georgia" in the Hall County section of this book.)

An article in an issue of the February, 1911 **Dahlonega Nugget** newspaper recorded the fact that one of Miner's accomplices in the robbery had eaten breakfast at the home of W.H. Early (brother-in-law of Merritt London) whose home still stands – as of this writing (2021) – on Long Branch Road just a short distance from the Georgia 400 – Highway 60 intersection. The article explains the outlaw had purchased tobacco and candy at McGuire's soda fountain in Dahlonega, as well as six boxes of snuff at J.W. Moore's store. The article goes on to explain that it was determined the man put the snuff in his shoes later to keep tracking dogs from finding him.

Miner and his two accomplices reportedly split up shortly thereafter. Miner was later captured in the Nimblewill community northwest of Dahlonega.

George W. Moore, Jr., the son of Mollie London and George W. Moore, operated the family coal business until 1980. He recalled attending a reunion at the old Merritt London homeplace when he was about seven years old and playing with some of his cousins there. He says the house was unpainted in those days, and there was a fence around it to keep out the livestock, since that was in the days prior to stock laws.

"I'm not sure when the London farm was sold, but (later owners of the property) found the sign from Grandpa Merritt's store and gave it to my brother and me," George explained. "It's made of a single board twelve feet long and three feet wide. Even after nearly a century, the black lettering 'M. M. London & Sons Cash Store' is still very legible."

Mrs. Hester Burns Rickman was born in 1897 and grew up just down the road from the Londons. "We could see the store from our house," she explained, "and Mama would send me to get things like sugar and coffee. Uncle Merritt had a long white beard that tickled when he hugged me. He wasn't really my uncle, but we called him that out of respect, because we were children and he was elderly."

Clara Belle Eades' daughter – Joyce Howard – of Stockbridge, still has an old ledger used to keep records in the London store in the late 1890s. It shows that bills were frequently not paid in cash but in other ways, such as "credit by 2 turkeys" (worth $1.35), "credit by 1 day's work killing hogs" (worth 40 cents), "credit by one day mowing" (worth 50 cents), and "credit by 8 gr gold" (worth 30 cents).

James A. "Jim" London was Merritt's younger brother. He also was born in Burke County, North Carolina, and he has a number of known descendants in Lumpkin County today. There are other signs of his passing too.

Dahlonega's Doug Cain remembers the Jim London house well, because his family lived in it from 1917 until 1949. It once stood less than half a mile from the Chestatee River, and was on the opposite side of the river from the Merritt

Old West Outlaw At The Old London Homeplace   Lumpkin County

One of the large gold-dredging barges which once plied the gravels of the Chestatee River on the London property is pictured. Workers on the barges often boarded at the London home. *(Photo courtesy of the GA Dept. of Archives & History)*

London homeplace. It faced the old wagon road to Auraria, and was torn down when Georgia Highway 400 was built in the early 1980s.

Jim's first wife – Martha A. Nicely – died in 1876 at the age of forty, leaving him with several young children. A little over two months later, he married a 25-year-old widow named Fanny Martin, who had four small children from her first marriage.

Jim and Fanny ultimately had seven children of their own – Thomas Jefferson, Floyd, Emma, Eva, James Albert, Clarence, and Myrtle.

Although Jim was five years younger than Merritt, he preceded him in death by several years. His will was probated in 1901.

An item in the February 5, 1892 issue of *The Dahlonega Signal* noted that James A. London *"is anxious to sell his farm at Martin's Ford, on the Chestatee River, and move his family to the Indian Territory,"* but he apparently never did.

In Merritt London's obituary, he was described as *"among our oldest citizens."* The newspaper account noted that he *"came to Lumpkin County in 1858 or 1859, where he took up the occupation of farming"* and that he *"had been a member of the Methodist Church ever since he was sixteen years of age."* He and Mary Neisler London are both buried at St. Paul's Church near the Lumpkin-Hall County line.

Today, well over a century after Merritt London's death, the area around the intersection of Highways 60 and 400 is still referred to as "the old London farm."

Mountain Stop-Over From Yesteryear:

Remembering Turner's Corner and Charlie's Bear, "Smoky"

Back when U.S. Highway 129 was a major thoroughfare "to the mountains," a unique little gas station/trinkets shop which had a real live wild black bear, was a stop most travelers simply could not pass up. And if they tried to pass without stopping, Charlie would flag them down.

In the earliest days of motorized travel into the Great Smoky Mountains, vacationers began stopping at Charlie Turner's little establishment for food, drinks, gasoline – and just plain entertainment. From 1925 when the road (U.S. 129 ultimately) was completed over Neel Gap right up until the day he had to quit, Charlie just had a knack for getting people to stop.

His motto was "Whatever it takes to get people to stop, I'll try it." Charlie was colorful and creative too.

Long before there was a bridge over the Chestatee River at Charlie's store, there was a ford for horse-drawn wagons and automobiles. "(In the early days) cars would get 'drowned out' when the water was high in the river," long-time area resident Oscar Cannon once explained. "They'd have to be pulled out of the river by a team of mules," and Charlie was always right there to pull them out

and then treat them to the wares in his little shop.

When he first opened his store, one of Charlie's tactics was to whistle and wave to passersby to telegraph his friendliness to the travelers. Sometimes it worked, and sometimes it didn't.

Then Charlie came up with an idea for a real crowd-pleaser. He started using animals.

"Charlie had a big bird dog named 'Jack'" Cannon continued. "He trained him to wear glasses and do tricks. Kids just loved it.

"When Charlie put a piece of candy on Jack's nose, the dog would flip the candy up into the air and then catch it." When word got around, everybody who stopped by (and lots of people did) just naturally wanted to buy some candy to watch old Jack work his trick. And of course both Charlie and Jack were more than happy to oblige.

It of course didn't hurt either that

Remembering Turner's Corner and Charlie's Bear, "Smoky"   Lumpkin County

Charlie was immensely entertaining and just naturally jolly to boot. He always enjoyed a good laugh, according to Cannon.

But above and beyond old Jack and Charlie's regular bag of tricks, the item which really "put him on the map" and earned him widespread acclaim undoubtedly was his pet bear "Smoky," a north Georgia black bear which Charlie raised from a cub.

Now wildlife officials and animal specialists will swear up and down that there is no such thing as "taming a wild bear," but you could not prove it by Charlie and Smoky. The big bear – who was absolutely terrifying in appearance – peacefully wandered about Charlie's premises for a decade or more.

It no doubt was rare, but Charlie had a friendly bear in spades, and he knew it and played it for all it was worth.

Smoky was so tame that children often rode on his back, and once word got around, no parent was going to be able to pass Charlie's store without stopping. At the very least they had to "see" the bear. Now whether or not they "rode" it was another matter. Regardless, business boomed at Charlie's little establishment.

Much of the time, Smoky was allowed to simply freely roam the river banks, such was his gentle nature. But despite the fact that he was tame as a housecat, his fearsome appearance often terrified some people, particularly strangers who weren't familiar with him.

When complaints began mounting – and eventually fearing for *Smoky's health* instead of the health of a human visitor – Charlie finally was forced to put Smoky in a cage. And there he remained for much of the remainder of his life, seldom being allowed to freely roam anymore.

For many years thereafter, however,

Turner's Corner – Charlie Turner (center) stands beside his beloved "pet" bear, Smoky. As far as is known, though he was fearsome looking, the bruin was docile, and never attacked a single person. *(Photo courtesy of Elizabeth Sparks)*

even though he was caged, Smoky was still quite the attraction, and many were the travelers who simply could not pass without stopping at Charlie's store, so the sales impact was almost the same.

When old Smoky finally died of old age – and he had lived for many years – poor Charlie was almost inconsolable. "He came to me and said 'Oscar, my bear's dead, and I need you to help me put it away.'" But even in a somber time such as the death of his old pet, Charlie could still "wheel and deal" with the best of them. Oscar remembers, that about the time he arrived with his shovel to help dig the big bear's grave, Charlie suddenly "remembered" something he had to pick up in Cleveland, Georgia.

"There I was," Oscar laughed in remembrance, "digging a five-foot-deep grave for this huge bear all by myself." In fairness, though, burying his old friend in the ground was probably just more than Charlie could bear – pardon the pun. (You knew a "bear" pun was bound to come eventually, huh?)

Charlie and his customers missed Smoky so much that the entrepreneur was forced to search for a replacement. He eventually located a man up over the

Two "Frenchmen" and Their Bears – A "wild but tamed" bear is a rarity to say the least, and actually doesn't exist at all if one asks a trained wildlife biologist. In the photo above, taken circa 1918, two "Frenchmen" with their dancing bears (undoubtedly captured and raised from cubs) provide a "show" on the town square of Dahlonega. *(Photo courtesy of the GA Dept. of Archives & History)*

mountain in Suches, Georgia, who had a bear cub whose mother had been killed.

To Charlie's great disappointment, however, the man explained he couldn't legally sell the cub to Charlie because there was a law against buying and selling wild animals. And it didn't help matters that the man was a game warden to boot.

But Charlie had "the inside track" on this deal. He'd actually been friends with the old warden for many years. He knew that patience and technique might yet allow him to strike a deal with the man.

"Well, if you *could* sell the bear, how much would you want for him?" Charlie persisted.

"I reckon he's worth $100," the man reportedly replied.

At that point, Charlie put a one-hundred dollar bill on a nearby stump, smiled and winked at the old fellow, picked up the bear and headed for home where he began raising the cub on a bottle. He named his new charge "Herman," after Governor Herman Talmadge who occasionally actually dropped in to visit with Charlie, a strong political supporter.

But the bear and old Jack the dog weren't the only featured attractions at Turner's Corner. Charlie's little mini-zoo also included a monkey and a whistling parakeet, both of which delighted visitors endlessly with their antics.

Though he was big on amusements, Charlie – who operated a service station there at his store – interestingly didn't actually know much about repairing cars at all. One time a customer asked him to adjust his carburetor and Charlie calmly replied, "I'll be happy to oblige, if you'll show me where it's at." Imagine

Remembering Turner's Corner and Charlie's Bear, "Smoky"   Lumpkin County

the perplexed look on his customer's face upon hearing that statement.

Once when Charlie was drunk – and he was known to take a drink or two fairly regularly – he was actually persuaded to sell Turner's Station. When he sobered up and realized what he had done, he called his Atlanta friends, Johnny and Elizabeth Sparks, and talked them into putting up the money needed to buy the place back.

The Sparkses amazingly agreed to actually become Charlie's business partners and eventually moved to the area. When once interviewed about Charlie, Elizabeth said she had many memories of working with him in the restaurant that he started.

"We served familystyle at first," she added, "and for 75 cents, you could get a meat, two vegetables, bread, a drink, and dessert."

Charlie was a bachelor, and Elizabeth and Johnny became his family for a number of years. One of Elizabeth's jobs was to keep Charlie sober, because everybody who knew him knew he enjoyed his liquor.

"Most of the time," Elizabeth said, "I was able to intercept Charlie's supply, but it took me a while to discover that a certain 'guest' was secretly leaving Charlie a bottle in the water tank of the commode in the restroom!"

As with all things, there is a beginning and an end. Charlie eventually passed away at the age of 75 in the late 1960s, and the little establishment was obviously never the same.

The Sparkses continued to operate Turner's Corner Restaurant and Station after Charlie's death, but it obviously just wasn't the same. Above and beyond the problem of losing Charlie, they had yet another big problem. They weren't able to get a replacement for the featured

Charlie Turner (l) popularized his automobile service station and restaurant in northern Lumpkin County with wit and charm for scores of years, but it was his "pet" bear Smoky who really stopped the traffic. The identity of the tentative passenger on Smoky is unknown today, but he looks none too happy with his adventure. *(Photo courtesy of Elizabeth Sparks)*

attraction – Herman, the bear – after he also succumbed to old age.

Following Johnny Sparks' death in 1972, Elizabeth ultimately just couldn't continue to operate the historic landmark by herself, so she put it up for sale. For the next few years, Turner's Station was run by a series of seasonal operators, but that didn't work out either.

The landmark establishment had been closed down for several years – much to the disappointment of travelers to the mountains – when Joyce Gowder, purchased it in 1991. Joyce grew up "just down the road," and some of her earliest memories are of Charlie Turner and his bear, which she remembers sitting on herself as a child.

Mystery & History in Georgia

Some things changed, but many things also remained the same as when Charlie had operated it.

After Joyce took over, things moved along at Turner's Corner Restaurant. Some things changed, but many things also remained the same as when Charlie had operated it. Folks aplenty still stopped by, and she still used the same stove on which Charlie cooked. Folks claimed she made wonderful biscuits, and she continued to offer many of the same dishes – grits and country ham or sausage for breakfast and a variety of entrees including fried or broiled trout for other meals.

The restaurant was also still heated by the same wood stove which provided warmth and comfort to Charlie's customers, and much of the decor inside the famed stop remained the same too.

Aside from the bear and mini-zoo, about the only thing that was really different was all the "doodads" with which Charlie liked to entice his customers. Little oddities like backscratchers and monkey piggy banks, whistles and rubber spiders, ceramic animals and other unusual handmade items.

When customers began dwindling a bit, Joyce said she seriously considered getting some live animals to continue the tradition Charlie had started, but the cages were too expensive, and the state wildlife management officials had established all sorts of rules and regulations with which Charlie had never had to contend. All he had to do was plop a $100 bill on top of a stump.

Despite the similarities, much in fact has changed over the years since Charlie Turner first opened his station at the little crossroads. The gas pumps no longer offer fuel to passing motorists; the highways have been widened and paved, and the cars which frequent the spot now are much faster and more sophisticated than their predecessors.

At last check, however, the Turner's Corner structure, atmosphere, mountain hospitality and delicious food continued to please the traveling public – and some locals as well. The unusual little attraction was still a good spot to stretch one's legs during a much-loved trip into or out of the scenic north Georgia mountains.

And if one watches the roadside close enough, he or she might just see another "Smoky" somewhere in the vicinity occasionally. Charlie, no doubt, would be pleased with his legacy.

Colorful Lumpkin County Native:

The Life and Legend of Captain Whit Anderson

He was a folk hero to those who knew him. He defended the "little man," was loyal to his friends, loved no one more than his family and the old South, and had the courage to stand toe to toe with an enemy on a city street, dueling in a shoot-out reminiscent of the Old West.

There are no monuments in Atlanta today for Captain "Whit" Anderson. The only memorial whatsoever is a crude tombstone in an Auraria, Georgia cemetery outside Dahlonega, Georgia, where he was buried. The lettering on the stone is unprofessional and the spelling imperfect. There is no date of birth and no date of death. But according to the late – and famed – former Atlanta historian Franklin Garrett, he was in fact "one of Atlanta's most colorful characters."

His full name was George Whitfield Anderson and he was born around 1822 in the Pendleton District of South Carolina, the son of Rueben Anderson and Susannah Welch Anderson. The exact year in which the family moved to Georgia is uncertain.

Dahlonega's Col. William P. Price, a close friend of Whit's, was being interviewed in 1894 for a news article about early Dahlonega. When describing Whit within that story, he told *Atlanta Constitution* reporter, P.J. Moran: *"His father, Rueben Anderson, brought him from South Carolina when a boy."*

This was evidently at approximately the same time as Georgia's gold rush, for Rueben's name appears in the *1830 Habersham County Census.* It is unknown for certain today if it was the Georgia gold rush of 1828 that attracted the family to Georgia, but Rueben apparently did move his family to the gold mining area. The *1850 Census* lists him as a miner living in the Auraria District.

A disabled veteran of the War of 1812, Rueben was an officer in the Georgia Militia. In 1840 he served as an Inferior Court Judge in Lumpkin County, so Whit sprang from solid stock.

In addition to Whit who was the oldest, and William Martin who was the youngest, Rueben and Susannah had four other children – David, John, Mary, and Nancy.

Muhlenbrink's Saloon – This historic site from the late 1800s – though forgotten for half a century or more – still existed beneath the blocks-long concrete viaduct which was paved over "railroad gulch" in old downtown Atlanta in 1906, allowing city streets to pass over the gulch. The historic building storefronts were "rediscovered" and converted into the attraction "Underground Atlanta" in 1969. The concrete and steel viaduct can be seen in the upper portion of this photo. Old Whitehall Street which passes beside Muhlenbrink's can be seen on the right. It was at this very site that Capt. Whit Anderson met Deputy Sheriff Tom Shivers for a pitched gun battle in the middle of Whitehall outside the saloon. When the gun-smoke had cleared, Shivers had departed this earth and Whit Anderson had entered the ranks of legend. *(Photo by Jimmy Anderson)*

According to Colonel Price, Whit grew up in what was known as "Nuckollsville," the original name of Auraria. Although the name seems to have accurately described the frontier atmosphere of the place – since street fights and brawls were quite common there – the town actually took its name from an early settler by the name of Nuckolls.

When U.S. Senator John C. Calhoun learned that the town near his gold mine was named Nuckollsville, he refused to allow the U.S. Post Office in the town to be known by what he regarded as a name too vulgar, and used his position and influence to have it changed to Auraria. Regardless of the official post office name, the town remained a wide open settlement, and in at least one of the many fights that took place there, Colonel Price maintained that Whit took a leading role.

The flashpoint for this early fisticuffs was an insult hurled by the manager of a circus which had set up at Nuckollsville. Whit and his younger brothers undertook to thrash the whole circus company in a wild free-for-all.

The Anderson brothers were acquitting themselves well too, but when reinforcements were called in, they decided that discretion was indeed the better part of valor, and they beat a hasty retreat. As it turned out, it was a fortunate withdrawal, as they soon discovered they would have been facing a large band of men, some armed with axe handles.

In 1846 as the Mexican War broke out, Whit helped to organize a company of Lumpkin County Volunteers. His obituary notes that he remained in Mexico until the war was over, adding, *"It was in the battles then fought that he first evinced that great bravery for which he was famous."*

Whit's official Mexican War records show that he was a lieutenant in Captain Nelson's Company, Calhoun's Mounted Battalion, Georgia Volunteers and that he was involved in the battles leading to the capture of Mexico City.

After the war Whit returned to Auraria, but he apparently didn't remain there long. News of the discovery of gold in California prompted many young men of Lumpkin County to leave for the California gold fields, and Whit was among them.

He appears in the *1850 Census of Sutter County, California*. His occupation: "miner." Of this time in California, his obituary states that he remained *"for* quite awhile and it was said by those who knew him intimately, (he was) the discoverer of the celebrated gold hills which have given up many fortunes." The obituary, however, adds somewhat ominously, "On account of a personal difficulty, however, he was compelled to leave California in 1856."

Since the exact circumstances of that "personal difficulty" are unclear today, one can only speculate, but Colonel Price, in his 1894 newspaper reminiscence, provides a clue. *"He was a firm believer in the rights of man: that the humblest man that lived had rights which should be accorded to him even at the cost of human life. That way of thinking made him at times wrangle about technical rights in a manner that frequently led to personal difficulties. In those affrays more than one man was killed."*

As if to soften any adverse reflection on his friend's character that such an observation might assign, the Colonel adds: *"He always befriended the friendless."* Price does not elaborate on the point specifically, but goes on to say that Whit was *"popular with the poor, as well as private soldiers, prisoners, and colored people."*

In 1859, according to an early Atlanta history published in 1902 by an organization called the "Pioneers of Atlanta," Whit was elected as a deputy marshal in Atlanta, a position he held until the outbreak of the Civil War. Helping to corroborate that bit of information is the fact that he appears in the **1860 Census of Fulton County, Georgia**. His age is given as 38 and his occupation as *"deputy marshal."* His residence is the *"Atlanta Hotel."*

As war erupted in 1861, Whit was commissioned a lieutenant in the First Georgia Regulars. He missed First Manassas, but was deeply involved in the

Pictured is the store of V.A. Higgins in Auraria, GA, circa 1910. It was in operation from 1833 to 1937, and was used as the first post office in Lumpkin County. It was located 2 to 3 lots below what was known more recently as "Woody Store" near the intersection of the town's main street (Gold Digger's Road) and Castleberry Bridge Road. Capt. Whit Anderson would have frequented this store in his travels to and from Auraria. *(Photo courtesy of the GA Dept. of Archives & History, Atlanta)*

Confederate victory on the same battlefield a year later. One has no idea of the terrors one might face, until service in hand-to-hand combat upon a battlefield becomes a requirement for honor and survival, and Whit undoubtedly faced his share.

In the official records of the *War of the Rebellion*, the First Georgia Regulars' activities at Second Manassas are described this way: *"From the nature of the ground and the impenetrable thickets of laurel and brush, none of the regiments except the First Georgia Regulars obtained a favorable position, but the Regulars succeeded in getting a good position and inflicted a very severe chastisement on the superior force of the enemy. The Regulars in this affair (officers and men) behaved with distinguished gallantry, and I only regret that our whole army is not composed of just such men."*

Whit was severely wounded in this battle and he returned to Georgia to recuperate. While he was recovering, he

Mystery & History in Georgia

Auraria, GA was photographed in the center of town on main street (Gold Diggers Road) circa 1908. In the mid to late 1800s, Auraria reportedly was still a substantial town. From one mile north of the site pictured here to a half mile south, it was one continuous "thick settlement" according to Professor Andrew Cain's **History of Lumpkin County 1832-1932**. (Photo courtesy of the GA Dept. of Archives & History, Atlanta)

was drawn into an episode that would stamp his name indelibly in Atlanta's history.

In February, 1863, while still on "wounded furlough," Whit became a candidate for his old job of deputy marshal against the incumbent, Tom Shivers. In those days, deputy marshals were elected by the Atlanta City Council, but on this occasion, the balloting resulted in a tie. Mayor James M. Calhoun broke the deadlock by casting his vote for Shivers, but the matter did not end there.

According to an account in the *Atlanta Journal Magazine* of April 29, 1923, Shivers and Anderson met accidentally the next day in a store on Whitehall Street *(the old downtown Atlanta section known later as "Underground Atlanta.")* They played a game of cards, and they quarreled. Shivers struck Whit on the head with a pistol and threw a bottle at him.

When the fight was finally broken up, Shivers said, *"Knowing you to be a brave man, Anderson, I suppose I will see you again."* Pointing a finger (which according to the *Journal* article) was *"dripping with blood,"* Whit, who was unarmed, replied, *"Just as sure as I live I will see you tomorrow."*

The next day -- February 2, 1863 -- Whit and Shivers met in front of Muhlenbrink's Saloon on Whitehall Street. *(Author's Note: Muhlenbrink's Saloon was among several blocks-worth of old Atlanta storefronts which had been forgotten for over half a century when the huge concrete viaduct was paved over "railroad gulch" in old downtown Atlanta in 1906 to facilitate traffic and commercial activity across the gulch. In 1969, the old storefronts and structures below the viaduct were "rediscovered" and converted into the entertainment complex "Underground Atlanta" which flourished from the 1970s to the turn of the century. In an earlier life, the old store-fronts had existed at "street level" along the railroad in the gulch.)* According to Franklin Garrett in his **Atlanta & Environs** Whit said to Shivers, *"I am now fixed up. Are you ready?"*

No other word was spoken. The two men drew their pistols and began firing. Shivers was struck twice and died within an hour. Whit was untouched.

Atlanta City Council minutes for its first meeting in February, 1863, note the death of Deputy Marshal Shivers, but provide no details. A resolution offered by Councilman James E. Williams and adopted by the council simply states: *"Resolved that the Mayor and Council do deeply regret the late and sad occurrence that deprived our Deputy Marshal Thomas Shivers of his life, and this City of an efficient officer, and that his wife and children have our sympathies in this, their great bereavement."*

Whit ultimately was indicted for murder by a Fulton County grand jury

Auraria After the Rush - Looking south down old Gold Diggers Road (present-day Hwy 9E) in Auraria. To the right on the vacant lot once stood the Paschal Hotel. The remnants of the two-story Graham Hotel built in the 1830s is visible in the distance. Capt. Anderson could have used either of these hotels when returning to Auraria, and would have frequented any number of the saloons which once fronted this road. *(Photo courtesy of the GA Dept. of Archives & History, Atlanta)*

in April, 1863. He plead *"Self Defense."* The April 11, 1863 edition of *The Southern Confederacy*, an Atlanta daily which did not survive the war, carries a terse account of the trial: *"Captain G.W. Anderson, charged with the killing of Thomas Shivers, late Marshal of the City in February last, was tried and acquitted by the Superior Court of this county now in session. The verdict which was rendered in a few moments after the case was submitted, justified the homicide."*

Whit apparently returned to military duty at some point in the summer of 1863, but the record of his service is unclear during at least part of that period. A letter in his service file to Confederate General P.G.T. Beauregard from an officer whose signature unfortunately is undecipherable, shows that Whit, still too weak for infantry duty, was seeking to raise a company of cavalry.

"General," the letter reads, *"Captain G.W. Anderson, a brave and chivalric officer who was among the very first to respond to the call of arms in defense of our country--and our inherent right--after serving through many severe conflicts was wounded at Manassas on the 30th of August, last, so badly that he is now unfit for active infantry service desires---in conjunction with W.C. Humphrey---a gallant soldier who fought bravely at the First Battle of Manassas and was taken prisoner--- to raise a cavalry company for active service and desires to obtain your approval of the same. I take leave to recommend these gentlemen to your consideration and hope that you will give your respect to their enterprise."*

There is no record in Whit's service file as to whether General Beauregard responded or whether Whit, in fact, ever even raised a cavalry company. But he evidently did return to the war. His obituary states that he was again wounded *"in the battles before Richmond in 1864,"* and his service record places him in the General Hospital at Atlanta on December 22 of the same year.

If Whit was in fact in a hospital in Atlanta at that time – and we have no absolute reason to believe he was not – it undoubtedly was a very crowded facility, since General William T. Sherman had burned most of the city just over a month earlier (November 18, 1864) in the Battle of Atlanta. How Whit Anderson even arrived in Atlanta at that time is a mystery today, since all of the rail lines into the city had been cut.

The able soldier and former lawman, however, cannot have been too seriously incapacitated, for an article by a reporter for the *Augusta* Georgia *Chronicle and Sentinel* which appeared in December, 1864, reported on the resurgence of Atlanta after Sherman's army had burned it to the ground. Among other news items appears the following: *"Many of the old citizens are returning, and the general watch-word is repair and re-build. Whit Anderson has opened a bar-room on Decatur Street where he serves his customers with dignity and grace..."*

The next published record of Whit's life appears in the 1866 edition of the *Journal of the Georgia Senate* (then meeting in the state capital at Milledgeville) which notes that Whit had been elected the Senate's "Sergeant at Arms," but he held this position for only a short time. In Atlanta it was time again for the election of city officers, and the City Council – apparently forgiving and forgetting Whit's volatile encounter with the unfortunate Tom Shivers – sent word of its desire to name him marshal of the city.

Whit returned to Atlanta to take the job and he continued to hold law enforcement positions there for the next decade and a half. For several years after the war Whit's life – as was the case with many Confederate veterans – seems to have been spent in clandestine resistance to the "carpetbagger" rule and Reconstruction government.

Colonel Price states that Whit was the leader of an Atlanta secret organization – presumably the Ku Klux Klan – and in August, 1870, was prepared to lead a band of some 200 armed men into the State Legislature (which had by then moved to the new capital of Atlanta) to prevent the enactment of a bill which would have extended the legislators' terms without the necessity of holding a popular referendum on the issue. The scheme apparently was organized by a group of what then were termed "Radical Republicans."

Colonel Price, a Democrat, discouraged Whit from taking such a desperate step in such a dangerous time. On a dramatic roll-call vote, with Whit and his unarmed friends seated in the gallery, the measure was lawfully defeated by a slim margin of ten.

Despite the accounts in the newspapers, Whit's post-war years apparently were not all spent with the tribulations of Reconstruction in Georgia. He had been an accomplished fiddler since his youth in the north Georgia mountains, and Atlanta historian Franklin Garrett wrote that *"he had been known as the best fiddler in Nuckollsville."*

At an October, 1870 fair in Fulton County, Whit competed his way into the finals in a contest to decide the best fiddler in Georgia. His last opponent was Thomas F. "Uncle Tommy" Lowe. The two men fiddled back and forth with renditions of *Arkansas Traveler* which were so stirring that, according to Garrett, they created "a veritable sensation."

When Lowe finally was declared the winner, Garrett writes, "Whit went up to him and said: 'Mr. Lowe, I want to say that having found somebody who can beat me playing Arkansas Traveler as bad as you can, I will never draw another bow.'" Adds Garrett, "And they say he never did."

The death of Whit's mother, Susannah, was a blow from which the now somewhat elderly lawman never fully recovered. A life-long bachelor, he was attached to his mother with a kind of Old South devotion that is endearing.

Colonel Price recalled visiting Whit once when he was sick and sleeping in a bunk at the Fulton County Jail. "His mind was as changeful as a kaleidoscope," Price says, "He talked of friends we both knew and sorrowfully of those who had bravely fallen in battle. Then he would speak tenderly of his mother and of the Democratic Party as the hope of the country. His mother always came first. The Democratic Party next. Sometimes," Price continued, "his turbulent feelings could be subdivided by the mere mention of her name... While a member of the legislature of 1877, I was requested by a majority of the population of Nuckollsville, to have an act passed to prohibit the sale of whiskey in that place...It escaped the watchful eye of Captain Anderson, who was not aware of the fact until he visited his hometown in the summer following and found that he had to send elsewhere for his whiskey. The next time he saw me in Atlanta, he expressed himself in no soft language about the matter. He said, 'Nuckollsville belongs to me and I should have been consulted before you dared to pass such a law. Prohibition may do for Dahlonega and other towns, but Nuckollsville should always be left free to have whiskey.'

By 1983, the historic Graham Hotel was almost beyond repair, and by 1993, it, unfortunately, had disappeared completely from the landscape. Built in the 1830s, this historic structure had housed such famous notables as South Carolina Senator and former Vice President of the United States John C. Calhoun who once owned a gold mine nearby. (Photo by Olin Jackson)

"I assured him that the act was passed at the request of many Nuckollsville people, some of whom had used liquor intemperately. He asked me to name some of the signers. I gave him the name of his brother, Dave. He scouted the idea of his brother's name as worth anything in such a case. He demanded other names. I added several old friends of his who were hard drinkers, but were sober when they signed the petition. 'Then,' said Whit, 'if they were sober, they were not in their right minds, and they should not be considered.' He wanted more names, which I gave him, and, lowering my voice, I gave him the name of his mother, Susannah Anderson. Tears came at once into the eyes of this strong man, who, putting his arm around

Historic Auraria Church was photographed here in 1983. Capt. Whit Anderson – along with numerous other notables – is buried in the cemetery on the rise behind this church. *(Photo by Olin Jackson)*

my shoulders said: 'Whatever my mother does is right. We will say nothing more about this matter now.'"

In January, 1881, Whit supported a rival candidate against Angus Perkerson in the campaign for sheriff of Fulton County. He apparently did so with the expectation of being named a deputy.

Perkerson, however, was elected and the loss was a bitter blow to Whit. Susannah had died only a few years earlier. With Atlanta law enforcement no longer an option after almost two decades of service, Whit was left "swinging in the wind."

It wasn't long after this time that he became ill and in October, at age 59, went back home to Nuckollsville.

"He sent for me in his last illness," Colonel Price wrote. *"He had come home to die. The message came too late for me to look on his face again in this life. More than twelve years ago it was, they buried him among the trees on this steep hill overlooking the little village which in life he had called his own."*

Whit's solemn tombstone, crafted obviously by one untrained in proper spelling, reads: "Captin Whit Anderson at Rest" No other information follows on the lonely marker.

On page 1 of the Nov. 22, 1881 edition of the *Atlanta Constitution*, a story headlined *"Captain Whit Anderson's Death"* concludes with these lines: *"When Sherman captured Atlanta he issued a proclamation outlawing Captain Anderson on account of his part in the capture of some Federal soldiers and this fact has handed his name to posterity in history. Since last January he has been gradually sinking and his death ended the life of as good and pure a man as ever breathed."*

So who, in truth, was Whit Anderson? In answering that, it may be easier to first say what he was not. He was not a pillar of Atlanta's emerging "New South" society. He was not a leader in business, trade or commerce. He was not a spell-binding orator, lawyer, or minister of the gospel.

Nevertheless, Henry W. Grady's *Atlanta Constitution* – though often reflecting somewhat overstated sentiments of the times, and sometimes even given to what could only be described as flights of fantasy – was right on the money with its assessment of Whit. He was a genuine folk hero to those who knew him, and a friend among friends, brave, loyal, and honest right to the end.

(Grateful appreciation is extended herewith to Robert E. Anderson who provided the factual information necessary for this article.)

Lumpkin County Folk Hero:

The Life & Legend of "Boney Tank"

Any way one cuts it, "Boney Tank" was an extraordinary individual and a fearless opponent if one ever chanced to oppose him. He joins a list of unusual personalities from Lumpkin County, Georgia, in the mid- to late-20th Century who rose to fame and legendary status in the state's history.

Ever heard of a person by the name of "Boney Tank?" Neither have a lot of people, but he nevertheless was one of the most colorful and legendary individuals in the history of the state of Georgia, chronicled in books, magazine articles, and news stories during and after his lifetime.

The American West has spawned a long list of characters who have been celebrated in song, story and major motion picture productions for well over 100 years now. Who, for instance, has not heard of such notables as John Henry "Doc" Holliday, Jim Bowie, and Meriwether Lewis?

All three of these individuals are deeply ingrained in the folklore and history of America. Despite this fact, however, few people today are aware that these men were Georgians before they were legends of the Old West. Many "legendary" characters came from the state of Georgia in the 19th Century.

Almost as famous, but just slightly more obscure, was "Boney Tank." Born with a name as incredible as the feats he accomplished, he was an adventurer, gold miner, wounded Civil War veteran, outrageous businessman, and fearless fighter of great renown in his day. His actual legal name was just as outrageous as he was: "Charles and Napoleon Bonaparte 'Boney Tank' Tankersley." "Boney" liked to be outrageous, for he sought nothing but adventure in his life.

At one time in the youthful years of America, the "western frontier" was what today is the state of Georgia. As "Manifest Destiny" and pioneer migration constantly pushed the American frontier farther and farther westward, Georgia gradually became more and more civilized, forcing out the Native Americans, and the adventurers who preferred a less restricted and uninhibited environment. By the 1840s, Georgia's "frontier" days – for the most part – were behind her, but there were exceptions. There were still pockets where

275

Mystery & History in Georgia

vestiges of frontier life still existed. One such spot was what today is known as Lumpkin County where gold had been discovered in 1828. This was where the story of Boney Tank began.

Until well into the 1870s, Lumpkin remained a lawless territory – particularly during and after the U.S. Civil War. It was a place which just naturally attracted opportunists and adventurers – and cut-throats. Just as with legends such as Texas's Judge Roy Bean, Boney Tank undoubtedly enjoyed fame and notoriety which exceeded his actual accomplishments and life experiences, but so also did many of the other famous personalities from yesteryear.

One Tankersley family legend maintains that Boney and his brother, "Tip," were twins born in a cave to a Cherokee woman who was hiding from the U.S. troops who were rounding up the Indians during the infamous "Trail Of Tears." The father of the two boys, as the legend goes, was a reporter and later editor of *The New York World* newspaper – forerunner of the later *New York Times*. Interestingly, when he died, Boney Tank was eulogized in *The New York World* as *"The Man Who Was Never Whipped"* with *"peace to his unconquered ashes,"* and other eloquent flatteries. How did they even know about him?

The family legend also maintains that the two brothers eventually had a bitter falling out after it was discovered that Boney had been involved in an affair with Tip's wife. Tip, according to the tale, abandoned Georgia and his wife and struck out for Oklahoma. The climactic conclusion to this story maintains that Boney – on his deathbed – married Tip's wife upon learning of Tip's death (Tip supposedly had never divorced his wife).

The actual circumstances of the life and times of Boney Tankersley were in fact considerably different, though no less captivating. Reality has a way of diminishing the luster of the exploits of most folk heroes, but even in reality, Boney Tankersley remains a remarkable personality.

After being abandoned by his mother and father at a young age, Boney left what today is known as Lumpkin County, Georgia, for the newly-emerging city of Atlanta. The site was fast becoming a railroad crossroads with rapid growth, and Boney apparently was eager to seek his fortune there.

There is some indication that Tankersley worked briefly as a policeman in Atlanta, but by 1859, he was employed as a laborer named Napoleon C. Tank in the Atlanta Rolling Mill, an enormous factory where railroad rails were manufactured and refurbished. It was extremely-hard work which could build a mountain of muscle upon a man.

Two years later, according to reports, Boney answered the call to duty, enlisting in Company K of the 7th Georgia Confederate Infantry Regiment. His unit fought at the Battle of First Manassas (also known as Bull Run) on July 21, 1861, the first major engagement of the U.S. Civil War.

In this hard-fought battle, Boney's leg was shattered by one of the huge .69 caliber minie balls fired from the large smooth-bore muskets so dominant early in the war. It was a miracle the leg did not require amputation. It was months before he could walk again, and thereafter, he was lame for the remainder of his life, with a painful wound which constantly festered and never completely healed. According to accounts, Boney also lost an eye in the battle, although no such injury is mentioned in his service records.

Shipped back to Atlanta, Boney had the honor of being among the first of thousands of wounded soldiers eventually sent to the Confederate hospitals of the city. As an early patient returning from the battlefield, Boney was treated to a hero's welcome, complaining years later that with all the parties and attention, he was nearly killed with kindness.

Wounds, however, could not keep Boney Tank out of action, and it was in these endeavors that his true mettle shined through. Discharged from the 7th Georgia Infantry as a result of his injury, he merely enlisted in Company D of the 1st (Galt's) State Line Infantry Regiment and then in Cavalry Company G (the famous "Fulton Dragoons") of Cobb's Legion (the unit of the mythical Major Ashley Wilkes in the major motion picture production *Gone With The Wind*.). He always enlisted as Charles N. Tank.

Thrust back into combat again in Virginia, Boney continued his fearless combativeness. A comrade later commented in remembrance that "no man took more chances in battle than Boney Tank." He was again wounded – once again in his bad leg – when his horse was shot from beneath him. Medical leave and want of a horse brought him back home and gained him temporary duty in Georgia with the Nitre Bureau (where he helped with explosives) and at another rolling mill making critically-needed horseshoes for the Confederacy.

Boney later returned from the war to Lumpkin County as a disabled veteran. Despite his courageous efforts in the war, he discovered to his disappointment that he had few prospects for a livelihood outside the military.

By 1870, however, Boney reappears as *"Napoleon Tankersley, liqour dealor of Auraria,"* living with Malissa "Eliza"

Charles and Napoleon "Boney Tank" Tankersley as he appeared in the later years of his life. *(Photo courtesy of GA Dept. of Archives & History, Atlanta)*

Lowe Tankersley and the couple's two children. Boney also apparently dabbled in the production of illegal whiskey "moonshining," since he was tried in federal court in 1873 as N.C. Tankersley. However, since the practice of moonshining was virtually akin to an honorable profession for mountain families, Tankersley's reputation undoubtedly was enhanced, rather than tarnished, by his encounter with the authorities.

Boney seems ultimately to have found his calling as an agent for the sales of cotton, whiskey and gold mines. The latter – usually sold to Northern interests – led to at least one charge of fraud for the sale of a "salted" mine, where the property in question had been doctored with a few gold nuggets and dust to make the mine appear more valuable. This practice of "salting a mine" was a time-honored profession among

Southerners, and indeed was undoubtedly considered "just desserts for Yankee carpetbaggers."

Boney's success as an agent eventually earned him acclaim across the country. One family story maintains that he was even invited to work in a group of mines in Africa, a deal which fell through like a ton of bricks when Boney saw the ocean for the first time. No way was he getting out on that endless body of water. Boney eventually was even successful as a financial agent – a feat later considered astounding, since he could neither read nor write.

In time, he became a respected leader of his little "kingdom" centered around the old mining town of Auraria (originally known as "Nuckollsville") near Dahlonega in Lumpkin County. An editor in Gainesville described him in 1896 as *"cool, serene, and imperturbable.... He still wears his hat cocked to the left side, over his absent eye, chews his tobacco on the same side, and has the same fascinating presence. When you talk with him you feel you are with a genius of his kind – that there is only one of him in the wide universe and you have found him."*

The *New York World* wrote that although Boney appeared in no *"Who's Who"* of local despotism, he was *"a giant, ruling his domain by his powerful fists, taking on any bully or any contender in Auraria."* The *World* called him *"the man who was never whipped"* and *"a Napoleon without a Waterloo."* Again, how did the *World* even know of him??

Despite his acclaim, and while acknowledging that there may be no rock in Auraria not thrown by Boney at someone at some point in time, his descendants also remember at least one incident in which Boney did taste defeat.

The circumstances involved one of the traveling salesmen who refused a time-honored tradition of a "treat" of a free shot of whiskey for a few regulars at a local gathering spot. Boney apparently attempted to persuade the fellow to honor the custom. The salesman, in return, reportedly unceremoniously dumped Boney into a meal barrel. Asked later about the incident, Boney merely replied honestly and good-naturedly that he *"had been taken to the mill for a good grinding."*

These types of incidents, however, apparently were few and far between, because aside from his tenacity as a fighter, Boney Tank also enjoyed an army of friends, and few if any enemies. His opinions carried great weight locally and the candidates he backed inevitably won in local elections.

It was in the years after the U.S. Civil War that Boney Tank truly emerged as a folk hero. His reputation was based upon real incidents reported in the contemporary issues of the Atlanta, Dahlonega and Gainesville, Georgia newspapers. The fact that Boney always made "good copy" didn't hurt either.

For example, in 1883, he made news as the defendant in *"the great mule case,"* wherein he was sued by another one-eyed man over a mule that had somehow had its tongue removed. Also in 1883, Boney fought his battle with a monster beaver that, when killed, proved to weigh sixty-nine pounds after being fully dressed – a huge specimen to say the least.

Despite his popularity and extraordinary charisma – feats of character which just naturally lend themselves to exaggerations – it goes without saying that one must closely examine the details of any incident involving an individual such as Boney Tank.

In point of fact, Augustus Henry "Tip" Tankersley was not dead nor was

Boney Tankersley on his deathbed when Boney married Eliza Lowe (on April 1, 1895) – who was already the mother of his seven children. It is also unlikely (though not impossible) that Boney Tank was born in a cave during the "Trail of Tears," nor is it certain that his father – Jim Tankersley – worked for *The New York World* (but that substantial news leader in the far-off reaches of New York somehow knew about the legendary Boney Tank).

Boney and his brother, however, do appear in the *1850 Federal Census of Lumpkin County* as *"Napoleon"* (age 11, born in Alabama) and *"Henry"* (age 8, born in North Carolina) *"Taonk"* respectively, living with *"Sally Taonk"* (age 27, born North Carolina) and a gold miner named *"James W. Lawrence"* (who was not the father of the boys.). That age places his birth at almost exactly the same time as the relocation of the Cherokees in 1838.

Interestingly, "Henry Taonk," living years later in Oklahoma as Augustus Henry "Tip Tank" Tankersley, filed a claim as a Cherokee Indian against the United States. He listed his mother as *Sarah Mahala "Mary" Narcissa Satterfield, the daughter of half-Cherokee Indian Lucy Ward* (Mrs. John Satterfield). He stated that his parents had split up after he was born and that his mother eventually married Rubin Moss. (As *Mary Moss*, the boys' mother appears in the *1884 Federal Census of the Eastern Cherokees* as living in Dawson County, Georgia.) Tip also claimed his mother died in 1885 and that his father was Jim Tankersley, born in Georgia and dead by 1851.

Testimony provided by Augustus Henry "Tip" Tankersley on other occasions, however, conflicts with information known about the family. In separate

Looking south down old Gold Diggers Road (present-day Hwy 9E) in Auraria. To the right on the vacant lot once stood the Paschal Hotel operated by Agnes Paschal. The two-story Graham Hotel built in the 1830s is visible in the distance. Boney Tank could have used either of these hotels when returning to Auraria, and would have frequented any number of the saloons which once fronted this road. *(Photo courtesy of GA Dept. of Archives & History, Atlanta)*

places, he is on record for having stated that he had no brothers or sisters, alive or dead, and that he was the only child of his mother.

Boney Tank, interestingly, also filed a claim as a Cherokee Indian. He even cited the claims of Tip's application for Cherokee citizenship in his (Boney's) application for Cherokee funds. In his testimony, Boney added that while he and his brother were young, his mother had married James Lawrence, and had left the two boys on their own *"without home or friends."* He stated that their own father, born in Georgia or North Carolina, had died around 1841. If he truly was "without home or friends," did he in fact spend time in some type of shelter other than a normal home?

Tip must have kept better tabs on his mother than did Boney, since Boney had reported her as having died in 1863. As for their Indian heritage, Boney claimed that his grandfather (sic? great-grandfather?) was James Mohannee (also called Ward), a full Cherokee who migrated west on the "Trail of Tears."

Pictured is the store of V.A. Higgins in Auraria, GA, circa 1910. It was in operation from 1833 to 1937, and was used as the first post office in Lumpkin County. It was located 2 to 3 lots below what was known more recently as "Woody Store" near the intersection of the town's Main Street and Castleberry Bridge Road. Boney Tank would have frequented this store in his travels to and from Auraria. *(Photo courtesy of GA Dept. of Archives & History, Atlanta)*

He also stated that James's wife abandoned him and "went into hiding with the couple's children in the area known today as Lumpkin County."

Boney Tankersley's last living daughter remembered him as a good father. The Gainesville, Georgia newspaper reported in 1883 of the troubles Boney was experiencing in raising his son Charley, Jr. The son apparently was a genuine "chip off the old block." In separate incidents, he nearly cut off his foot, broke his arm, had his throat cut in a knife-fight, and then shot himself in the thigh. Boney, however, wanted everyone to know that his son and namesake was still a "mighty good boy."

Never professing any religion, "the man who never was whipped," required ten days of the ministrations of Baptist preacher Joe Bell, before finally converting just before dying on April 23, 1908. He is buried in the Baptist Church cemetery in Auraria, Georgia, among many other legends of Lumpkin County's wild history, including such notables as Capt. Whit Anderson *(Readers see please see his information in this publication in the Lumpkin County section)* and "Grandma" Agnes Paschal, the "Angel of Mercy."

Because of his impact upon the social fabric of life in numerous communities in north Georgia, Boney Tank enjoys acclaim in a number of county histories. Today (2021), almost 115 years after his death, it is sometimes difficult to separate fanciful legend from factual legacy.

During the pioneer days when the western portion of our nation was still being settled, legendary characters inevitably emerged from the battle-tested and danger-experienced migrants who sought a new and better life. All too often, when the truth is uncovered, the persona of these folk heroes is diminished. In an ironic twist, Charles and Napoleon Bonaparte "Boney Tank" Tankersley is extraordinary in either fact or fiction.

Endnotes

Aside from the records of the National Archives and the Georgia Department of Archives and History, information in this article came from James E. Dorsey's The History Of Hall County, Georgia *(1991); Andrew W. Cain's* History Of Lumpkin County – 1832-1932 *(1934); and Andrew Sparks's "Bony Tank Was A Fighting Man,"* Atlanta Journal Constitution *Magazine, July 31, 1966, pp. 8ll.*

(Grateful appreciation is extended herewith to Robert S. Davis, Jr. for provision of the factual details used within this article. The author would also like to acknowledge the kind assistance provided by the late Madeline Anthony, Lumpkin County historian; by the late Franklin M. Garrett, Atlanta historian; by Indian genealogists Sarron Ashton and Weldon Hudson; and by Tim Lawson of Gainesville, Georgia.)

Murder Or Execution ?

The Tragic Civil War Graves on Bearden's Bridge Hill

During the last days of the U.S. Civil War, three men out of seven captives were either executed or murdered on a lonely hill outside Dahlonega, Georgia, in an incident which still disturbs investigators even today.

The Autumn of 1864 brought cool weather to the north Georgia mountains. Most of the area lay in ruins in the wake of General W. T. Sherman's three Union armies which had fought their way southward, mainly down the route along the Western and Atlantic Railroad from Chattanooga. The city of Atlanta, a major manufacturing center for the Confederate war effort, now lay in ruins and in Union control, its people in despair, wondering from whence might come their next meal. In other parts of north Georgia, some circumstances were even more desperate than this.

The Confederate Army of Tennessee under General John Bell Hood, severely beaten, starved and now mostly bare-footed, limped back northward to escape, yet still harassing Union troops whenever possible along the way, assaulting Sherman's supply line at Big Shanty, Allatoona and elsewhere along the railroad. Leaving his 20th Corps to hold Atlanta, Sherman took the rest of his forces temporarily northward in pursuit of Hood who finally turned southwestward, escaping into Alabama.

Desperate Circumstances

The more rugged terrain of extreme north Georgia held little strategic significance to the armies of the North, and they circumvented it. As a result, due to the absence of law enforcement – and even mature males to defend the homes, businesses and property – lawlessness was the order of the day in the north Georgia mountains. With almost reckless abandon, partisan guerrillas and Home Guard companies alike preyed upon each other and upon innocent civilians living in the remote northern reaches of the state. At the time, Lumpkin and Fannin counties were the two most dangerous counties in Georgia. *(Readers please see "Forgotten Union Guerrillas in the North Georgia Mountains" in this publication.)*

According to T. Conn Bryan's *Confederate Georgia*, Colonel G. W. Lee who was commanding the Atlanta post prior to its fall had earlier become aware of the disorder in the mountains, and telegraphed Governor Joseph Emerson Brown in Milledgeville: *"There is considerable trouble in northeast Georgia, especially in Fannin County,"* he stated *". . . supposed to be 150 Tories and deserters in a body and camped. They are plundering and burning. . . ."*

In Lumpkin County, known outlaw groups such as the Jeff Anderson and Moorland gangs of terrorists were raiding and killing innocent civilians in their homes almost at will. And farther north in the state, Captain John Gatewood's guerrillas were shooting and robbing suspected pro-Union sympathizers in Fannin County near the Polk County, Tennessee line.

Following the Confederate defeat in the Atlanta Campaign, a number of Southern troops began deserting their units. Many had already abandoned the Confederate cause at the Battle of Chickamauga in September, 1863, when the Union Army made its first major push into Georgia. Even though this battle was won by the Confederates, most of them could see "the handwriting on the wall" by this point.

Among these deserters was William A. Twiggs who slipped away on the night of September 19th after the first day of action at Chickamauga. Twiggs had been a private in Company "H," 52nd Georgia Infantry (C.S.A.). He had had his fill of the mayhem and gore, and decided that the Confederacy was unable to protect the homes of her own defenders, so he was going home to do it for them, since he was deeply worried about his wife and children who lived in Fannin County.

Iley T. Stuart, a Fannin County blacksmith, had watched the war from a distance for the past two years. He had somehow managed to evade the ever-present Confederate conscript officers – even while openly professing his strong loyalty to the Union. His wife, Margaret, would say of him in later years: *"He was a Union man from the first and cursed and abused the rebels for the way they did. . ."*

Finally, in September of 1863, Stuart followed a Captain Van Hook to Athens, Tennessee, where he then joined Company "G" of the 11th Tennessee Cavalry (U.S.). In early January, 1864, however, Stuart became ill and was hospitalized at Knoxville.

After he had recovered, Iley returned to his regiment which was at Strawberry Plains, Tennessee. There he informed Colonel Isham G. Young (U.S.) that he felt certain he could raise a company of men back in Fannin County if supplied with necessities and given the opportunity. Young filled out papers authorizing Stuart to recruit the troops he said were available in the mountains. Stuart reportedly then put the papers in his pocket and left the post shortly thereafter, headed back down to Georgia.

For unexplained reasons in 1864, Stuart was listed as a "deserter" on the rolls of the 11th Tennessee, even though he had papers confirming his commission from Colonel Young to raise troops among the loyalists to the Union cause in Georgia. This identity as "a deserter" would have an unfortunate serious impact not only upon his life and legacy, but upon his wife's future financial security as well. Historians are still perplexed with the designation even today.

Solomon Stansberry, a native of Burke County, North Carolina, had come to Fannin County at an early age.

He spent most of his life as a farmer and mechanic in north Georgia and had raised a family. At 34 years of age, he also was a strong loyalist to the Union, and joined Battery "D," 1st Tennessee Artillery Battalion (U.S.) in January, 1863. In March, 1864, he left the battalion in Nashville and returned to Fannin County.

William R. Witt was a family man, too. He had seen the Home Guard units riding through the mountains and had heard the stories of neighbors who had been attacked and whose homes had been ransacked, robbed and burned. In September, 1864, he left his wife Sarah and his five children to travel to Cleveland, Tennessee, where he joined Company "I," 5th Tennessee Mounted Infantry (U.S.). It was there that he met William A. Twiggs.

Twiggs' disenchantment with the Confederate cause had grown much deeper over the months since he had deserted his regiment at Chickamauga. Upon his return to Fannin County, he found that lawlessness prevailed in that territory, and innocent people were being killed merely on suspicion of pro-Union sentiments. He had no doubt heard the horrible story of Talitha Stanley who heard shots fired in her yard and ran out of the house to find her husband lying dead in a pool of blood with his baby in his arms. As she ran to him, soldiers of the Fannin County Home Guard clubbed her with their rifles, leaving her blind in one eye and deaf for the remainder of her life.

Pro-Union Recruits

Twiggs soon left Fannin County and went to Cleveland, Tennessee, himself, where the Union Army existed in strength and was recruiting regiments to operate as independent commands in the mountains of east Tennessee, western North Carolina and north Georgia. Many citizens had appealed to the Federal government for protection from the roving bands of Confederate guerrillas who were inflicting revenge on their enemies in these remote areas. In response, the Federal government decided to organize units like the 5th Tennessee Mounted Infantry to combat the Confederates in these areas.

At first, Twiggs joined Wood's Battalion. Then he learned that Colonel S.B. Boyd was organizing the 5th Tennessee Mounted Infantry. Boyd offered him recruiting papers to raise a company in Fannin County for his regiment, and Twiggs accepted, then returned to Fannin County sometime in the middle of September, 1864, where he began to assemble a group of men for his company. Witt had joined Twiggs in Cleveland in nearby White County, another hotbed of discontent, and returned to Fannin County with him.

Hearing that Iley Stuart was also recruiting troops for the 11th Tennessee Cavalry, Twiggs went to Stuart's place near Higdon's Store. Stuart had been ill most of the summer with jaundice and had only recently recovered. Twiggs asked Stuart to bring his recruits and join his company, but Iley was reluctant, since he had already nearly completed the ranks of his own company. Twiggs, who could have an imposing disposition when angered, told Stuart that if he didn't join his command, he would force him and his men to join.

It was late in the afternoon on September 25th, 1864, when Twiggs rode into Morganton. The afternoon shadows were long and the air had a slight autumn chill in it. Twiggs' men rode behind him, old muzzleloading rifles slung across their backs, old felt hats pulled low over their eyes. None of them had yet drawn a uniform issue, so they were still clad in their homespun clothes.

The men rode up to the old courthouse and dismounted. A small crowd began gathering to see the band of armed men, speculating whether they were Federal, Confederate or just another gang of bushwhackers.

Twiggs mounted the courthouse steps and turned around to face the crowd. The long ride into town from Green's Ferry had given him time to think about what he was going to say. He knew that many of these people had been victims of the Confederate "Home Guard" units and the guerrillas; their loved ones killed; their homes burned; their cattle and sheep driven off.

He also realized that these people had been promised protection time and time again by the Federal authorities over in Tennessee, but that help had never arrived. These people, Twiggs thought, will never join an outfit that will go off somewhere else to fight.

Of particular concern to Twiggs was the fact that he only had authority to "recruit" troops, not to engage in any type of open combat with them. Colonel Boyd had been very clear and pointed about this issue, explaining to Twiggs that he and his men would be outlaws if they went into any military engagements before they were legally mustered into the Army.

Twiggs' mind, however, was made up. The defenseless females and youngsters in these mountains needed protection and that was more important to him than worrying about the fine points of the law. As he spoke out, the solemn man took off his old felt hat and rested his hand on the butt of his Colt revolver. He started to speak in a heated, almost desperate manner:

"The Federal Army sent me here to help you. The people of Fannin County are tired of being attacked, molested and robbed by the rebel guerrillas. The time has come to drive them out of this country. If you will join my company, I will drive them out and make the country safe."

Some of the men in the crowd apparently looked more closely at Twiggs and his men and saw no regular soldiers in uniform. They began asking, "Where are the soldiers? We thought they were sending soldiers to protect us. How do we know you actually got authority to raise a company?"

Twiggs felt a sudden rush of fear in his heart before his anger began welling up. He knew he must win these people right here right now or else there would be no recruitment from the people of Morganton. It was as simple as that. Twiggs came down the steps and stood face-to-face with his hecklers.

"I've got authority alright, from the government of the United States and from Colonel Boyd of the 5th Tennessee," he said with fire in his eyes. "And if you don't join up, I'm authorized to conscript every one of you and make you join!," he responded menacingly.

The crowd no doubt became more reserved at this point. It is not known today just how long Twiggs remained in Morganton that day, but it is known that by the time he left, he was approximately 20 men stronger in number as they headed out of town back to Green's Ferry.

Meanwhile, Iley Stuart eventually received word of Twiggs' speech and made up his mind to join him as well. He told his wife Margaret as he was organizing a few things into his bedroll on his horse, "I can't just stay here." Stuart and his men ultimately joined Twiggs at Green's Ferry.

Shortly thereafter, the company reached the old McDonald Farm near the Dial community where they made camp. From there, squads of men made regular forays off into the mountains raiding Home Guard encampments and taking revenge on pro-Confederate citizens in the county. They didn't care that they were acting in just as lawless a manner as were the Confederate guerrillas.

Fateful Day

It was a clear, cool, sunny autumn day on October 20th, 1864. The woods along the Toccoa River were bright with the red sourwood leaves and the deep gold of the hickories mixed with the evergreen of the pines and hemlocks. The silent forest along the old wagon road came alive with the steady rumble of horses hooves as nine bewhiskered men armed with muskets rode toward the VanZant settlement from McDonald's farm.

Iley T. Stuart led the column of men, looking from side to side, ever-watchful for any odd movement or shadow that might betray the presence of a rebel sniper. Twiggs had gotten word earlier that there might be a rebel company patrolling the area from the south toward Gaddistown, and the Lumpkin County Home Guard headquartered in Dahlonega had been sending companies into the southern parts of Fannin and Union Counties to hunt bushwhackers and to keep a watch for approaching Union columns.

As the men cantered up to Lewis VanZant's old house, Stuart posted Willis Gilliam to guard the road to the north. VanZant, a wealthy blacksmith and farmer, stood on the front porch of his house, eyeing the newcomers with suspicion.

VanZant was getting well along in years by 1864. He had come to this valley in 1832 when the Indians were still camped there and had applied for a draw in the Sixth Land Lottery. In 1833, he won the land for which he had applied. In 1834, VanZant brought his family from North Carolina in a Conestoga wagon.

The war had brought trouble aplenty to the valley. Rebel and Federal guerrilla bands had both ridden up and down the valley shooting, burning and pillaging at will.

VanZant was suspicious when Stuart and his band rode up with guns out, all of them wearing an odd mixture of old mountaineer clothing. Stuart, wearing civilian clothes beneath an old blue overcoat, asked Mr. VanZant if he would let them use his forge to shoe their horses.

VanZant saw immediately that refusal might mean big trouble. He had a farm and a store that he had to protect, and a family, too. Not knowing for sure whether this group had Union or Confederate loyalty, he spoke sparingly. Finally he told Stuart to go ahead and use the forge.

Stuart and his men led their horses around back of the house to the old shed where the forge stood. They went to work building a fire, pumping the billows and raking the coals to bring a glow to the top of the forge. Soon the sounds of the hammer pinging against hot iron were heard ringing up and down the valley as the shoes were beaten out on the anvil.

Willis Gilliam continued his vigil from the side of the road, watching for any signs of Rebel patrols coming down the road. Because of Stuart's orders, he continued to watch to the north, never thinking that the enemy might appear from the open valley to the south.

Suddenly he heard shots ring out and men shouting. He broke into a run back down the road toward VanZant's house where he saw men on horseback, clad in gray. Hiding in some nearby brush, he watched breathlessly, knowing that he couldn't do anything to help.

The rebel soldiers of Captain Marion Williams' Company, Findley's Regiment had come up the valley past the old Chastain house. They had heard from a resident in the area that some bushwhackers were at old Mr. VanZant's house. They rode quickly to surround the house and the forge. One of Stuart's men broke and ran. Williams shouted "Halt, or I'll shoot!" The man quickly halted.

Stuart and his men had left their guns outside the forge, as they didn't want a round falling into hot coals. Without warning, the rebels had easily surrounded them. Williams demanded that they surrender immediately or they would all be killed. Seeing that they were out-manned and out-gunned, Stuart and his men surrendered and came out.

After collecting all the weapons of the men, the rebels commanded them to mount their horses. They then tied their ankles together with ropes under the horses' bellies and then led them back down the valley toward Gaddistown.

A shocked and shaken Gilliam witnessed it all. He wasn't certain just who had been captured, since he was watching from a distance, but he saw eight men being led off. After the men were gone, he quickly ran back along the road to McDonald's farm, a distance of a little over a mile. There he informed Twiggs of the incident.

Twiggs quickly summoned his men and they mounted their horses, riding hard back toward VanZant's place.

When they reached VanZant's, Twiggs and his men rode up and down the valley along the banks of the Toccoa trying to pick up the trail of the men. Try as they might, the trail, surprisingly, eluded them. By day's end, they returned to their encampment at McDonald's farm.

A Ride Into Eternity

Captain Marion Williams' company, escorting the eight captives, continued to ride until nightfall when they reached Gaddistown. Arriving at the home of Elishu Seabolt, the company pitched camp. The prisoners were dismounted and their hands tied behind their backs.

The darkness of the mountains eventually filled the camp and the embers of the campfire flickered low as silence descended upon the valleys. At that moment, Stuart and his men no doubt still had hopes that they might talk their way out of their predicament, but that hope was fading fast.

Exhausted from the long, hard ride through the mountains, prisoners and guards alike soon fell asleep. One of the prisoners, however – Thomas Anderson – remained alert and awake. Slowly, patiently Anderson worked at the ropes binding his hands until they began loosening. Continuing his efforts, Anderson soon had the rope just loose enough to slip one hand free, and that was all it took. He was free from his bindings.

Anderson now had to get past the guard who had been picketed to watch them. When he could not locate the man, he decided to simply slip away as quietly as possible. Crawling quietly on his belly, Anderson made for some nearby bushes. From there he moved into the woods and slipped away into the night.

After two days of wandering on foot and evading strangers, Anderson made it back to the McDonald farm encampment where he informed Twiggs that the rebels had Iley Stuart, Solomon Stansberry, W.R. Witt, Thomas Wilson, Sousby, Queen and Creasman, and they were headed for Dahlonega. It is unknown today why Anderson did not free his compatriots so that they might either overpower their captors, or simply flee together.

Captain Marion Williams was up early on Friday morning, October 21st. He wanted to make Dahlonega before nightfall and he knew it would be a long, treacherous ride down through the mountains. Counting the prisoners, he noted that one man was missing. He soundly cursed the private who had been assigned to guard the prisoners and threatened to punish him if any of their remaining captives escaped.

Once again, the prisoners were tied to their horses and the company set out to the south at a trot. The road down to Dahlonega wound round and round the steep mountains and then down into the valleys on the old turnpike road.

Williams watched the trees and bushes closely for any sign of Twiggs' men who might attempt a rescue. As the sun finally rose above the high hills and spread its light into the valleys, the soldiers rode through the west side of the Canada community near Governor Joe Brown's old home-place. On they continued, down through Cooper Gap, into the Hightower area, crossing Cane Creek and on toward Dahlonega.

Meanwhile, down in Dahlonega, Colonel J.J. Findley was worried. His regiment was camped about a block from the Dahlonega town square on the old mustering grounds not far from where the trail started up into the mountains. Captain Williams' company was an important segment of Findley's troops, and he needed them badly.

Findley made his headquarters in the Lumpkin County Courthouse (present-day Gold Museum in Dahlonega) which also served as a jail for deserters, bushwhackers and other military prisoners. Though modernized inside today, with paved streets and parking lots surrounding it, this structure otherwise has changed little from Civil War days.

It had been two or three days since Findley had dispatched Williams' company to Fannin County to round up Twiggs' men who reportedly were robbing farmers of their horses, mules and cattle as well as personal belongings. Had Williams run into one of the Federal units which were thought to be patrolling the area who had made their way down from Tennessee? Had he been ambushed by Moorland and his gang who had recently raided several homes in the Frogtown area? Findley could do nothing but wait.

Aside from Moorland and his ilk, Jeff Anderson's gang was still running loose in the hills too, stealing, burning, and destroying whatever Moorland and the Yankees overlooked. Only a month earlier, a company of the 10th Tennessee Cavalry (U.S.) had even ridden through Lumpkin County, burning and looting and driving off horses, cattle and sheep. Findley and his men had been called upon to repel that attack, and he knew the countryside was beginning to teem with pro-Union guerrillas.

Findley, no doubt, was very relieved when Captain Williams, his men, and his prisoners finally arrived in Dahlonega. By the time they reached the center of the little mountain town, it was late in the afternoon and the shadows had grown long across Dahlonega's town square.

Mystery & History in Georgia

Condemning Evidence

The rumble of horses' hooves probably startled Findley initially, but when he saw the gray column trotting across the mustering grounds with Marion Williams in the lead, his concern no doubt quickly melted away.

Williams rode up, dismounted and saluted. Findley returned the salute. Williams was tired and anxious to be rid of his charges.

"Colonel, we caught these bushwhackers at VanZant's place up near Morganton. Found these here papers on three of 'em – Stuart, Stansberry and Witt. Looks like they're reg'lar Yankee troops. Got plain old citizens' clothes on though. Could be spies, or deserters."

Findley looked at the papers then turned around to Lieutenant N.J. Gaddis. "Gaddis, take charge of the prisoners and lock 'em up!" Gaddis and L. W. Gilreath hustled the captives off their mounts and into the courthouse into the lockup.

Findley continued to study the papers from the Union Army commands. At least one of the documents may have been Stuart's papers signed by Colonel Isham G. Young, 11th Tennessee Cavalry, authorizing Stuart to raise troops for a company. Or perhaps it was the orders from Col. S.B. Boyd. We'll never know today – but we do know they had "papers."

Findley must have wondered if there was any connection between Stuart and the bushwhackers who had killed Jesse Turner near the Chestatee River only three months earlier. Moorland, the leader of that gang, had carried papers signed by a Colonel Young – and that, no doubt, is where the prisoners' troubles quite possibly became fatal.

Though it is unknown for certain today, Findley may also have found papers showing that Stansberry was a private in Battery "D," 1st Battalion, Tennessee Artillery (U.S.). And Witt was probably carrying papers which told Findley that he had joined the 5th Tennessee Mounted Infantry at Cleveland, Tennessee.

The hours between the evening of Friday, October 21st and early Saturday afternoon, October 22nd, are also shrouded in mystery today as regards the circumstances of these three men, but one assumption is obvious: The fact that they were the only individuals among the eight captives who had previous military records, coupled with the fact that due to their civilian clothing when captured within Confederate territory – as well as the fact they were conducting an illegal military operation – would have placed them outside the existing laws of war governing the treatment of prisoners. It is possible that Findley may have conducted a courtmartial proceeding that very night or the following morning and tried the three men.

Findley no doubt also suspected that the three men were deserters from the Confederate Army, as were many men during the closing days of the war. They certainly weren't in uniform. Indeed, Twiggs, the leader of the band from which these three were captured, had definitely deserted the 52nd Georgia Infantry at Chickamauga.

Based upon the later testimony of W.R. Crisson and several other individuals who knew the three men, as well as details gleaned from a search of Confederate muster records, there was no evidence whatsoever to show that any of these three had at any time in fact been enlisted in the Confederate Army. Nevertheless, at some point on the night of the 21st or the morning of the 22nd of

October, the decision was made to execute the three men.

Findley summoned Captain William R. Crisson, commander of Company "D," Findley's Regiment, and ordered him to take the three men out and execute them. Whether or not the three men imprisoned inside the Dahlonega Courthouse jail (present-day Dahlonega Gold Museum) had any idea of their fate is unknown today.

Captain Crisson and a squad of troops took Stuart, Stansberry and Witt from the temporary jail in the courthouse, tied them and mounted them once again on horses. The column rode out east along Main Street and along the Cleveland Road, crossing Yahoola Creek and then the Chestatee River at the fords. After a short ride further, they arrived on the windswept heights of Bearden's Bridge Hill overlooking the Chestatee River.

The captives were dismounted, blindfolded and forced to their knees on the edge of the steep incline. At that point, there almost certainly remained no doubt among these men that their lives were now forfeit and their days in this earthly realm were finished. One can only imagine their thoughts as they awaited their fate.

Meanwhile, seven rifles were being loaded for the execution squad – six with a powder charge and ball, and a seventh with powder only. The weapons were handed out to the squad.

John Baugus immediately handed his gun back to Captain Crisson, stating firmly that he wouldn't shoot them. Crisson took the gun from Baugus and handed it to another man.

Crisson then gave the commands. "Ready!" he barked.

Seven men, McKey Crisson, Hardy Forrester, Benjamin Van Dyke, Ferdinand McDonald, J.A. Hollifield, J.R. Pruitt and T.H. Worley brought their rifles to their shoulders to take aim, and the click of seven hammers pulled back in readiness broke the chilly stillness.

"Aim!"

Seven sights were trained on the three unfortunate soldiers.

"Fire!"

The blast of seven rifles spouting flame and lead sent Stuart, Stansberry and Witt into eternity. When the last echo of the gunfire had reverberated and then faded away into the valleys below, a windy silence returned to the desolate hilltop.

Captain Crisson then pulled out his revolver, walked over to the three lifeless-appearing bodies and examined them to be certain they were dead. Seeing no signs of life, he walked away. Shortly afterwards, the bodies were unceremoniously pitched over the embankment and left for the buzzards.

Deceit & Embezzlement

The executions of October 22, 1864 on Bearden's Bridge Hill were only the beginning of a much longer story which would not close completely until 1912. The families of these men would continue to relive the tragedy of 1864 repeatedly as a result of several later inquiries and investigations into the incident.

The men who carried out Colonel Findley's orders would continue to be reminded of the incident for years to come, first by the occupying Federal Army and a Lumpkin County Grand Jury, and later by various special agents of the Federal government.

Of particular note in this tragedy was the impact it had upon Margaret Hide Stuart, widow of Iley T. Stuart. Some 200 pages of documents on file in the National Archives, Navy and Old Army Records Section bear witness to the suffering which she endured for the remainder of her life.

Margaret and Iley were married in Gilmer County, Georgia on July 30, 1848 by John Thomas, a justice of the peace. The marriage was witnessed by Ellijay and Joseph Johnson.

Margaret and Iley ultimately had six children: Virgil, born November 2, 1849; Amanda M., born November 24, 1850; Sevada, born January 8, 1852; Cicero, born February 16, 1853; Elizabeth C., born December 21, 1854; Elem, born May 6, 1857. They were tragically impacted as well.

In 1869, Margaret Stuart was advised by Dr. Gilbert Falls, a prominent Fannin County physician, that she was entitled to pension money because of her husband's service and death. Falls was unable to locate the evidence required to prosecute the claim, so he sent Mrs. Stuart to John Wimpy, a Dahlonega attorney.

Wimpy was a prominent lawyer who had been elected to the United States Congress in the 1868 election, but because of the Reconstruction politics in place at that time, he was never seated. Nevertheless, he agreed to try and obtain a pension for Mrs. Stuart from the U.S. Bureau of Pensions which was administered at that time by the Department of the Interior.

It is unknown today exactly what transpired as a result of Wimpy's efforts, but several things are known. It is known for instance that a number of documents reportedly were forged without Mrs. Stuart's knowledge and signed with an "X" (a standard mark used by those who are unable to write their name). Also, affidavits of Wm. A. Twiggs and Nathan B. Long were forged. Long was a lieutenant in Company "H", 5th Tennessee Mounted Infantry and served under Twiggs *after Stuart's death*. However, the affidavit submitted by Wimpy with Long's signature falsely indicated that Long *personally knew Stuart and had personal knowledge of his service with Twiggs' unit.*

Based on the false testimony, the Pension Bureau awarded the requested pension in the amount of $8 per month plus a settlement sum of $760.00 in back pay and prior entitlements to Mrs. Stuart. Though these seem like paltry sums today, in 1869 when the pension and back pay were awarded, $8.00 was the equivalent of $156.00 in 2021 dollars, and in 1869, an individual making $156.00 every month could buy some serious groceries. Even better, the settlement amount of $760.00 which Mrs. Stuart received in 1869 was the equivalent of $14,800.00, which was a fortune.

Unfortunately, even though the pension and back-pay were awarded – and under false testimony no less – Mrs. Stuart never received any of the awarded funds. The award was made on September 13, 1869. Wimpy, as Mrs. Stuart's attorney, received the government draft.

Sometime later Mrs. Stuart found out that her pension claim had been granted and wondered why she hadn't received any of the money. In a later affidavit, she wrote: *"I repeatedly wrote him at Dahlonega, Ga., requesting him to come and settle with me. It was not until the 21st of August, 1870 that I succeeded in getting an interview with him. At that time, he denied having collected the money but that he expected soon to receive it, but as he had no power of attorney from me to draw my money, he had failed to get it..."*

As much as can be surmised today, Wimpy apparently managed to get Mrs. Stuart to sign a power of attorney and then proceeded to antedate the document to May 17, 1870. He promised Mrs. Stuart that she would *"have her money in a very few days"* if she would only sign the document. He also agreed to charge her nothing for his services. However, as of October 18, 1871 – well over one year later – records indicate Wimpy *still* had not sent Mrs. Stuart the money she had been awarded.

After repeated attempts to get Wimpy to pay her, Mrs. Stuart finally went to Col. W.P. Price, who agreed to take her case and get the money from Wimpy. According to further records, however, even as astute and prominent an individual as Col. William Pierce Price was also unsuccessful in obtaining the obligated money from Wimpy.

By this time, even the Pension Bureau had become aware of Wimpy's actions and it finally *forced* him to **repay** the money to the Federal government. At the same time, however, the Bureau unfortunately dropped Mrs. Stuart from the pension rolls when it was discovered that, according to records – which were false – Iley Stuart had **deserted** the Federal Army at Knoxville, Tennessee in January, 1864, and no record of his service with the 5th Tennessee Mounted Infantry, nor any copy of any orders issued to Stuart by Col. Isham G. Young (U.S.), was found in the files in Washington.

Mrs. Stuart, nevertheless, spent the next six years attempting to get her pension reinstated without success. Finally, in February, 1877, John N. Wager, a special agent of the Bureau of Pensions, took the extreme – and admirable – measure of coming to Dahlonega to collect evidence in Mrs. Stuart's case.

Wager interviewed a long list of people and took depositions from them: Margaret Stuart, William R. Crisson, Nathan B. Long, John Merrell, Thomas Wilson, James H. Beard, Martin Dillbeck, John Dyer, Thomas Anderson, Col. S.B. Boyd, and John Wilson. Wager's inquiry definitely ascertained that Wimpy had wrongfully received some $800.00 in pension money – the equivalent of approximately $13,000.00 in 2021 dollars. Wager also definitely established the circumstances of Iley Stuart's death and the deaths of Stansberry and Witt. However, the charge of desertion against Stuart still stood on the Army records and, once again, Mrs. Stuart's pension request was disallowed.

Undeterred by the latest in a series of disappointments, Mrs. Stuart continued to prosecute her claim. Over the next 26 years she submitted a number of claims for the money she felt was rightly hers. During the course of these years, she lost her eyesight and her home burned to the ground in Fannin County. The unfortunate widow finally moved to Mount Vernon, Tennessee.

Mrs. Stuart's, however, still was not finished, and she represents a case-point in indomitable will. In 1902, some 33 years after her original petition for a pension, her case finally came to the attention of the U.S. Congress. Following an extensive investigation of the service of Iley Stuart, the Congress passed a relief bill on March 3, 1903, which *finally granted* her a pension:

"Be it enacted by the Senate and the House of Representatives...that the Secretary of the Interior be, and he is hereby authorized and directed, to place on the pension rolls...the name of Margaret A. Stuart, widow of Iley T. Stuart, late of Company H, Fifth Tennessee Mounted Infantry and pay her a pension at the rate of twelve dollars per month."

By this time, Mrs. Stuart was 77 years old and had moved back to Blue Ridge, Georgia. Following her victory in Congress in 1903, she – no doubt

Photographed circa early 1900s, this view of Dahlonega from the Price Memorial Hall steeple at North Georgia College very closely approximates the circumstances in the small mountain town during the tragic final days of the U.S. Civil War.

to her undying delight – actually started receiving pension checks. After endorsing these checks, she turned them over one by one to her son Elam who, amazingly, then reportedly began depositing them *in his own personal account* at the North Georgia National Bank in Blue Ridge.

In 1908, Mrs. Stuart *again* communicated with the Pension Bureau seeking their assistance in the recovery of her money. Her son, Elam, had entered into a business agreement with a partner and had contracted a debt with W.G. Owenby and Company. Apparently the partnership had defaulted upon the debt to Owenby who obtained a judgement to *freeze* Elam's account. The money in the account amounted to $260, *"every cent of which is my pension money, not a farthing of it being my son's..."*, Mrs. Stuart wrote. The Bureau, however, had no other recourse but to send Mrs. Stuart their regrets, saying *"no assistance can be afforded you in connection with this matter..."*

On October 5, 1911, Margaret Stuart sadly passed away after nearly a lifetime of attempts to clear her husband's name of a desertion charge and collect her pension money. The file on Iley T. Stuart was finally closed on January 15, 1912, after the Bureau paid her son Cicero for his mother's burial expenses. Forty seven years after Iley T. Stuart died on Bearden's Bridge Hill, his case was finally permanently closed.

Filming "Fried Green Tomatoes" in Tiny Juliette, Georgia

The little whistle-stop community beside a railroad, with a scenic river dam and gristmill – all right out of the 1920s – had become a literal ghost-town until Hollywood found it.

Tucked back into the countryside north of Macon, Georgia, an actual little whistle-stop railroad depot and community right out of the 1920s exists alongside the very picturesque Ocmulgee River. If one happens upon this site by chance, the mind quickly responds with "I've seen this place somewhere before," and the truth is, you probably have if you are a movie-goer. It was the film site of a major motion picture which caused quite a stir back in the 1990s, called *"Fried Green Tomatoes."*

Much of the credit for the revitalization of this once-forgotten little milltown with its general store from 1927 (converted into the café) and other shops from even earlier times, is due to Fannie Flagg, author/producer of the movie which captured the attention of young and old alike. Miss Flagg reportedly rode up and down the railroad tracks at many sites in Georgia searching for a little town to use as the setting for the fictitious movie community – "Whistle-Stop, Alabama." Historic little Juliette, Georgia, finally caught her

Historic little Juliette, Georgia, finally caught her eye, and things have never been quite the same since.

eye, and things have never been quite the same since.

In the summer of 1991, Jessica Tandy, Kathy Bates, Mary Stuart Masterson, Cicely Tyson, Mary-Louise Parker, Stan Shaw, Chris O'Donnell, and the rest of the cast and crew for the movie descended upon the town to begin filming. Weeks later, when the movie had been completed and the stars had departed, so also did the glamour and activity with which the quiet little community had been infused.

Mystery & History in Georgia

Appearing just as it did in the major motion picture **Fried Green Tomatoes**, starring Kathy Bates, Jessica Tandy, Cicely Tyson, Mary Stuart Masterson, Mary-Louise Parker and Chris O'Donnell, the Whistle-Stop Café, though its hours sometimes are irregular, still provides delicious meals for travelers as of this writing (2021).

The movie company tore down many of the sets used in the production, and had not a few entrepreneurial individuals realized the continued money-making potential of the site, Juliette would no doubt have simply returned to its sleepy forgotten ghost-town status.

It was actually the movie-makers themselves, who hatched the idea of a tourist attraction at the site. "The director of the movie said we ought to consider opening the place as 'the Whistle-Stop Cafe,'" Jerie Lynn Williams, a resident of Juliette explained. She and Robert Williams (no relation) quickly began thinking about opening a real restaurant in the historic 1927-era hardware building which had been converted into the "Whistle-Stop Café" for the movie.

People in the area initially thought Robert was crazy. "Who are you going to feed?" some asked. Few were the individuals who thought a restaurant at the site could be successful.

Undeterred, Jerie and Robert started buying and renovating the old stores in the little town, their imaginations working overtime. Jerie says she bought old fixtures at auctions that give the interior of the café its authentic look.

And to top things off, Jerie didn't even know how to cook! She did, however, have a secret weapon – her grandmother's recipe for "fried green

Filming "Fried Green Tomatoes" In Tiny Juliette, Georgia — Monroe County

Visitors to Juliette will recognize a number of the filming sites from *Fried Green Tomatoes*.

Since the days when it really was a "whistle-stop" on the railroad, the steel rails which run through Juliette have played a dominant role in the community. Freight (but no longer passenger) trains still rumble up and down the tracks today.

Hoping to take advantage of the immense popularity of the movie, Jerie and Robert opened their "Whistle-Stop Café" for business on April 16, 1992.

Jerie smiled in remembrance, "when we opened for business and no one showed up." Nevertheless, as the popular maxim maintains, "Patience is a virtue," and the Williamses didn't give up.

"Eventually, (to our relief), newspaper and magazine writers *(with an appreciative nod to us)* and the publicity they created began attracting attention, and customers began appearing."

Once inside, guests are transported back to a bygone era. The restaurant, obviously, looks much as it did in the movie, with overhead fans, and the clapboard walls, dining booths, and tables covered with green-checked oilcloths.

They even kept a shattered window pane with a small bullet hole – which had been scripted and specially-created for the movie – and other movie memorabilia decorates the walls. The setting has some other "realistic" elements too, which is why it was selected for the movie.

"When a Southern Railroad freight train rumbles past, guests rush outside, because it's so near to the restaurant" she continued. "It's amazing. Almost as if people had never seen a train

tomatoes" (which Jerie keeps secret to this day, right along with her barbecue recipe. . .). She persuaded a cook from Mable's Table – the town's only real restaurant (which recently had closed due to lack of business!) to cook for her.

Hoping to take advantage of the immense popularity of the movie, Jerie and Robert opened their "Whistle-Stop Café" for business on April 16, 1992. Things, however, didn't go quite as smoothly as they had hoped. The "creation" of a tourist attraction is one thing; the actual attraction of the tourists, however, is quite another, as they discovered, to their abject disappointment.

"I think I cried the first ten days,"

295

before. The first time it happened, one woman thought we had staged the whole thing!"

The first thing one should do after arriving in Juliette is to write his or her name on the clipboard waiting list at the café's front door. If you're truly interested in dining in a site where a popular movie was filmed, don't be surprised if you have a one to two-hour wait to be seated, at least on weekends.

But never you mind. Just leave someone there to hear when your name is called out, and the rest of you can stroll down the little streets fronting the café in the meantime and look at the other movie props left behind.

To date, visitors to the site have traveled from all over the United States, and even from 44 different countries – some from as far away as Egypt and Iceland.

As a result of its current popularity via the movie, Juliette has literally returned from the dead. At one time, it boasted the largest water-powered gristmill in the world, but by the 1950s, gristmills had become a thing of the past, bringing operations at Dr. Glover's (former owner) enterprise to a close. When the mill ceased operations, the town's residents literally abandoned their homes and the shops and businesses in an almost wholesale move to find employment elsewhere. Within a year or two, Juliette had become a ghost-town.

For years thereafter, a handful of residents attempted to bring the community back to life in one way or another, all to no avail. Even the construction of nearby Lake Juliette proved fruitless.

A little Hollywood magic seems to have worked wonders for a town that was given up for dead in 1990.

Ironically, the very quality which was working against it – its isolated scenic, rural locale – was what ultimately appealed to the Hollywood moviemakers. The rest, as they say, is history.

Today, the big dam across the river in Juliette still offers the scenic quality that made it a highlight in a number of the movie's scenes. So also do a number of other manifestations of "rural flavor" which enlivened the production.

All of this, coupled with the Whistle-Stop Cafe, have combined to make Juliette a popular tourism destination. And in answer to the growing visitation to the site, other entrepreneurs have opened gift shops in the little town, selling everything from antiques and crafts to collectibles and candy up and down the tiny streets of the community, so be prepared for a measure of commercialism. One shop bears the name "The Ruth and Idgie House." *("The secret's in the sauce.")*

There is also "new" development of sorts in the community too. The old gristmill on the other side of the Ocmulgee River has been renovated into a substantial crafts mall with all manner of antiques, gifts and collectibles. It includes a substantial buffet restaurant too.

A little Hollywood magic seems to have worked wonders for a town that was given up for dead in 1990. One can only hope that the community's developers know when enough is enough.

(To reach Juliette, take Exit 61 off of Interstate 75, one hour south of Atlanta.)

The Mysteries Of Fort & Blood Mountains

The events in pre-history on these two mysterious mountain sites have puzzled researchers since the first investigations in the late 1800s. Today, they remain as historic sites with many unanswered questions.

North Georgia has been described as a land of magic and mystery, both natural and man-made. The "natural" creations are, for the most part, easily described and abundantly understood. Many of the "man-made" portions, however – some of which have their origins in a time far back in prehistory – were created by Native Americans when they first appeared on the American continent some 10,000 years ago, and have yet to be explained.

Some of the "natural" resources may include phenomena such as the large round crater-like depressions which are so large that they can only be identified from the air; yellow daisies which grow only on the granite mountain-tops in spots such as Blood and Stone mountains; and a strange form of cactus which also somehow survives the uncompromising climate of these mountains.

Examples of "man-made" phenomena include the Etowah, Kolomoki, Sautee, and other nearby Indian mounds; rock mounds that were once thought to be the work of Indians, but are now suspected by some researchers to have been made by nineteenth century farmers; strange rock carvings called petroglyphs, such as those at Track Rock Gap in Union County; a large renowned stone housed today at Brenau College in Gainesville, Georgia, that has been suggested to be a last message from the "Lost Colony" of Roanoke, Virginia; mysteriously-named north Georgia mountains; and strange stone forts on the summits of these precipices.

Fort Mountain

Perhaps the most famous of the "stone forts" genre of mysteries is the strange rock wall at Fort Mountain State Park in Murray County. A survey of the wall estimates that it is composed of thousands of local rocks ranging in size from a few pounds to several tons, stretching an amazing 928 feet or slightly more than 300 yards. Though this certainly is no "Stonehenge," it remains nevertheless as a suspected man-made phenomena of amazing proportions.

The height of the wall ranges from three to sixteen feet, and the width is from four and a half to sixteen feet. The wall is situated across the easiest approach to the top of Fort Mountain, and includes two gaps or "gates" along the length of the obstruction.

This wall or "fort" at Fort Mountain has inspired a number of interesting explanations over the years, none of which appear to have been based upon extensive historical or archaeological research.

Some tales describe the wall as a fortress and last refuge of a lost prehistoric people who used small enclosures or "pits" in the walls supposedly as "guard houses" in some stories and even as "honeymoon lodgings" in other explanations – both of which are preposterous to serious investigators. The wall, nevertheless, almost certainly is man-made, and continues to defy complete explanation.

Pre-Columbian Construction?

Still other stories credit the wall to a pre-Columbian Welsh colony, led by an early adventurer/explorer named Madoc. Some "authorities" even claim the wall was built by Hernando De Soto's Spaniards or a little later by the Spanish expedition of Juan Pardo and Boyano.

More cynical observers, however, have claimed that the wall is not man-made at all, but is in fact a natural formation. Still others, despite the explanation on the historical marker at the site, assume that the wall is the work of the State of Georgia's park authorities, to keep tourists from falling off the scenic mountain.

While no real archaeological excavations, professional or amateur, have been conducted at Fort Mountain, many facts about the site have come to light in the last two decades. This "enlightened" research has helped greatly in solving this north Georgia mystery.

It is now known that the wall at Fort Mountain is not unique, but only one of several similar constructions in the eastern United States. These include the smaller, circular walls atop Fort Mountain, in Union County, GA; the wall at Stone Mountain Memorial Park, DeKalb County, GA, which was partially destroyed in an earthquake in the late 1800s; and the walls at Alec Mountain, Habersham County, GA; Sand Mountain, Catoosa County, GA; Ladd Mountain, Bartow County, GA; Rocky Face Mountain, Whitfield County, GA; Pigeon Mountain, Dade County, GA; Brown's Mount, Bibb County, GA; Lookout Mountain, TN; De Soto Falls, AL; Manchester, TN; Fayette County, W.VA; and many other sites. The stone wall at Mount Alto, near Rome, GA, may also belong to this group, although this wall may actually be of modern construction.

Recent historical research has discredited the claims that the wall at Fort Mountain, Murray County, and the similar walls listed above were built by the Spanish. Although the tale of Madoc is revived from time to time, professional scholarship has not only proved that the Madoc story is a fanciful myth, but has seen fit to ridicule this presumption.

Even the original evaluations of the so-called small enclosures or "pits" in the walls of Fort Mountain, Murray County, have been re-appraised. The pits apparently were made only after 1893, and by treasure hunters searching for relics and buried gold. They could also have been made simply by trees which grew up in the wall in antiquity and then died, decayed, and disappeared. Such misguided individuals have vandalized a number of archaeological sites in Georgia over recent decades, particularly the rock carvings or petroglyphs, which these persons mistakenly believed were Cherokee Indian maps to buried caches of gold.

Scientific Findings

Modern researchers at Fort Mountain, Murray County, also question the accuracy of referring to the wall as a "fort," pointing out that the wall is actually poorly designed for defense, would require a large army to garrison, and does not account for protection of the other sides of the mountain peak that could be assaulted. Also, since there is no spring or other source of water at the summit, any group of people besieged there for any length of time would soon find themselves in desperate straits.

What then is the secret of Fort Mountain? The answer may lie in the extensive archaeological work conducted by Dr. Charles H. Faulkner at the Old Stone Fort near Manchester, Tennessee. His findings at this site – which is very similar to that of Fort Mountain, Murray County – strongly suggest that the stone wall at least was built by an Indian culture similar to the Hopewell Culture of Ohio, within the first few centuries A.D.

The research conducted by Dr. Faulkner and others at "stone wall" sites in the South strongly suggests that the walls on Fort Mountain, Murray County, Georgia, were built at almost the same time that the Hopewell Culture (400 B.C. to 400 A.D.) flourished and that the stone walls here, like the stone walls in Ohio, were built around the third century.

Similarly, the stone walls in Ohio and in the South tend to be void of any relics or other evidence which might suggest that they were used as places of habitation or as fortresses. Indeed, modern scholarship suggests that the walls actually enclosed ceremonial or religious areas rather than military strongholds.

Interestingly, Hopewell-type pyramids of rocks – used for marking burial sites – are often found near the stone walls in the South. These pyramid-shaped graves or cairns are common in north Georgia, the most well-known of which must be a site in Lumpkin

One of the oddities of the Fort Mountain stone wall is the circular pits found intermittently along its route. Just as with many other aspects of the wall, the origin and/or purpose of the pits are unknown today. Some researchers have suggested they may have been positions for astronomical observations.

County popularly known as "Trahlyta's Grave" at "Stone Pile Gap."

When one of these cairns near the wall at Ladd Mountain outside Cartersville was torn down for road material some years ago, human remains were discovered. Artifacts found in the grave included several large sheets of mica, a trapezoidal copper breastplate, two green stone celts, a copper celt, and other copper pieces. The presence of the copper celt, breastplate and other pieces could suggest contact with European explorers.

The actual builders of the wall at Fort Mountain in Murray County remain a mystery, but with modern archaeology, the answer may be known positively one day. In the meantime, one of the best theories that might be proposed, revolves around an Indian people who used the walls as part of their worship, and who left in their walls and pyramid rock piles vestiges of their former existence for all time.

Blood Mountain

Blood Mountain.... The mere uttering of the words conjures up visions of past violence and the mystery and mystique of the past. So what actually is the story of Blood Mountain?

During a recent search through part of the microfilm edition of Dr. Lyman C. Draper's collection of writings and research at the Robert W. Woodruff Library of Emory University, letters written to Draper from north Georgia in the 1870s are maintained. One of the letters, from Matthew F. Stephenson (presumably the same Matthew F. Stephenson of note from the U.S. Branch Mint in Dahlonega, Georgia), dated September 18, 1873, carried the following cryptic passage about Blood Mountain in Georgia's Union County:

"I read your last letter in due time and have examined all the localities; but find no defile corresponding to the one you mention. The country from Sautee to Frogtown is a partially cultivated wilderness; and on the plateau S.E. of the Appalachian Mountains about five miles distant, a broken undulating country; but in nowise answering to your description.

"In my investigations I am satisfied with regard to the battle at Nacoochee & Sautee Valley, etc. and the march to Frogtown; and the Blood Mountain where the Indians were effectively defeated and dispersed; about 600 were killed in the battles at Exutee(?) and on the retreat and half as many more at the Blood Mountain."

A letter Stephenson had written to Draper a week earlier, on September 10, 1873, also mentions the Blood Mountain battle:

"It was on Sautee, east of Nacoochee Valley instead of 'Chotee' as you have it. It is 16 miles N.E. of 'Frogtown'; and the scene of a hard-fought battle by Gen. Williamson & Pickens. The battle was at Lynch Mountain & Grimes Knoll, where the killed were afterwards buried by the Cherokees who lived there, amounting to 600. They retreated to the Blood Mountain, at the head of the Chestatee River, on the S.E. side of the Blue Ridge & the source of the Choestoe, a branch of the Notley River N.W. of the Ridge. It is a tributary of the Hiawasee River..."

Identity of Combatants at Blood Mountain?

To what does this battle of Blood Mountain refer? By consulting some histories of the Cherokees and the American Revolution, as well as the diary of militiaman Arthur Fairies in the Draper Collection, the facts seem to come together as follows:

In the early months of the American Revolution, British Indian Superintendent John Stuart was attempting to keep the southern Indians from going to war with the revolting colonies. He did not want the Cherokees and Creeks attacking the settlements until he could send white men with them to guarantee that only military targets were assaulted.

Stuart was particularly concerned because many of the frontier settlers were still loyal to the king. However, the Cherokees were angered by the Whites moving onto their lands, and in early July, 1776, attacked the back-country settlements from Georgia to Virginia, killing entire families and destroying crops and property left by fleeing frontiersmen. The refugees crowded into stockade forts, where disease and starvation were soon problems.

The colonists responded by sending thousands of militiamen into the Cherokee country to retaliate for the Indian attacks. Georgia had the smallest population of the colonies, and mounted the smallest offensive, although Burke County militiamen under Major Samuel Jack did destroy the villages in what is today Stephens County, and captured one of Stuart's agents.

Major Andrew Williamson of South Carolina led two expeditions against the Cherokees, the second of which he himself commanded 1,200 men. The South Carolinians destroyed the Lower Cherokee settlements and then, with General Griffin Rutherford and his North Carolina forces, laid waste to the Middle Settlements.

The last of the Cherokee towns, the Overhills, were destroyed by a Virginia army under Colonel William Christian. By the end of September, 1776, with their villages and crops destroyed, the Cherokees were facing extinction, and sued for peace.

The Stephenson letters to Draper in 1873 refer to this campaign and specifically to a battle Major Andrew Williamson, with his later famous subordinates Andrew Pickens and Thomas Sumter, fought with the Cherokees on September 19, 1776, at a place they called *"the Black Hole."* This pass was apparently in present-day North Carolina, but, according to the Stephenson letters, the battle only began there, and continued south into what is today Georgia, before the Cherokees made their last stand at Blood Mountain.

Origin Of The Name

Stories began appearing at least as early as 1874, that Blood Mountain was

The wall at Fort Mountain wanders for some 300 yards along the rear portion of the imminence and offers no suggestion whatsoever as to whether it was used as a defensive measure, for ceremonies of some type, for calendar development or anything else.

named for a battle fought there between the Creeks and the Cherokees. However, would a more logical origin for this name be the 1776 battle described by Stephenson?

The names of Blood and nearby Slaughter Mountain, obviously being White names, are more likely to have been given to those peaks by white men familiar with the Cherokees' battle against the invading militiamen, than a battle between the Creeks and Cherokees more than eighty years earlier. The name Blood Mountain, therefore, might presumably be a memorial to Cherokee heroism rather than a reminder of a gory clash between rival tribes.

Thinking along those lines, D.L. Swain wrote the following comments about the devastation of the Cherokee villages in 1776:

"....We can but feel that such an enterprise was necessary to check the dreadful havoc inflicted by the Indians. Yet that question will arise... Had we the right to force the poor occupants from their possessions and appropriate them to ourselves? Human nature may ever be too cowardly to interpose an objection to the titles

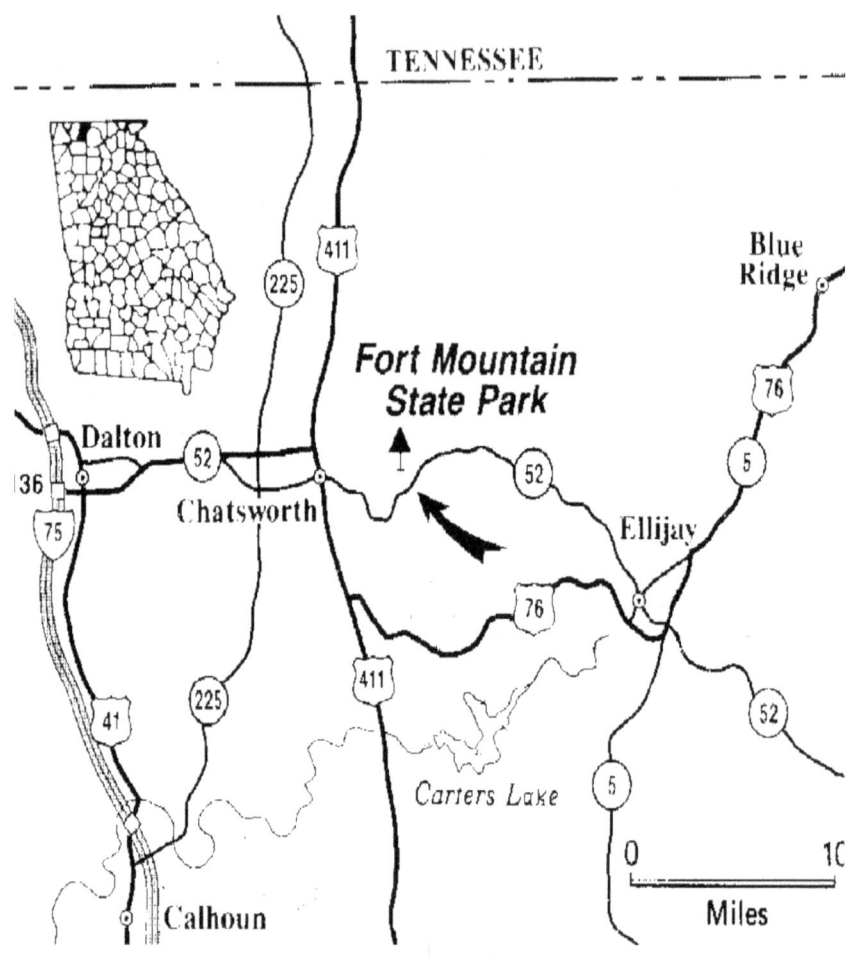

acquired by our fathers; but the time will come when retributive justice will plead the Indians' cause with more than an Angel's eloquence, and with far greater success than is ever witnessed in earthly tribunals."

Author's Note: Microfilm of the Lyman C. Draper Collection from which much of the above article is drawn, is available at the Robert Woodruff Library, Emory University, Atlanta, and at the University of Georgia Libraries in Athens, Georgia. See Josephine L. Harper, **Guide To The Draper Manuscripts**, (Madison, 1983). Other references included: The Thomas Sumter Papers, Draper Collection; D.L. Swain's "Historical Sketch of the Indian War of 1776," **Historical Magazine 2**, November, 1867; Ivan Allen's **The Cherokee Nation**; Bernard De Voto's **The Course of Empire**; Charles H. Faulkner's **The Old Stone Fort: Exploring An Archaeological Mystery**; Philip E. Smith's **Aboriginal Stone Constructions In The Southern Piedmont**, and Ruth E. Suddeth's "Land of Mystery and Magic: Cherokee Legends and Myths of the Georgia Mountains," **Georgia Magazine**, August, 1958.

Mystery of Cherokee John Martin Home Solved by a "Discovery" in Murray Co.

To imply that the historic Murray County structure known today as "Carter's Quarters" was not originally the home of Cherokee Judge John Martin, is the equivalent of a blasphemy to many residents of the area, but the simple fact of the matter is, it wasn't.

An impressive home located in the extreme southeast corner of present-day Murray County, Georgia, and known as "Carter's Quarters" is a historic puzzle still being sorted out after almost 200 years (as of this writing in 2021). New information which has recently come to light has enabled a huge part of the puzzle to be solved.

Cherokee Judge John Martin was a prominent Native American in north Georgia. The location of his very historic former home in what today is Murray County, however, had been lost to historians, most of whom had incorrectly identified a structure known as "Carter's Quarters" as also being the former Martin house. For decades, area residents and historians alike had simply assumed that the Carter's Quarters house and the John Martin house were one and the same.

The house known as Carter's Quarters has remained in the Carter family since Farish Carter (1780-1861)

– believed by some to be Georgia's first millionaire (Cartersville, Georgia, was named after him) – bought it from widow Sarah Bosworth of Clarke County, Georgia, on November 16, 1833, shortly after the departure of the first group of Cherokees from north Georgia. Bosworth had won the property (Land Lot 45, 25th District, 2nd Section) in the Cherokee Land Lottery conducted by the state of Georgia in 1832, but did not desire to live in nor even own it.

After purchasing the property, Farish Carter used the residence on the grounds as a summer home, residing most of the year at Scottsboro, near Milledgeville, Georgia. "Carter's Quarters" served as his headquarters for an enormous agricultural operation involving some 5,000 acres in Murray and surrounding counties – a major Georgia plantation by any description.

The construction date of the very aged home has never been accurately determined. An approximate date sometime between 1804 and 1806 has been suggested, but logic dictates the structure most probably was actually built in the 1820s with the help of nearby Moravian missionaries who were noted craftsmen.

The confusion between Carter's Quarters and the John Martin house apparently began when descendants of the Martin family corresponded with descendants of the Carter family concerning the Martin house. At some point in time, family members and residents alike eventually became accustomed to identifying Carters's Quarters and the John Martin house as one and the same, continuing the practice to the present. This incorrect identity erased – for all intents and purposes – any knowledge or known record of the existence of the true John Martin house, which in fact was a separate and very historic structure in its own right. Tragically, the real Judge John Martin house was not preserved since its historic significance was unknown at the time.

The suspicion that the Carter's Quarters house and the Judge John Martin house were two separate and distinct structures began when Nancy Carter Bland, owner of the Carter's Quarters house in the late 20th Century and the great-great-granddaughter of Farish Carter, remembered being told in her childhood of "an old house by the Coosawattee River" some three miles from Carter's Quarters. Mrs. Bland also remembered being told the Coosawattee house had once been "the other half of the house at Carter's Quarters," and that it had been moved the three miles to the river to serve as a river residence for the family. During the time of steamboat travel on Georgia's rivers and inland waterways, the house stood at the northernmost point reachable by steamboat traffic in Georgia – a strategic site for obvious reasons.

Even as a little girl, however, Mrs. Bland remembered doubting the "half of the Carter's Quarters house moved to the river" story, for she wondered how such a large two-story house could have ever been moved such a great distance in that day and time. Also, even if the house could have been moved, she couldn't help wondering why such an effort would have been made to provide a residence only three miles from the main house.

Mrs. Bland explained that "the Coosawattee house was a large structure which was rented out during my time, and was near collapse in 1970." At that time, the U.S. Army Corps of Engineers bought the property from the Carter heirs during construction of Carter Dam. Since no one was aware of the historic significance of the Coosawattee home, and since it was believed this home would be covered by the impounded waters of newly constructed Carter Lake, the home was simply demolished. And when the waters of the lake rose to their ultimate level, they very sadly did not rise over the former site of the Coosawattee – Judge John Martin home.

The answer to the puzzling question of the two houses finally occurred to Nancy Bland when she read the initial draft of this Carter's Quarters article being prepared for publication. Mrs. Bland proposed the theory that the Coosawattee house *was never actually part of the Carter's Quarters house*, but was, in actuality, a separate and distinct structure, and the actual original historic residence of Judge John Martin of the Cherokee Indians.

According to Cherokee genealogist Emmett Starr, John Martin was born October 20, 1781, the son of Susannah

Emory and Joseph Martin. He was a member of the Cherokee Constitutional Convention of 1827, and was the first treasurer and chief justice of the Cherokee Nation.

Martin was married to Nellie and Lucy McDaniel simultaneously who were sisters. He died October 17, 1840, and is buried at Fort Gibson, Oklahoma, to which he relocated prior to the "Trail of Tears."

Mrs. Bland's theory was researched and tested in the early 1990s by Rev. Charles Walker and Robert S. Davis, Jr., and ultimately proven to be correct, correcting a long-standing error. The Coosawattee River house – though very similar to the original portion of the Carter's Quarters house – was validated as having been in fact located on the property of John Martin on the Coosawattee River by *the field notes of the 1832 survey of District 25, 2nd Section, original Cherokee County (present-day Murray County) in the Georgia Surveyor General Department*.

Further corroborating the identification of the former site of the historic John Martin home is the fact the location also fits exactly in relation to an account of the Martin property as given in the memoirs of William Jasper Cotter, a resident of the area prior to the Cherokee Removal of 1838, who spent his first night in north Georgia in Carter's Quarters. And then there is of course the description of the Coosawattee house which almost exactly matches *the 1836 Federal Property Evaluation for John*

It is not difficult at all today to understand how the identities of the two homes could have become confused over time.

Martin's property at Coosawattee Old Town, on microfilm at the Georgia Department of Archives and History in Atlanta, Georgia.

It was at this point that Rev. Walker and Mr. Davis went to the Carter's Dam facility to search for records pertaining to the house. Resource Manager Joe Blackmon provided the two men with his memories of the old house, and invaluable maps.

It is not difficult at all today to understand how the identities of the two homes could have become confused over time. The Coosawattee house (the actual former residence of John Martin) was probably originally called "Carter's Quarters," while the house widely-known today as "Carter's Quarters" was originally known as "Rock Spring." These identities were even used by William Jasper Cotter whose own home in this neighborhood is still standing (as of this writing) almost within sight of Carter's Quarters.

Farish Carter owned all of this land, as well as the houses. His slaves replaced the blacks who had lived at John Martin's slave quarters near the Coosawattee house, and those slave quarters thus also became identified as "Carter's Quarters." Eventually, the name was attached to the whole area of Carter's enterprises, confusing matters even further.

As the years passed, however, the extensive agricultural endeavors at Carter's Quarters diminished almost yearly. Eventually, the name remained attached only to the house at Rock Spring.

And as to the suspected original

builder of the Carter's Quarters/Rock Spring house, William Jasper Cotter wrote in his memoirs that this house was the original home of half-Cherokee George Harlen who was *"part Indian and very dark,"* lending even more historic significance to this structure.

Cotter also indicated the house had been referred to as *"Rock Spring"* because a limestone spring existed on the grounds. He further described the two-story white building as *"the best house in that part of the country."*

The survey made of the property by the state of Georgia for the 1832 Land Lottery supports Cotter's claims. The surveyors list this lot as containing *"forty acres of improved land belonging to 'George Harlen.'"*

According to the **Cherokee Indian Letters**, a series of typescripts at the Georgia Department of Archives and History in Atlanta, Harlen was living in north Georgia at least as early as 1811. In 1818, he was listed as a native of Coosawattee, with four members in his household willing to move to Arkansas.

Cherokee genealogist Emmett Starr identifies Harlen's wife as Nancy Sanders, a member of the prominent Indian family of nearby Talking Rock which sponsored the Moravian Mission at Carmel. The Moravians, however, identified her as "Nancy Vann," a member of the prominent Vann family of Cherokee lineage, and wrote in 1813 of their failed efforts to redeem Nancy Harlen from her *"lusts."*

A few months after the Moravian diary entry on Nancy, she reportedly drove George from their house (Carter's Quarters?), and eventually took their children and left Harlen to become the wife of Ambrose Harnage, whose tavern near present-day Tate, Georgia, became a landmark on the Federal Road and later was the first white courthouse in north Georgia.

Cotter claimed that Harlen had excellent corn fields, apple and peach orchards, and seventy-five to one-hundred head of cattle that he, interestingly, reportedly would attract by covering himself in salt.

In 1815, the Moravians mentioned that Harlen remarried to a white woman. She was, however, actually mixed-blood Cherokee Anna May. Though probably light-skinned, Anna May was the daughter of a wealthy Cherokee, William May. From the union of George and Anna came a daughter named Almira who was married by the Moravians to Joshua Roach on May 5, 1830.

The Moravians further mention Harlen in 1830. He is described as being a merchant, owning a gristmill and a store; having slaves; and traveling regularly to Tennessee and to Augusta, Georgia, with herds of pigs and cattle.

Cotter wrote that Harlen and his family voluntarily left Georgia for the West in 1834. They probably did leave at that time, for they do not appear on the *1835 Census* or **Rolls of the Cherokee**.

Harlen's property is not included in the 1836 valuations of the Cherokee lands either, presumably because it had already been sold by that point. During the Cherokee Removal, the house was used as the headquarters of Army Quartermaster Col. Wm. J. Howard. The removal fort known as Fort Gilmer which was used as a stockade for the Cherokees in the area (during the *"Trail of Tears"* removal), reportedly stood across the road from the house.

Cotter also implies that the name "Carter's Quarters" actually comes from the village or "quarters" of the aforementioned eighty *"well-fed and clothed and not overworked"* slaves of the previously-mentioned Judge John Martin. Although located some three miles away from the house at Rock Spring, the village property was also acquired by Farish Carter and the whole area became known variously as "Carter's," "Carter's Quarters," "the Quarters," and "Rock Spring."

An active black community still resided in this vicinity well into the 20th century, many members of which were interviewed for their African-American songs by well-known folklorist/Professor Eber Perrow of Talking Rock.

The first Carter to actually live in the Carter's Quarters house year-round was Col. Samuel McDonald Carter (1826-1897), the son of Farish Carter and a one-time Murray County judge of the Inferior Court. Col. Carter added a bedroom wing to the rear of the house which was later removed.

In 1936, the original house became part of the expanded larger structure standing at this site as of this writing. Atlanta residential architect Louis Crook, famous for his buildings at Emory University in Atlanta, added sections to the older portion, creating a home much larger than the original building. And he did it in such a way that the older original structure appears to be only the south wing of the present-day house.

It is this older original portion of the house – built by the Cherokees – that continues to fascinate historians and architects today. It is a two-story plantation-style structure with two rooms on each floor.

The walls and floors are not of log construction, but heart pine, painted originally in the strong house colors of blue and maize also found at the Chief James Vann house near Chatsworth, Georgia. The mantels over the fireplaces are hard-carved and contain Cherokee symbols – as also does the Vann house.

A sophisticated cantilevered staircase – also a characteristic feature of the Chatsworth Vann house – provides access to the upper level in much the same fashion as is done in the Vann House. The staircase is actually mounted to the wall, giving the illusion of a staircase with no supports.

The doors are still mounted and fastened with the original hinges and other iron-work believed to have been produced in a metal-working or blacksmith shop on the grounds. Details of this house were copied in the replicas of the Cherokee buildings completed by the Georgia Department of Natural Resources at New Echota State Historic Site in north Georgia.

As of this writing, some of the original plantation out-buildings, including the kitchen, log cook's house, and trunk room, still stand on the grounds of the Carter's Quarters house. Also located nearby is the site of the rock spring which provided the impetus for the original occupation of the site by the Indians centuries ago.

Listed today on the *National Register of Historic Places*, Carter's Quarters is much more than just another historic site. It is a monument to the Cherokees who built the original structure as a portion of a valiant effort to assimilate into White culture. The home is also a credit to the Carter family which has maintained and preserved the site for future generations of history enthusiasts.

It can only be considered a tragic loss today, that the "Coosawattee - Judge John Martin Cherokee home" was not also preserved to be included in this valuable historic legacy.

The Alabama Roads
(Part I) (Upper Route)

In prehistoric America – when the southeast was still covered by virtually impenetrable forests and undergrowth – there were no highways upon which to travel. The best opportunity existed in the game trails which had been tramped down over millennia by migrating buffalo, elk, deer, and other hooved animals who instinctively followed the routes of least resistance around hills and mountains and across bodies of water. These crude early trails inevitably were adopted by the aboriginal natives of the southeast, and later – eventually – by pioneers to our great nation traveling westward who called the byways "the Alabama Roads."

After being organized as a territory in 1817, Alabama was the first general destination west of Georgia for pioneer travelers in the great "manifest destiny." Many who did so endured the arduous trip down the eastern seaboard and then across less mountainous South Carolina to arrive at Georgia, where the Appalachian range ended, allowing the pioneers to circumvent this mountainous obstacle. The next destination was Alabama Territory, and the routes they used to travel across Georgia to reach the West therefore became known as "the Alabama Roads."

Early travelers making this trip initially referred to the destination objective as the road "to the Alabama," since they were enroute to "the Alabama Territory." When the territory became a state in 1819, the term was shortened to "the road to Alabama," or simply "the Alabama Road," a term quite often still seen today on road signs identifying many modern (albeit actually very aged) routes to the West.

Prior to the European settlers, the Native Americans had gradually adopted (and re-shaped) over hundreds of years the early game paths of migrating hooved animals for use as "trading paths" and "war paths" etc. In order to reach their desired destinations, the natives slightly altered the paths, making use of available stream, creek and river crossings at spots such as shoals, falls, islands and shallows, so the paths understandably were seldom the most direct routes.

With European expansion into America and the adoption of the Indian trails by Whites as travel routes, an innovation known as the ferryboat soon came into use for fording the bodies of water which were encountered westward. This innovation substantially straightened the routes when the deep sections of streams and rivers, etc., could then be easily and safely forded – as opposed to traveling "out of one's way" in order to make use of one of the aforementioned shoals, falls, or island crossing spots established by the Indians.

This straightened line of travel reduced travel time from point A to point B, but it was tempered by the fact that though the ferryboats could cross much deeper water, they also required "calm" water for safety and success. As a result of all of the above, the "Alabama Roads" to the west today are essentially relatively straight thoroughfares which were sought out and heavily used by the pioneers.

Today, in many instances, the old Alabama Roads have been forgotten by the public. In the stretches where they are still used – and even occasionally identified as "Old Alabama Road" – they are nevertheless just accepted by today's travelers as yet another "modern road," instead of the user understanding that he or she is actually traveling upon a very old former pioneer trail. There are few markers to indicate these old routes today, and only rare historic tablets to remind citizens of the once conspicuous role these routes played in the settlement of our country.

Interestingly, it is the exception, rather than the rule today for these early routes to coincide with our modern roads and highways – for obvious reasons. Major emphasis in this article will not be placed upon the chronological development or history of these old roads, but rather upon a re-tracing of the actual routes as they originally existed.

A particular effort has been made to name old key points along these

Scudder's Inn - Alfred Scudder was one of the best-known individuals of the Hightower Crossroads area in north Forsyth County. His pioneer plantation home – known as "Scudder's Inn" – is pictured here, and once stood near the present-day intersection of GA Highway 369 and the Old Federal Road in Forsyth County. This structure tragically was burned circa 1941. Pictured are (l to r): Elie Sherrill (husband of Cynthia Heard Sherrill), Alice Paralee Heard (youngest child of Martha Paralee Hudlow Heard), Mattie G. Heard (with children: Pauline, Otto & Grace), George Bowman Hudlow (white-bearded family patriarch), Martha Paralee Hudlow Heard, and an unidentified young man. *(Photo courtesy of Don L. Shadburn)*

highways, with the hope that the information may prove of value to those interested in this type of historic information, and/or who may wish to learn of the various overnighting spots, ferries, homes of prominent leaders, and other details which may have impacted migrating forebears following these routes westward during the days of pioneer America. Though they are referred to as "the Alabama Road," there are any number of various alternatives to the road at various points across Georgia which have been used over time, and this article will address many of them.

The Alabama Road Via Rome and Coosa Valley

The most complicated former thoroughfares to trace westward across

Mystery & History in Georgia

Scudder's Trading House - Photographed circa 1890s at Scudder's Inn are (l to r): George Lumpkin, John Pinkney, Jefferson Seymour, James Linton, William Walker, Henry Arthur, and Charles Davis. The old Scudder Trading House (visible rear) served as a location for the headquarters for the U.S. Army in the 1830s, when the troops were collecting the Cherokee Indians of the area for relocation in the West. *(Photo courtesy of Don L. Shadburn)*

Georgia are the roads which utilized the natural gateway afforded by the Coosa River Valley. These old emigrant routes to the West are very interesting, because with the exception of stretches here and there, much of the original routes through the Coosa River Valley are still in use today. Significant portions of them are still known and described as "the Alabama Road."

The complexities in retracing the Alabama Roads arise from the fact that they began at a multitude of widely dispersed origins in northeastern Georgia, and ran westward until they merged together toward common destinations, so there are many different variations of the avenue known as the Alabama Road. The beginning of the route included a series of cris-crossing trails – also called Alabama Roads – which traversed from one main thoroughfare over to another.

The best-known of the Coosa River thoroughfares passed immediately above Rome, Georgia, into Alabama on the upper side of the Coosa River. It had a two-pronged beginning in northeast Georgia, with the first fork – known as "the Alabama Road" – commencing at Leathers Ford on the Chestatee River in extreme south Lumpkin County. This Leathers Ford entry point attracted travelers via a trail from Earl's Ford at the mouth of Warwoman Creek on the Chattooga River in eastern Rabun County, Georgia, which was a natural point of convergence for traveling pioneers. From there, this trail passed in the vicinity of the present-day communities of Clayton, Batesville, and the Nacoochee Valley, before moving down Lumpkin County to Leathers Ford.

Another route used by emigrants to reach the Coosa River Valley Alabama Road in west Georgia ran from Walton's Ford east of Toccoa on the Chattooga River, down to Clarkesville.

Although our description of this

The Alabama Roads (Part I) (Upper Route)   North Georgia

Alabama Road includes trails which began at the eastern boundary of Georgia, the Alabama Road itself did not physically begin at that point. A series of introductory byways ran along the piedmont sections of the Mid-Atlantic and southeastern states, all the way from Pennsylvania, Maryland and Virginia, to points southward. Emigrants on their way to the mid- or far-west used many of these piedmont routes which ran through Charlotte, Greenville and Spartanburg, in order to reach the Alabama Roads in Georgia.

Possibly the greatest users of the Coosa River Valley Alabama Road and its tributary connectors were not distant travelers from other states, but rather ex-gold miners from the Lumpkin, White, and Dawson County areas. When these settlers decided to give up their diggings and head West during the mid to latter portion of the 19th Century (and there were thousands of them), the Coosa River Valley route was the most logical path for them to take.

Because of the great importance of the many connectors to the Alabama Road, brief descriptions of them are provided herewith as follows:

Connection #1

This early access route began at the Chattooga River in Rabun County, east of present-day Clayton. Crossing the Chattooga River from South Carolina over Earl's Ford at the mouth of Warwoman Creek, Connection #1 paralleled and crossed Warwoman Creek a number of times on its way westward, continuing over Saddle Gap to reach Clayton.

Clayton, Georgia was originally known as "The Dividings" in the days of the pioneers, because a number of Native American hunting and trading trails crossed or "divided" there. Leaving The Dividings, Connection #1 continued southwestward along the same general route as present-day Georgia Highway 2, passing by present-day Fairview Church and crossing in the vicinity of today's Lake Burton. In Native American days, this trail was part of the "Tallulah Trail."

Connection #1 continued on, passing the site at which LaPrade's Fishing Camp once existed, passing into upper Habersham County where it followed the present-day route of GA 197. Continuing southward by Providence Church, the road left GA 197 to turn more southwestward and pass into present-day White County.

At the eastern end of the Nacoochee Valley at Sautee, Connection #1 joined the route of GA 105, which was another connector we shall call "Connection #2."

Connection #2

Connection #2 began at Walton's Ford on the Tugaloo River in eastern Stephens County. That location – northeast of Toccoa – in now under the waters of Lake Hartwell.

Connection #2 continued southwestward past LeTourneau Airport, following the route of present-day GA 17 in the eastern fringes of Toccoa. From there it continued westward on old "Locust Stake Road" (named after a locust stake placed by an early surveyor; locust has been known to occasionally sprout and actually take root from a simple stake or pole, the large durable trees creating very good boundary line markers) on the North Carolina/Georgia boundary north of present-day Dillard.

Continuing into Habersham County, Connection #2 passed through Chopped Oak, and then fell upon the route of GA 115 just east of Hills Switch

"Mule Camp Springs" – Photographed circa 1890s, a semblance of commerce exists on the old Gainesville town square – originally called "Mule Camp Springs" – where nothing but an intersection of dusty roads had prevailed barely 50 years earlier. One "connector" to the Alabama Road followed Highway 53 into Mule Camp Springs, passing through the town and continuing upon "Shallowford Road" on the other side of town which soon forded at a shallow spot on the Chattahoochee River west of the town. *(Photo courtesy of GA Dept. of Archives & History, Atlanta)*

School. It then continued through Clarkesville, following GA 115 until that highway intersected with GA 105. Connection #2 then passed through Harvest and Cool Springs to intersect with Connection #1 at Sautee.

Passing on through the Nacoochee Valley in present-day White County, the combination of Connections #1 and #2 turned southward on GA 75 to pass Yonah (Cherokee for "bear") Mountain and then through Cleveland. It was at Mountain View Church in this area that a historic fork in the road called "Gold Diggers Road" existed. Gold Diggers Road bore straight ahead at this point, while the combined Connections #1 and #2 continued on the route of present-day GA 115.

Gold Diggers Road is not a direct connection for the Alabama Road, but its route will be briefly described here since it has important historic significance.

This route was – as its name suggests – a way into the gold fields of present-day Lumpkin and White counties. It continued toward Dahlonega from Cleveland, passing just north of Dahlonega before falling upon the present-day route of U.S. 19 Highway just south of Concord Church. It passed through the western fringe of Dahlonega and then followed the present-day route GA 9-E, before finally ending at the old gold mining town of Auraria.

In its day, Gold Diggers Road was traversed by many rough-and-tumble hardy pioneers who were accustomed to an extremely harsh life, since they lived most of the time by camping out in tents and crude structures, enduring nature, vermin and the elements as they staked their claims and sought their fortunes. Some located just enough gold to encourage them to spent many years in Lumpkin County; some lucky few actually struck it rich and retired early, but many more endured frustration after frustration, eventually giving up and moving westward to California and Colorado, after learning of big strikes there in 1849 and 1859 respectively. Gold Miners Road was the route these miners took in this westward migration.

Back at the fork at Mountain View Church, Connections #1 and #2 remained on GA 115, passing Shoal Creek Church. Just east of Garland, the trail turned southward, passing Hickory Grove Church and St. Paul Church, both in southern Lumpkin County. At this point, Connections #1 and #2 crossed the Chestatee River at Leathers Ford, and then followed the route of present-day GA 9-E, passing into Dawson County. From there, the road ran through Landrum and by Dougherty. It was along this stretch that the route ceased to be a "connection," and actually

The Alabama Roads (Part I) (Upper Route)　　　　　　　　North Georgia

became commonly known as "the Alabama Road."

Connection #3

Connection #3 began at Hatton's Ford on the Tugaloo River northeast of Bowersville, and near today's Reed Creek Community, all in Hart County. The ford is now inundated by the waters of Lake Hartwell.

Connection #3 continued southwestward from its river crossing, close on GA Highway 51 through Reed Creek, where it was joined by another short connection. This latter connection ran from a crossing a short distance downstream on the Tugaloo known as Harrison's Ferry (later Andersonville Ferry), located at the site of present-day Lake Hartwell Dam. This short link ran southwestward to intersect Connection #3 about three miles north of Hartwell before the combined trails continued on into that city. From there, Connection #3 continued westward, close on present-day GA 77 for a short distance, before turning left onto GA 51.

Following this route, Connection #3 continued through Flat Shoals, Airline, and downtown Bowersville, passing New Franklin Church on its way to Carnesville. The latter portion of this stretch – from the North Ford Broad River and on into Gainesville – followed an old Indian trail known as "the Toogaloo Trail" (and sometimes "the Pickens Trail"). The word "Toogaloo" is actually a misnomer which has been perpetuated through time. The trail was so-named because it ran to the Indian town of "Tugaloo" (not "Toogaloo") situated on the stream of the same name. This section of Connection #3 earned the added identity of "Pickens Trail" from General Andrew Pickens who lived at the trail's eastern terminus in Oconee County, South Carolina, just across the Georgia state line.

Connection #3 continued on through Carnesville, following closely on the route of present-day GA 51. It passed the Indian Creek Church and Plainview before passing into Banks County. From there, it ran through Jewellsville, Cheap, Homer, and Mt. Carmel, before leaving the route of GA 51 to go into Gillsville.

Just south of Terrell Lake, Connection #3 followed the route of present-day U.S. 23 for a short distance before turning onto the route of GA 53 to pass into Gainesville. This stretch west of Gainesville was known as "Shallowford Road" (not to be confused with the Shallowford Road of Atlanta) in early days, because it crossed the Chattahoochee River at the shallow ford. A portion of this Shallowford Road still exists today in Gainesville.

"Big Savannah" / Dougherty

Connection #3 continued westward to cross the Chestatee River at Wooley Ford (later replaced by Bolding Bridge), still following the route of GA 53, and still known as Shallowford Road. Passing on into Dawson County, Connection #3 eventually intersected with present-day GA Highway 9-E just below Black's Mill, and continued northward to intersect with Connection #1 near the former community of Dougherty.

Landrum/Dougherty are/were located in virtually the same spot in a beautiful area of the Etowah River valley in Dawson County long-known as "Big Savannah." Anyone who has visited this section no doubt has noticed the fine river bottomlands which stretch away from the highway up and down the Etowah River. Prior to the removal of the native Cherokee Indians from Georgia, this spot was widely known as "Big Savannah," and was the home of a number of Cherokee families and white pioneers who had intermarried with them. It is known to have been the location of a large Cherokee town called "Tensawattee."

Co. Benjamin Hawkins, on his way in 1796 to take up his duties as Indian Agent, remarked that the Big Savannah area was "a large and beautiful savannah," and that portions of it were "the richest vale of land I have ever seen." In pioneer terminology, a "savannah" was a moist, open, meadow-like area with very rich earth where grass or reed cane proliferated. In a forested region like early Georgia, such sites were once highly prized spots for grazing stock and growing food, and were much-used for these purposes both by Indians and Whites alike.

It is interesting to note that a post office once existed at Big Savannah from 1869 until the community was renamed "Dougherty" in 1881. Records of the U.S. Postal Service indicate that the Big Savannah Post Office was established on August 9, 1869, with Harriet A. Barnett as the first postmistress. The Big Savannah post office was discontinued on November 7, 1881, after a nearby post office was established in Dougherty on October 19 of that year.

Robert A. Gober was the first postmaster of Dougherty. The Dougherty Post Office continued until January 31, 1955, at which time it was discontinued and the post office was transferred to nearby Dawsonville.

The name "Dougherty" has been in use in the Big Savannah area since Indian days, very likely a community name held over from the days of James Dougherty, Sr., who long resided in the Cherokee nation in that section. Dougherty and his wife died there in 1837, a year prior to the Cherokee Indian removal from that area.

Old Federal Road

As the Alabama Road continued westward by Salem Church and on through Barrettsville and Silver City, it intersected with the "Federal Road." That crossroads, located in extreme northwest Forsyth County, had great significance during late Indian occupation days, because it was a focal point for the U.S. Army under General Winfield Scott while initiating the Cherokee Removal program.

The fine river bottomlands at Hightower (sometimes identified as "Hightower Crossroads") caused a number of influential men and their families to settle in that area. Blackburn was a prominent name associated with the area, a name which also was attached to a settlement there.

Lewis Blackburn operated Blackburn's Public House (which once existed on the old Federal Road in Forsyth County). This ancient tavern was operated by Blackburn in the early 1800s, and the heavy log structure has survived some 200 years into the 21St century, and continues, as of this writing (2021) to exist. It had originally been built at the site later occupied by the old Sherrill home

Lewis Blackburn operated Blackburn's Public House (which once existed on the old Federal Road in Forsyth County).

The Alabama Roads (Part I) (Upper Route)　　　　　　　　North Georgia

"Dividings," GA – Photographed circa 1890s, Clayton was known as "The Dividings" in pioneer days in Georgia, because it was the site at which several major Indian trails crossed or "divided." Because of this convergence of "traffic," this vicinity became an excellent site for commerce to spring up – and it did. *(Photo courtesy of GA Dept. of Archives & History)*

on the Federal Road in Forsyth County. Following purchase of the property by the Sherrills, the aged public house was moved across the Federal Road to the opposite side, where it sat for many years, being used as a hay-barn.

At last check, this historic public house had been moved from the Sherrill property by possibly well-meaning individuals to the Cumming, Georgia, Fairgrounds where it was identified – with very little if any evidence – as the site of the murder of Cherokee Chief James Vann II in 1809. Though it (Blackburn's Public House) is an extremely historic structure in its own right, early maps of the area – and at least one eye-witness account of Vann's grave – strongly seem to identify this structure as Blackburn's Public House, and it is a matter of documented historic record that Vann was assassinated at a site known as Buffington's Tavern which, in turn, has been documented as being located farther up the old Federal Road toward Canton just inside the Cherokee County line.

A short distance away from this spot, the Alfred Scudder family which was probably the best-known of that area, operated yet another tavern/trading house. Scudder's trading house served as a headquarters for the U.S. Army during the mid-1830s when troops were collecting and removing the Cherokee Indians from the area. Just eastward on the Federal Road, about one and one-half miles from Hightower, Fort Gilmer was built at the same time as a stockade to house the Cherokees until they could be sent West. No remains at either spot of the former military occupation can be found today.

Through Cherokee and Bartow

From Hightower, the Alabama Road is much easier to trace, simply because much of it is still in use today, and is sometimes even identified in spots by the old original name. Continuing on westward on GA 20, the old road passed into Cherokee County, continuing by Etowah School, Ophir, Orange, and Buffington. The last-named community was originally "Fort Buffington," another of the Cherokee Indian removal stockades of the 1830s.

The namesake of the fort is not known for certain today, but he quite likely was Joshua Buffington, a prominent mixed-blood Cherokee who lived nearby in Indian days. Interestingly, this Buffington is also of the family which owned Buffington's Tavern once located just inside the present-day Cherokee County line on the right side of the Federal Road as one travels to Canton. This tavern, not Blackburn's Public House which is often confused with it, was the actual site – according to the best evidence existing today – of the assassination of Cherokee Chief James Vann II in 1809.

The Alabama Road continued on westward, following closely the current route of GA 20 through North Canton to a crossing on the Etowah River known during pioneer days as Downings Ferry. This crossing, now beneath the waters of Lake Allatoona, was just downhill (in the lake-bed) from today's Fields Church (located on the northern side of the lake).

After passing Fields Church, the Alabama Road again followed the route of present-day GA 20, past Laughing Gal, and on through a rugged region which must have been a very difficult portion of the road for travelers during pioneer days. Shortly thereafter, the road crossed Lick Creek (now Stamp Creek).

The Alabama Road next passed above Cartersville, crossing U.S. 411 at Felton Field to intersect U.S. 41 at the edge of Cass Station. Located at that place in Indian days was "Hawk's Store," where the Alabama Road crossed "New Town Road." New Town Road passed by the noted Sally Hughes' Ferry on the Etowah River just south of Cartersville. From this crossing, the Sally Hughes Road ran on northward to the Cherokee capital – New Echota. It is for this reason that the road earned the name "New Town Road." New Town Road also merits noting because it was also a cross-over from another Alabama Road running south of the Etowah River.

The pioneer mercantile business of Hawk's Store located at Cass Station in present-day Bartow County, was a trading post which was operated by Charles Hawks, a white man who of course was residing in the Cherokee Nation prior to the removal of the tribe. Hawks was appointed the first postmaster of Cassville when a post office was established there on July 12, 1833.

Major Ridge Home

From Cass Station, the Alabama Road (known at this point as "the Kingston Road" both in Indian days and today), went above Walker Mountain, but not on the course followed by U.S. 411 today. Instead, it ran south of the modern road to a point just east of Ransom School near the county line, and from there into Floyd County and on to "Chieftains," the former home of prominent Cherokee planter – Major Ridge – on the Oostanaula River in north Rome.

Ridge was intimately connected with the development of this old thoroughfare near his home, just as was James Vann II with the development of the Cherokee ("Old Federal") Road near his home. Ridge maintained a ferry across the Oostanaula River where the Alabama Road crossed near his home, just as did Vann across the Chattahoochee River.

Ridge's home – Chieftains – is still located in the original location – today's Chatillion Road in north Rome. The two-story house of milled lumber built around an earlier log cabin overlooked the Ridge Toll Ferry across the Oostanaula.

Major Ridge, and his son – John – both were signers of the *Treaty of New Echota* in 1835, and were assassinated for their roles in the removal of the Cherokee Nation from Georgia. Today, Chieftains is maintained as a very fine museum of Cherokee culture.

From Ridge's place, the original course of the Alabama Road is lost in a maze of modern roads and streets. It, nevertheless, continued westward, leaving the northern part of Rome, and, after a short distance, continued on the same route followed by GA 20.

Chief John Ross House

Before leaving the present city limits of Rome and near the intersection of Burnett Ferry Road and GA 20, the Alabama

The Alabama Roads (Part I) (Upper Route) — North Georgia

"**Chieftains**" – The Coosa River Alabama Road crossed the Oostanaula River at the site of the home (Chieftains) and ferry of Major Ridge, once a prominent leader of the Cherokees during the early 1800s. Ridge was later assassinated by a Cherokee Death Squad for his role in the Treaty of New Echota and the subsequent displacement of the Cherokees to the West. Just as were other prominent Cherokee planters, Ridge was intimately involved with the development of the Alabama Road near his home, profiting greatly from the commerce it brought for the sale of his products and the use of his ferryboat by travelers on the road who crossed the river. *(Photo courtesy of Rome Area History Museum)*

Road was intersected by a road from the forks of the Etowah and Oostanaula Rivers. This junction, which represents the beginning of the Coosa River, is the center of present-day Rome, and formerly the site of Chief John Ross's home.

This connecting road at this site is of significance because it was also called an Alabama Road, and was a link between the Alabama Road below the Etowah and Coosa Rivers and the upper trace under discussion. The crossing in what today is downtown Rome bears nothing because it was the site of the "Widow Fool's Ferry," so-named for one of the two Cherokee women who operated river crossings (the other was the previously-mentioned Sally Hughes).

The Brainerd Road

The Alabama Road continued westward on GA 20, passing today's village of Coosa, the site during pioneer days of the Creek Path Missionary Station. Just beyond this point, the Alabama Road was joined by a prong of "the Brainerd Road," another Alabama Road from Tennessee.

The main Alabama Road continued westward on GA 20 which became AL Highway #9 when it reached that state and ran on to Jeffersonville, now Cedar

Bluff in Cherokee County, Alabama. Just before reaching the latter city, a fork bore off to the right (approximately along the route of AL 35) to go to Gaylesville where it intersected another Alabama Road from Brainerd and Calhoun County, Tennessee.

The Brainerd Road was so named because it was one of the routes used to reach the Brainerd Missionary Station and School, located on Missionary Ridge in east Chattanooga, TN. That station was the headquarters of all the missionary stations in the Cherokee Nation. The only sign or indication that this mission ever existed at all is a historical marker and a small cemetery at the edge of a modern shopping center.

The Brainerd Road (also called "the Tennessee Road" when followed northward from Alabama) was an Alabama Road and is so labeled on numerous maps – even today. It was important as a main thoroughfare for reaching Alabama across the northwestern tip of Georgia from Tennessee.

The Brainerd Road entered Georgia at two places on the Tennessee state line. One of these connections – known as "Old Calhoun Road" (from Calhoun, Tennessee) came into Georgia above Ringgold via present-day GA 151 and intersected the Cherokee Federal (Old Federal Road) at that place. The combined roads continued a short distance before the Alabama Road turned southward along the route of today's GA 151.

The other fork of the Brainerd Road entered Georgia at Graysville, Catoosa County, Georgia. It also intersected the Federal Road and ran eastward to a point just west of Ringgold, where the road from Calhoun branched off. These two trails combined to form the Alabama Road. The combined union ran southward into Catoosa County, as does GA 151 by way of Pleasant Grove Church, Wood Station, and Bethel, before passing into Walker County. The road did not go directly through LaFayette, but ran just east of there through Naomi.

Five miles further, immediately above Cane Creek, the road forked. The left fork continued on southward into Chattooga County, down the east side of the Chattooga River and along the foot of Taylor's Ridge. It passed Holland, Tulip, and Sprite, before going into Floyd County, following very nearly the route of present-day GA 100. It intersected the old main Alabama Road shortly thereafter near Coosa and the Creek Missionary Station.

The right branch of the Alabama Road from Tennessee bore west at Cane Creek for a short distance before turning south to strike U.S. 27 at the first fork below Oakton. From there, the road skirted the eastern fringe of Trion – not following U.S. 27 into town – before continuing on through Summerville. At that city, the old road left U.S. 27 and followed GA 114 along the edge of Berryton and on through Lyerly and Chattoogaville before continuing on into Cherokee County, Alabama and on to Gaylesville via AL 75.

(Special thanks is due to the late Marion Hemperley for providing much of the material used in the above article. Marion served with the Georgia State Surveyor-General Department for 30 years, 10 years of which included service as Deputy Surveyor-General. He is the author of numerous books and articles of historic research, and researched and documented many of the historic maps and archival materials currently on file at the Georgia Department of Archives and History in Atlanta, Georgia.)

Trails Of The Pioneers:

Re-tracing The Alabama Road
(Part II) (Lower Route)

Travelers on some roads in Georgia today occasionally encounter roads called "Old Alabama Road." This pioneer trail had many different branches, connections, and beginnings and ends with two things in common: the collective roads were originally ancient trails cut by migrating wildlife, then adopted by the Indians, and then still later by White settlers. And though there were any number of them, the roads all ended in "Alabama."

Many people think the early pioneers and explorers just hopped into a covered wagon and headed west upon a well-established road, but it of course didn't happen that way. In the beginning, if they were lucky, these ambitious adventurers were able to follow small game trails and Indian paths which gratefully traversed the contours around the hills and through the valleys, always following the route of least resistance. If, however, they were unlucky, these pioneers were forced by necessity to hack their way through intense undergrowth and thick forests and to seek out navigable spots at which to ford the countless streams, creeks, and rivers to continue the westward march. It was an arduous task.

These routes westward invariably initially required these brave souls to travel down the eastern seaboard of the United States until they reached the flatlands of South Carolina and Georgia in order to circumvent the almost impenetrable barrier of the Appalachian Mountains range.

Some of the travelers might also initially land by ship at Savannah, Georgia, and then make their way northwestward across the state. As a result, there ultimately were a number of different pioneer trails across the state, all of which were called "the Alabama Road," because they inevitably led to the great state of Alabama – the next destination after Georgia on the road westward.

One of the first settlements in north Georgia was created as a result of the gold mania sweeping across the landscape following the discovery of the precious yellow metal in that locality. The community which sprang up upon a ridge between the Chestatee and

Etowah rivers in northeast Georgia was called "Nuckollsville." Here, in 1832, William Dean built a cabin, followed by Nathaniel Nuckolls who opened a tavern and gave the community its name.

The community's main street extended along the ridge of land between the Chestatee and Etowah rivers, and everything of importance fronted on it. A stage coach line had been established from Athens, Georgia, by way of Gainesville, for a tri-weekly run to Leathers Ford across the Chattahoochee River then up to "Gold Diggers Road" as the north-south avenue from Nuckollsville to Cleveland, Georgia, was called.

This rutted red-clay trail through Nuckollsville quickly became an important feeder for one of the several "Alabama Roads" which the pioneers used to travel westward across Georgia. During times of heat and dry weather, Gold Diggers Road boiled with dust, and when the rains came, it just as quickly became a gooey quagmire which made travel almost impossible.

After deciding that the name "Nuckollsville" wasn't the most pleasant-sounding or attractive name for a community, the town fathers eventually renamed it "Auraria," which, roughly translated in Latin means "gold mine."

Gold Diggers Road was a vibrant artery of traffic moving into the bustling town, and later, of miners and travelers moving ever westward, reaching for new opportunities on the horizon. Drovers brought in hogs and turkeys to feed the growing population. The animals were herded noisily through town and then penned up on the outskirts until they could be made ready for the table.

From the earliest days, the nearby community of Dahlonega was the rival village of Auraria. When a blight was discovered upon the land lot numbering system in Auraria, the county seat was removed to the more stable locale of Dahlonega. When the all-important Bank of Darien also selected Dahlonega for its new branch, a decline in population began almost immediately in Auraria. Lawyers moved their practices to the new seat of justice, and other businesses gradually followed.

In 1838, when the United States Branch Mint was built in Dahlonega, the death knell was sounded for Auraria. In less than ten years, the city of gold went from a rambunctious gold mining town to a quiet village, its brief moment of glory passed.

With this diminished community status, so too diminished the traffic on Gold Diggers Road through Auraria. In contrast however, traffic on the Alabama Roads across Georgia was surging by the mid-1800s, as the rush for new opportunities westward was beginning in earnest.

In the following article, we will focus upon the Alabama Road via present-day Warsaw and Cave Spring, a route also known as the "**Lower Alabama Road**." There are several other "Alabama Roads" across Georgia which will be covered in a later article.

The Warsaw/Cave Spring route of the Alabama Roads began near the community of Warsaw on the west side of the Chattahoochee River in "Old Milton County," (present-day North Fulton County). This ancient byway, by means of connections at its beginning and through tributaries which joined it on the way, received traffic from widely different areas of Georgia.

The exact date at which the Alabama Road via Warsaw came under general use by pioneer settlers is not known today. Suffice it to say, however, that this route was in use at least as early as 1825,

Re-tracing The Alabama Road (Part II) (Lower Route) — North Georgia

because at about that time, one George Waters moved to the western or Cherokee side of the Chattahoochee River and began operation of a ferry at the spot.

Following his marriage to a Cherokee woman, Waters settled in the rich river-bottomlands there where he farmed and raised a family of mixed-blood children. In the Cherokee Removal of the 1830s when all of the Cherokee Native Americans were forced to abandon their homes and farms in Georgia, the Waters family was also compelled to depart.

Shortly thereafter, however, when the area on the western (present-day Fulton County) side of the Chattahoochee was opened for white settlement, Waters, as a white man, returned, as was his right, to settle once again upon his former home and acreage. However, his efforts to reclaim his former home site proved to be in vain, due to the fact that it had been claimed by a new owner after being abandoned.

Waters, nevertheless, was able to purchase land across the Chattahoochee River on the eastern or Gwinnett County side. He and his family lived in that area for the rest of their lives, and are buried in the cemetery of the Presbyterian Church there.

The ferry operated by Waters was first known as "Water's Ferry," but in later years, it became known as "the Warsaw Ferry," after the town which had blossomed in that area. This old crossing point is now spanned by Georgia Highway 120 and McClure Bridge.

On the western side of the Chattahoochee, the Alabama Road westward began just above present-day McClure Bridge. The stretch of the former road leading away from the old ferry site does not exist today, but it once mounted the hill in front of the old Howell house before turning westward. The road did not go through today's Warsaw, but passed several hundred yards to the south of the community.

Just below the Howell house, this Lower Alabama Road continued westward across the state, its course virtually unaltered by modern highways except for a few significant stretches and minor relocations. The road is still well-known today in numerous spots across the state, including north Fulton, Cobb, Bartow, and Paulding counties where, in various sections, it still retains its original name as "Old Alabama Road."

Leaving Warsaw, the Alabama Road – still identified with its original name today on much of this section of the route – passed Pleasant Hill Church and School, before going through Newton and adjoining what today is known as Holcomb Bridge Road. Holcomb Bridge Road (or Rockbridge Road, to use its older name) was an out-growth of the well-known Hightower Indian Path which was the dividing line between today's Gwinnett and DeKalb Counties.

From its juncture with Holcomb Bridge Road, the Alabama Road continued westward on what today is Georgia Highway 140, by Lebanon Mills and Lebanon, and passed north of old Roswell to follow what is now called Woodstock Road (GA Highway 92). That same road today is also known as Crossville Road, so named because it runs through what once was a tiny community of that name.

Leaving Fulton County, the Alabama Road continued across the extreme northeast tip of Cobb County before entering Cherokee County. Continuing to follow present-day Georgia Highway 92, the road ran past Little River Church and what once was the tiny community of Trickum (located at the intersection of Trickum Road and Georgia 92.

321

The Shallow Ford Across the Chattahoochee – Shallowford Road in modern-day Roswell is quite familiar to many Atlantans. It achieved its name from the fact that it was the portion of the Alabama road to and from the shallow fording spot across the Chattahoochee River at which ox and mule-drawn wagons (and foot traffic) could easily cross (in normal to dry weather). The actual fording spot was approximately at the site at which the present-day Roswell Road Bridge between Roswell and Sandy Springs crosses the Chattahoochee (where the river has deepened in recent times). This photograph, taken circa 1900, shows the same site after it had been spanned by a covered bridge. Shallowford Road, which is a feeder road into the old Alabama Road, continues on up the hill toward present-day Highway 92. The structure to the right in this photo was the Roswell Hotel. The buildings to the left were a portion of the Ivy Woolens Mill complex. *(Photo courtesy of GA Dept. of Archives & History)*

Continuing westward, the Alabama Road crossed Georgia Highway 5 just south of Woodstock at an intersection known as "Bulloch's Barn," and continued to a fork near Carmel Church. At that point, the Alabama Road was joined by its second important tributary – Shallowford Road – also known as Bell's Ferry Road. The latter name was derived from the site at which the road crossed the Etowah River at Bell's Ferry, located a few miles north of the Alabama Road junction.

The name "Shallowford Road" owes its origin to the "shallow ford" on the Chattahoochee River, a noted crossing point which allowed for the passage of ox and mule-drawn wagons across the river when the water was at a normal level. The actual crossing spot was located just below the present Roswell Bridge where Georgia Highway 9 now spans the Chattahoochee just south of Roswell. "Shallowford Road" can still be found across stretches of the road from the Chattahoochee River all the way to Bell's Ferry Road.

Back up in Cherokee County, the Alabama Road, after its juncture with Shallowford Road, continued directly westward, passing through Oak Grove community, before turning more northwestward just beyond the intersection with Hunt Road. That stretch is also still officially identified today as "Old Alabama Road." The old route continued from that point through Payne before turning directly west on New Hope Road and continuing on into Bartow County.

The Alabama Road passed New Hope Church before crossing Allatoona Creek over a stretch which today has been inundated by the backwaters of Lake Allatoona. Shortly thereafter, at Emerson, the Alabama Road diverged. One fork, as "Shallowford Road" (yes – the same road from the shallow ford on the Chattahoochee River) turned right and continued northward where it crossed the Etowah River at Sally Hughes' Ferry.

Sally Hughes was one of two noted Cherokee women who owned and operated ferries in the Cherokee Nation. She was living in the Indian community of Etowah in 1796, (as recorded in the notes of Indian Agent Col. Benjamin Hawkins when he visited that place.). The town was located at the site of the present-day Etowah Indian Mounds Historic Site southwest of Cartersville.

Sally's ferry site was slightly upstream of the mounds, near the site of the present-day Cartersville city water works. Sally's residence in 1832 was a short distance upstream from her ferry. Her home was a simple log cabin on the north side of the Etowah River.

In 1832, it is interesting to note that Sally suddenly encountered competition in her ferry operation. Her competitor was a man named "Dawson." The official state surveys of that year show Sally still living at the ferry site, but just north of her cabin, "Dawson's Ferry" has appeared as a business operation.

Sally apparently was extremely upset by this drain on her income, and forwarded a letter to the governor of Georgia in complaint. This letter is still on file in the Georgia State Archives, and it interestingly was mailed in the Cherokee Nation after being written by another person and then signed by Sally with an "x". Sally could not write or sign her name in English, as was the case with most Cherokees at that time. In all probability, her plea fell upon deaf ears, because it was shortly thereafter that all Indians were expelled from Georgia.

Continuing on northward past Sally Hughes' place, a turn-off road called Newtown Road closely followed the course of U.S. Highway 41 to intersect yet another "Alabama Road" option via Rome. This route, called "the Upper Alabama Road," was just north of Cass Station.

The Newtown Road went on northwestward to New Echota, the Cherokee capital prior to 1838 near present-day Calhoun, Georgia. Travelers to north Alabama or Mississippi would have logically used this connection from the lower Alabama Road to the upper Alabama Road, because it would have saved distance for them.

Back at the other fork at Emerson, the lower Old Alabama Road continues to be relatively easy to trace, because it is also clearly identified on road signs there today. The many persons living along that stretch will assure you that they live on THE Alabama Road, and interestingly enough, few of these individuals know of the other Alabama Road via Rome and the Coosa Valley.

One of the mysteries of the former Cherokee Nation in Georgia has been the identification of the exact location at which the "Etowah Mission," established near Etowah in the early nineteenth century, once existed. The mission, established by Moravians, almost certainly was located on the Alabama Road, directly across the Etowah River from the settlement of Etowah (today's Indian mounds historic site).

In the valuation of Cherokee property by the U.S. prior to the Cherokee Removal, Etowah Mission is listed as "Pumpkinvine Mission," so called for Pumpkin Vine Creek that empties nearby into the Etowah River (directly across from the large mounds and the former town of Etowah). The same valuation lists a "stone-lined well" from which water was obtained for the mission. A well which is almost certainly that well remains today in the front yard of a fine country home on the Alabama Road near the Mounds.

This home with the well and its adjacent large field are almost certainly located almost exactly on the old mission site, but confirmation of this fact has not been secured. One of the out-buildings of this home is a log structure with an exceptionally large aged stone hearth and chimney which probably date from Cherokee days. Although the stone fireplace and chimney are very old, the existing building quite possibly is somewhat newer, having probably been built sometime in the 20th century.

From this point, the Alabama Road continued westward. The road, clearly marked with its original name, branches off from Highway 61 just prior to the intersection of Highways 61 and 113. At Richland Creek, the road fell on Georgia Highway 113 for a short distance.

The road, again marked with its original name for more short distances, continued through the center of Stilesboro and passed just above Taylorsville before passing into Floyd County. Col. Benjamin Hawkins was traveling through that section in December of 1796 on a trail that crossed the later Alabama Road about Stilesboro. Hawkins' route ran directly from Stilesboro through the center of present-day Taylorsville, whereas the Alabama Road passed just above Taylorsville.

Hawkins' travels bear mentioning at this point, since his notes describe a visit with a prominent Cherokee chief – the Terrapin – sometimes known as "Old Terrapin," who lived between today's Stilesboro and Taylorsville. The Indian chief's farm was on Euharlee Creek, which was called Limestone Creek in pioneer days.

Hawkins' journal entry for December 3, 1796, states that his party was "... continuing on 6 miles to the Old Terrapins, (we went) across a creek and passed thro' some good lands southwest by west to his house, he was from (not at) home. I visited his wife, informed her who I was, and directed her to inform her husband of it, and to deliver him a present of paint which I brought him. The old fellow lives well, the lands he cultivates are lined with small growth of saplins for some distance, his farm is fenced, his houses comfortable, he has a large stock of cattle and some hogs. He used the plow."

Benjamin Hawkins did not get to see Old Terrapin that day, but the next morning, the chief caught up with Hawkins' party and they conversed through an interpreter. It is interesting to note the thoughts of an older, and probably very wise, Cherokee during that period (the 1790s).

Hawkins records that The Terrapin "... told me he was glad to see me. He knew me and rejoiced when he was informed in the talk with the President (George Washington) that I was to superintend their affairs. That their nation had been under much embarrassment from the uncertainty of their existence as a nation, as the encroachments of the whites were constantly growing against them, notwithstanding their treaties and the repeated promises made to them to the contrary by the agents of the government."

The Terrapin was well-informed in political matters since he had been one of the chiefs who attended the Grand Cherokee National Council of 1792, held in the Cherokee capitol of that day – Ustanali (Oostanaula).

After leaving the Taylorsville area, the Alabama Road turned northwestward to go through Wax and by Chambers to Silver Creek, before skirting through the lower edge of Lindale (known as Courtsey in former days).

Between Lindale and Cass Station (above Cartersville, Bartow County), old maps show a cross-over linking the upper and lower Alabama Roads. Settlers going from South Carolina and northeast Georgia via Mulecamp Springs (Gainesville) and Leathers Ford (Auraria/Dahlonega, GA) on their way to eastern Alabama, would have found it shorter to use this cross-over.

From Lindale, the Alabama Road

intersected U.S. Highway 411 just below today's Six Mile. At this place in Indian days, there was a public stop or inn called "Wests." There, the Alabama Road was joined in early days by another Alabama Road coming south from the "Widow Fool's Ferry" (the other Cherokee Indian female, who, like the previously described Sally Hughes, owned and operated a ferry in Georgia) which was located at the forks of the Oostanaula and Etowah Rivers (present-day center of Rome).

Today, we know virtually nothing about the Widow Fool, other than the fact that she operated some type of boat which she used to convey passengers across the three-pronged delta formed by the junction of the Etowah and Oostanaula Rivers (which combine to form the mighty Coosa) in present-day Rome. The name "Fool" was a rather common one among Cherokee men, and did not imply that the person carrying the name was in any way foolish. Instead, the name ironically was an honored war title signifying that a warrior was so brave, that he was reckless in battle.

Following the route of present-day U.S. Highway 411, the Alabama Road turned southwest and continued through Vann's Valley by Cunningham (also known as Agate) and the settlement of Vann's Valley, before reaching Cave Spring.

David Vann (1800-1863), the nephew of notorious Cherokee Chief James Vann of Spring Place, lived at Vann's Valley in the vicinity of Cave Spring in Indian days. David was also a wealthy planter, but unlike his uncle, he was a very well-liked Cherokee. David planted 200 acres, owned 13 slaves and 17 houses on Cedar Creek in Vann's Valley. Local folklore in the area maintains that the stone foundation of one of his out-buildings

Former Home of a Pioneer – This two-story log home was built circa 1830s and was a focal point for the Rucker family of Crabapple, Georgia, for generations. It still exists as of this writing (2021) and is located at the intersection of Broadwell and Rucker Roads near the community of Crabapple. The Alabama Road passed very near this structure, bringing much foot and ox and cart traffic for generations. *(Photo by Olin Jackson)*

remains today under a more modern structure there.

Just beyond Cave Spring near Rehobeth Church, the Alabama Road forked, with the left branch turning southwestward into Polk County, passing Jones Church. For a short distance, the exact route of this road has been lost through time, but it was certain to have skirted around the eastern and southeastern side of Indian Mountain, a rather large prominence located on the Alabama/Georgia state line.

After passing above the community of Aetna, this fork of the Alabama Road turned westward to run on into Cherokee County, Alabama, where it passed Tecumseh and Bluffton, before falling onto another main trail just east of Spring Garden. That main route, known at that time as "the Cedartown Road," ran westward from Cedartown, Georgia, and closely followed the route of today's U.S. Highway 278 through the Piedmont, Alabama area.

The right fork of the Alabama Road

Mystery Mission – Due west of the small community of Emerson, the old Alabama Road is clearly marked, passing quite near the Etowah Indian Mounds in Bartow County. One of the mysteries of the Cherokee Nation in Georgia which has long plagued historians has been the identification of the exact location of the "Etowah Mission" established near Etowah in the early 19th Century by Moravian missionaries. The mission is believed to almost certainly have existed on the Alabama Road near the Etowah Indian Mounds, but the specific site has eluded historians. Nevertheless, a very aged stone-lined well (pictured here) is strongly believed to be the one which existed at the mission as identified in the valuation of the Cherokee property here by the U.S. government prior to the Cherokee Removal in 1838. (Photo by Olin Jackson)

(just west of Cave Spring) continued on the route of present-day U.S. Highway 411, entering Alabama one mile or so beyond Rehobeth Church and extending to Centre via Forney, Key, and Bomar, remaining on U.S. 411 all the way. At Bomar, there was a left turn to old Coloma, a prominent community before the advent of railroads.

At Centre, an additional Alabama Road bears mentioning. It was a short, but very important link from Rome, Georgia. This road began at the forks of the Oostanaula and Etowah Rivers (again, today's downtown Rome) and ran along the south bank of the Coosa River as the "Black Bluff" or "Bluff Road." It passed Brush Arbor Church and ran just below Cedar Creek Church before crossing Big Cedar Creek at a ford located just below an old mill site known as Foster's Mill.

The Black Bluff Road continued westward by State Line Church, before entering into Alabama by an early place known as "Blood." From there, it ran on by Kirks Grove, Alexis and Blaine, before reaching Centre. Today, it is known as the Rome-Centre Road. Although this road was not included on the original Georgia and Alabama surveys, it bears the tradition of being an Alabama Road, and is so indicated on later maps.

From Centre, the old road went on to cross the Coosa River at Hampton's Ferry, and proceeded into present-day Leesburg. At this point, some travelers took the "Old Georgia Road," (present-day U.S. Highway 411) to the important section which developed around Gadsden. Others bore right and northwestward through Bristow to intersect the arterial route from Gaylesville and Cedar Bluff to the Tennessee Valley or to Cotton Gin Port or Columbus, Mississippi. The juncture of these historic thoroughfares occurred at what is now a nondescript road fork between Collinsville and Sand Rock, the intersection of present-day Alabama Highways 68 and 89.

(The late Marion R. Hemperley who provided virtually all of the information used in this article, served with the Georgia State Surveyor-General Department for 30 years, 10 years of which included service as Deputy Surveyor-General. He is the author of numerous books and articles of historic research, and documented many of the historic maps and archival materials currently on file at the Georgia Department of Archives and History in Atlanta, Georgia.)

Three Prominent Cherokee Families and a GA Legacy

Their progeny were among the most talented and successful leaders of the Cherokee Nation in Georgia during the crucial decades prior to the unfortunate "Trail of Tears." They were early Scottish traders who married Cherokee females, earning the right to become full citizens in the Cherokee Nation. Over the ensuing 100 years, they were all interrelated by marriage. Today, the remains of their stately homes and other signs of their passing preserve them for posterity.

The Vann Family

Sometime before 1720, a young Scottish nobleman named James Clement Vann fled Scotland following a duel over a woman. He was charged with murder, and quite possibly would have been convicted, due to the popularity of the dead man. The British colonies in America became his new home.

James first made his way to South Carolina, living there until further legal entanglements forced him to ride northward into the Cherokee Nation of what today is encompassed by the state of Georgia. Arriving at Spring Place (near present-day Chatsworth, GA), he met and married a half-blood Cherokee woman named Ruth Gann, and was promptly accepted into the Cherokee Nation as a full citizen.

Through his trading and leadership abilities, James Clement Vann soon prospered. He and Ruth established, by way of their five children, a dynasty that played an important role in Georgia history for well over a hundred years. Most important of the offspring was James Clement Vann I, born in 1735.

The Vann fortunes continued to ascend, even during the bellicosities of 1740, when the Cherokees furnished Georgia with over 1,000 warriors to fight the Spanish at St. Augustine, Florida. The elder Vann vastly increased his plantation land and black slave holdings. He began a system of practical education and he imported professional agriculturists to establish large-scale farming.

Tall and handsome, James Clement Vann I eventually took over the reins of his Scottish father's empire, adding to the family's wealth. He married a Cherokee chieftain's daughter, WaWiLi (later

Stand Watie (1806-1871) – This courageous Cherokee was the younger brother of Buck Watie (Elias Boudinot). He was a plantation owner in Cass County and also a member of the Treaty Party. By a stroke of luck, he was absent from his home the day an assassination attempt was made on him by angry Cherokees. His uncle Major Ridge, John Ridge and Buck were not as fortunate, dying a gruesome death at the hands of the warriors. Stand Watie later became the highest ranking Indian officer in the U.S. Civil War, rising to the rank of brigadier general in the Confederate Army. *(Image courtesy of Western History Collection, University of Oklahoma Library)*

Buck Watie (1802-1839) - Also known as Elias Boudinot, Buck was editor of the *Cherokee Phoenix* newspaper. His support for the Removal Treaty caused him to be replaced as editor of the paper, and later, to be brutally murdered at his new home in Park Hill, Arkansas. His younger brother was the legendary Stand Watie. *(Image courtesy of Western History Collection, University of Oklahoma Library)*

renamed Mary Christiana), and eventually became chief of the Cherokees in his vicinity.

Vann traveled to his father's native homeland of Scotland and returned with plans to build a mansion. His plans, however, were postponed by the outbreak of the disastrous English-Cherokee War of 1759-1760, a conflagration which nearly destroyed the Cherokee Nation following the Cherokee destruction of Fort Loudoun at the confluence of the Little Tennessee and Tellico rivers. Amazingly, the Vann holdings emerged from the war intact, and WaWiLi gave birth to her first son in 1768. His name was James Vann II.

By the time James II came of age, he was a powerful man, both in physical prowess and wealth. His six-foot-five stature, aided by a penetrating dark-eyed stare, was imposing, as was his unflinching courage in the face of adversity. He, too, became a Cherokee chief, and interestingly, was the brother of Avery Vann, the great-grandfather of famous American humorist, Will Rogers.

At the height of his powers, James II owned a mansion, taverns, stores, and ferries, as well as over 60 slaves on a plantation spread over hundreds of acres of prime farmland. He moved back and forth across these holdings, closely monitoring each and increasing his wealth daily.

Wealthy though he was, this latest Chief Vann suffered from a Jekyll-and-Hyde personality. Warm, kind and generous when sober, he was a veritable monster when inebriated. He was, even according to the Moravian missionaries whom he welcomed at Spring Place, "... . feared by many, loved by few."

In his sober periods, half-blooded James Vann II accomplished many admirable undertakings, including the importation and support of the Moravians, allowing them to build a mission and educate Cherokee children so that they might assimilate into the White population. He had judged correctly the circumstances necessary to preserve his race in the face of the White onslaught. He just didn't count on the destructive power of greed after gold was discovered in the state.

James II was also instrumental in the development of the Federal Road built between Nashville, Tennessee and Augusta, Georgia. Just prior to construction of the road, Vann had completed the construction of the impressive brick mansion planned by his father, the only such dwelling ever built by an Indian in Georgia. Today, Vann's mansion still stands, an important historic landmark in the state.

James Vann II had two wives, much to the dismay of the Moravian brothers. One of them was a mixed-blood woman named Elizabeth Thornton who lived in a rough-hewn log cabin some distance from the mansion. Little is known today about the Thornton family prior to Elizabeth, but it is known that she bore

John Ross (1790-1866) – As principal chief of the Cherokee Nation from 1828 until his death, Ross nevertheless both appeared to – and in fact did – have much more White blood than Cherokee. He was an eighth-blood Cherokee. He also was unflinchingly opposed to the treaty which would cede the Cherokee lands to the Whites, and oversaw the assassination of the members of the Treaty Party. *(Photo courtesy of Western History Collection, University of Oklahoma Library)*

James Vann one child – the beautiful and important Delilah Amelia (1785-1838).

Vann's other wife, Margaret, or "Peggy," as he called her, lived in the mansion with their five children, including Joe, who was often later referred to as "Rich Joe Vann," to distinguish him from another quarter-blood individual of the same name.

Though fortunate in health and welfare, James Vann II ultimately became a victim of his own over-indulgence. He was assassinated from ambush at a tavern in 1809 at the age of 43. *(Readers please see "The Murder & Burial of Chief James Vann" in this publication.)*

Mystery & History in Georgia

Final Cherokee Capital in the East - Following the removal of the Cherokees in 1838, the town of New Echota, former capital of the Cherokee Nation in the Southeast, fell into ruin and the land reverted to agricultural usage. In the foreground in this photo, the last remains of the Buck Watie aka Elias Boudinot home are visible – a few foundation stones and the outline of the old well. Buck, who was the older brother of Stand Watie and first editor of the **Cherokee Phoenix** newspaper, constructed a large two-story home on this site in 1827. *(Photo courtesy of Joe Griffith)*

Vann's Last Will & Testament left the mansion and most of his other possessions to Joe, but the other Cherokee chiefs later partially overturned the Will, distributing some of the possessions to Vann's wives and other children.

James Vann II was a big man, standing at least six-foot, five-inches, perhaps taller. Interestingly, most everything which he ordered to be built for and installed at the Spring Place mansion was intentionally constructed "over-size" for that reason. Everything, that is, except the third level of the home which was originally designed as a nursery.

The cabin where Elizabeth Thornton lived and raised Delilah until her father's death rotted and disappeared long ago. The site where it once existed, however is still known. The mansion – constructed of solid red brick fired on the premises – has stood the test of time, even weathering a fire on the landing of the stairwell in the 1830s, after the home had been vacated by the Vanns and was coveted and being contested by rival Whites.

Rogers Family Line

John Rogers (1774-1851), often called "Nolichucky Jack" by the Indians, was born to John and Nancy Rogers, a family which had come from the Surry County sections of Virginia. John, Sr. had waged war on the side of the patriots during the U.S. Revolutionary War, so the younger John had been thoroughly indoctrinated with the concepts of personal freedom in his early years. He set off at an early age to make his own way in the world, ultimately settling in the Cherokee Nation just east of the Chattahoochee River in Georgia.

There, the younger John met and fell in love with Sarah Cordery (ca. 1785-1842), the oldest daughter of Thomas Cordery (a Scotch trader) and Sonicooie Cordery (a fullblood Cherokee who was later renamed Susannah).

Sarah was, of course, half-Cherokee. Soon after the marriage, John built a fine home near the mouth of Suwanee Creek (not far from presentday Suwanee, Georgia), where he began what eventually became a remarkably-profitable

John Rogers (1774-1851) - The son of a veteran of the American Revolution, John Rogers became an Indian countryman, marrying Sarah Cordery, a half-blood Cherokee Indian. John lived almost 50 years on the Chattahoochee River near the boundaries of present-day Forsyth and Fulton Counties, and his former home still stands there today. *(Photo courtesy of Don L. Shadburn from a miniature portrait.)*

William Rogers (1805-1870) - William was the second son of John Rogers and Sarah Cordery. He was a one-quarter blood Cherokee, and became a strong champion of Indian rights in Georgia during the last decade of the tribe's existence in the Southeast. This profile of William was sketched by an unknown artist of Rogers' day. *(Print courtesy of Don L. Shadburn)*

farming operation. During a 50-year span of time, he amassed a small fortune, and was able to give all his children, including sons William and Johnson, good educations.

William and Johnson soon figured prominently in Cherokee affairs. During the War of 1812, particularly the portion involving the "Red Stick" Creek Indians uprising, John served on the staff of General Andrew Jackson. He rode a very dangerous mission from Fort Strother to Monticello, Georgia, and fought at the Battle of Horseshoe Bend.

Interestingly, to the surprise of many people, the original home built by William Rogers – "Oakland" – still exists today in north Fulton County, and at last check, was owned by a descendant of the family – Michael Rogers.

A short distance from William's home, the former home of John Rogers also still exists on a tree-sheltered hilltop facing the wide floodplain of Suwanee Creek. At last check, this property was owned by a young artist and her husband who preferred anonymity.

William's home has been significantly renovated, right down to the floor stenciling, and continues to be a valuable resource to the family. Will Rogers, Jr. has even utilized the site in past years for film work.

McNair Family

It was during the campaign against the Creek Indians that David McNair (1774-1836) was introduced to John Rogers, an acquaintance which would later prove noteworthy. McNair was a prominent and respected citizen of the

The former home of Indian countryman John Rogers still stands in north Fulton County. *(Photo by Olin Jackson)*

Cherokee Nation, having come into the nation in 1800, according to testimony recorded in 1829. He owned a beautiful farm in the rolling hills near the Conasauga River in Tennessee, approximately one and one-quarter miles beyond the Georgia border.

McNair built his tall, beautiful wife – Delilah Amelia (daughter of James Vann II and Elizabeth Thornton) – a very handsome brick home, complete with intricate Indian-carved fireplace mantles, brick smoke houses, and brick houses for his numerous slaves. McNair prospered, and Delilah gave him six healthy, handsome children.

To reach the site of the former McNair home, one must travel on U.S. Highway 411 north into Tennessee. A historic marker will soon be encountered which explains the former site of "McNair's Stand" was once located near there, just to the west of the highway. Visitors to the site today are immediately impressed with the stark beauty of the rolling farmland.

A neat impressive home has been built in recent years atop a low hill at the end of a long, gracefully-curving drive. Just inside the gate to the property, the walled gravesite of David and Delilah McNair may still be seen today.

The McNair mansion itself still stood near the road until 1936, when it was destroyed by a tornado. Bits and pieces of the home, such as a mantle survived, and are still in the possession of area residents. The brick foundation of the once-impressive home also still exists, but all else has disappeared.

McNair was a staunch friend to both the Cherokees and Whites, performing yeoman service in the struggle to preserve the Cherokee homeland in Georgia. He acted as superintendent of the Cherokee Nation at tribal voting; gave religious leaders free transportation to do their work; and he, just as the Vanns, was supportive of the Moravian missionaries, giving them free lodging for three years when they were forced out of Georgia by the state legislature. He also provided them with a small brick building so they could conduct education classes for young Cherokees.

McNair's house, surprisingly, was only 18 miles north of James Vann's "Spring Place," so he was a frequent guest at the Vann mansion.

He also kept up his acquaintance with his old war companion John Rogers, and eventually, John's son – William – became enamored of McNair's daughter, Mary Vann McNair. In 1828, he married her, and began construction of his home, which he called "Oakland."

William and his brother Johnson, were educated at the Lawrenceville Academy in Gwinnett County, Georgia. Their father was personally acquainted with various governors of Georgia, as well as with the leadership of the Cherokee Nation. The two sons, therefore, were very knowledgeable of governmental affairs. William was particularly adroit in that area.

By 1829, when the Georgia State Legislature passed a series of laws designed to remove the Cherokees' citizenship rights and to appropriate their land, William Rogers was 24. He and his brother worked tirelessly for the Cherokee interests, both in Georgia and in Washington.

In 1830, after passage of the Indian Removal Bill by the U.S. Congress, William and Johnson became outspoken critics of Cherokee Chief John Ross, and joined the so-called "Treaty Party," along with Major Ridge, a full-blood Cherokee, and Elias Boudinot, editor of the remarkable *Cherokee Phoenix* newspaper, the first of its kind for Native Americans.

By 1834, a storm of change had descended upon the Cherokees. William Rogers and his associates had become convinced that it would be better for the Cherokees to be removed under their own terms than to be forced out under military pressure. He exerted all his efforts to convince the other Cherokees of this necessity, but he failed.

Finally, the *Treaty of New Echota* (the Cherokee Capitol) was signed on December 29, 1835. William and his brother joined Stand Watie (another prominent Cherokee leader) in signing the treaty that John Ross and his faction considered to be fraudulent. Because he had signed the treaty, numerous threats (and even attempts) were made on William's life. Johnson Rogers left Georgia to go to Washington, where he worked diligently for the Cherokees until his death at age 61.

In spite of William's optimism, the Cherokee Removal of 1838 was a nightmare for the Indians. While awaiting transportation across the Hiwassee River on the first leg, Delilah Vann McNair died of a stroke, becoming one of the first of over 4,000 Cherokees to perish during the terrible forced march.

In a demonstration of a semblance

Michael Rogers, the great-great-grandson of William Rogers, stands in front of his forebear's former home. The property remained in the Rogers family from the 1840s to the 1950s when it was sold to an outside interest. In 1980, the Rogers family was able to re-acquire the property. *(Photo by Olin Jackson)*

of compassion, the army allowed the McNair children to return Delilah's body for burial next to her beloved husband who had died two years earlier. Their remains exist there in the same spot today on their cherished homeland.

William Rogers paid $150.00 for inscribed grave markers for both the McNairs. A short time later, on September 1, 1839, William's wife, Mary, was killed in a horse accident, leaving William with four small children to raise.

Like many other mixed-bloods and Indian "countrymen," William and his family had opted, under the Treaty of New Echota, to become citizens of Georgia. They were granted citizenship on December 29, 1838. William accordingly lived out his life at his home with his second wife, a Moravian teacher named Louisa Ruede. He died peacefully at Oakland on April 12, 1870.

The Mysterious Night Riders of the Mountains of Pickens

In the years following the U.S. Civil War, strange individuals in still-stranger garb, patrolled the mountainous region of what today is Pickens County. They were vigilantes whose sole purpose in life was to rid the area of U.S. Revenue agents.

In 1889, some twenty odd men in the Sharptop Militia District of Pickens County, Georgia, gathered around a blazing fire in a secluded area back in the mountains. They were vigilantes who had dubbed themselves *"The Honest Man's Friend and Protector"* (hereinafter referred to as HMF&P), and for the next two years, they provided Pickens with a period of unwanted statewide notoriety.

Dressed in *"weird and terrifying black cloaks and hoods,"* the men always gathered under the cover of darkness. Their existence was generated out of a self-described need *"to fight the revenue laws for the good of the country and ourselves."*

The men all swore to protect each other, even if it meant perjuring themselves in court. They would help each other *"in bearing the business of life,"* and promised death to any member who divulged their secrets.

Members of HMF&P did not use their own names in signing their bylaws, but assumed the names of local law enforcement officials and the men who testified against "moonshiners" for rewards (called "reporters"). Members who failed to appear when summoned for a meeting or task were fined fifty cents. Members arriving drunk at a meeting were tempered with the whip.

North Georgia has a history of such groups. Vigilantes helped remove the Cherokees in the 1830s. Before the Civil War, secret political societies such as the "Know Nothings" and related organizations also existed. Later, groups of mountain men banded together to fight for or against the Confederacy. And the well-known Ku Klux Klan (KKK)

The Pickens County night riders were not concerned with racial circumstances.

334

served as a model for later secret societies in the mountains after the war.

Although identified then and since with the KKK, the members of the HMF&P were not Klansmen. The Pickens County night riders were not concerned with racial circumstances. Their one and only objective was the elimination of the revenue agents who were depriving the mountaineers from their main source of income – untaxed mountain whiskey, better known as "moonshine."

During the first half of the 1860s, the Confederacy had prohibited the distillation (production) of alcoholic beverages, in order to conserve foodstuffs such as the corn used to make the liquor. After the war, the federal government continued the trend, imposing licenses and taxes on the "luxury" and "vice" of alcohol.

This "luxury," however, was the only real source of income available to many small farmers in the mountains, since tillable land was very limited in the area, and rich river-bottom sediment capable of growing substantial crops was almost nonexistent. The federal taxes being imposed upon the alcoholic beverages of the mountaineers – to put it bluntly – were more than they could afford.

Faced with the choice of losing their livelihoods or carrying on their occupations in secret by working "blockade stills," many mountain men in Pickens County and elsewhere chose the latter. They had little choice.

On a Sunday night on November 10, 1889, the HMF&P had reached a fever pitch in Pickens. They gathered in the "Sea Field" to organize their first raid.

The laws were forcing them to become outlaws.

The United States Treasury responded with a system of paying local citizens a fee for "spying" on their moonshining neighbors. Persons later arrested were taken to Atlanta for trial, leaving their families with no alternative but the sale of family possessions for the payment of legal costs. If convicted (and virtually all were convicted), a moonshiner would be sent to prison while his family struggled to survive on little more than charity.

The situation to the mountaineers/moonshiners therefore was an extremely serious matter – even to the point of dying if necessary. Violence against the revenue agents – and the neighbors who became spies – became a common affair.

In neighboring Murray County in 1888, and almost immediately afterwards in Pickens, Gilmer, Whitfield, and Gordon counties, this resistance had reached the level of organized vigilantism. There is no doubt they were desperate individuals, but beyond their illegal moonshining endeavors, most were far from criminals. No record of previous illegal activity has been uncovered for any of the Pickens County vigilantes.

The federal commissioner of Pickens at that time testified at one point that the Pickens County vigilantes – with whom he apparently was familiar – were men of good character. They reportedly included five former or current county officials, but the acts they eventually committed marked them as criminals for life.

On a Sunday night on November 10, 1889, the HMF&P had reached a fever pitch in Pickens. They gathered in the "Sea Field" to organize their first raid.

The following Tuesday, they entered the house of a man who, despite their warnings, was in Atlanta testifying against their moonshining brethren. After robbing the man's home of food, some of which they scattered down the road, the HMF&P burned the house, sparing only a stack of hay and a cow and a calf. The owner's family was not home at the time.

The situation was different on December 3, when the HMF&P came down Sharptop Mountain, passing around a bottle en route to a rendezvous at a nearby church. From there, dressed in bizarre and terrifying disguises (their captain wore "blacking" on his face, a white moustache, purple coating on his chin, and an oil skin coat), they walked to a house on Jones Mountain to pay a visit to another man testifying in Atlanta.

The wife and children of their intended victim were at home asleep when the HMF&P stormed the farm from two sides. The wife was awakened by the noise of the stable burning. Running outside into the freezing cold night, she was met with gunfire, shouts and laughing. The house was burned next, while the frightened mother gathered her children. The leader of the vigilantes mocked the baby's crying.

The HMF&P's of Pickens County eventually burned the homes of at least three men who testified in Atlanta. Folklore and local legends have exaggerated the burnings of the group over the ensuing years to *"100 houses in the Marble Hill area."*

Activities such as these were common in north Georgia during this period, as small, desperate but otherwise law-abiding farmers fought for what they considered to be their chief means of supporting their families. In Pickens County, however, the activities of the HMF&P were quelled after a brief two-year stint.

When the incidences of arson began on November 12, 1889, a posse of deputies were organized. Local lawmen and federal agents began a practice of rounding up the persons against whom testimony had been rendered in Atlanta. In the first instance of these arrests, the men were brought before the justice of the peace in the Sharptop District, but were strangely released. (The agents didn't know the JP himself was one of the house burners.)

Despite this fact, the posses – whose numbers were increased – continued increasingly to disrupt the activities of the HMF&P. Some of the night riders fled to other states to assume new identities and lives. Other members remained, but were forced to post "lookouts" and patrols to avoid capture, a necessity which began draining their resources.

In one gun battle

In one gun battle with a posse, one member of the HMF&P was seriously wounded.

with a posse, one member of the HMF&P was seriously wounded. Other members were eventually captured, and to avoid prosecution, they began informing on their comrades.

A copy of the bylaws of the organization – along with a black cloak and hood – was recovered from a hollow tree following the confession of one participant. The leader of the vigilantes was arrested with another member and confined in the Pickens County Jail in Jasper. A group of their friends helped them escape during a storm on the night of February 13, 1890, but they were soon recaptured.

The conviction of these "night riders" proved to be much more difficult than the arrests. In May, 1890, seven men *"who a year ago were put down as staunch and respectable,"* were tried for arson. Evidence and witnesses (principally HMF&P members who turned state's evidence) could only be obtained for a single house burning incident.

The *Atlanta Journal* reported that there *"was never such excitement over the trial of criminal cases in Georgia or the South. Hundreds of men and women thronged the courtroom and the town."*

The seven men ultimately were sentenced to life in prison. Following the close of the U.S. Civil War, and all the damage wrought by General William T. Sherman's infamous "March To The Sea," in which town after town was put to the torch, Georgians had become significantly sensitized to the crime of arson. As a result, though it was often difficult to obtain the proper evidence for an arson conviction, when suspected criminals in fact were finally convicted, they were punished with a maximum sentence.

At the time of this trial, these seven men were reported as the largest single

Individual resistance to the revenue laws however, continues, even to this day.

group sent to prison in the state's history. The convicted men ultimately were sent to work in the coal mines of Dade County, Georgia. Among them was the leader of the HMF&P and his son. He was killed and his son seriously wounded in the Coal City mutiny of June 21, 1891.

Ironically, the son escaped from prison on January 5, 1893, and returned to Pickens County long enough to inspire a number of stories. He subsequently moved to another region where it is assumed he changed his name and began life anew.

Ten other members of the HMF&P were tried in Atlanta for conspiracy before the Federal Circuit Court of May, 1891. Certain of a conviction, their lawyers were announcing plans for an appeal even before a verdict had been rendered by a jury. One can only imagine their surprise when a verdict of *"Not Guilty"* was announced. Despite this fact, five of the defendants were almost immediately tried and convicted for defrauding the federal government of alcoholic beverage taxes.

The persistence of federal officials eventually ended the HMF&P throughout north Georgia. Individual resistance to the revenue laws however, continues, even to this day.

The Shocking 1923 Pickens County Jail Break

The small-town lock-ups and "calabooses" from yesteryear have virtually disappeared from the landscape as newer, larger, and more modern facilities have been built. Some, however, can still be found – unused of course – in small-town historic tours. One such aged county jail still exists in the north Georgia township of Jasper, where, on a sunny afternoon in 1923, the old Pickens County Jail became the site of quite a bit of excitement.

Most accounts of legal incarceration, by nature, are tragic, but at least one chapter in the history of the old Pickens County Jail (now listed on the *National Register of Historic Places*) includes more than a touch of comedy, and a fair amount of heroism as well.

At 5:00 P.M. on May 23, 1923, Pickens County Sheriff D.P. Poole climbed the stairs to the cells on the second floor of the jail to bring his prisoners the usual bucket of fresh water and to lock them in their individual cells for the night. A seasoned lawman such as Sheriff Poole normally would have exercised more caution in such a situation. On this day, however, Poole apparently misjudged the criminals confined in his "accommodations."

Among the "guests" on the second floor that day, was an individual by the name of Ralph King, accused of *"assault with intent to commit murder,"* and his accomplice, Fred Hill. The latter had escaped from this same jail hardly a month earlier via a route which surprisingly had been used by several previous prisoners. The bars in the windows of the cells apparently had not been sturdily installed, and Hill had found it quite simple to loosen and remove one of the bars, and then slide quietly down to the back porch roof.

The Jails

As is obvious from the above, the Pickens County Jail was not the most dependable of lockups in the 1920s. It had some age on it and was showing some "wear and tear." In the 1920s, however, small towns such as Jasper were lucky to even have a prison as sturdy as the one used on this day.

The first Pickens jail was built in the 1850s. It was two stories tall and made of logs. It was burned amidst the chaos of the U.S. Civil War – probably by some of the "law-abiding" hangers-on who were following the troops of General William T. Sherman through the state.

The second jail – built after the war

338

– was made of rock and existed behind the presentday courthouse. The construction of new jails historically was not a priority for the Pickens County citizens and government. If a criminal was unfortunate enough to be captured and incarcerated for a crime in Pickens County, then he – or she – simply had to suffer the consequences of what in the late 19th and early 20th Centuries were very inhospitable circumstances.

By 1906, the then "old jail" had apparently absolutely reached the end of its useful life, and a new structure was built. It was described in April of 1907 as "... *constructed with all of the modern conveniences, both to the health and good keeping of the prisoners.*" However, fifteen or twenty years of wear and tear by unruly prisoners quickly takes a toll on any jail, and the 1907 facility was no exception.

Assaulting The Sheriff

On the day that Fred Hill escaped from the jail for the first time, he had been visited by his wife earlier that morning. For reasons unknown today, she had mentioned in passing to one of the guards that she would be staying with her parents, so the pursuing lawmen had a relatively good hunch where they might recapture Hill.

Interestingly, despite being surprised by lawmen on the premises of his wife's parents' home, the determined fugitive nevertheless eluded his captors once again as he lit out across a swamp. He was later apprehended some 50 or 60 miles away in Rome, Georgia, and had been back in jail only a week, when he and King decided to attack Sheriff Poole in order to escape once again.

Despite the background of these two men, Poole apparently did not consider them dangerous. He didn't even holster a handgun as he ascended the stairs to tend to them for the night.

At the top of the stairs, the two men – who by then had escaped from their cell – jumped Poole. One of them had a brick which he had worked loose from the jail wall, and the other had a bottle. Poole fell to the jail floor after being struck by the men, and pretended to be unconscious.

While the men searched him for a weapon, Poole recovered and began fighting back. The prisoners attempted to drag Poole into a cell, but the determined sheriff continued to struggle. With exhaustion near at hand, the two men finally decided flight was their best option, and abandoned the determined sheriff.

They turned to run down the stairs to Poole's living quarters on the first floor of the jail, but the sheriff was anything if not a brave lawman. Never one to be easily conquered, he latched onto the two prisoners with all his might, apparently hoping to slow them down long enough for help to arrive.

Help On The Way

By this time, Poole's wife had heard the commotion and obvious struggle taking place upstairs, and had run to the bottom of the stairs, screaming like a banshee. Though obviously in shock, she at least was raising enough of a ruckus to draw attention to the situation from outside the jail.

Jasper resident Oscar Champion lived next door to the jail at that time. (His home existed on the spot occupied, as of this writing, by the automated teller banking machine.) Mrs. Poole's screams had been effective, for Champion had been alerted and had run onto the back porch of the jail. Realizing that a prisoner escape was in progress, he ran into the sheriff's living quarters and found Poole's pistol.

By this time, the two prisoners had finally reached the bottom of the stairs and were only inches away from freedom. King finally broke free and leaped from the jail porch, heading towards a cotton field (a site occupied today by the Jasper Elementary School) and freedom.

Criminal Flight Interrupted

Oscar Champion had never fired a weapon at anyone before (or since) in his life. However, on this day, he closed his eyes, pointed the pistol at the escapee, and ordered the fleeing man to stop.

When the man failed to halt, Poole yelled at Champion to shoot. Oscar squeezed off a round from the big pistol and the countryside around the normally peaceful mountain community resounded from the discharge.

According to Mr. Champion, despite the fact that King was running at an incredible clip, he almost fell backwards in his immediate effort to halt and raise his hands. He then marched quietly back to the jail as the sheriff subdued the other man.

This, however, was not the conclusion of this tale. Things were just beginning to get interesting....

Determined Prisoners

The sheriff, as one might imagine, assumed the desperate attempts at freedom were at an end, and that he would simply return his two escapees to the lockup with the rest of the prisoners on the second floor. By this time, however, the general population of remaining prisoners had been exposed to a taste of freedom as well, and were reluctant to acquiesce so easily.

According to reports, the detainees began raining a shower of bricks, soft drink bottles and disinfectant upon anyone who attempted to reach them, refusing to allow the sheriff access back into the facility. By this point, Poole's patience was exhausted, and he responded to this revolt with another heavy round from the revolver.

The prisoners, however were not so easily deterred. Many of them had been fired upon previously – some of them many times. They responded with still more bottles and bricks.

By this point, however, some fifty or sixty men, most of them armed, gathered around the jail and one of them – Felix Allred – directed the prisoners to give up or die (All things being equal, prison revolts and negotiated settlements simply did not exist in those days.) In 1923, Pickens County was barely beyond frontier status, and frontier justice therefore still prevailed. The disgruntled prisoners, realizing they had little choice, finally succumbed, but remained restless and agitated.

Ironically, the two escapees from that day were eventually found *"Not Guilty"* of the original charges for which they were being held, but were each sentenced to two years in prison for the attack on Sheriff Poole.

Seeking a New Profession

Poole, by this time, had decided to pursue a profession other than law enforcement. He chose not to seek reelection to his position, no doubt strongly encouraged to depart by his wife whose nerves were shot.

The late Oscar Champion subsequently decided to put some distance between himself and the jail as well, moving to nearby Tate, Georgia, and living to be over 100 years of age.

Legendary Lawman from Pickens :

County Policeman Lee Cape Murdered Over "Moonshine"

The folklore associated with the Southern Appalachian Mountains is replete with descriptions of "moonshine" and the violence often associated with this former staple of the uplands. The murder of Lee Cape, a fabled lawman in north Georgia's Pickens County, undoubtedly will be remembered as one of the more grisly chapters in this enduring saga.

Of all the information associated with Pickens County, no single episode remains as controversial as the gruesome 1927 murder of County Policeman W. Lee Cape. On a sunny September 17 afternoon of that year, the respected lawman lost his life in one of the most heinous murders in Pickens County history.

Pro-Cape accounts (including those of the newspapers of that day and from interviews of persons who knew him well) contend that Cape was guilty of nothing more than law enforcement, an effort for which he paid the ultimate price. Other suspicions, however, maintain that he was excessive and over-zealous in the performance of his duties, and that in the final analysis, he simply became careless and fell victim to a wanton murderer. At the very least, he was excessively confident of his safety in what normally would be considered very dangerous circumstances.

Interestingly, as a simple county policeman in 1927, Cape's annual salary was anything if not modest. The budgets of rural mountain counties in north Georgia were exceptionally small – as therefore were the salaries paid to county employees such as Cape. Nevertheless, Cape owned what could only be described in his day as a very fine home in Hinton, Georgia, which, as of this writing, still stands. He also possessed other luxuries such as a fine automobile.

Lee Cape 'On the Take?'

In an assessment of the circumstances today, one has to wonder how Cape managed to obtain the relatively-expensive items he possessed, which, in that day and time, were only possessed by the wealthy. Was Lee Cape "on the take" in his monitoring of the "moonshine" (untaxed liquor production) in his region? One cannot help but wonder about that possibility today, when considering all the facts, but absolutely nothing either before or after his death even hinted of dishonesty.

The system of enforcement of the federal revenue laws involving untaxed liquor definitely did not help the situation. Revenue agents and deputy U.S. marshals such as Cape were not paid salaries, but rather fees based upon the number of illegal distilleries or "stills" they captured and the number of arrests they made.

As a result of this system, the agents were often accused of making fraudulent arrests to pad their fees, and their incomes reportedly were often supplemented by bribes, and even by profiteering from the illegal sale of captured stills back to their former owners after they were in the custody of law enforcement officials. Such was the environment in which Cape worked, and the reason mountain moonshiners could quickly react in a violent manner.

Early Life

Born in South Carolina on June 5, 1862, during the height of the U.S. Civil War, Lee Cape was orphaned at an early age. He undoubtedly learned to be self-sufficient and independent at an early age. By 1880, he was living with his grandmother Cape in Pickens County, Georgia.

By 1927, Lee Cape had spent more than forty years in law enforcement, and was a respected citizen and policeman. Those who knew him agree he was determined in his efforts to enforce laws against the trafficking of the untaxed liquor ("moonshining" and "bootlegging") which was so prevalent in the north Georgia region at this time.

The "Roaring Twenties" was a time of firearms, illegal liquor, and violence. In general, Chicago was – and remains today - the symbol of these times, but in point of fact, the social ill was a nationwide phenomenon. Much of the illegal liquor was produced in remote mountain regions, and Pickens County was as active as any locale.

It was during these times that the counties added extra deputies and county police (such as Lee Cape) to ease public fears and to beef up rural enforcement efforts in what had become an American guerrilla war against those persons who made and transported the illegal liquor.

Lee Cape reportedly was one of the more active county policemen who pursued the illicit traffickers. As a result, he was a sharp thorn in the side of many mountaineers who depended upon the production of illegal liquor for income. He therefore would also have been a very obvious target for a bribe.

Dangerous Profession

Nevertheless, as early as 1890, Cape's name was discovered on a list of law enforcement officials targeted by Pickens County vigilantes known as "The Night Riders" (also known as "The Honest Man's Friend & Protector"), who were burning and raiding homes of law enforcement officials and others in retribution of the enforcement of the liquor laws by local authorities. The Night Riders, however, were apprehended before they were able to savage Cape's home.

Despite the threats on his life and property, Lee Cape eventually advanced in service and was appointed as a deputy United States marshal. To put this in perspective, the famed gunfight behind the O.K. Corral in Tombstone, Arizona, which involved another deputy United States marshal – Virgil Earp – and his deputy, Wyatt Earp, had occurred only a few years earlier in 1881.

Policeman Lee Cape Murdered for "Moonshine"

In 1893, Lee Cape reportedly was apprehending and bringing in moonshiners almost daily. According to records, he even arrested his own sons on occasion, so his diligence and effectiveness is a matter of record.

Family History of Violence

Cape's sons, in fact, frequently appeared in the Pickens County court records, and were the subject of almost as much sensation as Cape's untimely death. In 1924, Levi, amazingly, was sentenced to life in prison (he was paroled in 1934) for killing his brother, Hobert, and leaving Lee Cape for dead in Hinton where the family lived. The third son, Waldo, was killed in 1942 in Hinton, during a drunken brawl.

It can only be considered ironic today, that despite his heroic effort at the elimination of illegal alcohol in the Pickens County area, much of Lee Cape's family was erased by the illicit substance – their lives snuffed out by excessive consumption, violence, and the violence of the times in which they lived.

Cape took his job of law enforcement – particularly as involved the illegal liquor trade – very seriously. Law enforcement during these times in north Georgia was an extremely dangerous occupation, yet Cape, surprisingly, never expressed any concern or gave any indication that he feared for his life. He frequently traveled unarmed, and his "deputies" in his raids, more often than not, were his wife or his young grandsons.

Despite the extreme hazards and physical requirements of such an occupation, Cape always seemed up to the task. Even as a middle-aged man, he was known to be fleet of foot, able to out-run most fleeing offenders.

To some, Cape was reckless; to others, he was simply relentless. Almost invariably, however, he was respected. As late as 1922, he was described as having never harmed anyone in the pursuit of his duties. Even in the testimony in the trial of persons accused of his murder, including that of the men later convicted of the crime, Cape was described as well-liked and even as a friend of the very individuals he often arrested.

Accidental Homicide

Cape's neighbor, Tom Evans, however, remembered that Cape was once given a rude awakening late in his career. According to accounts published at the time in the *Pickens County Progress*, at 11:00 A.M. on Friday, April 7, 1922, Cape, with the sheriff and other county policemen, had been working a road-block all night, successfully arresting bootleggers at the Aiken Cemetery, three miles north of Jasper.

The lawmen had just arrested thirty-three-year-old Willie Pickett McFarland of Keithsburg Community in Cherokee County. McFarland's buggy had been obviously overloaded, and upon inspection, had revealed a load of contraband whiskey. When the bootlegger had attempted to escape, he and Cape became involved in a struggle. In the midst of the fight, a pistol which Cape had confiscated from another prisoner accidentally discharged, killing McFarland.

The victim was described as an honest, hard-working, peach-grower, with a wife and two children. His mistake, according to the paper, had been an attempt to supplement his pitiful income with proceeds from illegal whiskey trafficking. The paper exonerated Cape, describing him as *"fearless, truthful, and always self-possessed."* Tom Evans, however, remembered that Lee Cape was "never the same" after the McFarland shooting.

McFarland's widow subsequently

moved to Alabama. Interestingly, by crossing the state line for her residence, she was able to sue Cape in federal court for the death of her husband and her loss of income. She won $1,273.00 of the $35,000.00 she sought in damages for Cape's "recklessness."

Relentless Lawman

Lee Cape, however, remained relentless in his pursuit of moonshiners and bootleggers. With his usual disdain of personal safety, he departed Hinton on what would be his last raid on September 17, 1927, at 7:30 A.M. His open "Touring Car" was driven by his sixteen-year-old grandson, Surber Cape, and they were accompanied by Surber's young friend, Will Evans (Tom's brother). The boys carried a shotgun; Lee Cape had a pistol.

According to later testimony, the group reached the top of nearby Henderson Mountain near the Cherokee County line approximately half an hour later. Lee Cape stepped out of the car and instructed the boys to search the western slope of the mountain. They agreed to fire shots if anyone in the group discovered anything. They were to meet at a nearby house at 3:00 P.M.

At 12:30, the boys discovered a large illegal liquor operation ("still") which had been set up for fermenting beer and producing liquor. They fired the shotgun as instructed, but Cape did not answer. They then drove to the rendezvous point. An hour later, when Cape still had not appeared, the boys drove around the mountain searching for the lawman.

According to later court testimony, at approximately 3:30 P.M., the boys encountered three men – Lindsey Evans, his brother Hoyt Evans, and C.L. Smith – who were blocking the narrow road with their car. Lindsey Evans recognized the boys' car as Lee Cape's vehicle, and the men angrily charged up to the boys yelling and cursing, apparently guessing that the youngsters were helping Cape search the neighborhood for moonshine operations.

Surber, realizing he was in danger, quickly attempted to shift the vehicle into reverse, but when the stubborn machine wouldn't comply, the boy sprang from the car and ran. The by-then enraged Evans reportedly grabbed young Will Evans (no relation to Lindsey or Hoyt Evans) by the head and attacked him with a knife, cutting one of his fingers. The younger Evans broke free, however, and fled also.

Young Assistants Assaulted

Surber, shortly thereafter, arrived at the home of Dott Pharr, a local bailiff, and reported the attack. Pharr reached Cape's automobile as the Evans brothers and Smith were fleeing, having stolen the boys' shotgun.

According to the courtroom testimony, the three men stopped at the home of Lindsey Evans who went inside to retrieve his own shotgun. Evans then checked his weapon – firing both barrels – then climbed back into the car.

Meanwhile, Lee Cape was oblivious to the circumstances unfolding around him. He had not heard the boys' signal shot because he had left the mountain to explore nearby Salacoa Creek. At some point after 12:00 noon, he began to walk back towards the scheduled rendezvous with the boys – a walk which would prove to be Cape's last.

R. Seab Newborn saw the county policeman as he trudged down the road, and then, thirty minutes later, on the same road, saw the car and the three men who had accosted the boys. Newborn later testified that twenty to thirty minutes later, he heard shots.

On their initial encounter on the road, the three men reportedly passed Cape without attempting to harm him, but Lindsey Evans angrily demanded that they turn around so he could confront Cape. The driver of the vehicle, Hoyt Evans, however, continued on, apparently preferring to avoid further problems.

Unbeknownst to Hoyt however, the spot he picked to eventually park the vehicle (the Evans family home on old Goshen Road, one and one-half miles below the former site of the community of Talmadge) was the very spot at which Cape was scheduled to rendezvous with his two young assistants. Lindsey Evans was later quoted in court as stating "Me or old man Lee Cape one is going to die, when he comes out the road."

Date With Destiny

As he hiked up the road that day, Lee Cape reached the men in the car and in his usual inquisitive manner, inquired as to the owner of the vehicle. Cape, familiar with the men and apparently suspecting something amiss, began casually searching behind the vehicle's seats – undoubtedly for illegal liquor.

At this point, Lindsey Evans reportedly warned Cape that he would have to pay for any damages to the vehicle. Had he known of the danger afoot, Cape undoubtedly would have reacted differently, but he had no reason to suspect the murderous circumstances which were slowly unfolding around him. His reply to Evans's statement reflected Cape's usual fearless (and some would say reckless) demeanor.

"Well that would be very easy done I guess," Cape was quoted as saying. "You've been tryin' to run ablazin' around all the time; nobody ain't scared of you."

Those words proved to be Cape's last. Witnesses at the scene later testified that Evans quickly took out a shotgun (specifically whose shotgun was never proven) and fired three shots point-blank into Cape, killing the famed lawman almost instantly. He fell onto the side of the roadway, dead from multiple wounds.

Hoyt Evans, at this point, grabbed the weapon from his brother and pleaded with him to stop. Eyewitnesses at the scene ran into the Evans home.

The killer, however, was unrepentant, and threatened to shoot his fleeing neighbors as well as his brother. Cape's body was stuffed into the trunk of the men's automobile and the two brothers then drove off.

Any hope of an unwitnessed disposal of the body was virtually wasted, for in their panic, the two men careened up the road from Fairmount to Adairsville at an incredible rate of speed. Their reckless driving and open touring cars (they drove two vehicles to dispose of the body) made identification easy for the numerous individuals who later testified against them.

Disposal of the Body

Grisly and varying accounts of what next transpired have been circulated for years. According to court testimony, the corpse was mutilated in a twisted hope that this would in some manner render identification of the body impossible (For reasons unknown today, the fact that the crime had been committed in full view of several witnesses seemed to have been lost upon the Evans brothers.).

Whatever the circumstances, at what is still (at the time of this writing) a lonely dirt crossroads five miles south

It was Lee Cape's perceived destruction of an illicit production site for untaxed liquor in Pickens County, which is believed to have ignited a vendetta against him that cost him his life. *(Photo courtesy of the GA Dept. of Archives & History)*

of Adairsville, the body of Lee Cape was dumped. Horrifyingly, Cape's head was severed from his body and mutilated by shotgun blasts which rendered the face unrecognizable. The head was then thrown to the opposite side of the road from the remainder of the lawman's body. The body was also stripped naked before being abandoned – for what reason is unknown today.

News of the murder traveled swiftly. The following morning, when the brothers paused for a meal at a Fairmount road-house, a crowd gathered around their automobile searching for grisly signs of the murder. By that evening, a crowd of more than one hundred had gathered at the home of Lindsey Evans, hoping to cash in on the $500.00 reward already offered by the Pickens County commissioner's office for information leading to the identification and capture of Cape's murderers.

Coincidentally, one of the first persons at the scene when Cape's body was accidentally discovered by T.R. (Rex) Sherman two days later was C.H. Peacock of Canton. Peacock had administered to Cape years earlier when the lawman had been wounded by his drunken son. Peacock had no trouble identifying the body then and later for the court.

Lee Cape was given a hero's funeral, attended by more persons than any previous funeral in Pickens County history. The old lawman was laid out in an open casket (although his head was concealed). Marble magnate Sam Tate gave the eulogy.

Two men subsequently were appointed to fill Cape's position as county policeman, but filling his shoes was no small feat. According to an editorial in the *Pickens County Progress* newspaper, doubts existed: *"Can Pickens County get another Lee Cape? Do you know any man that will lay out all night in the cold, sleet and rain that people might enjoy full protection? . . . At public gatherings, he was usually on hand, and when he came up, everybody knew there would be no disturbance, no matter how large the crowd. . . He didn't know the meaning of the word 'fear.'"*

Over the years, numerous bizarre tales have been circulated regarding the motive for Cape's murder. The most likely explanation, however, and the one supported by the trial transcript, maintains that the killer was enraged because he mistakenly suspected Cape had discovered his moonshine still, and that he (the perpetrator) was about to be arrested for the production and possession of illegal liquor (moonshining), a highly volatile issue in the mountains of north Georgia. In a rage, perhaps enhanced by alcohol intoxication, the assailant committed an unplanned act of violence.

Killer Never Caught

During the trial for Cape's murder, no evidence was presented which in any way indicated any dislike whatsoever of Cape by his killer, Lindsey Evans. Surprisingly, despite being indicted for the horrifying murder, Evans managed to avoid capture by the authorities. He was never brought to trial.

Twenty years after the murder, an individual held in a Texas jail was suspected of being Lindsey Evans. However, when representatives from the Pickens County Police arrived in Texas, they were unable to make a positive visual identification, and other criminal investigation tools such as fingerprinting,

etc., had not been used in Pickens County in 1927. Lindsey Evans remained at large.

A Jasper, Georgia physician later claimed to have administered to Evans in the 1950s, as the wanted man lay dying.

Four other men were subsequently brought to trial for participation in the Cape murder. Despite being ably defended by Atlanta attorneys, C.L. "Seal" Smith and Hoyt Evans were convicted and given life sentences. Smith later escaped from prison and was never recaptured. The other two defendants – Carter Wilson and Carter Jones – pleaded *"Guilty"* and were given twelve-month sentences each.

An illegal liquor still near the site of Cape's death is presumed to have been the motive for his murder. The still was destroyed the day after his shooting.

The men convicted for Cape's murder were also found to be guilty of the possession and production of illegal liquor. Their sentences for this crime were added to the sentences for Cape's murder.

Little more than verbal accounts remain of the sites associated with Cape's murder today. The roads and communities associated with the murder have either been considerably changed, or have disappeared completely.

In Hinton, Lee Cape's prominent home still stands as of this writing. It has been nominated for inclusion on the *National Register of Historic Places*. Across the road, in Hinton Cemetery, Lee Cape's monument is easily recognizable. On his headstone, a final epitaph is chiseled: *"Through The Performance Of His Duty In The Enforcement Of Law He Sacrificed His Life."*

Lee Cape, undoubtedly, would have been proud.

The 1876-'77 Federal War on Georgia 'Moonshine'

The north Georgia mountains have long been a refuge and home for descendants of those hardy early pioneers who chose that environment, and who, as a result, were continuously dependent upon the production of untaxed liquor ("moonshine") as a cash crop. When the federal government "outlawed" the production of their liquor, it was essentially a declaration of war – and there was indeed, considerable fighting.

In contrast to many other countries of the world, the United States, by and large, has historically been very reluctant to use regular army troops against its own civilian population. There have, however, been some rare exceptions, and considering the mixed results of even these few incidents, a strong argument could be made for confinement of the Army's duties solely to the defense of the nation from "external" enemies.

A good example of one of these failures was the misuse of the army in an abortive attempt by U.S. agents to enforce taxation laws involving alcohol and tobacco in the north Georgia mountains in the 1870s.

The federal revenue laws that taxed alcohol and tobacco manufacturing through the requirement of licenses were first passed during the U.S. Civil War, and imposed a tremendous hardship on Appalachian families, many of whom depended upon their production of spirituous liquors as their main cash crop. Ironically, it was many of these same mountain families who took their lives and livelihoods in their hands to defy the Confederacy during the Civil War as they adamantly supported the federal government.

Due to their isolated highlands homes where extensive productive farmland and commercial endeavors were practically nonexistent, mountain families turned to the production of whiskey and tobacco, since these items were virtually the only marketable cash commodities which they could produce. Their ancestors had been producing home-made liquor for hundreds of years in Scotland and Ireland, prior to coming to the American colonies.

Further exacerbating the already volatile situation was the fact that the federal revenue laws did not (and still do not to this day) distinguish between alcohol and tobacco used for home needs (such as medicinal remedies) and that used for illegal sale on the public market.

The "licenses" required for the "legal" sale of these commodities invariably cost more than the average mountaineer could afford to pay, and therefore, thousands of otherwise honest citizens were driven into criminal activity. By 1876, cases involving the prosecution of revenue law violations virtually monopolized the docket of the Federal District Court in Atlanta, Georgia.

The system of enforcement of the federal revenue laws made matters infinitely worse too. Revenue agents and deputy U.S. marshals, unlike the more highly regarded Justice Department commissioners, were paid based upon the number of illegal distilleries or "stills" captured and the number of arrests made. The agents were often accused of making fraudulent arrests to pad their fees, and their incomes reportedly were also supplemented by bribes, blackmail, and profiteering from the illegal sale of captured stills.

And as time passed, the situation began to feed upon itself in worse ways too. Residents of the areas under surveillance were often hired to spy upon and testify against their neighbors. Personal and political vendettas from the Civil War and even earlier often became motives for "reporting," which could and did cause an incendiary situation to burst into criminal flames.

The revenue agents also carried a reputation for being brutal, profane and heartless. When an individual was arrested for violating the revenue laws, he or she was immediately taken to Atlanta for confinement and trial. Innocent mountain families could – and often did – lose everything in an attempt to pay the accused's legal fees, even if he or she was found to be innocent.

A strange twist to this situation was also discovered in the charge that some of the revenue agents who, although working for Republican administrations (who created and enacted the untaxed liquor laws), were in fact Southern Democrats who were using the law to persecute the mountaineers, many of whom had turned their backs on the Confederacy just a few years earlier in the 1860s. Memories of those disloyalties, coupled with the pains still being suffered by the South from Reconstruction, added incentive as well as momentum to the revenue agents' inflictions of pain upon their disloyal mountain brethren.

As efforts to eliminate the illegal liquor increased, many of the mountain men decided to organize in order to fight back. The north Georgia counties of the late 1870s were the most violent of the Southern Appalachian mountain region, with more than twice the number of alleged revenue agent casualties as those reported in second-place Tennessee. The U.S. government in turn responded by using federal troops to protect its agents during raids as early as 1872.

In what may have been a signature incident that year, U.S. Deputy Marshal Charles B. Blacker, accompanied by a Lieutenant Wolf of the 2nd U.S. Infantry, was

The revenue agents also carried a reputation for being brutal, profane and heartless.

349

fired upon in the Fightingtown (Boardtown) area of Fannin County, Georgia. In 1876, citing the preposterous loss of $500,000.00 annually in federal taxes and the reports of bands of moonshiners firing upon revenue agents, the Republican administration of then-President Ulysses S. Grant ordered increased use of U.S. Army troops for the support and protection of revenue officials. "U.S." Grant had no problem punishing the South.

One such patrol led by Deputy Marshal Blacker at Santa Luca in Gilmer County, visited the home of the elderly John Emory (formerly of Pickens County) on the night of January 14, 1876, and arrested – without warrants – four men who were waiting for daylight at Emory's still house. When Emory emerged from his house to investigate the cause of the commotion outside, he was shot in the face (almost exactly between the eyes) and killed instantly without warning or provocation by Private William O'Grady, a federal soldier.

With two other soldiers – Edward P. Wells and Frederick E. Newman – Private O'Grady concealed Emory's corpse in a nearby creek where Emory's grief-stricken widow discovered it the next morning.

On February 13, United States Deputy Marshal James A. Findley and his men fired upon Lafayette Southern seven times on a raid in the nearby Cartecay District. They captured two of Southern's stills, a wagon and a team, and 120 gallons of untaxed illegal whiskey. Findley and his crew then arrested and carried off James Sitton – who was in bed in ill health – simply because he resided nearby.

Gilmer Countians immediately organized a written protest to the Governor of Georgia. The Georgia State Legislature was in session at that time and William Robert Rankin of Gordon County introduced resolutions in the Georgia House which culminated in a demand that Governor Smith authorize a full investigation of the outrages committed by revenue agents in north Georgia.

A warrant was issued almost immediately by Gilmer County Justice of the Peace M.A. Berry for the soldiers responsible for John Emory's death. O'Grady and his colleagues were arrested in Atlanta, but before they could be tried in Gilmer County, a Writ of Habeas Corpus from no less than the President of the United States himself authorized a transferral of the trial to the U.S. Federal Circuit Court in Atlanta.

The federal government attempted to hire Blue Ridge District Solicitor General Charles D. Phillips to defend the soldiers. Phillips, however, declined the opportunity, choosing instead to be the prosecutor, and taking as his fee no income other than "Mrs. Emory's tears." However, a largely black, and allegedly politically-pressured jury subsequently found O'Grady and the other two soldiers *"Not Guilty."*

Adding still more fuel to the growing inferno was the fact that revenue agents in the area used this incident to reinforce their calls for more federal troops and still more irresponsible violence by these troops, contending that Emory's

They captured two of Southern's stills, a wagon and a team, and 120 gallons of untaxed illegal whiskey.

350

death had encouraged organized resistance and even revenge against federal officials. Surprisingly, had the agents known just how well-founded their fears had been, they may have been even more vocal, for the events leading up to the night of February 10, 1877, had already been set in motion.

Federal troops from McPherson Barracks in Atlanta and revenue agents left Cartersville, Georgia, on February 1, 1877. They made camp at Ellijay, Georgia, the county seat of Gilmer County. From there, they dispatched detachments with instructions to raid moonshiners and illegal tobacco manufacturers in Gilmer, Pickens, and Fannin counties.

Deputy Marshal Blacker, with a party of revenue agents and soldiers, left Ellijay at noon on February 9. They arrived at the home of a Mr. Ayers Jones at 2:45 A.M. the next morning. They were in the Frog Mountain region of western Fannin County (although they were close enough to the county line to believe they were in Gilmer County) on the headwaters of Conasauga Creek.

Having seen the light from Jones' cabin, the men initially suspected that they had chanced upon a moonshine distillery. Upon closer inspection however, they discovered the cabin contained only Mrs. Jones and seven children huddled around a fire, trying desperately to stay warm.

According to Mrs. Jones' later deposition, the men had burst into the cabin unannounced, with no warrant and with weapons drawn. They questioned her at length, and when she could not, or would not tell them where her husband was or the location of his stillhouse, Blacker became very profane.

According to her further later testimony, Mrs. Jones repeatedly asked the men to leave her cabin, and one of the soldiers, apparently taking pity on the poor family, even supported her, urging that he and his fellow troops withdraw. But Blacker, continuing with his swearing, announced that he would stay as long as he pleased. Mrs. Jones and the children, some of whom were sick, remained in the cabin with Blacker, Corporal Calloway, two guides, and Lieutenant Augustine McIntyre, while the remainder of the party left to search for the stillhouse.

According to reports of the incident, approximately fifteen minutes had passed since Blacker and his men had arrived, when footsteps were heard outside by the men inside the cabin. It was assumed by the men inside that the sounds they were hearing were from the return of their compatriot soldiers and agents dispatched to search for the stillhouse.

Imagine the surprise of those soldiers inside the cabin, who upon opening the front door to what they thought were their own men outside, were confronted instead by a fearsome group of very angry and revenge-minded strangers. A stout, dark-haired man with whiskers, nearly six feet tall, stood in the doorway with a large pistol.

Shouting "Stand, God damn you. . . You're in the wrong place tonight!," the stranger fired his pistol, sending soldiers and Blacker scurrying for cover. Corporal Calloway, standing by the cabin hearth, fired his carbine and then put out the lamp on the hearth. A pine knot still burned in the fireplace, but reportedly did not shed enough illumination to give the attackers any view of the inside of the cabin.

Shortly thereafter, Ralston and Anglin who had served as guides for the soldiers, fled out the back of the cabin, closing the door behind them, leaving

Callaway, Blacker, and McIntyre to face the music alone. The mountain men stormed the house four times, firing shotguns, pistols, and rifles. Both sides emptied their guns through the doorway. Blacker reportedly told McIntyre repeatedly to take cover behind the bedstead, but he refused, fearing that the children might be hit by a stray bullet.

On the fourth volley from the attackers outside, Lt. McIntyre was wounded. He reportedly cried out: "Blacker, I'm shot through the heart."

With their ammunition running out, the lieutenant, corporal, and Blacker fled out the rear door. McIntyre, now weak from his wound, stumbled and fell off the rear steps of the cabin. When Blacker attempted to help him, the lieutenant, apparently realizing his wound was mortal, urged the deputy marshal to save himself.

Shortly thereafter, Blacker retreated, leaving McIntyre behind. Shouts in the distance were soon heard to the effect of: "Oh yes, we've got one of the damned son of a bitches," and ".... We'll fix you!"

The next morning, Blacker and five men returned to the cabin. McIntyre's body still lay grotesquely where he had fallen earlier that morning. Blacker found Mrs. Jones and her children still in the cabin in bed.

When the men questioned Mrs. Jones about the attackers, she pleaded ignorance. The men began cursing her. Blacker reportedly warned her that they were out for revenge, and would in three weeks burn all the cabins in the area.

During Blacker's tirade, one of the men suddenly exclaimed "Look out!" Stepping outside, Blacker saw before his eyes a forest filled with armed men, some behind rocks no more than 300 feet away. He ordered his men to once again withdraw immediately, surprisingly leaving McIntyre's body behind once again.

At 3:00 P.M. that afternoon, twenty-two soldiers under Lieutenant James Ulio finally recovered McIntyre's corpse, carrying it out on a horse, since the terrain was far too rugged for a wheeled wagon or cart. This group was also fired upon by a party of men from a ravine 200 yards away.

According to an article entitled "Gilmer's Guerrillas," published in the February 13, 1877 issue of *The Atlanta Constitution*, three of the mountaineers were killed in the recovery of Lt. McIntyre's body. McIntyre's corpse had been robbed, and a hob-nail boot print was found on his forehead.

Federal retaliation was swift and decisive. On February 23, revenue agents, accompanied by soldiers, arrested seventy to eighty individuals, both men and women, simply because they lived or were apprehended within fifteen to twenty miles of Frog Mountain. They were carried to Cartersville, using old arrest warrants or no warrants at all. Many of the persons arrested were seized in the middle of the night while asleep in bed, and subsequently subjected to conditions of hunger and exposure from which some were not expected to recover.

For some of the prisoners, their odyssey did not end until

With their ammunition running out, the lieutenant, corporal, and Blacker fled out the rear door.

they eventually were set free in Atlanta, forcing them to make their way back home on foot in the dead of winter, a distance of more than 130 miles. On March 13, 1877, the *Atlanta Constitution* reported that on March 12, sixty-nine of the persons arrested for revenue violations were released in Atlanta after pleading *"Guilty,"* and receiving suspended sentences. And in the week just prior, 247 prisoners had been similarly sent home. With other arrests, the total number eventually exceeded 500 persons.

Due to the fact that it had become a target for federal revenue officers, the Frog Mountain area was gradually abandoned by its families, as men who had escaped the dragnet hid out or fled to neighboring states.

Some residents remained however. The *Atlanta Constitution* reported that the local people were stockpiling powder and shot for self defense against another raid.

The quest for justice in the murder of Lt. McIntyre did not die easily either. Rewards were offered by the Governor of Georgia as well as by the federal government for the killers. James Holt and his three sons were arrested in Nashville, Tennessee, for McIntyre's death, but were released when it was revealed that the only evidence against them was the fact that they were former Frog Mountain residents preparing to move to Texas.

Embarrassed by this mistake, federal authorities quietly and cautiously spirited their next group of suspects – John Davenport and five of his neighbors – into Atlanta. The only evidence against these individuals was reported to have been the testimony of a lone female. Following a hearing, Davenport and his friends were also released.

The U.S. Army believed that the man who had appeared in the doorway of the Jones cabin had been Ayers Jones himself, and even claimed that the whole incident, including the light from the cabin and the women and children, had all been an elaborate plot to lure McIntyre and his party into an ambush. The army claimed that the Jones family members were part Indian and had moved to Frog Mountain after fleeing the mountains of western North Carolina during the Cherokee relocation of 1838.

Ayers Jones' wife and son were later arrested, but subsequently also released. It seems the government simply could not find enough evidence or witnesses to make a case against any suspects whatsoever.

Ayers Jones himself, and his brother Tom, were not caught until 1879. They were not tried for murder, but were indicted for conspiracy to avoid the service of a warrant by Blacker. They were eventually tried and found *"Not Guilty,"* again, due to a lack of evidence and witnesses. Papers in their case file in the National Archives, Atlanta Branch, shed some interesting sidelights on the death of McIntyre and details of the incident.

Informants in the incident apparently claimed that a Elijah Johnson had been in the Army's camp. Acting as a spy, Johnson had sent three men to Frog Mountain to warn the mountaineers of the impending raid.

The Jones family and their neighbors subsequently armed themselves and banded together. Prior to the raid by the agents and soldiers on Jones' cabin, the mountaineers apparently were actually attempting to avoid confrontation, but decided instead to storm the cabin after over-hearing the abuse being heaped upon Mrs. Jones by Blacker.

The National Archives papers

further indicate that one witness testified that a W.H. Green who was related to the Jones family, was in possession of McIntyre's pistol and knew where his watch could be found. And later, during a daring rescue of a fellow moonshiner, Ayers Jones allegedly boasted that his pistol had killed McIntyre.

Ayers Jones however, was also described as being *"as pure a specimen of a child of nature as can be imagined,"* so illiterate and backward that he had never even seen a railroad. He was however, a substantial landowner, with some 700 acres in the 980th District of Fannin County. He, ironically, was himself later murdered by his son – John – in nearby Chattooga County on September 11, 1893.

In 1877, mass meetings were being held in Gilmer and Fannin counties (more than 100 persons attended the Fannin meeting) where declarations were signed and sent to newly-elected Governor Alfred Colquitt. The resolutions condemned the killing of Lt. McIntyre and the persons violating the revenue laws. However, they also charged that the revenue agents were, in actuality, the root of the current crisis. The declaration called the agents *"men without any social standing, without honor, or integrity, and who themselves have been, up to the present time, without a single exception, the most persistent violators of the law in our midst."* The *Atlanta Constitution* also blamed McIntyre's death on the revenue agents themselves, describing them as *"a hungry pack of remorseless and heartless spies and vampires."*

When the Georgia State Legislature was again in session, Rep. B.C. Duggar of Gilmer County and Lemuel J. Allred of Pickens introduced new resolutions which were passed, requesting that Governor Colquitt investigate the situation in north Georgia. The House also passed resolutions condemning the internal revenue laws on alcohol production and the system designed to enforce those laws.

Colonel Samuel C. Williams was sent to north Georgia by Governor Colquitt to conduct the investigation. He arrived in Ellijay on February 28. Traveling through Pickens, Gilmer, and Fannin counties, he collected more than 130 depositions, many of which were later published in the *Atlanta Constitution* of May 8, 1877.

Not satisfied with only "looking into the matter at hand," Williams recorded information on the events and persons going back to 1872. He personally visited the places involved, including Frog Mountain and the Jones cabin. Everywhere, he received "not only a willingness, but a desire to help," as men even left their work to aid him in his investigation.

Williams' report was a lengthy condemnation of the entire revenue enforcement system in north Georgia, and of the men who ran it. He collected dozens of depositions of people arrested without warrants who were compelled to hire lawyers at considerable expense to clear themselves of nonexistent charges, and of brutal revenue agents who extorted blackmail, took bribes, and sold liquor distilleries captured in raids. Army officers interviewed were no less negative about the revenue agents, and expressed their regrets in being forced to help these men.

Col. Williams' investigation of the death of Lt. McIntyre was no less revealing. He discovered that had the "guerrillas" actually wished to wipe out the entire party of agents and soldiers, a successful ambush could have been easily carried out by two men at any of several places on the narrow trail to the cabin.

And the Jones' cabin itself, could have been a tremendous kill site had the mountaineers wished to truly exact revenge. It was described as *"an oak log pen, 12 by 14 feet in size, neither chinked nor daubed."* The attackers would have needed to do little more than to fire through the three to five-inch cracks between the logs to have killed Blacker and his entire party as they stood in the cabin.

Clearly, Williams concluded, the attackers had not intended to massacre the raiding party or to harm the soldiers. As for the mass arrests, Williams reported that McIntyre's commander believed that the attackers were not thirty men, but only four or five.

In the interim following this incident, Deputy Marshals Blacker and Findley, accompanied by troops, were still actively inciting ill will with their tactics in north Georgia. Starting from Dawson County, they and a posse arrested a Harrison Barker of Forsyth County at his home in March, 1877. In their account of the daring and dangerous capture, Blacker and Findley described Harrison Barker as a legendary north Georgia moonshining "Jesse James" of many a daring escape and blazing gun battle.

Barker, who was subsequently captured and tried, turned out to be little more than a wiry man of average height who claimed never to have been convicted of moonshining or charged with any "mean thing." He speculated that his notoriety as a legitimate tavern keeper in Cumming may have led to his being singled out by Blacker and Findley.

Whatever the circumstances, Barker nevertheless took flight after wounding Blacker in the arrest attempt. Blacker and Findley later pursued him to Kentucky where they re-captured him, bringing him back to Atlanta for trial.

Barker eventually lived up to his notorious reputation, escaping from the prison in which he was being held. He, however, remained peacefully at home, until dragged out of his bed by Findley early one morning in 1877. Barker eventually plead *"Guilty"* to selling moonshine, and was given a suspended sentence. He had also been indicted for shooting Blacker in 1873, but was never tried on this charge.

On April 10, 1877, the U.S. Army finally left Ellijay and Gilmer County. In 1879, an act of Congress prohibited the use of troops to aid civilian authorities in making arrests.

So ended what came to be known as *"the North Georgia Moonshine War of 1876-1877."* The official score stood at one civilian and one officer killed, with an untold number of other casualties among the moonshiners and revenue agents.

Contrary to the hopes of the mountain people, the revenue laws, the revenue agents, and the local resistance all continued through to the days of the *"whitecaps,"* also known as *"the night riders,"* and on to the more recent moonshining days of *"Thunder Road."*

Some headway was made against moonshiners by such federal agents as Commissioner of Internal Revenue Green B. Raum, who, in the 1880s, used what Dr. Wilbur R. Miller has called "a systematic strategy combining force and restraint," built both on persistence and on winning local support. That moonshining has been greatly reduced in north Georgia, however, is due not to law enforcement, but to the rising cost of sugar, new economic opportunities in north Georgia, and affordable, "taxed" liquor.

Murder In The Mountains

The Strange & Tragic Case of Kate Southern

Pickens County, Georgia, in its earliest settlement days was a very rural – and sometimes very primitive – place for family life. The struggles were many, and it was not unusual for a simple family or friend disagreement or jealousy to explode into violent rage.

In the last decades of the 19th century, the mountainous northeastern region of Pickens County carried a very unsavory reputation for immorality and flash violence, many times involving violent individuals left over from the Civil War. On February 10, 1877, a sensationalized murder which involved two women – instead of men – and a vicious sex triangle, is still occasionally discussed by distant relatives of the principal characters and long-time natives of the area.

Criminals and violence-prone individuals were frequently involved in horrendous deeds in Pickens during this period. Legends and tales abound in the county where strange "goings-on" have occurred for 100 years or more.

The murder and subsequent trial in 1877, focused national attention upon the county, as if the area hadn't already attracted enough attention. Here was the home of house-burners and night riders of the 1860s, '70s, and '80s, who were involved in many illegal activities.

And in 1884, Democrats in Jasper – the county seat – celebrated Grover Cleveland's presidential victory by exploding two anvils full of gunpowder, making a racket so loud that it caused area resident Clark McClain to comment, "*They are having this joyful noise away over at Sharp Top Mountain, where there's neither God nor law.*"

Interestingly, the area around Sharp Top, the volcano-shaped peak that can be seen so clearly from Jasper, also produced its share of preachers and lawmen – almost as if in response to the lawlessness. However, the community there was secluded, and involved a very different culture from the hill people or "flatlanders" of nearby Jasper.

The natives of Sharp Top were the southernmost extension of that reclusive, isolated, Appalachian personality that so often represents the stereotypical mountain member of a clan. They usually had no greater problems than any other group, but unfortunately, they far too often resorted to violence to "solve" their problems, and the news about them therefore that reached the ears of outsiders was never anything but "bad."

Set-Up For Crime?

In 1877, John Hambrick lived on land lot 111-5-2 in the "Lansdown," a wooded valley in northern Pickens County near the Gilmer County line named after the area's most prominent family. The Lansdown was always isolated, and is even more so today.

Hambrick had a wife and four daughters – all nearly grown. One frigid evening in February, 1877, he decided to have a party, which, in those days for unknown reasons, they called a "play." Such an event sometimes included wild activities, but more often than not, just dancing and music (fiddling), and other such common actions, just as do present-day parties.

However, the fact that the elder Hambrick himself had planned such a get-together can only be viewed as strange today, particularly in view of the fact that his daughter, Kate, would later claim that it was *"the first time I ever seed a reel (dance) run."* Perhaps he was concerned about the future of one or more of his daughters, and a seeming inability to find a husband in the deep woods of north Pickens. We'll never know.

Hambrick's role in what happened at this party depends very much today upon which newspaper and/or trial testimony version of the account is read. Whatever the

circumstances, his initiation of the event will carry suspicious overtones as long as the memory of this incident exists.

Nineteen-year-old Catherine or "Kate" Hambrick Southern was married to Robert Southern, and she was angry at one of the invitees to the party – Narcissa "Sis" A. M. Fowler – for spreading rumors that Kate had been seeing a man named "Woods" for lewd activities in the nearby cane swamp.

Accounts of the main characters indicate Sis Fowler herself was no angel. She had been the subject of a great deal of gossip as well. She was married to Taylor S. Cowart by whom she had a daughter.

In 1873, Sis tried to divorce Taylor for adultery – and for having held her head firmly between his legs while he gave her a good beating. Sis had angered her husband – ironically – for openly carrying on sexual relations with Robert Southern. Cowart apparently eventually decided that Sis wasn't worth the trouble he was enduring, so he eventually just deserted her.

Rachel Bramlet would later testify in court that she had heard Kate threaten in July of 1876, to *"cut Sis's haunch out,"* even if she had *"to do it at a church meeting"* if her father did not sue Sis for slander. The reason for Kate's outrage undoubtedly was her jealousy over her husband's affair with Sis.

At noon on that Saturday, which was the day of the dance, Mary Mealer was at the Hambrick home. She also later testified

Accounts of the main characters indicate Sis Fowler herself was no angel. She had been the subject of a great deal of gossip as well.

against Kate, stating that she (Kate) had remarked – to no one in particular – that if Sis Fowler was at the party, she (Kate) was going to kill her. (Other persons present would later surprisingly testify that these comments never occurred.)

Deadly Party

If these threats reached Sis Fowler, she quite possibly was not terribly worried. She and Kate were about the same height (5 ft., 5 in. tall), but while Sis was very stout and healthy, Kate was thin and sickly, weighing only 110 pounds, thirty pounds less than even her younger and shorter sister Amazilla Hambrick. What Sis Fowler apparently did not anticipate, however, was a fight with the whole Hambrick family – with one member carrying a deadly weapon.

John Haynes, Kate's brother-in-law, set out for the party with a group of his friends. "Someone" suggested that Sis Fowler be invited, supposedly to insure that enough women were at the dance, and because she was known to be "a good hand." Haynes had a mule-drawn wagon and was traveling around the backwoods picking up the party participants, and therefore stopped at Sis's house where she climbed quickly aboard.

It was not until Haynes pulled up for the party at the Hambrick house that Sis reportedly realized that the "play" or dance was not going to be held at the Haynes's house as she had thought. At this point, she expressed a reluctance to go into the house, but Kate's parents warmly invited Sis in and peer pressure no doubt encouraged her to go ahead.

Her choice to relent and attend the "party" was a decision which haunted her family for the remainder of their lives. A Pickens County prosecutor would later refer to the Hambricks as *"welcoming her with hospitable hands to a bloody grave."*

The dance reportedly went on for hours to the music of fiddler William Bramlet. Witnesses guessed that from a dozen to twenty people were present in a room that was between 14 x 14 feet and 16 x 18 feet in size. To say the least, the room was completely filled with people, and as things "heated up," John Hambrick passed around a bottle of whiskey.

Space for actually dancing (square dancing) at this event was at a premium, because the two beds and other furniture normally in the room were still there, since the only alternative would have been to drag them out into the woods. As a result of the close quarters – and since it was late at night, with the only light provided by the fireplace and a small brass lamp on the mantle – visibility was very poor.

Kate was on one of the beds with her husband, Bob. She went outside and asked her father for the loan of his pocket knife to trim her nails and to cut some "tooth brushes" (black gum twigs used by the girls.) She left the house but came back a few minutes later, and the stage was set for disaster.

Cold-Blooded Murder

As midnight approached, Sis was dancing with James

Her choice to relent and attend the "party" was a decision which haunted her family for the remainder of their lives.

Honea. He would later testify that she stumbled and then complained that for the third time that evening, Kate had tripped her.

Sis, at this point, reportedly warned Kate not to trip her again. The music then stopped, and all eyes turned to the two women, no doubt because most of those present had anticipated this fight from the outset.

According to testimony, there was silence for a few minutes. Kate then approached Sis and said something only they could hear.

Sis then openly challenged her to "Come ahead."

Kate replied "Oh yes, God damn you," and the fight was on.

Sis quickly pulled Kate to the floor, yanking her hair while clubbing her over the head. She fully intended to give Kate a good old-fashioned country beating. What she didn't know, however, was that Kate was armed.

Amazilla, (Kate's sister), then joined in the fight by grabbing Sis by the hair and beating her over the head, in order to give Kate a chance to regain her feet. At that moment, Kate pulled herself up by Sis's shirt tails and started landing some stout blows herself.

Weak and sickly, Kate presumably was tiring quickly, and needed any advantage she could obtain. According to later testimony, she and Sis continued grappling near one of the beds, and then tumbled over into a dark corner, rolling out near the fireplace and finally to the door. No one moved to stop the fight.

The brawl, however, suddenly stopped of its own accord near the door, when Sis suddenly just strangely collapsed over on her side. Even in the poor light of the room, blood could be clearly seen pouring out of her breast.

At that point, Honea reportedly attempted to pull Sis to her feet, but it was too late. She had been devastatingly wounded by the knife Kate had wielded, and she was already in her death throes.

Honea, who apparently had been attracted to Sis, then stood in front of the door and loudly instructed everyone to remain where they were, since Sis clearly appeared to be dead and it was obvious a murder had occurred.

Kate, by then in a murderous rage, screamed at him to get out. When he refused to move, her husband, Bob, reportedly then pulled out a revolver and forced Honea – at gunpoint – to leave.

Within the confines of the dark room, there was no one who actually saw Kate use the knife on Sis, but no one doubted what had happened either. Since she had obviously been holding an opened knife the entire fight, Kate had cut both of her own hands, particularly her right hand, where she had nearly severed a little finger.

Amazilla was heard to ask Kate if she was sorry for having killed Sis, to which Kate reportedly replied that she did what she wanted to do.

Murder Investigation

News of the murder quickly reached Jasper. Kate, to her disservice – and stupidity – reportedly openly bragged that she was the "man" who had killed Sis Fowler.

According to a traditional account told by Jasper resident Dallas Byess, when Sheriff John Lindsay arrived the next day to search the Hambrick house, both the Hambricks and Southerns were washing blood from their clothes. Though the lawmen wanted to question Kate, they failed to find her, reportedly because she had hidden in the arch of the chimney. The fact that there was no immediate indictment allowed the

Hambrick family the time they needed to take flight.

Kate and her husband, Bob, were not captured until well over a year after the crime had occurred. They nevertheless were indicted – along with the rest of the Hambrick family – for murder at the next term of the Pickens County Superior Court.

Susan Petit, a make-shift undertaker in the vicinity, was called ten to eleven hours after the murder to remove the body. Why it took that long to take the body to prepare it for burial is unknown today.

Petit reportedly took the corpse by wagon to Sis's father's home and dressed the deceased for burial later that same day. In Pickens County Superior Court, she would later serve as a coroner of sorts, a capacity in which she served surprisingly well.

When called to testify in court, Petit stated that Sis was about twenty to twenty-five years of age; a very stout woman and larger than Kate. She explained that the body had not one, but a total of six knife wounds – one on the temple, one on the jaw, one under the collar bone, one below the breast, and two others in the chest.

Apparently unbeknownst to those in the room, Kate had been delivering wound after wound to the unfortunate Sis, with more than one, no doubt, being fatal. Petit explained that the wounds appeared to have been made by a knife that was pushed straight into the chest.

Petit described other evidence as well, being very thorough. Hair which Petit said she found in Sis's hands at the Hambrick house and at the Fowler house, looked like Kate's hair.

Since she assisted her in the fight, Amazilla, Kate's sister, was also tried, and on May 31, 1877, was sentenced to two years in prison for her part in the murder.

Flight From Justice

As explained above, Kate Southern had taken flight following the murder. Alfred H. Colquitt, having taken office on January 12 of 1877, offered a reward of $150.00 (the equivalent of roughly $3,000.00 in 2021 dollars) and Sis Fowler's family – who apparently were reasonably wealthy for that day and place, considering the reward they made available – offered another $250.00 (the equivalent of approximately $6,300.00 in 2021 dollars) for Kate's arrest.

The Southerns, nevertheless, remained at large for over a year, at which time, it was decided that more sophisticated help would be needed to locate them. Men like Walter Webb (W. W.) Finley were called "mountain trackers," although tracking, in the usual sense, had little to do with their work. They were really north Georgia detectives.

These lawmen, sometimes working as sheriffs or deputies, and at other times as freelance posses, knew the mountain roads and the mountain people. They knew who to ask for information, what to ask, and what to believe and not believe. With common sense, experience, and patience, they enjoyed a high rate of success in the apprehension of criminals.

Ex-Sheriff Walter W. Finley of Fannin County was one of these men. Once hired for the case, Finley set the wheels of justice for Kate Southern into motion.

In late January, 1878, after considerable research, patience, and dogged effort, he finally learned the Southerns were living on a farm near Franklin, North Carolina. With two other men, Finley arrived at the farm only minutes after the Southerns, accompanied by Bob Southern's father and two brothers, had left in an ox-drawn wagon, headed in the opposite direction for northern Alabama.

Undeterred, Finley and his men set

out in pursuit. After riding most of the day and following night, the three men finally closed within a few minutes of their quarry at Murphy, North Carolina.

Leaving his party at a hotel, Finley scouted the Southerns' camp. He decided to make his move at 4:00 a.m. the next morning.

Early the following day, despite the dark and a miserably-cold rain, the Southerns again broke camp just minutes in advance of the posse. They either possessed incredibly good intuition, amazing luck, or simply unbelievable timing.

This time, however, Finley was able to close on his quarry. After riding hard to make up for lost time and sensing that he had almost reached his quarry, he slowed his horse to a trot and calmly rode up the trail past the Southerns – who were totally unaware of the lawman's identity – in order to get men situated on both sides of the Southerns.

The mountain detective and his men then made their move, surrounding the fugitives from front and rear, taking them prisoners before they could use their two long-guns, pistols, or knives. The Southerns clearly were well-armed and prepared to resist violently.

Bob Southern's father, William, and two brothers, James and Miles, were turned over to a local bailiff for having passed through the gate at the Western North Carolina Turnpike without paying the toll, while Finley took Bob, Kate, and their recently-born baby to a nearby house for breakfast.

No sooner had everyone started to eat, however, than William Southern and his sons, having escaped from the bailiff, attempted to free Bob and Kate. According to accounts of the incident, Finley and his men, however, were far and away the better of the match-up, ultimately disarming the attackers, taking two more pistols and a knife from them and avoiding any injuries. Just under a week later, Bob, Kate, and their baby were in the Pickens County jail.

Old man Southern and his sons would later claim – to no avail – that they had persuaded Bob and Kate to surrender to the authorities and were on the way back to Jasper to collect the reward to give to Kate's mother when Finley arrested them.

Media Frenzy

The *Atlanta Constitution* did not report the murder in its February, 1877, issue, although it could have reprinted the account from the *Marietta Journal*, which did report the incident. The trial and conviction of Kate's sister, Amazilla, also went unnoticed and unreported by the *Constitution*.

The first account whatsoever of the incident to appear in the *Constitution* was a reprint from the *Ellijay Courier* which described Finley's capture of the Southerns. A news editor at the *Constitution* apparently realized at last that somewhere in this tidbit of information, a story could be found (or made).

Almost a year to the day after the murder, the *Constitution* published a lengthy – and decidedly distorted – story of the whole affair. The article was run in the February 14th (St. Valentine's Day) issue.

Contrary to the facts of the incident, the *Constitution* story "*The Fatal Dance*" added some twenty-five pounds to the skinny, sickly Kate Southern, to make her "*one of the prettiest girls in the up-country,*" and the simple fiddling at the Hambrick house suddenly became a "*ball.*" Here, Kate caught husband Bob "*in a cotillion*" with Narcissa Fowler, now described as a former girl friend. In a fit of jealous rage, Kate, according to the article, pulled out the knife and shouted *"You have danced enough,"* killing the very plump Narcissa with a single blow to the neck that cut all the way to the heart.

As a hedge, the **Constitution** printed the disclaimer that *"the tragedy was committed in the heart of Pickens County, beyond the reach of newspapers, and what we know of it is received through mere hearsay."* However, the newspaper's version, faulty even in describing the Pickens County geography and in ignoring the coverage by the **Ellijay Courier** and the **Marietta Journal**, would be the version that the national press, both pro-Kate and anti-Kate, would use to build their own feature stories on the incident.

Even the local tales of this murder would be based at least in part upon this romantic fiction. If the **Constitution** had failed to find the truth (and had not even looked very hard for it), it at least had apparently found a money-making story. For several issues, Kate Southern articles were featured, frequently on the front page.

Trial For Murder

In Pickens County, however, officials were looking for the truth. Kate Southern, her husband Bob, her father John Hambrick, her mother Sarah, and brother-in-law John Haymes had all been indicted for the murder in 1877, and were now all crowded by Sheriff Lindsay into Pickens County's rock jail (demolished in the 1960s; not the restored and now historic 1906 brick jail which is still standing as of this writing).

On April 23, 1878, Kate Southern finally stood trial for her crime. Thirty-six extra jurors had been summoned to guarantee that an impartial jury could be picked.

The testimony of the witnesses in this case, in the trial of Amazilla, and in the trial of the rest of Kate's family, has survived. In none of this material did any witness suggest that Bob Southern even knew Narcissa Fowler, much less that he had danced or was having sex with her, contrary to the sensational stories being published in the **Atlanta Constitution**.

Kate's real motive – offered by only one witness and suggested in the questions put to most all the witnesses – was actually nothing more than the gossip Narcissa reportedly had been spreading about her. The witnesses variously also explained how Narcissa then had been provoked into what appeared to be a fair fight, not knowing that Kate had concealed a knife. The prosecution tried to prove that the "dance" was *"a deliberate and willful conspiracy, that was planned by the Hambricks"* and their friends, to set up the circumstances for the fight and possibly even for the murder itself.

Opening and closing arguments were not recorded, but nothing in the **Ellijay Courier**'s report of the trial supported the love triangle or jealousy motive stated in the **Atlanta Constitution**. S.A. Darnell, J.C. Allen, and T.F. Greer represented the state, and the defense was composed of D.P. Lester, W.T. Day, Carey W. Styles, and W.H. Simmons.

Both sides would be credited with making strong cases. Seven arguments were heard, besides the opening argument. The testimony took up a day and a half, the arguments required much the same, and the jury took twenty-four hours to render a verdict which found Kate Southern guilty but with a recommendation of mercy, if possible.

Judge George N. Lester had seen his share of death on Civil War battlefields, but he announced that the verdict he was about to render – the only one that law allowed him to make – was the saddest moment in his life. On Saturday, April 28, he told Kate to make peace with her God, and, while he openly wept, sentenced her to be hung by the neck until dead between the hours of 10:00 a.m. and 3:00 p.m. on Friday, June 21.

Kate's lawyers announced that they would appeal for a new trial at the June term of the Gilmer County Court. However, Judge Lester met with an accident that left him incapacitated and, on May 10, the June term of court was postponed until July.

This was bad news for Kate, but for the *Atlanta Constitution*, matters could not have taken a better turn. A photographer from Canton was hired to make photographs of Kate, her husband, and her baby. The photographs were copyrighted and then printed, not for publication in the *Constitution*, but for sale to the public at the *Constitution's* offices and to other newspapers. A discount was offered if all three photographs were ordered. The *Constitution* advised that *"the history of this remarkable case cannot be thoroughly understood until these pictures have been seen."*

Media Distortions

On May 3, 1878, the *Constitution* reported the trial and its outcome in *"A Woman's Sin,"* which was hardly more than a rehash of the earlier *"Fatal Dance."* Previous inaccuracies were actually expanded. The very plump Narcissa Fowler was now described as *"a beautiful young lady, one of those handsome country girls who, knowing her charms, delighted in making conquests of men."* The *"ball"* was now explained as being given to celebrate Kate's marriage to Bob Southern and described as attended by *"all the belles and beaus of the neighborhood."*

Beyond the pronouncement of a death sentence, very little of the actual trial was mentioned in the *Constitution* rehash. The story did add Congressman H.P. Bell to the defense team, and Kate was described as holding her baby in her arms while the sentence was read. The paper even misspelled her name as *"Sothern,"* an error that was continued in the later articles.

The *Atlanta Constitution* ended its coverage of the trial of Kate Southern by pointing out the censure that former Governor James M. Smith had received for not commuting the death sentence of Susan Eberhart and that the present *"Gov. Colquitt will have to be thoroughly convinced of the justice of the sentence before he will allow her to hang."*

As inaccurate as the stories were that appeared in the *Constitution*, even stranger was the *"Atlanta Special"* that appeared in the *Chicago Times* newspaper on May 12, 1878. The fatal dance was described in that account as having happened during a public Christmas ball held in Jasper in December, 1876. The former Kate *"Hambright,"* *"acknowledged belle of what is known as the mountain counties"* was described as recently married to Bob Southern, and *"better fitted for breaking hearts than for any practical business."*

The *Times* went on to state that after an angry confrontation with Bob's ex-girlfriend Narcissa Cowart, in the *"dressing room,"* Kate, in this version, reportedly caught Narcissa and Bob dancing. The jealous wife then entered the dance floor and, after shouting *"You have danced enough!"* plunged a knife to the hilt into Narcissa's shoulder, severing an artery. Not finished, however, the paper then had Kate slashing Narcissa across the breast, cutting through the heart. Finally, with an effort worthy of

Jack the Ripper, she, *"like an infuriated tigress, jumped upon the dead body, ripped open the abdomen, and would have literally hacked it to pieces, had not someone attracted her attention."*

Through such publicity, Kate Southern became a national pariah, and the *Atlanta Constitution* became the forum for a debate on whether she should or should not be hung, publishing letters and reprinting editorials about the sentence. However, these pieces were based upon the romantic fiction in the *"Fatal Dance"* and other stories published in the *Constitution*, not upon the actual court case testimony or the local newspaper accounts.

The *New York Herald* published an editorial that cited the Southern case as an argument for exempting women from capital punishment, while the *New York Globe*, refusing to comment on the reported circumstances of the case, argued against any *"discrimination in hanging on false and sentimental grounds."* The *Constitution* claimed that of the numerous petitions and letters that the governor had received from Georgia and elsewhere concerning Kate Southern, no one had written urging that the death sentence be carried out.

Saviour For Kate?

In the midst of this ink war, Kate eventually acquired an anonymous white knight. Writing under the pseudonym of *"Mortimer Pitts,"* a lengthy letter in opposition to the hanging of any woman, and particularly under the circumstances reported for Kate Southern, appeared on the front page of the *Constitution*. Pitts reported that Kate Southern's case would be heard by the Georgia State Supreme Court in August, and possibly retried before Judge Lester in Pickens County in September. At the earliest, Pitts felt Kate could be hanged in November. He argued that the people of Georgia would do all that they could to prevent that from happening.

Pitts's letter drew a number of responses and a few days later, another article he had penned appeared, again in the *Constitution*. In a story headlined *"Mrs. Sothern's (sic) Neck,"* Pitts argued that women are instinctively unable to commit murder except under the influence of whiskey or while otherwise not in full control of their senses. In Kate's case, Pitts claimed that she had suffered three epileptic fits the Monday before the murder, and was sick from her pregnancy which, with the noise of the party and the provocations from the victim, left her unbalanced.

S.A. Darnell of Atlanta, one of the prosecutors in the case, later responded that Kate Southern had been examined in Pickens County Jail by physicians who were prepared to testify on her behalf as to a plea of *"Guilty By Reason Of Insanity"* because of the epilepsy. Darnell felt that the defense, having refused to plead insanity at the trial, should not be allowed to do so now. The defense attorneys subsequently withdrew the plea, opting instead to enter a plea of *"Not Guilty."*

Kate also suddenly found her image being completely white-washed. She was described by Mortimer Pitts as *"an active church member"* and as a person who had *"never attended a dance prior to the one held on the night of the murder."* He explained that she only happened to be staying with her parents that evening because of her ill health.

Pitts also reported that Kate's attorneys had decided against any further appeals in court, and that they were going directly to the governor. He added that Kate Southern was again (somehow)

The Strange & Tragic Case of Kate Southern — Pickens County

pregnant, and that the baby would be due in October if Kate didn't hang in June.

In a postscript, Mortimer Pitts announced the impending arrival in Atlanta of Kate's attorney – Col. Carey W. Styles – who intended to see the governor on her behalf. It is the defense of Southern by Col. Styles which remains as one of the mysteries of the trial. Styles was from extreme south Georgia, but was well-known throughout the state as a soldier, politician, and newspaperman. Among the twenty-two newspapers with which he was associated, was the *Atlanta Constitution*, which he had founded. He was a lawyer, but had practiced little or no law.

As of this writing, at least one Pickens County native still recounts the tale of Kate Southern and other legends of the mountains, as they have been handed down to him. According to this individual, on the day of her scheduled execution, Southern rode from the old rock jail behind the Pickens County Courthouse, sitting in her coffin, carried in a wagon. Beneath a tree across from the Norton Cemetery, a gallows had been erected. Just prior to the scheduled execution, however, a rider on a black horse supposedly raced the short distance from town to announce that the hanging had been canceled; the governor had commuted the sentence.

Sentence Commutation

Due to circumstances such as that described in the above paragraph, it is not difficult to see how some individuals believed the hanging had actually taken place. In actuality, however, Gov. Alfred Colquitt had commuted the sentence on May 22, a full month before the execution was to have happened, and the executive action was reported almost immediately in the *Marietta Journal* and

Henry W. Grady was a staunch proponent of what he termed "the New South," advocating southern endurance of whatever hardships might be imposed by the federal government as a result of the outcome of the U.S. Civil War. It was also Grady writing under the pseudonym of "Mortimer Pitts" in the Atlanta Constitution who advocated mercy for cold-blooded murderess Kate Southern simply because she was a female. (Photo courtesy of GA Dept of Archives & History, Atlanta)

the *Atlanta Constitution*, newspapers that were distributed and read in Pickens County. It is therefore highly doubtful that even something as unthinkable as a mock execution could have been carried out in order to teach a lesson, even if these officials had been so inclined.

Gov. Colquitt had made a tough decision, despite the pressure by the news media and letters from the public on Kate's behalf. His term came near the end of what historian E. Merton Coulter characterized as *"the golden age of Georgia hangings."*

Colquitt maintained his decision was based upon additional written testimony by respected Pickens County citizens... testimony which was not used in the trial. He also noted a petition signed by all of the jurors which stated that they would not have found Kate guilty had they known she would be sentenced to die. Gov. Colquitt ultimately reduced the original sentence to ten years in prison.

No lesser a journalist than Henry W. Grady of the *Constitution* covered the reprieve. The only known account of his article, *"Mrs. Sothern's Neck Feels Relieved,"* is located in Grady's scrapbook at the Woodruff Library of Emory University. This piece is the nearest the *Constitution* came to a balanced account of the murder of Narcissa Fowler.

Grady described the affidavits that Col. Styles presented to Gov. Colquitt in great detail, and then followed with a much briefer account of the county's case against the Hambricks. Three of the signed statements dealt with Narcissa's bad character, including one *"the details of which cannot be published."*

A deposition by Kate's husband Bob, claimed that his relations with Narcissa were "criminal," and the affidavit by Bob's father stated that Fowler frequently came to the fields when Bob was working and took him away, usually for all night.

Other statements implied that shortly after Bob and Kate were married, Narcissa and Bob stayed alone together late into the night after a corn shucking, a story that had reached Kate. Several depositions claimed that Narcissa had threatened Kate's character and life.

So, under the circumstances, it appears that Miss Fowler might possibly have been anything but the innocent party-goer that she was formerly believed to have been. The actual circumstances will never be known.

Amazilla's Destiny

A short time later, the *Atlanta Constitution* reprinted an interview with Amazilla Hambrick, Kate's sister, from the *Sandersville Courier*. Amazilla had turned sixteen and seventeen while serving her sentence for helping Kate murder Narcissa Fowler. A note beside Amazilla's name in the convict registers at the Georgia Department of Archives and History reads: *"young and pretty; ought not to be sent to the penitentiary."*

At the time of Amazilla's conviction, Georgia did not have a prison for females, and sent convicts to county work camps or leased them to private individuals and companies as laborers. Amazilla had been lucky enough to be sold to Colonel Jack T. Smith's work farm in Washington County.

While at the farm, Amazilla did light work as a domestic for Smith's wife, and learned to read and write as well as to cut and sew garments.

In her interview with the *Courier*, Amazilla repeated the story that Narcissa had been trying to take Bob Southern back from Kate, and added that Narcissa's husband had left her because she was having sex with Bob. Narcissa was even quoted by Amazilla as having said at the dance: *"I knew Bob before you did and have as good a right to him as you."*

Amazilla added that her sister Kate did not approve of dances, did not know that the dance was even being held until the visitors started to arrive, and had been persuaded to stay. She described her family as land-owners who all worked together in the fields.

Amazilla also claimed that she had pulled both Kate and Narcissa apart and had only tried to stop the fight. In the end, Amazilla ironically had no interest in being pardoned, and even indicated that she hoped she could stay with the Smiths after her sentence expired in twelve months.

Amazilla's account of the murder

does not correspond with the court testimony, any more than did the stories in the *Constitution*, but coming from Amazilla Hambrick, this version suggests that the story of Narcissa's affair with Bob Southern may have been an invention by the Hambrick family to help Kate or to save themselves from being prosecuted as co-conspirators.

Regardless of the circumstances, Kate Southern was a cold-blooded murderess who quite possibly was caught up in a love-triangle, whether it involved sex between all the parties concerned, or not.

Kate Joins Amazilla

On May 28, 1878, in a front-page announcement, the *Atlanta Constitution* informed its readers that Kate Southern would arrive in Atlanta en route to confinement at Col. Smith's prison farm in Washington County. She would be carried sixty miles in an open buggy to the railroad

In a story entitled *"The Woman In Black: A Greeting To The North Georgia Murderess,"* Henry W. Grady reported of her arrival and the near riot at the train station. A mob of the curious, *"probably the largest crowd ever assembled in Atlanta so late at night,"* pursued her to the women's saloon at the train station and appeared ready to storm the building. Men and boys climbed over each other at the windows to see her. Some of the crowd reportedly stood on top of the train cars to catch a glimpse of the woman in black as she went by.

They undoubtedly didn't see much, however, because Kate wore a dark hat and black veil. Having earlier described her as robust and beautiful, the *Constitution* shortly began reversing its glowing description of her beauty, admitting tactfully that in reality, she *"was not particularly striking, being tall and slender and with rather delicate features."*

The *Columbus Enquirer* was less kind, writing *"Kate Southern is not pretty even"* but only *"passably good looking"* and *"very ignorant, can hardly read and write,"* and speaks with *"the twang of a north Georgia cracker."*

With her was her baby and her husband. Captain J.W. Nelms, keeper of the state convicts, had secured a position of light duties for Kate cooking and washing for the prisoners at the same farm where Amazilla worked. He even arranged for Bob Southern to be employed there as a guard.

An unknown individual from Atlanta donated Bob's train fare. Shortly thereafter, Kate Southern and her little family pulled out of Atlanta on the train for Sandersville.

At this juncture, the *Atlanta Constitution* apparently decided that public interest in the story was exhausted. No mention whatsoever was made in the *Constitution* of the trial in the April, 1879 term of Pickens County Court in which Bob Southern and the Hambricks were tried for their alleged part in the circumstances which led to the murder of Narcissa Fowler. A verdict of *"Not Guilty"* was handed down in this case.

The last Kate Southern story to appear in the *Constitution* was printed on the last page of the March 26, 1882 issue, and carried an account of her pardon by Governor Colquitt. In his executive minutes, the Governor cited petitions for Kate's release from all parts of the state and her ill health, a case of nervousness brought on by another pregnancy. (She bore at least one and possibly two children during her stint at the prison farm.)

So ended what the *Constitution*

proclaimed as *"one of the most noted cases ever in the courts in Georgia; one that created perhaps more interest and excitement than any ever known in the state."*

After Kate reached the prison farm, the **Macon Telegraph** obtained a copy of the testimony in her trial from the Governor's Office, and printed the entire text. The **Columbus Enquirer** then reprinted the same and added in an editorial that was copied by the **New York Times**: *"On reading this evidence one feels utterly disgusted with the amount of sentimental twaddle that has been expended on the case. We do not believe there is a single woman, no matter how warm and sympathetic her heart may be, who, after reading this sworn testimony, will sign a petition for Kate Southern's pardon."*

The Later Years

Some mysteries to the Kate Southern story remained for a number of years. The identity of the individual who wrote under the pseudonym of *"Mortimer Pitts"* and who helped to create the sensational account which made Kate Southern's plight a national issue, is now known to have been Henry W. Grady.

Years later, when Grady won worldwide fame as the champion of the *"New South,"* adamantly preaching that the South must learn to live under the yoke of the North, no matter the circumstances, he frequently made reference to a fable which he had invented about a funeral in Pickens County where the deceased was buried with tombstone, coffin, clothes, etc. purchased from outside of the South, even though all the identical raw materials for these products existed in his native Pickens County. Grady had chosen Pickens County - a place about which he knew little, and quite possibly had never even visited - as his example of all that was wrong with the thinking of his beloved South.

We cannot prove that Grady orchestrated the campaign to save Kate Southern. However, as Grady would often answer when pressed about the truth of his Pickens County funeral story, *"Why be hampered by the facts? It could be so!"*

After the trial, the Southerns announced they would never again return to Pickens County to live, but eventually, they did. The "sickly," epileptic Kate Southern lived to have at least eight children. She raised her brood among neighbors who undoubtedly, in one way or another, revealed her dark past to them all.

Kate must have known a great deal of unhappiness in the remainder of her life. At least two of her children died before the age of seven. One of her daughters reportedly discovered her father's pistol under his pillow, and was killed when the weapon went off as Kate was trying to extricate it from her daughter's grasp.

In the final analysis, Kate Southern seemed never able to escape a legacy of violence and misfortune. Interestingly, one of her granddaughters remembered her as *"the best grandmother anyone could have."* It is sometimes amazing how forgiving a child can be.

Author's Postscript: According to records, Kate and Bob Southern were living in the Lansdown after 1900, raising a large brood of children almost in sight of Long Swamp Cemetery where Narcissa Fowler is buried. Two of their children are buried at Burnt Mountain Baptist Church Cemetery near Jasper. The Southerns eventually moved to Winston County, Alabama, where Kate died on February 15, 1927. Her grave can be viewed there today. Robert Southern died there on October 9, 1930.

Railroad Destination to Utter Devastation:

The Horrible 1926 Rockmart Wreck

Exactly two days before Christmas of 1926, a lot of the passengers upon the northbound Ponce De Leon passenger train in northwest Georgia had happy plans for the upcoming holiday season. They not only would never enjoy those plans, they would never see Christmas on this earth again.

"I heard the shrill whistle and saw the headlights ahead, but the northbound was not slowing.... When I saw the collision was certain, I slammed on my brakes and called to my fireman to jump."

-Arthur M. Corrie
Engineer of the Royal Palm

The tiny township of Rockmart, Georgia, in the northwest quadrant of the state was very sparsely-settled in 1926. It was a very uneventful place where a major disaster had simply never occurred. That changed on December 23rd of that year as two immense passenger trains crashed head-on in one of the worst disasters in U.S. railroad history.

Interestingly, though it was a tiny town, Rockmart had enjoyed passenger rail service since the 1870s, when philanthropist Seaborn Jones, according to tradition, donated land to Southern Railway for a rail line right-of-way through the county at no cost – with the stipulation that Southern would guarantee passenger service to Rockmart as long as the company existed. It was the strict timetable required for this passenger service which quite possibly became the catalyst for disaster in 1926.

That December evening was a dark and rainy night in the foothills of north Georgia, as are many days in the autumn and early winter months of that region. Despite the miserable weather and gloom outside, the Pullman coaches in the Ponce De Leon were nevertheless filled with warm diners and, no doubt, lively Christmas cheer.

369

Mystery & History in Georgia

According to tradition, an early philanthropist, Seaborn Jones of Rockmart donated land for the rights-of-way for the railroad through the town in return for one stipulation, that being the railroad would always supply Rockmart with passenger service. Despite the ultimate elimination of passenger service in the 1960s, freight trains still roar down the same track (photographed here in 2021) upon which the 1926 disaster occurred. Some prognosticators say it's only a matter of time before another accident occurs, due to the speed at which the behemoths speed down the incline from the Braswell Mountains into the town. *(Photo by Olin Jackson)*

The rustic downtown area of Rockmart was photographed in the early 1900s. A trestle for the Southern Railroad approximately three-quarters of a mile north of the 1926 accident site is visible in the distance. The first large building below the trestle is the old Commercial Hotel which once existed in Rockmart. The building in front of it is the original (first) Seaboard Depot in the town. The old city hall building exists on that site today. *(Photo courtesy of GA Dept. of Archives & History, Atlanta)*

Both the Royal Palm and the Ponce De Leon were crack passenger trains of Southern Railway, and were regularly patronized by many travelers, since the 1920s was a time when the rapidly-growing network of railroads in our nation dominated the travel industry. Both trains were renowned for their good food, accommodations, and timely schedules. December 23rd was no exception, as both trains hustled to remain on schedule.

It was at a long sidetrack at Rockmart that the Royal Palm and the Ponce De Leon regularly passed each other on this route, so it was a common occurrence. The Southern railroad through Rockmart was not doubletracked, so the sidetrack a short distance from the Rockmart depot made it possible for these two luxury trains to pass each other and then continue on to their destinations in opposite directions.

In order to prepare for this maneuver, Engineer Arthur M. Corrie on the Royal Palm had throttled back to slow his big locomotive down to approximately 4 miles per hour to give the Ponce De Leon ample time to take the siding. All seemed normal until Corrie realized to his shock that the on-coming train was not slowing at all; nor did it seem that engineer Robert M. Pierce of the Ponce even intended to take the siding at all. To the contrary, a horrified Corrie realized that the Ponce was bearing down directly toward the Royal Palm at an incredible rate of speed.

For many years, engineers negotiating the Braswell Mountains just prior to Rockmart had become accustomed to increasing speed down the leeward side into the little town. This was particularly true – and to a greater degree – when there was no oncoming train requiring

The Horrible 1926 Rockmart Wreck

The site of the 1926 disaster at which the Royal Palm and Ponce De Leon passenger trains collided was photographed in 2021. *(Photo by Olin Jackson)*

A rail siding photographed here in 2021, still exists today in almost the identical spot at which the fateful side-track in the 1926 rail disaster existed. *(Photo by Olin Jackson)*

a pause on a side-track. All the engineers were constantly working to stay on schedule, because a timely delivery of passengers and postal materials meant "money."

As could best be determined in the after-accident report, the engineer of the Ponce apparently was simply unaware of the need to take the siding at Rockmart, and was taking advantage of the acceleration opportunity down from the Braswell Mountains in order to make up for some lost time on his schedule. That misunderstanding, coupled with the poor visibility caused by the drizzling rain and fog, led to a disaster of immense proportions.

The late Leonora (Mrs. Robert Henry) Mintz was seventeen years of age on the day of the accident. Prior to her death, she lived not thirty feet from the tracks of the Norfolk-Southern Railroad (formerly Southern Railway) in Rockmart for many years, and approximately one mile from the scene of the terrible 1926 disaster. When interviewed in the early 1990s, she stated that she could still clearly remember that fateful Christmas.

"At that time, we lived on our family farm (near the site of present-day East Side Elementary School) in Rockmart," Mrs. Mintz explained. "We heard the crash all the way from there. It was so loud, we thought it was thunder."

As an experienced trainman, Corrie knew that he had just enough time to yell a warning to his fireman, pull on the whistlecord as another warning to his passengers, and then to leap from the train to attempt to save himself. After he had jumped, the next thing Corrie heard was the horrendous blast from the collision, the grinding of metal, and the horrible screeching of the train trucks on the twisting, ripping rails.

According to reports, Corrie later told Interstate Commerce Commission (ICC) investigators that he turned and watched as the Ponce De Leon, traveling at approximately fifty miles an hour or better, crashed headlong into his beloved Royal Palm.

"I will never forget it," Corrie later stated. "It sounded like the heavens had split open. I don't want to ever hear anything like that ever again."

Despite the enveloping darkness and miserable cold rain on the fateful evening, the noise of the crash immediately brought local residents running to the crash site. The provision of help to the injured and dying proved a challenge for the citizens of the tiny,

The Southern Railway Depot in Rockmart was photographed in the early 1900s. A locomotive very similar in class to that of the Royal Palm or Ponce De Leon is stopped at the station. *(Photo courtesy of Polk County Historic Society)*

The site at which the Southern Railway Depot formerly existed in Rockmart, photographed in 2021. *(Photo by Olin Jackson)*

poorly-equipped community, for the carnage at the wreck site was absolutely overwhelming.

"When the Royal Palm and the Ponce De Leon collided, we weren't allowed to go up there to see it, because it was just too horrible," Mrs. Mintz explained emphatically, still shaken by the tragedy. "A friend of mine told me she and some other friends went to the wreck, and she said they saw the best-looking gentleman in a car. All of a sudden, it seemed like his head just rolled off his shoulders. He had been decapitated.

"Rockmart was a very rural area back then," Mrs. Mintz continued. "People were begging for help. We had no ambulances here at that time. Some people were carried in private automobiles to Rome (Georgia); others were carried as far away as Atlanta. It was just chaos."

One can only imagine today the misery and pain endured by the injured as they were carried out of the wrecked train cars and laid upon the ground in the rain until they could be huddled into automobiles for what then was a long, bumpy ride on dirt roads to a hospital many miles away. It is not known today how many victims died of their injuries "enroute" to hospitals and doctors, but there no doubt were many.

Mr. Hal Clements, a retired educator and a native of Rockmart said he was a lad of 11 at the time of the disaster. He and his family resided on Bluff Street in Rockmart. He remembered traveling with his father to the wreck shortly after it occurred.

"It happened just east of (what today is the former) Goodyear Mill complex in an area we used to call 'Barber's Woods,'" Clements explained. "I was only eleven years old, so I don't remember a lot. One of the things I do vividly remember, however, is the steam that was still rising from the locomotives. And I remember later that they brought a lot of boxes down to Cochran's Funeral Home.

"My father drove immediately to the accident, because he wanted to help in any way he could," Clements continued. "As I remember, I held onto my father's hand the whole time. I knew instinctively that there were a lot of bodies in those crushed cars."

Much of the horror of the disaster was caused by the Pullman cars of the Ponce De Leon which had "telescoped" into each other when they met the immovable force of the huge locomotive

The Horrible 1926 Rockmart Wreck — Polk County

Photographed shortly after the collision, the heavy damage inflicted upon the Ponce De Leon (r) is visible. The Royal Palm, however, due to its slow rate of speed, suffered far less damage. Rescue workers stand over a covered body beside the Ponce De Leon, possibly that of deceased Engineer Robert M. Pierce. *(Photo courtesy of Atlanta Historic Society)*

Arthur M. Corrie was the engineer of the Royal Palm on the night of the accident. His counterpart on the Ponce De Leon, Robert M. Pierce, was killed in the wreck. Corrie leaped from the engine cab at the last moment in a bid to survive and watched in horror as the two huge engines collided. He provided much of the eye-witness testimony on the accident. *(Photo courtesy of Atlanta Historic Society)*

which suddenly had come to a halt. The impact was horrendous – a crushing and mutilation of passengers – as the heavy cars smashed one into the other and then were each crushed as the heavy wooden housings collapsed, piling up against the locomotive.

After the shock of the initial crash had passed, the screams and moans of the dying and injured passengers – many of whom were trapped beneath the huge weight of the wreckage – horribly filled the night. The *Associated Press* reported *"The screams of women pinned beneath the wreckage were mingled with the hoarse shouts of men and the prayers of a Negro waiter when he was released, uninjured, from a hole in the side of the dining car."*

According to the *Rome* (Georgia) *News-Tribune*, *"The scene. . . . tested the strength of strong men. Bodies of victims crushed and mangled beyond description were . . . unreachable because of tons of weight upon them. The roof of the diner was rolled up like paper. The body of one man was hanging from a window, his legs pinned beneath the heavy weight."*

Most of the residents of Rockmart were unprepared for the trauma involved in a disaster of the magnitude of the 1926 wreck. Some rescuers went about their work numbly; others found themselves simply unable to continue as the shock set in.

Most sources today agree there were approximately 20 fatalities as a result of the collision. The official Interstate Commerce Commission report, filed January 11, 1927, reported that 11 passengers, 7 Southern Railway employees, and 1 news agent were killed (a total of 19 deaths as of that date; others may have died at a later date as a result of their injuries.). The report went on to explain that 113 passengers, 4 Southern Railway employees and 6 Pullman employees were

Mystery & History in Georgia

The day-coach of the Ponce De Leon which telescoped into the dining car was the site of many mutilated bodies. *(Photo courtesy of Atlanta Historic Society)*

injured in the wreck. It was miraculous that the death toll was not higher.

On December 24, the front page of the *Atlanta Georgian* trumpeted *"18 Dead In Wreck."* Due to the confusion which reigned at the scene of the accident and the inaccuracies in news reports of that day, several variations of the death count were published.

The dead in the Ponce De Leon included Road Foreman of Engines, Robert M. Pierce, who had assumed the engineer's duties from the regular engineer shortly before the crash. An arm and a leg were amputated from Pierce in a futile effort to save his life, but he succumbed shortly thereafter. Also dead was the fireman in the engine with him – H. R. Moss – who was killed instantly. W.H. Brewer, the baggage-master, died a few hours later.

Others listed as dead in the December 24, 1926 issue of the *Atlanta Georgian* were:

- Dr. P.T. Hale, 69, a professor of evangelism at Southern Baptist Seminary in Louisville, KY.
- W.L. Dynes, 56, an Atlanta real estate developer who lived at 951 Courtney Dr.
- J.E. Frost of 509 Foster St., Chattanooga, TN.
- L.B. Evans of Lebanon, KY, Kansas City and Jacksonville, FL addresses.
- Mrs. J.W. Whitaker of Chattanooga, TN.
- Goldie Williams, the infant daughter of Mrs. Alice Williams of Detroit, MI.
- J.W. Whisenhunt of Aragon, GA.
- W.I. Dowie, Jr. of Jacksonville, FL.
- A young boy, age approximately 8 years, believed to have been the son of Mrs. George Hardy of Toronto.
- A young girl, age approximately 10 years, with the initials H.M.H. on a bracelet, believed to have been the daughter of Mrs. Hardy.
- Six other individuals were unidentified: two white and four Negro.

Those listed as injured in the same article were:

- Mrs. George Hardy of Toronto.

The Horrible 1926 Rockmart Wreck   Polk County

Residents from miles away traveled to Rockmart to view the disaster for several days. *(Photo courtesy of Atlanta Historic Society)*

Some of the curious posed for photographs at the fateful site. A sheet formerly covering a body lies on the ground beside him. *(Photo courtesy of Atlanta Historic Society)*

- J.W. Dosser of Chattanooga, TN.
- F.W. Swann of Bolton, GA.
- Will Kuhn of St. Louis, MO.
- L.I. Seibert of Chattanooga, TN.
- Corporal Gus Rusts of Ft. Oglethorpe, GA.
- Dan Lobrugh of Cincinnati, OH.
- Robert Hilty of Lansing, MI.
- Edward Wiseman of Louisville, KY.
- H.E. Bullis of Lexington, KY.
- R.L. Bateman of Macon, GA.
- Mrs. J.J. Finlay of Chattanooga, TN.

As for the Royal Palm, the injuries were much less severe, and there were no fatalities. Much of this was due undoubtedly to the slow speed of the Royal Palm as its heavy engine impacted the Ponce De Leon.

"The hand of providence guided the destiny of the Royal Palm last night," Corrie told a reporter at his home Friday morning following the accident. "I was barely moving, pulling my engine along about 4 miles per hour as I neared the switch at the siding.

"I was obeying orders to await the Ponce De Leon which was to pull up and go into the siding so I could pass. When I saw the collision was certain, I slammed on my brakes and called to my fireman to jump.

"I jumped to the ground and rolled down a steep embankment. I don't suppose I was 30 feet away when the two engines met. . . . I fully expected the engine and cars to topple over and roll down upon me, but they didn't."

The Royal Palm consisted of one club car, five regular Pullman sleeping cars, one dining car and two Pullman sleeping cars of all-steel construction. They were pulled by Engine #1456.

The Ponce De Leon consisted of one combination car (half baggage & half coach), one coach, one dining car, and seven Pullman sleeping cars, all of steel construction, pulled by Engine #1219.

Following the impact, both engines were derailed, but somehow remained upright. Engine #1219 (Ponce De Leon) was badly damaged and its tender was torn from its frame and thrown down the embankment on the inside of the curve. The combination car was telescoped at its forward end nearly the length of the baggage compartment. The coach immediately following it telescoped into the dining car.

Though there has been much speculation, the positive cause of the accident is still not known to this day – or if it is, it has not been reported – and many questions linger:

Mystery & History in Georgia

Amazingly, despite the damage to the Ponce De Leon apparent in this photo, both locomotives from the collision were repaired and put back into service. *(Photo courtesy of Atlanta Historic Society)*

What about the switch controlling the entrance to the siding? Much speculation has centered around this device. It is not known today if it (the switch) was even open to admit the Ponce De Leon to the siding, but even if it had been open, the Ponce De Leon was moving at an incredible rate of speed far in excess of that which would have allowed it to negotiate the arc of the turn leading into the switch.

Another question centers around the speed of the Ponce De Leon. The descent down from the Braswell Mountains into Rockmart can be a perilous route. As recently as 1961, another train – this time a freight – was derailed in almost the identical spot as the 1926 disaster, causing an immense catastrophe in its own right. Speed and a lack of familiarity with the incline from the Braswell Mountains into Rockmart quite possibly played a role in that accident, and are suspected as prime catalysts in the 1926 disaster as well.

Just a few moments prior to the 1926 accident, S.J. Keith, the regular engineer, was directed by Pierce to *"go back into the train."* According to Keith's later statement, Pierce was running behind time, and therefore had advanced the speed of the Ponce De Leon to an excessive rate, *"dropping down off the mountain below Rockmart."*

According to the 1927 Interstate Commerce Commission report on the accident, *"When it (the Ponce De Leon) stopped at McPherson, 11.4 miles south of Rockmart, for the purpose of meeting an opposing train, Road Foreman of Engines Pierce, who had been riding in the combination car, boarded the engine and took charge of it, Engineman Keith going back to ride in the combination car.*

"Train first No. 2 (the Ponce De Leon) departed from McPherson at 6:23

The Horrible 1926 Rockmart Wreck — Polk County

Another view of the 1926 collision and derailment, looking from Goodyear Mill. *(Photo courtesy of Rockmart Library)*

p.m., 15 minutes late, passed Braswell, 6.4 miles from McPherson, at 6:35 p.m., 16 minutes late, passed the south passing track switch at Rockmart and collided with train #101 while traveling at a speed believed to have been approximately 50 miles per hour."

Some individuals have speculated that the blinding rain, coupled with Pierce's unfamiliarity with a newly-installed switchhead, were responsible for the tragedy. Others have maintained that in the driving rain, Pierce mistook a freight engineer's signal from a siding further up the line as the Royal Palm's signal that all was clear. This, at the very least, might provide a measure of explanation for Pierce's obvious decision to continue on at top speed without instead taking the side track.

The Interstate Commerce Commission report, however, concluded that the wreck occurred because Road Foreman of Engines Pierce, who had relieved Engineman Keith, either failed to have a thorough understanding with the engineman as to the contents of Train Order #92 (requiring him to take the siding), or else simply forgot it.

The true reason for the tragedy may never be known, since this information departed with Robert M. Pierce when he succumbed to his injuries shortly after the wreck. However, over the ensuing years of time, there have been some long-time former employees who have developed interesting opinions and theories concerning the accident.

Mr. H.D. "Cowboy" Mintz, a retired Southern Railways senior conductor and the son of Mrs. R.H. Mintz of Rockmart, says passenger train crews always consisted of the oldest men on the seniority list. Therefore, most of the Southern Railway employees from the Ponce De Leon and the Royal Palm who were involved in the accident were either deceased or retired by the time he was employed by Southern in the mid-1940s. However, "a few were still around," he said, and they – from time to time – shared their thoughts with him.

"I worked with Nath Turner, an engineer on the Royal Palm; Henry Sorrells, the conductor; and Harry Smith, the flagman," Mintz related. "Harry told me he and Henry were up in the cupola on the caboose on the rear of the Royal Palm, and they could hear the Ponce De Leon 'still working steam' as it was approaching. The whole train should have been coasting down the grade by that point. He always thought Bob Pierce was attempting to make up the lost time the train was suffering from."

377

Heavy-duty rail cranes labor to re-rail the locomotive of the heavily-damaged Ponce De Leon. *(Photo courtesy of Rockmart Library)*

But Mr. Mintz also says there have been rumors over the years of a personal vendetta between Keith and Pierce, and speculation regarding the possibility that this may have played a role in the disaster.

When Keith was relieved of control of the engine by Pierce at McPherson, could he (Keith) possibly have intentionally neglected to inform Pierce that the Ponce De Leon was to take the siding in Rockmart? Surely Keith would have known that failure to communicate these instructions to Pierce would have meant almost certain death or injury to himself.

The Interstate Commerce Commission report however, states unequivocally, that *"After the accident, Mr. Copeland assisted in removing Road Foreman of Engines Pierce from his engine and he said the road foreman asked him how the accident had occurred. When told that he had failed to take the siding for train #101 (the Royal Palm), he replied that Engineman Keith, Fireman Moss and everyone concerned had told him that he was to hold the main track."*

"Harry Smith's personal observation, Engineer Keith's statement that he explained the conditions of the orders to Pierce, and the theory of a personal vendetta between Keith and Pierce will always add to the mystery of the Rockmart wreck," Mr. Mintz added. "We'll never know the answer for certain."

Today (as of this writing), trains – albeit freight trains – still pass swiftly down this same single-tracked railroad from the Braswell Mountains into Rockmart. They often are moving at what almost anyone would deem to be an excessive rate of speed, causing automobile drivers at the Rockmart track intersections to cautiously stop far in advance of the crossings.

And to the rear of the former Goodyear Rubber Company building in Rockmart, a lone siding still exists today in virtually the identical location as the 1926 siding, almost as a harbinger of the terrible 1926 disaster, and reminding the trainmen to "slow down."

A Mysterious Cherokee Photograph, And The Naming of Collard Valley

His name has long been associated with a very fertile valley in present-day Polk County, Georgia, but most people never knew it. This Cherokee and his family were swept up in the shameful "Trail of Tears" incident in 1838, but an aged photograph may prove they survived the trauma.

The road winding through Collard Valley near Cedartown, Georgia, has not changed in well over 150 years. A few old-timers there like to tell new-comers that the area was named after a Cherokee Indian chief, but until just recently, no one was ever really convinced or knew any additional details.

A few residents can even point out where they think "Chief" Collard actually lived approximately 200 years ago, and according to U.S. government property valuations of the dispossessed Cherokees of this area in 1836 and '37, much of the speculation undoubtedly is true. Collard's home, according to the aged records, once existed where the main road crosses the creek that drains the valley.

History, unfortunately, has not been kind to Collard. There even is no proof today that he was ever a actually a "chief" or "headman" of his area despite anointment of the title over the years.

Virtually all official records of him have vanished, with the exception of the obscure property valuations and other brief mentions. And even in the valuations and other references, he has been forced to suffer the indignity of being addressed by his anglicized name "Collard," rather than his formal Cherokee name.

In order to wring every clue from the remaining circa 185-year-old (as of 2021) Indian property valuation records, one must do a bit of extrapolating to guess how the Native American earned his English name.

"Collard" is a corruption of the word "colewort." This ancient vegetable came early to North America, and at the time of this writing, the state of Georgia was growing some 10,000 acres of it. When Indian agent Col. Benjamin Hawkins travelled through the Cherokee Nation in 1798, he dined with a "Mr. Bailey" and his household of three Indian women, consuming a Christmas dinner of pork and coleworts.[1] He

Mystery & History in Georgia

According to records, the sons of a Native American Indian described as "Chief Collard" visited the spot known today as Collard Valley shortly after the U.S. Civil War. They presented this photo to Mrs. Martha Cordelia Whatley Whitehead, daughter of pioneer settler W.O.B. Whatley and grandmother of Miss Annie Jane Zuker of Rockmart, GA, who kindly made the print available for reproduction here. The date and specific identity of the three Native Americans pictured have been lost through time. *(Photo courtesy of Annie Jane Zuker)*

also described how the Indians were *". . . growing collards"* in this area in his writings. It may represent one of the first corruptions of the colewort name, and offer a glimpse into the origin of the Indian's name, since he undoubtedly grew the food.

The 1830 Census of this area (which at that time was a portion of Paulding County) lists *"Colewart's wife"* with three boys, also *"John,"* adjacent to an entry for *"Greenwood,"* which suggests Collard's wife and son, John, may have been living in *"Cedar Town"* (as it was written in pioneer days) near another individual named Greenwood.

Interestingly, "Greenwood," as it turns out, was a full-blooded Cherokee himself, farming a tract of land outside Cedar Town. He apparently was more successful than Collard, because he appears much more prominently in the historic records of this spot. *"He was tall, handsome and of commanding presence. He rode horseback when he went out dressed in a broadcloth suit and 'plug' hat, sometimes called beaver, but more correctly silk."*[2]

Greenwood lived below Judkins Mill[3] according to early Cedar Town histories. His claim, recorded in 1836 by the valuating agents, was for two parcels of property totaling some 40 acres valued at $1,540.[4]

The survey of 1832 places Greenwood on Lot 88724, along East Cedar Creek south of Cedar Town. On today's map, this lot includes the junction of east-running Pumpkin Pile Creek and north-running Cedar Creek.

Despite the prominence of Greenwood in today's records associated with Collard Valley, "Chief" Collard's star may be rising, thanks in part to the late Miss Annie Jane Zuker of Rockmart, Georgia. For a number of generations, Miss Zuker and her family have been in possession of a remarkable photograph from which they claim Collard and his sons proudly gaze forth.

"After the Civil War, his two sons travelled back from Oklahoma to visit Collard Valley. They arrived by train at Cave Spring (a rail line that was taken up many years ago) and walked nine miles to visit Grandma *(Martha Cordelia Whatley Whitehead, the second daughter of Wilson Ornan Burwell Whatley who was one of the first pioneers in the valley in the early 1830s),"* Miss Zuker recalled.

Collard and his sons apparently had posed for a photograph at some point in time and, during their visit with Mrs. Whitehead, the two surviving sons had proudly presented the photograph to her. This photo has been handed down in the family from generation to generation, and finally into the possession of Miss Zuker who is the great-granddaughter of W.O.B. Whatley.

It is unknown today just when or where the photograph was made, but it almost certainly was made after the terrible *"Trail of Tears."* Collard and his sons were among those Native Americans in the "Cedar Town" area who were imprisoned in "Fort Cedar Town" prior to being sent to the reservation in the West in 1838. They disappeared from the Cedar Town area at that time, and their property was listed in the U.S. government property valuations of Cherokee possessions in 1837.

As a result, the photograph undoubtedly was made after Collard and his sons had been re-settled in the west, quite possibly by one of the many photographers of that day recording the then-peaceful Native Americans on film. Since Collard himself apparently did not accompany his sons back to Cedar Town during their visit, it must be assumed that he was either too elderly, or deceased. Whatever the circumstances, the photograph is a strong indicator that he survived the "Trail of Tears."

In 1832, (at the time of the first Cherokee treaty and the relocation of the first group of Cherokees from Georgia who traveled voluntarily to a reservation out West), W.O.B. Whatley married Elizabeth Lumpkin, the daughter of Georgia Governor Wilson Lumpkin. The pioneering couple came to the rich bottomlands known today as Collard Valley to lay claim to vacated property

Photographed in 1970 is the historic W.O.B. Whatley home. It was this structure that Cherokees in the mystery photograph visited in 1837 to pay their respects to the first-born of the Whatley family. It was also to this house that the two Cherokees of the Collard family came when visiting shortly after the U.S. Civil War. This home, unfortunately, was erased in the flicker of an eye in 1978 by a vicious fire.

and carve out a plantation. Their first house was a small log cabin – a primitive start on the frontier to be certain for the daughter of the state's chief executive.

At that time, there possibly were still 20 to 30 Indians such as Collard in the valley outside Cedar Town who were yet living in defiance of the demand by the state of Georgia for them to relocate to the West, but only three other White families – aside from the Whatleys – lived along the 16-mile stretch of valley road.

Whatley, undoubtedly with the aid of his slaves, "cut the timber on the farm, stacked it, and let it age for two years," according to his great-grandson, Wayne Gammon. He then built a fine two-story plantation structure next to his Indian neighbor – Collard.

The home apparently was well-built – and a "lucky" structure to boot – because it survived Indian times, the U.S. Civil War, and the ravages of nature and the elements right up to the late 20th Century. After enduring all those harsh years, however, in 1978, it was erased in a flicker, as a vicious fire reduced it to ashes. Nothing remains today, aside from a windlass from the well, which was rescued by Mr. Gammon as the historic structure burned.

Chief Collard's dwelling was not nearly as grand – due of course to no fault of his own – nor did it survive as long as the Whatley home. According to the valuations mentioned above, it was a simple 16-foot square log cabin – as was customary with most Indian homes of that era, and, due undoubtedly to a lack of care by later owners following his departure, it soon fell into disrepair and decay.

Though his designation as a "chief" or "head man" is in question today, Collard nevertheless appears to have been a full-blooded native Cherokee. Unfortunately, his recorded accomplishments apparently were few in number, so the historic record of him is thin. He obviously was not one of the successful mixed bloods, such as James Vann, the McNair family, or the Rogers family, who variously cultivated large plantations with slaves and/or owned public houses and public ferries across the rivers and earned positions of authority in tribal councils. Collard was just a simple farmer, as were the majority of the Cherokees at that time.

Interestingly, the federal agents who made the assessments in 1836 did not list Collard among the five Cherokee farmers in Cedar Town, nor even among the fifteen Indians listed in Cedar Valley. Nor did the surveyors list Collard's 7-acre improvement four years earlier in the district in which Collard Valley was located when they surveyed the area. They undoubtedly followed lot lines, and sometimes simply overlooked improvements which should have been included in their notebooks.

Nevertheless, one year following the "Treaty of New Echota" in which all Cherokee property improvements were supposedly tallied, Indian Agents Shaw and McMillin retraced the Cherokee Nation for overlooked improvements. They eventually were guided through Cedar Valley by the proprietor of a Cedar Town trading post – L. H. Walthall – who had first scouted the area in 1826 and appears prominently in the county's history. This time, the searchers did find Collard, as well as his son. They found them not in Collard Valley, however, but along Cedar Creek.

According to Charles K. Henderson's writings in 1897, one hundred fifty Indian huts occupied an area south of Cedar Town called *"Char'le* (or Charley) *Town."*[5] According to the Paulding County map in Don L. Shadburn's *Cherokee Planters*, Char'le Town was "apparently a settlement slightly above Cedar Town, where Char'le (or Chai'le'te), a headman or spokesman for the people, owned improved land and a few tenements.[6] It is not known today if the name Collard could also be an anglicized derivative of this Char'le or Chai'le'te, but due to the absence of records, it is a possibility which must be considered.

In 1837, Indian agents listed the holdings of Collard: *"7 acres of upland with a valuation of $147, including two log cabins each 16 feet square and a stable 12 x 16 feet."* The record appears to show Chief Collard's signature; as his "mark" was made next to his name with a plus sign.

The next valuation in the agents' records is for *"John, son of Collard,"* who had *"8 acres of half-cleared land for a total value of $32.7"* (Note: As of this writing (2021), one dollar in the late 1830s would be worth approximately $28.79 in 2021 dollars. Therefore, the pay-out for Collard's property in 1837 would have been the equivalent of $4,232.00 in 2021 dollars – a tidy sum – and the pay-out for John's properties would have been worth approximately $921.00 in 2021 dollars. Those amounts of money would have easily enabled them to obtain a luxury such as a photograph in the late 1830s.)

Another note in the Indian agents' report – sadly characteristic of pioneer Georgia – described how Collard had been dispossessed of 7 acres in 1836, and was entitled to $21 in rent. This undoubtedly is the reason his place of residence changed from the Collard Valley area to Cedar Creek. His earlier site of residence may possibly have been taken over by Whites – a common occurrence, as the Cherokees were being relocated by this point – forcing him to move from the valley bearing his name.

The striking photograph of Collard with his two sons does not include the visage of the wife and mother, but gives us an interesting glimpse of the social fabric of life of the men. Collard wears two Christian crosses on his necklace, and one son (possibly the one with the Christian name of John) wears a cross near his throat. Clues such as these indicate the missionaries who had been working the territory since 1801 quite probably had swept up the Collards in their net. It is interesting to note that Collard's "mark" on the Indian agents' valuation record was also a "cross."

The cost of the studio portrait of the Indians may have been paid in cash or with credits from government compensation. Each of the three men appears to have a jacket on his lap, maybe for a hard Oklahoma winter after surviving the harshness of the "Trail of Tears."

One can only speculate today, and imagine how cheated and violated the Cherokees must have felt, particularly

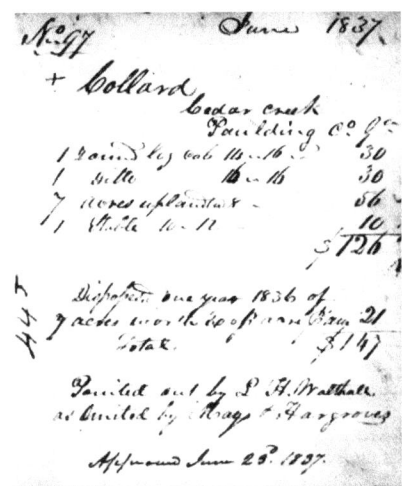

Proof of Existence – The federal valuation (#97) recorded by Indian agents Shaw and McMillin in June of 1837, confirms the existence not only of the property of Collard, but Collard himself near what today is known as Cedartown, GA. Collard's possessions and improvements are listed and valued, and the location identified as "Cedar Creek, Paulding (present-day Polk) County." Note how the valuation explains that Collard was "Dispossessed one year 1836 of 7 acres worth $3 an acre each," with the verification of "Pointed out by L.H. Walthall as omitted by Mags & Hargroves." *(Valuation record courtesy of the GA Dept of Archives & History, Atlanta)*

after the considerable efforts they made toward assimilating and co-existing with White settlers in such harmony and dignity for several decades prior to the removal.

One legend in the Gammon family suggests that Chief Collard must have been quite neighborly in his relations with the Whites. In 1837, the firstborn of the Whatleys – Lucy Ann – arrived. *(Gammon family lore includes recollection of an earlier child who died of fever.)* The Collard family reportedly stopped by to see their neighbors' new baby. However, the strangers crowding

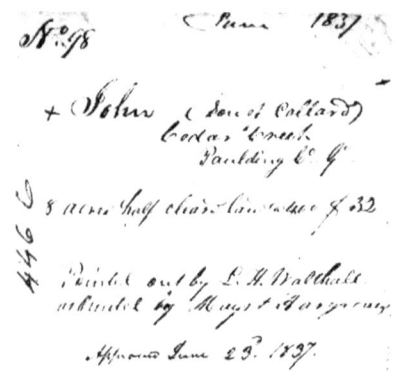

Proof of Son's Existence – This valuation, conducted at the same time as was Chief Collard's, indicates positively that he had at least one son who owned property in the same vicinity as he. *(Valuation record courtesy of GA Dept. of Archives & History)*

into the parlor, and speaking in a strange tongue, succeeded only in frightening the new mother who almost refused to show them her baby.[8]

The aged Whatley house which burned in 1978, quite likely was the scene of Collard's visit to the newborn baby in the 1830s. Located in the yard where the house stood is the family cemetery with a marker on the grave of Elizabeth Lumpkin Whatley – daughter of the former governor of Georgia – who died and was buried there January 10, 1872.

Another bit of family recollection maintains that Collard might even have been a bit too neighborly. According to accounts, a horse would occasionally disappear mysteriously from the Whatley farm. W.O.B. Whatley and a few of his farmhands would then simply mount up and ride down to the creek to pay the old chief a visit. No mention was ever made of the missing horse, but when the visitors were ready to leave Collard's cabin, they would always be greeted by the horse outside, ready and waiting to be returned home. According to the tale, no horses were ever lost permanently – just periodically "borrowed." The theft of horses was a long-time tradition among Native Americans, and a successful theft was a way for them to demonstrate superiority.

It can only be considered ironic that Collard undoubtedly did not know of the identity of the mother when he visited the newborn child at the Whatley home. Had he known that the child's grandfather was Governor Wilson Lumpkin, the visit by Collard to the Whatley home might not have been nearly so friendly.

It was Lumpkin who had ignored a U.S. Supreme Court mandate (which legally protected the lands of the Cherokees – for the Cherokees – in Georgia) and ordered the surveying of the land in the Cherokee Nation in Georgia, so that it might be distributed to white settlers in a state lottery. It was an act of defiance and illegality which ultimately was responsible for the dispossession of Collard and his kinsmen.

The removal deadline for the Cherokees had been set as May 24, 1838, and according to one official just months prior to that date, *". . . the whole of the Cedar Town Indians belong to the Ross party and oppose emmigration."*[9] In other words, the Cherokees in Cedartown were among the portion which supported Cherokee Chief John Ross and who refused to leave until forced to do so – which ultimately is exactly what happened.

A few years earlier, a similar plea to the governor by a White settler complained that *"The Cherokees have become much more impudent and hostile than they were before and say the Creeks are willing to aid them in killing up the white people and taking their land back again.*

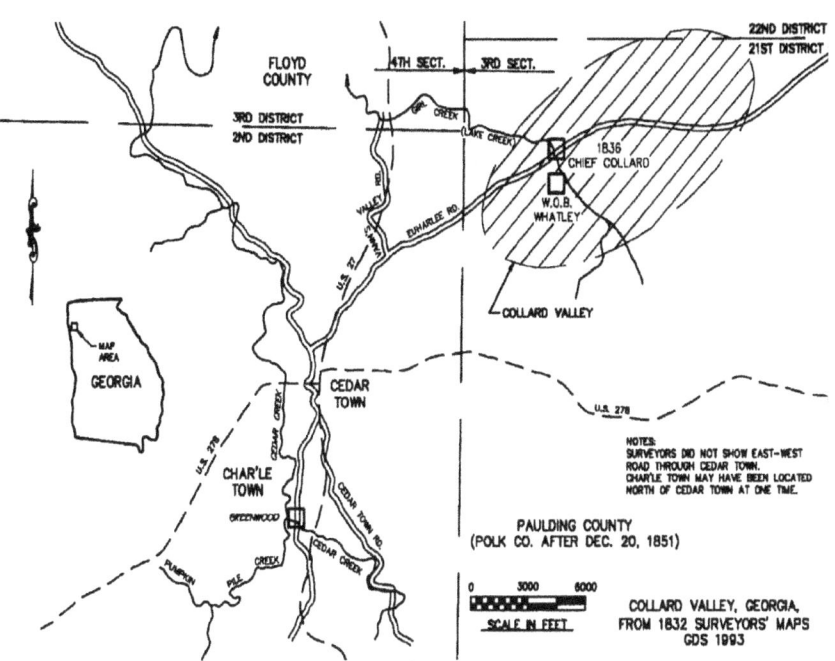

They have been continually robbing and plundering....[10]

Just days before the removal date, however, another official was more optimistic in another complaint to the governor – this time about the local militia's drunkenness and hostility toward the Indians: *"... the Cherokees in this part of the country (Cedar Town) remain as friendly as they ever were...."*[11]

Despite the seeming calm demeanor of the vast majority of the Cedar Town Cherokees, area officials no doubt maintained a wary vigil, monitoring the dispositions of the Cherokees, since their society had not progressed to the point beyond which an unannounced attack was to be discounted. As recently as the earlier 1830s, a number of vicious Indian raids in the area had in fact occurred. The *Savannah Georgian* carried an account of a Cherokee raid south into Cedar Town in 1830. It reported that in nearby Vann's Valley, 35 houses occupied by whites were burned. A party of 23 pursuing whites followed the 30 armed Indians south to Cedar Town but were too late to save it from the flames.[12]

As the removal date approached for the Cherokees, it is not known for certain what circumstances were faced by Collard. General Winfield Scott commanding some 4,000 militia and 2,500 regulars, ordered stockades to be erected for use as concentration camps. For Paulding County (which included most of today's Polk County) with 750 Whites, "Fort Cedar Town" was built to house the 200 Indians which were to be rounded up.[13]

The exact site of this stockade – just like the logs of the palisades around it – has long since been lost to history. Chief Collard and his family undoubtedly were herded into this inhumane enclosure with the rest of the Cherokees in the area, and in June, proceeded with an early detachment to Gunter's Landing

385

Mr. Wayne Gammon and daughter examine the grave marker of his great-grandmother near the former site of the W.O.B. Whatley home in Collard Valley near Cedartown.

on the Tennessee River where they were force-marched westward to their new home.

The state planners of the Cherokee relocation estimated the wagon trains could cover the 800 miles in 80 days, but to the contrary, the detachments each took from 104 to 189 days. Nearly 17,000 Native Americans in all were driven – at cruel bayonet point – along the Trail of Tears, and some 4,000 reportedly perished enroute. Collard and his son were among the lucky who survived. The aged photograph in the possession of the Zuker family almost certainly proves it.

As the forlorn exodus was beginning, Maj. Gen. Scott offered a revealing glimpse into his obviously very twisted perspective on the terrible project: "... I am confident that it will be found that among every thousand individuals, taken in families, without selection, there are at least 500 strong men, women, boys and girls, not only capable of marching twelve or fifteen miles a day, but to whom the exercise would be beneficial...."[14]

(The generous sharing of family stories and materials by the following individuals is gratefully acknowledged: Miss Annie Jane Zuker, Mrs. Georgia Wyatt, Mr. and Mrs. Wayne Gammon, Mr. and Mrs. Ralph Ayers, and the many other individuals who assisted with the information necessary for this article.)

Endnotes:

1. Hawkins, Benjamin, "Letters Of Benjamin Hawkins, 17961806," *Collections Of The Georgia Historical Society, Volume III*, Part I, 1848, Reprinted, 1982, pp. 21, 48.

2. Henderson, Charles K., *Polk County Persons And Things*, May 27, 1897, Chap. 3.

3. Ibid, Chap. 2

4. Shadburn, Don L., *Cherokee Planters In Georgia, 18321838*, p. 271.

5. Henderson, Charles K, *Polk County Persons And Things*, Chap. 3.

6. Shadburn, Don L., *Cherokee Planters In Georgia, 18321838*, p. 270.

7. Shaw and J.W. McMillin, *Cherokee Valuations, Alabama and Miscellaneous (Alabama, Georgia, & Tennessee)*, No. 97, (Collard) and No. 98 (John, son of Collard), Appraised June 23, 1837. Microfilm Drawer 242, Box 23, Surveyor General Dept., Georgia Department of Archives & History.

8. Gammon, Mrs. Beth, "Whatley, Cedar Valley Pioneer," *The Cedartown Standard*, October 14, 1976.

9. Adair, W.H., "Letter to Gov. George R. Gilmore" (Gilmer), Dec. 15, 1837, *Cherokee Indian Letters, Talks, & Treaties, 17861838*, Surveyor General Dept., Georgia Department of Archives & History.

10. "Letter To Gov. Wilson Lumpkin, May 27, 1834," *Cherokee Indian Letters, Talks & Treaties*, 17861838, Surveyor General Dept., Georgia Department of Archives & History.

11. Witcher, Lacy, "Letter to Gov. George R. Gilmer, May 21, 1838," Georgia Department of Archives & History.

12. *Savannah Georgian*, March 1, 1830, p. 2, c2, Microfilm Drawer 78, Box 45, Survey General Dept., Georgia Department of Archives & History.

13. Forts Committee, "The Cherokee Removal Forts," *Georgia Magazine*, (JuneJuly, 1970), p. 29, quoting Walker Messenger, November 5, 1915.

14. Gregory, Jack, and Rennard Strickland, Starr's *History Of The Cherokee Indian*, p 101.

Polk County's Asa Prior Family:

Frontier Fighters From Yesteryear

If one rides through Polk County today, the name "Prior" can still occasionally be seen on a street name here and there, and in scattered news accounts, marking them as a once-prominent family. They were hardworking, honest, and law-abiding citizens, and when a criminal element threatened their lives and livelihood during the war, the criminals seriously misjudged their adversary.

The area of northwest Georgia known today as "Polk County" was originally settled as a portion of Paulding County. It had abundant natural resources, one of which was (and continues to be) the rich farmland in Cedar Valley. Following the Georgia land lottery of 1832, large numbers of adventurous and ambitious white settlers began moving into the area and taking over the former lands of the Cherokee Indians. One of the earliest settlers in this area was a family by the name of Prior.

The Priors were led by family patriarch Asa, and they enjoyed a natural inclination toward accumulating capital. They prospered not only from farming, but also from the buying and selling of property.

Sometime around 1826, two scouts – Linton Walthall and Hampton Whatley – visited the Cedar Valley area along Cedar Creek. Both men envisioned a bright future for this fertile area.

After the state legislature created ten new counties from the Cherokee lands in 1832, land lotteries were conducted to distribute the land to new owners. Settlements were springing up and developing into towns such as Cedartown, with farms, shops, schools and churches, roads and post offices.

Walthall and Whatley established trading posts in the vicinity of the beautiful valley they had discovered. Walthall located his post above one of the largest springs in the territory, and Whatley chose a spot near Tanyard Branch, a little creek south of the new village already beginning to take shape along Cedar Creek.[1]

The Asa Prior Family

Asa Prior had made his home in Morgan County, Georgia, near the town of Madison before moving to Cedar Valley. He had laboriously built a

John T. Prior was photographed in 1899 in Cedartown. Pictured with him are his mother Ann M. Prior (far right), and his daughter, Anna Lou Davis. *(Photo courtesy of Polk Co. Historic Society)*

blacksmith shop there, working long and hard hours as the village smithy before deciding the pull up stakes and head to Paulding (later Polk) County in northwest Georgia.

Over a 25-year period, "Sally," as Prior referred to his beloved wife, bore him 14 children. Three of these children had died in infancy, and one had married by the time the Priors moved to Paulding.[2] According to county records, the *blacksmith from Morgan County* was among the very first settlers in Paulding, arriving in 1832.[3]

The living conditions for the newcomers undoubtedly were exceedingly primitive and exhausting for the first few years, in spite of the availability of slaves for the heaviest labor. The hardy settlers found abundant game, timber, and water, but farm land had to be cleared, planted and maintained. It was a long and arduous process, but the Priors knew how to work hard and make money.

When W.O.B. Whatley arrived about 1832, his family lived in a crude log cabin as well for two years until he could construct their fine home. *(Readers please see: "Mysterious Cherokee Photo & the Naming of Collard Valley" in the Polk County section of this volume.)*

It is not known today exactly where the Priors first lived in Cedar Valley, but in 1848, Asa reportedly built a substantial structure in the center of the new community, not far from the Big Spring. That house still stands as of this writing, but Asa Prior would not recognize it today.

Mrs. J.W. Pickett, a later owner of the Prior home, had the house jacked up and rotated 90 degrees, all accomplished by lowering the house onto logs lubricated liberally with grease. Instead of fronting on East Avenue as originally constructed by the elder Prior, the house was turned to face North College Street. After still more changes by later owners, the house gained a considerably different appearance. As of this writing, it serves as a mortuary called Gammage Funeral Home.

Early-on in his relocation to Cedar Valley, Asa suffered a grievous loss. His wife, Sarah, who was indescribably dear to the elder Prior and who had borne him so many children, passed away suddenly on January 2, 1838, at the somewhat young age (even for that day) of 54.

Sarah's mortal remains were buried in a spot apart from the site of the latter-day Prior home-place. She was laid to rest in a little family cemetery a mile south of the center of town – possibly near the site of an earlier temporary home prior to construction of the finer home in downtown Cedartown or the plantation on the outskirts.

Sarah's tombstone, undoubtedly the first in the little cemetery in which she rests for eternity, still can be seen today, but the weather and elements and the passage of time have virtually erased from the stone the date and touching epitaph which Asa ordered inscribed therein:

Sleep on my loving wife sleep
This world shall thy memory keep
But deeper on my heart is graven

The thought that we shall meet in heaven.[4]

The Priors were not strangers to tragedy. Several of their children died at a young age, and five of the fourteen had been born deaf. One can only imagine the anxious parents gently tinkling a little bell or some other attention-getter near the ear of the latest newborn, waiting patiently – but in vain agony – for a response from the infant.

Throughout his life, Asa Prior was deeply concerned with caring for his handicapped children. His last will and testament is a tangible reminder of his angst. In this document, he provides a lifelong income for each of his deaf children, no doubt filled with pain and pity as he carefully identified them as *"deaf and dumb."*[5]

Prior Landmarks

Asa Prior appears to have been a charter member of Cedartown's Baptist church. In 1835, the Baptists rented a building located on a knoll above Tanyard Branch which served as both a church and school. *(This site may have coincided with the little cemetery where Asa's wife was buried.)*

After a period of ten years, the congregation decided to build a proper church. A tract of property with a beautiful grove along what would become Main Street and West Avenue was donated for the purpose. One acre for the site of the new church and graveyard was donated by Asa,[6] and the adjacent acre was contributed by William E. West.[7]

The church and graveyard once stood where the First National Bank of Polk County stands (as of this writing) on West Avenue near Main Street. *(Author's Note: When workmen were preparing a parking lot for the bank, they reportedly discovered pioneer gravesites and* had to reconsider their plans.) A second church on a new site replaced the first in 1891, but today, both of the old churches have disappeared, replaced by a handsome modern structure.[8]

The one building most often associated with Asa Prior – his gristmill – still stands as of this writing in Cedartown. Somewhat surprisingly, there were in fact several gristmills in the Cedar Valley area just a short ride from Asa's mill.

These early mills were a staple and high necessity in pioneer American communities, but there normally was only one – or possibly two such mills – for each locality. This was due to the fact that the large millstones for a mill were exceedingly difficult and expensive to obtain, and in each locality, there was only so much grain that needed to be ground. The gristmills competition for grain clients in Asa's day must have been keen indeed.

The fact that there already were several gristmills in the area apparently did not discourage Asa Prior in the least. According to Charles K. Henderson's *Polk County Persons And Things*, written by Henderson and first published in the *Cedartown Standard* newspaper starting on May 27, 1897, *"Greenwood, the Indian, owned the mill located at the junction of Big and Little Cedar,"* (later known as Judkin's Mill).[9] John Wilson had a mill at Hightower Falls in 1832, later owned and operated by Elias Hightower. On upper Big Cedar Creek yet another mill was operated by George Watts.

To build his gristmill on Cedar Creek, Prior reportedly hired Milton H. Hanie of Cave Spring about 1849. This structure, amazingly, somehow survived the U.S. Civil War, when most of the remainder of Cedartown was burned by Union troops. For almost 100 years,

The third Polk County Courthouse on this site (l) and the Jail (r) were photographed in the early 1900s. In 1852, Asa Prior sold 19 acres to the city for development of the town. *(Photo courtesy of Watson Dyer Collection)*

Cedartown residents took their corn to this facility to be ground into meal.

Asa's mill later changed hands and became known as "Benedict Mill," and finally, in 1945, the little enterprise fell victim to progress, as were gristmills all over the country at this time. Electricity and the industrial age had ushered in a new era of modern electrically-powered facilities, and fresh meal and flour suddenly were offered in abundance in shops and grocery stores everywhere. Operations at Prior's old mill ground to a halt – no pun intended.

In 1960, the aged mill underwent a rejuvenation of sorts, when Robert L. Stevens and his wife, who had operated a restaurant in Cartersville, Georgia, purchased Prior's old mill and opened what they called *"The Old Mill Restaurant."* The site quickly became a popular dining spot, lasting for thirtyone years, before closing. Many families in the area had fond memories of many a happy Sunday dinner at this facility, while watching the water gushing down the millrace.

During his days in Cedartown, Prior reportedly accumulated an amazing six thousand acres of land and 500 to 600 slaves. By the 1840s, he had a sizeable plantation approximately eight miles west of town.

Asa's son – Haden – lived in a fine home at that site, and managed the plantation for his father. Asa maintained his residence in town.

When the Southern Railroad laid rails from Rome, Georgia, to Birmingham, Alabama, a railroad depot *"Prior Station"* was established on Prior plantation. A number of these former Prior establishments are commemorated for posterity in street and road names and city parks today.

Cedartown – The Early Days

Much of the property in the central portion of what today is downtown Cedartown was once owned by Asa Prior. Knowing that the town would need room to grow and prosper, and a reliable and abundant source of fresh water to supply to the citizenry, Asa sold 19 acres to the city of Cedartown for $1,200.00 in 1852. Though that was quite a lot of money in that day and time, the sale not only included the very important 19 acres, but the rights and access to the Big Spring as well.[10]

A courthouse ultimately was built on the site. When completed, the large brick and granite structure housed offices on the first floor and a courtroom on the second. This structure, however, and most of the rest of the town, were put to the torch by Kilpatrick's cavalry of Gen. William T. Sherman's army during the Civil War. It was therefore, rebuilt in 1869.[11]

Another courthouse was built in 1891. Today, on the same site as the original courthouse in the 1852 town plan, the Polk County Courthouse built in 1954 now stands.

Prior to the Civil War in the 1850s, Cedartown increased in importance

Frontier Fighters From Yesteryear Polk County

when it became the county seat of government. Polk County had recently been created (primarily by taking a portion of Paulding County), and needed a more centrally-located seat of government. Van Wert, formerly the seat of Paulding, was now in Polk, but it was near the edge of the new county, and thus was unsuitable as the new county's government seat.

With the loss of its status as county seat, Van Wert withered and died. The courthouse, bank, saloons, hotels, and other structures disappeared from the landscape over the years. Some were burned by the same cavalry unit from Sherman's army. Today, virtually nothing remains of Van Wert except for a state historic marker, the old Methodist Church and a portion of the old jail.

Despite his plantation and businesses, and the vigorous growth being experienced in the community he had helped found, Asa Prior surprisingly pulled up stakes in Georgia sometime around 1850. Did he see trouble on the horizon for the South and move out west to escape it?

Whatever the reason, Asa abruptly moved to Sabine County, Texas, purchasing a new spread not too far from his son, Andrew, who had been bitten by wanderlust earlier, settling in nearby Rusk County.

A Changing Of The Guard

Asa's son, Haden, remained behind in Georgia to maintain the Prior plantation and land development businesses there. He, quite likely, was one of the most prosperous planters in the area. It, unfortunately, was a reputation which later would prove fateful to Haden.

Asa Prior may merely have been visiting Cedartown from Texas, when he made his last will and testament dated

This 1864 illustration by W.D. Matthews for *Harper's Weekly* shows a vigilante raid on a Southern plantation during the lawless days of the U.S. Civil War. Records indicate circumstances in the north Georgia area – including Cedartown – were this bad and much worse during the days of the Prior family in the area.

October 13, 1853. In this document, he left instructions for the disposition of the Prior properties both in Cedartown and Texas, upon his death.

It is unknown today whether or not Asa knew of or suspected his impending death. Whatever the circumstances, a few months later, on July 2, 1854, the man who had done so much to foster the growth and development of the city of Cedartown, Georgia, passed away. He was buried in far-away Sabine County, Texas.

The enterprises and investments of the Priors undoubtedly continued to flourish throughout the 1850s, but came to a screeching, grinding halt with the advent of the 1860s, and the onslaught of the horrors which divided the Northern and Southern states.

War Comes Southward

Asa had one son and one grandson who enlisted on the side of the Southern cause in the Civil War, joining the Confederate Army in 1862. William H.C. Prior went off in June with a Polk County company. John left Rome on April

Mystery & History in Georgia

Though burned by Union forces during Gen. W. T. Sherman's engagements through Georgia in 1864, Cedartown was eventually able to rebound as shown in this circa 1899 photo. *(Photo courtesy of Watson Dyer Collection)*

5th with 65 other cavalrymen in a Cave Spring company,[12] but was able to return home a few months later after he hired a substitute.[13]

John reportedly was convinced there was no hope of the Confederacy winning the war, and thus did not strongly support the cause. It would not be long, however, before he would be confronted with a war of his own, one which would test his endurance.

As the Civil War drew to a close, affairs in Polk County were going from bad to worse. Sherman's troops had swept through the area on their "March To The Sea" and had burned Cedartown and nearby Van Wert to the ground. Outlaw raiders, many of whom were inveterate criminals, but also Confederate deserters and even "Home Guard" troops, laid waste to what little was left in the countryside.

Lawlessness prevailed during this period, mainly because virtually all law-abiding men – including law enforcement personnel – and even young boys barely big enough to carry a weapon, eventually were serving in the Confederate Army, as the war progressed and the casualties mounted. It was a situation ripe for crime. Homes were looted and residents who did not readily hand over their valuables were persecuted, maimed and murdered.[14]

Outlaws so terrorized the citizenry during the war that the state of Georgia organized what came to be known as "home guards," which were militia companies intended to provide law and order in the trouble spots, but who, more often than not, took advantage of the circumstances to become lawless bandits themselves. For the Cedartown district, however, Governor Joe Brown appointed a very capable and law-abiding citizen – Haden Prior – to command that company.

Prior's standing in the community apparently out-shined what had been, at most, a lackluster support of the Confederate cause. By the closing days of the war, however, Haden no doubt had become outspoken and active in the revolt against the North. A few months earlier, Union soldiers had burned his barns and warehouses and carried off whatever cattle and provisions were available.

Out of pure desperation, Haden and several of his sons were inexorably drawn into the vortex of these events in the last years of the war. It was a preoccupation which eventually would cost Haden his life, erupting into one of the bloodiest vendettas in Polk County history.

Plagued By Outlaws

The story of the events which follow was documented by a reporter in an 1897 Rome, Georgia newspaper following an interview with John Thomas Prior, Haden's son. Needless to say, the events precipitated by the feud are still told in old-timer circles in Cedartown to this day.

At some point in the mid-1860s, word reportedly reached Haden and his

392

militia that an outlaw group led by an individual named Jack Colquitt was raiding local farms in Cedar Valley. The local Home Guard militia, including Haden and his son, John, promptly set out to hunt the men down, per their instructions from the governor of Georgia.

After picking up the outlaws' trail, Haden and his Home Guard troops soon caught five of the raiders on the road between Cave Spring and Prior Station. One of the outlaws reined in his horse, quickly turned him around and made the mistake of trying to escape. John Prior drew a bead on the fleeing horseman and fired, knocking him out of the saddle with one shot. He was the first of six men John would ultimately kill in a personal quest against the Colquitt gang.

Following a successful first stage in eliminating the lawless riffraff from Polk County, the posse brought back the four men they had captured and lodged them in the Cedartown jail. Within a few weeks, however, all four surprisingly had been released – possibly for lack of evidence, but also possibly due to a breakdown in civil order and law enforcement. Regardless of the circumstances, the criminals were soon back terrorizing the citizens of the county.

Eight Slugs From A .44

"A fellow named Phillips was very bitter," John Prior explained in later years to the Rome reporter. "Colquitt's gang put out the word that they would kill my father for having them arrested, but he never took it seriously."

Determined to arrest Colquitt and bring him to trial before he and his gang could carry out their threat or inflict more suffering upon innocent farmers, John and his brother, James (who was also a member of the Home Guard), set out to search for Colquitt one night. It is not known today why the Prior brothers decided to search for the renegade at night, or if in fact they were simply availing themselves of an opportunity of which they had learned.

Whatever the circumstances, the two men appeared at a Cedartown grocery store that night where they found the outlaw in a drunken stupor, lying on the store counter. Colquitt did not know it at the time, but his final day on earth was quite near at hand.

"When we aroused him," John later stated for the newspaper reporter, "he was very quarrelsome and cursed loudly. We let him rave, but when he reached for his pistol to shoot us, ... I (put) a bullet through his heart."

George Battey, in his seminal *A History Of Rome and Floyd County*, added some details to John Prior's account. According to Battey, when the shooting began, both brothers fired at Colquitt, putting a total of eight bullets into him.

It seems apparent from the description of the incident, that the brothers wanted to make certain Colquitt did not move from the spot – at least not without being carried out. John later told a friend, "I was so close when I fired my first shot that I saw smoke coming out of his mouth."

The killing of Jack Colquitt, however, did nothing to dampen what by then had become a bloodlust among his men, particularly regarding Haden Prior. It was a scene very reminiscent of the circumstances which led up to the now famous gunfight behind the O.K. Corral in Tombstone, Arizona, some 16 years later.

Undeterred by their leader's demise, members of the Colquitt outlaws bided their time, waiting for just the right opportunity for revenge. It finally came on April 6, 1865.

Mystery & History in Georgia

One of the oldest structures in Polk County remains in excellent condition today, but its former owner – Asa Prior – undoubtedly would not recognize it due to substantial alterations. *(Photo courtesy of Gordon Sargent)*

As events in Cedartown were boiling over, the final curtain on the U.S. Civil War was being drawn. On that Sunday, two army chieftains, one in blue and one in grey, met at a tiny town called Appomattox Court House for an epic surrender. The following Friday, an event at Ford's Theatre in Washington City (D.C.) would further stun a nation that was already reeling.

Haden Prior Murder

In the spring of 1865, Haden Prior was visiting a Mr. Hampton about two miles from his Prior Station home. Haden was accompanied by an adolescent Negro servant.

As Haden was leaving the Hampton residence, four of the Colquitt gang-members apparently confronted him not a hundred feet from the front gate of the Hampton home. According to later accounts of this incident, Phillips, the leader of the party, exchanged a few words and then drew his pistol and shot Haden through the heart, killing him instantly. He also killed the servant.

Around noontime, Haden's son, John, learned the shocking news of his father's violent murder. He immediately saddled up and rode out to the Hampton property where he learned the details of the crime.

John Prior has been described as "tough as nails" when necessary – about five feet and eleven inches in height, and thin and wiry. His slight stature was said to have been deceptive, however, for he reportedly had a muscular physique, and rawboned determination in any objective set before him.

The feature, however, which most impressed those who knew John, was his eyes. They were said to have been small, gray, and glittering like jewels. Stranger still, there reportedly was no white around the glassy gray iris. John Prior's eyes literally were hypnotic in appearance.

John once stated, "I never center my eyes on anybody but a person I hate, because I know their effect on people. I never stare at anybody because it would frighten them."

John Prior's anguish upon the discovery of his father's crumpled body can only be imagined today. It is known that he wasted no time in setting out with a few friends to hunt down the killers.

The members of the Colquitt group responsible for shooting Haden Prior in cold blood may not have known it at the time, but John Prior "was coming," and hell was coming with him.

Deadly Pursuit

By sunup the next day, the trackers had found first one and then another home plundered by the bandits whose blood-lust seemed to be growing by the hour. John and his men, however, knew that they could be only a few hours ahead.

The trail led due-west into Alabama and the area of Piedmont. There, however, the trail grew cold.

As John Prior later recalled, *"We*

rode on rapidly across the Alabama line to Ladiga (presentday Piedmont), for which point we thought they would make, but we could learn nothing of them. Baffled, but never despairing, I rode three miles to Cross Plains, a point lower down. Here, I could find no clue."

Returning to Ladiga, John remembered another road leading out of town. He questioned some young boys at a school on the road and fortunately received a good description of the men they were hunting. They were able, once again to pick up the trail, and rode north for several miles.

"It was between 11 or 12 o'clock when just beyond Coloma, Alabama, I rode up in front of the Widow Lane's house and saw two men sitting under some trees and three horses tied nearby. I remember the pink and white blossoms of the peach trees. The house, situated as it was at the foot of the Wiseman Mountains, made a most inviting place.

"The men, I think, saw me about the same time I saw them and both sides were somewhat surprised. One of them made a movement to reach for his gun. I jumped off my horse, cocked my double barrel shotgun, and fired before he raised his.

"One of them fell over riddled with buckshot, while the other ran around the house. I drew my pistol and ran after him, but just around the corner came upon his dead body where he fell."

The third man fired and fled into the woods. Prior quickly caught up with him and, unwilling to leave the situation to a decision by a "fixed jury," gunned him down on the spot. John Prior apparently was deadly with almost any type of firearm. Later, he said, "They were not the murderers of my father, but doubtless belonged to the same gang."

Within twenty-four hours of his father's murder, John Prior had found and killed three of the gang. Together with the earlier shooting of Colquitt and the gang member who had tried to escape when threatened with arrest, the death toll had now reached five men. However, the actual killer of Haden Prior – Phillips – and his two henchmen who had been identified as Montgomery and Bishop, were still at large.

Four Horsemen Of The Apocalypse

"I learned that Phillips, when not on a freebooting excursion, lived on a farm down in Haralson County," John continued to the newsman. "It was early July that (I with) one of my brothers and two friends started out about nightfall for Phillips' home with the determination of killing him. We surrounded his home somewhere about 3 o'clock in the morning."

Early the next morning, John cornered his quarry. Phillips had emerged from his house and walked to a nearby field to begin a day of plowing.

John Prior later explained it was an easy matter to get close enough to surprise Phillips. John said he rode to the top of the hill above Phillips, dismounted, then eased down to the edge of the field, concealing himself in the undergrowth. He then waited until Phillips plowed to the end of a row, and then just as he was about to turn his horse, John said he stepped out of the woods and covered the man with his pistol.

"Phillips," he said, "I want you."

"Let me go to the house first to see my wife," Phillips reportedly pleaded. He had to have known by then what had happened to the other members of Colquitt's criminal group. He had to know that his final moments on this earth were upon him.

"No. I want you right now," Prior replied harshly.

"Well, let me unhitch my horse from the plow."

"All right. Go ahead, but be quick about it."

John could see the bandit's women and children in the distance running out of the house. They, no doubt, had seen members of John's party and also suspected the worst, running to Phillips to warn him. However, it was too little too late.

"I knew that unless I killed him pretty quick, the women and children would all be crying around me very shortly," John later explained.

Probing for a confession, John asked, "Phillips, who killed my father?"

Phillips responded with the name of a man who John knew had no connection with the murder.

"I have the best evidence that you did the killing," John replied, and with that, Phillips reportedly fell on his knees and began to beg for his life.

"You needn't expect any mercy from me," John added. "I'm going to kill you."

Desperate and realizing that his end was near at hand, Phillips reportedly broke into a run. John merely took careful aim and, without compunction, shot him in the back.

Phillips fell on his side and then rolled over on his back. With the women and children watching a short distance away, John walked over and shot Phillips through the heart at close range.

After making certain that his quarry was too dead to even kick again, John remounted his horse and set out in search of Montgomery, another of his father's murderers. After killing six men, there were two more left to hunt down.

Just as had Phillips, Montgomery had also heard what had happened to his partners in crime, and he (Montgomery) was not going to hang around to give John Prior an easy target. He had fled the district, but it made no difference. John Prior was relentless. After following clues for a length of time, he finally discovered the man in Arkansas, but for reasons unknown today, he relented and spared his victim this time.

Perhaps John had seen enough killing. Maybe he just had compassion for Montgomery. The exact circumstances have been lost through the passage of time. Montgomery, nevertheless, died about five years later in Arkansas, so his days were shortly numbered anyway.

John Prior still was not finished though. There was one left – a man by the name of Bishop. John told the newspaperman that he tracked Bishop many, many miles, no doubt making his life miserable.

John Prior again was relentless. When he finally reached Bishop's location, he learned the man had died of natural causes. If I had to guess, I'd say the last two men on John Prior's list had died prematurely from sheer terror. Whatever the circumstances, the hunting and killing was over.

The manhunt and ultimate murders of men – without benefit of a legal trial by jury – may seem horrific to a reader in modern times. However, during the U.S. Civil War and its immediate aftermath, the southern United States was a lawless area, besieged by cutthroats and criminals of all makes and descriptions. It was a brutal and bloodthirsty time, when many men lived by the gun. Violence was a way of life.

There were also many "kangaroo courts" and opportunities for criminals to slip through the cracks if they could demonstrate to a northern-dominated jury or sympathetic northern judge that they, the criminals, had actually committed no crime, since they were merely a continuation of the then-accepted abusive system designed to punish the South of the mid- and late-1860s. John Prior was not about to allow any such system to deny him the justice he felt he deserved.

Peace At Last

Following this series of horrendous events, John Thomas Prior enjoyed a surprisingly quiet and uneventful life. He was never charged with any crimes for the shootings and the men he had killed. It is quite possible that many residents of Polk County in fact wanted to honor him, instead of prosecute him.

Six months after John Prior's story appeared in the Rome, Georgia newspaper in 1897, his son, George Prior, married and moved away, settling in Roseburg, Oregon. John and his daughter later moved there to live with him in 1906.[15]

Two years later, John's daughter married, and around 1910, the proud old avenger posed for a photograph with his new granddaughter, Georgia M. Davis.[16] That same year, John T. Prior reached the age of 70, and died peacefully at his daughter's home.

John's cause of death was attributed to *"the direct infirmities attendant to old age."*[17] He was buried in the old Masonic Cemetery, now Memorial Gardens in Roseburg, Oregon.

Back in Cedartown, Georgia, it wasn't too many years after the Civil War and the infamous murder of Haden Prior, that the pleasant residence of Prior Station was finally completely abandoned by the Priors. The final disposition of this property out of the Prior name is unknown today.

Through investments and good business acumen, the Priors possibly had become financially independent and simply were no longer in need of the

The former site of Asa Prior's (and later Haden Prior's) plantation, known as "Prior Station," leaves much to the imagination today. The only remaining remnant here of the Prior home or out-buildings, is the sadly-overgrown and unkempt Prior Family Cemetery (undergrowth, left) where Haden Prior is buried. *(Photo courtesy of Gordon Sargent)*

property. Or perhaps it was in fact sold out of the family by the last Prior in the family to own it. Whatever were the actual circumstances involved in that sale likely will never be known, since today, there are no records back that far.

Most of the remnants of the Polk County Prior family ultimately drifted off to the West, always west. Haden Prior and his mother and a few other deceased Priors, however, remained behind in gravesites in Polk.

Today, descendants of Asa Prior can still occasionally be found in Cedartown, but few with the Prior name. And as for Prior Station, all traces of the once-grand plantation have vanished.

In more recent years, a home and dairy occupied the site where the Prior plantation house once stood. The railway depot and rail line near this site also disappeared years ago. Nothing remains today except the small overgrown Prior family cemetery surrounded by an iron fence – ironically with a gate facing westward – always westward.

The city built by a blacksmith, and protected by his sons and grandsons, still thrives today. And sometimes, when

Mystery & History in Georgia

Built in 1849, Prior Mill continues to weather the years. In more recent times, it has been the site of a popular restaurant on several different occasions. *(Photo courtesy of Gordon Sargent)*

native sons of the community gather to reminisce about area folklore, the life and times of the Asa Prior family inevitably become a topic of conversation.

Acknowledgements

The generous sharing of Prior family materials by the following is gratefully acknowledged: Miss Matilda West, Cedartown; Mrs. Marjorie Brown, Longview, Texas; Mrs. George O. Marshall, Jr., Athens, Georgia; and Ms. Eileen Talburt, Douglas County Genealogy Society librarian, Roseburg, Oregon.

Endnotes

1. Whatley, George Fields, "Cedartown's Big Spring," *Georgia Life*, Spring, 1978, p. 2021.

2. Georgia DAR Book 8, 194950, *Bible Records Of Revolutionary Soldiers*. William H.C. Prior family Bible. Prior file in genealogical records at the Georgia Department of Archives & History, Atlanta, GA. In the various records, the spelling of the family name changed with Haden although the records appear to be consistent otherwise. Fourteen children with their birthdays are listed for Asa Prior.

3. Floyd County Deed Record Book C, p. 6. Deed records of Paulding County go back only to 1848, but Floyd County records show Asa Prior was a resident of Paulding County who was buying and selling numerous lots in Floyd County. His earliest recorded transaction was November 8, 1832.

4. Brown, Marjorie Maxwell, various Prior family materials.

5. Prior, Asa, October 13, 1853, recorded last will and testament in Record of Wills, Book A, Polk County, Georgia, pp 2627.

6. Paulding County Deeds, Record Book X, p. 579. It is interesting to note that the 1832 survey shows the road which would become Main Street, although it had several twists in it which have disappeared.

7. Paulding County Deeds, Record Book X, p. 580. The surveyor noted that one fortyacre lot included Judge Witcher's yard and field and another 160 acres included Witcher's farm. By 1845, this farm was owned, at least in part, by William E. West.

8. Johnson, Larry G., *A History Of The Polk County Missionary Baptist Association*, Nashville, TN, 1977, p. 98.

9. Henderson, Charles K., "*Polk County Persons And Things*," Chap. 11 from the series appearing in the *Cedartown Standard* starting on May 27, 1897. Henderson observed that the mudsills of Greenwood's mill could still be seen. The state survey of 1832 noted the Indian, Greenwood, and his mill on Lot 887 on "East Cedar Creek." This lot appears on a current Polk County map at the junction of Cedar Creek and Pumpkin Pile Creek.

10. Polk County Deeds, Record Book A, p 191.

11. Henderson, op. cit., Chap. 2.

12. Kinney, Shirley Foster and James Paul Kinney, *Floyd County Confederates* (and surrounding counties), Vol. VIII, SFK Genealogy, Rome, Georgia, 1992, p. 215.

13. Battey, George Magruder, Jr., *A History Of Rome And Floyd County, Vol. I*, Atlanta, 1922, p. 384385. It may have been no coincidence that the company commander was Capt. M.H. Hanie the same individual who had built the gristmill for Asa Prior.

14. Battey, op. cit., pp. 205208.

15. Marshall, Mrs. George O., Jr., Athens, Georgia.

16. U.S. Census of 1910, Deer Creek District, Douglas County, Oregon.

17. Obituary of John Thomas Prior, *Umpqua Valley News*, November 7, 1910, Roseburg, Oregon.

Early Den Of Iniquity:

High Times & High Crimes at Polk County's Esom Hill

Since the earliest days in the county, tiny Esom Hill was known as a place where a person could go to "get a drank of likker," and have some high times.

The people of west Georgia in the vicinity of present-day Polk County never hesitated to travel wherever necessary in that region since the county's earliest days, but there was one little spot which earned a reputation early-on as a place to which outsiders simply did not go. It was called "Esom Hill."

As an example, on one occasion in years past, a neatly-dressed stranger from an out-of-town company was examining a lot upon which his firm had contracted to build a home for a local resident. Suddenly, a man with a shotgun walked up. "Get out of Esom Hill," he rasped at the builder. "You ain't got no bizness here." After a glance at the barrel of the deadly weapon, the builder had to agree, and left in a cloud of dust.

Such was the reputation for the little state line community in northwest Georgia's Polk County for well over a century – an image fostered by a long record of illicit activities such as "moonshining," gambling, and even darker crimes like murder. And surprisingly, it seemed the stronger the criminal element became in the township, the less visible became law enforcement.

Despite its infamy, Esom Hill, according to many residents, is nevertheless a friendly community today with caring neighbors and a bad name circulated by "outsiders." Just like many situations, the truth lies somewhere in the "grey area" in between.

Early History

Settlers in this westernmost edge of present-day Georgia, in what once was Cherokee Indian Territory, interestingly were among the *last* to arrive in Paulding County, Georgia, since it was reorganized as a part of Polk County in 1851. The beginnings of "infamous" Esom Hill ironically occurred with the founding of the "very religious" Shiloh Baptist Church[1] in 1848 and the "very law-abiding" first post office[2] in 1850.

Partly as a result of its close proximity to the Georgia-Alabama state line and partly due to its generally remote circumstances away from the watchful eyes

Law enforcement officials destroy an illegal distillery ("still") in Esom Hill circa 1928. Untaxed corn liquor was an extremely important "cash crop" to rural settlers of north Georgia, particularly in the mountain regions, during the 1920s and '30s, when a terribly depressed economy left many families with no other options. Esom Hill in northwest Georgia – just as Dawson and other counties in northeast Georgia – has enjoyed a long-standing reputation as a center of moonshine production. *(Photo courtesy of Mrs. Brenda Bentley)*

of law enforcement, Esom Hill somewhat naturally gravitated toward lawlessness and controversy. Local tales describe – tongue-in-cheek – how bootleggers escaped law enforcement officers by moving their liquor from one room in a building (in Georgia) to another room in the same building (in Alabama).

Another claim even maintains the first Esom Hill, "Georgia" post office was actually established in Alabama (1847) and then later moved to Georgia (1849) after the discrepancy was discovered.[3] This possibly could be explained by the fact that the first postmaster – Benjamin Wheeler – lived in Alabama and actually operated the post office there from his home or store. Today, no one really knows for certain, nor cares.

Local folklore maintains the name of the little community sprang from an old trading post once operated by an Indian named "Esom" or "Easom," possibly prior to the removal of the Cherokees from the territory. The "Hill" apparently was added later, and no one knows today to what it originally referred – nor, once again, cares.

Another version of the origin of the town name claims it came from an early settler now buried in Shiloh Baptist Church cemetery beneath an unmarked fieldstone. Whatever the origin, the name and fame of Esom Hill aren't just "local." The reputation of the tiny township has spread far and wide over the years, and always accompanied by its dark reputation.

A book entitled the *Georgia State Gazeteer*[4], published way back in 1881, lists Esom Hill as a community of 169 people with five general stores, three churches, a school and a saloon. The village also boasted a steam gin, a water-powered gin, and a sawmill. The year 1881 was the same year, interestingly, as the famous Old West gun-fight behind the O.K. Corral between the Earps and Clantons, just to put things into perspective.

Early Commerce

Four years earlier in 1877, when Amos West founded his Cherokee Iron Company in Cedartown, Esom Hill must have shared in the prosperity as mining operations grew (supported by plentiful iron ore deposits in the area). Farming, of course, undoubtedly also figured prominently as a professional pursuit, but according to early records, there surprisingly were quite a few small

businesses in the "up and coming" little community as well, suggesting a very self-sufficient environment:
- W.P. West, postmaster
- J.P.S. Brewster, general store
- Rev. V.A. Brewster, Baptist pastor
- A.A. and J.W. Camp, saw mill
- Dukes and Pearson, blacksmith
- H.A. Edmonson, notary and J.P.
- Jeremiah "Jerry" Isbell, general store
- M.E. McCormack, tax collector and teacher
- J.S. Mercer, general store
- Nobles and Adkins, blacksmith
- T.J. West, general store
- W.P. West, general store
- West and Hackney, grist and saw mill
- C.M. Wheeler and son, saloon

Today, many of these original residents of Esom Hill rest in Shiloh Cemetery, and many of their descendants still live in the same community.

The general stores of Brewster and Isbell are still remembered particularly well – one in the village center and the other three miles east at Akes Station. Brewster's original building reportedly burned, and he built a new store across the street in 1901, a structure which, as of this writing, still functions today as the Esom Hill Trading Post.[5]

Jeremiah Isbell's country store operated out of the front room of his home[6] and was still standing until a few years ago when it was demolished. The Brewsters and Isbells were among the original families to settle in Esom Hill.

In 1860, the Rev. Vann Allen Brewster left Haralson County and moved to Esom Hill with his family.[7] Jeremiah Isbell finally made it back to Floyd County at the conclusion of the Civil War in 1865, only to find that his family had "refugeed" to Polk County.[8] Rome having been largely destroyed and occupied by Union troops was an inhospitable environment, and the Isbells – though they made it no further than "west Georgia" – had joined many Georgia residents who were headed to Texas and other parts westward, looking for new opportunities.

The Brewster and Isbell children grew up together as nextdoor neighbors in Esom Hill. The families were formally linked in 1879 when a son and daughter married – Joseph Proctor Screven Brewster to Laura Jane Isbell. From this union came twelve children, contributing to the family of the proud grandfather, and making these two families among the largest and most prominent in the community.

Jerre Isbell boasted in his eighty-first year: "There are now living, and physically and mentally strong, not an idiot nor invalid nor a deformed one, in whose total reaches 198."[9]

The Brewster Mercantile Company became one of the first in the county to have electric power when Brewster installed a "Delco System" to generate power for lights in his store and in his home across the road.[10] The little generator charged a system of batteries during the day, and at night, when it shut down, the bank of batteries took over providing electricity. The store carried everything from toothpicks to two-horse wagons to serve the farmers in the surrounding area.

A counter and post office boxes were located behind swinging doors at the back of the store.[11] The enterprising Joseph P.S. Brewster also served as postmaster. (Later, his son, Fred, would become postmaster when he and brother Gordon succeeded their father in the operation of the store.[12])

Mail deliveries from the Esom Hill Post Office were carried over two mail

Mystery & History in Georgia

Joseph Proctor Screven Brewster (1856-1913) – Brewster was one of the original pioneers of Esom Hill. He built the Brewster General Store in town in 1901.

routes. In 1928, when Jack Phillips began carrying the mail, he covered two routes (Routes 1 and 2) which apparently were combined into one route at about that time. According to Cora Belle Honea, Phillips drove a car to make his deliveries.

Prior to Phillips' tenure, Ben Griffith had driven Route 1 and Jim Woods had done Route 2, both of them using a horsedrawn postal buggy. In the beginning, Phillips also reportedly drove a horse-and-buggy to deliver the mail, but when his first horse, Maude, grew too old and slow, he bought another faster horse which he named "Dammit." The frisky beast would often trot too fast, necessitating a "Whoa, Dammit!" much to the amusement of any bystanders."[13]

As a rural mail carrier, Jack Phillips provided some services totally unavailable today. As he made his rounds, he could be persuaded to carry eggs from one farm to another, or a basket of fruit to a shut-in. This courier might even delay the swift completion of his appointed rounds by stopping to read – or even write – a letter for someone needing assistance. Phillips reportedly even helped one elderly lady to order a corset and some batteries for her radio from the Sears Roebuck catalogue – even to the point of installing them when they were delivered (the batteries of course, not the corset).[14]

Moonshine & Murder

It was from this bucolic-sounding setting that the illicit activities of Esom Hill eventually evolved, and the community, in many instances, did nothing to diminish its reputation or discourage the activities – often even reveling in it. At one point many years ago, alongside the approach road and next to the railroad crossing, the town name and population were even proudly and boldly inscribed across the face of a decommissioned moonshine still, much to the delight of many.[15]

The production of untaxed whiskey – i.e. "moonshine" – eventually grew into big business in the hills and hollows between Esom Hill and Borden Springs, five miles to the west in Alabama. Brokers lined up orders for the spirituous liquor, distributing it freely in a wholesale operation. During Prohibition (1920-1933), huge trailer trucks reportedly transported literally thousands of gallons of illegal whiskey from these hills northward to thirsty markets such as Chicago. Cars and small trucks could be fitted to handle loads of 100 to 150 gallons to make deliveries. Moonshine was big-bidness in Esom Hill.

When law enforcement officials stepped up arrests and crackdowns on the production of un-taxed whiskey in northwest Georgia in the 1950s, they, for obvious reasons, began their efforts at Esom Hill. One group drove out to the Treat Mountain area south of Esom Hill to search for illicit distilleries, parking their car alongside the road. While they were searching, their car mysteriously caught fire and burned to the axles. The insult so stung the officials that they opened a local office and dedicated it to the eradication of Polk County moonshining.[16]

Because it often involved so much money and represented the main source of income for so many rural citizens, any destruction or interruption of moonshine operations could – and often did – result in violent consequences. Just like the Hatfields and McCoys of old, disputes between neighbors at Esom Hill frequently got out of hand and became a deadly conflict.

Of the many storied shootings at Esom Hill – and there have been quite a few of them – the day in April of 1933 that Warren Bailey fatally wounded Robert Hackney undoubtedly stands out prominently in the memories of some old-time residents.

According to the *Cedartown Standard* of that day[17], *"Deputy Sheriff Stone was called to the scene early Sunday night and found the body of (Robert) Hackney alone in the Bailey home. He had been shot through the body by a Winchester rifle and death was believed to have been instantaneous.*

"Investigation by Mr. Stone revealed that Hackney held a pistol in his right hand under his body and that the pistol had been recently fired twice. Alvin Bailey, son of Warren Bailey, claims to have been an eye witness to the affair and states that Hackney entered the home under the influence of liquor and shot at his father with the pistol and that the elder Bailey

Jeremiah Marion Isbell (1829-1913) was another original pioneer in Esom Hill.

then grabbed the rifle and killed him. The rifle load indicated it had been fired one time."

The shooting apparently took place in the Bailey home. The "liquor" which Hackney had consumed was of the Esom Hill variety. Prohibition did not end until December 5, 1933.[18]

Warren Bailey ultimately was acquitted of the charge of murder by a grand jury. Three years later, however, in another notorious incident, he was killed by his nephew, Clayton Bailey.[19] "He who lives by the sword...."

"Bell Tree" Smith

Of all the liquor legends floating around Esom Hill, the most popular one by far involves an individual named Will Smith, better known as "Bell Tree" Smith, the moonshine king. Over the years, the legend almost certainly has mushroomed, and Will's son, William Smith, and his family in fact do maintain that much of the information about his father in the tales simply is not true.

Despite the disclaimer, it is known for a fact "Bell Tree" Smith had a unique method of selling his corn liquor – a system which somehow seemed to protect him from detection by law enforcement officials.

It actually was very simple in design. Not far from his still, Smith rigged a dinnerbell in a large oak tree, attaching a rope from the bell so that it could be rung by customers. A buyer would set his empty jug and money by the tree, give the rope a tug to ring the bell, and then leave the premises. When the bell rang again, the buyer would return to the old oak tree to find his jug filled with "shine" and the proper change left, all accomplished without any sign of the proprietor.

The tree under which all this activity took place was eventually dubbed – you guessed it – the "Bell Tree," and over the ensuing years, Will Smith became known as "Bell Tree" Smith.

Although Esom Hill today proudly lays claim to the Bell Tree legend, the former site of the old oak was not even in Georgia. The Bell Tree itself died and rotted away years ago, but by most accounts, it stood in Alabama near the Georgia line, in a hollow formed by a stream draining the south side of Flagpole Mountain north of Tecumseh, Alabama.

Will Smith's family today strangely "does not recall" any ties the elder Smith might have had with Esom Hill, or even the location of the infamous old oak tree.[20] Though many of the tales concerning Bell Tree Smith may vary, his ultimate demise is known for certain. On a warm Sunday in August of 1908, the legendary Smith became yet another Esom Hill crime statistic, when he was killed – according to police reports – by an individual named Will Chandler.[21]

According to a description of this incident, Smith reportedly had attended an all-day church singing in Borden Springs, Alabama. Gradually, the men had separated from their womenfolk after eating lunch, and had drifted off to a field near the Borden Springs Post Office.[22]

Bell Tree and Will Chandler – with Will's brother Joe Ben – got into a heated argument over payment for two yearling bulls. It has also been reported that Smith was attempting to stop the Chandler brothers from roughing up a young friend who happened to be present.

Will Smith was recognized as a community leader, accustomed to being called upon by neighbors to help keep the peace. In those days, the sheriff normally took an hour to reach these parts, and many times he would arrive too late to help.

On this fateful day, Smith stepped into the fracas and proceeded to subdue the attackers. As he left the fray and climbed into his buggy, a stone reportedly was thrown by one of the Chandlers. It struck Smith, stunning him, and before he could recover, Will Chandler reportedly shot him, killing him instantly.

An unusual twist to this story occurred when Will Chandler was tried for the crime. He ultimately was convicted, but strangely was only sentenced to one year in the Alabama State Penitentiary. And before he served even a single day of his sentence, young Will received a sudden inexplicable pardon from none other than the governor of the state himself.

Today, William "Bell Tree" Smith lies buried in the Salem Baptist Church Cemetery in Bluffton, next to his father, Melton. A simple but eloquent inscription on Bell Tree's tombstone reads: *"A light from our household is gone. He was a kind and loving son and affectionate brother."*

Frank Lott Murder

One of the most infamous crimes ever associated with the Esom Hill area occurred more recently in 1974, with the

The Bailey family – These hardy early residents of Esom Hill were probably captured on film by an itinerant photographer circa 1919, and offer a glimpse of the violence which once prevailed in this community. Warren Bailey (behind his mother) killed Robert Hackney in an argument in the family home (rear) and was later killed himself in another dispute. Also pictured are: Silas Clayton Bailey (seated), Minerva Owens Bailey (seated), and standing (l to r) Will Bailey, Dave Woodward, Warren Bailey, and Andrew Bailey. *(Photo courtesy of Billy Bailey)*

murder of prominent Polk County Sheriff Frank Lott, Sr.

In the late 1960s and early 1970s, much of the illicit activity at Esom Hill had been interrupted by investigations and arrests carried out by Lott, when, as the newly-elected sheriff, he began cleaning up the county. As a result of his uncompromising efforts in law enforcement, Lott undoubtedly made his share of enemies in Esom Hill. It was inevitable.

Though no direct link has ever been established between his murder and a "payback" from bootleggers at Esom Hill, much public speculation about just such a connection has surrounded the incident. Lott's son, however, disagrees.

"When Dad went in (to the Esom Hill area just prior to his election as sheriff), a lot of the bootleggers asked him, 'How are you going to be if you're elected?'" explained Frank Lott, Jr. "Dad told them, 'My advice to you is if you're doing something illegal, you need to find another line of work.'

"(As a result), a good many of them did change their line of work. Some of them didn't though, and in time, Dad caught them, but he was always straightforward with them and I don't think they would have hurt him."

Frank, Jr., says that on the evening just prior to the murder, some of the family had gone with his father to Rome for dinner. Upon returning from such a trip, he says his dad always went by the jail at night to make certain everything was in

Griffith's Cash Store and Post Office – This establishment was photographed in June of 1934, and once stood where the present-day post office now exists. *(Photo courtesy of Kathleen Griffith)*

order. On this particular night (June 23, 1974), Lott reportedly was making his check on the jail when a silent alarm indicated a burglary was in progress at Cedartown High School.

"There was a trustee at the jail that night," Lott, Jr. continued. "He had a drinking problem and was serving some weekend time. He went with Dad (to the burglary), and when they got to the school, Dad drove around (to the back) where they saw a man getting into a car.

"When Dad got out of his car, the (burglar) got out too. Dad asked him 'What's going on here?'

"Dad started approaching the (burglar) and got between the cars (where) the lights probably blinded him. The (burglar), while he was standing there, apparently had a gun in his hand, and he came up firing and hit Dad three times." The gunman, according to reports, then jumped into his car and sped away.

"(Later), the boy that was with Dad was put under hypnosis," Lott added. "He was certain about the (burglar's) car – a Ford *Torino*. A vehicle fitting this description was later found burned around Esom Hill."

The prime suspect in the crime was described as a white male with long hair and driving a car with an Alabama license plate. When asked if the individual was from Esom Hill, Frank Lott Jr. would only reply, "They thought he was a psychopath. He later killed himself. After (the killing of the sheriff), nobody would have anything to do with him. Some of them at Esom Hill that had been friends with him didn't even want anything to do with him."

Hoyt Dingler retired from the Polk County Sheriff's Department following

30 years of service. He maintains that he and others in the department knew who committed the crime, but that there simply was never enough evidence to make a case against the killer, described also by Dingler as an Alabama man.

Dingler also maintained that the murder was not a setup – at least not as far as Sheriff Lott was concerned. "There's no way they could have known that Frank would have answered the call that night, because ordinarily, he wouldn't have," Dingler explained. "At night, it would have been the county police that answered a burglary alarm at the high school. And it was also a fenced-in area with only one gate out. A person is not going to fence himself in to commit a murder."

As a result of its netherworld activities, Esom Hill, according to Dingler, is pretty widely known. "I've been in other parts of the country, and when people want to know where I'm from, and when I reply Cedartown, Georgia, they often say they've never heard of Cedartown, but they've heard of Esom Hill."

Today, Esom Hill is like any other rural northwest Georgia crossroads community. Most folks are friendly and accommodating, and you'd be hard-pressed to find any visible sign of criminal activity. Despite this seemingly peaceful demeanor however, one can't help but sense that just below the surface in this crossroads fiefdom, the action is still bubbling in Esom Hill.

Endnotes

1. Johnson, Larry G., *A History Of Polk County Georgia* (GA) Missionary Baptist Association, Curley, Nashville, 1977, p. 7.

2. U.S. Post Offices, Polk (and Paulding) County, U.S. Records, Microfilm Drawer 281, Box 32, Surveyor General Dept., Georgia Department of Archives and History, Atlanta, GA.

3. Stewart, Mrs. Frank Ross, Alabama's Cleburne County, Centre, AL, 1982, p. 68.

4. *Georgia State Gazeteer* (sic) *& Business Directory*, 188182, Atlanta.

5. The date of construction was once inscribed in the concrete on the front step, but is no longer legible today.

6. Hoyt Dingler interview, August 17, 1994.

7. "A Pioneer Dead," *The Cedartown Standard*, October 28, 1897.

8. Jeremiah Isbell served in the U.S. Civil War with his eldest son. His father, Pendleton Isbell (18061873), served also, as did eight of his sons and three of his grandsons. All returned home safely, except one son and one grandson, who were killed.

9. NW Georgia Document Preservation Project, 1993. Microfilm SHC156, Brewster/Isbell Papers.

10. Brewster, Phil, Sr., Cedartown, Georgia, video interview, August 7, 1988.

11. Honea, Cora Belle, Cedartown, Georgia, letter to Dennis Holland, August 31, 1992.

12. NW Georgia Document Preservation Project, Op. Cit.

13. "Vacancy At Esom," *The Cedartown Standard*, c. June 29, 1971.

14. IBID

15. Hoyt Dingler interview, August 17, 1994

16. Hoyt Dingler interview, August 17, 1994

17. "Warren Bailey Is Held For Murder In Hackney Death," *The Cedartown Standard*, April 20, 1933.

18. Distilled spirits were taxed from 1862 onwards to help pay for the Civil War. Georgia voted out whiskey in 1907 and Alabama the next year. Prohibition went into effect in early 1920. Dabney, Joseph Earl, *Mountain Spirits*, Charles Scribner's Sons, New York, 1974, pp. 74, 103.

19. "Clay Bailey Is Held For Killing Of Warren Bailey," *The Cedartown Standard*, August 1, 1935.

20. Smith, William E., Tecumseh, Alabama, interview on July 29, 1994.

21. "'Bill' Smith Is Killed," *Cleburne News*, August 20, 1908.

22. Charlie Collins, Muscadine, Alabama, letter, March 4, 1994, interview, March 7, 1994.

Boarding School From Yesteryear:

Old Piedmont Institute And A Famous Author

No sign of the stark stone building which once dominated the skyline in Rockmart, Georgia, exists today. It disappeared years ago, but at one time, this education institution was the pride of northwest Georgia. It also possibly is the site at which a famous author once wrote at least a portion of a best-selling book which became a major motion picture.

Piedmont Institute, which once stood at the approximate site of today's old Rockmart High School building (present-day Rockmart City Hall complex), first opened its doors to the students of the community almost 150 years ago as of this writing in 2021. The curriculum proved rigorous, and the graduation rate therefore, was quite low, but those who did graduate carried their diplomas with an extra bit of pride.

Today, the graduates of Piedmont have all passed from the scene, but their descendants still speak reverently of this former private academy's high standards of excellence – and maybe not so reverently of the discipline demanded within its halls.

In 1889, public education in Rockmart was limited to six elementary grades. The town was only a few years old, having been founded several years previous. At that time, there simply was little demand for substantive educational training.

In that day and age, there were no child labor laws, and children, even very young ones, were needed to help provide income for the survival of a family. Many worked long hours on farms. Others worked equally hard in factories. As late as the turn of the century, in Polk County... children eight years old and up were employed by one factory.[1]

Those parents who longed for a better life for their children promoted private academies through their churches.[2] When the membership of the Rome District of the Methodist Church[3] met in Cave Spring on July 24, 1889, the attendees resolved to establish a school somewhere in the piedmont area.[4]

At that time, the church leadership

408

Old Piedmont Institute And A Famous Author Polk County

Old Piedmont Institute – The date of the photograph as well as those pictured at this institution in Rockmart, Georgia, are unknown today. *(Photo courtesy of GA Dept. of Archives & History, Atlanta)*

made the decision to leave the location of this new education facility to the best inducement by any town in the bounds of the Rome District. Civic-minded leaders in nearby Rockmart felt they were just as entitled – and likely – to gain the new institution as any of the other towns, and through her perseverance – and contributions from civic leaders – they got it.[5]

Though several other communities strongly competed for the right to become the location of the Institute, Rockmart's town fathers offered not only a five-acre plot for the building site, but the building materials and labor for a new brick building to house it. The total value of the two were estimated at $10,000 – a considerable sum in 1889.

After the town fathers of the city of Rockmart were notified that they had won the bid for the new educational facility, the funds were quickly raised. The five-acre site on a commanding knoll was reportedly donated by Rockmart patriarch Colonel Seaborn Jones, who had also contributed the land necessary to bring the railroad to the little town.

Though period newspapers of that time credit Jones for the donation of the land for the Institute, others have claimed over the years that the land was actually donated by Judge Wiley Crawford Barber, whose name reportedly was inscribed on the cornerstone of the new building. An inspection of the Polk County deeds of 1880 (when the donation reportedly was made) revealed no record of this beneficence by Judge Barber; the donation, however, could have occurred in another year.

Regardless of who donated the property, the Methodists, eager to get their new program up and running, reportedly did not wait for their new building to be constructed. When the first term began on January 20, 1890, classes were held in nearby Myers Academy with a faculty consisting of the Rev. E.W. Ballenger assisted by the Rev. G.J. Orr, Mrs. Orr, and Miss Eula Stubbs heading the music department.

The closing ceremonies of the Institute's very first term were held on June 10, 1890. Of interest is the fact that the Institute's leadership were wise enough to schedule the school term from January through May, in order to avoid interfering with the agricultural growing and harvesting seasons as much as possible while still allowing enough time for the students to be taught the various subjects reasonably well.

The Rev. Ballenger was the first head of the Institute. According to the June 12, 1890 issue of the *Cedartown Standard*, he laid the facility's cornerstone which held *"various tokens of value and interest,"* and which was inscribed *Piedmont Institute 1890*, on one face and on the other the names of the building committee – Messrs. E.W. Ballenger, W.B. Fambro, W.C. Barber, M.L. Troutman, and J.A. Peek.

The May 8, 1890 issue of the *Cedartown Standard* described the Rev. Ballenger as an educator and Methodist preacher who *"was more instrumental in (the Institute's) establishment than any other one man."* The article went on to explain the Rev. Ballenger was *"a splendid instructor and a fine disciplinarian."*

Ballenger obviously was a natural choice as president of the new Institute – well-suited for the task ahead. The coming years would prove the wisdom of his selection.

Ballenger and his governing board had chosen strict rules of conduct which left little to chance or choice. Discipline was to be rigid, although the school authorities were quick to point out the school was not intended to serve as a reformatory. The Rev. Ballenger, in his role as dispenser of discipline, apparently did not shirk his duty nor spare the rod.

Today, with corporal punishment having long ago been relegated to the junk-heap by liberal education administrators and limp-wristed government leaders, one can only imagine some sturdy farm lad awaiting a caning and wondering why he should submit to this little man, but submitting to him nonetheless. Not only was Ballenger small in stature, but he also walked with a faltering limp, the result of an injury he had suffered early in life. But if his stature was slight and his disability obvious, the Rev. Ballenger made up for his shortcomings with the heart of a lion.

Ballenger had joined the Confederate Army at an early age (he was born in 1847), and while in this service, he quite possibly had contracted malaria. While recovering from this illness in a field hospital, he somehow fell from a second-story window, breaking his leg. The ill-healed limb left him with a permanent limp. He also suffered from recurring bouts of malarial fever throughout his life.

Following the U.S. Civil War, the University of Georgia was re-opened. One-armed and one-legged veterans were a common sight among the students.[7] When Ballenger joined his fellow veterans at the university, his limp, no doubt, drew little attention.

Before attending the University in 1874, Ballenger apparently taught school for several years.[8] He later joined the North Georgia Conference of the Methodist Church. He first served as an itinerant circuit rider and eventually as minister to various churches. He was serving the Rockmart Methodist Church when

Old Piedmont Institute And A Famous Author — Polk County

the Conference agreed to sponsor Piedmont Institute in 1889.

In 1890, a handsome two-story building was erected using local products: limestone, slate and brick. Each classroom was fitted with electric bells and furnished with patented desks – quite modern for that day and age. The main building also included an office, music room, library and, of course, a large chapel.[9]

Piedmont Institute must have been an unusually imposing structure in its day, with a belfry and steeple looking out over Euharlee Valley. The belfry surely had a bell which undoubtedly pealed out a regular reminder to students, hurrying them on to their classes.

In 1901, an annex was added to the main building. This increased the number of recitation rooms and almost doubled the size of the chapel.

Directly across Piedmont Avenue from the Institute, a home was built for President Ballenger and his family. When he moved in, he and his wife of fifteen years – Louisa Elizabeth Upshaw of Cassville – had three daughters (Mrs. Mabel Ballenger Klunder, Mrs. Ludie Ballenger Morgan, and Mrs. Mayme Ballenger Haney).[10]

These daughters, according to family lore, reportedly were the source of considerable excitement when the Ballengers first arrived at the Rockmart train depot (later known as the old Southern Railway Depot just off College Street) in 1888. The news of their arrival had preceded them with an announcement which noted the family included not one, but three lovely daughters.

When the train pulled into the Rockmart Depot, young men transported by horse-and-buggy and on horseback were swarming around the site, much as they would have done for some

The Rev. E.W. Ballenger was the minister of Rockmart Methodist Church, and first head of Piedmont Institute. He seems almost caught at an awkward moment in this photo. Old Ballenger Hall, the only remnant left of the former institute in Rockmart was originally constructed as his home. Ballenger Street in Rockmart was named for him.

famous celebrity of that day. The crowd, no doubt, evaporated quickly when it was realized the Ballenger girls were aged 10, 7, and 4.

Though no sign of Piedmont Institute remains in Rockmart today, one associated building, unbeknownst to today's residents, does remain. The old Ballenger home, later used as the girls' dormitory, still stands on Piedmont Avenue, and is privately-owned today. Ballenger Street, running from Piedmont Avenue to Jones Avenue, was named for Professor Ballenger.

A girls' dormitory – Young Harris Hall – was built on the campus, and named for its benefactor – Judge Young L.G. Harris of Athens, Georgia – who donated $750 toward its construction. The male students originally were required to find accommodations "off-campus." Eventually, the Ballenger home was converted into a dormitory for use by the female students and renamed "Ballenger Hall." Young Harris Hall then became the men's dormitory.

By this time (1898), Rev. Ballenger,

Mystery & History in Georgia

Downtown Rockmart was photographed circa early 1920s. The parents of prospective students of Piedmont Institute were reassured by the Institute staff that "barrooms are not tolerated in or near the town." This view up South Marble Street shows the old Rockmart Bank building (far right) and old City Drug Co. building in the distance (left), as well as other structures which still stand as of this writing (2021). *(Photo courtesy of GA Dept. of Archives & History, Atlanta)*

who was in poor health, was forced to turn over the reins of his beloved Institute to the Rev. O.L. Kelley. Ballenger was able to serve the ministry in Austell for a few years. While filling in as minister of nearby Fairburn Methodist Church after the death of the pastor there, Ballenger himself suffered a stroke in the pulpit. After a few months at a retirement home in Milledgeville, he died on Friday, June 24, 1904.

Today, Rev. Ballenger's somber gravestone, shaped like a pulpit with an open Bible, stands prominently in Rose Hill Cemetery in Rockmart, flanked by the graves of his wife and daughter.

After Ballenger's departure from the scene, Piedmont Institute, continued to flourish for a time, and its discipline remained just as strict. In the early 1900s, Rockmart had a population of about one thousand residents and parents of students at the Institute were reassured by the fact that barrooms were not tolerated in or near the town, though they had operated in abundance in the town's original center – Van Wert – for many years.

Boarding students came under the watchful eyes of the faculty members, usually two assigned to each dormitory. Famed author Corra Harris, a prolific writer from her earliest days, began her writing career while she and her husband lived in the girls' dormitory where they supervised the females. As such, she may well have written at least a portion of her best-selling book – *A Circuit Rider's Wife* – at this site in Rockmart.

Interestingly, though no historic marker identifies it as such today, old Ballenger Hall – now weathered and forlorn – still stands on Piedmont Avenue directly across the street from the present-day Rockmart City Hall complex (old Rockmart High School). Its credentials include not only having been the residence of a nationally-famous author, but quite possibly also the site at which at least a portion of a nationally-renowned best-selling book was written, which later spurred the filming of a major motion picture starring an internationally-famous actress by the name of Susan Hayward, the movie itself having been filmed in northeast Georgia.

It is unfortunate that this structure has not been preserved and its historic significance chronicled in a historic marker of some form or fashion. Time and circumstances do not favor the aged structure either. This is understandable, however, since it was built as a simple clap-board home well over a hundred years ago.

After publication of her book, Corra Harris went on to become Georgia's first woman writer to gain national prominence. Her husband, the Rev. Lundy Howard Harris, was a teacher of Greek and Latin at the Institute.[11]

Piedmont Institute prided itself on being affordable, but the financial management of the Institute later proved to be its undoing. Monthly tuition in 1911 ranged from $1.50 for the lower grades to $3.50 for the upper two high school levels. Board cost $12.00 per month, music and elocution $3.00 each, and washing was estimated at $1.00.

In its early years, the Institute basically served as a junior college. A diploma from Piedmont granted a student admission – without examination – to the sophomore class of such colleges as Emory, Mercer, Wesleyan, and LaGrange.

The requirements for graduation from Piedmont included four years of English, four years of Latin, two years of French, four years of social science, one year of botany, and one year of chemistry. An average of seventy percent was required in scholastics, deportment, and society work.

Despite its best efforts, by 1912, the Institute was forced to close as a result of a large accumulation of debts. The fact that the cost for admission was so

Church Street in Rockmart was photographed in the 1890s during "horse-and-buggy" days. Rev. Ballenger of the Institute was pastor of the Methodist Episcopal Church (distance in photo). Virtually all of these structures still stand today in the old downtown section of Rockmart. *(Photo courtesy of GA Dept. of Archives & History, Atlanta)*

inexpensive, coupled with the extremely strenuous curriculum which discouraged all but the most talented students, proved to be its undoing.

In its 22 years of existence, the Institute had graduated some 94 students (with 16 more prospects waiting in the wings when the school closed in 1912). An average of roughly five students per year were graduated from its halls, and the income from such a limited student-body simply could not keep the Institute funded. Despite the rigidity of the curriculum, many Rockmart descendants of former students still speak reverently of the old facility even today, years after the last graduates have vanished into the mists of time.

Shortly after its closure, the Institute building was purchased by the city of Rockmart and it subsequently became the community's high school building. By coincidence, the same year Piedmont Institute had closed, the Georgia legislature had authorized funds for the creation of public high schools in the state. Since Rockmart already had the old Institute building, it made a quick and easy

Mystery & History in Georgia

transition into publicly-funded higher education.

However, it was a short-lived revitalization for the old Institute building. The structure which was constructed of stone and brick and considered practically fireproof in 1889, burned to the ground in 1915. Amazingly, it was completely rebuilt the next year, and, just as amazingly, was burned to the ground once again in 1940. That same year, a new high school building was built on the site, and though it served as Rockmart High School for over 60 years, it was converted into the Rockmart City Hall complex after a new Rockmart High School was built a few miles away.

Piedmont Institute Graduates

1893
Lula B. Caldwell
J.S. Davitte, Jr.
Mrs. Hocker Smith (nee Davitte)
W.W. Mundy
Mrs. W.J. Nix (nee Davitte)
J.J. Simpson
Kate Stephenson
J.J. Waits
R.P. White

1896
Mabel Ballenger
Mrs. C.C. Bass (nee Montgomery)
Mrs. Eugene Cook (nee Simpson)
M.L. Harper
J.L. Ingram
Walter P. Jones

1897
Rev. T.J. Branson
Mrs. W.E. Everett (nee Ballenger)
Mrs. C.E. Pearce (nee Lawson)

1898
Ollie Allen
F.P. Branson
Philip A. Kirton
T.E. McBryde
O.L. Wozencraft

1899
Jessie Branson
Joe Dean
Kittie King
Rev. P.A. Kellett
Mrs. F.D. Lane (nee Lewis)
Mrs. I.F. Mundy (nee Algood)

1901
A.D. Barber
W.W. Morgan

1902
Jno. W. Brooks
Mrs. B.J. Fisher (nee Morgan)
Ruby Johnston
Loyd Perryman
S.T. Sims

1903
Fannie Bulloch
Annie Camp
Mrs. Geo. Dansby (nee Ferguson)
Mrs. Allen Davis (nee Perryman)
Minnie Hendrick
Annie Williamson

1904
Ada Camp
Mrs. J.W. Fincher (nee Davitte)
Van Hunter McCormick
Smiley Nichols

1905
Mrs. Chas. Jones (nee Conally)
Mrs. M.D. Jones (nee Bullock)
Milton D. Jones
Ernest Mundy

1906
Mrs. Allsman (nee Simmerville)
Mrs. Tom Clements (nee Williamson)
Mrs. T.B. Crawford (nee Davitte)
Aileen Fambro
Jennie Hubbard
James McBryde
Lula McRae
Parker Moseley
Conley Strange
Ozzie Strange

1907
Mrs. B.F. Burnette (nee Davitte)
Ezra Carleton

Old Piedmont Institute And A Famous Author — Polk County

Mattie Carlton
Charlie McGarity
Hugh McRae
Mattie Mundy
Hopkins Perryman
Sara Ramsaur
Jasper Tilly
Lucy Williams

1908
Leo Bidez
Willie Belle Cannon
Mrs. Irby Henderson (nee Mayhew)
Roy Hendrick
Robt. Peacock
Key Perryman
Bessie Sigler

1909
Roger Dodd
Hattie Hall
Annie Phinizy

1910
Gertrude Blakeley
Flossie Cannon
Myrtle Cumming
Pauline Hubbard
Lula Nichols
Ruth Tramelle
Edgar Williams

1911
Ruth Adair
Dovie Carleton
Howard Fambro
Roy Fambro
Marion Fambrough
Hermie Lane
Wendell Williams

1912
Though their scholastic achievement and subsequent graduation status is unknown today by this writer, the class of 1912 might have graduated part or all of the following students:
Auzy Adams
Jehu Beasley
Laura Calhoun
Fannie Cannon
Lallah Cowden
Florine Everett
Davitte Hammond

Katye Harris
John Harris
Evans Hubbard
Ida B. Huckaby
Elma Jones
Mary Jones
Mattie Lane
Lamar Lewis
Hugh Morgan

Acknowledgements

The generous sharing of family stories and materials by the following individuals is gratefully acknowledged: Mrs. Elizabeth Herring Colquhoun, greatgranddaughter of the Rev. E.W. Ballenger; Mrs. Leonora F. Mintz; Mrs. Harold Hurt; and Mrs. Hugh M. McRae, Jr.

Endnotes:

1. Hepburn, editor, *Contemporary Georgia*, Carl Vinson Institute, University of Georgia, 1987, p. 209.

2. The first private school to be established in Polk County (Paulding County at that time) was the Raccoon Creek Academy in 1836, followed by Cedartown Academy in 1837 and Williams Academy in Van Wert in 1838.

3. Rome District, North Georgia Conference, M.E. Church, South.

4. *Cedartown Standard*, August 1, 1889.

5. *Cedartown Standard*, September 26, 1889.

6. Ballenger, Grady Woodfin, editor, *The Ballenger Family Of Oconee County, Seneca, South Carolina*, 1956, p. 8.

7. Nixon, Raymond B., *Henry W. Grady, Spokesman For The New South*, New York, 1943, p. 42.

8. Alumni records, University of Georgia, Athens, GA.

9. *Piedmont Institute Annual Catalog*, 190506.

10. Mabel Elizabeth (Mrs. Mabel B. Klunder); Mamie Lucille, Class of 1897 (Mrs. Mamie B. Haney); and Ludie (Mrs. B.T. Morgan). Mamie had been the wife of Mr. William B. Everett, a Rockmart banker, and after he died she married Mr. Haney, who left her widowed again. From *The Ballenger Family Of Oconee County, South Carolina*, op. cit.

11. Mintz, Leonora Ferguson, Piedmont Institute photo caption in *World's One and Only Rockmart*, *Georgia Life*, Spring, 1978.

French Huguenots ?

The Gravatt Family And A Polk County Connection

The late Goldie Evelyn Jordan Hill of Sunland, California, stated emphatically in a letter to her niece, Marilyn Jordan Jackson of Rockmart, Georgia, on July 20, 1964, "My mother's family (Gravatt) is of French Huguenot ancestry." Proof of this heritage, however has been difficult – if not impossible – to obtain.

There has been ample speculation, genealogical research, and further investigations for decades into the origin of the Gravatt family which ultimately wound up in the Allegheny Valley north of Pittsburgh, Pennsylvania, in the 18th Century. Much of this research and investigative effort by family descendants has been met with abject frustration, since the Gravatts were not avid records-keepers, but research is "on-going."

Recorded variously as "Grevatt," "Gravatt," "Gravet," "Gravat," and "Grevet," it has become accepted that this is an English surname, but in actuality, it quite likely is of Norman French origin. The name itself is somewhat rare, but there interestingly are a fair number of individuals with this name in Georgia.

Research indicates there are actually three possible origins for the name:

The first is that of a medieval diminutive of the occupational name "Graff,"

This surname is amply-recorded as well in the surviving church registers of the diocese of Greater London from Elizabethan times.

a derivative of the pre-7th Century French word "grafe," meaning "a quill," and therefore referring to "a clerk" or "scribe," *(which this writer, a descendant, finds oddly amusing).* To this has been added the diminutive suffix "-et," meaning "son of Graff."

A second possible origin of the name is from the ancient Germanic name of "Creiz." Also, in "Norman"-French this was "Grev," and again to this was probably attached the diminutive suffix "et" to also denote "son of Grev."

Other possibilities which cannot be dismissed are from the pre-7th Century Olde English words "graeve" or "graefe" or "greve," denoting a wood, or perhaps more likely referring to a steward, and hence an occupational name of medieval origin. This surname is amply-recorded as well in the surviving church registers of the diocese of Greater London from Elizabethan times.

It is into the vortex of all of these possibilities that any search for the accurate origin of this particular family line, and the reason(s) for their emigration to America, will fall. Such research is further complicated by the almost clannish nature of this family.

In one union, the Gravatts intermarried with the Jordan family, yet another line of possible Norman-French origin, and both ultimately found settlement in "the new world" north of Pittsburgh, Pennsylvania, in the Allegheny and Perry counties areas.

It is interesting to note that the township in Allegheny County in and around which the Gravatts and Jordans resided offers direct evidence that these families quite possibly hailed from Holland, or, from France by way of Holland (which is a more likely possibility), arriving in the fledgling United States prior to the U.S. Revolutionary War. That township in Allegheny County ultimately became known in county records as "Dutch Hill."

But this is one place where things can get a little messy if one isn't cautious. Many family researchers assume "Pennsylvania Dutch" automatically indicates

Three generations of Jordans appear in this photo from yesteryear, quite probably taken at the Jordan home in San Bernardino, California, when grandmother came for a visit circa 1900. Pictured (L to R) are: Goldie Evelyn Jordan (Guy Jordan's sister); Mary Melinda Gravatt Jordan (Goldie's and Guy's mother); and Barbara Ann Pollard Ferguson Jordan (Goldie's and Guy's grandmother and father Alvin Gilmore Jordan's mother). The late Guy Jordan was a resident of Rockmart, Georgia, from the 1920s to 1946 when he was tragically killed in an industrial accident. The late Marilyn Jordan Jackson, a native of Rockmart, long-time resident and teacher, was his daughter. There are many Jackson, Hughes/Busby, Bradley and other native Georgia families descended from this Gravatt/Jordan line. *(Photo from author's files. All rights reserved)*

That township in Allegheny County ultimately became known in county records as "Dutch Hill."

Mystery & History in Georgia

This obviously-posed photograph shows Goldie Evelyn Jordan and her mother, Mary Melinda Gravatt Jordan, probably taken in San Bernardino, California, circa 1894. Mary Melinda Gravatt Jordan was also the mother of the late Guy Jordan of Rockmart, Georgia. (Photo from author's files. All rights reserved)

an origin from Holland or the Netherlands – which could possibly be the case, but not necessarily. This Pennsylvania "Dutch" designation ironically could also refer to "Deutsch" instead of "Dutch," thereby indicating an origin from Germany – by way of Holland shipping – rather than Dutch or French ancestry. It is for this reason that many of the early settlers in Pennsylvania – including the Amish, Mennonites, and others of that area – speak *German*, not Dutch.

Allegheny County in which these Gravatts chose to settle was organized in 1788, but deeds to property and possessions did not begin to be officially recorded there until 1842. The Gravatt family farm near Logan's Ferry was recorded in 1846.

On October 24, 1967, Mrs. Goldie

Evelyn Jordan Hill, a descendant of both the Jordans and the Gravatts of Pennsylvania, wrote to her niece – Marilyn Jordan Jackson of Rockmart (Polk County), Georgia – stating *"My cousin Mildred and her husband were here for a short visit. She is the one who has given me most of the information that I have about the Gravatt family.* She had (conducted) *rather extensive* (research) *about 25 years ago because she thought that she might become a member of the Daughters of the American Revolution.*

"Most of the information she (Mildred) *collected I believe has come through word of mouth (and family lore) from one generation to the next,"* Hill added. *"The records in the Gravatt family Bible were obliterated by it becoming soaked* (at some point) *by water – I suppose during a flood which sometimes happens in the Allegheny Valley* (where they lived in Pennsylvania).

"There were three brothers (who originally immigrated to America), and the names of two of them were Robert and Samuel," Mrs. Hill said. *"These three brothers were driven from France at the time of the Huguenot persecution under Louis XIV. They went either to England or to Holland, and from there to New Jersey (perhaps stopping first in Nova Scotia). Evidence seems to indicate they came with Dutch colonists directly to New Jersey and settled in Monmouth County in Upper Friebold Township – a well-known Dutch settlement in America."*

Here again, things are somewhat difficult to sort out. There is of course the obvious tie-in with the "Dutch," clearly reinforcing the known fact that Holland was a dominant force in the merchant shipping industry at this time, and that the Gravatts were taking advantage of this travel option to come to America. But again, were the Gravatts "Dutch," or "Deutsch," or "French," or what?

But again, were the Gravatts "Dutch," or "Deutsch," or "French," or what?

Robert Gravatt was born 1708 in Monmouth, New Jersey. According to family tradition and notes passed down by the late Mrs. Hill, a "Robert Gravatt" was brought across the mountains from New Jersey later in life to live with Johnson Gravatt at the Gravatt home at Logan's Ferry near present-day Kensington, PA (or possibly it was to the later Gravatt farm at nearby Fawn Township), Allegheny County, PA. It is not known for certain today if this Robert Gravatt was **Johnson's father or grandfather,** but he quite possibly was his grandfather, since conflicting records seem to indicate Johnson's father died at a relatively young age and was buried in New Jersey. Johnson's grandfather, (Robert Gravatt the elder), who also was born in New Jersey, apparently died in Allegheny County, PA, and is believed to have been buried in the old Gravatt family cemetery in Fawn township, Allegheny County, PA.

Johnson (or "Johnston" on some census and other records) Gravatt was born in 1754 (some records indicate 1755) in Monmouth, New Jersey, and married Sarah Percy Pierce in 1780. Sources also indicate that both Johnson and his father, Robert, possibly served under Gen. George Washington during the Revolutionary War, participating in the Battle of Trenton.

"Records indicate that Johnson served in the army at the age of 24," Hill continues. "It seems that at that time, soldiers enlisted for one or two months at a time. He served in the Monmouth County New Jersey Militia in April, May and June of 1778, and in July and August of 1780.

"Johnson migrated to western Pennsylvania, near the present-day town of Kensington, probably in 1780, since **his son John** was born there on August 25, 1781."

Contrary to the above information, however, according to the ***American Genealogical-Biographical Index*** which is an international online database accessed through ***Ancestry.com***, John W. Gravatt was born in 1790 (not 1781) in New Jersey (not Pennsylvania), a date and location which obviously conflict with the other associated datelines for his birth, etc.

In the late 1700s, the shores of the Allegheny and the Monongahela Rivers were one vast wilderness, broken only by occasional patches of land cleared by the sparse settlers who braved that wilderness. Johnson Gravatt is credited with construction of the first schoolhouse in the Allegheny Valley which came to be known as "Percy School," after his wife, Sarah Percy.

Johnson Gravatt is credited with construction of the first schoolhouse in the Allegheny Valley which came to be known as "Percy School," after his wife, Sarah Percy.

In later years, being afflicted with asthma and wishing to move to higher ground, Johnson obtained title to land in Fawn Township about five miles north of Tarentum. This property ultimately became known as "the old Gravatt farm," and remained in the family until about 1870 when Johnson's grandson, Daniel, sold it.

Records indicate Johnson's son – John – served in the War of 1812. John, as characterized by many of these Gravatts, died young at the age of 58 on January 7, 1839. He is buried in the third grave in old Gravatt Cemetery, Fawn Township, Allegheny County, Pennsylvania.

John's son – **Daniel Gravatt** – and his twin sister were born to John and wife Sarah Kennedy Gravatt on September 8, 1827, in Fawn Township, Allegheny County, PA. Daniel married Martha Jane Girt on April 22, 1851. The Girts came to the Pennsylvania area circa 1840. Daniel and Martha had eleven children, one of the older of whom was **Mary Melinda Gravatt**.

Daniel was a veteran of the U.S. Civil War, enlisting as a captain in 1864 and serving in Battery D, 6th Heavy Artillery Regiment, Pennsylvania until the end of the war. He died at the ripe age of 82 on April 6, 1909 and was buried in Knox Chapel Cemetery at Cabot, Butler Co.

Daniel was the last heir to own the old Gravatt farm in Fawn Township, Allegheny County, PA. He sold it circa 1870, retaining title only to the old Gravatt family cemetery. It is unknown by this writer if this cemetery continues today to be owned by the Gravatt family. It is known, however, that it is located within private property in old Fawn Township (Brackenridge), Allegheny County, PA.

The following graves have been identified in the old Gravatt family cemetery:

1st Grave: Robert Gravatt. [It is not known for certain today if this grave is occupied by Robert the elder (Johnson's grandfather) or Robert the younger (Johnson's father).]

2nd Grave: Johnson Gravatt. (Died 1837)

3rd Grave: John W. Gravatt (Died January 7, 1839)

4th Grave: John Kennedy. (He was the father of John's wife, Sarah Kennedy, and has an interesting history of service in the Revolutionary War.)

5th Grave: Sarah Percy Gravatt (Mrs. Johnson Gravatt) (Died 1845)

6th Grave: Sarah Kennedy Gravatt (Mrs. John W. Gravatt) (Died circa 1872)

(The late Marilyn Jordan Jackson, formerly of Rockmart, Polk County, Georgia, and her children, Patricia, Olin, David, the late Mary Jackson Oettinger, and the late Guy Jackson of Rockmart (Polk County), Georgia, are among the Georgia descendants of the Allegheny Valley, Pennsylvania Gravatts and Jordans.)

Daniel was the last heir to own the old Gravatt farm in Fawn Township, Allegheny County, PA. He sold it circa 1870, retaining title only to the old Gravatt family cemetery.

Built By The Civilian Conservation Corps:

Memories of Walasi-Yi Center at Historic Neel's Gap

Built in the 1930s, the cozy old lodge in the heart of the north Georgia mountains is now almost 100 years old. To the surprise of many visitors to the gift shop today, the site once served as a mountain inn serving up delicious food, and offering rooms in which honeymooners once delighted.

For a number of years now, the very rustic stone building at Neel Gap has been a site of welcomed relief to the multitudes of hikers on the Appalachian Trail which literally passes right through the structure known as Old Walasi-Yi Center. In fact, the Center has become an oasis of sorts – even allowing a number "beginner" hikers to realize the error of their ways and overnight in the hiker hostel portion of the Center to wait for a ride back home.

By the time they've crossed Blood Mountain and are descending the Trail into Neel's Gap, most hikers pretty much know if their gear is too heavy, their shoes are too tight, their sleeping bag is too thin for the frosty conditions they are encountering – or if they've just "bitten off more than they can chew."

Luckily for the hikers, the Center serves as a temporary hostel, allowing hikers to re-group and refresh themselves with any needed supplies.

Unbeknownst to many, however, this historic building, was actually serving as a rest stop long before it became a hiker hostel on the Trail.

The sturdy structure was built originally as an inn and a restaurant in the 1930s by the Civilian Conservation Corps (C.C.C.) during then-President Franklin D. Roosevelt's "New Deal" program. It sits near the summit of Blood Mountain, and enjoys a sweeping view down Neel's Gap.

A historic marker in front of the Center denotes the opening of the state highway passing through the north Georgia mountains at that point, elevation 3,108 feet. The gap is named after former Georgia highway engineer, Warren Rabun Neel, who was instrumental in the opening of the road (Highway 129) in 1925.

But there is much more history in the area beyond the old building. Prior to construction of the highway or the

Viewed from the Appalachian Trail (AT) which crosses U.S. 129, Walasi-Yi Center was constructed as a mountain lodge by the Civilian Conservation Corps (CCC) in the 1930s. Today, it serves as a stop-over for hikers on the AT who begin their trek at Georgia's Springer Mountain, the southern terminus of the trail.

building, evidence has been discovered which indicates that the Cherokee Indians had an encampment very near to the site of the Center. Some hikers still occasionally discover ancient arrow points once used by the Native Americans as they descend Blood Mountain. *(Readers please see "The Mysteries of Fort and Blood Mountains" in the Murray County section of this book.)*

The name "Walasi-Yi," in fact, is derived from the Cherokees. Early settlers in the area translated the Indian words Walasi-Yi to mean "frog place." During the days prior to construction of the highway, Neel's Gap was called "Frogtown Gap" by early pioneers in the area.

Records indicate the Walasi-Yi Center property, and the property of nearby Vogel State Park, up to the top of Blood Mountain, was once owned by Vogel Leather Tanning Company, based in Milwaukee, Wisconsin. The tanning company used the tannic acid from the bark of the seemingly endless supply of chestnut trees in the area for tanning their leather. That is, before a great blight began wiping out the noble trees.

When the chestnut trees had all been either harvested or killed by the blight, the property became worthless to Vogel Leather Tanning Company, and it then took a nice tax write-off by donating the property to the state of Georgia in the late 1920s. It is for that reason that a piece of "state property" exists right in the middle of a National Forest. Just another little footnote making the Walasi-Yi Center special.

The 1930s witnessed the budding of the U.S. National Forest management program, coupled with Roosevelt's "New Deal" programs. A large C.C.C. work camp once existed nearby at present-day Goosecreek for the construction of Vogel State Park and the Walasi-Yi Center.

Some thirty C.C.C. workers were involved in the construction of Walasi-Yi from 1933 to 1937. Its massive design includes 18-inch thick stone walls. It is the immenseness of the structure that took four years to build. Not only did the workers hand-form the stones themselves, they blasted the rocks from a ridge several miles south of the Center and then pulled the huge stones back to the construction site.

If they know where to look from the lookout balcony of the Center, visitors can still see a substantial rock face exposed on the second ridge below the Center. The C.C.C. workers constructed a roadway from the Center to that rock face to obtain the rock for the Center. Former C.C.C. workers who have returned to the Center over the years have explained the boulders were hauled on trucks, drug behind tractors, and even transported with the use of mules.

It was an immense task which undoubtedly will keep the Center around long after any visitors to the site have disappeared from the face of the earth. Aside from the stonework, the captivating building is constructed of huge hand-hewn virgin chestnut and pine timbers, making it an architectural wonder. Some of the timbers are several feet wide and span 16 to 18 feet.

Most of the iron door hinges, latches, and even the lamp holder over the massive double front doors were hand-forged by the workers at the Goosecreek work camp. By today's standards, such workmanship is a marvel and a virtual lost art. Despite all its historic background, Walasi-Yi Center was once slated for demolition after being closed down and abandoned in the 1960s. Thankfully, today it has lasting protection by being listed on the *National Register of Historic Places*.

Designed originally as a restaurant and an inn by the state of Georgia, Walasi-Yi apparently was very popular in its early days. Visitors trekked substantial distances – occasionally from as far away as Atlanta – just to have dinner in the inn, then return home, and that was in the days before the road up the mountain was even paved.

Despite all the visitation and former popularity of the inn, no one has yet located a photo of any patrons from yesteryear dining in the former eatery. Nevertheless, returning visitors have occasionally made statements to the effect of "This is our 40th anniversary, and we had dinner under the bay window here after our wedding night, and stayed in room number three."

Regretfully, no photographs of the old building from its heydays are known to exist either, even after searches at the Georgia Department of Archives and History or the Georgia Department of Natural Resources in Atlanta. And that is part of what makes the history of Walasi-Yi somewhat elusive.

In addition to the structure which exists today, there apparently once were several stone cabins to the rear of the Center. Only their foundations remain today, so the stone from them must have been used elsewhere on the premises.

As time passed, state funds for the operation of Walasi-Yi diminished. Visitation dropped off too, as more and more travelers to the mountains began using other newer and faster highways and the new "interstate highways." As a result, Walasi-Yi finally was closed during the 1950s.

The Center enjoyed a revival of sorts in the 1960s, when potter Phil Mayhew – who eventually moved away himself to Tennessee – operated a north Georgia crafts cooperative at the site. Since that time, several other "Mom and Pop" operators have come and gone over the years.

As of this writing (2021), Walasi-Yi is an exceptionally well-appointed hiking shop, offering the latest technology in light-weight and heavy gear. It offers a small library of naturalist and mountain-oriented publications. Shelves and racks in the store are literally filled with mountain and hiking clothing, beautiful knit sweaters, colorful brushed cotton shirts, and souvenir T-shirts too. Backpacks, sleeping bags, camp stoves, tents, lanterns, canteens – you name it, and it quite possibly can be found in this shop. The Center also offers a variety of foods, including the light-weight freeze-dried versions preferred by backpackers.

Forest Ranger Extraordinaire:

The Life & Times Of Ranger Arthur Woody

The state of Georgia enjoys the distinction of having hired one of the first forest rangers in the United States. Ranger Arthur Woody, however, was much more than a simple forest ranger. He enjoyed a level of fame which has seldom previously been achieved. Arthur Woody literally was a legend in his own time.

To put it bluntly, William Arthur Woody was a pragmatist, and he did not suffer fools lightly. He was on a life-long mission to save what remained of the north Georgia wilderness and wildlife, and today, the state is imminently wealthier and more advanced in this realm as a result of his hard and honest work.

Woody's native home was located in the upper reaches of north Georgia known today as the Chattahoochee National Forest. He was intimately familiar with this wilderness, having grown up in it and hunted and fished all across its domain. He eventually realized this magnificent natural resource was slipping away and being destroyed by mismanagement and neglect.

Woody's purpose in life became a quest to establish a new and progressive era in forest and wildlife conservation, implementing many practices which still significantly impact the preservation and management of American forestry resources today.

"Each time I go deer hunting in this game preserve," the Rev. Waldo Brookshire once reflected, "I remember Arthur Woody's struggle to restock the mountains with deer." It broke Woody's heart to know the beautiful deer which once graced the magnificent mountains had literally almost been hunted to extinction.

As a result, Woody became determined that he would not be denied the revitalization of his beloved Blue Ridge Mountains, in particular, those of his native Union County. He was able to do it in part because he was ever vigilant, determined, and because he commanded the respect of his fellow man by sheer force of personality.

Woody was born April 1, 1884, in a log cabin in the tiny community of Suches, Union County, Georgia. He was the son of parents Abraham Lincoln and

Eliza Ingram Woody. His great grandparents were John Wesley Woody (born in 1820 in South Carolina), and Axey Seabolt Woody.

Raised in the mountains and roaming at will all his life, Arthur Woody was at home with the forest that surrounded the Woody cabin. He loved the undulating hills, the sparkling mountain streams, the cry of the whippoorwill, and the beauty of each passing season that painted variegated landscapes on the canvas of his mountains.

Just as most all mountain children, Arthur worked with his father in the management of their mountain farm. Their cattle ranged free in the mountain recesses. There were no fences to contain them, but each family knew which cattle were theirs and where to find them almost at will.

When it came time to market these cattle, they were rounded up from the mountains and driven to market in Gainesville or Atlanta or other sites via the early mountain passages such as the Logan Turnpike. In those days, the trip took about ten days over the rough trails.

These early experiences taught Woody independence, industry and perseverance, attributes that would serve him well in later years. Since he and his family essentially lived off the land, he was intimately aware of the fact that many aspects of the wildlife and other resources were essentially disappearing.

As a result, Arthur became resolved early in life to halt the deteriorating condition of the mountains and wildlife around him. He was particularly determined to restock the Blue Ridge peaks with the deer which had been almost completely extinguished by over-hunting. Other wildlife such as the turkey, elk, mountain lions, buffalo, and many of the fishes in the streams had already disappeared completely.

"I saw Pa kill the last deer out of these mountains when I was just a kid," Arthur Woody reportedly told Charles N. Elliott, then director of the Georgia Game and Fish Commission. "I thought about that for a lot of years, and made up my mind that some day I would put back what he and the mountain men of his time had took away."

It took quite a while for that resolution to materialize, but eventually it did. First came his education. Arthur went to local country schools in Suches through age sixteen. He then entered North Georgia College in Dahlonega, an institution which his great-grandfather had helped to found.

After one year in college however, Arthur decided the world of academics simply was not for him. His world and theater of education was the great outdoors. He returned to Suches and helped his father farm and drive cattle for a few more years.

Arthur next took himself a bride. He married Emma Abercrombie, whom he affectionately called "June," possibly after a pleasant memory they shared of that month. To them were born three children: Walter W. Woody, born July 13, 1902; Clyne Edward Woody, born April 30, 1905; and Mae Woody, born July 15, 1907.

On October 1, 1912, Arthur Woody began working for the United States Forestry Service. His first job was as an axeman on a baseline crew. From this humble beginning, he gained first-hand knowledge of forest fire management and control.

Woody's first advancement was to "surveyor." In this capacity he was responsible for surveying the new lands acquired by the Forestry Service in his area.

Mystery & History in Georgia

Already something of a mountain celebrity, Arthur Woody takes a break from his labors in game and forest management in Suches, Georgia.

Surveying is a unique skill, requiring mathematics skills, knowledge of surveying techniques, good eyesight, and general endurance.

On May 1, 1915, according to records, Arthur was sworn in as a newly-appointed "forest guard." His main responsibility in this capacity was the protection of the National Forest – which he had helped to establish – against trespassers and fires.

And on July 1, 1918, Woody finally was promoted to "forest ranger," the first such designation in Georgia, and one of the first in the nation. His area of responsibility now was the Blue Ridge District (later named the Chattahoochee National Forest).

In order to become a ranger, Arthur was required to pass an examination which, among other things, tested his practical knowledge of basic existence and survival in the forest. The exam inquired about his knowledge of saddling a horse, building a campfire with no tools other than flint and sticks, and tying various knots with rope – all things with which Arthur of course was intimately familiar, having grown up in the backwoods of north Georgia.

After he was established in a profession in which he knew he could finally have an impact upon the preservation of the forests and wildlife he so cherished, Arthur went to work with a flourish. He first acquired three western mule deer from Wisconsin left behind by a traveling circus. Then he bought five fawn from the Pisgah National Forest in North Carolina.

Arthur cared for and bottle-fed the young deer religiously in a special pen built at his home, keeping regular midnight and 6:00 a.m. feedings. He personally mixed their formula from canned milk.

Arthur understandably became fond of his wildlife initiates, naming the deer Nimble, Bessie, Billy, Nancy and Bunnie-Girl. They became regular Woody pets, one even learning to open the screen door of his mountain cabin and come inside, much to the delight of the mountain ranger.

Eventually, the deer reached adulthood, able to survive on their own, so Woody released them into the forest. He kept adding more and more deer to the herd, carefully protecting them from hunters.

One day, Arthur, by chance, discovered a large bear track, perfectly formed, from which he hatched an ingenious plan. He decided to make a plaster cast of the imposing track. He kept this cast in his truck, and as a result of his never-ending wit and resourcefulness, fell upon the idea of using it as a deterrent against poachers. Wherever he thought poachers might try to take advantage of the deer he was cultivating in the national forest, Woody left an ominous trail of "bear tracks."

"Them bear tracks do more to discourage poachers than three game wardens," Woody once declared proudly.

Authur remained true to his original goal, particularly early-on, when deer populations were still thin in the mountains. To forestall the first deer hunting season and give his young charges time to mature, he reportedly slyly guided inquiring wildlife specialists from the Georgia Game and Fish Commission to the side of Rock Creek Lake, a spot which he knew had few natural deer signs. By this action, he was able to get the first controlled deer hunting season postponed for yet another year until 1941, giving the animals ample time to multiply and gain strength.

By 1941, Woody had cultivated the deer population into numbers exceeding 2,000 head in his area, sharing the beautiful forest preserve with increased numbers of foxes, wild turkeys, quail, grouse, opossums, woodchucks, squirrels, rabbits and some black bear.

Hunters, forestalled as long as possible by the resourceful Woody, eventually took to the woods in seasonal hunts to harvest the wildlife once again. It was a situation which the preservation-minded Woody both deplored and mourned, but over which he had little control. He also knew it was necessary to maintain the proper strengths of populations of the various wildlife.

Nevertheless, as he was working at a hunting "checking station" one day, inspecting the kills of various hunters, Woody reportedly was moved to tears as one fine deer was weighed and listed. "That's old Nemo," he said. "I've been seeing him almost every month since I put him in these woods years ago. But never no more."

In addition to the preservation and re-stocking of the deer, Ranger Woody wanted the streams and lakes to have ample fish too. Rainbow and speckled trout received special attention, but brook trout, which he called "specs," were his favorite. Like his pet deer, he gave the big trout names, observing, "I know the big trout by name, and if I'm smart, I can get them on a hook."

In order to re-stock the many depleted streams and rivers once again with ample fish, Woody applied new innovative techniques. He had the first rainbow trout shipped in from Denver, Colorado, in 1918.

"Dad met the train in Gainesville at 3:00 a.m.," Arthur's son, Clyne Woody, later recalled. "He hauled the fish by truck to the foot of the mountain, transferred them to a wagon, then hauled them across Grassy Gap, and then put them in the streams around the community."

Herman Caldwell of Lumpkin County also reminisced about the fish Ranger Woody brought to the mountain streams. "In those days, there were no fish in the streams except minnows and horny heads," he explained. "Then Ranger Woody told Daddy (Monroe Caldwell) how he could order trout from the state of Washington. My brother Pool rode with Daddy in a two-horse wagon loaded with 60-gallon barrels to Gainesville to pick up the fish when they came in (on the train). My other brother, Henley, and I helped put five or six little trout in every creek hole we could find. Five years later, people were catching trout as long as your arm."

Ranger Woody was also particularly proactive in forest fire prevention too, since he had seen over and over how

Mystery & History in Georgia

Woody enjoys some good-natured "ribbing" from friends as he shows off his archery skills.

entire forests – and the wildlife therein – could be decimated by negligent hunters, moonshiners, and trappers. Though he didn't necessarily follow orthodox methods, Woody's efforts and outstanding achievements in forest fire prevention, game restoration and preservation, land reclamation and timber management, paved the way for today's advanced methods used by the forest service all over America.

Lucy Justus, writing about Woody in an article in the *Atlanta Journal & Constitution* "Magazine" on February 16, 1969, noted that he was the *"father of wildlife management in the South. His conservation theories are still being taught in colleges and universities."*

The secret to Woody's success lay in his totally practical approach to any problems at hand. He had no patience with government "red tape" and the quagmire of bureaucracy, and became ever-more resourceful in working around these obstacles as the years passed.

In many instances, though a government action or approval was necessary before he could act on a particular situation, Woody acted on his own judgment alone, rather than lose time awaiting some official dictum. He thought through each situation, appraised local reaction, and then arrived at the best solution.

Woody's ranger district was one of the largest and most forest-fire prone in the United States, yet he set a national record for fire prevention, with only a four-acre tract burned in a year. His resourceful and admirable efforts were eventually noticed by upper level officials.

As his successes mounted, Woody was finally called to Washington, D.C. where he was to receive a special award for his many successes in forest fire prevention. When queried as to the method in which he attained his outstanding accomplishment, he responded simply by saying "Wal, you just have to know your people. I kiss all the babies and buy them candy, tell all the women if I weren't married I'd be in love with them, and I go fishing with all the men." After pausing a moment, Woody reportedly added with a chuckle, "And I keep a trained bloodhound chained to my back door."

His wry sense of humor and charm were legendary long before he passed away. According to outdoor writer Charles Elliott, Woody refused to wear shoes around his house or office, despite Forest Service regulations to the contrary. Woody's regional forest supervisor eventually paid him a visit to "lay down the law" about the dress code. Later in the evening, the supervisor's assistant drove up with a message for his boss. He discovered the man – along with Woody – sitting on the front porch, their feet on the railing, both as "barefooted as a yard dog."

During the period of President Franklin D. Roosevelt's "New Deal" programs, when the Civilian Conservation Corps was active, Ranger Woody used many of the young men to build forest service roads, telephone lines, and other civil engineering projects.

One such example was Dockery Lake near Suches. Woody sent a crew of men to build, according to his specifications, the dam to the lake. Months later, irate government officials whose engineering skills and technical expertise had not been sought for the project, explained hotly that the dam would not hold. The engineers immediately built two additional dams further down the stream below the lake, following federal guidelines for construction of the impoundments. Later, during floods, each of the later government-built dams broke, but Woody's original Dockery Lake impoundment held firm.

Basic construction was yet another skill learned and passed down through the Woody family. Stone Pile Gap is a historic site of long renown in the mountains just south of Suches. According to tradition, the aged pile of stones at this site mark the grave of a former Cherokee Indian princess.

When the road from Stone Pile Gap to Suches was completed, it was a dream come true for Woody. Charles Elliott was with Woody one day at the gravel quarry where stone was being crushed for the road. Picking up several pieces of rock, Woody studied them thoughtfully and put them into his pocket.

Several weeks later, the two were together again, driving over the road. Woody explained to Elliott that he had taken the stones to be assayed and had discovered the gold content to be thirty dollars a ton.

"Why didn't you stop them from putting it on the road?" Elliott wanted to know.

"Wal," Woody drawled, a glint of mischief in his eyes and his wit in high gear, "I wanted at least one government road in this country to be worth what it cost."

Ranger Woody was anything if not resourceful, and eventually became one of the wealthiest men in the north Georgia mountains. Not solely dependent upon his salary as a forest ranger, he was an entrepreneur and a trader. He dealt in cattle, land and loans.

To keep constituents within the Chattahoochee National Forest area aware of his preservation measures, Woody firmly followed foreclosure procedures on mortgages of the property of any who hunted out of season. Many parcels of land reportedly were added to the National Forest by such foreclosures on promissory notes.

A large man in stature, Arthur Woody was six feet tall and weighed in at an imposing 250 pounds. But inside his large frame was literally a heart of gold. He reportedly returned home one day from the funeral of a mountain farmer. Shuffling through legal papers, he found a document, read it, tore it up and burned the scraps. When his wife inquired about what he had done, she was told, "When the widow woman comes inquirin' about the mortgage, tell her it was cleared up before her husband died."

Noted for his homespun philosophy and wisdom, Woody once counseled Charles Elliott who was distressed over a problem. Looking to the mountains surrounding his home, the ranger mused, "These mountains must be

A much younger and "svelte" Ranger Woody enjoys some of the deer he was raising to release into the Blue Ridge Mountains to repopulate the white-tail deer in that region.

a little human. They go through spells of being cold and dark, and it looks like night won't never end. But I been watching it for nigh onto 60 years, and it always does."

Using roads as a metaphor, Woody said, "Everybody's life is crossed with roads. Some of them don't go nowhere. Sometimes you got to hunt around for a spell to find the one that does. Yesterday you took the wrong road, but the sun over yonder jest gave you a whole new day t'git on another."

As a father, Ranger Woody was firm in discipline, but companionable in nature. Sons Walter and Clyne and daughter Mae remembered nevertheless that their father never spanked them.

"He found other means of discipline without laying a hand or a whip on us," Clyne recalled. The Woody children were introduced at an early age to hunting, fishing and camping in the mountains. Both sons also had careers as forest rangers, and grandson Richard became a fire control engineer in the Atlanta Regional Office of the U.S. Forest Service.

A monument to Woody's vision for a better life for mountain children is the Woody Gap School at Suches, Georgia. Opened in 1941, this kindergarten through twelfth grade school has been the pride of the community for almost fifty years, and is a model of education today.

The citizens of Suches successfully campaigned to keep Woody Gap School in operation, despite a concerted effort to consolidate it with the schools of Blairsville. It is one of the few remaining isolated schools allowed to operate in Georgia.

The main portion of the now-aged Woody Gap School was constructed of fine granite from Arthur Woody's own quarry and lumber sawed at his mill. Situated on land donated by Woody, the school not only bears his name, it continues to perpetuate high ideals and excellence in education.

Though tall, and at one time almost as strong as an oak, Woody eventually proved not to be as durable. He was confined to Georgia Baptist Hospital in Atlanta in February of 1945, in what he described as "taking a rest, city-fashion... because my tired ticker needs a little rest." The "tired ticker" became obvious after a slight stroke which Woody had suffered on September 18, 1944.

The stay in the hospital was an effort to eliminate some of Woody's body weight, to prevent strain on an overtaxed heart. Woody, jovial as ever with nurses and doctors, threatened to have his wife June bring in spare ribs to substitute for the chicken gruel on which he was being forced to subsist.

On September 30, 1945, Woody retired from the U.S. Forest Service, after realizing that his physical condition was preventing him from attending to his duties in the manner he felt necessary. A retirement party was held at Woody Gap

School, and colleagues presented him with his forest service badge – which he had worn so proudly for thirty years and which for him they had gold-plated.

Even though his health continued to deteriorate following his retirement, Woody retained his sense of humor to the very end. He penned verse which he titled *"I'm Retired"* shortly before his death:

"No fires to fight, no diaries to write,
No J.F.s to teach the poplar from beech;
No tools to grind, no desks to shine - Ah, this is the life for me!
For the rest of my life I'll stay with my wife,
Just sit on my rear, watch those who are near;
'Cause my battle is done, my race has been won.
Independent? That's what I be!"

Death for the great ranger came on June 10, 1946. He had given generously to have a new church building erected at Mount Lebanon Baptist Church, so there "would be a place large enough for my funeral." The crowd on that day, however, must have exceeded even Woody's expectations, for over 1,500 people turned out to bid him farewell at the small church nestled in the shadow of Black Mountain in Suches. The great man was laid to rest in Mount Lebanon Church Cemetery.

The Woody monument rises today among the sentinel trees. Beside him are buried his wife, Emma June, who lived to be almost ninety-six (1877-1973). Nearby are the graves of forester sons Walter Woody (1902-1986) and Clyne Edward Woody (1905-1984), and daughter Mae Woody White Pidgeon (1907-1986).

Today, on Route 180 between Suches and Vogel State Park, Sosebee Cove bears mute testimony to the accomplishments of Ranger Arthur Woody. The 178-acre scenic forest site was dedicated as a memorial to him on September 21, 1958. Within the confines of this lush spot exist beautiful stands of poplar, buckeye, black cherry, oak, hickory, white ash, basswood, black birch, cucumber, butternut, American chestnut, hemlock, service berry, silverbell, dogwood, persimmon, sassafras, black locust, maple, pine of several varieties, black gum, ironwood, holly, sourwood and more. Plants such as Dutchman's breeches, showy orchid, wild ginger and St. Andrew's Cross make the spot a botanist's dream.

Arthur Woody surveyed and negotiated the sale of this land on February 16, 1925, from F. Alonzo Sosebee. The sale price: $1,523.40. The cove was added to what was then the Blue Ridge District of the Cherokee National Forest (later named the Chattahoochee National Forest in Georgia.)

Dr. Philip F.C. Greear, head of the Biology and Earth Science Department at Shorter College in Rome, Georgia, wrote in October, 1976, in "Letters to the Editor," in the ***Atlanta Journal & Constitution*** *Sunday Magazine*, of the inspiration he had derived from two related Woodys: *"Events and people interact in fascinating ways. Olene Vandiver Woody was my fourth grade teacher in Helen, Georgia. I recall that in 1935, her father-in-law, Arthur Woody, the 'father of forestry in Georgia,' took me to Sosebee's Cove to see the great buck-eye and tulip trees. Miss Olene and Arthur Woody had much to do with shaping the direction of my life."*

Today, because someone cared about the forests and fought to preserve them for posterity, we enjoy their beauty and benefits. Only this continuous preservation will be a fitting tribute and a lasting reminder of a tall man among tall timbers – William Arthur Woody – forest ranger extraordinaire.

Mysterious Petroglyphs At Track Rock Gap

The unusual petroglyphic engravings in the large soapstone boulders at this secluded spot in the north Georgia mountains have defied explanation since their first discovery by Native Americans and pioneer settlers.

The six micaceous soapstone boulders scattered in the secluded gap in Union County, Georgia – the largest about 10 feet long and 3 feet high – are covered with mysterious petroglyphs or "stone writings" that have not only defied interpretation, but so far, have defied accurate dating as well.

Though the markings may have been made in pre-history by the Cherokees, none of the Cherokees who lived in what today is the state of Georgia in the early 1800s could explain the strange engravings. They are thought to at least be pre-Columbian in origin, and therefore very likely already in existence when the Cherokees arrived in Georgia in the 1500s.

Conversely, the symbols may have been carved by the native Creeks or their predecessors who were here before the Cherokees, or they may have been made by Indians from the Mississippian period (mound builders) who inhabited this area from the time of Christ to the 1500s, or even by the Woodland Indians who preceded them. Today, they are simply a great archaeological mystery – one of Georgia's many wonders – which must be protected.

According to Jack Wynn, archaeologist with the U.S. Forest Service which is responsible for protecting the site, petroglyphs are normally dated by cross-referencing with other similar patterns whose date of origin is known. But the patterns carved at Track Rock Gap are an isolated case, and currently have not been identified on any pottery or other artifacts which might help to identify and date the inscriptions.

There are a few other occurrences of prehistoric rock inscriptions in Georgia, Tennessee and Alabama, but those at Track Rock Gap are by far the largest and, unlike any of the other sites. They located in a strategic gap in the mountains by which the Indians, and later the white man, moved north and south.

"(The symbols) are as likely as not to have been made 3,000 years before the time of Christ," said Wynn, who feels that the markings may have been made in the mid-Archaic period, from 3,000 to 5,000 B.C. He bases this guess on the fact that it was during that era that prehistoric peoples of this region worked with stone, building stone structures, and making utensils, such as bowls from soft soapstone like that found at Track Rock.

"Forest Service surveys of the gap area have revealed nothing helpful, however," Wynn says. He explains that the markings may have had some meaning as part of a hunting or religious ritual, or they may simply be "prehistoric graffiti," carved by the Indians for their own amusement while resting in the gap, but that is pure supposition at best.

Though the Cherokees may not have made the markings, they did create and pass down through generation after generation of their own culture several stories which they maintained were an explanation for the petroglyphs' existence. They referred to the place as *"Datsu nalas gun vi,"* or "place where there are tracks."

Some Cherokees believed the markings had mystical origins and were made by a great army of humans and animals which crossed the gap in a great migration to escape some pursuing danger from the west. The tracks, supposedly, were retained because the earth's surface was still new and soft at that time.

Another Cherokee explanation resembles a "Noah's Ark"-type theory, in which the world was once flooded and all animals and mankind were destroyed except for one family, and some animals which survived in a great canoe. Their tracks were retained in the softened rocks as they disembarked from the site. This theory seems at least a little less far-fetched when one realizes that these rocks lie on the surface of the world's oldest mountain chain – the Appalachians.

The stone today is soft and could easily have been carved with prehistoric implements, particularly other stones. It is the softness of these stones, however, coupled with modern man's irreverent and disrespectful tendencies, which may prove to be the undoing of this remarkable prehistoric site.

Regardless of whether the Cherokees made the markings, they left the stones undamaged, and appear to have revered the site. It may have been the Cherokees, in an effort to discourage the white man's vandalism, who initiated the superstition that it always storms when a white man visits the spot because the Great Spirit is provoked by the intrusion.

In contrast to the Cherokees' respect for the site, the white men who entered the area in the early 1800s were not so careful to preserve it. One of the first white men known to have visited the site was a self-confessed vandal, and became but one of the many who would mar the carvings in the modern era.

Matthew F. Stephenson, one-time assayer of the U.S. Branch Mint which once existed at nearby Dahlonega, reports in his diary that he and a party left Nacoochee Valley in what today is White County on the morning of September 3, 1834, heading for Track Rock gap *"for the purpose of verifying those traditions which for the last half century have created so much interest and curiosity in the minds of speculative philosophers."*

In his diary, Stephenson described the events that followed:

"At six a.m., we arrived at the summit of the mountain. As we approached it, the heavens, which before for several days and nights had worn a brightened countenance, began to scowl and threaten; we advanced with a quickened pace to the foot of the rock and spread out our breakfast on the 'table of stone,' poured out a libation to appease the wrath of Jupiter, drank a few appropriate sentiments, and then, with

433

In an effort to curtail the defacement of the curious petroglyphs at Track Rock, heavy iron cages were constructed over the large boulders many years ago, but the senseless defacement continues nonetheless.

chisel and hammer, commenced the resurrection of one of the tracks.

"Notwithstanding, I believe I possess as little superstition as anyone, yet, I could not suppress a strange sensation that pervaded me... No sooner did we arrive on the consecrated ground, than it began to threaten, and the first stroke of the hammer in the sacrilegious act of raising the track of a human being was responded to by a loud peal of thunder; the clouds continued to thicken and condense, attended with the most awful lightning, when soon a deluge of rain was precipitated upon our offending heads. I continued, however, to labor incessantly until I succeeded in disintegrating the impression of a youth's foot, which I carefully wrapped up, and sounded a retreat, still however, looking back... in momentary expectation of seeing a legion of exasperated ghosts issuing forth to take their vengeance upon the infidel who would presume to disturb the relics of the dead. As soon as we passed the confines of the mountain, rain ceased, the sun broke out, and all nature resumed her cheerful aspect..."

Despite his vandalism, however, Dr. Stephenson did preserve some observations about the stones as they appeared that day, only two years after Union County, in which the stones lie, was organized. He counted 136 defined impressions on the stones, *"some of them quite natural and perfect, others rude imitations."* Even so long ago, Stephenson found that *"the effects of time"* had *"obliterated"* most of them.

Stephenson also noted that the *"human tracks"* ranged from 4 inches long to a track of the *"great warrior"* which measured seventeen and one-half inches long by seven and three-quarters inches across. He noted that, except for the great warrior, whose track showed six toes *"proving him to have been a descendant of Titan,"* all the other human prints were natural. Of the 26 human footprints, only one seems to have been wearing a moccasin, Dr. Stephenson reported.

Near the great warrior's footprint was a *"fine-turned hand, rather delicate"* which Stephenson presumed to be that of the warrior's wife. He noted many horse tracks, some small and one measuring twelve and one-half by nine and one-half inches, which he said the Indians speculated was the track of the great warrior's horse. Stephenson also noted the tracks of *"a great many"* turkeys, turtles, terrapins, a large bear's paw, a snake and two deer.

On later examination of the parcel of stone which he removed, Dr. Stephenson concluded that the impressions were made in *"an imperfect species of soapstone, which, more than any other circumstance, induced us to believe it to be a production of art."* Thus, Dr. Stephenson recorded his disappointment in the product of his vandalism.

The stones of the gap, which originally lay on an Indian path later used by white settlers, now lie immediately beside a paved county road in a lonely and easily-overlooked spot, marked only by a historical marker. Visitors today will note with sadness that the impressions are in fact slowly fading as they are "weathered" away.

The 20th century, and particularly modern man, have not been kind to these ancient signposts from yesteryear. For many years, great dense forests sheltered the stones from pelting rainfall, sleet and other elements, but in the 1920s and 30s, man denuded the mountains of the forests in this region as he harvested the trees for timber. The forests that have reclaimed this spot today do not shelter the rocks as completely.

Nevertheless, time and erosion are not the stones' worst enemy.... That culprit would be the simple vandal.

In more recent times, strong iron bars were placed across the rocks by the Forest Service in an effort to discourage vandalism, but it is still too simple to slip a hand between the bars and mar the ancient petroglyphs, as numerous crudely-carved modern initials on the rocks attest today.

For those who stop to view the historic Track Rock petroglyphs with respect today, however, there is no doubt that there is something of value here, something that beckons from the dim shadowy recesses of man's unwritten pre-history. Who carved these symbols into these boulders in north Georgia? Why and when did they do it? And what meaning did these symbols carry for the ancients who made them?

The world may never know the answers to these questions or solve the mystery of the petroglyphs, but it will at least be able to admire the ancient site and wonder about them as long as these artifacts remain. Here, in a forgotten corner of north Georgia, lies a mystery that may well remain unsolved forever; its cold gray boulders mutely denying us a glimpse backward into man's prehistoric past.

Ironically, one of the early defacers of the petroglyphs at Track Rock was Matthew F. Stephenson, famed assayer in the 1830s of the U.S. Branch Mint which once existed in Dahlonega, Georgia. In 1834, he recorded a specific incident in which he chiseled and broke off a section of one of the stones with a glyph to take back to Dahlonega to study. *(Photo courtesy of GA Dept. of Archives & History, Atlanta)*

(Grateful appreciation is extended to Jack Wynn for his assistance in the production of this article.)

References

"Vandals Mar Indian Rock Carvings" by John Harmon, Atlanta Journal/Constitution, Sunday, June 29, 1986

Sketches of Union County History, Vol. II, by Bryan Webb and Jan Devereaux

"Engraved Rocks" by Jim Miles, Rural Georgia magazine, November, 1984

"Land of Mystery and Magic - Cherokee Legends and Myths of Georgia Mountains" by Ruth Elgin Suddeth, Georgia Magazine, Aug.-Sept. 1958

Victim of the Devastation of War:

Col. James Hall Nichols Rebuilds His Devastated Life in North Georgia

Today it is a prominent historic landmark in an area where historic landmarks flourish – the Nacoochee Valley in north Georgia's White County. Colorful stories – including tales shrouded in mystery and tragedy – have surrounded the large mansion since the days of the U.S. Civil War.

For many years, the Italianate villa built by Col. James Hall Nichols shortly after the close of the U.S. Civil War was encumbered in a family estate. Some decades, the impressive home at the junction of U.S. Highway 17 and Georgia Highway 75 in northeast Georgia's White County was in use by family members, and in other decades it sat empty, forlorn, and silent. The mere fact of its age and origin lend it a cachet of historic significance.

Peopled for centuries by Native Americans, then by pioneers in the early 19th Century, the earliest White settlers would often stumble across prehistoric relics and remains in the broad Chattahoochee River valley. The immense beauty and rich natural resources of the valley were the impetus for the settler Nichols and the huge villa which he constructed and named "West End."

If it wasn't gold being discovered in the area, it was relics which appeared to have originated from an ancient bygone era – remnants of the conquistadors and Spanish explorers who are known to have traveled in the region. The Nacoochee Valley, hidden away in the northeast Georgia mountains, has been home to Native Americans in ancient times, and then home to others seeking escape in more modern times. Such a person was Col. Nichols.

He was born in Milledgeville on February 17, 1835. His family lived in the Midway community of that town, no doubt moving to and settling in Milledgeville due to its "up and coming" status as the state capital of Georgia.

On April 30, 1856, just a few short years prior to the devastation wrought by the U.S. Civil War, Nichols – who was a druggist by trade – married a beautiful young lady by the name of Kate Latimer. The two no doubt had plans and envisioned a long happy life together in Milledgeville. It, however, was not to be.

Immediately prior to the war in 1861, James and Kate Nichols became the proud parents of a daughter they named Anna Ruby whose moniker has found a lasting permanence in its attachment to the nearby (and now famous) tempestuous mountain waterfall a few miles north of Nacoochee Valley (in present-day Unicoi State Park).

War's Devastation

At the outbreak of war, just as did many young men of his day, Nichols answered the call, and raised a company of soldiers to which he was elected captain. Just as many of their day, they were all eager to engage Northern opposing troops.

Nichols's unit was the elite "Governor's Horse Guard," – a cavalry unit – which ultimately saw action in northwestern Virginia and then along the South Carolina coast. It no doubt was that coastal duty at which Nichols first contracted the malaria which would plague him the rest of his life.

In early 1862, the Capt. Nichols's unit was moved to a site near Richmond, where it became Company A of Phillip's Legion, Stuart's Cavalry, in the Army of Northern Virginia. Nichols was in Virginia when the tragedy that was to darken his life even more than the malaria occurred.

In November of 1864, Gen. William T. Sherman, his militant troops, "bummers" and general thieves and pillagers burned Atlanta, setting off the infamous general's campaign to "make Georgia howl." According to accounts, when Union troops neared Milledgeville, two blue-coated soldiers forced their way into the Nichols's home in Midway. Young Anna Maria Green, a resident of the area, penned the following lines in her diary that November which indelibly described the day:

"The worst of their acts was committed to poor Mrs. Nichols... an atrocity committed that ought to make her husband an enemy unto death. Poor woman, I fear she has been driven crazy."

Rape was a subject which polite 19th Century Georgians did not discuss. Insanity was another. And from the time of her tragic misfortune in Milledgeville, right up until her death, Kate Latimer Nichols virtually disappeared from the public scene, receding almost into myth. And insanity resulting from her rape was her destiny.

The actual details of what occurred to young Mrs. Nichols are unknown today, but in those lawless times – the darkest of the war – rape, murder, theft, assault, and virtually any other crime known to man was committed by the "troops," pillagers, thieves and other criminals which followed Sherman into Georgia to take advantage of the many opportunities which existed.

The wealth of the South and the subsequent opportunities for criminals in those terrible times were almost endless. The evil riff-raff who followed the armies of the North, and even the oft-presumed "safe" members of many Confederate "Home Guard" troops, knew the "pickings would be ripe" since virtually all of the former male residents of the many plantations, farms, businesses, and homes along the way were off fighting in the war or already dead. There almost always was no one home to protect the innocent and usually defenseless females and children.

By April 9, 1865, when he surrendered with the rest of the troops at the tiny community known as Appomattox

The Nichols-Hardman home ("West End") as it appears today in the Nacoochee Valley. (Photo by Olin Jackson)

Court House, James Nichols had advanced to the rank of colonel of the cavalry unit he commanded. Weakened from the debilitating effects of malaria, and scarred by defeat, Nichols no doubt struggled to return on the long slow trip homeward – walking most of the way from Virginia.

One can not imagine today the abject horror Nichols must have experienced after returning home to Milledgeville to find his beautiful wife despoiled by Yankee invaders and verging already upon insanity. The public record carries no hint of his reaction to the terrible discovery of his wife's tragedy, nor of his own pain and suffering thereafter. One can only surmise his abject despair.

From war's end until 1868, records indicate Nichols remained at his Milledgeville home, recuperating in both health and fortune, and caring for his wife and daughter. Though his business no doubt was destroyed with virtually everything else – since Milledgeville had been burned by the troops – he at least had a trade as a druggist which he could fall back upon.

Although legend credits malaria with Col. Nichols's eventual removal to the mountains, Kate's condition may well have been a factor in his decision to relocate the family residence to the isolation of the Nacoochee Valley. According to one anonymous account, Nichols was visiting a popular resort of the day outside Gainesville, Georgia, called White Sulphur Springs when his malaria flared again, forcing him to his sick-bed. He reportedly lingered on the point of death for weeks before recovering.

The exact details have been lost to history, but Nichols quite possibly was well-enough versed in medicine to understand the environment necessary in order for one to endure the constant trials involved in malarial afflictions – or perhaps he was advised by a physician to move to the cool environs of the mountains.

Whatever the circumstances, intent upon pushing into the Blue Ridge Mountains for health reasons, Nichols eventually reached the beauty of the Nacoochee Valley and advanced no further. Later, with funds from a family fortune which had fallen into his hands through the death of an unspecified relative, he purchased his property in the Nacoochee.

Author George Chapin's description of the valley in 1892 probably closely coincides with what Nichols felt: *"A view of this lovely valley bursts upon us - a view once seen, never to be forgotten..."*

Beginning in November of 1868, Nichols began purchasing the land that would ultimately comprise his 2,600-acre estate which he named "West End." And on February 17, 1869, he purchased the 473 acres in the Nacoochee that were to be the center of his mountain empire and the fabric of his social life for two decades.

The exact date of the construction of Nichols's Nacoochee home is unknown today, but it is unlikely that he completed it before 1870. George W. Williams's *Sketches of Travel In The Old And New World*, (1870), describes the Nacoochee in detail, but does not make any mention of West End. For an impressive home such as that built by Nichols to go undescribed in such a publication would be unusual.

To build his captivating dwelling, Nichols demolished a homestead which already existed on the site that had been constructed years earlier by a settler by the name of Daniel Brown. Interestingly, a substantial prehistoric Indian mound existed (and still does today) in the pasture just south of the home. Nichols leveled the top of this historic relic in order to build a "summer house" at the site.

It is quite possible today that Nichols modeled his West End home after his former residence in Midway. It rises majestically, cushioned into the edge of the hillside. The villa-style country residence is weather-boarded and painted white, with a distinctive square central cupola, and includes ultra-fine detailing throughout.

The residence enjoys fresh mountain water from a spring at the rear of the home. Italian marble filled the rooms of the home at one time; marble basin and wash-stand lavatories graced each bedroom, as did an unusual abundance of closets.

Twenty-two years later, George Chapin admired:

"The dwelling is spacious, surrounded by broad piazzas, over which are entwined flowering vines, and here Captain Nichols has gathered around him everything that makes life pleasant, a large farm, well-stocked rich fields, trained hounds, and plenty of game, fish ponds, a choice library, billiard room, pure spring water throughout, greenhouse, fountains, and near by on a rise of land, shaded by beautiful oaks, the captain has erected a charming little church finished in natural woods from the trees of the forests of Nacoochee Valley, comprising many different shades and colors which beautifully harmonize, and this gem of a church Captain Nichols has deeded to the trustees of the Presbyterian Church... many acres of rich interval are now in waving crops, presenting a scene of rare loveliness... The whole forming one of the most perfect country seats in the South."

A raised, covered walkway led to the one-story kitchen at the rear of the Nichols home, and a bridge connected the house to a nearby two-story game room with its scalloped wood-working. When completed, West End also included a magnificent two-story dairy barn, game pens, servants' quarters, a spring house, a gristmill, and more. Nichols operated the dairy, as well as his gristmill which was nearby on the river, while farming the fertile river-bottomlands.

On the Indian mound, Nichols's summer house was basically a small roofed enclosure with table and chairs for reading, writing, and reflecting. From the spring and the willow-draped pond, he amazingly piped water out to the mound. It is unknown today what happened to the water after it reached the mound.

While plowing near the mound in June of 1870, Nichols discovered a number of large stone slabs several inches below the surface of the field. After removing the slabs, he discovered three stone graves *(Readers please see the associated article in this publication entitled "Early Spanish Explorers in White County?")*.

Charles C. Jones studied the site and discussed it in ***Antiquities of the Southern Indians***. "So far as we are informed, these are the first ancient stone graves which have been observed within the geographical limits of Georgia," he wrote.

Breath-taking and soothing, the Nacoochee Valley also no doubt suited Nichols's purposes by being an isolated paradise. Mail was delivered only once a week. Farming and gold mining were the major occupations.

Nichols assumed the role of patron of his domain, perfectly happy to be reduced in rank back to the title of "Captain" as he was known by the hardy mountain residents, and charmed by their respect for him.

From Midway, Nichols brought his Scotch coachman and three black and one white house servants. Augusta Latimer, Kate's mother, lived also at West End, and designed the lovely flowers and gardens there... and probably served as caretaker for her daughter as well.

Kate, by this time, quite likely bordered on madness, yet the Captain was a Sphinx to his neighbors. Invariably, the few recorded accounts of him throughout his life raise more questions than they answer. One visitor to West End likened James Hall Nichols to Orion, the mythological hunter.

Resident George Walton Williams termed Nichols *"that liberal-hearted Christian gentleman... who has expended more than a hundred thousand dollars in making this valley 'as lovely to the eye and hand of Art, as it comes to Art beautiful from the hands of Nature.'"*

A stable-keeper – John Jones – of Clarkesville once was quoted as declaring: *"Ah sir. Captain Nichols is a good man. God, I think, never made a much better one. He is not one thing to one man and another thing to another, but the same today as yesterday, and an honest man to all!"*

Captain Nichols was an avid hunter with hounds, and had at one time a game park – including bear pens (the heavy steel bars are still in place in the basement of the horse barn) – and hunting trophies inside West End. His abundance of leisure-time pursuits were in keeping with those of a man of his wealth and social standing.

Of note is the fact that Nichols also served as a trustee of the lunatic asylum in Milledgeville, a preoccupation which some of his contemporaries undoubtedly considered unusual for a man of wealth who resided a substantial distance away in north Georgia. His undoubted concern with his wife, and no doubt a presumption of his need for her incarceration in the facility in the future – and are inescapable.

In acknowledgment of the fact that he would not live forever and wished to make certain of the provision for his loved ones, in July of 1879, Nichols granted the house and grounds of West End to Kate and Anna Ruby, with the provision that he was to serve as trustee and retain possession during his natural life.

In 1885, Anna Ruby married George Frederick Payne of Macon, and what almost certainly had been the light of Nichols's life – his daughter – was suddenly gone. The magic of West End, no doubt, was now quickly diminishing with each passing year for Nichols.

Kate, undoubtedly, was worsening by this time too. Was she mad enough that Nichols kept her hidden now? How much did Anna Ruby know about her mother? Of these questions, one can only surmise the answers. Nichols's own health may at that point have also been more of a concern.

Whatever the circumstances, on July 24, 1893, Nichols apparently had decided another change was necessary. He sold 604 acres in White County, including the house and grounds, 18 head of cattle, growing crops, farm implements, wagons and harness, and *"all household and kitchen furniture except bed and table linen,"* for $22,500, to Calvin W. Hunnicutt of Atlanta.

Though that sale price seems like a pittance for such a magnificent and extensive estate, it would be the equivalent of $72,768.00 in today's dollars. But even at that price, the sale would still have been a tremendous bargain for Hunnicutt. Suffice it to say that Nichols obviously was more than ready to leave, and had found a willing and able buyer.

Nichols took his funds and, in the now-burgeoning town of Atlanta, purchased two lots on Linden and Williams Streets, and one on West Peachtree Street – including the C.W. Hunnicutt home-place on Spring Street, opposite the Baltimore Block. Hunnicutt was a former Fulton County commissioner, and wealthy gas and plumbing fixture dealer with Hunnicutt & Bellingrath.

Tannie Williams Lumsden recorded the event and the area's emotional attachment to Nichols for posterity, writing:

"I suppose you have heard Capt. Nichols has sold his home in the Valley. I think that he exchanged it for property in Atlanta. Captain has lived here so long we will miss him very much when he leaves."

Perhaps the Nacoochee Valley was losing the charming isolation that Nichols had craved initially. In the 1890s, the mail was delivered daily, and there was talk of a rail line (which ultimately would in fact exist in the years ahead, and pass quite near to West End) being built in the near future. Summer boarders now filled the handsome cottages strung along the Unicoi Turnpike, and the haunting loveliness of the valley in the shadow of the Blue Ridge Mountains was no longer a well-kept secret.

Early Gristmill – Pictured here is a rare period photograph of the gristmill originally built by Daniel Brown in 1824, and later owned by James Nichols (present-day Nora Mill on the Chattahoochee) adjacent to the Nichols-Hardman home in Nacoochee. *(Photo courtesy of Libby K. Tucker)*

Today, much of what is remembered about Kate in the old home centers around a hook suspended from the upper bedroom ceiling.

Perhaps also, Nichols's decision to leave hinged upon the stability of his wife and his own increasing loneliness. On August 5, 1895, he was appointed guardian for the person and property of Kate L. Nichols, who, according to the *1895 White County Estate Records*, was *"now in the Lunatic Asylum."*

Today, much of what is remembered about Kate in the old home centers around a hook suspended from the upper bedroom ceiling. Local folklore

Mystery & History in Georgia

Photographed in 1912, saw-milling had become big business in the Nacoochee Valley, soiling the rivers and streams with sediment run-off, and obliterating the forests and beautiful views. Virtually all of the virgin timber which had once graced the mountainsides and valleys in this area was eventually wiped out, reducing the Sautee-Nacoochee Valleys – once a dreamland – to a barren wasteland that has only just recovered in recent years. *(Photo courtesy of GA Dept. of Archives & History, Atlanta)*

maintains that Kate's cot reportedly hung from this hook, and that she often was confined in this spot. Additional details concerning her illness and the circumstances of her years at West End have faded into the mists of time.

Captain Nichols, following the move, involved himself in Georgia's exhibit in an exposition in Nashville, Tennessee in the summer of 1897. The malaria that had first driven him to the Nacoochee Valley struck again in Tennessee. By the time the exposition closed and he arrived back in Atlanta, he was in extremely feeble health.

In an apparent bid to repeat his earlier remedy, Nichols decided to return to West End to restore his health. The site of his residence this time is unknown to this writer.

At first, Nichols did in fact seem to recover, but on a cold Wednesday evening on November 23, 1897, after eating a hearty supper, he reportedly suffered a massive heart attack, and died within minutes.

Nichols's remains were returned to Milledgeville where his life – and the tragedy which would haunt him for the rest of his life – had originated all those years ago. He was interred in the family vault there. Accompanied by his son-in-law, they arrived at 3:00 p.m. on Friday. Some of Nichols's old cavalry comrades served as his pall-bearers. The *Union Recorder* reported:

"*Captain Nichols was a noble cultured Christian gentleman - a gallant soldier, an upright citizen, a noble man.*"

Dr. Lamartine G. Hardman, a

future governor of Georgia, purchased West End from Hunnicutt in November of 1903. He renamed it *"Elizabeth On The Chattahoochee"* in memory of his mother. During his tenure as governor (1927-1931), the site served as the summer governor's mansion.

It might almost be considered poetic justice that James Hall Nichols departed this life prior to the turn-of-the-century, for he undoubtedly would have despaired the destruction of the beauty he so enjoyed in his beloved Nacoochee Valley. Sawmilling, which plundered the beautiful mountainsides, soon spoiled the lovely land for many years.

The first big mill came in 1907, and primarily because of the mills, tracks for the Gainesville and Northwestern Railroad were laid into Nacoochee in 1911, passing approximately 100 yards from Nichols's former home.

The advent of the railroad into the region only increased the fury of the logging industry there. The mills stripped the hills and mountains bare, violating the once breath-taking beauty of the valley.

After the timber was gone, the railroad departed with it. The tracks were pulled up from the Nacoochee Depot in 1931, and a measure of peacefulness descended upon the valley once again.

Interestingly, in 1912-13, St. Louis-born John E. Mitchell had laid out a tiny new community not far from Nacoochee Depot. In 1915 the Mountain Ranch Resort was built there, setting the stage for later growth in the little community which came to be known as "Helen." Ironically, rampant development today in Helen poses what could be a renewed threat to the scenic beauty of West End.

For the Nichols family however, the future in the Nacoochee Valley ended long ago. Anna Ruby and George Frederick Payne became the parents of a single child. And she, when her husband died, was left childless.

At the junction of U.S. Highway 17 and GA Highway 75 today, the old white weather-boarded villa still looms behind the huge magnolias. Immense, impressive, and silent... its past shrouded in a mist-like secrecy forever.

(Editor's Note: Nichols's former gristmill at West End – Nora Mill – also still exists today, and is a popular stop for travelers and tourists. In the 1950s, it was one of the filming sites for the major motion picture "I'd Climb The Highest Mountain," starring Susan Hayward, William Lundigan, and Rory Calhoun. For more information, please read the article entitled "I Remember When Hollywood Came To North Georgia" in this publication.)

References:

(1) *The Diary Of A Milledgeville Girl, 1861-1867*, from the diary of Anna Maria Green, edited by James C. Bonner.

(2) *Health Resorts Of The South, 1892*, by George Chapin.

(3) *Health Resorts Of The South, 1892*, by George Chapin.

(4) *Nacoochee And Its Surroundings, 1874*, by George Walton Williams.

(5) *Augusta Chronicle*, July 20, 1883.

(6) *Estate Records of White County, 1860-1895.*

(7) *The Lumsden Papers*, Josephine Hardeman.

(8) *Estate Records of White County, 1860-1895.*

Also: **Lumsden Family History**, Susan Lumsden. *History Of The Nacoochee Valley, 1979*, by Tom Lumsden. *Sautee-Nacoochee Valley National Register Nomination* information, Georgia Department of Natural Resources. *Sketches Of Travel In The Old And New World, 1870*, by George Walton Williams.

"I Remember When Hollywood Came Filming In North Georgia"

In the 1950s in northeast Georgia, one former lucky participant remembers when Hollywood "came-a-callin'" to film – on location – not one, but two movies set in the Blue Ridge Mountains of north Georgia.

In the early 1900s in north Georgia, virtually all of the towns and villages were dusty little crossroads communities with a very slow and sleepy existence. Life progressed day to day with very little fanfare. In the 1950s, however, that quiet country scenery became the setting for two major motion pictures starring the cream of Hollywood's actors, and one of the native participants – the late John Kollock – remembered it well.

As of this writing (2021), author Corra Harris has now been gone for almost 100 years, but her most famous work – *A Circuit Rider's Wife* – is still read by young and old alike, and was once a best-selling novel. *(Readers please see "Bartow County Phenomenon: The Author of A Circuit Rider's Wife" in the Bartow County section.)* The book is focused around the career of a young minister and his new bride, and their first church in the Blue Ridge Mountains.

In 1949, the popularity of Harris's book led Hollywood producers to purchase the film rights in order to produce a major motion picture entitled *I'd Climb The Highest Mountain*. The movie was filmed in northeast Georgia near Cleveland.

The book, interestingly, was written as a memorial to Harris's own experiences as the wife of a Methodist minister, and contains many snippets of her life with her husband in their early years in north Georgia. It is not known by this writer all of the locales where Corra and her husband, Lundy, spent their earliest years, but one such spot which is known, is Rockmart, in northwest Georgia's Polk County.

The Harris family moved to Rockmart after Lundy received a teaching position at the community's Piedmont Institute, and it was here that it is believed that Mrs. Harris began work on her best-selling novel. It was the book's originality and heart-tugging drama which captured the attention of the movie-makers, and led them to select the north Georgia locale as the location for filming.

Back over in northeast Georgia,

I Remember When Hollywood Came Filming — White County

though movie-making in the 1950s certainly was a rare event, silent movies, in fact, had been made around nearby Dahlonega, Georgia, several decades earlier, but few people remembered back that far. For most of these north Georgians, the film-making around Cleveland was an exciting new experience.

Heading up the cast in this new movie were then-famous actors Susan Hayward, William Lundigan and young new-comer heart-throb, Rory Calhoun. Alexander Knox, Gene Lockhart, Barbara Bates, Jean Innis, and Lynn Bari rounded out the cast.

To fill out the small "bit-parts," a call went out for local aspiring actors and actresses to come to Atlanta to "read" for parts. One such participant was a young art and theatre major – John Kollock – who would later gain renown in the area for his historically-oriented paintings, books, and other creations.

Kollock was among many applicants who trooped past casting directors and other decision-makers in these heady days, but he was ultimately deemed "too old" for one part, and "too young" for any of the others. Nevertheless, since he lived near the area anyway, John decided to just go to Cleveland (Georgia) where one of the assistant directors – a Mr. Jack Suntag – was organizing extra talent for things like "crowd scenes" in the movie.

After poking around the set a day or two and offering wherever possible to help in other areas, John learned that Mr. Suntag had instructed that he (John) be placed on the studio list of "extras," which for John, was a huge break. "Before I knew it," the late Kollock explained in an interview in the 1990s, "I, and a sizeable contingent of local residents from White, Habersham, and surrounding counties, were being

In the summer of 1950, *20th Century Fox Film Corp.* brought production personnel and film crews to White County to film the major motion picture *I'd Climb The Highest Mountain*, starring Susan Hayward, William Lundigan, Rory Calhoun and other Hollywood celebrities. Here, on the Chattahoochee River at present-day Nora Mill outside Helen, Georgia, a scene is being set up. *(Photo used with permission)*

introduced to the magical world of movie-making."

In that day and time, "extras" received six dollars for a day's work. "We might not work at all," Kollock said, "but as long as we were 'on-call' for a location, we reported 'in costume,' and hung around the set to see if we would be needed. They filmed six days a week, so in a good location, I would make thirty-six dollars by Saturday. I had worked a lot harder for a lot less."

The Art of Filming

As an "extra," one of the first things John learned was that if he wanted to keep working in the movie, his objective strangely became to "avoid the camera." "If you were an extra and you wanted to keep your job," he explained, "it was prudent to remain as anonymous as possible. If you accidentally appeared in a 'close-up,' you became 'established' as a character, and the directors therefore might decide not to use you again, because they couldn't have an 'extra' interfering with the audience focus upon the stars."

A young Rory Calhoun and Barbara Bates enjoy a moment of "down-time" prior to filming a scene in *I'd Climb The Highest Mountain*. (Photo used with permission)

Such an occurrence was the last thing John wanted to have happen, since he had worked so hard to become accepted by the film-makers. "Needless to say, I became a very good crowd-mingler," he added.

One day, to his great fortune, John was asked if he could handle a team of horses. The director it seems needed someone to drive one of the buggies full of people along the road to the picnic scene in the movie.

"I of course replied that I absolutely could, and from then on, I was put to work driving buckboards, wagons and other rolling stock whenever such were needed in the background for 'atmosphere.'

"With this new responsibility, I was able to work most of the outdoor location shoots," Kollock continued. "In Mossy Creek *(a rural locality near presentday Cleveland, Georgia)*, we spent several weeks filming around the minister's home. One day, they enveloped the whole exterior of the house in a giant tarpaulin to make it dark enough to shoot a night scene in the yard. The interiors of the house were shot on sets built in the old Cleveland School gymnasium."

The church chosen for much of the main action in the movie was in Robertstown *(just north of presentday Helen, Georgia)* across the Chattahoochee River. "In one scene, a large group of us were gathered between the church and the cemetery to say goodbye to the minister," Kollock smiled. "This scene later became the end of the movie."

Kollock explained that immediately following the filming of this church scene, the "extras" were broken into smaller groups to shoot the scenes which became the early portion of the movie. "We quickly realized why actors, directors, etc., needed scripts to stay organized. When Gene Lockhart came forward to say his line to Bill Lundigan at the farewell scene, I heard the director say 'Now smile. You like each other in this scene.'"

On another day, Kollock says the set designers draped the windows of the church with blackout curtains so the inside could be used for a night scene when the community was sick with fever and the building was serving as a hospital. "I appear in this scene as a shadowy figure fanning a little girl lying in her crib," he added with another grin. "She delighted in trying to make me laugh by making faces at me."

Kollock says the daily life of moviedom in the north Georgia shoot was actually more like a social gathering than the intense business of film-making. "Folks sat under the trees and relaxed and visited with each other until they were called for a scene.

"Harvey Hester, the owner of *Aunt Fannie's Cabin Restaurant* (which was a popular restaurant in Atlanta in the 1950s and '60s), would climb into a buggy that wasn't being used in a scene and doze the afternoon away. Men hunkered down and discussed their crops."

Since almost all these "extras" were

I Remember When Hollywood Came Filming   White County

just local country folks, they continued the social mores they had been practicing since childhood. The ladies "talked family" and kept the small children out of the way of the technical people. "Looking back, I think it was part of that low-key approach which gave much of the real flavor to the film," Kollock added. "The credit for this must go to the director, Henry King. His career in films reached back into the very early days of silent movies. He loved atmosphere and seemed to have a special knack for bringing out the spirit of the times.

Special Flavor

"Mr. King would often shoot extra footage in order to linger on the local people who were so much a part of the story. One day, he positioned kids along both sides of a long picnic table, and placed a mouth-watering slice of watermelon in front of each one. He then instructed them to begin eating, and left them alone, all the while leaving the camera rolling until they were done.

"Unfortunately, most of this sort of footage was left on the 'cutting room' floor in order to focus upon the main story of the preacher and his bride, but snippets of it often found their way into the body of the movie, adding 'flavor.'"

According to Kollock, bits and pieces of this north Georgia hill country flavor often appear in this film. When the extras were gathered on a set, they didn't have to be instructed on acting techniques. They simply behaved naturally as the north Georgia country folks behaved, adding instant credibility to the movie.

"When a group of us gathered to sing *In the Good Old Summer Time* to be dubbed in over the soundtrack portion of the scene in which the people are traveling to the picnic, we just sang naturally.

As it turned out, it sounded natural too. Not great singing, but very natural... not a 'canned' Hollywood production.

Amusingly, it seems a few of the females objected to their period costumes, apparently not understanding the purpose of the clothing. "Don't know why we got to wear these old-timey clothes," complained one lady. "We've got good Sunday clothes at home we could wear to have our picture took."

Kollock went on to explain how one wonderful old gentleman from Chimney Mountain Road back in the mountains kept trying to come to the filming without his false teeth (dentures). His wife always made him wear them "for the picture folk." "One day he appeared with a broad gummy grin," Kollock laughed in remembrance, "and announced mirthfully to his cronies that he had 'hid the danged things from her.'"

Special attention reportedly was paid to making the stars look neat, especially the ladies. Also, since William Lundigan usually appeared in a dark suit, he was constantly being dusted off for lint and other natural particles that might settle upon him.

"The clouds of dust that arose every time a car passed were a particular problem," Kollock said. "The rest of us, however, were allowed to collect as much dust and lint as possible for 'atmosphere.' I wore the same costume for the better part of three months without laundering. Needless to say, by the time the production 'wrapped,' I was a bit. . . . no, I was VERY 'gamey.'"

Kollock says the north Georgia weather was a constant problem as well. "The Californians were accustomed to clear skies day after day. The summertime Blue Ridge Mountains thundershowers would send the cast and crew scurrying for cover and change the

447

Director Henry King gives instruction on "the drowning scene" filmed along the Chattahoochee River in White County in 1950. *(Photo used with permission)*

appearance of a location from a dry, ochercolored dust, to bright red mud in a matter of minutes."

Patience Is A Virtue

"One day while we were shooting in the pasture at Helen, Georgia, Mr. King took refuge under my wagon where its passengers were trying to stay dry during a sudden rain shower," Kollock continued. "He seemed to keep his frustration under control, despite the fact that several hundred expensive performers and technicians were crouching under trees and picnic tables while the rain drenched everything in sight. Once the cloud had passed however, he led a frantic rush to get the shot done before the next shower hit.

"On another day at Nora Mill, the billowing clouds were causing an excess of tension. It was the only time I saw Henry King explode. They were filming the scene in which the small boy drowns in the mill race.

"I was in the 'mingling group' which gathered after the boy fell into the water and failed to reappear. This first portion went well. We extras mingled hurriedly and acted dreadfully concerned. At this point however, the clouds once again began to gather overhead. Time and again, we would wait and watch as the daylight was wasted.

"Finally, the shot in which Rory Calhoun jumps into the river to search for the body was begun. Rory was dressed beautifully in coat, tie and cream-colored slacks for the picnic scene, and just as he hit the water, someone in the crowd of spectators (who often stopped along the roadway to watch the film-making) gave a loud laugh. Mr. King turned upon the visitors and, with a few restrained but nevertheless emphatic words, banished them from the set for the remainder of the day. Rory retired to dry off and change into a duplicate costume, while the rest of us watched still more clouds begin to roll in.

"On another day, we were shooting at a country crossroads store in Mossy Creek. It was for a winter scene just before Christmas, but in actuality, we were shooting the scene on a hot day in July. I was driving a two-horse wagon for 'background' in a scene with William Lundigan and Gene Lockhart. I was bundled up in a heavy jacket and wool hat. After about half a dozen trips, circling the store and driving a quarter of a mile down the road in the background of the scene, I was getting just a bit warm. *(Reader's Note: The country store described above and below was an actual store which existed for many years in Mossy Creek at a crossroads, but was demolished circa 1970s.)*

"We finally finished that scene and then began shooting an interior sequence with Lundigan and one of the 'bit players' arm-wrestling on the store counter. Mr. King, as usual, decided to pad the scene to provide a lead-in. Since I was handy, and had never actually been 'on-camera' as a character, I was called upon to wrestle first with the boy who was playing the jilted boyfriend of Barbara Bates.

"As Mr. King began to embellish this arm-wrestling scene, he decided I should put up my side of the wager. The prop man gave me a large coin which was a 'period coin' to fit the scene. I casually dropped it into my pocket, forgetting all about the other 'modern' coinage I already had in that pocket. When it came time for me to bet, I discovered to my horror that the prop coin was mixed with my 1950s-era change. I stood there with the camera rolling as I fumbled wildly in my pocket trying to identify the correct coin to flip on the counter.

"I knew full well that if I dropped a shiny 1949 dime into the scene I would be out of a job. Finally, after a painful lapse of time, Mr. King stopped the filming and explained that if it took that long for me to bet, we would have very little time left for the rest of the picture. I finally found the coin, and when filming continued, I palmed it tightly in my fist as I faked the motion of its retrieval from my pocket. We made the scene on the second 'take,' but like so many other shots, this one was cut out of the picture, leaving only the preacher winning his part of the match. In the background of this scene in the movie, however, I can be seen smiling broadly, supposedly at the preacher winning. *(Actually, it was sheer joy at having found the coin in time.)*

"An interesting sidelight to that day was the fact that I had been given a line to say on-camera. At the beginning of the wrestling, I was told to say 'Set,' (as in 'ready, set, ...'). For this I was promoted from an 'extra,' to a 'bit-player' for one day. I got paid eighty dollars for this honor instead of the usual six and received a temporary membership in the *Hollywood Screen Actors Guild*. I was overcome with this newfound wealth,

DARRYL F. ZANUCK
Presents

I'D CLIMB THE HIGHEST MOUNTAIN

COLOR BY
TECHNICOLOR

STARRING

SUSAN HAYWARD

and

WILLIAM LUNDIGAN

Directed by
HENRY KING

Produced by
LAMAR TROTTI

Screen Play by
LAMAR TROTTI

From a Novel by
CORRA HARRIS

CAST

Jack Stark	Rory Calhoun
Jenny Brock	Barbara Bates
Mr. Brock	Gene Lockhart
Mrs. Billywith	Lynn Bari
Glory White	Ruth Donnelly
Mrs. Brock	Kathleen Lockhart
Salter	Alexander Knox
Mrs. Salter	Jean Inness
Dr. Fleming	Frank Tweddell
George Salter	Jerry Vandiver
Bill Salter	Richard Wilson
Martha Salter	Dorothea Carolyn Sims
Pike Boys	(Thomas Syfan
	(Grady Starnes
Martin Twins	Kay and Fay Fogg

A
20th CENTURY-FOX
PICTURE

(and 'fame'), and five years later, it would inspire yet another encounter on my part with Hollywood.

Walt Disney Comes To Town

"In 1955, yet another Hollywood movie-making giant came to north Georgia to film – on location – another movie set in north Georgia's Blue Ridge Mountains," Kollock continued. "*Walt Disney Productions* was a name known to every youngster who watched *The Mickey Mouse Club*, and *The Wonderful World of Disney* on television, not to mention the numerous Walt Disney movies. This famous company was now

Mystery & History in Georgia

Actress Susan Hayward speaks her lines in a scene from *I'd Climb The Highest Mountain* being filmed at the tiny community of "Mossy Creek" just outside Cleveland, Georgia. The country grocery being used in this scene was an actual store in Mossy Creek for many years before going out of business circa 1960, and unfortunately being demolished. *(Photo courtesy of 20th Century Fox Film Corp)*

Actor Rory Calhoun prepares to jump into the Chattahoochee River at the gristmill known today as "Nora Mill" in White County, during filming of "the drowning scene" in *I'd Climb The Highest Mountain*. *(Photo courtesy of 20th Century Fox Film Corp)*

in our town to film '*The Great Locomotive Chase*,' a historic account of a genuine historic event which occurred during the U.S. Civil War.

"One of the reasons which northeast Georgia had been chosen for the filming site – aside from the obvious breath-taking natural scenery – was the Tallulah Falls Railroad (TFR), a short-line from Cornelia, Georgia, to Franklin, North Carolina. At the time, I was working as a freelance artist, but the opportunity to try out for a real 'bit-part' was just too tempting to turn down."

Kollock explained that the movie was based upon a true incident which occurred during the war when a Northern spy named James J. Andrews commandeered a Confederate locomotive and set out to wreck the important rail line – the Western & Atlantic Railroad – from Marietta, Georgia to Chattanooga, Tennessee.

"Most of the filming of this movie was scheduled to be done on the TFR between Tallulah Falls, Georgia, and Franklin. Some of the old railroad depots were dressed up to look like the actual locations. At other sites, sets were built along the track in spots where the background was appropriate. Many of the wonderful old wooden trestles of the Tallulah Falls Railroad have been preserved for posterity in the footage of this movie."

For the train itself, Walt Disney shipped in period locomotives and cars to Cornelia where they were put on the track and then driven up the Tallulah Falls line to Clayton. Disney, himself a big train buff, traveled from Hollywood to join the Georgia crew for a while to enjoy the fun and watch the old locomotives on the beautiful TFR trestles, which today are long gone, having sadly been dismantled and removed in the 1960s when the railroad went bankrupt.

"A talent call was announced for the

I Remember When Hollywood Came Filming   White County

Television and entertainment impresario Walt Disney brought his movie production company to the Tallulah Falls Railroad in Rabun County, Georgia, and Otto, North Carolina, to film the major motion picture *The Great Locomotive Chase* on the scenic railroad line in 1955. Pictured here is motion picture star Fess Parker – portraying James J. Andrews – giving instructions to a locomotive engineer who in real life is a young John Kollock, native of Rabun and, later for many years, a renowned artist and writer in northeast Georgia. *(Photo courtesy of Walt Disney Studios)*

movie, and area hopefuls came to 'read' for the movie," Kollock says. "This time, I decided to apply only for a bit-part, bypassing any opportunities for work as an extra.

Once again, Kollock says a parade of aspiring actors appeared before the casting director, producer and assistants who were housed in a hotel suite in downtown Atlanta where the casting-call was held. "I read the assigned part in my best native accent," he smiled. "The California visitors had been listening to an assortment of the well-modulated voices of radio announcers and performers from the Atlanta scene, all expecting to easily obtain a part. I apparently sounded strangely twangy, and must have been just what they were seeking. The production people muttered to each other a bit and finally one of them asked if I really talked that way all of the time. When I assured him that I did, I, to my great delight, was awarded a bit-part and instructed to stop cutting my hair. I learned my lines, let my hair grow, and reported to Clayton in high spirits in October. I was officially 'an actor!'

"I think this was perhaps the first time a film company had swallowed up a whole community in this part of Georgia," Kollock continued. "The hotels and restaurants immediately began experiencing a bonanza with all of the late fall flow of ready cash."

Due to its location and antique style, the Clayton Depot became the make-up room and was also used as one of the sets in the movie. "We began each morning at 6:00 A.M. when we were costumed and plastered with 'pancake' make-up," Kollock added. "I was given a drooping mustache which came loose every time the steam from a cup of coffee hit it. At 7:00 A.M., the bits, stand-ins

Mystery & History in Georgia

Another view of a scene from *The Great Locomotive Chase*, starring Fess Parker, Slim Pickens, and others, being filmed in Otto, North Carolina, on the Tallulah Falls Railroad. *(Photo used with permission)*

and 'atmosphere' *(as the extras were now called)* were loaded into a bus and driven to the set.

A Whistle-Blower

"As a bit-player, I was only involved in one location. This took place above Otto, North Carolina, where the crew had constructed a 'railroad station,' and even a siding track which were to represent Kingston, Georgia *(site of a portion of the actual historic Civil War event)*. My part was that of the engineer on the south-bound locomotive which blocked Andrews' train from traveling north toward Chattanooga."

The *Great Locomotive Chase* was particularly captivating for any young boy of the 1950s, since it starred none other than Fess Parker, fresh from his role in the *Walt Disney Production "Davy Crockett."* Parker was portraying the main character – James J. Andrews.

"In this particular scene in which I was involved," Kollock said, "Mr. Parker was pretending to be a Western & Atlantic Railroad official under special orders. My lines called for me to express doubts about his ability to get his train through, at which point I then dutifully removed my train (via the sidetrack) in order to let him pass."

Kollock says that in reality, he had nothing to do with the actual driving of the locomotive in this scene. A special technician lay on the floor of the cab between his feet and did the work. "Nevertheless, I did get to blow the whistle as we came in," he smiles.

The filming of this brief moment of glory took over a week to accomplish. The procedure with any scene was to assemble everyone who might be involved. These actors and actresses then sat until they were called for their scenes.

"Every morning after costumes and make-up, we rode off into the early fog along the Little Tennessee River to Otto. Once we arrived at the set, speculation began as to when the fog would lift. In October, the fog did not choose to dissipate until around 11:00 A.M. in the morning. We usually sat around several small campfires of scrap wood, letting the dew settle in our makeup and watching the technicians set the lights and camera while the executives fidgeted over the delay. When the weather complied, we shot until lunch at noon.

"In the afternoons, we made better time until the long yellow light of early evening made it impossible to match scenes with those which had been shot in full light. On one of these occasions in which the light was changing, the crew was trying to get a single close-up shot of the stationmaster telegraphing down the line. He had only a short line in this scene, but for some reason, the actor just couldn't get the line out.

During filmmaking, every shot is marked with a chalkboard indicating the scene and the 'take' number. Then a wooden clapper is snapped to synchronize the picture and sound and the action begins. Unfortunately, every time

Hollywood movie-maker Walt Disney pauses to speak with production staff filming *The Great Locomotive Chase*. He is photographed at the old Clayton, Georgia, depot of the Tallulah Falls Railroad, which had been converted for filming purposes in several scenes. Sadly, this depot was demolished many years ago after the Tallulah Falls Railroad ceased operations in 1961. *(Photo used with permission)*

Another photo of the always-genial Disney who paused while eating a meal in a restaurant in Clayton, Georgia, in 1955. *(Photo used with permission)*

the clapper snapped in the face of the actor portraying the stationmaster in this scene, he blew (garbled) his line. In the final film, there is a slightly golden glow to that shot, because it was finally mercifully finished just before sunset.

"After about a week of these unhurried times, I finally received a rush call to get into my engine. We loaded up, backed up the track, and on cue, came puffing and tooting into the depot. The movie crew then set up a camera for a medium shot of Fess, the train and myself. They framed a close-up of me, then we did it again – after the make-up man had been called to lock down my wayward mustache. They then took the train away and I stood on a platform as they shot a close-up of Fess. It was all over in about an hour.

"Shortly after the shooting of this scene, the producer called me over and very kindly explained that he was pleased with the work I had done and that if I wanted to come to California, he could write a small part for me in an upcoming movie entitled 'Johnny Tremain' which was scheduled for production later in the year. These words undoubtedly would have been music to the ears of most anyone else interested in an acting career, but by this point, I had come to realize that I was not enough of a gypsy to be able to laconically follow the theatre. My roots were just too deeply planted in red clay to transplant elsewhere."

Kollock, however, says his Georgia movie-making days did cause him to have one regret. . . . "In all the years that the wonderful old Tallulah Falls Railroad rumbled through the hills of north Georgia, I never once took the time to ride it," Kollock says with a sigh. . . "that is, except for one hour in Otto, North Carolina. But then again, I did ride in the cab, and I did get to blow the whistle."

(The late John Kollock was a renowned professional artist and author of numerous books for many years in Georgia. His many works of art – usually done with a historic theme – are still widely sold in shops in the north Georgia region, and internationally via the internet. Among his many accomplishments is the civic design and theme of today's "Alpine" Helen, Georgia in White County.)

I'd Climb The Highest Mountain ... Again!

Northeast Georgia's White County is booming with development and tourism today, but in 1950, it was a very isolated mountainous region populated by a sprinkling of true country folks. These conditions were exactly what famed Hollywood director Henry King needed to create a motion picture based upon Georgia author Corra Harris' best-selling book, "A Circuit Rider's Wife." The end product was a major commercial success for King, and provided an experience many White County residents never forgot.

Virtually every state in America has served as the backdrop for a Hollywood motion picture at some point in the past 100 years of movie-making. New Yorkers have been thrilled by the likes of *An Affair To Remember* with Cary Grant and Deborah Kerr. Pennsylvanians have swelled with pride every time the movies *Rocky* and *The Philadelphia Story* have graced the screen. In the state of Georgia, *Gone With The Wind* wins – hands-down – as the most popular movie ever filmed about the state, but another major motion picture, released in 1951, also captivated audiences with its appeal, and continues to earn a four-star rating in television movie guides even today.

When renowned Hollywood director Henry King of *20th Century Fox Film Corporation* came to north Georgia in 1950, his mission was to capture on film the story, scenic beauty, and rich

The late John Kollock, artist and writer from Clarkesville, Georgia, was known for his historic recreation paintings and prints of northeast Georgia. Hired by *20th Century-Fox Film Corporation* as an actor in *"I'd Climb The Highest Mountain,"* he witnessed first-hand almost all the filming of the feature-length movie. He painted this depiction of the drowning scene in the movie from memory and from photographs he took as the filming was occurring. *(Illustration by John Kollock and reprinted with permission. All rights reserved.)*

I'd Climb The Highest Mountain . . . Again!   White County

It was the scene in which young George Salter was drowned at the old mill that riveted the attention of movie-goers in 1951 when *"I'd Climb the Highest Mountain"* was released to audiences nationwide. The mill at which this sequence was filmed still stands today just outside Helen, Georgia. The late Jerry Vandiver (pictured) who portrayed Salter paused at the site in 2000, to reflect on that day half a century earlier, when he and rising star (the late) Rory Calhoun acted out the drowning scene. Very little has changed at this site since the filming. *(Photo by Olin Jackson)*

Lovely Crescent Hill Baptist Church in the Sautee-Nacoochee Valley near Helen, Georgia, was the first choice of Director Henry King for use in the filming of the church scenes in *"I'd Climb The Highest Mountain."* Unfortunately, the membership of the church at that time declined to open the facility for Hollywood movie-making. *(Photo by Olin Jackson)*

rural flavor of the area described in author Corra Harris' book, *A Circuit Rider's Wife*. This work was a semi-autobiographical account of Harris' experiences with her Methodist minister husband as he preached in churches across the northern realm of Georgia. The book includes rich depictions of the people, places and lives of late 19th Century and early 20th Century residents of the north Georgia hill country, and Henry King wanted that same rich earthy theme in his movie.

The movie was to be titled *I'd Climb the Highest Mountain*, and the locale King picked out for the filming sites closely approximated the north Georgia vicinity described in Harris' book. As a bonus, King found that the rural north Georgia mountains included local residents who had continued to pursue their daily lives in much the same manner as had Harris' characters in her book. In 1950, north Georgia had very few highways which extended into the mountains, and much of the post-war "progress" being experienced in Atlanta and environs had not yet filtered up into the state's isolated mountain region.

King thoroughly enjoyed the north Georgia mountains, and seemed to think the red Georgia clay was one of the prettiest sights he had ever witnessed. *"I hope they never pave these red clay roads,"* he once said admiringly, during filming of the movie. He often wet down the clay thoroughfares prior to filming a scene, just to make them appear a brighter red in the movie.

Recognizing the value in using local residents as bit-part actors in the movie,

The adjoining graveyard at Chattahoochee United Methodist Church in Robertstown, Georgia, contains the last remains of many Vandiver family members. The late Jerry Vandiver who portrayed the youngster George Salter who was drowned in the millrace in the major motion picture *"I'd Climb The Highest Mountain,"* pauses at the grave of one of his relatives in 2000. Several of the scenes in the movie were filmed at this church. *(Photo by Olin Jackson)*

Old U.S. Highway 129 leading up into the north Georgia mountains was a popular thoroughfare for tourist traffic in the 1940s, 50s and 60s. It originally passed right beside the Cleveland Deluxe Cottages just outside Cleveland, Georgia, which provided overnight accommodations. In 1950, the cast and crew filming *"I'd Climb The Highest Mountain"* had accommodations here for the several months it took to film the movie. Pictured above is the former lobby building from this establishment. *(Photo by Olin Jackson)*

King arranged for try-outs in Cleveland, Helen, and Atlanta, to seek out talent. One of the individuals who earned a role was the late Jerry Vandiver of the Mossy Creek vicinity of White County where much of *I'd Climb The Highest Mountain* was filmed. His character quickly became etched in the minds of movie-goers as "the little boy who was drowned at the mill."

"It was an exciting time in Cleveland and Helen and for much of the surrounding area," Vandiver said in an interview in 2000 prior to his death, as he described the mood of the residents of Helen upon learning of the impending arrival of the Hollywood film company. "We had heard that Hollywood was coming to make a movie, and we suspected that we wouldn't be having our usual lazy, hazy, slow-paced summer that year."

At the time of the interview, Vandiver was still mildly reminiscent of the youngster from his movie role, even though at the time of this interview in 2000, it had been over 50 years since the movie was filmed in north Georgia. It was released in 1951 to national audiences. "Where has the time gone?" Vandiver said. "I still can't believe that Susan Hayward, William Lundigan, Rory Calhoun and the others were once right here in our back yards."

Sadly, all of the stars and many of the bit players from *I'd Climb The Highest Mountain* are gone today, having been claimed by advancing age and health infirmities. The most recently demised star

Former cast member Jerry Vandiver points to the spot on the opposite bank of the Chattahoochee near Edelweiss Street in Helen where the watermelon-eating, singing, and other scenes were filmed in 1950. "It was at that little brook over there that the scene with Barbara Bates and Rory Calhoun at the picnic was filmed," Vandiver said. *(Photo by Olin Jackson)*

Highway 254 (foreground) was one of the many red clay roads so admired by Director Henry King during the production of *"I'd Climb The Highest Mountain"* filmed in 1950 around Cleveland and Helen, Georgia. M.A. Cooley's General Store in Mossy Creek which was transformed to portray "Brock Store" in the movie, once stood in the grassy area (right foreground). This historic structure – where the arm-wrestling, fabric-buying and other scenes were filmed with Susan Hayward, William Lundigan, Gene Lockhart and others – unfortunately was demolished circa 1972. *(Photo by Olin Jackson)*

– Rory Calhoun – passed away in 1998. In 1950, however, they all were among the jewels of America's Hollywood royalty, and they shone with a brilliance that only Tinseltown can create on the silver screen.

Susan Hayward, already a big star in 1950 and a breathtakingly-beautiful actress, gave an outstanding performance in the north Georgia production. According to Jerry, she moved easily among the Helen and Cleveland residents in the movie, and seemed to identify with them.

Miss Hayward's "ease with the common folk" would come as no surprise to those who truly knew her. She started out in life as Edythe Marrener in poverty-ridden circumstances in Brooklyn, New York. Though she ultimately became rich, beautiful and famous, she never forgot who she was and from whence she had come. As a result, she treated everyone equally, showing compassion and kindness with all the locals in the area during production of the movie. That, reportedly, simply was her style and personality.

Though she probably did not know it at the time, Miss Hayward was destined to become a Georgia resident herself a few years later in 1957, when she married Eaton Chalkley, a Carrollton, Georgia attorney and businessman. The couple made their home in Carrollton where Miss Hayward lived until 1967. Tragically, Eaton Chalkley died in 1966 from a hepatitis infection contracted while on a trip he made with Miss Hayward to Rome, Italy.

Even more tragically, fate was not kind to Miss Hayward later in her own life either. In 1972, she was diagnosed with multiple inoperable brain cancers, and though she struggled on bravely in life, she passed away on March 14, 1975. She was buried in her adopted north Georgia homeland of Carrollton, with her husband.

Jerry Vandiver said he was

Mystery & History in Georgia

This rare photo shows M.A. Cooley's General Store in Mossy Creek as it appeared prior to being transformed into "Brock Store" for filming purposes in the major motion picture *"I'd Climb The Highest Mountain."* Today, virtually nothing remains from this one-time landmark. *(Photo courtesy of Jerry Vandiver)*

A photographer caught this opening scene from *"I'd Climb The Highest Mountain"* at old Demorest, Georgia Depot on the now long-departed Tallulah Falls Railroad. The Demorest Depot building (as of this writing) is one of the few such structures remaining in existence from the former railroad and is visible (far right) in this view looking south down the line as the train arrives. *(Photo courtesy of Jerry Vandiver)*

particularly captivated by Miss Hayward. "In the scene in which my character is drowned," he smiled, "they had placed me in the back of the wagon, and Miss Hayward was sitting up front on the buckboard. There was a break in the filming, and she was relaxing for a moment. She told me she thought I had the cutest little nose, and that she just had to kiss it, and she did. I'll never forget that."

The production of *I'd Climb The Highest Mountain* required lots of extras, and Jerry explained that these locally-obtained actors were paid $6.25 a day. Some of the locals had "speaking parts," and as such were required to be under contract with *20th Century Fox*.

"A local lady was hired to obtain a social security card for each of the 200 to 300 people who did get hired," Jerry explained. "At that time, a person wasn't required to have a social security number unless he or she had a job.

"I was one of the people who needed a number," Jerry continued. "There were also some people hired to round up horses, buggies, wagons, and other necessities of the movie. I do remember that Kay and Fay Fogg, twins from

Atlanta, were chosen for singing parts during the filming of the reception scene for the new pastor's wife."

Others in the movie who still resided in the White County area at the time of this interview in 2000 with Mr. Vandiver include Shirley Black McDonald of Cleveland, Georgia, who was Miss Hayward's stand-in for the movie. "I remember when I saw Shirley standing in front of the camera during a lighting test, I thought there were two Susan Haywards, and that Hollywood must be able to do *anything*," Jerry laughs today. "A twelve-year-old's mind is an amazing thing."

Jerry says he vividly remembers the bit-part try-outs in Helen. The talent-search was conducted at the old Helen Grammar School, a site which later was converted for use by Orbit Manufacturing Company. Also at the time of this interview, the old grammar school site was being used as a portion of the Alpine Antique Auto & Buggy Museum in Helen. Interestingly, this museum

I'd Climb The Highest Mountain . . . Again! White County

Looking north, this view of old Demorest Depot was photographed in 1991, and clearly shows the depot agent's window. In 1950, the Tallulah Falls Railroad was still very active, and the track lay along the right side of the building. The structure (right-rear) is a more recent addition, having been built after 1961, when the line fell into receivership and rail operations were abandoned. *(Photo by Olin Jackson)*

This 20th Century-Fox Film Corporation publicity print shows the scene in which William Lundigan (as Rev. Thompson) and Susan Hayward (as his wife) invite the Salter children – portrayed by the late Jerry Vandiver (l) and Richard Wilson (r) – to a church picnic as Mr. Salter (portrayed by Alexander Knox) looks on disapprovingly. The structure used to portray the Salter home in the movie was in the Mossy Creek community just outside Cleveland, Georgia. *(Photo courtesy of 20th Century-Fox Film Corporation)*

included a 1961 Cadillac once owned by Susan Hayward when she lived in Carrollton, as well as a 2-seater surrey used in the movie.

"At the ripe old age of 12, I thought that I would try out for a small part," Jerry said, in remembering that special day so long ago. "I thought maybe, just maybe, I could get a small role.

"They started out with about 500 children," he continued. "They eventually narrowed it down to twelve. They brought those twelve back for more screen tests later. I was small for my age, and I remember some of the movie people asking my teacher, Mrs. Theresa New, if I really was twelve years old. She finally convinced them of my age, and they gave me the role of George Salter.

"I was under contract with *20th Century Fox* for $175 a week, as were the two other 'Salter children,'" Jerry added. "I don't know what the other locals with small speaking parts were paid."

Alexander Knox, a well-known actor of that period portrayed Mr. Salter, an atheist and father of the children.

The opening scene of the movie had a unique setting. It was filmed at the Demorest, Georgia, depot of the now-historic Tallulah Falls Railroad which was still active in 1950.

Mrs. Salter was portrayed by Jean Inness, another well-known Hollywood actress. Aside from Jerry who portrayed the eldest Salter son who downed, Richard Wilson of Atlanta played the other son, and Dottie Sims Jackson of Helen portrayed the daughter.

The opening scene of the movie had a unique setting. It was filmed at the Demorest, Georgia, depot of the now-historic Tallulah Falls Railroad which was still active in 1950. The train comes rolling to a stop on the siding at the Demorest Depot, and the circuit riding preacher – portrayed by William Lundigan – and his new bride (Miss Hayward) step down dramatically from the passenger car.

The Tallulah Falls Railroad – with its breath-taking grade up the side of Tallulah Gorge – sadly does not exist today. It slipped into bankruptcy and finally ceased operations entirely in 1961. Though the tracks were taken up years ago, the old railroad bed still exists, as do a few of the old depots on the line, including Demorest Depot at the time of this writing. It sits quietly beside the old road bed today, seemingly lost in time.

There are no trains chuffing into Demorest Depot any longer, nor travelers milling about the site as they scurry to reach summer getaways in the mountains. These depot activities have drifted away into the mists of time. Everyone travels by automobile or modern jet travel today.

The ground around old Demorest Depot, however, is now hallowed ground ... a place where Hollywood royalty of yesteryear once strode and spoke their lines for the audiences of the world... a place where an Academy

Award-winning actress once moved with grace and charm as she stepped down from the old Tallulah Falls Railroad train.

Jerry remembered a number of details of the filming of many scenes in this still-popular movie. He offered to take me around to the sites so we could see what still exists today.

The old grist mill – where Jerry portrayed the drowning George Salter – is known today as Nora Mill. It still stands on the banks of the fabled Chattahoochee River, and when last checked, was even still in operation, grinding corn for tourists and area residents.

I drove Jerry down to the spot where the drowning scene was filmed. Though half a century had passed (in the year 2000 when this interview was conducted), the site is little-changed today. There is a new dam holding back the waters of the Chattahoochee, but the old millrace is still in place, and even the aged bent tree beneath which the scene was filmed still stands.

Rory Calhoun, a major Hollywood star in his own right during the 1950s and '60s, jumped into the Chattahoochee at this spot in an attempt to rescue young George. When the movie is seen today, Calhoun – just as the other Hollywood stars in the movie – appears so young and full of life. It's almost hard to believe that he's now gone.

Many of the filming sites have disappeared too... victims of time, natural disasters, and "progress."

There are no trains chuffing into Demorest Depot any longer, nor travelers milling about the site as they scurry to reach summer getaways in the mountains.

Lobby Cards used to promote *"I'd Climb The Highest Mountain"* were widely circulated in 1951 by *20th Century-Fox Film Corporation*. This card shows "the preacher's house," filmed at the E.B. Hunt family home in Mossy Creek, with (l to r) Rory Calhoun, Gene Lockhart, Barbara Bates, William Lundigan and Susan Hayward among others in the confrontation scene outside the home. This structure unfortunately was destroyed by a fire in the 1990s. *(Photo courtesy of 20th Century-Fox Film Corporation)*

Some, however, like Nora Mill continue to thrive.

Interestingly, Jerry told me that according to some sources, the lovely little Crescent Hill Baptist Church just around the corner from Nora Mill was the site first selected for the filming of the church scenes in the movie. "It is my understanding that the pastor of the church at that time did not feel it was appropriate to allow a Hollywood film company to shoot a movie inside the church," he explained, "so Crescent Hill ultimately was not used."

This seems somewhat ironic today, particularly considering the religious theme of the movie. As a result of the misgivings of the membership of Crescent Hill, the church scenes were moved to nearby Chattahoochee United Methodist Church in Robertstown, north of Helen.

Founded in 1860, this historic structure – which still stands today – was exactly the filming site for which Henry King had been searching. Within its confines, the hospital scenes were filmed, as was the scene in which Rev. Thompson introduced his new wife to the congregation. Outside this church, the burial scene for Preacher Thompson's son was filmed. Several other film sequences were also staged at this site.

Jerry says the Sunday School picnic in the movie took place where the parking lots, an apartment building and several Bavarian-styled shops exist today in Helen (to the rear of the buildings fronting the main street at the Chattahoochee River). In 1950, this area was little more than a broad undeveloped pasture area in Helen.

A little further back, near present-day Edelweiss Street where a small brook flows into the Chattahoochee, the watermelon eating, singing, and other scenes were filmed. Jerry says this was also the spot at which Rory Calhoun and Barbara Bates met and talked with each other during the picnic filming scene.

I next drove Jerry out to the Mossy Creek community to revisit those filming sites and see what remained of the structures there used in the movie. We went first to the former site of Cooley Store, identified in the movie as "Brock Store," owned by "Mr. Brock," portrayed by Gene Lockhart. This late 19th Century mercantile business once located at an intersection on Highway 254 in Mossy Creek, tragically, was torn down in the 1970s. It would be a valuable property today, but in the 1970s, it was just another worn-out store in what then was still a fairly rural area that had not yet experienced the tourism onslaught currently being experienced (and generating income) in northeast Georgia.

Susan Hayward (center) celebrates her birthday on the set of *"I'd Climb The Highest Mountain"* with (l to r) William Lundigan, Gene Lockhart, and Rory Calhoun. *(Photo courtesy of Jerry Vandiver)*

In 1950, however, Cooley Store was exactly what Henry King needed for the portrayal of a general store. It was used for the filming of the arm-wrestling and fabric-purchasing scenes.

Today, little, if anything, remains of Cooley Store. At last check, an old well and a couple of stone columns which once supported the porch of the store still existed, but these are probably long gone by now as well. Everything else has been erased by man and the passage of time – even memories of the famous actors who once performed here for Hollywood's cameras. Susan Hayward, Gene Lockhart and William Lundigan spoke their lines and portrayed their characters here, but very few people – including even the present-day owner of this property – seem to be aware of this today.

Interestingly, another north Georgian, well-known in Georgia artistic and literary circles for many years, made his silver screen debut in Cooley Store. The late John Kollock was familiar to many north Georgia residents prior to his death in 2014. He is also credited as the primary designer of present-day "Alpine" Helen. His water-color paintings of scenic and historic sites in north Georgia are highly sought today by collectors.

In 1950, however, Kollock was fresh out of college and urgently in need of a job. He ultimately was selected as an Extra in *I'd Climb The Highest Mountain*, earning $6 a day six days a week. As he once stated, "At that time, I had worked a lot harder for a lot less."

"One day we were shooting at Cooley Store," Kollock reminisced in a 1998 interview. "It was for a winter scene supposedly just before Christmas, but in actuality, we were shooting the scene on a hot day in July. I was driving a two-horse wagon for 'background' in the scene with William Lundigan and Gene Lockhart. I was bundled up in a heavy jacket and wool hat. After half a dozen trips, circling the store and driving a quarter of a mile down the road in the background of the scene, I was getting just a bit warm, and worrying that my sweat might start showing through my clothing.

"We finally finished the scene and then began shooting an interior sequence with Lundigan and one of the "bit" players arm-wrestling on the store counter," Kollock continued. "Mr. King, the director, decided to pad the scene to provide a lead-in. Since I was handy, and had never been on-camera, I was called upon to arm-wrestle first (prior to Mr. Lundigan) with the boy who was playing the jilted boyfriend of Barbara Bates.

"As Mr. King began to embellish the scene, he decided I should put up a wager on my prowess at arm-wrestling. The

This home, owned by the Autry family of Mossy Creek, was used to portray the Salter home in *"I'd Climb The Highest Mountain."* The Autrys reportedly were paid a sizeable fee for the use of their home by *20th Century Fox Film Corporation.* Shortly after filming wrapped for the movie, this structure was demolished for construction of a new home. *(Photo courtesy of Jerry Vandiver)*

prop man gave me a large coin which was typical of the period. I dropped it into my pocket and we began the scene. When it came time for me to bet, I found to my horror that the coin was mixed with an assortment of my 1950s-era change.

"With the camera rolling interminably, I fumbled wildly in my pocket trying to identify the correct coin to flip on the counter. I knew full well that if I dropped a shiny new 1949 dime into the scene, I would be out of a job. Finally, after a painful lapse of time, Mr. King stopped the filming and explained that if it took that long for me to bet, we would have very little time for the rest of the movie.

"I finally found the proper coin," Kollock laughed in remembrance, "and when filming continued, I palmed it tightly in my fist as I faked the motion of its retrieval from my pocket. We made the scene on the second 'take.' Like so many other shots, this one was cut from the movie during the final edit, leaving only the preacher winning his part of the match. In the background however, I can be seen smiling broadly, apparently at the preacher winning the bet. (In actuality, my smile was an expression of sheer joy at having found the coin in time.)

Cooley Store is not alone when it comes to film sites that have disappeared. As Jerry Vandiver and I drove on down Highway 254 in Mossy Creek, Jerry showed me the site at which the old E.B. Hunt family home had once existed. This structure, identified in the movie as "Rev. Thompson's home" was used for many scenes, including one very humorous sequence in which "Mrs. Billywith" comes to discuss the *Bible* with the preacher, and incurs the wrath of his wife.

Today, this old home sadly is also gone, having fallen victim to a fire in the 1990s. The site once occupied by the structure is an empty grassy knoll today, with the exception of a bright sprinkling of jonquils in the springtime. The spirits

Actress Lynn Bari ("Mrs. Billywith") enjoys a break on the set during filming of *"I'd Climb The Highest Mountain."* (Photo courtesy of Jerry Vandiver)

of Susan Hayward and William Lundigan no doubt linger at this site on occasion too.

The day-to-day activities associated with the filming of the movie eventually became very low-key according to Jerry. He says he still remembers one incident involving himself and Henry King which was somewhat comical.

"I wasn't in any of the scenes being filmed one day, so I had made other plans for that afternoon," Jerry says, still amused at the memory. "Mr. King called me over to where he was sitting in his director's chair and asked me if the clothes I had on were the ones to be used in my next part. I just told him 'No,' and explained the clothes were my own and that I was going fishing. He was taken back somewhat by his mistake, but he also had a good laugh at his error too."

King seemed to greatly appreciate the history, culture and landscape of the southern Appalachians. It was because of this that he used as much native stock such as the surreys, clothing, actual homes and businesses in the area as possible for the filming of scenes in the movie.

Jerry says that not long ago, he was afforded the privilege of viewing one of the surreys – or what was left of it – used in the movie. Cobb County businessman Jody Hill, who restored author Corra Harris' home near Pine Log, Georgia, was attempting to purchase the surrey for display purposes at Harris' former home. At that time, the historic conveyance was missing two front wheels and the fringe on top was in barely salvageable shreds. Henry King, no doubt, would have been disappointed.

"Time stands still for no man," as the saying goes. Today, many of the local Cleveland, Georgia, residents who were extras and bit-part actors in the famed movie have also gone on to the "the great beyond" with their Hollywood counterparts. "All three of us who portrayed the Salter children now have children of our own, and ... yes.... even grandchildren of our own," Jerry smiled at the time.

If by chance you are lucky enough to catch *"I'd Climb The Highest Mountain"* on one of the cable channels, or even to rent it, the movie is just as enjoyable today as it was when it premiered in 1951. . . possibly even more so for long-time White County residents. They can see – first-hand – the many changes wrought by the march of time in their community, and remember how things were over 70 years ago, when Hollywood came to town for one bright shining moment.

Mysterious Remnants of Early Spanish Explorers?

After the discovery of gold in Georgia's White County in the 1830s, miners discovered a series of mysterious underground structures for which no one had an explanation – not even the native Cherokee Indians, who had lived in the region for hundreds of years. Those structures remain unexplained today.

When gold was discovered in the floodplain along Duke's Creek in present-day White County in 1829-1830, everyone was surprised, but many were even more surprised at a series of strange and ancient underground "shelters" for which there seemed to be no logical explanation. When the native Cherokee Indians who still resided in this region were queried about the structures, they also had no explanation. There were, however, a handful of discoveries inside the structures which possibly provided an explanation.

There was plenty of gold in and around Duke's Creek. There was placer gold in the bed of the creek and in the alluvial deposits along its banks. And there was saprolite gold in the hills on either side, from whose veins of quartz the placer gold undoubtedly originated.

In 1834, a scant five years since the yellow metal had been discovered in the bed of the creek, the entire length of the stream from where it entered the gold belt just below the present-day site of Alternate Highway 75, to its junction with the Chattahoochee River in Nacoochee Valley, was buzzing with activity. One aspect of this activity involved the diversion of the creek waters through canals cut across the alluvial flats of the narrow valleys.

These canals served several purposes. They allowed miners to extract gold-bearing sand and gravel from the pot-holes and ledges of the ancient streambed. The canals many times also provided a source of water for the operation of sluice boxes – usually at the lower end of the canals where the water returned to the creek.

And finally, in as much as the canals were often dug through gold-bearing gravels (left by ancient meanders of the creek), they provided a source of ore which the gold seekers did not neglect to wash in their sluices and pans.

One party of miners at what was known as the "Eaton Diggings" were excavating for just such a diversion when they stumbled upon a mystifying puzzle. They found logs beneath the earth, stacked and notched at the corners as if for a cabin.

As the miners dug further, they

465

discovered that this first "cabin" was connected to yet another, and then yet another. This line of interconnected log structures reportedly very nearly followed the route of the miners' prospective ditch, so the miners excavated each one. By the time they had finished, they had uncovered a long line of the structures, the total number of which was amazingly recorded as "thirty-four."

To compound the mystery, according to reports, it appeared as if the logs had been worked with iron axes, and by all accounts, the site itself had been covered with an old growth of timber, variously estimated to be one hundred and fifty to two hundred years of age. The antiquity of the structures was further revealed by the fact that, once exposed to the air and allowed to dry, the wood crumbled to dust.

From Mysteries To Legends

The science of archaeology was in its infancy in the early part of the nineteenth century, and the prospectors of Duke's Creek, to say the least, were not among its practitioners. Nevertheless, it can safely be assumed that the dirt and gravel from these ruins received a thorough sifting and washing in the sluice boxes and pans of the miners whose curiosity must have definitely been aroused by this curious site.

The exact nature of their eventual discoveries during this impromptu excavation is a matter of conjecture today, since all of the published accounts from the era lean heavily upon second and third-hand information, and tend also to reflect the speculation of the respective authors as to the origin and description of the artifacts.

Most accounts however, maintain that at least one large manual item was discovered at the site. It was described variously as a "double mortar," "sand crucible," and a "stone trough." Some authors report that only fragments of pottery and baskets of Indian manufacture were found at the site.

Today, no known relics from this site exist anywhere. Any information involving them were maintained strictly in the scattered reports of that day. It is quite possible that the builders of these log structures left little if anything behind, and therefore, no actual evidence from the site exists today.

If the underground structures did once exist as described in various personal letters and reports of that day – and there is no reason to suspect that anyone would manufacture such a creative fiction – it is highly unlikely that any of the wooden enclosures would have survived their disinterment and the subsequent mining activities which were visited upon Duke's Creek in successive waves throughout the nineteenth and early twentieth centuries. In the absence of solid proof – or even precise descriptions – speculation thrives today, and in the case of "the underground village at Duke's Creek," there is no shortage of theories. Some of these theories do not stand up well to cold reason, however appealing they may seem.

The author of the ***Gazeteer of Georgia*** published in 1837, flatly stated that the ruins were of a *"subterranean Indian village,"* and in doing so, evidently was not aware that the *"cabins"* were without evidence of roofs, and many were only three or four feet high.

Also, this theory neglects to account for the fact that the structures were very close to the waterline – perhaps even below it at the time of their discovery – and as such would have been uninhabitable. This site of the structures also is hardly a likely location for an Indian village, since all aboriginal natives wisely kept their habitations well away from the flood plain of any creeks or rivers.

It is also worth noting that though the native Cherokees had long traded with white settlers and were therefore eventually in possession of iron tools, the preponderance of evidence – circumstantial as it may be – points away from an aboriginal origin of the structures, though this possibility cannot be entirely discounted. Despite all of the above, there is very convincing evidence that early European-created artifacts and even the possible remains of a European were discovered at this site.

Vestiges of De Soto?

In a letter written in August of 1870, George W. Williams, the son of Major Edwin Williams who was an early pioneer in the nearby Sautee Valley, offered the following report: *"It is very certain that this region was settled by a race in civilization far in advance of the Cherokees, as they (the Cherokees) were unable to give any account, even by tradition, of the numerous fortifications and tumuli which were found here.*

"The strongest fortifications lie between the Chattahoochee and Sautee, in the eastern portion of the valley, not far from the point where Sautee enters the Chattahoochee.

"As a means of defense, the situation was well-chosen. The adjacent heights are naturally so formed and disposed, as with but little expense and military architecture, to be rendered almost impregnable.

"Many Indian relics have been found here. In 1834, the miners, while searching for gold, disinterred a subterranean village, numbering some forty houses, which had been buried, judging from the forest trees which covered the city of the dead, a **century or more***. The logs were hewn and notched as at the present day;* **war-like instruments were found in the buildings***.*

"A discovery was also recently made in Nacoochee Valley, on the farm of Captain Nichols (today a historic site near Helen, Georgia), *that interested me very much, and which must interest every lover of antiquity. A ploughshare struck a hard substance near the base of an Indian mound* (located in front of the Nichols home); *the ploughman, while attempting to remove it, ascertained that it formed a portion of a regularly walled sepulcher, the bottom being paved with stones.*

"The tomb contained many skeletons; in one of the recesses **was found that of a 'giant,' or a man much larger than the present race of Indians***. In the sepulcher were also immense conch shells, pipes, tomahawks, and many curious pieces of workmanship; but* **the most remarkable relic was a piece of in-wrought copper***. As the natives were ignorant of the art of working in copper, the question naturally arises (as to) what period the huge men, skilled in art, lived. The tomb itself showed that the builders understood the use of tools."*

The reports of "leaden plates" and the "crucible" also offer evidence that the ruins were of an ancient settlement of European explorers of pre-Columbian origin. Madoc the Welshman (or another of the ancient mariner-adventurers suspected of possibly visiting the interior of our state) has been also offered as a possibility, eventually possibly moving on from Duke's Creek to Fort Mountain, where local folklore and some historians maintain he may have made his last stand behind the piled-up rock wall from which the mountain derives its name.

The mainstream of historical scholarship, however, does not support this supposition. A more convincing argument, however, can be made for Spanish explorer Hernando De Soto. The

Spanish explorer's existence, at least, is not open to serious question. Also, he has long been thought by many to have come through Nacoochee Valley in the sixteenth century as he searched for a golden kingdom to conquer.

An authenticated ancient sword of European origin which quite likely was used by one of De Soto's men, was discovered in northwest Georgia in 1982. The location was a field near Rome, in Floyd County.

On the day of the discovery, the men knew they had a high likelihood of finding at least some minor historic relics. The field they were searching alongside the muddy Coosa River is a documented aboriginal Indian village site within a large loop of the river known as "Foster Bend." The origin of the sword was later authenticated by authorities, and associated with a later documented battle which involved the Spanish explorer and his men in nearby Alabama.

The proposal of Spaniards as the most probable builders of the strange underground structures remains a popular contention today, particularly in view of the discovery of the sword in nearby Floyd County. Circumstantial evidence, at least, tends to support that contention. For one thing, if contemporary estimates of the age of the remains can be trusted, the structures appear to have been built in or around the time of De Soto.

The De Soto theory also received a boost from one of the early observers of the remains – one of the only eye-witnesses to record in his own words what he saw. By happy coincidence, this individual happened also to have some training as a scientific observer.

An Englishman of Letters

George William Featherstonaugh was the name of this early traveler who chanced through the Sautee-Nacoochee Valley shortly after the underground log structures had been discovered. Should that name seem like too much of a mouthful to pronounce, it may be shortened with a Cockney slur to "Fanshaw."

His personal opinions aside, Mr. Featherstonaugh remains one of the keenest observers to report on the American frontier in the early nineteenth century. The records of his journeys therefore make interesting reading for those interested in the America of Andrew Jackson and Martin Van Buren.

Featherstonaugh first happened through Nacoochee Valley in August, 1837, as he traveled the old stage coach road from Dahlonega to Clarkesville. Bearing the weighty title of "United States Geologist," he had been dispatched by the newly-formed *Bureau of Topographical Engineers* to survey the gold-bearing regions of the Southeast.

While staying overnight at one "Mr. Richardson's," Featherstonaugh heard about the Duke's Creek find. He was even allowed to examine a "micaceous stone trough" said to have been unearthed at the strange site. Although his curiosity apparently was somewhat aroused, causing him to devote several paragraphs in his journal to the find, he did not visit the ruins at this time.

Instead, Featherstonaugh proceeded with his planned journey to Franklin, North Carolina, and from there to Whiteside Mountain, thence back to Murphy and on to Red Clay, where he attended the last, sad meeting of the Cherokee Nation prior to the removal of these people from their native land in 1838.

While in the neighborhood of Murphy, Featherstonaugh heard about some other cryptic remains and paid these a visit as well. He reported that from the appearances at hand, a number of individuals had attempted a mining operation in the neighborhood of the Valley River. The ruins there appeared to him to be several hundred years old, though many particulars of his account make this dating open to question.

At any rate, among the ruins at the Murphy site, Featherstonaugh claimed to find another stone trough similar to the one he had witnessed at Nacoochee. He also found the remains of what seemed to be a furnace for the smelting of ore, and from his reports, the smelting of iron had been attempted, though he concluded that the people who had attempted the venture did not really know what they were doing. Lacking limestone for flux, they had evidently attempted to use quartz and thus had failed in their efforts.

Probing further, Featherstonaugh and his companions reportedly discovered a number of skeletons buried beneath the rocks at the bottom of some of the excavations. It was not difficult to arrive at the conclusion that these were very likely the remains of the miners themselves.

Featherstonaugh also reported from hearsay a story told by an aged Cherokee woman of some "yellow-complexioned people who visited the area" during her remote ancestors' time. According to the report, the visitors undertook the mines, and upon their return with more and more companions, eventually provoked enough uneasiness among the resident aborigines to cause them to murder the intruders.

After a roundabout journey, Featherstonaugh once again found himself back in the vicinity of Duke's Creek in north Georgia. This time, he made it a point to visit the Eaton Diggings where the underground log structures existed, in order to see the strange underground structures for himself.

Unfortunately, three years had passed since the ruins had first been exposed, and there reportedly was little left for Featherstonaugh to see. He procured only a small specimen of wood which crumbled to dust when it dried.

From the looks of the site, and from the reports that Featherstonaugh had heard, he concluded that the "pens," as he called them, were never used as habitations, and that they were intended as a storage cache of some kind – though exactly why anyone would have needed a cache of this size in this spot, he neglected to say.

At any rate, with the memory of the sites in North Carolina and Georgia fresh in his mind, it apparently was not difficult for Featherstonaugh to notice the similarities between the two. With the knowledge that De Soto had been through the mountains in this region, it also was not hard for him to reach the conclusion that these remains were connected in some manner with the famous conquistador.

The Verdicts of History...

There are, for the modern scholar, a few problems with the De Soto conclusion. Although there is some disagreement concerning De Soto's route through the Appalachian Mountains, Dr. Charles Hudson of the University of Georgia, concluded the Spanish adventurer's path was no closer than Swananoa, North Carolina, a far piece from Murphy, and further yet from Nacoochee. At the time, however, he did not have the benefit of the ancient sword discovery in northwest Georgia's Floyd County.

Hudson also was of the opinion that De Soto, a veteran of the conquest of the Inca nation, had definite ideas of how he wanted his gold. Hudson maintained that De Soto was looking for a product which had already been extracted from the ground and refined into portable quantities. It therefore seems unlikely that anyone directly associated with De Soto's party would have attempted such works as those found on the Valley River in North Carolina or at Duke's Creek in north Georgia.

If we seek, however, further authoritative opinion on the subject, we need not go too far from Nacoochee Valley to find it. One of the foremost authorities on the history of Nacoochee and its surroundings existed in the person of Dr. Thomas Lumsden, a life-long resident of Clarkesville. Surgeon, general practitioner, gentleman and scholar, Dr. Lumsden studied the history of the valley for many years.

Dr. Lumsden also had the benefit of an ancestor – his great-great-great-grandfather – directly involved with the log ruins. He reportedly helped excavate the ruins, and based upon his research, Lumsden maintains that any theory today concerning the origin or intended use of the site is largely speculation, for obvious reasons. That warning aside, he goes on to state that it is his opinion that the ruins were probably of Spanish origin.

Dr. Lumsden speculates that someone in the Spanish settlements of Florida or the Caribbean learned from survivors of De Soto's expedition, or from some other source, of rumors of gold in the mountains of what is now north Georgia and North Carolina. These individuals then presumably mounted a less-publicized expedition (on a smaller budget) in an attempt to retrieve gold directly from the creeks and rocks of the country, rather than from the Indians whose disinterest in the yellow metal had already been established.

If this is indeed the case, the enterprising adventurers were on the right track when they began work on the banks of Duke's Creek. And the mystery then becomes one of determining why they were unsuccessful. Were they simply too ignorant of mining? Were they repulsed by defending aborigines or perhaps even politely instructed to leave?

The last possibility seems the most likely, considering the fact that few artifacts from these Spaniards seem to have been left behind. As to the particulars of the structures which seem so hard to explain, perhaps we need only to note that newcomers to a foreign land do not always behave in a rational manner – particularly if they are inexperienced in the necessities of homesteading.

Perhaps even these same people then went on to the Valley River in North Carolina to meet their final fate there. These two sites could have been part and parcel to the same expedition as Featherstonaugh speculated.

These are questions and possible answers which obviously defy definitive answers today. We do know however, that if their purpose was to extract great treasure from the ground of north Georgia, they failed in that attempt. If they meant to found a nation, they failed in that attempt as well.

Apparently, these early entrepreneurial explorers left no written records of their efforts, not to discount the small possibility that an account resides within the confines of a distant archive in Spain or elsewhere. The only known legacy of these explorers in Georgia is the mystery they left in the soil of the earth. And even those remains have been largely erased, leaving only puzzling fragments of written history and an enduring, if untidy, legend.

Old England Gold Mine, Bottomless Pit of Waste

A gold mining venture which has been an investment "filled with crap" for much of the 140 years that it was actively mined, was once located on property which very fittingly is today occupied by the waste treatment facility in Alpine Helen, Georgia.

Of the many previous investors in the historic "Old England" Gold Mine in Alpine Helen, Georgia, dating as far back as the day Daniel England sold it in 1831, only a small handful have enjoyed financial success in the venture. Even though the Old England Mine did at one time produce quantities of gold, it, nevertheless, was basically a "millstone around the neck" of most all of its investors.

Four years prior to the Georgia Gold Rush of 1829, Richard England purchased – for $1,500.00 – a 250-acre tract, including the property on which the England mine later existed. Mr. England, however, wasn't interested in gold mining. He intended to farm on the site, and he cleared the land and planted crops in the rich floodplain between the old Unicoi Turnpike (which once passed through what then was a wilderness in what today is Helen, Georgia) and the Chattahoochee River. Ironically (and we'll explain why shortly), the site of England's former property is occupied today by Helen's "Twin Lakes" sewage treatment plant.

By the time the Georgia gold rush had begun in earnest, England's farm was already a productive enterprise, yielding corn and other crops in a plentiful bounty. By this time, England had also purchased an adjoining 40 acres of land, paying for it with 55 bushels of corn.

Despite the presence of gold in the mountainsides and streams around England's farm, no mining had occurred on his property prior to 1831, nor on the property since he had purchased it. England just didn't believe in "get rich quick" schemes. The countryside around him, however, was being overrun by prospectors and digging operations seeking such wealth.

It was about this time (the summer of 1831) that John Humphries, an area resident, figured out that there were rich gold deposits in the lower portion of England's fields and in the steep, rocky ridges across the Chattahoochee River. He agreed to pay $10,000.00 to England for a half-interest in a mine he wanted to open on this site, giving England $5,500.00 in cash and a mortgage note on his home in the amount of $4,500.00.

In 1831, the amount of $5,500.00 was the equivalent of $157,142.00.

Though it may sound like a rather paltry sum today, in 1831, $10,000.00 was the equivalent of almost $300,000.00 in 2021 dollars. In short, it was a lot of money.

Just as with a modern borrower, Humphries made a promise to pay the balance due on the mine, hoping to "strike it rich" in order to easily pay off his indebtedness to England and retain ownership of his home. And just as with a modern creditor, Richard England could, if need be, force the sale of the above-described home to collect the note. No other property was involved.

England apparently trusted Humphries fairly implicitly, since he (Humphries) was a former sheriff of Habersham County, a profession which would logically lead one to assume that he would be a dependable and law-abiding individual. To the contrary, however – and unbeknownst to England – Humphries had actually been involved in numerous brushes with the law recently, so his credibility was much less than it appeared. In 1830, he was charged with *"false imprisonment."* In 1831, he was charged with *"obstructing a constable in the execution of his office."* The record shows these were not the last of Humphries' legal problems either.

Three other men eventually joined Humphries in the real estate purchase from England. For the sum of $9,000.00 they purchased from England, the remaining half-interest in the 100 acres co-owned by England and Humphries, and which ultimately became known as "the England vein," or "the England Mine."

A ditch was dug through the middle of England's former field to carry water for placer mining operations. A dam was built across the river and a stamp mill was set up to crush ore from a mine shaft dug into the side of the ridge opposite the nearby Chattahoochee River. Hard rock mining of the "England Gold Vein" began in earnest, and England's once-peaceful fields were suddenly abuzz with activity.

Meanwhile, with a pocketful of money and his fields a mess, Richard England pulled up stakes and moved about a mile up the river, where he obtained new property near his relatives.

Shortly thereafter, in 1832, records of the area indicate an individual named Archibald McLaughlin arrived on the scene. McLaughlin had been hired by Daniel Blake, a prosperous Savannah planter, to make investments in gold properties. For the sum of $2,500.00, McLaughlin purchased a one-sixteenth interest in the England Vein property from one of Humphries' partners, then transferred the interest to Blake.

Daniel Blake was born in England in 1775, and educated at Cambridge University. He was married in 1800, and moved first to South Carolina, then to the Savannah, Georgia area.

Blake's fine upbringing seems to have prepared him favorably for the gentlemanly enterprise of managing a plantation, but his good judgement apparently was blinded by a bad case of gold fever. He undoubtedly was accustomed to the orderly business affairs of a planter, where men were generally honorable – a professional preoccupation quite apart from the rogues and scoundrels of the north Georgia gold region in the 1830s.

Blake's first problems arose with Archibald McLaughlin. The two had signed an agreement whereby McLaughlin, using funds supplied by Blake, would serve as a purchasing agent for the planter. The apparent intention of the agreement was to create a situation in which

McLaughlin would secure promising real estate and gold mining deals solely for Blake.

McLaughlin, however, violated their agreement by trading extensively for his own account, and in some cases by buying property (with Blake's money) and then secretly transferring the property to Blake at a higher price than he (McLaughlin) had actually paid. To his credit, Blake eventually caught onto the ruse, and brought criminal charges against McLaughlin for "cheating and swindling" and dissolved their relationship.

Blake nevertheless maintained ownership of his one-sixteenth interest in the England Mine. At the time, the site with its dam, water ditch and stamp mill, was yielding a steady stream of productive ore. In 1832, with the mine in a profitable mode, Blake sought to increase his personal holdings in the property. He bought out Humphries' three partners, paying them more than twice what they had originally invested in the mine.

Thereafter, for the next two years, the patrician Mr. Blake and the tough ex-sheriff were equal partners in the England Mine. Both men apparently supplied slaves for labor in the mine, and both men also invested in numerous other endeavors in addition to the England Mine.

The winter of 1834 found John Humphries in Lumpkin County where he was awarded a contract for construction of that municipality's new courthouse. As low bidder at $7,000.00, he was awarded the project and promised to complete the building in 18 months. He was advanced $2,500.00 towards expenses. In 1834, a payment of $2,500.00 was the equivalent of approximately $73,529.00 in 2021 dollars. Again, we're talking about a lot of money.

Martin England was photographed in his later years. His father, Joseph, was Richard England's (original owner of the Old England Mine) uncle. Martin was one of the first pioneers in White County and is believed to have been the first body buried in England Cemetery in Helen, GA, near where the Helen Sewage Treatment Plant exists today.

In December of 1834, Daniel Blake suddenly died in Savannah. The administrator of his estate found that the deceased had, along with his numerous other mining properties, a number of Negro slaves and *"other personal effects"* scattered all over the gold region. He also found that the titles to the mines were *"in many cases wanting or not to be found among the papers and in others the claim of title appears to be defective."*

By 1835, the wheels had come off of John Humphries' mining operations at the England Mine, and the local authorities had begun seizing his gold properties to pay his mounting debts. The original England vein had been lost and none of his other investments were paying well enough to keep him afloat. Daniel Blake's two sons purchased Humphries' half-interest in the mine for $2,501.00

Though the landscape more resembles a western gold mine than north Georgia, this photo demonstrates how denuded the landscape had become following heavy gold mining in the area. This view shows a gold mining operation in White County, Georgia, circa 1890s which is believed to be the Old England Mine. A water flume for washing ore is visible upper left. *(Photo courtesy of GA Dept. of Archives & History, Atlanta)*

on the steps of the Habersham County Courthouse in Clarkesville.

Richard England, meanwhile, had filed suit against Humphries for the unpaid $4,500.00 mortgage taken in partial settlement of the England property sale four years earlier. With this final collection, Richard England – the salt-of-the-earth farmer and pioneer – had received a total of approximately $19,000.00 from the sale of the mine – a sum the equivalent of $542,857.00 in 2021 dollars, which, in 1835, was definitely a fortune. As it turns out, this original owner of the property on which the England Mine was opened – a person who never mined the property himself – ultimately made a fortune from it, but he was one of the few.

Meanwhile, former sheriff Humphries' problems didn't end with England. Back in Lumpkin County where he had contracted to build the courthouse, Humphries still had done no work at all on the new building, despite having been advanced $2,500.00. When county officials attempted to have him arrested for breach of contract, they received a surprise. A record of the incident described it as follows:

"In attempting to serve the within writ, the defendant, John Humphries, stood in defiance, armed with a pistol, which he drew, so he could not be served and after I had summoned the posse comitatus he had concealed himself and has absconded from the county of Lumpkin. Fifteenth day of October, 1835.
John D. Fields, Jr.,
Deputy Sheriff."

Humphries involvement with the England Mine officially ended shortly

Old England Gold Mine, Bottomless Pit of Waste — White County

thereafter in March of 1836, when his house and three-quarters of an acre in England's old field were sold on the courthouse steps in Clarkesville.

By this time, Richard England also had died, but if he was looking down from heaven, he undoubtedly had the last laugh in this real estate transaction. His widow, Martha, and oldest son, Athan, were high bidders for the property, buying the place back for a grand total of $28.25.

Still mired in legal entanglements, the England Mine languished thereafter. The heirs of Daniel Blake advertised a public sale of mining properties to be held at the Habersham County Courthouse in May of 1836.

On the day of the sale, it suddenly became clear that Blake had lost a fortune in the gold region. One mining interest for which he'd paid $500.00 was sold for $5.00, and another for which he'd paid $1,000.00 was sold for $20.00.

The half-interest in the England Mine for which Daniel Blake had paid Humphries' partners over $20,000.00 was sold for $300.00, and would have brought less had it not been for the intervention of Daniel's two sons and a family friend who purchased it. With this transaction, the Blake family owned the mine outright, and controlled it until the 1890s.

As is evidenced today by the number of mine shafts and deep chasms cut by hydraulic-powered water hoses, the mine has been extensively worked since the days of Daniel Blake and John Humphries.

In 1882, an individual by the name of G.W. Sylvester purchased an interest in the mine from a Blake descendant, carrying on still further mining operations thereafter for several years. Sylvester, however, suffered the same fate as had Humphries, with the exception that his interest was sold on the courthouse steps in Cleveland, Georgia, instead of Clarkesville, since by that time, the county lines had been altered and the property existed in White County instead of Habersham County.

The England Mine seemed destined to be regularly peddled on the courthouse steps, making yet another appearance in 1891 when it was purchased by Jay Mitchell of Jackson, Michigan for $990.00.

By 1895, the mine was again in operation, run this time by Procter Pettingill and the Plattsburg Mining Company of Plattsburg, New York. They, amazingly, paid $15,000.00 for the property, and by the summer of 1896, true to the spirit of the England Mine, the new owners were also experiencing difficulties, with no less than thirty-two liens filed against them.

Like many north Georgia gold mines, the Old England Mine has been the scene of much hard work and the final resting place of more than a few broken dreams. With the exception of Richard England and a few later owners who acquired the property inexpensively, the mine has represented a bottomless pit into which owners poured untold sums of money.

And then of course there's modern-day Albert and Ursula Wiesner of the 1990s, who effectively converted the old mine into an attractive "tourist destination" instead of a mining venture. They also undoubtedly would have confirmed that it's much less laborious (and a lot more fun) to have flocks of tourists handing you money to view a piece of history, than to prospect for the illusive precious yellow metal in the bottomless pit of waste once known as the old England Mine.

The Murder Of Joseph Standing

The founding fathers of the United States of America viewed religious freedom as sacrosanct and a cornerstone of our nation's freedoms. On a warm summer morning in 1879, on a lonely mountain road in northwest Georgia, an appalling act of violence – with religion as its impetus – took the life of an innocent man.

Joseph Standing awoke with a start, worry creasing his otherwise seamless brow. He reportedly had been dreaming, and the image in his dream had been so vivid – so real – that it shocked him. Had he witnessed his last day? According to his dream, he had.

The next morning, the 26-year-old Mormon elder and missionary, visibly agitated, shared his premonition with his 22-year-old partner, Rudger Clawson. "I thought I went to Varnell's Station, when suddenly, clouds of intense blackness gathered overhead and all around me," Standing told Clawson.

"I visited a family who were connected with the Church, and the moment I entered their house, the most extreme consternation seized them, and they made it clear beyond any possibility of doubt that my presence was objectionable," he explained. "They appeared to be influenced by a sense of great fearfulness. There was no clearing away of the clouds nor abatement of the restlessness of the people, when I suddenly woke, without my being shown the end of the trouble."

Though troubled by the revelation, Clawson no doubt did his best to hide his concern. It was the summer of 1879, a time of great strife for Mormons all over the country, and especially in the southern United States where Protestantism dominated the religious landscape.

In the small rural towns of Georgia, fundamentalist ministers preached with fanatical zeal against the Mormons and their polygamous beliefs which the Protestants found abhorrent. The Ku Klux Klan tried to scare Mormons from backcountry neighborhoods, and they were clearly unwelcome wherever they went.

One Mormon missionary wrote in *The Desert News* in Salt Lake City, *"In our travels we frequently find sign seekers who request us, as a proof of our ministry, to drink deadly poison, to carry serpents in our bosoms, to walk on the water and to fly through the air."*

Joseph Standing, an intense, stout young man with light brown hair who had been called to north Georgia the year before, was becoming increasingly concerned about the air of open hostility toward Mormons. Sent to the area in 1878 because of his gentle disposition, maturity and experience, he had quickly founded a branch of the church in Varnell Station (also known as Red Hill, Varnell's Station or simply Varnell) in north Georgia's Whitfield County, a frequent stopping place for Mormon missionaries traveling through Georgia.

The Atlanta Constitution newspaper reported that the hostility against the Mormons gathered in Varnell Station actually began in late 1878 *"when two Methodist preachers and two or three Baptist preachers who were residing at short distances from the place, came in and commenced circulating false reports which usually form the staple of arguments of their tribe against 'Mormonism' and incited that people to drive out the elders by violence."*

Other missionaries were being attacked by armed mobs. By June of 1879, Standing had become concerned enough to write and ask the governor for protection. J.W. Warren, secretary to Gov. Colquitt, responded with a promise to look into the matter. According to state records, the governor never attempted to answer Standing's request.

On Sunday, July 20, 1879, Standing and Clawson set out on foot for a conference in Rome. It was near 9:00 p.m. when they stopped at Varnell Station, but the men felt certain some church members they knew would give them a place to rest for the night. When they got to the house, however, their "friends" were anything but hospitable.

"They said that threats had been made against the brethren, and the feeling toward them in the neighborhood was bitter and murderous," chronicled *The Journal of Church History*, a daily organizational diary kept by the Mormon Church historians. *"They declined to allow the two men to stop overnight, because if anything happened they would have to share the trouble."*

It is not known how Standing reacted, but it is said that Clawson shivered in recognition of the similarity of this situation to his partner's dream.

The missionaries did ultimately find shelter that night at the home of a non-Mormon named Henry Holston. Despite being hospitable, however, their host told them the same thing: *"There is danger in the air threats of mobbing, whipping and even killing."*

Joseph Standing harbored an intense, almost obsessive fear of being beaten. Anxious and pale, and even though totally opposed to violence, he slept that night with an iron bar propped by his bed.

The next morning, which, by church accounts was *"clear and beautiful,"* Standing and Clawson headed back to the first family's home to retrieve some belongings they'd left there in their hasty departure the previous night. The road was densely wooded on both sides, and the pair had traveled only a short distance when suddenly a mob of twelve men – three mounted on horseback – appeared in the road. They were armed.

The bloodthirsty crew cursed the two missionaries and commanded them to follow them. Standing and Clawson pleaded with the kidnappers. "It is not our intention to remain in this part of the state," Standing reportedly told the men, then added, "We use no inducements to persuade people to join our church."

The mob, however, was unmoved, and continued to taunt the young Mormons, striking them from behind with

Mystery & History in Georgia

Rudger Clawson (l) and Joseph Standing (r) as they appeared during their travels in Georgia. *(Photo courtesy of GA Dept. of Archives & History)*

blunt weapons. Clawson later told reporters that at one point, one of the men said smugly, "The government of the United States is against you, and there is no law in Georgia for Mormons."

Twice the group passed other travelers – first a local man named Jonathan Owensby, then Mary Hamlin, the daughter of a Mormon family who had been sent too late of course to warn Standing and Clawson of the potential danger.

Three members of the mob temporarily veered off from the gang and the remaining members led the captives to a secluded spring near Elledge's Mill. According to later reports of the incident, the apparent leader of the group – James Faucett – was approximately 60 years in age, and spoke from his mount. "I want you to understand that I am the captain of this party, and that if we ever find you in this part of the country we will hang you by the neck like dogs."

There are several accounts of what transpired next. Clawson first told authorities that Standing was shot down when he seized a pistol from one of the mobsters. Clawson, however, later testified at the trial that Standing was merely attempting to bluff the mob into thinking he had a weapon.

According to Mormon Church records, Standing jumped up, commanded the gang to surrender, whereupon *"a man seated close to him pointed his pistol at him and fired."* Standing was shot through the eye. An article in the ***Southern Star*** dated December 31, 1898, stated that the young man died instantly, while other accounts indicate Standing was unconscious but still alive for some time.

As soon as Standing had fallen, one gang member pointed at Clawson and declared "Shoot him." Clawson, however, amazingly maintained his composure, and was able to convince his captors that someone needed to bury the body. *"It is a burning shame to shoot a man down in this way and leave him to die in the woods. Either go and get help or let me go,"* church records quote him as saying.

Following his release, the shaken but courageous young missionary then made his way back to Holston's where he borrowed a horse and rode to the coroner's office. He arrived in Salt Lake City ten days later, with Standing's body, which had, by the time Clawson retrieved it from the murder site, been riddled with more than 20 bullets. Standing was buried in the old Salt Lake Cemetery amid much ceremony and mourning.

Back in Georgia, a jury ordered the

A brick enclosure covers the freshwater spring where the mob paused with Standing and Clawson. A small marker (far left foreground) marks the spot at which Standing died.

arrest of David D. Nations, Jasper N. Nations, A.S. Smith, David Smith, Benjamin Clark, William Nations, Andrew Bradley, James Faucett, Hugh Blair, Joseph Nations, Jefferson Hunter and Mack McClure. A Whitfield County Grand Jury later indicted Jasper N. Nations, Bradley and Blair on charges of "First Degree Murder," "Manslaughter" and "Riot," and set bail at $5,000 each.

Area newspapers, hardly objective in those days, carried conflicting accounts of the murder and the circumstances surrounding it.

"It appears that two Mormon preachers have been in that portion of the county for several weeks proclaiming their plurality of wives doctrine, with a view to working up a colony of women to send back to Utah," wrote one reporter for Dalton's ***North Georgia Citizen*** in an article which appeared July 24, 1879, three days after Standing's death. *"The boldness with which they proclaimed this doctrine incensed the men of that neighborhood against them, so much so that they were warned to leave the county."*

The ***Daily Constitution*** in Atlanta which had previously described the murder as a *"cold and premeditated one, no cause having been given other than that the Mormons had made some converts and created some disturbances in families in the neighborhood,"* did an about-face on August 24 when it ran an un-bylined story entitled *"The Lustful Lout."* In this article, Standing is accused of having *"succeeded in accomplishing the ruin"* of two women in Walker County. In example after example, he is cited as a seducer of young ladies, including a daughter of one of the murderers.

The ***Catoosa Courier*** also rationalized the killing: *"Mr. Standing's* preaching and teaching have been of such an immoral character that the good citizens.... could not stand any longer the bad influence that his preaching had upon the female portion of the neighborhood."

A few news accounts, however, were much less unbiased, perhaps even a bit sympathetic toward Standing and his fellow Mormon missionaries in Georgia. "Their policy is not, as has been supposed, to take all their converts to Utah," wrote a reporter for *The Macon Telegraph and Messenger*. "They do not attempt to practice under Georgia laws the polygamic part of their creed."

A Dalton correspondent of the *Chattanooga Daily Times* wrote, "So far as the reports in regard to Standing's immoral influence over his female converts is concerned, I find no proof to support the rumor."

Several months after the murder, Clawson was summoned back to Dalton to testify against Nations, Bradley and Blair. So many Whitfield County residents were reluctant to testify against the three men that 150 people were interviewed before a jury was selected.

On October 16, the first day of the trial, Whitfield County Superior Court was packed with curious onlookers eager to hear the case against Nations. To Clawson's dismay, as well as the rest of the Mormons in the area, the jury rendered a *"Not Guilty"* verdict.

Later that same week, the prosecution dismissed the murder charges against Bradley and Blair. On Thursday, October 23, the last charge of *"Riot"* was dismissed. Sadly, in far too many instances in our nation's history, one's cultural and ethnic identity can make it difficult to obtain a fair trial in the U.S. legal system.

Today, a memorial park lined with maples, poplars and weeping willows

The site remains much as it might have been when Standing and Clawson traveled this winding backroad near presentday Varnell.

marks the spot where Standing was killed. The site remains much as it might have been when Standing and Clawson traveled this winding backroad near presentday Varnell.

The spring where the mob stopped with their young Mormon captives still trickles over a mossflanked bed of rocks. At the park's entrance, an unobtrusive dark wooden marker, low to the ground, reads simply: *"Joseph Standing Monument."* Further on, a small square stone with the initials *"J.S."* identifies the spot where Standing reportedly died.

Dalton resident W.C. Puryear donated the tract of land to the Mormon Church in the early 1950s, and in May of 1952, a special church ceremony was held at the spot to honor the first Mormon missionary killed in the U.S.

The story of Standing's murder is occasionally retold at the site by members of the Mormon chapters in Chattanooga and Dalton. Today, the hidden park, which has been beautifully maintained by the Chattanooga ward since the 1970s, offers a haven for modern-day Mormons to remember and honor their past.

Northwest Georgia Rail Disaster:

The Wreck of the W&A at Willowdale

A group of picnickers from Calhoun, Georgia, set out on a special excursion train for an afternoon of adventure, bound for Chattanooga, Tennessee. They never made it. On a section of the track near Willowdale, fate turned a happy afternoon into a frightening trip into destiny.

"Onward thundered 179,
With hundreds of souls on behind.
Faster and faster it sped the rail,
'Til it reached a place called Willowdale."

(From "The Wreck Of The Willowdale" by T.B. Kendrick)

On the morning of June 12, 1912, a beautiful summer day dawned for a group of some 400 residents from Calhoun, Georgia, who were heading for the Western & Atlantic Railroad's (W&A RR) Train Number 179. The occasion was a picnic for members of the Knights of Phythias Lodge with their friends and families. For one of this group and two of the trainmen, it would be their last day on this earth. They just didn't know it yet.

Travel by train in the 19th and early 20th Centuries was the rough equivalent of air travel of today. And when disaster struck a train, it was just as compelling as are the air-travel tragedies of today.

When the excursion was planned, a special passenger train had been hired for the day. The group planned to visit the Civil War battlefields in Chattanooga. At that point, the war had ended only a mere 47 years earlier, and there were still many relics left on the huge battlefield – at that time free for the taking. Unfortunately, the only memories this group would retain of this day would be of suffering and death.

A cross-section of Gordon County was represented that morning as the train departed the Calhoun station amid much jubilation. Spirits were high. All indications pointed to a very memorable day. As things turned out, it was indeed memorable – just not the type memories one wishes to have.

The group departed Calhoun early, and by 8:00 a.m. were on the siding in Dalton some 20 miles north in Whitfield County. A southbound train was due through Dalton at 8:08, and once it

481

Mystery & History in Georgia

The shocking destruction which occurred in the wreck of the Western & Atlantic Railroad passenger cars and locomotive at Willowdale on June 12, 1912. *(Photo courtesy of the GA Dept. of Archives & History, Atlanta)*

had passed, the Chattanooga delegation continued their journey.

Approximately two miles north of Dalton, in an area known locally as Willowdale, a work crew was performing routine maintenance on the tracks. At the sound of the approaching northbound passenger train, the three men – Arthur Pilcher, Bill Richards, and John Shuman – quickly ceased working and moved with their tools to an area they presumed would be safe, waiting for the train to pass.

As the train neared the workers, the locomotive suddenly erupted from the tracks without warning. The cars which followed gyrated into tangled masses of splintering wood and buckling steel, their crumpled remains scattered about the hillside on either side of the tracks.

The horrified three unsuspecting maintenance workers were immediately engulfed in the avalanche of wood, iron, and spewing debris. Richards and Shuman, amazingly, were not seriously injured by the wreckage. Section hand Pilcher, however, was killed, a victim of traumatic injuries from which he could not recover.

The fireman of the ill-fated #179 – Claud Holcomb of Resaca – was horrifyingly completely buried beneath the engine of the train. He reportedly died instantly of massive injuries.

Though there was understandably an intensive investigation into the cause of the tragedy, the explanation was met with doubt and even outrage from some. The investigators had suggested the cause of the accident was *"a spreading of the rails at the point of derailment."* It was speculated that the high temperatures of the week previous could have been the culprit.

Skeptics, however, were quick to point out that the Willowdale curve had in fact been the scene of many serious wrecks in the past. Though none of the previous wrecks had equaled the magnitude of this disaster, it was reasoned that all the mishaps could not have been the result of "spreading rails," and many of the trains sped down that section of track much too swiftly.

Other doubters noted that the engine pulling No. 179 had earlier been in a serious accident south of Dalton. Could there have been a problem with it which caused it to initiate the accident by jumping the rails?

Eyewitness accounts of the wreck stated that immediately following the crash, the passengers showed great calmness and presence of mind. Within minutes, a make-shift emergency ward was assembled on the hillsides adjacent to the disaster site.

Within an hour, as soon as word had reached Dalton, all available physicians were rushed by special train to the Willowdale area. Much of the credit for this quick response was given to the local telephone exchange which voluntarily took the responsibility of locating the doctors and advising them of the needs involved.

Those victims most seriously injured were returned to Dalton on the train which had carried the physicians to the wreck site. Many victims interviewed in later days emphasized that it was the sight of so many injured bodies being loaded onto the train that brought the scope and magnitude of the catastrophe home to them.

In Dalton, all available hotel rooms were quickly occupied. There were in fact so many serious injuries that the local First Baptist Church was pressed into service as a hospital, as was the city park downtown, where rows of cots and litters revealed an all too graphic scene of injury and despair.

Scores of Dalton females volunteered their services as nurses for the injured, and as babysitters for the children – both injured and unscathed – who had been on board, since many of the parents of those children were hospitalized.

This was back in the day when in times of emergency, everyone volunteered to help. No one just stood around watching. One such lady, a Mrs. Statem whose home was in the vicinity of the derailment, donated her entire supply of linen for bedding and bandages. The *North Georgia Citizen*, Dalton's weekly newspaper, reported that *"Mrs. Statem busied herself, despite the fact that she was in a 'delicate condition' (emphasis added), in assisting in caring for the injured, her work and generosity showing the noble woman she is."*

In all, four cars jumped the tracks that fateful day. The baggage car followed the engine down the eastern slope of the steep embankment, while the other cars fell to the right.

Engineer Charlie Kitchens was at the throttle and stayed his post, escaping with only a badly bruised and lacerated head and a broken arm. The conductor, A.W. Hill, escaped uninjured.

Those most seriously injured were evacuated to Dalton first, with a second run following shortly thereafter.

Meanwhile, back in Calhoun, word was filtering back via a special long distance telephone line established by the Dalton Telephone Company. This courtesy was extended to the victims without charge, and allowed the two cities to remain in uninterrupted communication.

In Calhoun, rumors were as rampant as fact, and a sense of shock pervaded the town. According to accounts in the next day's *Calhoun Times*, townspeople were *"completely stunned by the news."* Later dispatches during the ensuing days detailed how the town seemed unable to come out of the stupor thrown over it by the serious injury to so many of its distinguished citizens.

In the aftermath of the disaster, the presence of "ambulance chasers" and other profiteers – those who attempt to turn another's tragedy into their personal gain – abounded.

One enterprising photographer filmed stereopticon views of the horror only a few hours after it happened. Calhoun people reportedly turned out in record numbers to see the show, just to see how close they themselves had come to serious injury, even death.

Another scavenger, who, incidentally was never identified, went about the wreck site collecting edible food items from the many picnic baskets and undamaged items of passengers' personal property. He later was seen hawking his bounty around the wreck site and about Dalton during the days which followed.

"Enterprising" individuals unfortunately seemed to abound at the wreck site. One small girl, amazingly judged to be only about ten years of age, reportedly busied herself helping those critically injured, and then helping herself to their jewelry at the same time!

Two young boys who had escaped unscathed, evidently were determined not to miss the picnic they had been promised. Reports indicate that they collected a picnic basket and a blanket and spread their repast on the hillside amidst the pallets of the suffering.

Thankfully, more numerous than those who sought to profit from the wreck were those who gave unselfishly in this time of need. Many deeds of heroism were recorded, and physicians who were first on the scene credited many of the passengers with saving the lives of many who might otherwise have perished.

In all, eight individuals out of a passenger manifest of some 400 people were considered seriously injured. Of those, Mrs. John A. Ray, who sustained a serious back injury, was the only passenger who died. Others considered seriously injured were Dr. G.A. Anderson, a representative to the state legislature from Gordon County, and prominent Calhoun matron Mrs. Kate Littlefield. It was judged amazing that more passengers were not seriously injured or killed, such was the extent of the destruction.

First-hand reports from those who experienced the horror tended to be the most reliable. One account was rendered by Captain A.H. Hill, surprisingly a Civil War (Confederate) veteran: "I was at Gettysburg, but believe me, it was nothing like this. I'd rather go through another such battle as that one than to be in another accident like this."

Miss Tilla Rooker, who with her brother Bart and sisters Ola Belle and Maude operated Calhoun's famous Rooker Hotel, was a passenger on the train. Accompanying her for the day's outing was her brother and Joshua Hamilton, Mr. Rooker's Negro man-servant. "It (the train) was just going too fast around a curve near Willowdale... and went off the rails," she explained some 77 years later. "Joshua in the baggage car was killed (and) my brother was injured. I was not injured, just scared half to death." That day, she would later testify, was her "most exciting event."

Once the initial shock of the tragedy had subsided, Calhoun residents began efforts to repay those Whitfield Countians who had so generously given of their time and resources. A purse containing nearly $100.00 was collected in Calhoun for Mrs. Statem who had donated all her linens. Though that seems like a paltry sum today, in 1912 it was a significant amount of money, the equivalent of $2,711.00 in 2021.

Another view of the terrible derailment and wreck of the W&A at Willowdale. *(Photo courtesy of the GA Dept. of Archives & History, Atlanta)*

The city of Calhoun, led by Mayor J.F. Allison and the aldermen; Col. J.G.B. Erwin, superintendent of the M.E. Sunday School; H.J. Roff, chancellor-commander of the Calhoun Lodge No. 264, Knights of Pythias; W.L. Hines, superintendent of the Baptist Sunday School; and Mrs. C.C. Harlan, president of the Calhoun Woman's Club, presented the city of Dalton with a formal resolution which concluded that the heroic, benevolent actions of many in Dalton had demonstrated *"for us and yourselves, woman in her gentlest and truest and man in his noblest aspects."*

Regarding the officially-stated cause of the accident, follow-up investigations were conducted – such as could be done – but no definite cause other than "the spreading rails" was ever declared the culprit in the accident. Today, most prognosticators would surmise that simple excessive speed was the actual cause.

The tracks northward to Chattanooga remarkably were cleared and repaired that same day, and by nightfall, it was "business as usual" for the W & A.

Despite the severity of the wreck, the engine from the train was judged to not have been damaged irreparably. On Friday following the wreck, the locomotive was raised from the ravine where it lay, and by noon, it was at rest on a side track, awaiting shipment to the factory where it would be rebuilt for further service in the W&A network.

That same Friday afternoon, the body of fireman Holcomb, having been prepared for burial, was shipped south to his home in Resaca where funeral services were held shortly thereafter. Mrs. Ray, the only fatality among the passengers, died several days later and was buried in a family cemetery in Gordon County. No report exists on where section hand Pilcher lived or where he was buried.

And of the victims who survived the wreck, their first-hand accounts and written recollections over some three-quarters of a century indicate that the Willowdale wreck was not something that was easily forgotten. It was, in fact, a haunting memory which most of those 400 individuals carried to their graves many years after they first cheated the *Grim Reaper* at Willowdale on a sunny morning in June, 1912.

About The Author

R. Olin Jackson – for all intents and purposes – was born for a career in journalism and history. As a youngster in the 1960s, he was the person searching the plowed fields of his father's farm after warm spring rains for arrow tips, spear points, broken bits of pottery, and other relics of the Native Americans who once inhabited northwest Georgia. He was the person picking up minie balls which had been fired from U.S. Civil War muskets in that war, and treasuring a rusty bayonet from that conflict which had been uncovered from a plowed field on his grandfather's farm. He was the person admiring – year after year – a beautiful black Native American tomahawk discovered on his great-uncle's farm, until his great-uncle took pity and left it to him in his Will.

Since those days, Olin has moved on to different "pastures." In December of 1971, he volunteered for service in the United States Army where he was trained as a military policeman, and assigned to the security detail for the U.S. Army commander of NATO in Heidelberg, Germany – a task which required him to travel throughout Europe. In his spare time, he sought out the historic battlefields and relics from World War II.

In his three-year tour of duty, Olin was decorated for his service, and with his obligation completed in December of 1974, he returned state-side to complete his goal of higher education at Georgia State University in Atlanta, where he earned the Bachelor of Arts degree in journalism.

In 1980, following stints as a speechwriter and public relations specialist for the Georgia Commissioner of Agriculture, Olin was hired as the Director of Media Services at North Georgia State University in Dahlonega, Georgia, where he managed the public relations and sports information programs, and earned the Master of Education degree in political science history in some of his off-hours there. In his remaining free time, Olin haunted the old 1800s-era gold mines and countless other historic sites in and around the former gold rush town of Dahlonega, searching for relics and writing often of his experiences, cataloging details and information for a career he planned to pursue at a later date.

In 1984, Olin was hired as the senior Account Executive at a major public relations firm in Atlanta where he was responsible for the promotion and publicity of a variety of clients both local and national.

Seeking to manage a business of his own, Olin founded Legacy Communications, Inc. in 1987, with *North Georgia*

Journal magazine becoming his centerpiece. He ultimately captained that publication into status as the top travel, history, and lifestyles magazine in Georgia, writing, editing, and publishing countless articles, and, ultimately, numerous spin-off books on subjects involving travel and history in the state. Along the way, Olin converted *North Georgia Journal* into *Georgia Backroads*, a state-wide travel, history and lifestyles magazine which eventually earned numerous journalistic awards from the Magazine Association of Georgia.

The books written, co-written, edited, and published by Olin include *A North Georgia Journal of History, Volumes I, II, III* and *IV*; *Moonshine, Murder and Mayhem in Georgia*; *Georgia Backroads Traveler*; *Georgia's Doc Holliday*; *Tales of the Rails in Georgia*; and *Old Mills in the Georgia Hills*.

After approximately 20 years of ownership and management of Legacy Communications, Olin sold the profitable business to a buyer in Rome, Georgia, where *Georgia Backroads* magazine is still published today for a readership that continues to increase weekly. Olin, meanwhile, has embarked upon a new business venture, founding Whippoorwill Publications, LLC in 2021.

Supplemental Bibliographical References

1/ Amerson, Anne Dismukes, *Dahlonega, Georgia: Site of America's First Major Gold Rush* (2013), Chestatee Publications
2/ Bartow County Genealogical Society, *Bartow County Heritage Book* (1995)
3/ Battey, George MacGruder, *History of Rome and Floyd County* (1979), Cherokee Publishing
4/ Bouwman, Robert W., Travelers Rest and Tugaloo Crossroads (1980), Georgia Dept. of Natural Resources
5/ Cain, Andrew, *History of Lumpkin County, 1832-1932* (1979), The Reprint Company Publishers
6/ Chapman, George, *Chief William McIntosh* (1988), Cherokee Publishing
7/ Coulter, E. Merton, *Auraria: The Story of a Georgia Gold Mining Town* (1956), UGA Press
8/ Dabney, Joseph E., *Mountain Spirits* (1974), Bright Mountain Books
9/ Davis, Donald E., *The Land of Ridge and Valley, A Photographic History of the Northwest Georgia Mountains*, (2000), Arcadia Publishing
10/ Dickens, Jr., Roy, *Cherokee Pre-History* (1976), University of Tennessee Press
11/ Dillman, Caroline M., *Days Gone By: Alpharetta and Georgia* (1992), Chattahoochee Press
12/ Ehle, John, *The Trail of Tears* (1988), Anchor Books
13/ Foster, Jr., W.A., *Paulding County: Its People and Places* (1983), W.H. Wolfe Associates
14/ Furnas, J.C., *The Americans: A Social History of the United States, 1587-1914* (1969), G.P. Putnam's Sons, New York
15/ Garrett, Franklin and Rice, Bradley, Atlanta Historic Society, *Atlanta History, A Journal of the South* (1980)
16/ Glover, V., James Bolan; McIntyre, Joe; and Rebecca Nash Paden, *Marietta 1833-2000*, (1999), Arcadia Publishing
17/ Harris, Corra, *A Circuit Rider's Wife* (1998), University of Georgia Press
18/ Head, Sylvia Gailey, *The Neighborhood Mint* (1986), Gold Rush Gallery
19/ Hicks, John D., *The Federal Union (Second Edition), A History of the United States to 1865* (1952), Houghton Mifflin Company / The Riverside Press Cambridge
20/ Jackson, III, Ralph Olin, *A North Georgia Journal of History, Vol. 1* (1989), Legacy Communications, Inc.
21/ Jackson, III, Ralph Olin, *A North Georgia Journal of History, Vol. 2* (1991), Legacy Communications, Inc.
22/ Jackson, III, Ralph Olin, *A North Georgia Journal of History, Vol. 3* (1995), Legacy Communications, Inc.
23/ Jackson, III, Ralph Olin, *A North Georgia Journal of History, Vol. 4* (1999), Legacy Communications, Inc.

24/ Jackson, III, Ralph Olin, *Moonshine, Murder & Mayhem in Georgia* (2003), Legacy Communications, Inc.
25/ Jackson, III, Ralph Olin, *Tales of the Rails In Georgia* (2004), Legacy Communications, Inc.
26/ Kloeppel, James E., *Georgia Snapshots* (1994), Adele Enterprises
27/ Kollock, John, *These Gentle Hills* (1976), Copple House Books
28/ Lyle, Katie Lecher, *Scalded to Death by the Steam* (1988), Algonquin Books
29/ McRay, Sybil, *A Pictorial History of Hall County* (1985), Taylor Publishing
30/ McRay, Sybil and James Dorsey, *Windows of Memory, The Hall County That Was* (1989) Chestatee Regional Library
31/ Mooney, James, *Myths of the Cherokees and Sacred Formulas of the Cherokees* (1982), Charles & Randy Elder Booksellers
32/ Reeve, Jewell, *Climb the Hills of Gordon* (1962), Southern Historic Press
33/ Ritchie, Andrew Jackson, *Sketches of Rabun County History*, 1819-1948, Copple House Books
34/ Roswell Historic Society, *Roswell: A Pictorial History* (1985)
35/ Sargent, Gordon, Polk County Heritage Committee, 2000, *The Heritage of Polk County, 1851-2000*
36/ Sawyer, Gordon, *Northeast Georgia: A History*, (2001), Arcadia Publishing
37/ Shadburn, Don L., *Cherokee Planters in Georgia, 1832-1838*, (1989), W. H. Wolfe Associates
38/ Shadburn, Don L., *Pioneer History of Forsyth County, Forsyth County Heritage Series, Vol. 1* (1981), W.H. Wolfe Associates, Roswell, GA
39/ Sherman, Gen. William T., *The Capture of Atlanta and the March to the Sea* (2007), Dover Publications, Inc., Mineola, New York
40/ Tate, Luke, *History of Pickens County* (1987), The Reprint Company Publishers
41/ Walker County Historic Society, *Walker County, Georgia Heritage, 1833-1983* (1984), Taylor Publishing Company
42/ Webb, J.A., *History of New Holland, GA* (1985)
43/ Wells II, Ridley, *Old Enough To Die* (1996), Hillsboro Press, Franklin, Tennessee
44/ Whitfield-Murray County Historical Society, *Murray County's Indian Heritage* (1987), W.H. Wolfe Associates
45/ Williams, David, *Georgia Gold Rush* (1993), University of South Carolina Press
46/ Williams, Harry T.; Current, Richard N.; and Freidel, Frank; *A History of the United States to 1876* (1959), Alfred A. Knopf, New York

Name Index

A
Abercrombie, Emma 425
Adamson, Bill 115
Adamson, Susan 115
Alexander, Arthur 118, 121
Allen, J.C. 362
Allen, David 252
Allen, Jesse 252
Allen, Ollie 414
Allison, J.F. 485
Allred, Elias R. 254
Allred, Felix 340
Allred, Lemuel J. 354
Anderson, Amelia Gaines 29
Anderson, Anna 31, 44
Anderson, Edward 224
Anderson, Ella 44
Anderson, Frances E. 224
Anderson, Dr. G. A. 484
Anderson, Mrs. Garland 224
Anderson, George (Bill Miner) 184, 185, 186, 189, 256
Anderson, George Whitfield "Capt. Whit" 267-274
Anderson, Grover 99
Anderson, Hepatia Bowden 32
Anderson, Isaac 28
Anderson, Isaac, Jr. 28
Anderson, James 28
Anderson, Jeff 282, 287
Anderson, Jimmy 32, 245, 268
Anderson, John W. 252
Anderson, Julia Margaret 31, 44, 45
Anderson, Laura 32, 45
Anderson, Martha Bell 28
Anderson, Oliver Davis 28-32
Anderson, Robert 28
Anderson, Robert E. 274
Anderson, Rueben 267

Anderson, Susan Gaines 45
Anderson, Susannah Welch 267, 273
Anderson, Thomas 286, 287, 291
Anderson, William 104
Anderson, William, Jr. 253
Anderson, William, Sr. 253
Anderson, Woodrow 99, 100
Anderson, Woodville B. 254
Andrews, Cleveland 250
Andrews, James J. 72-81
Antoinette, Queen Marie 5
Armstrong, Don 22
Armstrong, John 22
Arthur, Henry 310
Ash, Henry 252
Ash, Wallace 14
Ashworth, Dr. John A. 251
Ashworth, Col. J.H. 255
Autry, William S. 123
Aycock, Roger 153

B
Bailey, Alvin 403
Bailey, Andrew 405
Bailey, Billy 405
Bailey, Clayton 403, 407
Bailey, Jesse 139
Bailey, Minerva Owens 405
Bailey, Silas Clayton 405
Bailey, Warren 403, 405, 407
Bailey, Will 405
Ballenger, Rev. E.W. 26, 410, 411, 412, 413, 415
Ballenger, Mable 414
Baltzelle, Addie 8
Baltzelle, Capt. James P. 7, 8
Baltzelle, Julia 7
Bandy, Mrs. B.J. 135, 136

Barber, A.D. 414
Barber, Judge Wiley Crawford 409, 410
Barker, Gladys Opal 224
Barker, Harrison 355
Barker, Robert 140
Barnett, Harriet A. 314
Barnsley, Adelaide 7
Barnsley, Godfrey 1-9
Barnsley, Jr., Godfrey 3
Barnsley, George 7
Barnsley, Harold 7
Barnsley, Julia Henrietta Scarborough 2, 3, 4
Barnsley, Lucian 7
Bari, Lynn 445, 464
Bates, Barbara 167, 445, 446, 449, 457, 461, 462
Bates, Kathy 293, 294
Bates, Samuel 104
Bateman, R.L. 375
Battey, George M., Jr. 128, 153, 154, 393, 398
Baugus, John 289
Beard, James H. 291
Bearden, Ancil 254
Bearden, Jackson 138
Bearden, Nelson 253
Bearden, William M. 254
Beauregard, Gen. (C.S.A.) P.G.T. 271
Beck, John 104, 253
Bell, Francis 182, 183, 196
Bell, Congressman H.P. 363
Bell, Jane 180, 183, 195, 196, 204
Bell, Joe 280
Bell, Martha 28
Bell, Mellie 182
Bell, Sarah "Sallie" Carolina 145
Bell, Thomas 182

Mystery & History in Georgia

Benton, Thomas Jefferson 181
Bernard, George N. 19, 20
Berry, M.A. 350
Berry, Milas 254
Berry, Martin P. 252
Berry, William A. 254
Bevins, Bessie 31
Bingham, J.F. 138
Bird, Georgia 51, 56
Bishop, Arch 111
Bishop, Wiley T. 110
Black, Dessie 112
Black, Dick 112
Blacker, U.S. Deputy Marshal Charles B. 350, 351, 352, 353, 355
Blackburn, Jesse W. 253
Blackburn, Lewis 130, 131, 134, 135, 136, 314, 315
Blacker, Charles B. 349
Blackmon, Joe 305
Blackwell, Daniel 252
Blackwell, Sidney 252
Blair, Hugh 479, 480
Blake, Daniel 472, 473, 475
Blakely, Robert L. 128
Bland, Nancy Carter 304, 305
Boone, Nancy 113
Booth, Hoyt T. 240
Borden, Lizzie 58
Bosworth, Sarah 303
Boudinot, Elias 142, 143, 144, 145, 146, 147, 150, 151, 152, 153, 328, 330, 333
Bowden, Hepatia 32
Bowie, Jim 275
Boyd, Kenneth W. 154
Boyd, Col. (U.S.) S.B. 283, 284, 288, 291
Boyd, Weir 236, 238
Box, Dr. J. Brent 151, 154
Bradley, Andrew 479, 480
Bradley, Flora 225
Bradwell, I.G. 73, 81
Bramlet, Rachel 357
Bramlet, William 358
Braselton, J.J. "Seif" 181
Bray, Bannister 151, 154
Brewer, W.H. 374
Brewster, Fred 401
Brewster, Gordon 401
Brewster, Joseph Proctor "J.P.S." 401, 402
Brewster, Rev. Vann Allen "V.A." 401

Brice, W.M. 218, 223
Brittain, John C. 243
Brooke, Jule 44, 47
Brooks, Alexander 254
Brooks, Aaron T. 253
Brooks, Hiram 250
Brooks, John W. 414
Brooks, Mamie 224
Brooks, Zack 253
Brookshire, Rev. Waldo 424
Brown, Claude 224
Brown, Daniel 439, 441
Brown, Col. James G. 249, 250, 251
Brown, Jim 162
Brown, Gov. Joseph Emerson 23, 71, 72, 73, 74, 80, 81, 240, 241, 287, 392
Brown, Marjorie 398
Brown, Melvin 118, 119, 121
Brown, Rodney Hilton 73, 81
Bryan, T. Conn 282
Bryant, Wilson 138
Bryant, Winnie 224
Buell, Don Carlos (Gen.) 74, 75
Buffington, Joshua 315
Buffington, Tom 130, 131, 132, 133, 135, 136, 315
Bullis, H.E. 375
Bundy, B.J. 134
Burns, Ken 42
Burrell, Bertha 175, 176
Byess, Dallas 359

C

Caffrey, (Agent) Raymond J. 15
Cain, Prof. Andrew W. 233, 235, 236, 270, 280
Cain, Doug 260
Caldwell, Herman 427
Caldwell, Lula B. 414
Caldwell, Monroe 427
Calhoun, Mayor James M. 270
Calhoun, Sen. John C. 169, 268, 273,
Calhoun, Laura 415
Calhoun, Rory 25, 164, 167, 443, 445, 446, 448, 450, 455, 456, 457, 460, 461, 462
Camp, Aida 414
Camp, Annie 414
Camp, J.W. 401
Campbell, Duncan G. (Col.) 67, 68
Campbell, William 75

Candler, Allen D. 80
Candler, Martin 224
Cannon, Fannie 415
Cannon, Flossie 415
Cannon, Oscar 262, 263
Cannon, Willie Belle 415
Cape, Hobart 343
Cape, Levi 343
Cape, Surber 344
Cape, Waldo 343
Cape, W. Lee 341-347
Carmichael, Pete 189
Carney, Absolem 253
Carney, Edmond 254
Carney, L.B. 254
Carney, Mary 195
Carney, S. 254
Carroll, Henry L. 249, 252
Carson, Kit 109
Carter, Clyde 224
Carter, Clyde B. 223
Carter, Farish 303, 304, 307
Carter, Nancy 304
Carter, Col. Samuel McDonald 307
O.A. Carter 223
Castner, Officer Ralph 14
Cauthen, Rainey 118, 119, 120, 121
Chalkley, Eaton 457
Champion, Oscar 339, 340
Chandler, Joe Ben 404
Chandler, Will 404
Chapin, George 439, 443
Christian, Col. William 301
Christiana, Mary (WaWiLi) 328
Clark, Benjamin 479
Clark, Hubert Henry 224
Clawson, Rudger 476, 477, 478, 479, 480
Clayton, Elias 253
Clayton, John 18, 20, 21, 22
Clements, Hal 372
Clements, Tom 414
Cleveland, Grover 44
Cofer, Carl H. 9
Coker, Clint 2, 7
Cole, J.W. 120
Collard, "Chief" 379-386
Colquitt, Gov. Alfred 477, 354, 363, 365, 366, 367
Colquitt, Jack 393, 394, 395
Colston, "Aunt Fannie" 5
Conkle, Ellen 15, 16

Name Index

Connoly, John 3
Cook, Carrie Merrill 227
Cook, Mrs. Eugene 414
Cook, Lemuel 254
Cook, Lucious Riley 230
Cooper, Journey
Cooper, Sheriff 53, 57
Cooper, Simon 58
Cooper, Thomas 182
Coppe, Carl 98
Cordery, Sarah 330, 331
Cordery, Sonicooie "Susannah" 330
Cordery, Thomas 330
Corey, Bill 9
Corrie, Arthur M. 369, 370, 371, 373, 375
Corse, Gen. John M. 20,
Cotter, William Jasper 305, 306
Coulter, E. Merton 365, 59
Cowan, Lillie Woolfolk 55, 58
Cowart, Fances M. 254
Cowart, Narcissa 363
Cowart, Taylor S. 357
Cowart, Thomas A. 254
Crane, Fannie Moore 49, 55, 58, 59
Crane, John Ross 49, 59
Crawford, D.A. 40
Crawford, T.B. 414
Crisp, William 138
Crisson, McKey 288, 289
Crisson, Capt. (C.S.A.) William R. 288, 289, 291
Crittenden, James 112
Crook, Louis 307
Crow, Patsy 180
Crow, Sheriff W.A. 188, 193
Cunningham, Frank 153, 154
Cunningham, Robert 254
Curtis, "Aunt Mollie" 7
Curtis, MG Samuel R. 148

D

Da Vinci, Leonardo 4
Dalton, Beecher 157
Dalton, Catherine 157, 158
Darby, Bessie 16
Darnell, Elias 254
Darnell, S.A. 362, 364
Darnell, Thomas 253
Davenport, John 353
Davis, Abner 117, 118, 119, 120, 121
Davis, Allen 414

Davis, Anna Lou 388
Davis, Benjamin 252
Davis, C.C. 192
Davis, Carrie Louise 225
Davis, Charles 310
Davis, Charles C. 192
Davis, Dan 237
Davis, Daniel 112, 237
Davis, Georgia M. 397
Davis, Gordon 192
Davis, James 255
Davis, President Jefferson 246
Davis, Jim (Sheriff) 188, 189, 192
Davis, Joe 189, 192
Davis, Joseph C. 237
Davis, Lorenzo Dow 237
Davis, Mary Nelle 225
Davis, Jr. Robert S. 251, 255, 280, 305
Davis, Rufus Tilman "R.T." 189, 192
Davis, Capt. W.C. 57
Davis, William S. "Bill" 192
Davison, Robert E. 191
De Baillou, Clemens 135
De Soto, Hernando 123, 125, 126, 127, 128, 467, 468, 469, 470
Dean, Joe 414
Dean, Mary 112
Dean, William 320
Depratter, Chester 128
Dexter, Amory 237
Dill, Milton 138
Dillbeck, Martin 291
Dillard, Alec 163
Dingler, Hoyt 406, 407
Disney, Walt 164, 168, 169, 449, 450, 451, 452, 453
Dosser, J.W. 375
Dougherty, James, Jr. 112
Dougherty, James Sr. 314
Dougherty, Sarah 112
Dowdy, Alfred J. 240
Dowdy, Anna Johnson 244
Dowdy, Dwane 224
Dowdy, James R. 252
Dowdy, Rev. John M. 244
Dowdy, Julia Ann 244
Dowdy, Sidney 240
Dowdy, William Taylor 244
Dowie, W.I. 374
Downing, Nellie 112
Downing, Sam 112

Draper, Dr. Lyman C. 302
Duke, David 130
Duggar, B.C. (Rep.) 354
Dunagan, George 181
Dutton, Oscar 118, 119, 120, 121
Dyer, John 291
Dyer, Watson 390
Dynes, W.L. 374

E

Eades, Clara Belle 258, 260
Eades, Jesse C. 224
Earle, Col. Richard 6
Early, William H. 257, 259, 260
Echols, Elmer 13
Echols, Emily Elizabeth Gaines 13
Echols, Mamie 13
Edmonson, H.A. 401
Edmonson, Thomas 252
Edmonson, William 252
Elliott, Bill 94, 95, 96, 97
Elliott, Charles N. 425, 428, 429
Elliott, Chase 96, 97
Ellis, Clarence Osgood 224
Ellis, Frank 120
Elrod, James 258
Emory, John 350
England, Daniel 471
England, Joseph 473
England, Martin 473
England, Richard 471
Epps, Joe Monroe 244
Erwin, J.G.B. (Col.) 485
Evans, G.M. 254
Evans, Hoyt 344, 345, 347
Evans, Hubbard 415
Evans, John 253
Evans, L.B. 374
Evans, Lindsey 344, 345, 346, 347
Evans, Mary Hudgins 224
Evans, Mirey 254
Evans, Ralph 224
Evans, Tom 343
Evans, Will 344

F

Fairies, Arthur 300
Falling/Fawling, Nancy 131
Falls, Dr. Gilbert 290
Fambro, Aileen 414
Fambro, Howard 415
Fambro, Marion 415

Mystery & History in Georgia

Fambro, Roy 415
Fambro, W.B. 410
Fant, David J. 185, 186
Farmer, William C. 140
Faucett, James 478, 479
Featherstonaugh, George William 468, 469, 470
Fields, Elizabeth "Betsy" 145
Fields, Sheriff John D. 474
Findley, Catherine 137
Findley, Col. (C.S.A) James Jefferson 137, 138, 250, 286, 287, 288, 289, 350, 355
Findley, James 137
Findley, Walter Webster "Web" 137, 138, 139, 140
Finlay, Mrs. J.J. 375
Flagg, Fannie 293
Floyd, Charles Arthur "Pretty Boy" 10-16
Floyd, Duff 13, 16
Floyd, E.W. 13
Floyd, Fannie Mae 16
Floyd, Jack Dempsey 14
Floyd, Katheryn 16
Floyd, Katheryn Murphey 11
Floyd, Patience Pinson 11
Floyd, Redding 11, 12, 14, 16
Floyd, Samuel 11
Floyd, Walter 13, 16
Fog, Fay 458
Fog, Kay 458
Ford, Henry 4
Ford, John 252
Forrester, Hardy 289
Fortenberry, Bill 128
Foute, Anna 45
Foute, Augustus Marcellus 32, 44, 45
Foute, Augustus Marcellus, Jr. 45
Foute, Julia 45
Foute, Laura Anderson 45
Foute, Mary 45
Foutes, Claude 224
Fowler, James B. 255
Fowler, Johnson 252
Fowler, Narcissa A.M. "Sis" 357, 358, 359, 360, 361, 362, 363, 366, 367, 368
France, Bill 100
Franks, Kenny A. 153-154
Freeman, Robert 3, 4
French, Maj-Gen S.G. 19, 20, 21, 22
Fricks, John D. 138

Frost, J.E. 374
Fuger-Babenhausen, Prince Hubertus Fuerst 8, 9
Fuller, William A. 21, 72, 74, 78, 80
Fultz, Chief John 15

G

Gaddis, Lt. (C.S.A.) N.J. 288
Gaines, Amelia 29
Gaines, Emily Elizabeth 13
Gaines, H.L. 222
Gaines, H. Leon 224
Gaines, Herman L. 222
Gaines, Katherleen Gertrude 222
Gaines, Kathleen 224
Gaines, Mary Kathryn 16
Gaines, R.J. 228
Gaines, Susan 32, 45
Gambold, John 153
Gammon, Beth 386
Gammon, Wayne 381, 382, 383, 386
Gandee, Officer Sherman 14
Gann, John (State Senator) 85, 87
Gann, Ruth 327
Garner, John 211
Garrett, Franklin 267, 270, 272, 273, 280
Garrett, Joseph 252
Garrett, Martin 252
Garrett, Robert 252
Garrison, William 229
Gideon, Martha "Patsy" 181
Gilliam, Willis 285, 286
Gilreath, Jeffie 35, 38
Gilreath, L. W. 288
Girt, Martha Jane 420
Gist, Nathaniel 155
Glore, Harold 87, 88
Gober, Robert A. 314
Gold, Harriet 144
Gore, Vilwon Cook 227
Grady, Henry W. 365, 366, 367, 368, 415
Grant, President Ulysses S. 350
Gravatt, Daniel 420
Gravatt, John 419, 420
Gravatt, John W. 419, 420
Gravatt, Johnson/Johnston 419, 420
Gravatt, Mary Melinda 417, 418, 420

Gravatt, Robert 418, 419, 420
Gravatt, Samuel 418
Gravatt, Sarah Kennedy 420
Gravatt, Sarah Percy 420
Greeley, Horace 109
Green, Anna Maria 437, 443
Green, Garland S.D. 254
Green, W.H. 354
Greenwood (Native American) 380, 389, 398
Greer, T.F. 362
Griffith, Ben 402
Griffith, Joe 72, 147, 148, 150, 152, 154, 330
Griffith, John 252
Griffith, Kathleen 406
Griffith, William 252

H

Hackney, Robert 403, 405, 407
Hale, P.T. 374
Hall, Roy 96, 99
Hally, David J. 128
Hambrick, Amazilla 358, 366, 367
Hambrick, Catherine "Kate" 357
Hambrick, John 357, 358, 362
Hamilton, Gary 123
Hamilton, Joshua 484
Hamlin, Mary 478
Hampton, John 104
Handford, James 187, 190
Haney, Mayme Ballenger 411, 415
Hanie, Milton H. 389, 398
Hansell, Gen. Andrew I. 238
Hardgrave, Wilma Ruby 14
Hardman, Dr. Lamartine G. 438, 441, 442
Hardy, Elizabeth 112
Hardy, Emily Norvell Tant 89, 90, 91, 93
Hardy, Mrs. George 374
Hardy, Oliver Norvell 89-93
Hardy, Oliver, Sr. 89
Hardy, Dr. Weston C. 39
Hardy, Dr. Wilson 38
Harlan, Mrs. C.C. 485
Harlen, George 306
Harlen, Nancy 306
Harnage, Ambrose 306
Harris, Bob 128
Harris, Corra 24-27, 454, 455, 464

Name Index

Harris, Elizabeth 196, 197, 199
Harris, Elizabeth Clementine 200
Harris, John 415
Harris, John M. 232, 233
Harris, Katye 415
Harris, Lundy Howard 25, 26, 27, 413
Harris, Mary P. 232
Harris, T.B. 117, 120
Harris, Woodrow 119
Harris, Judge Young L.G. 411
Harvey, Granny 175
Harvey, Gussie 175, 176
Harvey, J.D. 175
Hawks, Charles 316
Hawkins, Col. Benjamin 314, 322, 324, 379, 386
Hawkins, Jane 69
Hawkins, Samuel 62, 63, 65, 66, 67, 68, 69
Hawless, (FBI Agent) 16
Haynes, John 358
Hayward, Susan 25, 164, 167, 413, 443, 445, 450, 456, 457, 458, 459, 460, 461, 462, 464
Head, Joe F. 21, 22, 23
Heard, Alice Paralee 309
Heard, Grace 309
Heard, Martha Paralee Hudlow 309
Heard, Mattie G. 309
Heard, Otto 309
Heard, Pauline 309
Hemperley, Marion 67, 318, 326
Henderson, Charles K. 386, 389
Henderson, Mrs. Irby 415
Henderson, Mrs. Jamie 224
Henderson, Lillian 81
Henry, Alexander 253
Herron, Kenny 9
Hester, Harvey 446
Hicks, Charles 132
Hicks, Eli 145, 152
Hicks, Isabella 145
Hightower, Elias 389
Hill, A.W. 483, 484
Hill, Bud 138
Hill, Elizabeth Ann 37
Hill, Fred 338
Hill, Goldie Evelyn Jordan 416, 418, 419
Hill, Jody 27, 464
Hill, Louise Biles 81
Hilty, Robert 375

Hines, W.L. 485
Hodden, John 194
Hodge, W.W. 120
Holcomb, Claud 482
Holcomb, Sargent M. 255
Holliday, Dr. John Henry "Doc" 102, 103, 275, 488
Hollifield, J.A. 289
Holston, Henry 477
Holt, James 353
Holt, R.A. 243
Honea, Cora Belle 402, 407
Honea, George M. 254
Honea, James 359
Hood, Gen. (C.S.A.) John Bell 281
Hood, Lt. Gen. (C.S.A.) John G. 19
Hood, Samuel 254
Hood, Tate 254
Hope, A.A. 258
Hope, Charlie 258
Hope, "Doc" 258
Hope, Mary Annie 257
Horn, Althea 92
Houston, Pvt. Andrew Jackson 23
Houston, Sam 156
Howard, John L. 254
Howard, Joyce 260
Howard, Major Dewitt C. 248, 251, 255
Howard, Mattie E. 50
Howard, Samuel 254
Howard, Col. William J. 306
Hudgen, James Beverly a.k.a. "Bevely" 195, 196
Hudgen, Jane Bell 195
Hudgen, John 195
Hudgens, H.E. 185
Hudgeons, Beverly 182, 196
Hudgins, Albert 200
Hudgins, Arabella Pettyjohn 196, 197, 198, 200
Hudgins, Carl 198, 200, 202
Hudgins, Clyde 199
Hudgins, Cora 200
Hudgins, Daisy 199, 200
Hudgins, David 199
Hudgins, Dessie 183
Hudgins, Dorothy 194, 201, 202
Hudgins, Elizabeth Clementine Harris 196, 197, 200
Hudgins, Essie 183, 198, 202
Hudgins, Francis Bell 183, 196

Hudgins, Holder 183, 196
Hudgins, Hugh 195
Hudgins, Iverson Daniel 183
Hudgins, Iverson Delaprierre
Hudgins, James Beverly a.k.a. "Bevely" 180, 182, 183, 196, 204
Hudgins, James Beverly, Jr.
Hudgins, James Zacheus 183, 196, 197, 198, 199, 200, 201, 202, 203
Hudgins, Jane Bell 180, 182, 183, 196, 204
Hudgins, Jim 183, 196
Hudgins, John 194
Hudgins, Lucy May 197, 199
Hudgins, Margaret 196, 197
Hudgins, Margaret "Peggy" Major/Majors 196, 197
Hudgins, Marjorie 202
Hudgins, Mary 196, 197
Hudgins, Mary Lou 199, 204
Hudgins, Raleigh 200
Hudgins, Ralph 200
Hudgins, Richard 197
Hudgins, Richard Bennett 195, 196, 199
Hudgins, Richard Braselton 199
Hudgins, Robert 195
Hudgins, Sarah 201
Hudgins, Sarah "Sallie" Elizabeth Tanner 196, 197, 198, 200, 201, 202, 203
Hudgins, Silas Arthur 197, 199
Hudgins, Thomas 195
Hudgins, Zacharia/Zacheus/ Zaccharia/Zachus/ 183, 195, 196
Hudlow, George Bowman 309
Hudson, Dr. Charles 128, 469
Hudson, Weldon 280
Hughes, Patricia Jackson 183, 204, 417, 420
Hughes, R.V. 138
Hughes, Sally 316, 317, 322, 323, 325
Humphrey, W.C. 271
Humphries, John 471, 472, 473, 474, 475
Hunnicutt, Calvin W. 441, 443
Hunt, E.B. 461, 463
Hunt, Frank Cleveland 244
Hunt, Molly Margaret 244
Hunter, Charlie 187
Hunter, Jefferson 479

Hunter, Jeffrey 168
Hunter, Jim 38

I
Innis, Jean 445
Isbell, Jeremiah "Jerry"/"Jerre" 401
Isbell, Laura Jane 401, 403, 407
Itson, Larry 123

J
Jack, Nolichucky 330
Jackson, Gen. Andrew 23, 63, 143, 146, 155, 331, 460
Jackson, David Anderson 183, 420, 183, 204, 420
Jackson, Dottie Sims 460
Jackson, Elizabeth Ann Hill, 37
Jackson, Elizabeth Ann Patterson 33
Jackson, Frederick 33, 39
Jackson, George 34, 38
Jackson, Guy Jordaner 420
Jackson, Isabelle Neel 44, 45
Jackson, Marilyn Jordan 39, 47, 204, 416, 417, 418, 420
Jackson, Mary Lynne 420
Jackson, Milton C. 33, 34, 35, 36, 37, 38, 39
Jackson, Jr., Ralph Olin 39, 47, 204
Jackson, III, Ralph Olin 18, 26, 34, 35, 36, 38, 106, 108, 111, 114, 115, 131, 134, 180, 183, 186, 187, 193, 204, 273, 274, 325, 326, 332, 333, 370, 371, 372, 420, 438, 455, 456, 457, 459, 487
Jackson, Thomas Frederick 33
Jackson, Thomas Patterson 35
Jackson, William Anthony ("Willy/Billy") 35, 38
Jackson, Zimri Wilson 33, 34, 35, 36, 37, 38, 39
Jefferson, Eliza 243
Jefferson, President Thomas 212
Johnson, Abda 12, 40, 43
Johnson, Annie E. 87
Johnson, Elijah 353
Johnson, Ellijay 290
Johnson, Joseph 290
Johnson, Larry G. 398, 407
Johnson, Rufus 185
Johnston, Col. L. 249, 250
Johnston, Ruby 414

Jolley, Clyde 36
Jones, Ayers 137, 351, 352, 353, 354, 355
Jones, Carter 347
Jones, Mrs. Charles 414
Jones, Charles C. 439
Jones, Elma 414
Jones, John 440
Jones, Lizzie 225
Jones, Mrs. M.D. 414
Jones, Mary 224, 414
Jones, Milton D. 414
Jones, Col. Seaborn 369, 370, 409
Jones, John 224
Jones, Sam 46
Jones, Walter P. 414
Jordan, Alvin Gilmore 417
Jordan, Barbara Ann Pollard Ferguson 417
Jordan, Essie Hudgins 183, 198, 202
Jordan, Goldie Evelyn 417, 418
Jordan, Guy Wilfred 417, 418
Jordan, John G. 254
Jordan, Mary Melinda Gravatt 417, 418
Justus, Lucy 428

K
Keith, S.J. 376, 377, 378
Kelley, Pollard 253
Kelley, Rev. O.L. 412
Kelley, William 253
Kellogg, Col. (U.S.) John Azor 250
Kendall, Elbert 189
Kennard, Moody 67
Kennedy, Ambrose 181
Kennedy, John 420
Kennedy, Sarah 420
Kerlin, Sheriff Tom 117, 118, 120
Kimsey, William 140
King, Henry 167, 447, 448, 449, 454, 455, 456, 457, 461, 462, 463, 464
King, Kittie 414
King, Ralph 338, 339, 340
Kitchens, Charlie 483
Klunder, Mabel Ballenger 411, 415
Knox, Alexander 121, 445, 459
Kollock, John 444, 445, 446, 447, 448, 449, 450, 451, 452, 453, 454, 462, 463

Korstian, Mary Kathryn Gaines 16
Kuhn, Will 375
Kurtz, Jr., Henry H. 81
Kurtz, Wilbur G., Sr. 80, 81

L
Lamar, Mirabeau B. 156
Lancaster, Dr. Homer 202
Lancaster, Martha 202
Landrum, Charles 112
Landrum, James 112
Langston, James C. 117-121
Latimer, Augusta 440
Latimer, Kate 437
Laurel, Stanley 89-93
Lawrence, H.G. 40
Lawrence, James W. 279
Lee, Col. (C.S.A.) G.W. 282
Lee, Gen. (C.S.A.) Robert E. 7
Lesberg, Sandy 16
Lester, D.P. 362
Lester, Judge George N. 362, 363, 364
Lewis, (Pastor) Iverson 195
Lewis, Lamar 415
Lewis, Meriwether 275
Lewis, Tarleton 134
Lindsay, Sheriff John 359, 362
Linton, James 310
Little, Keith 124, 125, 128
Littlefield, Kate 484
Lobrugh, Dan 375
Locket, Green 51, 52, 53, 56, 57
Lockhart, Gene 167, 445, 446, 448, 457, 461, 462
London, Alice 258
London, Annie Kemp 188
London, Ben 258, 259
London, Bob 258, 259
London, Clarence 258, 261
London, Dave 258
London, Elizabeth Conley 258
London, Emma 258, 261
London, Eve 258, 261
London, Fannie Martin 261
London, Floyd 258, 261
London, Frank 188, 258, 259
London, George 260
London, James 260, 261
London, James A. "Jim" 258, 260, 261
London, James Wadkins 258
London, Jim 258
London, Julia Martin 258

Name Index

London, Mary Neisler 188, 258, 259, 261
London, Mattie 259
London, Merritt M. 188, 189, 256, 258, 259, 260
London, Mollie 260
London, Myrtle 258, 261
London, Thomas Jefferson 261
London, Willie 259
Long, Bernard G. 99
Long, Connord 252
Long, Henry 252
Long, James, Jr. 252
Long, James, Sr. 252
Long, James M. 252
Long, Jasper 138, 252
Long, John 252
Long, Joseph 252
Long, Nathan B. 290, 291
Long, Nathaniel 252
Long, William 252
Longest, Mary 195
Lott, Frank, Jr. 405, 406
Lott, Sheriff Frank, Sr. 404, 405, 406, 407
Lott, J.J. 183, 196
Lott, Jesse, Jr. 181
Lott, Jesse, Sr. 180
Lowe, Malissa "Eliza" 277, 279
Lowe, Thomas F. "Uncle Tommy" 272, 273
Lumpkin, Elizabeth 381, 384
Lumpkin, George 310
Lumpkin, Gov. Wilson 381, 384, 386
Lumsden, Susan 443
Lumsden, Tannie Williams 441
Lumsden, Dr. Thomas 443, 470
Lundigan, William 25, 164, 167, 443, 445, 446, 447, 448, 456, 457, 459, 460, 461, 462, 464
Lynch, J.M. 237

Mc

McAfee, John M. 234
McAfee, Joseph 104
McClain, Clark 356
McClatchey, Juliet Anderson Neel 45
McCormack, M.E. 401
McDaniel, Gov. 47
McDaniel, Lucy 395
McDaniel, Nellie 305
McDonald, Ferdinand 289
McDonald, Shirley Black 458
McEver, W.A. 181
McFarland, Willie Pickett 343
McIntosh, Chief William 60-69
McIntosh, Chilly 63
McIntosh, Hogey 68
McIntosh, Peggy 67
McIntosh, Susannah 67, 68
McIntyre, Lt. Augustine 351, 352, 353, 354
McClure, Mack 479
McClure, Robert 114
McClure, Robert B. 114
McClure, Widow 114
McCrary, Capt. (U.S.) George W. 251, 252
McCrary, Julius 254
McCrary, Samuel 225
McLaughlin, Archibald 472, 473
McLoughlin, William G. 153, 154
McNair, David 331, 332, 333, 382
McNair, Delilah Vann 332, 333
McNair, Mary Vann 332
McNeal, Az 199
McPherson, Gen. James B. 6, 7
McReynolds, Zacharia 31
McWhorter, Frank 229

M

Mahone, Walter 39
Major, Mamie 199
Major/Majors, Margaret "Peggy" 195, 196
Manes, Officer Harland F. 14
Martin, Asbury 87
Martin, Candler 224
Martin, Fanny 258, 261
Martin, John (Cherokee Judge) 303-307
Martin, Joseph 305
Martin, Julia 258
Martin, Lucy McDaniel 305
Martin, Nancy 180
Martin, Nellie McDaniel 305
Martin, Roy 224
Martin, Susannah Emory 304-305
Martin, William 254, 267
Masterson, Mary Stuart 293, 294
Mathews, David S. 128
Mathews, Thomas N. 252
Mathis, Susan 243
Matthews, Jasper 243
Matthews, W.D. 391
May, Anna 306
May, William 306
Mealer, Mary 357
Medford, Rachel 236
Meeks, Martha 182
Mercer, J.S. 401
Meriwether, James 67, 68, 275
Merrell, John 291
Merrill, Carrie Lee 227, 229
Merrill, Ella 230
Merrill, Georgia A. 227, 230
Merrill, Henry Albert "Bit" 227, 229
Merrill, Lee 227
Merrill, Lula Miller 227
Merrill, Robert 227
Merrill, Sarah J. 230
Miller, Althea 92
Miller, Henry Clay 87
Miller, Vern 15
Miller, Walter B. 186
Miller, Dr. Wilbur R. 355
Miller, William "Baby-Face Billy" 14
Miner, Bill 184-193
Mintz, H.D. "Cowboy" 377, 378
Mintz, Leonora 371, 372, 377, 415
Mitchell, Jay 475
Mitchell, John E. 443
Mitchell, Brig-Gen (U.S.) Ormsby 75
Mohannee, James 279
Mooney, Walter T. 186
Moore, Fannie 49, 59
Moore, G.W. 258
Moore, George 258, 260
Moore, George W., Jr. 260
Moore, Joseph 252
Moore, Col. Robert Hughes 258
Moore, Susan 48
Moore, Thomas 48
Moore, Tom H. 191
Montgomery, Esther 182
Moran, P.J. 267
Morgan, Mrs. B.T. 415
Morgan, George 184
Morgan, Hugh 415
Morgan, Ludie Ballenger 411
Morgan, W.W. 414
Morrow, Elizabeth 8

Mystery & History in Georgia

Moss, Fannie Mae Floyd 16
Moss, H.R. 374, 378
Moss, John 254
Moss, Louise "Kittie" 225
Moss, Mary 279
Moss, Rubin 279
Mulcahy, Lucy Josephine Cunyus 40
Munford, Lewis Martin 39
Murphey, C.M. 12
Murphey, Frances 11
Murphey, John 11
Murphey, Catherine 11
Murphey, Matthias 11
Murphey, Roger, Jr. 10
Murray, Gov. (Oklahoma) 15
Murrell, John A. 205-208
Murrell, Rev. William 206
Myers, Camille 35, 36
Myers, Joe L. 35, 36
Myers, Joel 35

N

Nash, Frank 15
Nations, David D. 479
Nations, Jasper N. 479
Nations, Joseph 479
Nations, William 479
Neel, Amelia Gaines Anderson
Neel, Anna Anderson 44, 46, 47
Neel, Blanche Hall 45
Neel, Bob
Neel, David W. 44
Neel, Ella ("Aunt Neely") 44, 45
Neel, Fred 45, 47
Neel, Frederick Donald 45
Neel, Gladys 45
Neel, Isabelle ("Izzie") 44, 45
Neel, James Monroe 29, 31, 32, 44, 45, 46, 47
Neel, James Monroe, Jr. ("Uncle Syl") 45, 47
Neel, James Monroe, III 47
Neel, Joseph Francis 44, 45
Neel, Joseph Norris 45
Neel, Capt. Joseph Lockhart 29, 40, 41, 42, 43, 44, 45, 46, 47
Neel, Julia Margaret Anderson 44, 45, 46, 47
Neel, Julia Anderson 45
Neel, Juliet Anderson ("Aunt Dootz") 45
Neel, Leonora 43, 44, 46
Neel, Mary Ann Swain 46
Neel, Mary Ella 45

Neel, Oliver Anderson ("Uncle Poly") 44, 45, 46
Neel, Robert William ("Bob") 45
Neel, Roland Hall 45
Neel, Susan Gaines Anderson 45
Neel, W.J. 44
Neel, Warren Rabun 421
Nelms, Capt. J.W. 367
Newberry, Cub 138
Newborn, R. Seab 344
Newton, Ebenezer 133
Nicely, Martha A. 261
Nichols, Anna Ruby 437, 438, 440
Nichols, Capt. James Hall 436-443, 467
Nichols, Kate Latimer 437, 438, 440, 441
Nichols, Lula 415
Nichols, Smiley 414
Nickel, Dr. Helmut 125
Nixon, Patricia Jordan 183, 204, 420
Nixon, Raymond B. 415
Neisler, Daniel 257
Neisler, Frances "Fannie" 257, 259
Neisler, Mary 188, 257, 258, 259, 261
Newman, Frederick E. 350
Newman, James 255
Nuckolls, Nathaniel 268, 320

O

O'Donnell, Chris 293, 294
O'Grady, Pvt. William 350
Orr, Rev. G.J. 410
Owenby, W.G. 292
Owensby, Jonathan 478

P

Palmour, Aaron 113, 116
Palmour, James Barnes 224
Palmour, John 113
Palmour, John D. 112, 113, 114
Palmour, Mary 113
Palmour, Nancy
Palmour, Silas 106, 111, 112, 113, 114, 115
Palmour, Silas B. 111
Palmour, Solomon 113
Pardo, Juan 126, 298
Parham, J.H. 229

Parker, Fess 168, 451, 452,
Parker, Mary-Louise 293, 294
Parker, Moseley 414
Parks, Benjamin 212
Parks, Joseph E. 73, 80
Parks, Raymond 96, 100
Parrot, John W. 40
Pauley, William C. 87
Payne, Ambrose 254
Payne, George Frederick 440, 443
Payne, George W. 252
Payne, John 252
Payne, Thomas 254
Payne, Thomas W. 254
Peacock, C.H. 346
Peacock, Robert 415
Pedro, Emperor Don 5
Peek, J.A. 410
Peeples, Oscar 39
Percy, Sarah 419, 420
Perkerson, Angus 274
Petit, Susan 360
Pettingill, Proctor 475
Pettyjohn, Arabella 196, 197, 198, 200
Pharr, Dot 344
Phillips, Charles D. (Gen.) 350
Phillips, Jack 402
Phillips, Mrs. Jesse L. 225
Pickens, Andrew 301
Pickens, Slim 168
Pickett, Mrs. J.W. 388
Pierce, Robert M. 370, 373, 374, 376, 377, 378,
Pierce, Sarah Percy 419
Pilcher, Arthur 482, 485
Pilgrim, Alice 243
Pinkerton, William 191
Pinkney, John 310
Pirkle, Jr., Gordon 94
Pirkle, Sr., Gordon 94, 95, 96, 97, 98, 99, 100,
Pirkle, Sanford 137
Pittenger, William 75, 76, 77, 78, 79, 80, 81
Pool, William 255
Porch, Rosa 120
Potts, Grover 15
Price, Col. William Pierce 267, 268, 269, 272, 273, 274, 291, 292
Prior, Andrew 391
Prior, Ann M. 388
Prior, Asa 387, 388, 389, 390, 391, 394, 397, 398

Name Index

Prior, George 397
Prior, Haden 390, 391, 392, 393, 394, 395, 397
Prior, James 393
Prior, John Thomas 388, 392, 393, 394, 395, 396, 397, 398
Prior, Sarah "Sally" 388
Prior, William H.C. 391
Pritchett, Emma 4
Pruitt, J.R. 289
Purvis, (FBI Agent) Melvin 16
Puryear, W.C. 480

Q

Quinn, Mary 6

R

Rackley, Willis 140
Ralston, Lewis 104, 112
Rankin, William Robert 350
Raum, Green B. 355
Ray, Archable 252
Ray, Archibald 253
Ray, Mrs. John A. 484, 485
Ray, Joseph 252, 253
Ray, John D. 252
Ray, Martin 252
Ray, Thomas 255
Raymond, Jeffrey 123
Redden, Steve 123
Reed, Dr. Clinton 87
Reed, John 253
Reed, J.T. "Thomps" 181
Reed, Robert G. 253
Reeve, Jewell B. 151, 154
Reid, Alexander 210, 211
Reid, Elisha 211
Reid, Josephus 211
Reid, Templeton 209-216
Rice, John W. 87, 88
Rice, Parker M. 87
Rice, Zachariah Armistead 88
Richards, Bill 482
Richardson, Gene 123
Richardson, John Henry, Jr. 224
Richardson, L.W. 216
Richardson, Mrs. Lilly 225
Richetti, Adam "Eddy" 15
Rickman, Hester Burns 260
Ridge, John 143, 145, 147, 151, 153, 316, 328
Ridge, Major 142, 143, 144, 145, 146, 147, 148, 151, 152, 153, 316, 317, 328, 333
Ridge, Susannah 144

Ridley, Harmon 227
Riley, Callie 244
Riley, Charles 243
Riley, Clarence 244
Riley, David Sherman 244
Riley, Goliath 243
Riley, Grace 244
Riley, H.W., Jr. 244, 245
Riley, Harrison W. 231-245
Riley, Hattie 244
Riley, Henry 243
Riley, Isaac 234
Riley, Jesse L. 232, 234
Riley, Jesse T. 243
Riley, Josephine 244
Riley, Julia 243
Riley, June 243
Riley, Lonnie 244
Riley, Marley 244
Riley, Mary 233, 243
Riley, Rial 243
Riley, Roy 244
Riley, Sarah Ann 243
Riley, Susan 232, 243
Riley, William 232
Riley, William H. 234
Roach, Hal 93
Roach, Joshua 306
Roberts, Bud 138
Roberts, MacClennan 80, 81
Robinson, Andrew J. 254
Robinson, George R. 250, 254
Robinson, Mrs. Henry 223
Robinson, Lillie Onie 225
Roe, Ancil C. 255
Roe, Solomon 104
Roff, H.J. 485
Rogers, Carl 166
Rogers, Jean 202
Rogers, John 330, 331
Rogers, John Stewart 224
Rogers, John "Nolichucky Jack" 330
Rogers, Johnson 333
Rogers, Joseph 252
Rogers, Mary Vann McNair 332
Rogers, Michael 331
Rogers, Nancy 330
Rogers, Sarah Cordery 331
Rogers, Will 328
Rogers, Will, Jr. 331
Rogers, William 331
Rooker, Tilla 484
Roop, Benjamin Josephus "Ceph" 227, 228, 229

Roop, Bula 227, 230
Roop, Ella 227, 230
Roop, Homer D. (H.D.R.) 227, 230
Roop, Georgia A. Merrill 227, 229, 230
Roop, Martin 227
Roop, Thomas 227, 228, 229
Roper, W.A. 214
Ross, Mrs. Frank 407
Ross, "Chief" John 144, 145, 146, 147, 149, 154, 316, 329, 333, 384
Ruckart, Gordon 85, 88
Ruddell, Clifford 131, 134
Ruede, Louisa 333
Ruff, Henry Clay 85, 87
Ruff, John Wesley 87
Ruff, Martin Luker 82, 83, 84, 86, 87
Ruff, Robert Daniel 83
Russell, Benjamin H. 106
Russell, Charlie 106
Russell, Elizabeth M. 106
Russell, Frances 106, 107
Russell, James 101
Russell, Jane 107
Russell, John 102, 103, 104, 107, 108, 109, 255
Russell, Joseph Oliver 101, 102, 103, 104, 106, 107, 109
Russell, Levi 101, 102, 103, 104, 105, 106, 107, 109, 116
Russell, Meager 255
Russell, Susan 106, 108, 115
Russell, Thomas 106
Russell, William Greenberry "Green" 101, 102, 103, 104, 105, 106, 107, 108, 109, 114, 115, 116
Rusts, Corporal Gus 375
Rutherford, Franklin 243
Rutherford, Gen. Griffin 301
Rutherford, John C. 55, 56, 57
Rutherford, Julia 243

S

Saloshin, Madelyn 93
Samuels, George B. 121
Sanders, Nancy 306
Satterfield, John 112
Satterfield, Mrs. John 279
Satterfield, Sarah Mahala Mary Narcissa 279
Saye, Dr. John 173, 174

499

Mystery & History in Georgia

Saylor, Addie 8
Saylor, B.F.A. 8
Scarborough, Julia Henrietta 2, 3, 4
Scarborough II, William 2, 3
Scott, Father Phillip Paul 14
Scott, Dr. Thomas 88
Scott, Gen. Winfield 314, 385, 386
Scudder, Alfred 309, 310, 315
Seabolt, Elishu 286
Seay, Garnett 99
Seay, Lloyd Grayson 94, 96, 99, 100
Sergeant, Sheriff John 189, 192
Seymour, Dexter C. 209
Seymour, Jefferson 310
Shackleford, Floride Woolfolk Edwards 55, 58
Shadburn, Don L. 111, 112, 130, 131, 133, 136, 153, 154, 309, 310, 331, 386
Shaw, Dorothy Hudgins 194
Shaw (Indian Agent) 382, 383, 386
Shaw, Ray 186
Shaw, Richard 199
Shaw, Stan 293
Shelton, Bill 83
Sherman, T. Rex 346
Sherman, Gen. William T. 18, 19, 23, 34, 36, 41, 49, 115, 248, 251, 272, 274, 281, 338, 437
Sherrill, Cynthia Heard 309
Sherrill, Elie 309
Sherrill, Ernest 130, 131, 133, 134, 314, 315
Shirley, C.H. 186, 187
Shivers, Tom 268, 270, 271, 272
Shope, Roy 166, 169
Shuman, John 482
Seibert, L.I. 375
Silvertooth, Dennis 155
Simmons, S.J. 138
Simmons, W.H. 362
Sitton, James 350
Smedlund, William S. 71, 81
Smith, A.S. 479
Smith, "Bell Tree" 403, 404, 407
Smith, C.L. "Seal" 344, 347
Smith, Charles 138
Smith, Chester 16
Smith, Collins 254
Smith, David 479
Smith, Harry 377

Smith, Mrs. Hocker 414
Smith, J.R. 120
Smith, James F. 151, 153
Smith, Gov. James M. 350, 363
Smith, Marvin 128
Smith, Mrs. Shiloh 225
Smith, Tommie 225
Smith, Verna Cook 229
Smith, Will 403, 404, 407
Snyder, Buck 163
Snyder, John 163
Sorrells, Henry 377
Sosebee, F. Alonzo 431
Sosebee, Gober 96, 97, 98, 100
Southern, Catherine "Kate" Hambrick 356-368
Southern, James 361
Southern, Miles 361
Southern, Robert 357, 360, 361, 362, 363, 366, 367, 368
Southern, William 361
Sparks, Andrew 237
Sparks, Elizabeth 263, 265
Sparks, George 138
Sparks, Johnny 265
Spencer, Col. Thomas 22
Standing, Joseph 476-480
Stanley, Braxton 252
Stanley, Elisha 252
Stanley, Reculious 252
Stanley, Samuel 252
Stanley, Talithla 283
Stanley, William 252
Stanley, William, Jr. 252
Stansberry, Solomon 282, 287, 288, 289, 291
Starr, Emmett 304, 306
Steedman, Gen. (U.S.) James B. 249
Stephenson, Kate 414
Stephenson, Matthew F. 300, 301, 433, 434, 435
Stevens, Robert L. 390
Stevens, Talmadge DeWitt 224
Stowers, Ophelia 113
Stratigos, James 100
Strickland, Hattie 224
Strickland, Irvin, Jr. 180
Strickland, Irvin, Sr. 180
Strickland, John 180
Strickland, LeRoy 225
Strickland, Loyd 180
Stuart, Iley T. 249, 282, 283, 284, 285, 286, 287, 288, 289, 290, 291, 292

Stuart, John 300
Stuart, John A. 138
Stuart, Margaret Hide 289, 290, 291, 292
Stubbs, Eula 410
Styles, Carey W. 362, 365, 366
Sumter, Thomas 301, 302
Suntag, Jack 445
Swain, D.L. 301
Swain, Mary Ann 40
Swain, W. Jesse 43
Swann, F.W. 375
Sylvester, G.W. 475

T

Tankersley, Charles and Napoleon "Boney Tank" 275-280
Tankersley, Charlie, Jr. 280
Tankersley, Jim 279
Tankersley, Malissa "Eliza" Lowe 277, 279
Tankersley, Augustus Henry "Tip-Tank" 276, 278, 279
Taonk, Henry 279
Taonk, Napoleon 279
Taonk, Sally 279
Tandy, Jessica 293, 294
Tanner, David 182, 197
Tanner, George Washington 198
Tanner, Gladys 224
Tanner, Matthew, Jr. 182
Tanner, Rebecca Hawkins 201
Tanner, Sarah "Sallie" Elizabeth 196, 197, 204
Tant, Emily Norvell 89, 90
Tant, Sam 91
Tate, Grace 225
Tate, Sam 346
Teague, William 138
Tench, Rev. Hoyt 157-164
Tennille, Amelia 92
Terrapin, Old 324
Thomas, Gen. (U.S.) George H. 249, 251
Thomas, Joe, Sr. 237
Thomas, John 290
Thomas, Mary Addie 224
Thompson, Howard 190
Thompson, James 252
Thompson, Joe 225
Thornton, Elizabeth 329, 330, 332
Tierney, Luke 104, 105
Tilly, Benjamin M. 138

Name Index

Todd, Captain Isaac L. 240
Tollison, A.B. 134, 136
Townsend, David 255
Townsend, Ken 126
Trimble, A.C. 40
Trippe, Robert B. 44
Troup, Gov. George 60
Troutman, M.L. 410
Turner, Charlie 262-266
Turner, George H. 254
Turner, Jesse 288
Turner, Nath 377
Turner, O.P. 253
Turner, Tandy W. 254
Turpen, Jim 177
Turpin, Drucy 175, 176
Tustinugee, Tom 63
Twiggs, William A. 249, 282, 283, 284, 285, 286, 287, 288, 290
Tyson, Cicely 293, 294,

U

Ulio, Lt. James 352
Upshaw, Louisa Elizabeth 411

V

Vandiver, Jerry 455, 456, 457, 458, 459, 462, 463, 464
Van Dyke, Benjamin 289
Vandergriff, J.W. 138
Vann, Avery 328
Vann, David 325
Vann, Delilah Amelia 329, 332, 333
Vann II, James 129-136, 307, 315, 316, 325, 328, 329, 330, 332, 382
Vann, James Clement 327
Vann, James Clement I 327
Vann, J. Raymond 133, 134, 136
Vann, Joseph "Rich Joe" 133, 329
Vann, Mary 332
Vann, Nancy 306
VanZant, Lewis 285
Van Dorn, MG Earl 148
Vaughters, Lindsay 250
Vaughters, Linza 254

W

Wager, John N. 291
Walker, Bert 14
Walker, Brawner 163
Walker, Rev. Charles O. 133, 305
Walker, Mary Page 93

Walker, William 310
Waller, Charlie 118, 121
Waller, John 117, 118, 120, 121
Waller, Lula 121
Walthall, Linton H. 382, 383, 387
Ward, James Mohannee 279
Ward, Lucy 279
Ward, Noah 162
Warren, J.W. 477
Warren, Jeremiah 255
Washington, Gen. George 324, 419
Waters, Ellen 225
Waters, George 321
Waters, Ruth Smith 181
Watie, Buck 328, 330
Watie, David 141, 143, 145
Watie, Elizabeth 145
Watie, Eleanor 145
Watie, Isabella 145
Watie, Sarah 145
Watie, Stand 141-154
Watie, Susannah 145
Watkins, Elias 255
Watkins, Sam 41, 42
Watts, George 389
Watts, John B. 191
Weaver, Daniel 236
Weaver, James M. 255
Weems, Charley 97, 98, 100
Welch, Susannah 267
West, Amos 400
West, Ben 225
West, Columbus J. 255
West, Matilda 398
West, T.J. 401
West, Temperance 52, 55, 59
West, W.P. 401
West, William E. 389, 398
Whatley, Elizabeth Lumpkin 381, 384
Whatley, George Fields 398
Whatley, Hampton 387
Whatley, Martha Cordelia 380
Whatley, W.O.B. 380, 381, 384, 388
Whatley, Wilson Ornan Burwell 380
Wheaton, Steve 9
Wheeler, Benjamin 400
Wheeler, C.M. 401
Whisenhunt, J.W. 374
Whitaker, Mrs. J.W. 374
White, Kathryn Gray- 59

White, Gaz 39
White, Mae Woody 431
White, R.P. 414
White, Robert 22
White, Samuel 138
Whitehead, Lois 225
Whitehead, Martha Cordelia Whatley 380, 381
Whitley, Henry 80
Whittle, J.W. 191
Whittle, John 120
Whittle, Ora 118, 121
Wiesner, Albert 475
Wiesner, Ursula 475
Wiggins, W.M. 192
Williams, Mrs. Alice 374
Williams, Carrie Lee 225
Williams, Edgar 415
Williams, Edgar Lee 225
Williams, Edwin 467
Williams, George Walton 440, 443, 467
Williams, Goldie 374
Williams, J.R. 149
Williams, James E. 270
Williams, Jeri Lynn 294
Williams, Lucy 415
Williams, Capt. (C.S.A.) Marion 286, 287, 288
Williams, Mollie Butts 225
Williams, Robert 294
Williams, Col. Samuel C. 354, 355
Williams, Tannie 441
Williams, Wendell 415
Williams, William W. 253
Williamson, Maj. Andrew 301
Williamson, Annie 414
Williamson, Mrs. Tom Clements 414
Wilson, Carter 347
Wilson, John 291, 389
Wilson, John A. 81
Wilson, Lorene 224
Wilson, Richard 459
Wilson, Thomas 287, 291
Wimpy, John 290, 291
Windencamp, W.J. 192
Windham, Melvin 118, 119, 121
Winn, Elisha 182
Wiseman, Edward 375
Witherow, Alfred H. 243
Witherow, Alice 243
Witherow, John 243
Witherow, Kirby 243

Witherow, Lorena 243
Witherow, Nancy 243
Witt, William R. 283, 287, 288, 289, 291
Wofford, W.T. 44
Wood, Byrd 229
Wood, Elizabeth "Eliza" 240, 244
Woods, Jim 402
Woodward, Dave 405
Woody, Abraham Lincoln 424
Woody, Axey Seabolt 425
Woody, Clyne Edward 425, 427, 431
Woody, Eliza Ingram 424, 425
Woody, Emma June Abercrombie 425
Woody, John Wesley 425
Woody, Mae 425, 431
Woody, Robert 252

Woody, Robert P. 139, 140
Woody, Walter W. 425, 431
Woody, Ranger William Arthur 424-431
Woolfolk, Annie 52, 53, 54
Woolfolk, Charles H. 52, 55, 59
Woolfolk, Floride 49, 55, 58
Woolfolk, Georgia Bird 51, 56
Woolfolk, Lillie 49, 55
Woolfolk, Mattie Howard 50, 51, 52, 55
Woolfolk, Pearl 52, 55, 56
Woolfolk, Richard, Jr. 52, 55, 59
Woolfolk, Capt. Richard Franklin 48, 49, 50, 52, 55, 58, 59
Woolfolk, Rosebud 52, 55
Woolfolk, Susan Moore 48, 49, 59
Woolfolk, Thomas (the elder) 48

Woolfolk, Thomas G. "Tom" 48-59
Woolfolk, Thomas Moore 48
Wordsworth, William 9
Worley, T.H. 289
Wynn, Jack 432, 433, 435

Y

Yeager, Wayne 133, 134, 135, 136
Young, Col. (U.S.) Isham G. 282, 288, 291
Young, Wilson Abercrombie 255

Z

Zuker, Annie Jane 380, 381, 386
Zbar, Jack 134, 135, 136

Subject Index

A
A Breed Apart 97
A Chump at Oxford 93
A Circuit Rider's Wife 24-27, 444
A City Laid Waste 218
Adairsville 10, 31, 42
Agate (Vann's Valley) 325
Agents That Fly 97
Alabama Road 63, 105, 180, 308-326
Alabama Territory 308
Alcohol, Tobacco & Firearms 97
Allatoona Dam 22
Allatoona Mountain Range 17
Allatoona Pass 17-23
American Numismatic Society 209
American Polearms 73
American Revolution 195
American Textile Company 47
Anderson, Capt, Whit, gunfight 268-270
Anderson, Capt. Whit, death of 274
Anderson (SC) Independent Mail 58
Anderson's Ferry 313
Annals of Athens 59
Anti-Treaty Faction (of *Treaty of New Echota*) 142-153
Appalachian Trail 421
Archaeology 122-128
Arkansas Gazette 155
Army of Tennessee 41
Assassinate 232, 236
Assayer 210
Assault & battery 235, 236
Athens Southern Banner 81

Athens Weekly Banner Watchman 58
Atlanta Conservatory of Music 91
Atlanta Constitution 54, 217-225, 228
Atlanta Journal 27, 85, 133, 188, 217-225
Atlanta, Muhlenbrink's Saloon 268, 270
Atlanta Rolling Mill 276
Attempted murder 237
Auraria 101, 268, 270, 271, 279, 320
Auraria Cemetery 267, 274
Auraria Church 274
Auraria, Graham Hotel 271, 273, 279
Auraria, Paschal Hotel 271, 279
Auto races/racing 94-100

B
Baldwin Hotel 91
Ballenger Hall 24-25
Bank of Darien 320
Bank robberies 13-16
Barnsley Gardens 1-9
Barnsley Gardens, "Woodlands" manor 3, 4
Barton's Brigade 41
Bartow County Courthouse 35
Bartow County Genealogical Society 37
Bartow County Heritage Book, Volume I 34, 37
Bartow History Center 35
Battle of Allatoona Pass 17-23
Battle of Atlanta 41, 43, 272
Battle of Chattanooga 41
Battle of Chickamauga 41, 247

Battle of First Manassas 271, 276
Battle of Horseshoe Bend 143, 155
Battle of Kennesaw Mountain 41
Battle of Mabila 127
Battle of Missionary Ridge 41
Battle of New Hope Church 41
Battle of Peachtree Creek 41
Battle of Resaca 29, 41
Battle of Ruff's Mill 85, 87, 88
Battle of Second Manassas 269
Battle of Shiloh 41
Battle of Vicksburg 43
Bears 262-266
Bears dancing 264
Besser Hotel, Dahlonega 242, 245
Bibb County 48
Bible 27
Big Savannah 102, 105, 108, 109, 110, 112, 113, 115, 313, 314
Big Savannah Post Office 314
Big Shanty 19, 40, 70, 72, 73, 76, 77, 78
Bill Elliott Day 96
Bill Elliott Museum 95
Bill Elliott Street 95
Black Diamond Railroad 169
Black Fox 132
Blackburn Cemetery 129-136
Blackburn's Public House 130, 131, 132, 133, 314, 315
Blood Mountain 297-302
Blue Mountain Masonic Lodge 103
Blue Ridge Railroad 169
Bog gardens 9
Bolding covered bridge 205, 206, 313

503

Bolding house 205, 208
"bootlegger" 121
Brainerd Missionary Station 318
Brainerd Road 318
Brazil 7
Brenau College 217, 220
British consulate 7
Brown's Bridge Road 217
Buffington's Tavern 129-136, 315
Bulloch's Barn 322
Button Gwinnett Hotel 91

C

C.V. Nalley Company ruins 219
"Cabin District" 66
California gold coins 209
Camp McDonald 40, 70, 71, 72, 73, 74, 75, 76, 77, 78, 80
Camp meetings 208
Camp Fires of Georgia's Troops, 1861-1865 81
Cape, Lee, murder and decapitation 345-346
"carpetbagger" 272
Carroll County Times 228
Carter Lake 304
Carter Lake Dam 304
Carter's Quarters 303-307
Cartersville 13, 17
Cartersville City Directory 47
Cartersville Daily Tribune 36
Cartersville Depot 22
Cass Station 316
Cassville 12, 28, 32
Cassville Cemetery 39
Castleberry Bridge Road, Auraria 269
Cave Spring 325
Cedar Town 379-384
Cedar Town Baptist Church 389
Cedar Town Big Spring 388, 390
Cedar Town, Char'le Town, Indian town 382
Cedar Town, "Charley Town" Indian town 382
Cedar Town burned 391-392
Cedar Town Cherokees 385
Cedar Town Cherokee Indian raids 384, 385
Cedar Town Cherokee Indian raids in Vann's Valley 385
Cedar Town Cherokees removal to the West 385-386, 387

Cedar Town Cherokees stockade 385
Cedar Town, Greenwood's gristmill (later Judkin's Mill) 389, 390
Cedar Town, Greenwood's residence 380
Cedar Town, Walthall, L.H., trading post of 382
Cedar Town, outlaws 392-396
Cedar Town, Prior, Asa, gristmill (later Benedict gristmill) 389-390, 398
Cedar Town, Prior Station 390, 397
Cedar Town, Watts, George, gristmill 389
Cedar Town, Wilson, John, gristmill (later Elias Dorsey Hightower gristmill) 389
Cedartown, Civil War 391-393
Cedartown, Civil War outlaws at 392-394
Cedartown, Colquitt gang in 393-394
Cedartown, "Old Mill Restaurant" in 390
Cedartown, Sheriff Frank Lott murder 404-405
Central City, CO 105, 107
Champion's Hill 41
Chattahoochee High School, Clermont 200, 201, 203
Chattahoochee River 60-62
1836 Cherokee Valuations 306
Cherokee, blood law 146, 147
Cherokee, Death Squads 141-153, 317
Cherokee, destruction of Lower Settlements 301
Cherokee, destruction of Middle Settlements 301
Cherokee, destruction of Overhill Settlements 301
Cherokee, genealogy 306
Cherokee Advocate 132
Cherokee Constitution 145, 305
Cherokee Constitutional Convention 305
Cherokee Coosawattee River House 304-309
Cherokee Council 144
Cherokee County Home Guard 250
Cherokee Indian Letters 306

Cherokee Mounted Volunteers 147
Cherokee National Capital 144
Cherokee National Counsel 132
Cherokee Phoenix 150, 151, 152, 156, 330
Cherokee Planters in Georgia, 1832-1838 111
Cherokee Police 144
Cherokee Supreme Court 145
Cherokee valuations 382-384
Cherokee violence 384-385
Cherokees 3, 10, 28, 29, 101, 104, 108, 109, 112, 129-136, 141-153, 279, 300, 305, 310, 327, 379-386, 382-384
Cherokees, Red River, Texas, resettlement in 149-150
Cherokees Removal of 1838 305, 321, 379-386
Chestatee River 205, 208, 257
Chestnut Mountain 179-183
Chief Collard 379-386
Chief Collard and sons, photo 380
Chief Collard and sons, photo description 383
Chief Collard, dispossession 383
Chief Collard, dwelling description 381
Chief Collard, name origin 379, 380
Chief Collard, property valuation 379, 382, 383
Chief Collard, son, property valuation 382, 384
Chief Collard, sons return to Cedar Town 380-381
Chief John Ross House 316-317
Chieftains 148, 316, 317
Choctaw Nation 205
Cincinnati Enquirer 54
Clayton-Mooney House 18-23
Clermont, Hudgins Store 199, 201, 203
Clermont ("Miller's") Hotel 202
Cliff House 174, 177
Climb The Hills of Gordon 151
Cobb County 82-88
1851 Cobb County Tax Digest 84
Coin-maker 209-216
Collard Valley, Georgia, 1832 Map Survey 385

504

Subject Index

Collard Valley, Georgia, name source 379-386
Colonial Churches of Tidewater Virginia 195
Colorado Rocky Mountains 101
Company Aytch 41
Concord Baptist Church 85, 201
Concord Baptist Church Cemetery 203
Concord Covered Bridge 82-88
Concord Manufacturing Company 86
Concord Woolens Mill 84
Confederate Army 17-23, 29, 48, 70-81, 141, 232, 246-255, 269
Confederate Army desertion 281-292
Confederate Conscription Act of 1862 246
Confederate guerrillas 281-292
Confederate "Home Guard" 246-255, 281-292
Confederate Georgia 282
Confederate Veteran 73
Confederate war bonds 6
Confederate War Department 71
Cookson Hills 13
Cooper Manufacturing Company 221
Cooper Pants Factory deaths 221, 223
Coosa River Valley 309-310, 311
Courant American 36
Covered bridges 205-208
Creek Indian Nation 60-69
Creek Indians 60-69, 142, 143
Creek Indians, "Red Stick" faction, 143
Creek War of 1813 155

D
Daffodil Farm 151
Dahlonega, GA 292
Dahlonega, Chestatee Street town lots 234-235
Dahlonega, Eagle Hotel 235, 242, 245
Dahlonega, gold coins minted 239
Dahlonega, Gold Diggers Road 102, 269, 270, 271, 279, 312, 320
Dahlonega, gold dredging barge 261
Dahlonega, Hope house 258
Dahlonega, Old Lumpkin County Courthouse 287-289
Dahlonega, W.H. Early house 259
Danish Battle of Wisby 126
Daring and Suffering 81
Dawson's Ferry 323
Dawsonville, Gober Sosebee Street 96
Dawsonville Highway 217
Dawsonville Poolroom 95, 96
Daytona 500 95, 96, 97
Daytona Beach Race 98
Daytona International Speedway 95
De Soto, Hernando 122-128, 298, 468-470
De Soto, Expedition 128, 468-470
De Soto Trail Study 128
Denver, CO 101
Diesel-Electric ("Dinky") Mail Car 161
Diary of an Illinois Soldier 6
"The Dividings" 311, 315
Dixie Hunt Hotel 188, 190
"Double Cabins" 66
Doublehead Gap 137, 138, 139
Dougherty, GA 112, 312, 313, 314
Dougherty Post Office 314
Downing's Ferry 316
Dr. A.C. Hendrick Memorial Bridge 57
Draper Manuscripts 301-302

E
Earl's Ford 310, 311
East Tennessee Railroad 75
Ebenezer Newton's Diary 131, 133
Echols family photo 12
Electric chair 14
Elliott Family Parkway 96
Elliott, Bill, *Winston 500* win 95
Elliott, Bill, *Winston Cup* win 95
Elliott, Bill, *World 600* win 95
England 4
English boxwoods 5
Erie County Penitentiary 139
Esom Hill, "Bell Tree" Smith 403-404
Esom Hill, "Moonshine" violence 402-403
Esom Hill, "Prohibition" 402-403
Esom Hill, Bailey family 405
Esom Hill, Brewster General Store 401
Esom Hill, Brewster Mercantile Company 401
Esom Hill, GA 399-407
Esom Hill, Griffith's Cash Store 406
Esom Hill, iron ore industry of 400-401
Esom Hill, Isbell General Store 401
Esom Hill, Mercer General Store 401
Esom Hill, moonshine 399-407
Esom Hill, post offices 401-402
Esom Hill, Sheriff Frank Lott murder 404-405
Esom Hill, Shiloh Baptist Church 399-400
Esom Hill, Shiloh Baptist Church Cemetery 401
Esom Hill, West & Hackney Gristmill 401
Esom Hill, Wheeler Saloon 401
Etowah Indian Mounds 44, 297, 323, 326
Etowah River 101
Etowah River Road 112
Etowah River Valley 313
Etowah Valley Historical Society 21, 22, 36, 38
Excavation 134-135

F
"fat lighter," use of 63
FBI 15, 16
Federal Building, Gainesville 222
1820 Federal Census, Hall Co. 180, 182, 196
1830 Federal Census, Habersham Co. 267
1830 Federal Census, Paulding Co. 380
1834 Federal Census, Lumpkin County 234
1835 Federal Census Rolls of the Cherokees 306
1838 Federal Census, Lumpkin County 234
1850 Federal Census, Cass Co. 29
1850 Federal Census, Gordon Co. 40

1850 Federal Census, Hall Co. 182
1850 Federal Census, Lumpkin Co. 267, 279
1850 Federal Census, Muscogee Co. 216
1850 Federal Census, Sutter Co., California 268
1860 Federal Census of Arkansas 11
1860 Federal Census, Cass Co. 29
1860 Federal Census, Fulton Co. 269
1860 Federal Census, Lumpkin Co. 243
1870 Federal Census, Bartow Co. 35
1880 Federal Census, Bartow Co. 32
1884 Federal Census, Eastern Cherokees 279
Federal Property Evaluation of 1836, Cherokee Lands 305
Federal Road 129, 130, 133, 180, 181, 306, 309, 314, 315, 329
First Georgia Regulars 269
First National Bank of Cartersville 47
Floyd, Charles Arthur "Pretty Boy," Kansas City Massacre involvement 15
Floyd, Charles Arthur "Pretty Boy" photo 11
Folsom, GA 14
Fort Buffington 315
Fort Cedar Town 385
Fort Gilmer 315
Fort Mountain 297-302
Fort Smith Road 106
Foster Bend 122-128
Foster's Mill 326
Fra Diavolo 93
Fried Green Tomatoes 293-296
Fulton County Jail 273

G

7th Georgia Confederate Infantry Regiment 276
1936 Gainesville Tornado 217-225
1936 Gainesville Tornado, deaths 217-225
1936 Gainesville Tornado, destruction of Gainesville Midland Railway yard 225
1936 Gainesville Tornado, disaster report(s) 217-225
1936 Gainesville Tornado, freaks of 223
1936 Gainesville Tornado, town square destruction of 220
1936 Gainesville Tornado, victims of 223
1936 Gainesville Tornado, West Spring Street devastation from 218
G.W. Moore Coal Company 258
Gainesville Mint 209, 210
Gainesville-Northwestern Railroad 201, 203, 443
Gamblers 233
Gann House 85
Garden of Valhalla Memorial Park 93
Georgia forestry management 424-431
Georgia forestry management, Charles Elliott 428
Georgia forestry management, Ranger Arthur Woody 424-431
Georgia General Assembly 232, 237
Georgia gold 208-213
Georgia Gold Rush 212
Georgia Historical Quarterly 59
Georgia House of Representatives 239
1st Georgia Infantry Battalion 251
40th Georgia Infantry Regiment 40, 41
41st Georgia Infantry Regiment 40, 41
42nd Georgia Infantry Regiment 40, 41
43rd Georgia Infantry Regiment 40, 41
52nd Georgia Infantry Regiment 40, 41, 238
1st Georgia State Cavalry 250
1st Georgia State Line Infantry Regiment ("Fulton Dragoons") 277
1st Georgia State Line Troops 31
1st Georgia State Troops Volunteers 249, 250, 251
Georgia Journal 211
Georgia Land Lottery 84
Georgia Military Academy 91, 92
Georgia Military Institute 74
"Georgia Pike" 72
Georgia Racing Hall of Fame 94
Georgia Railroad 30, 89
Georgia State Bar Association 44, 47
Georgia State Legislature 40, 47, 85, 96
Georgia State Penitentiary 140
Georgia State Railroad 75
Georgia State University 126
Georgia Supreme Court 55, 56, 57
Georgian Terrace Hotel 93
Germany 8
Gold bullion 240
Gold clock 4
Gold coins 209-216
Gold mining 101-109, 231, 256-261, 702
Gold rush 231, 234
Gothic Revival architecture 34
Governor Wilson Lumpkin and Cherokee dispossession 384
Grand Cherokee National Council of 1782 324
Gravatt family, French Huguenot ancestry of 416-420
Gravatt family, Jordan family connection with 416-420
Gravatt family, Pennsylvania ancestry of 417-420
Gravatt family, Pennsylvania family cemetery 420
Gravatt family, Polk County, GA 416-420
"Great Freeze of 1892" 32
Great Locomotive Chase, filming of 70, 79, 80, 168, 450-453
Great Locomotive Chase, Walt Disney Productions filming of 449-453
Greek Revival architecture 4
"Grey Fox" 191, 192
Grimes Knoll, Indian battle of 300
gunfight 137, 231, 242, 268, 270, 271

H

Hall County Police 188
Harmony-Hall Baptist Church 200

Subject Index

Harpers Weekly 6
Harrison's Ferry 313
Hatton's Ford 313
Hawk's Store 316
Hazel Creek 159
Heard County 226
Henry Clay Ruff House 87
Hightower Crossroads 309, 314
Hightower Indian Path 321
Hillabatchee Creek 226-230
Hills Switch School 311-312
Historic Bartow County, Circa (1828-1866) 38, 40
Historic Buildings Survey 235
History of Lumpkin County, (1832-1932) 233, 235, 236
Hollywood 25, 89, 93, 444-464
Hollywood film-makers in north Georgia 444-464
"Honest Man's Friend and Protector (HMF&P)" 334-337
Honey Creek 153
Hong Kong 7
Hope House 258
Hopewell Culture 299
Hudgins Store 199, 201, 203
Huerfano Valley 108

I

I Wandered Lonely As A Cloud 9
I'd Climb the Highest Mountain, Autry family home filming site 463
I'd Climb the Highest Mountain, Chattahoochee United Methodist Church filming site 461
I'd Climb the Highest Mountain, Cooley General Store filming site 458, 461-463
I'd Climb the Highest Mountain, E.B. Hunt family home filming site 461, 463
I'd Climb the Highest Mountain, filming of 24-27, 164, 167, 444-450, 454-464
I'd Climb the Highest Mountain, Nora Mill drowning scene filming site 460
I'd Climb the Highest Mountain, Old Demorest Depot, opening credits filming site 460
I'd Climb the Highest Mountain, Sunday School picnic filming site 461

illegitimate children 234
"In The Valley" 26-27
Indian agents Shaw and McMillin 382
Indian Creek Church 313
Indian Removal Bill 333
Indian Spring 66
Ireland 210
iron ore mining 400
Ivy Woolens Mill 322

J

James Vann II, home 327
James Vann II, *Last Will & Testament* 330
James Vann II, murder 329
"Joe Brown Pike" 72, 73, 74, 80
Judge John Martin house 304-307
Joseph E. Brown and the Confederacy 81

K

Kansas 15
Kansas City Massacre 15
Kansas Territory 103
Karankawa Indians 155
Kennesaw House 76
Kennesaw State University 27
Kentucky 14
"King Site" 122-128
Kingston Parish, Virginia 194
Kingston Parish Register, Virginia 194, 195
Kingston Road 316
Kolomoki Indian Mounds 297

L

L.H. Walthall trading post, Cedar Town 382
Laboratory 8
Lacy Hotel 70, 72, 76, 79
Lake Lanier 206
Lakemont 169
Lakewood 100 99, 100
Lakewood Speedway 99, 100
1832 Land Lottery of Georgia 84, 306
Landrum 312, 313
Laurel & Hardy 89-93
Laurel & Hardy, Atoll K 93
Laurel & Hardy, Babes in Toyland 93
Laurel & Hardy, Flying Deuces 93

Laurel & Hardy, Hal Roach Studios 93
Laurel & Hardy, Hardy House 90
Laurel & Hardy, Harlem, GA 89
Laurel & Hardy, Pardon Us 93
Laurel & Hardy, Putting Pants on Philip 93
Laurel & Hardy, Saps at Sea 93
Laurel & Hardy, Sons of the Desert 93
Laurel & Hardy, Turnell-Butler Hotel 89, 90, 91
Laws of the Cherokees 132
Leather's Ford 101, 310, 312, 324
Liberty Church 66
Library of Congress 235
Limestone (Euharlee) Creek 323
Liverpool 3
Locomotive *General* 21, 70, 72, 78, 79
Locust Stake Road 311
London Cash Store 260
London, Jim, family 258
London, Merritt, family 258
Long Branch community 257
Long Branch Road 257, 259
Lookout Mountain, Tennessee 76
Lost Colony of Roanoke 297
Lott, Sheriff Frank murder 404-405
Louisville & Nashville (L&N) Railroad 47
"Lower Alabama Roads" 319-326
Lucy Cobb Institute 56
Lumpkin County Volunteers, Mexican War 268
Luna Expedition 125-126
Lynch Mountain, Indian battle of 300

M

M.M. London & Sons Cash Store 260
Macland Cemetery 14
Macon Evening News 54, 55, 56
Macon Telegraph 52, 53, 57, 58, 59
Madison Grammar School 91
Manifest Destiny 275
Marietta 17

Mystery & History in Georgia

Marietta House 77, 78
Marietta Journal 86
Marietta Railroad Depot 76
Martin Feed & Grain 87
Martin's Ford, Chestatee River 261
Mathews Baptist Church, Virginia 195
Mathews County, Virginia 195
McClure Cemetery, Dahlonega 106
McGuire's Soda Fountain, Dahlonega 260
McIntosh, Chief William, murder of 60-69
McIntosh Ferry 66
McIntosh Reserve 66-67
McIntosh Road 66
McNair, David, grave 333
McNair, Delilah Vann, grave 333
McNair Stand 332
Medford's one-cent pipes 237
Memory Hill Cemetery 193
Merrill-Roop Cemetery 228
Merrill's Mill Disaster 226-230
Methodist minister 24-27
Mexican War 233, 268
Michigan International Speedway 95
Mill Grove 85
Milledgeville 89, 90, 91, 436
Milledgeville Argus 211
Milledgeville, Midway community 436
Miner, Bill, robberies and escapades 184-193
Miner, Bill, burial, Memory Hill Cemetery 193
Missionary Ridge, TN 318
135th Mississippi Regiment 23
Missouri 14
Missouri State Penitentiary 14
"Money Panic of 1857" 103
"Moonshine" 94-100, 117-121, 137, 277, 334-337, 341-347, 348-355, 399-407
"Moonshine" arrests 348-355
"Moonshine" distillery 117, 138, 341-347, 348-355, 399-407
"Moonshine" informants 335-337, 348-355, 399-407
"Moonshine" violence 334-337, 341-347, 348-355, 399-407
Moore Hall (originally Harrison Riley's Eagle Hotel) 245

Moore, J.W. Store 260
Moravian Mission, Brainerd 318
Moravian Mission, Carmel 181, 306
Moravian Mission, Etowah 323, 326
Moravian Mission, Oothcaloga 144
Moravian Mission, Pumpkin Vine 323, 326
Moravian Mission, Spring Place 329
Moravian Mission School 143
Moravian Missionaries 132, 136, 304, 306
Mormons, hostility against 476-480
Mormons, murder of 478-480
Mormons shunning Mormons 477
Morrow Cemetery 153
Motorsports Hall of Fame of America 96
Mt. Vernon Church 66
Muhlenbrink's Saloon, Atlanta 268, 270
Mule Camp Springs 312, 324
Murder in Pickens County 345-346, 348-355, 356-368
Murders 15
Murrell gang 205-208

N

Nacoochee, battle of 300
Nacoochee Indian Mounds 297, 439
Nacoochee Valley 312, 436-443
Nacoochee Valley, antiquities/artifacts 439
Nacoochee Valley, Daniel Brown gristmill 441
Nacoochee Valley, Col. James Hall Nichols, death of 442
Nacoochee Valley, Col. James Hall Nichols departure 441
Nacoochee Valley, Nichols-Hardman home 438-439
Nacoochee Valley, saw-milling 442
NASCAR 94
NASCAR *Brickyard 400* 95
NASCAR "Most Popular Driver Award" 95
NASCAR Nationwide Series 97
NASCAR Racing Hall of Fame 100

Napoleon and His Marshals 56
Natchez Trace 207
National Climatic Center 218
National Mint 210
National Register of Historic Places 82, 83, 84, 87, 88, 307, 338, 347
National Society for the Preservation of Covered Bridges 88
Native American artifacts 9
Neel & Peeples 44
Neel's Gap 262, 421-423
Neel's Gap and Appalachian Trail 421
Neel's Gap and Vogel Leather Tanning Company 421
Neel's Gap, name origin 421
Neel Pleading Act 47
Neisler's Ford 259
Neisler's Road / wagon trail 257
New Echota 136, 144, 150, 156, 316, 330
New Echota State Historic Site 307
New Holland 217, 220
New Hope Road 322
New Orleans 3
New Town (Newtown) Road 316, 323
New York Independent Magazine 24
New York Times 54, 276
New York World 276, 278
Nichols-Hardman home 438
Nickajack Creek 82
Nickajack Post Office 86
"Night Riders" of Pickens County 334-337
North Carolina & St. Louis Railway (NC& St. L) 47
North Georgia "Moonshine" War of 1876-'77 348-355
Northeast Georgia Medical Center 217
Nuckollsville 268, 273, 278, 320

O

Oak Hill Cemetery 39
Oconee River Navigation Company 211
Ohio 14
Oklahoma 14, 15
Old Alabama Road 194, 308-326

508

Subject Index

Old Dawsonville Highway 208
Old England Gold Mine, White County 471-475
Old England Gold Mine, White County, litigation of 473-475
Old Federal Road 309, 314, 316, 318
Old Fort Wayne 147, 153
Old Hall County Courthouse 222
Old Liberty Methodist Church 183
Old London home-place 256-261
Old London home-place store 256-261
Old Lumpkin County Jail 192, 193
Old Madison Alabama Stage Road 66
Old Milton County 320
Old Piedmont Institute, Rockmart 408-415
Old Rockmart High School 25, 408
Old Settlers 146
Old West legends 275
Old West outlaw 256-261
Old Whitehall Street, Atlanta 268, 270
Oothcaloga Baptist Church 31
Oothcaloga Moravian Mission 145, 152, 153
Orange Hill Cemetery 58
outlaws 205-208, 256, 276, 334-337, 338-340, 341-347

P

1923 Pickens County Jail-break 338-340
Paintings 4
Palmour Gristmill 112
Panther Creek Trestle 159
Pardo, Juan Expedition 126, 298
Park Hill 153
Paschal Hotel 271, 279
Path Killer 132
Paulding County, Civil War in 391
Paulding County, Van Wert, town of 391
Peachtree Street 93
Pennsylvania College of Medicine & Surgery 102

Perry Rifles 57
Petroglyphs at Track Rock Gap 432-435
Petroglyphs at Track Rock Gap, Matthew F. Stephenson visit to 433-435
Petroglyphs at Track Rock Gap, origin of 432, 433
Petsworth Baptist Church, Virginia 195
Petsworth Parish, Virginia 195
Petsworth Parish Episcopal Church, Virginia 194
Philadelphia Mint 215
Pickens County "Moonshine" 341-347
Pickens Trail 313
Pictorial History of the Great Rebellion 75
Piedmont Institute, bankruptcy of 413
Piedmont Institute, graduates of 414-415
Piedmont Institute, Rockmart, GA 24-26, 408-415
Pike's Peak Gold Rush 101, 105, 107
Pinkerton Detective Agency 191
Pittsburgh Dispatch 58
plantation owners 231
Polk County, GA, frontier days of 387-398
Polson Cemetery 153
Ponce De Leon, train wreck of 1926 369-378
Ponce De Leon, train wreck of 1926, causes of 375-378
prehistoric aborigines 122-128, 299
prehistoric artifacts 299
Price Memorial Hall 216
Prior, Anna Lou, photograph of 388
Prior, Ann M., photograph of 388
Prior, Asa, burial of 391
Prior, Asa, departure from Georgia 391
Prior, Asa, family in Paulding (Polk) County, GA 387-398
Prior, Asa, gristmill, Cedar Town, GA 389, 395
Prior, Haden, murder of 394
Prior, John T., death of 394
Prior, John T., photograph of 388

Prior, plantation site 394
Prior, Sarah, burial of 388
Prison escapees 338-340
Prohibition 98
Pruitt-Barrett Hardware Company ruins 219

Q

Queen's Trestle 161

R

Railroad boxcar 28-30
"Rails To Trails" 166
Ralston's Creek 104
Rare gold coins 209-216
"Reconstruction" 137, 272
Red Cross 218, 219, 221
Red River, Texas resettlement 149-150
"Red Stick" Creek Indians 143
Reid, Templeton, coining mint 209-216
Reid, Templeton, gold coins 209-216, 239
Reid, Templeton, ten-dollar gold coin 209
Revival 208
Revolutionary War 195
Rhododendron gardens 9
Rice House 88
Rice Station 87
Ridge Cemetery 153
Ridge Toll Ferry 316
Riley, Harrison, burial of 245
Riley, Harrison, death of 245
Riley, Harrison, hidden gold 232, 239, 240
Riley, Harrison, hotel 235, 242, 245
Riley, Harrison, illegitimate children of 241, 242, 243
Riley, Harrison, *Last Will & Testament* 239, 243, 244
Riley, Harrison, tavern 235
Riley, Harrison, treasure of 232, 239, 240
Ringgold Church 66
"Rock Spring" 305-306, 307
Rock House 87
Rockbridge Road 321
Rockmart, Ballenger Hall 411
Rockmart, Ballenger Street 411
Rockmart, GA 24-26, 412
Rockmart, GA and best-selling *A Circuit Rider's Wife* 412-413

509

Rockmart, GA and famed author Cora Harris 412
Rockmart, GA and major motion picture *I'd Climb the Highest Mountain* 412-413
Rockmart train wreck of 1926 369-378
Rockmart train wreck of 1926, causes of 375-378
Rockmart train wreck of 1926, fatalities from 373-374
Rome Georgia Light Guard 7
Royal Palm train wreck of 1926 369-378
Royal Palm train wreck of 1926, causes of 375-378
Rucker Family Home 325
Ruff & Daniel Mill 87
Ruff Family Cemetery 86
Ruff's Gristmill 82-88
Russell brothers gold-mining, Gregory Gulch 107
Russell brothers gold-mining, Ralston's Creek 104
Russell brothers gold-mining, "Richest Square Mile on Earth 105
Russell brothers gold-mining, Russell Gulch 105

S

Sally Hughes' Ferry 316, 317, 322
Sally Hughes' Road 316
"salting a mine" 277
Sanfernando 156
Saturday Evening Post 26, 27
Sautee, battle of 300
Savannah 3, 8
Savannah Plantation 102, 103
Scotland 28, 210
Scudder's Inn 309, 310
Scudder's Trading House 310, 315
Scull Shoals 211
Seaboard Airline Railroad 47, 87
Seaboard Railroad 86
Seay, Lloyd, *Lakewood 100* champion 99, 100
Secession Convention 237
Secessionist 137
"Sergeant-at-Arms" of the Senate 272
Sequoyah 155-156
Shallowford Road 312, 313, 322
Sherman, Gen. William T., *March To The Sea* 19, 34

Sherrill home-place 129-130
Shirley Hotel 173
Sigma Alpha Epsilon (SAE) fraternity 49
Silversmith 210
Silversmiths of Georgia 211
slaves/slavery 232, 234
Smithsonian Institution gold coins 215
Southern 500 95
Southern Banner 73
Southern Confederacy 271
Southern Railroad 86, 157, 164, 369-378
Southern Railroad Depot, Rockmart 369-378
Southern Railway, Ponce De Leon 369-378
Southern Railway, Train #36 185-188
Southern Recorder 210
Spanish conquistadors 122-128
Spanish explorers, artifacts/ archaeology of 465-470
Spanish explorers, artifacts in Nacoochee Valley 465, 466, 467, 468
Spanish sword 122-128, 468, 469
Spring Place 129-136, 327
steamship 1, 304
steamship travel in Georgia 304
stock-car racing 94-100
Stone Mountain, GA 30
Stone Pile Gap 299
Stonewall Limited Partnership 9
Stovall's Brigade 41
swindlers 233

T

Talladega 95
Tallulah Falls, City Hall 175
Tallulah Falls, firestorm of 1921 172-178
Tallulah Falls, Glenbrook Hotel 176
Tallulah Falls Railroad 157-176, 178
Tallulah Falls Railroad, Wiley Junction 171
Tallulah Falls Railroad, Wiley Trestle 159, 163
Tallulah Falls Railroad Depot – Clayton 168

Tallulah Falls Railroad Depot – Demorest 167
Tallulah Falls Railroad Depot – Lakemont 168, 169
Tallulah Falls Railroad Depot – Tallulah Falls 167, 168
Tallulah Falls School 178
Tallulah Gorge 167
Tallulah Gorge State Park 163
Tallulah Lake 163, 168
Tallulah Trail 311
Tanner's Mill 182
Templeton Reid gold coins 209-216, 239
Templeton Reid Mint 213
Ten-dollar Reid coin 209
1st Tennessee Infantry Regiment 41
5th Tennessee Mounted Infantry 249
Tensawattee 314
The First Hundred Years: A Short History of Cobb County in Georgia 81
The White House 91
Time-Life Series – The Civil War 42
Toochalar 132
Toogaloo Trail 313
Towes Chapel 12
Track Rock Gap petroglyphs 297
Trahlyta's Grave 299
Trail of Tears 28, 40, 156, 276, 279, 305, 327, 379, 381
train wreck 369-378
treasure 232, 239
Treaty of Indian Spring 60, 61
Treaty of New Echota 141-153, 316, 317, 333
Trickum Road 321
Triple-murder (1838) 233-234
"triplet" tornadoes 217-225
tuberculosis 2
Tugaloo 313
Turner's Corner 262-266
Turner's Corner Restaurant 265-266

U

U.S. Army Corps of Engineers 18, 83, 304
U.S. Army Federal Pension 290-292
U.S. Branch Mint 213, 216, 240, 241, 320

Subject Index

U.S. Civil War 5-6, 11, 17, 28-32, 40, 41, 42, 44, 45, 46, 47, 48, 82-88, 103, 105, 107, 112, 115, 137, 141, 147, 148, 149, 181, 240, 269, 276, 277, 281-292, 328, 334-337, 391-392, 436-438
U.S. Civil War, graves from 281-292
U.S. Civil War, outlaws in 240, 281-292, 392-394, 436-438
U.S. Civil War, relics from 9
U.S. Mint 210, 213
U.S. Postal Inspector 120
U.S. Postman 117-121
U.S. Revenue Agent 120, 334-337
U.S. Treasury Department 97
U.S. Weather Bureau 218, 219, 220
U.S.S. Savannah 1-2
"Underground Atlanta" 268, 270
Union Army 17-23, 181, 246-255
Union Army guerrillas 246-255, 281-292
Union Church 66
Union County 248
Union Hill 248
Union Jack 6
"Unionist" 137, 138, 139, 248, 281-292
University of Georgia 48, 56
University of Kentucky 44
untaxed whiskey 348-355
untaxed whiskey arrests 348-355
Upper Cabin Road 66
Ustanali (Oostanaula) 324

V
V.A. Higgins Store, Auraria 269
Van Wert, town of 391
Vann House 307, 327, 328
Vann's Ferry 180
Vann's Tavern 133, 136
Vann's Valley 325
"Veach Guards" 40

W
W.G. Owenby & Company 292
W.H. Early House 259
W.O.B. Whatley cemetery 384
W.O.B. Whatley home, Polk County, GA 380-381
Walasi-Yi Center, Civilian Conservation Corps construction of 422-423
Walasi-Yi Center, Neel's Gap 421-423
Walasi-Yi Center, original construction of 422-423
Wallis-McElreath Builders 37-38
Walt Disney Productions 168, 169
Walthall Trading Post, Paulding (Polk) Co., GA 387
Walton's Ford 311
War of the Rebellion: Official Records of the Union and Confederate Armies 81, 269
Warwoman Creek 310
Water's Ferry 321
water-ram 4
Watie, Buck (Elias Boudinot) home-place of 330
Watts, George, gristmill of 389
Wayne Street Hotel 91
Wellsville Police Dept. 15
Western & Atlantic Railroad 3, 17, 23, 29, 31, 32, 34, 70, 71, 74, 84

Western & Atlantic Railroad, Train #179 wreck at Willowdale 481-485
Westview Cemetery 93
Whatley Family Cemetery 384
Whatley Trading Post, Paulding (Polk) Co. 387
Wheeler's Confederate Cavalry 250
Whistle-Stop Café 293-296
White County's Old England Gold Mine 471-475
White County's Old England Gold Mine litigation 473-475
White Sulphur Train Station 186
Widow Fool's Ferry 317, 325
William Rogers' home ("Oakland") 332-333
Wilson, John, gristmill of (later Elias Hightower gristmill) 389
"Woodlands" manor 3, 4
Woody's Store, Auraria 269
Wooley Ford 313
Wordsworth 9
World Almanac 218
World Guide To Covered Bridges 88

X

Y
Young Harris College 91

www.ingramcontent.com/pod-product-compliance
Lightning Source LLC
Chambersburg PA
CBHW051415290426
44109CB00016B/1303